D0148043

Jesus Is Lord!

An Introduction to the
New Testament

Jesus Is Lord!

An Introduction to the
New Testament

KENNETH SCHENCK

Triangle Publishing
Marion, Indiana

Jesus Is Lord! An Introduction to the New Testament
by Kenneth Schenck

Direct correspondence and permission requests to one of the following:

Triangle Publishing
Indiana Wesleyan University
4301 South Washington Street
Marion, Indiana 46953

Web site: www.trianglepublishing.com
E-mail: info@trianglepublishing.com

Unless otherwise noted, all Scripture quotations are from the *Holy Bible, New Living Translation*, copyright ©
1996. Used by permission of Tyndale House Publishers, Inc., Wheaton, Illinois 60189. All rights reserved.

Scripture quotations marked NIV® are from *The Holy Bible: New International Version*®. NIV®. Copyright ©
1973, 1978, 1984 by International Bible Society. Used by permission of Zondervan Publishing House. All rights
reserved.

Scripture quotations marked NRSV are from *The Holy Bible*: *New Revised Standard Version*, copyright, 1989,
by the Division of Christian Education of the National Council of the Churches of Christ in the U.S.A. Used by
permission. All rights reserved.

Scripture quotations marked KJV are from the Authorized King James Version, 1611.

Classical quotations are from The Loeb Classical Library®, Harvard University Press.

Quotations from the Pseudepigrapha are from James H. Charlesworth, ed., *The Old Testament Pseudepigrapha*,
2 vols. (NY: Doubleday, 1983, 1985).

Quotations from the Dead Sea Scrolls are from *The Dead Sea Scrolls Translated: The Qumran Texts in English*,
trans. Florentino Garcia Martinez. Translated into English by Wilfred G.E. Watson (Leiden: E. J. Brill, 1994).

Schenck, Kenneth
Jesus Is Lord! An Introduction to the New Testament

ISBN: 1-931283-03-6

Copyright © 2003 by Triangle Publishing. All rights reserved. No part of this publication may be reproduced,
stored in a retrieval system, distributed or transmitted in any form or by any means: electronic, mechanical,
photocopy, recording or any other, except for brief quotations in printed reviews and as permitted under the
United States Copyright Act of 1976, without prior written permission of the publisher.

Cover and graphic design: Susan Spiegel
Illustrations: Eric Wieringa

Printed in the United States of America
Evangel Press, Nappanee, Indiana

To Angela, Stefanie, Stacy, Thomas, and Sophia

Contents

Unit 4: Acts – Chapters 29–35

Unit 5: Paul's Letters – Chapters 36–50

Unit 6: Hebrews, General Letters, and Revelation – Chapters 51–53

Epilogue

Glossary

Index

Preface

This book has arisen from a number of concerns. Perhaps the greatest is the incredible gap that often exists between the academy and the pew. The developments and agreements that are common knowledge among scholars often take decades to filter down to the layperson. Sometimes by then the scholars have even changed their minds!

Even worse is setting up our youth for faith crises because we stake Christianity on something inappropriate, like a particular version of the Bible or on the possibility of harmonizing the gospels. How often we forget that the living, exalted Christ stands at the heart of the matter. It is to Him that the Bible points! This book shows that we too often have let the skeptic set the terms of debate over the Bible. When we let the Bible's world set its own terms, many of these "problems" disappear.

It is also my passion to turn Christians on to seeing the Bible as God first revealed it. The Bible embodies the fact that God speaks to humans, and He speaks so that we can understand Him. As one line in the hymn "Spirit of God, Descend upon My Heart" puts it, God is a God who repeatedly "stoops to my weakness," meeting us wherever we are in our understanding. If you get anything from this book, I hope it will be that long before this collection of writings spoke to us, these books were individual instances of God meeting His people "where they were at," in their categories, and in their situations.

The danger lies in selfishly assuming that the words are ours without first listening to what God was saying to the original audiences—and why He was saying it. While many Christians assume that applying the words of Scripture directly to today honors God, the gap between "our time" and "that time" can actually imply the opposite. It is possible that the church would actually be resisting God's will if it did things exactly as the Bible says (e.g., with regard to slavery)!

Yet I remain committed to the Bible as a "sacrament," a divinely appointed meeting place where God makes the words say what we need them to say, even when those meanings differ significantly from anything the original authors understood. The expertise of scholars and the distance of ancient texts can easily discourage Bible students. To them I offer the advice to "Misinterpret boldly, that the Spirit may come!" If your heart is right, God will make His will known.

I also have written this book with the conviction that most New Testament surveys and introductions do not meet the learning styles of contemporary society. In our day of self-help books and "Idiot's Guides," students need snippets and snapshots rather than long discourses. I have tried to keep the chapters to ten pages at most. Each one is meant to be a self-contained unit that can read in any order. I do not require my students to read the entire book, often letting them read chapters in a completely different order than that in which I have arranged them here.

For example, I have incorporated the background chapters into appropriate places in the course rather than having students read them in isolation, when they have little idea what their relevance might be. Many New Testament professors also may want to treat the New Testament books according to the order in which they were written (e.g., Mark before Matthew, 1 Thessalonians before 1 Corinthians), rather than in the arbitrary order in which they now appear in the canon. With this fact in mind, I have numbered Paul's letters according to one reconstruction of their original order. In this way the student will get a better feel for how Paul's teaching developed as he matured in his understandings and experiences.

This approach naturally leads to some repetition within the chapters. I have done this consciously. Not only does it keep the text flexible from a teaching standpoint, but we all know that repetition is one of the greatest keys to learning.

Now may the grace of our Lord Jesus Christ, and the love of God, and the fellowship of the Holy Spirit be with us all, evermore. Amen.

Kenneth Schenck
August 8, 2002

Acknowledgements

Countless individuals have had an impact on this final work. They have bequeathed this book its strengths. In my "brief" thirty-some years on the earth, I have had countless positive influences on my spiritual and intellectual understanding. I would like to go on record with thanks to my parents, broader family, and former teachers for their impact on my life.

Numerous colleagues have read one or more chapters. Dr. David Smith and Dr. Steve Lennox checked my content for plausibility and accuracy, although they did not always agree with me. David in particular read the entire manuscript. I must take responsibility for the ideas as they now stand.

Dr. Keith Drury and Dr. Bud Bence provided me with helpful spiritual and practical advice. Keith more than anyone else has helped me aim at always building up the body of Christ and avoiding anything that might be a stumbling block. I share his priority that our hearts are far more important than our heads. Beyond the spiritual, I also have him to thank more than anyone else for any skill I might have as a teacher. It is hard to imagine the level of pain I might still inflict on my students if his office were not next to mine!

I want to thank my students these last few years at Indiana Wesleyan University. They have labored under photocopies and loosely bound editions, oral reports, and written evaluations. They have made me a better teacher and, I trust, this book a better introduction to the New Testament.

Bobbie Sease has done an incredible job editing the project. I have improved tenfold as a writer from her suggestions. Nathan Birky and Triangle Publishing have been models of patience and support. Graphic designers, other readers, and many other unnamed individuals deserve immense thanks.

Most of all I would like to thank my family for their incredible sacrifice of time and my attentiveness. They surrendered innumerable hours so that I could work at a computer. My wife Angela also waded through numerous chapters and made excellent suggestions toward making the book more helpful and readable. Stefanie, Stacy, Thomas, and Sophia lost hours of fun and play with their Dad, who wasn't always patient and rested. It is to my family that I dedicate this book.

Kenneth Schenck
June 24, 2003

Abbreviations

General Abbreviations

A.D.	"in the year of our Lord"
B.C.	"before Christ"
ca.	"around"
cf.	"confer"
e.g.	"for example"
i.e.	"that is"

Bible Translations

NLT	New Living Translation
NIV	New International Version
NRSV	New Revised Standard Version
RSV	Revised Standard Version
KJV	King James Version

Old Testament Books

Gen.	Genesis	Eccles.	Ecclesiastes
Exod.	Exodus	Song of Sol.	Song of Solomon
Lev.	Leviticus	Isa.	Isaiah
Num.	Numbers	Jer.	Jeremiah
Deut.	Deuteronomy	Lam.	Lamentations
Josh.	Joshua	Ezek.	Ezekiel
Judg.	Judges	Dan.	Daniel
Ruth	Ruth	Hos.	Hosea
1 Sam.	1 Samuel	Joel	Joel
2 Sam.	2 Samuel	Amos	Amos
1 Kings	1 Kings	Obad.	Obadiah
2 Kings	2 Kings	Jon.	Jonah
1 Chron.	1 Chronicles	Mic.	Micah
2 Chron.	2 Chronicles	Nah.	Nahum
Ezra	Ezra	Hab.	Habakkuk
Neh.	Nehemiah	Zeph.	Zephaniah
Esther	Esther	Hag.	Haggai
Job	Job	Zech.	Zechariah
Ps.	Psalms	Mal.	Malachi
Prov.	Proverbs		

New Testament Books

Matt.	Matthew	Heb.	Hebrews
Mark	Mark	James	James
Luke	Luke	1 Pet.	1 Peter
John	John	2 Pet.	2 Peter
Acts	Acts	1 John	1 John
Rom.	Romans	2 John	2 John
1 Cor.	1 Corinthians	3 John	3 John
2 Cor.	2 Corinthians	Jude	Jude
Gal.	Galatians	Rev.	Revelation
Eph.	Ephesians		
Phil.	Philippians		
Col.	Colossians		
1 Thess.	1 Thessalonians		
2 Thess.	2 Thessalonians		
1 Tim.	1 Timothy		
2 Tim.	2 Timothy		
Titus	Titus		
Philem.	Philemon		

Unit 1:
Introduction

Chapters 1–5

CHAPTER 1

Why Read the New Testament?

Many are convinced that the Bible is the best, perhaps even the only way to find God and ultimate meaning.

The Bible has had an immense impact on the history of our world, especially on Western culture. Its use in American courtrooms provides just one small example. Before testifying, a witness takes an oath to tell the truth by placing his or her right hand on a Bible. The Bible has long been a symbol of honesty, truth, and the highest values of Western culture.

Those who read the Bible give various reasons for doing so. For some it may simply be the fact that it is classic literature. The Bible continues to outsell all other books in today's competitive market. One reason is that Christianity has been the dominant religion of the Western world for over 1,500 years. Those of us who live in this hemisphere can learn about ourselves through these pages, even though they were written in another time and cultural mind-set. We will find ourselves amazed at how often we have heard the words and thoughts of the Bible in everyday circumstances, sometimes without even realizing their origin.

On the other hand, the Bible is not just a window on Western culture. Those from other cultures might be surprised at how well it also reflects the highest values of their world. Some of them may come to realize what many

New Testament: The second part of the Christian Bible; literature relating to God's people after the coming of Christ.

Old Testament: The first part of the Christian Bible; literature relating to God's people before the coming of Christ.

1

Westerners themselves do not—that the Bible was not actually written in the categories of Western culture. Some read the Bible—in particular its second part, the **New Testament**—to learn more about Christianity, one of the major religions of the world. For those seeking something beyond our passing existence in this life, the New Testament is on the list of essential reading. Millions of individuals have claimed to find God on this path.

Indeed, many are convinced that the Bible is the best, perhaps even the only way to find God and ultimate meaning. For Christians, the Bible holds important keys to becoming better individuals and to finding strength beyond ordinary means to handle life's challenges. Many read the Bible when they are facing a situation beyond their control, especially death, which is perhaps the ultimate challenge of our earthly existence. In both the **Old Testament**—the first part of the Bible—and the New Testament, they find comfort and hope.

This book is based on the story of Jesus Christ, Christianity's founder. In one early Christian statement of faith we read, "He was crucified, dead, and buried . . . On the third day he rose again from the dead." In that statement, Christians express their belief that Jesus Christ not only overcame death, but that He can help us do the same.

While we cannot begin to cover every topic, it is my hope that you will find in this book a way to think about certain pivotal aspects of the New Testament. I invite you to view this survey of the New Testament as a collection of "snapshots" in a photo album. Whether you are already familiar with the New Testament or not, try to see these pictures as if you were looking at them for the first time.

Within the pages of the New Testament, you will find the ultimate concerns of humanity. Why are we here? What is the purpose of our lives? Is there anything beyond death? These are the kinds of questions the New Testament addresses, questions that are just as relevant today as they were two thousand years ago.

Things to Think About

Key Terms:
New Testament
Old Testament

1. What value do you think reading the Bible might have for you?

2. What expectations do you have as you approach the New Testament, and how do you think these expectations will affect what you see there? Are you a skeptic? Do you feel you already know what the New Testament teaches? If you find that the Bible contradicts something you currently believe, how open would you be to changing your beliefs?

CHAPTER 2

How to Read the Bible As a Christian

Christians today largely do not read the Bible in terms of what it originally meant. We much more often read it for the significance it might have for us today.

The Problem

The sheer number of different churches thriving in the Western world today is mind numbing. On a random city street in America, you might find any number of different groups worshiping almost side-by-side—Roman Catholics, Orthodox, Episcopalians, Lutherans, Presbyterians, Baptists, Methodists, or any one of a host of other "denominations." Walk into one of these churches and you will find that it differs significantly from the others. Even two churches in the same denomination can differ dramatically in worship style and teaching. "If the Bible is the path of ultimate truth," one might ask, "why is there so much disagreement on what it means?"

In one respect, the diversity of interpretations is easy enough to explain. Words mean different things when read in different ways. And the Bible has many, many words! It is comprised of over sixty books authored by writers from varied backgrounds over a long period of

At a Glance

• Many Christians read the Bible "personally," applying its ancient words directly to themselves.

• Christianity has often reinterpreted the words to have more universal meaning.

• Denominations often reinterpret the Bible's words according to their particular emphases and situations.

• The original meaning of the Bible is a function of how these words were used back when they were first written.

• The Bible consists of over sixty books written over a long period of time under many different circumstances.

inerrant: With regard to the Bible, without errors, including scientific or historical errors.

infallible: With regard to the Bible, without error in any matter of faith or doctrine.

revelation: Truth conveyed or "revealed" from God to humanity.

inspiration: The process by which God conveyed truth through human authors into the written text of the Bible.

time under vastly different circumstances.[1] Relating the ideas from so many different contexts to one another is not an easy task, especially since we often lack important information about the original contexts. And we are reading these words at least nineteen hundred years after they were written, meaning that our words usually have significantly different connotations than they did back then. When you consider all these factors, it is no wonder people often disagree over what the Bible means.

Thankfully, Christian tradition does hold many interpretations of the Bible in common, such as the belief that Jesus' death and resurrection hold the key to life. But people will always disagree to some extent over what the Bible means. Thus, it is very important that we find common ground so Christians can talk to one another profitably. This goal will require us to know what is really going on when we read the Bible.

Of course, many individuals read the Bible strictly as good literature or because of historical interest. The Bible may hold no particular authority for such people, who read it simply as historians or students of literature might read it. Others believe the Bible to have great significance for their Christian faith—they may even consider it to be **inspired** or divinely **revealed** to some extent—but may not give it absolute authority. A number of Christians believe that Christ rose from the dead, yet are not sure the writers of the New Testament were always correct in their teachings.[2] On the other hand, many Christians believe that the entire Bible holds absolute authority. Christians often use words like **inerrant** and **infallible** when they discuss the Bible, implying that it does not have errors. Those who use the word inerrant often mean that the Bible has no errors of any kind, including matters of science and history. The word infallible usually implies that the Bible has no errors in terms of faith or doctrine, allowing for mistakes of a historical or scientific nature. As the rest of this chapter will show, these categories often start our discussions off on the wrong foot and rarely lead to common ground.

For example, presuming that *our* categories of science and history are those of God himself is a questionable practice.[3] Yet this is exactly what some Christians subtly imply when they use the word inerrant. They define errors according to the standards of modern historical writing or the categories of modern science. They expect the biblical authors to speak of the world as a globe and for the book of Acts to give us something like a documentary of words and events. They fail to realize that these are the ways *we* talk about history and the world, not the way the first authors and readers of the Bible did. These Christians assume that modern methods of writing about science and history go about things the right way—God's way—and ignore the possibility that God might meet people of all times in their own categories.

Those who first heard the writings of the Bible, for example, no doubt understood those writings from the standpoint of their own worldviews. After all, it was God's word to them long before it was God's word to us. Their ancient worldviews thus provide us with a much more appropriate starting place for understanding the Bible's words than do our current views of the world. For these reasons, terms like inerrancy and infallibility, because they often are used in an anachronistic way, are not the best starting points for finding common ground among Christians.

One thing that *is* extremely helpful in reaching this common ground is the realization that the Bible basically can be read in two different ways: (1) we can read it for what it actually meant to those who first wrote and heard it, or (2) we can invest its words with some other meaning. While this distinction seems obvious and perhaps even pointless, it is extremely important because

Christians today largely do not read the Bible in terms of what it originally meant. We much more often read it for the significance it might have for us today.

We might call what the Bible originally meant to its authors and first readers the **original meaning**.[4] The meanings of words originate from how people use them at any particular time and place. While these meanings often overlap significantly from language to language and from place to place, the connotations many times do not carry across from one historical/cultural context to the next. This is one of the reasons translations of the Bible frequently render the same Greek or Hebrew sentence in significantly different ways—it is often difficult to capture the precise meaning of a sentence from one language to another. To understand the original meaning of the Bible, we will need to have extensive knowledge of the history, literature, and culture of the ancient world. In other words, we will need to understand the "dictionaries" from which the Bible's words derived their original meanings.

> **original meaning:** Reading the Bible's words for what they meant when they were first written, using what the words and concepts meant 2,000 years ago.

Needless to say, the "dictionary" from which the average reader today draws meaning will not be an "original-meaning dictionary." The dictionary of the person who knows little about Christianity will consist almost completely of what the words in his or her English Bible mean in contemporary American culture. If someone comes from some Christian tradition—perhaps they are Roman Catholic, Baptist, or Methodist—they no doubt have learned further "definitions" for the Bible's words. Is it any surprise that a person with a "Baptist dictionary" will often think the Bible clearly teaches Baptist doctrine, or that a person with a "Methodist dictionary" would think the Bible teaches the beliefs of Methodism? When we realize the difference between these approaches to the Bible's meaning and the original meaning, we can begin to find common ground for using the Bible as Christians.

Reading the Bible "Personally"

Growing up, one of my favorite verses was Joshua 1:9: "Be strong and courageous! Do not be afraid or discouraged. For the LORD your God is with you wherever you go."[5] I took this verse as a promise from God directly to me—I did not need to be afraid of the circumstances of my life because God was always with me. It was one of many verses I memorized as a child for reassurance and in order to learn the basics of Christian belief. The King James Version of the Bible (KJV), the Bible I used as a child, listed every verse by number, making it easy for me to see individual verses as self-contained statements of truth.

However, it does not take much reflection to see that in its original setting, Joshua 1:9 was not written to me or to any other human being alive today. God spoke these words *to a man named Joshua* as he was about to conduct a military campaign in Canaan. God promised that Joshua would be victorious in battle throughout his conquest of the land. Nothing in the immediate context of Joshua 1:9 indicates that anyone else should apply that verse to his or her life. While I still believe that the meaning I drew from that verse is true for me as a Christian, I am now aware that it is not what the verse really meant.

This way of interpreting the Bible gives its words a "**personal" meaning**. The words are brought directly from the Bible into *my* world and given

---

Finding Verses in the Bible

• The book of the Bible is listed first (e.g., Matthew).

• The chapter number comes next (e.g., Matt. **1**)

• The verse number comes after the colon (e.g., Matt **1:1**)

• See the Table of Contents in your Bible to find the arrangement of books.

• Remember the Bible has at least two parts: the Old and New Testaments (some also have the Apocrypha).

9

personal meaning:
Finding meaning in the Bible's words without regard to their original meaning; interpreting the Bible from the "dictionary" in your head, as if its words were written directly to you and not to people who lived 2,000 years ago in a far different historical and cultural context.

meaning in *my* context without careful consideration of what they might have meant originally. Sometimes the interpretation parallels the original sense closely, as in this case; sometimes it goes quite far afield.

On the one hand, it would be easy to dismiss such interpretations, since they often have nothing to do with the actual meaning of the words when they were written. And this approach to Scripture can be extremely dangerous if you do not realize you are reading the Bible out of context. In fact, this approach to the Bible is the stuff of which cults are born—cult leaders like David Koresh and Jim Jones read the Bible this way. Since the words are not limited to their original meaning, they can come to mean almost anything, depending on who is reading them.[6]

On the other hand, Christians are regularly programmed to read the Bible in this manner, as if they are always the "you" addressed by its words.

In one sense, not a word of the Bible was written to anyone alive today.

However, it takes little thought to realize that the immediate audiences of the Bible were the Israelites, Romans, Corinthians, Thessalonians, and others to whom it was first written. *In one sense, not a word of the Bible was written to anyone alive today.* While the message of God to these individuals relates to us today in an indirect way, it is often inappropriate—and can actually be contrary to God's purposes—to take its words and apply them directly to ourselves.[7]

It does the doctor no service if his or her patient takes someone else's medicine. A person who has high blood pressure will not make the doctor happy by taking medicine prescribed for someone with low blood pressure. In the same way, it does not necessarily honor God to do what He told the ancients to do, without prayerfully and thoughtfully considering what He would say directly to our context. Could it be that in our situations God would sometimes require us to do exactly the opposite of what He commanded the ancients?

Before we completely dismiss personal interpretations of the Bible, we should remember how extensively God seems to minister to His people through this approach to the Bible's words. Since the Bible became available in nearly everyone's language, people of all stripes and backgrounds have heard God speaking to them through the words of Scripture. In a sense, Scripture has become a **sacrament** like baptism or communion, a divinely appointed meeting place where God can "stoop to our weakness" and meet us where we are. As ordinary bread and wine are supercharged to signify the body and blood of Jesus in communion, so the ancient words of the Bible seem to be a catalyst for God's Spirit to speak to His people—even out of context.

> **sacrament:** A "means of grace," a divinely appointed path by which to meet God and experience His love (e.g., communion, baptism).

Since so many Christians experience God through the Bible in this way—in fact, far more frequently than through its original meaning—we must accept personal interpretations as potentially valid ways of meeting God through the Bible. However, it is important for those who read the Bible in this way to realize that the authority of their interpretations depends on whether or not they are truly hearing God. Like ancient prophecy, any individual's "spirit interpretation" is subject to the critique and testing of his or her fellow Christians (cf. 1 Cor. 14:32; 1 John 4:1).[8]

Reading the Bible in Church

A visit to a few churches quickly demonstrates that different denominations often have their own unique interpretations of the Bible. While some of this

Christians have often taken words that were closely related to a particular ancient situation in the Bible and given them more contemporary or universal meanings for the church.

community meanings: The meanings that various groups of Christians see in the Bible.

diversity comes from genuine ambiguity within the pages of Scripture itself, a great deal of it also comes from reading the Bible out of context. *Christianity in general has often taken words that were closely related to a particular ancient situation in the Bible and given them more contemporary or universal meanings for the church.* We might call such interpretations **community meanings** of the Bible, because they are meanings that various Christian churches or communities see in the text.

The book of Romans is an excellent case in point. The apostle Paul, a famous early Christian, wrote this letter in part to defend his mission to those who were not Jews, that is, the **Gentiles**. He argued that keeping the Jewish Law by doing such things as circumcising your son would not keep anyone from destruction when God came to judge the world. God had found another way of escape; He sent Jesus Christ to pay the penalty for this breaking of the Law by both Jew and Gentile. All one needed to do was trust in what God had done

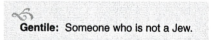

Gentile: Someone who is not a Jew.

through Jesus. God had not thrown the Jews away, like some said Paul taught. God had found a way not only to save the Jews, but the Gentiles as well.

If you found the previous paragraph a little boring or somewhat removed from the concerns of your life, you may find the following rendering easier: Everybody in the whole world has done wrong, so no one will get to heaven by doing good things. The punishment for doing wrong is death and hell. God loves us, though, and does not want us to go to hell, so He sent Jesus to die in our place.

All you have to do is believe that all this is true, and you will go to heaven.

This last rendition is an excellent example of how churches throughout the centuries have sometimes taken the Bible just a little out of context to make its teaching more contemporary or universal in focus. Not that the second paragraph is untrue—it is, in fact, a fairly close parallel to Paul's original message. But it has subtly changed the original meaning in the process of making the message more universal in scope.[9] This shows how the church, in attempting to address the ongoing concerns of Christians in the world, has often, without even realizing it, slightly changed the Bible's meaning.

One reason the Bible has such a "transferable" quality is that so much of it is story. Stories by their very nature can be told in numerous ways with differing emphases. For example, take the story of the "prodigal son," which is found in Luke 15. As chapter 22 of this book will discuss further, you probably will not hear this story told in church with the specific meaning Jesus had in mind—that the characters in the story represent the various ways in which the Jews had received His message of restoration for Israel. Yet it is so easy to see this as a story about new beginnings for those who have messed up and want to start again.

In the course of this book, you will see many instances in which Christian denominations have taken biblical verses to worlds the original authors never imagined. Many of the disagreements among churches actually come from these "over-readings" of the text. These observations lead us to an important conclusion: Churches—even those that claim to be "Bible-based"—often use the Bible far more as a mirror to see what they already believe than as the true source of their beliefs. Realizing the implications of what it means to read the Bible according to its original meaning is the first step toward finding common ground among Christians. Reading the Bible in terms of its original message also helps tremendously in the appropriate application of its message today.

Reading the Bible for its Original Meaning

Many Christians have taken a keen interest in the original context of the Bible. In the last few decades, a lot of books have been published about the historical background of Scripture, many of which have availed themselves of these original resources. Many churches publish study guides and "Sunday School" material meant to help the members of their congregations move closer to the Bible's original meaning. Countless Christians have visited the Holy Land to retrace the steps of Jesus and other biblical figures. When these pilgrims return, they usually have a better appreciation of the Bible's meaning than they did before their trips.

Even with all this attention to history, however, many Christians only go part of the way toward really reading the Bible in terms of what it originally meant. The tendency to make sense of the Bible's words according to our own worldview—even our current "Christian" worldview—is strong and understandable, since the ancient significance will often seem strange and foreign to our world. Cultural differences are sometimes very subtle and easily missed, clouded as they are by the cultural "glasses" through which we see our own world.

> When we read the Bible in terms of what it originally meant, it becomes a witness to how God has revealed himself to His people in the past—in fact, in the most important moments of all history.

Since the books of the Bible were God's revelation to ancient Israelites, Romans, Corinthians, and other people, it makes sense that He would reveal himself in terms they would understand. Why would He speak to ancient people using modern categories of expression? To be sure, humans hold many experiences in common: love, suffering, death, and joy, to name a few. These common human experiences that God addresses in Scripture are another reason Christians have so easily and directly applied the Bible to today's realities.

The pages of the Bible address so many issues common to human experience that its words sometimes seem to "hit two birds with one stone"; that is, the meanings that spoke to their concerns centuries ago seem to speak just as directly to ours today.

But we should also realize that even something as "obvious" as love had somewhat different connotations to the first audiences of the Bible than it has to contemporary audiences. Often these basic categories, the ones

---

Applying the Bible Today

Phase One: The Bible

1. What did the passage mean originally?

2. Why did it say what it said? What are the principles behind it or what does it say about the character of God?

3. What do other Scriptures say on the topic?

Phase Two: The Church

1. What have Christians through the ages said about this topic?

2. What are my fellow Christians saying now?

3. What do I believe the Holy Spirit is saying?

---

we could not imagine being different, will cause us to misread the Bible in the most subtle ways—like our understanding of sexuality, what it means to be divine, or even what defines a person. We should not be surprised that the disciples thought heaven was straight up (Acts 1:10) or that Paul pictured Paradise in the third layer of the sky (2 Cor. 12:2). Why would God present himself in the context of what *we* think of the universe when He was working in *their* context?

It is also difficult for many Christians to read the Bible as a collection of books rather than as a single book. The different authors of the Bible's books do not always use the same words in the same ways. We cannot necessarily use a verse in Paul's writings to clarify a verse in Matthew, for these two individuals used words differently. John says Jesus performed countless "signs" (John 20:30); Mark says he gave none (Mark 8:12). James says God accepts us because of "actions" [works] (James 2:24); Paul says He does not

(Gal. 2:16). In these examples, the different authors are using the same words in a different sense.[10]

The difference between reading the Bible according to its original meaning and reading it "personally" has quite significant implications for how we appropriate the authority of the Bible. When individuals read the Bible as a direct word from God to them or when churches universalize the Bible's message, the Bible seems to immediately take on a timeless and authoritative character.[11] Some Christians speak of "absolute truth" or of a "biblical worldview" when referring to the Bible in this context. Many denominational statements of faith arguably refer to Scripture in this way. We should not rush to dismiss these kinds of interpretations, even if they often do take the words of Scripture out of context. Surely these are the dominant ways in which God has spoken through Scripture to His people throughout the ages. However, it is important to realize that these readings of the Bible really are God speaking *through His Spirit and the church* more than through the Bible itself.

Reading the Bible in terms of its original meaning changes the way we appropriate its message. *Rather than a direct revelation from God to us, it becomes a witness to how God has revealed himself to His people in the past— in fact, in the most important moments of all history.* When we use the Bible in this way, we cannot assume that God wishes us to do exactly what the people of the past did or to think the way they thought. Today we must look for the underlying principles of what God told them to do (in their terms) and then conceptualize these truths as they would apply to us. We do this when we look both for continuity in the character of God and for points of contact between our context and theirs.

We can apply the original meaning of the Bible today by way of a two-phase process. The first phase is the scriptural phase. Determine what the particular passage at which you are looking meant in its original context. Then ask why it said what it said. What principles are at work? What was God doing? What do other Scriptures say on the topic in their individual situations?

The second phase involves other Christians—God's church. One of the things a full understanding of the Bible's original meaning does is to help us realize just how much we need one another—as Christians listening to God's Spirit in order to work out what Christianity should be today. The Bible addresses problems *similar* to ours, but usually not exactly the same as ours. Bridging the distance between then and now is a bigger task than any one Christian can handle. What have Christians said on this topic throughout the centuries, and what are they saying now? What do I believe the Holy Spirit is saying to me directly? It is by prayerful and thoughtful work like this that Christians will "work out your [plural] salvation with fear and trembling, for it is God who works in you to will and to act according to his good purpose" (Phil. 2:12-13 NIV).

Things to Think About

1. Why do you think Christians have different beliefs? After all, they are using the same Bible.

2. What does it mean to you to say that the Bible is *inspired*? Do you think it is appropriate to call it inerrant? Infallible?

3. Do you agree with the claim that Christians largely do not read the Bible in terms of its original meaning? Or do we mostly read its words the same way its first audiences did?

4. How do *you* read the Bible? Personally? Following what you have learned from your church? For its original meaning?

Key Terms
community meanings
Gentile
inerrant
infallible
inspiration
original meaning
personal meaning
revelation
sacrament

5. Identify the following as either a "personal" interpretation, a "community" interpretation, or an interpretation in terms of the original meaning:

• I sat by the bedside of my dying father, wondering whether it was God's will for him to die now or whether God would miraculously heal him of his cancer. As I read my Bible, I came across Acts 20:25: **"Now I know that none of you . . . will ever see my face again."** I suddenly felt a strange peace that my father was going home to be with God. Like Paul, he was leaving on a victorious note after a life full of goodness.

• When Paul said, **"[Y]our body is a temple of the Holy Spirit"** (1 Cor. 6:19), he used the plural word for "you" in Greek. He was telling the Corinthian church as a whole that they *together* made up the body of Christ, the temple in which God's Spirit lived. Therefore, an individual in the church who would visit a prostitute at the temple of Aphrodite not only was taking his physical body, but also was taking the "body" of Christ with him.

• My church does not allow smoking. Further, my pastor tells me it is wrong to drink too much coffee, go excessively without sleep, or get fat—because 1 Corinthians 3:16 says that **"you are God's temple."** Why would I want to harm my body if it is the temple of God's Spirit?

endnotes

1. Most Protestant Bibles have sixty-six books, while Roman Catholic and Orthodox Bibles include an additional group of writings known as the "Apocrypha," books that come roughly from the period in between the Old and New Testaments. See chapter 3 of this text.

2. Some Christians present belief in the Bible's authority in terms of a false alternative: either the Bible is without error in every way or Christianity is false. The heart of Christian belief, however, is surely the saving death and victorious resurrection of Jesus Christ—an event in history rather than words on a page. Thus, the truth of Christianity does not rise or fall on the veracity of even the majority of the Bible's words.

3. I will occasionally refer to God in this book by way of masculine pronouns such as "He" or "Him." I do so because this is the most typical way the Bible itself refers to God, not because God is literally male. The Old Testament in particular makes it clear that God does not have genitalia of any sort.

4. Of course, this phrase—the "original meaning"—is somewhat vague, for those who first heard the biblical texts probably differed among themselves from time to time in their understanding. Further, when books of the Bible have incorporated or developed sources, the texts sometimes came to imply things no author anticipated. The meaning of a text is often a slippery thing, even to its very authors and readers.

5. Unless otherwise noted, all biblical translations in this book come from the New Living Translation of the Bible (NLT). When all the letters of "LORD" are capitalized, it means that the proper name for God, Yahweh, stands in the Hebrew behind the translation.

6. Some read the Bible out of context intentionally rather than accidentally. "Feminist" readings, for example, intentionally read the words of the Bible devoid of the patriarchal and "sexist" aspects of ancient culture, thus representing the concerns of a female reader. "Black" and "liberationist" readings do the same, with a view to concerns for social justice. All three of these are examples of a method of interpretation known as "reader-response criticism," in which the reader of a text is allowed to take the words in whatever way s/he sees fit. The theory behind this approach argues that the meaning of a text is unstable and, thus, that any reading of a text is as good as any other.

7. For example, it is possible to biblically support the practices of polygamy and slavery, since the Bible nowhere prohibits these practices in principle. The role of women is another subject about which straightforward transfer of the Bible's teaching to today's culture would, I believe, actually work against the Spirit of Christ. Is it possible that like the Pharisees of the gospels—who followed the

words of the Old Testament so closely—some who claim to follow Scripture are actually striving against God's purposes for His people today?

8. For the abbreviations of the books of the Bible, as well as for the various translations used in this book, see the abbreviations page after the table of contents.

9. I see at least six points in which this paragraph disagrees with Paul's original message. (1) Paul was not talking about good works or wrongdoing of a general sort but, instead, about keeping the Jewish Law. (2) Accordingly, the focus of the second paragraph is off. When Paul said, "All have sinned" (Rom. 3:23), his focus was on all ethnic groups—i.e., both Jew and Gentile—rather than on all people as individual human beings. (3) Paul never mentioned hell in Romans. In fact, he never used the word in any of his writings. (4) Similarly, he did not mention heaven as our eternal destiny in any of his writings. He barely even hinted that heaven is the ultimate destination for those in Christ (maybe 1 Thess. 4:17). Paul's message concerning salvation and judgment focused on Christ's return to earth, not on the afterlife. (5) Paul thought of Christ's death as a sacrificial offering and as something I participate in mystically, not as a substitution for my own death. (6) The second interpretation makes Romans 9–11 somewhat irrelevant and tangential to Paul's earlier argument since these chapters deal with Israel as God's people (I did not even mention these chapters in my "church" reading of Romans). In context, they are the climax of the preceding argument, the proof that God has remained faithful to his covenant with Israel.

10. The NIV and NLT remove the problem somewhat for the English reader by translating the same Greek words differently. Here is another example of interpreters "contemporizing" the Bible's words.

11. Of course, it does not actually become timeless; its meaning is transformed to a meaning that is still time conditioned, but conditioned to our time rather than theirs.

CHAPTER 3

An Overview of the New Testament

The Bible is more like a library of books than a single volume.

The Christian Bible is divided into two parts: a group of books called the "Old Testament" and a group called the "New Testament." For Protestants, the Old Testament is comprised of thirty-nine different books. The Old Testament of the Roman Catholic and Orthodox churches includes some additional documents called the **Apocrypha**.[1] In all Bibles, however, the New Testament is made up of twenty-seven books. It is all too easy to think of the Bible as one book. In fact, some refer to it as "the good book." You can even buy a Bible that is titled *The Book* (NLT). But the Bible was not originally one book. The word *Bible* itself originally meant "little books"—over sixty-six "little books" when the word was first coined. The Bible is actually more like a library of books than a single volume.

Initially, these writings were not bound together but were written in different places by different authors

At a Glance:

• The books of the New Testament should be read individually—each author used words in a unique way to address different situations.

• A number of different genres appear in the New Testament. Ancient genres did not always function like our genres today.

Apocrypha: A group of writings included in Roman Catholic and Orthodox Bibles but not in the Bibles of most Protestants.

> **gospels:** From our perspective, the genre of the four presentations of Jesus in the New Testament—Matthew, Mark, Luke, and John. In their own world, most look like ancient biographies, although Luke may be considered a history.

for different purposes over perhaps as much as a thousand years. Eventually, they came to be grouped together in various ways and recorded on scrolls. Sometime after all the books of the Bible had been written, Christians gathered them together into one big book—more like the Bible as we now know it.

> **genre:** A type of literature or literary form, such as a novel, a personal letter, an eviction notice, a diary, etc. Such forms create certain expectations in a reader before s/he even starts reading.

We mentioned that the Bible was more of a library than an individual book. In a library, of course, there are many different kinds of books—novels, history books, science books, magazines, and scholarly journals, to name a few. These different types of literature are called **genres**. No one would read a comic strip in the same way as a math book, nor would anyone read a novel in quite the same way as a history of World War II. We have learned over the years to have different expectations of a comic play and a book on the Holocaust.

The same is true of the library of the New Testament. Of its twenty-seven books, there are at least four different kinds of basic genres in use, probably more. The first four books—Matthew, Mark, Luke, and John—are called **gospels**. Each in its own unique way presents what it considers to be important events and teachings from Jesus' life on earth. The gospels look similar to what we think of as biographies, but there are some significant differences.

The fifth book, called Acts, looks a little like a **history** book to us, although we should not assume that ancient history writing followed the same rules used by a modern historian. This book takes us from the last days of

Jesus on earth to a time over thirty years later when Paul arrived in Rome to stand trial before the emperor.

There are also a number of letters or **epistles** in the New Testament. Thirteen of

> **history (ancient):** A genre of literature presenting the story of a group or the circumstances surrounding a key period of time. Ancient histories varied somewhat in their precision and in general allowed for greater creativity than modern histories do.

> **epistle:** Basically a letter, although some scholars only use the word to refer to a somewhat official letter that circulates to a broad audience.

these have Paul's name on them, although the situation may be a little more complicated than it seems. There is also an anonymous "epistle" named Hebrews, which may actually be an early Christian sermon. The remaining seven letters are called the *Catholic* or *General Epistles*, since they seem to have in mind a general audience.

The final book of the New Testament is of a genre completely unfamiliar to most of us. It is an **apocalypse**, and to many it will no doubt seem an extremely strange book. The word "apocalypse" means that the book is the

revelation of hidden things, which is why it is also called the book of Revelation. We will have to learn a whole new set of expectations from the ancient world if we want to hear this book as it was first heard.

> **apocalypse:** A type of writing in which a heavenly being brings a revelation to an authority figure, both about things going on in the heavenly realm and about things that are going to happen in the near future. Placed on the lips of a famous figure from the past, these messages usually were written in a time of crisis and foretold how God would make everything right in the world.

As you are beginning to see, reading the Bible for what it originally meant is a lot more involved than you might have thought. It involves learning a whole new set of assumptions about things that seem obvious to us—like what it means to be the author of a letter. Before we are done, we will have to shift our thinking on matters as basic as what a father is or what it means to be poor. This shift is necessary if we want to have any chance of understanding what Jesus or Paul or any of the New Testament personalities were really saying.

Basic Genres of the New Testament

Gospels
Matthew, Mark, Luke, John

History
Acts

Apocalypse
Revelation

Letters/Epistles
- *Pauline Epistles*
  Romans, 1 and 2 Corinthians, Galatians, Ephesians, Philippians, Colossians, 1 and 2 Thessalonians, 1 and 2 Timothy, Titus, Philemon

- *Hebrews* (possibly a sermon)

- *General Epistles*
  James, 1 and 2 Peter, 1, 2, and 3 John, Jude

Things to Think About

1. What are the two parts of the Christian Bible?

2. What section do Roman Catholics and other Christian traditions include that Protestants do not?

3. What are the four basic genres in the New Testament?

4. If some artistic license were taken for the genres of ancient history or biography writing, can we consider them legitimate today?

5. Into what genre might Hebrews actually fit?

6. Which letters are included among the Pauline Epistles? Which books are included in the General Epistles? Which book was an apocalypse?

Key Terms
Apocrypha
apocalypse
epistle
genre
gospel
history (ancient)

endnotes

1. The term Apocrypha most often refers to the seven books included in the Roman Catholic Bible but not in most Protestant Bibles: Tobit, Judith, 1 and 2 Maccabees, the Wisdom of Solomon, Ecclesiasticus (also known as Sirach), and Baruch. In addition, the books of Esther and Daniel in the Catholic Bible include extra material. A few other books appear in early manuscripts of the Greek Old Testament (e.g., 1 Esdras, 3 and 4 Maccabees, Odes of Solomon). Sometimes these books are also considered apocrypha.

CHAPTER 4

Who Chose These Books?

If you believe God had a hand in the formation of the canon, then He must have been in this process, directing things toward their final result.

Introduction

Since the Bibles we buy come as a single book, it is all too easy to assume that the group of books we call the New Testament has always been bound together. This is not the case. As we pointed out in the previous chapter, the books of the New Testament were written and circulated independently for the most part. The earliest manuscript we have that contains all the books of our New Testament comes from the A.D. 300s, and it includes other books that ultimately did not end up in the Bible. Before then smaller collections had been in circulation, like Paul's writings or the four gospels. But the development of the New Testament **canon**—the group of early Christian writings considered to be authoritative for Christians—took several hundred years to reach its current form.[1]

At a Glance

- The writings of the New Testament were not written in the order in which they appear in our Bibles.

- The writing process took place over a number of decades.

- Paul's letters were collected first.

- By the late A.D. 100s, the four gospels were the gospels of the mainstream church.

- With regard to the remaining Christian books in circulation, churches debated which were authoritative enough to be considered "Scripture."

- The first list of authoritative books known to correspond to our New Testament list was made in A.D. 367.

canon: The group of writings that Christians consider to be authoritative on the level of Scripture.

Early Christians debated which books belonged in the canon. To be sure, mainstream Christians agreed early on concerning the majority of the writings. But they were uncertain whether other books (such as Hebrews and Revelation) were authoritative enough to be considered Scripture. Similarly, some books did not make it into the canon (such as the Shepherd of Hermas or 1 Clement) that many Christians thought should be included. The discussion continued well into the A.D. 300s. The first list we have that contains exactly the same writings found in our current Bible was part of an Easter letter sent out in A.D. 367—some two and a half centuries after the last books of the New Testament were written. The Council of Carthage in A.D. 397 gave this list official approval (at least for half of the church), accepting these twenty-seven writings as the "New Testament."

Collecting the Books

The books of the New Testament were not written in the order in which they now appear. For example, the gospels, which appear first in our New Testament, were written later than many of the other books. The writings of the apostle Paul were the earliest, although some think the letter of James was early as well. Even Paul's letters were not written in the order in which they appear in our Bibles. (They were arranged by length, going roughly from longest to shortest.) Either 1 Thessalonians or Galatians was the first book of the entire New Testament to be written.[2]

Either 1 Thessalonians or Galatians was the first book of the entire New Testament to be written.

Paul's writings began to circulate together rather early. The letter to the Colossians indicates that churches were sharing Paul's letters with one another within his lifetime or soon thereafter (Col. 4:16).[3] Second Peter also shows that Paul's writings had been collected together from early on and could be read as a group (2 Pet. 3:15-16).

> **Scripture:** A writing or collection of writings considered to be authoritative in some way for a particular religious group.

Aside from 2 Peter's mention of Paul's writings as **Scripture**, the first clear reference to a New Testament book as authoritative in this way comes in the mid-second century (about A.D. 150) in an anonymous sermon known as 2 Clement.[4] There, a quotation from the gospel of Matthew is apparently referred to as "Scripture," that is, on the same level as the Old Testament. This trend toward creating a second body of authoritative writings alongside the Hebrew Scriptures would continue and expand in the days to come. Soon, not only the "Old Testament" was referred to as "Scripture," but the "New Testament" was as well.[5] We do not know for certain when Christians began making lists—called "canon lists"—of the books they considered to be authoritative Scripture. Some think the whole process was started in response to a man

> "After you have read this letter, pass it on to the church at Laodicea so they can read it, too. And you should read the letter I wrote to them."
> **Colossians 4:16**
>
> "The Lord is waiting so that people have time to be saved. This is just as our beloved brother Paul wrote to you with the wisdom God gave him—speaking of these things in all of his letters. Some of his comments are hard to understand, and those who are ignorant and unstable have twisted his letters around to mean something quite different from what he meant, just as they do the other parts of Scripture ..."
> **2 Peter 3:15-16**
>
> "And another Scripture also says, 'I came not to call righteous, but sinners' [quotation of Matthew 9:13]."
> **2 Clement 2:4**

named Marcion, whose list was so unsatisfactory that it led more mainstream Christians to make better ones.[6] We know that mainstream

Christianity was fairly united by the end of the A.D. 100s in considering the four gospels of the New Testament to be the only ones the church should use. Many of the

> Marcion's (ca. A.D. 150) list of authoritative books included only "mutilated" versions of some of Paul's writings and the gospel of Luke, edited to his liking.

other writings in the New Testament were also accepted, but a discussion about the precise list would continue over the next few centuries.

We should point out that the question these Christians were debating was not necessarily whether these books were good or bad. No doubt some did object to books like Hebrews and Revelation because they thought these books taught inappropriate things (e.g., in Hebrews, the impossibility of returning to Christ after you have left Christianity). But more often than not, the issue was

> The "Muratorian Canon" at the end of the A.D. 100s included the four gospels, Acts, all of Paul's letters, James, 1 and 2 John, Jude, Revelation, and two other works—the Revelation of Peter and the Wisdom of Solomon. Hebrews, 1 and 2 Peter, and 3 John were not included.

whether these were just good books in general or whether they were authoritative *Scripture*. No one, for example, thought that 1 Clement was a bad letter; indeed, some thought it should be a part of the canon. In the end, it was excluded from the New Testament because the church did

not think it was *as* authoritative as, for example, Paul's letters were.

Further, we should not think that some committee just sat down one day and took a vote on these matters. The decision of the Council of Carthage in A.D. 397 simply affirmed what had come to be the general consensus of the church at large. We should think of this process of "canonization," as it is called, as a long process of dialogue among Christians in authority around the ancient world.

What Qualified a Book as Scripture?

Several different factors came into play as the church was deciding which books were authoritative for Christianity. Who the author was, how long the book had been around, whether it taught the right things—these factors played an important role. But the process was no doubt more complicated than these questions might suggest. For example, the criteria of the second century may have been slightly different from that of the third. Group dynamics came into play as well, including tensions between groups. Such conflicts no doubt led some groups to resist books accepted by others.

If you believe that God had a hand in the formation of the canon, then He must have been in this process, directing things toward their final result. If so,

> Some of the key criteria for accepting a book into the canon were authorship, antiquity, and orthodoxy. The author should be linked in some way to an original apostle, the book should be written by one of the earliest Christians, and it should teach correct ideas.

was it important that the intentions and thought processes of the church be correct in order for us to accept their conclusions as legitimate? Or did God direct the process toward its ultimate conclusion despite the understandings *or misunderstandings* of the humans involved? These are interesting questions for Christians to ask.

The Christians of the A.D. 100s do not seem to have been as definitive as later generations would be in considering standards for what constituted a book as Scripture. Two of the gospels in our New Testament are attributed to Matthew and John, followers of Jesus while he was on earth—Jesus' **disciples**.[7] The belief that Matthew and John wrote them assured these books a place in the canon; they had the right authors. Mark and Luke were not Jesus' disciples, but their gospels were connected respectively to the apostles Peter and Paul. Perhaps the longstanding use of these four gospels by the church—that is, their antiquity and connection with mainstream Christianity—

disciples: Followers of Jesus while He was on earth.

would have ensured their canonicity regardless of their authors. Nevertheless, a concern arose to connect them with important **apostles**, followers of Jesus who led the way in the spread of Christianity. This connection ensured their place in the canon.

Paul's writings were collected and used even earlier than the gospels. Indeed, we have no record of any ancient Christian debating their authority. Even in regard to 1 and 2 Timothy and Titus—the Pastoral Epistles—we have little debate, although they do not appear in the literature of Christianity until the middle of the second century (the A.D. 100s).[8] Many scholars believe these books to have been written by a second-century Christian, perhaps to address a perceived lack of order in

apostles: A group of early Christians who saw Jesus after He rose from the dead. The New Testament primarily refers to Jesus' disciples by this term, but the word can also be used of others like Paul who took leading roles in the spread of Christianity.

some churches. Using the name of a deceased authority figure as a pseudonym was a fairly common practice at that time, and some scholars believe the church of that day was open to this practice—as long as it was done by an appropriate authority with an appropriate teaching.[9] Whether pseudonymous or not, we have no evidence that the Pastoral Epistles faced opposition by the mainstream of Christianity.

The last books of the New Testament—Hebrews, the General Epistles, and Revelation—gave rise to the most debate. It is in regard to these and other writings of the period that questions of authorship, antiquity, and orthodoxy seem to have become most important in the A.D. 200s and 300s. Nevertheless, many of these books were quickly accepted—even books like 1 John and 1 Peter.

The book of Hebrews gives us a good illustration of the factors involved in the process of canonization. Hebrews is anonymous—it nowhere names its author—although in the second century it increasingly came to be associated with the apostle Paul. That is, at least the Eastern Mediterranean part of the church came to believe Paul authored it. Most Christians in Rome and the Western Mediterranean considered it to be a good book, but they resisted the idea that Paul wrote it. Eventually the decision about its authorship seems to have played a role in its acceptance as Scripture. The Eastern half of the Roman world, for example, seems to have had no problem with its "canonicity." It is probably no coincidence that the Western half also accepted Hebrews into the canon at about the same time they accepted Paul as its author.

This example demonstrates some of the dynamics involved in the decision-making process. On the one hand, there was the question of authorship and the desire to link the writings of the New Testament with the original apostles. On the other hand, group dynamics were at play as East and West disagreed in part just to disagree.

orthodoxy: Correct teaching as it is understood by the mainstream, as opposed to **heresy**, which is incorrect teaching.

A further issue is the question of **orthodoxy** or "correct teaching." This is in contrast to **heresy** or "incorrect teaching." Passages in Hebrews seem to teach that one cannot return to Christianity after one has committed **apostasy**—that is, made a definitive break with Christianity. This issue was hotly debated in the middle A.D. 200s when some Christians betrayed their communities to the government by renouncing Christ and turning in fellow Christians, some of whom were killed for

apostasy: Abandoning or rejecting Christianity after having previously been a Christian.

their beliefs. Many did not wish to take such traitors back after the persecution died down, but others argued that God would forgive the apostates.

Eventually, the church made it policy to take them back. In this light, we can see why some questioned the orthodoxy of Hebrews.

The book of Hebrews thus raises the question we asked earlier about the whole process of canonization. Authorship seems to have played an important role in the church's discussion concerning whether or not to include Hebrews in the canon. It very well may have been the belief that Paul authored it that secured its place in the canon. And yet it is nearly the unanimous verdict of scholars that Hebrews was not written by Paul. Did Hebrews get in, therefore, on the basis of a mistake? One might claim that the hearts of the early Christians knew it should be included—they simply found a way for their heads to agree, even though their thoughts were incorrect. But Hebrews raises the question of God's direction in the process. Did God work not only with the understandings of the church, but also around its misunderstandings?

deuterocanonical: "In a second canon" to the other books of the Old and New Testament.

A final issue is worth mentioning. Many Christians consider the Bible to be the ultimate authority on any matter of faith and practice. But many of these same Christians downplay the significance of the church and their fellow Christians as sources of authority as well. Yet, as we can see, those who believe the Bible to be authoritative must also believe that God led the church in the right direction in the process of canonization. That is, there would be no Bible if there had been no church. What does this say about the role the church has played (and still plays) in determining the authority of Scripture for Christians?

For some readers, this whole process will seem very human. It involves personalities, groups, ideas, and traditions, all interacting with one another in a series of causes and effects. For others, this process demonstrates God's church carefully verifying the inspiration of the books it was already using as authoritative, doing so with a care and caution befitting a sincere seeking of

God's will. Perhaps a third group will strike a middle position and see in this process God stooping to the weakness of His people once again, a God-directed process that worked despite whatever human politics and misunderstandings might have been involved. The important thing was the end result toward which God was working.

Things to Think About

1. Were the books of the New Testament written in the order in which they now appear?

2. Were they written all at once or over a period of several years?

3. How long after the books of the New Testament were written did it take before someone came up with exactly the same list of authoritative books for the New Testament that we now believe is correct? Which books were most debated? What are some other books that did not make the final "cut"?

4. In deciding which book of the New Testament was written first, what are the top two candidates?

5. What individual's poor collection of books may have inspired other Christians to move toward an authoritative list of "canonical" books?

6. What were some of the criteria that played into the church's decisions about whether a book qualified as Scripture or not?

7. Do you think it is possible that some books of the New Testament got "in" on the basis of misunderstandings—e.g., did Hebrews get in because early Christians thought Paul wrote it? Does God work through human misunderstanding as well as through human understanding?

Key Terms
apostasy
apostle
canon
deuterocanonical
disciple
heresy
orthodoxy
Scripture

8. Which came first—the Bible as Scripture or the church? Given that Protestants often try to eliminate the role the church plays in the authority of Scripture, what do we make of the fact that it was through the church that God "created" Scripture? Does this place more authority in God's church than in the text of the New Testament?

endnotes

1. The process of setting limits on the Old Testament canon was longer and more complicated. On the one hand, the books the Jews came to consider authoritative are the same as the books most Protestants today accept as the books of the Old Testament. However, for over a thousand years Christians also used several additional books, a group of books known as the Apocrypha. The man responsible for the most important Latin translation of the Bible, Jerome, placed these writings in a second category as **deuterocanonical**—in a "second canon" to the other books of the Old and New Testament. While he believed they were uplifting and beneficial, he considered their authority to be secondary to the other books. The Roman Catholic Church made its official decision about the canonicity of these at the Council of Trent in 1545, accepting seven books not contained in the Jewish canon, as well as several additions to the books of Daniel and Esther. The Greek Orthodox Church accepts even more books as canonical than those accepted by Roman Catholics.
2. First Thessalonians was written ca. A.D. 50; "ca. 50" means "around the year 50."
3. Some scholars do not believe that Paul himself wrote the letter to the Colossians.
4. This is one reason some scholars think 2 Peter is pseudonymous—written in the name of Peter but not by Peter. There are no other Christian writings before the middle of the A.D. 100s that clearly refer to New Testament writings as Scripture.
5. The terms "Old Testament" and "New Testament" are obviously Christian in origin (see chapter 3 of this text). No non-Christian Jew would refer to the Hebrew Scriptures as the "Old" Testament. The earliest clear reference to two Testaments in this way dates from the early Christian Tertullian, who wrote in the late second/early third century. However, traces of the idea can be found earlier.
6. Marcion believed that the God of the Old Testament was not the same being as the Father of Jesus Christ. Since Marcion held that matter was evil, he could not believe that the Creator of the world could be the same being as the Father to whom Jesus prayed. Marcion's teachings are one variety of the second-century heresy known as Gnosticism.

7. All four of the gospels are technically anonymous, since the names of their authors appear nowhere in their texts. The titles were attached to them after they were written.
8. They do not seem to have been on Marcion's list, for example.
9. Conservative scholars strongly tend to reject the notion of pseudonymous writings in the New Testament.

CHAPTER 5

Why Are There So Many Different Bibles?

*We need not be troubled about the original wording of the Bible—
scholarship has done its homework.*

The "Real" Bible

It would not take long at your average bookstore to realize the incredible number of Bibles available in today's market. Not only do we have the old favorite, the King James Version (KJV), but we also have the New King James (NKJV), the New American Standard (NASB), the New Revised Standard (NRSV), the New English Bible (NEB), the New International Version (NIV), not to mention the version used for quotations in this book—the New Living Translation (NLT). But this list just scratches the surface. There are countless other translations of the Bible in English alone, as well as English "Study Bibles" galore, which are Bibles equipped with all kinds of study tools for better understanding the Bible.

At a Glance

• We do not have the "first editions" of any New Testament book.

• The copies, or manuscripts, of the New Testament that we do have sometimes differ significantly from one another.

• Some translations, such as the King James Version, differ from other versions because they rely on different manuscripts.

• Other versions differ because they try to express the ancient words in ways we can more easily understand today.

• There is often ambiguity in the original meaning that makes possible more than one translation of the same words.

Among these are the Serendipity Bible, the Max Lucado Bible, the NIV Study Bible, the Thompson Chain Reference Bible, and the list goes on. The uninitiated could get really confused—will the real Bible please stand up?

If you were raised on one of these versions, like the King James Version, other surprises await you when reading a modern translation. Perhaps you grew up saying the Lord's Prayer and happen to run into it while reading Matthew 6 in a modern translation. You start quoting it aloud and are all ready to say, "for thine is the kingdom and the power and the glory forever"—until you realize it is not in the version you are reading! Perhaps you are reading Mark 16 in the NIV and suddenly come upon this bracketed comment: "The earliest manuscripts and some other ancient witnesses do not have Mark 16:9-20." And an observant reader of Acts 8 may just notice that the story goes straight from verse 36 to 38—what happened to verse 37?

Textual Criticism

These minor variations reflect one aspect of the process by which we came to have the Bible as we know it today. The New Testament was originally written in Greek. But the "original **manuscripts**"—the very first copies of such books as Matthew, Mark, Luke, and John— almost certainly disintegrated into dust long ago. We have thousands of manuscripts of the New Testament books, but these are copies of copies of copies of copies. And no two of these manuscripts have exactly the same words as the others. Most of them were copied between the years A.D. 900–1500, a thousand years after the books were first written.

manuscript: An ancient document written by hand. Over five thousand handwritten Greek manuscripts, copies of portions of the New Testament, have survived to today.

It can be unsettling to hear of the diversity of manuscripts and the variations among them. This information can make those Christians who base their

Christianity on the Bible a little nervous, to say the least. Those looking for ammunition use this fact to argue against the Bible as a true authority. Others retreat into a "King James Only" stance, seeing in the more recent translations a conspiracy to corrupt the true faith.

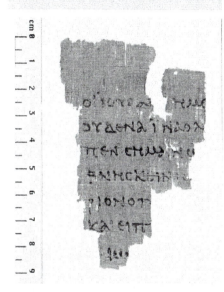

textual criticism: That branch of New Testament studies that aims at recovering the exact wording of the original texts of the Bible.

But not to worry—scholars are actually very confident about the overwhelming majority of variations among the manuscripts we have. A branch of New Testament studies called **textual criticism** is devoted to the science of figuring out what the first editions likely said.[1] Thus, there is no need to be troubled about the original wording of the Bible—scholarship has done its homework.

While most of the manuscripts we have are late, copied over a thousand years after the New Testament was written, we do have a number of very old manuscripts. For example, the oldest one is a tiny fragment of John

The oldest New Testament manuscript, dating to ca. A.D. 125.
(Reproduced by courtesy of the Director and Librarian, the John Rylands University Library of Manchester.)

18 that may date as early as A.D. 125, about thirty years after the original letter was written. It is not really that unusual for the oldest surviving manuscript of an ancient work to have been copied hundreds or even a thousand years after the original. After all, do you think the letters you write would survive a thousand years? The earliest copies of Plato's writings, for example, come well over a thousand years after Plato lived, yet no one would seriously question whether these manuscripts are at least basically accurate.

Further, most of the variations among the biblical manuscripts are insignificant and have resulted from simple errors that were inevitable as each manuscript was copied by hand. Maybe two lines ended with the same word and the copyist's eye skipped from one line to the next, causing him to omit a line. Since many manuscripts were copied in halls as a reader read them aloud to a group of copyists, sometimes a copyist would mishear and write down the wrong word. Sometimes someone would smooth out or edit a rough or ambiguous original. Others relied on their memories rather than the text they were copying. Copyists might take comments someone had written in the margins and put them somewhere in the text. Still other copyists, faced with more than one reading in the manuscripts in front of them, combined them into one long passage.

> The general rule for finding the original wording of a passage from the New Testament is to choose the wording that best explains how the other variations among the manuscripts would have come into existence.

There were countless, predictable reasons for many of the mistakes that were made. Being aware of these common ways in which variations arose, scholars can make good decisions about how the original probably read. The general rule is to choose the wording that best explains how the other readings in the manuscripts came about. Those who translated the Bible into English in the 1500s, as well as those who completed the King James Version in 1611, had only "late" copies of the New Testament at their disposal. A man named Erasmus referred to about a dozen Greek manuscripts in deciding what the New Testament originally said. However, the earliest of these had been copied in the A.D. 900s—over eight hundred years after the New Testament was written. Since the 1500s we have discovered copies of New Testament books

> Because of the discoveries of the last century and a half, we can now determine the wording of the original Bible more accurately than ever before.

that predate by a thousand years most of the copies he used. Modern versions are thus based on the earliest manuscripts we have available.

When you have grown up using a Bible like the King James Version, it is easy to think the modern versions have taken words out of the Bible. After all, some of the words you grew up with are not in these modern versions. In reality, the King James Version is based on manuscripts that *added* verses that were not in the first copies of the New Testament. The KJV is based on Greek manuscripts that had embellished the original text by adding words that made the New Testament clearer and smoother.

A minority of scholars still defends the Greek text behind the King James Version as being more original. This text is closely related to the Greek and Latin text the church used from the A.D. 300s on. Since most of the earliest copies of the New Testament have long since disintegrated, it is understandable that the majority of manuscripts read this way, since most of these were copied in the late Middle Ages. But scholars who defend this form of the text maintain their position based on theological reasons rather than on the evidence. They do not believe God would have allowed the majority of manuscripts to deviate from the originals, even on details that do not change the overall meaning. Some of you may share their concerns and want to do some further research on the topic.

Therefore, one reason we have so many different Bibles is because we have

> Modern translations do not take words out of the Bible or change them. Rather, older versions like the King James Version were based on traditions that had embellished and added to the original text.

different approaches to the various manuscripts available. The King James Version and the New King James (which updates the earlier English of the King James) are based on the textual tradition that the church used from the 300s to the early 1800s. Other versions utilize older, more recently discovered manuscripts to recreate the original text with more accuracy.

Different Approaches to Translation

Chapter 2 of this text explains some of the reasons why just *one* translation is impossible when going from one language to another. Sometimes Christians assume that knowing Greek or Hebrew will clear up all questions about a verse they do not understand in English. Take the verse in which the apostle Paul says, "I thank God that I speak in tongues more than all of you" (1 Cor. 14:18). Some would say that "tongues" here means human languages, while others believe that Paul referred to angelic languages unintelligible to the human ear. The Greek does not make the meaning any clearer: the word *tongues* simply means "languages." The Greek word does not tell us what kinds of languages are meant—or even if Paul meant the word *languages* to be taken literally.

As this example illustrates, it is often possible to translate the same word in different ways. Take these two translations of Romans 3:25:

The New Living Translation:
"God sent Jesus to take the punishment for our sins and to satisfy God's anger against us."

Today's English Version:
"God offered him, so that by his sacrificial death he should become the means by which people's sins are forgiven . . ."

These two versions do their best to bring out the meaning of the verse. But they have expanded the original wording and meaning to try to help us understand it.

The translations in the column on the next page stick more closely to the original wording. The first two of these versions no doubt leave most people wondering what "expiation" or "propitiation" means. Most English speakers do not use words like these. Yet these versions come the closest to the words of the original Greek.

These passages reflect two basic approaches to translation. One tries to stay as close as possible to the sentence structure and words of the original Greek. These are what might be called **formal equivalence** translations. Versions such as the Revised Standard or the New American Standard Bible present the reader with a fairly good look at the way the Greek text was arranged.[2] Yet, these versions are often difficult for today's average reader to understand.

On the other hand, **dynamic equivalence** translations attempt to find words that convey the spirit of

> **The Revised Standard Version:**
> "[Christ Jesus], whom God put forward as an expiation . . ."
>
> **King James Version:**
> ". . . whom God hath set forth to be a propitiation . . ."
>
> **The New International Version:**
> "God presented him as a sacrifice of atonement . . ."

> **formal equivalence:** The attempt of a translation to stick closely to the wording and sentence structure of the original languages.
>
> **dynamic equivalence:** The attempt to catch the spirit of the original meaning in readable English that makes sense on our cultural terms.

the original meaning in terms we can understand in our culture. The New Living Translation and New International Version, for example, have tried their best to bring the basic meaning of the original into English. Of course, these versions can thus be somewhat deceptive, since the precise meaning of the Bible cannot be expressed exactly in our cultural terms. These versions can only approximate the spirit of the original meaning at best.

Things to Think About

1. Do we have any of the original copies of the books of the New Testament?

2. Of the thousands of New Testament manuscripts that we have, do any agree completely with one another?

Key Terms

dynamic equivalence
formal equivalence
manuscript
textual criticism

3. Which translations of the Bible do most scholars think are based on manuscripts whose wording in Greek and Hebrew comes closest to the first copies of the Bible? Would they select versions like the KJV and NKJV, or those like the NRSV, NIV, NLT, etc.?

4. Where the Greek and Hebrew texts behind the various translations are the same, which versions stick most closely to the original wording and sentence structure: formal equivalence translations like the KJV and NRSV, or dynamic equivalence translations like the NIV and NLT?

5. What is the general rule for deciding the original wording of the New Testament?

6. If God allowed the wording of the Bible to change over time—in fact, allowed the church to use a different text for over a thousand years—does this imply that God is not concerned with the exact words of Scripture, but with its overall message instead?

7. Why do you think some continue to maintain that the Greek and Hebrew texts behind the KJV are more original?

8. Why do you think so many churches and scholars today seem to locate the authority of Scripture in its original wording rather than in the text God allowed the church to use for over a thousand years? Should the story of the woman caught in adultery in John 8 stay a part of Scripture, even though it probably was not originally in John? After all, the church has used this story for over fifteen hundred years.

endnotes

1. The word criticism in this context does not mean that one "cuts down" or is critical of the Bible. Textual criticism has to do with making decisions about the text of the New Testament, not with being critical of it.

2. The King James and New King James Versions are also excellent formal equivalence translations. While they are based on manuscripts that are not as accurate as those used by other translations, these two versions stick closely to the Greek and Hebrew of the manuscripts upon which they are based.

༄

For Further Study

Introductions to the New Testament
- Achtemeier, Paul J., Joel B. Green, and Marianne Meye Thompson. *Introducing the New Testament: Its Literature and Theology.* Grand Rapids: Eerdmans, 2001.

- Brown, Raymond E. *An Introduction to the New Testament.* New York: Doubleday, 1997.

- Gundry, Robert H. *A Survey of the New Testament.* 3d ed. Grand Rapids: Zondervan, 1994.

- Guthrie, Donald. *New Testament Introduction.* Downers Grove, IL: InterVarsity, 1970.

- Harris, Stephen L. *The New Testament: A Student's Introduction.* 4th ed. Boston: McGraw Hill, 2002.

How to Read the Bible
- Caird, G. B. *The Language and Imagery of the Bible.* Grand Rapids: Eerdmans, 1980.

- Fee, Gordon D. and Douglas Stuart. *How to Read the Bible for All Its Worth.* 2d ed. Grand Rapids: Zondervan, 1993.

- Thompson, David L. *Bible Study That Works.* Nappanee, IN: Evangel, 1994.

The Genres of New Testament Books
- Aune, David E. *The New Testament in Its Literary Environment.* Philadelphia: Westminster John Knox, 1987.

The New Testament Canon
- Bruce, F. F. *The Canon of Scripture*. Downers Grove, IL: InterVarsity, 1988.

- von Campenhausen, Hans. *The Formation of the Christian Bible*. London: Adam and Charles Black, 1972.

- Wegner, Paul D. *The Journey from Texts to Translations: The Origin and Development of the Bible*. Grand Rapids: Baker, 1999.

Texts and Translations of the New Testament
- Aland, Kurt and Barbara Aland. *The Text of the New Testament*. Translated by Erroll G. Rhodes. Grand Rapids: Eerdmans, 1987.

- Metzger, Bruce M. *The Text of the New Testament: Its Transmission, Corruption, and Restoration*. New York: Oxford University, 1968.

- Wegner, Paul D. *The Journey from Texts to Translations: The Origin and Development of the Bible*. Grand Rapids: Baker, 1999.

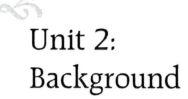

Unit 2:
Background

Chapters 6–12

CHAPTER 6

The Story Behind the Story: From Abraham to Moses

The early Christians did not see themselves as part of a new religion but as the true ending to the Jewish story.

Stories That Tell Who We Are

Although you may never have thought about it, we identify who we are to a great extent by the stories we tell about ourselves. Your life is one long story with numerous episodes. Some of those episodes capture who you are better than others, although our stories can be told in many different ways. We usually focus on episodes that compliment us when we are presenting ourselves to others. Someone else might focus on events that embarrass us or bring out our weak points. In either case, a person without a story is to some extent a person without an identity.

Western culture differs from other cultures in that we tell far more stories about ourselves as individuals than we do about the groups to which we belong. We want someone to judge us on our own merits, not because of what we look like or who our family is. To us,

---

At a Glance

• The story behind the story of the New Testament begins with a man named Abraham. The twelve sons of his grandson Israel gave rise to twelve tribes.

• God led these twelve tribes out of slavery in Egypt to a land He had promised to their forefather Abraham.

• God made a solemn agreement—a covenant—with Israel at Mt. Sinai. We refer to this covenant as the Law.

• Since God chose Israel exclusively from all the nations to be His people, they were to serve Him alone. He promised to prosper them if they would keep this agreement.

stereotypes often involve prejudice, which we consider highly inappropriate.

However, the ancients identified themselves extensively by the **groups** to which they belonged—by things like gender, race, and family background. This **collectivist culture** is still the case in most places outside the Western world today. In the world of the Bible, someone who was an "independent thinker"—something we prize—was a misfit, a danger to society.

group or "collectivist" cultures: Cultures in which identity is primarily a function of the groups to which an individual belongs—such as one's race, family, or gender.

It surprises some people to learn that Jesus and the first Christians were Jews. An understanding of the New Testament's original meaning is incomplete without knowing something about the Judaism that preceded it. Christianity sprang from the roots of Judaism, and the words of the New Testament constantly draw from that background. Therefore, we must know something about the Jewish story—the story that Jews of Jesus' day told to identify who they were as a group—in order to understand the New Testament appropriately. The story of the Jewish people is thus the "story behind the story" of the New Testament.

Beginnings

The story behind the identity of ancient Jews started with a man named Abraham. According to the story, God picked out Abraham from all the people of his day some 2,000 years before the birth of Christ (Gen. 12:1-3). After bringing Abraham out of his home to a foreign land, God promised to make his offspring into a great nation. God even promised to give Abraham's descendants the very land in which Abraham then found himself a stranger, a land later called Palestine.[1] Finally, God gave Abraham a special symbol of their relationship, **circumcision**. All of the male descendants of Abraham were to be circumcised soon after they were born (Gen. 17:1-14).

> **circumcision:** The cutting off of the foreskin; a sign of the special relationship between God and the sons of Abraham.

Abraham's grandson Jacob was later renamed "Israel." The nation of **Israel** and the Jews would eventually descend from this man. Jacob himself had twelve sons, who gave rise to twelve tribes, twelve different clans of people who would eventually inherit twelve distinct regions of land in Palestine.[2] Because of a famine,

> **Israel:** Originally the name of Abraham's grandson, it would become the name of his descendants and the nation they constituted.

the family of Jacob migrated to Egypt where food was available (Gen. 46:1-7). At first they lived there peacefully and comfortably, but soon they found themselves slaves to the Egyptians and to Egypt's ruler, the Pharaoh.

In these early stories, the Jews found some of the most basic aspects of their identity. For example, they called themselves "Israel" after Jacob

> **Yahweh:** God's proper name in the Old Testament, usually translated LORD in all capital letters.

and the twelve tribes that descended from him. They also identified themselves as "sons of Abraham," even arguing among themselves at times about who the "true" sons of Abraham were.

Circumcision was perhaps the most important indicator that a male was a Jew. At the time of Christ, it also stood as one of the biggest obstacles for someone who was thinking about "converting" to Judaism.[3] It is thus no surprise that one of the biggest debates in the early years of

Christianity was whether non-Jews needed to be circumcised before they could become Christians.

The Exit from Egypt

Some of the most significant events in the Jewish story occurred when the Israelites escaped from slavery in Egypt and made their way through the desert toward Canaan, the name by which Palestine was known before Israel inhabited it.[4] In the story, God guided them out of slavery through the leadership of an Israelite named Moses.[5] At first Moses negotiated with Pharaoh so that Israel could offer sacrifices in the desert to Israel's God, whose name was **Yahweh**. But even after God brought nine plagues—including such things as frogs, lice, darkness, and blood in the drinking water—Pharaoh refused to let them go.

The tenth and final plague was the one that convinced Pharaoh. Moses instructed the Israelites to kill a lamb and place some of its blood on the doorposts of their houses. At midnight, the "angel of death" went through the land of Egypt, killing the firstborn sons of any house not marked in this way, including the house of Pharaoh. When the angel found a house with blood on the doorpost, he "passed over" that house. For this reason, Jews today

Passover: The most important Jewish festival, Passover celebrates the day when the death angel "passed over" the sons of the Israelites before they escaped from Egypt.

celebrate a yearly feast called **Passover** to commemorate the fact that God saved their sons from death and rescued them from slavery.[6]

Pharaoh finally released the Israelites, only to change his mind after they had left. Before they had traveled far, they discovered that Pharaoh's army was bearing down on them. Many of you will be familiar with the story of how the Israelites crossed the Red Sea.[7] God enabled Israel to cross this sea on dry ground by piling up the water on both sides of them like walls. But God allowed the army of the Egyptians to drown when he returned the waters to their original place.

This departure from Egypt is known as the **exodus**, which basically means "exit." For Jews, it symbolizes the power of God to deliver them out of oppression, as well as His love for them above all the peoples of the earth. Even further, it came to define Israel's attitude toward the oppressed. Some of ancient Israel's laws commanded kindness toward foreigners who might find themselves living outside their homeland (e.g., Deut. 24:17-18).

This part of the Jewish story is especially significant as it relates to the New Testament. Christianity makes an important connection

exodus: The victorious departure of Israel from Egypt to freedom.

between Passover and Easter, the day that Christians believe Jesus came back from the dead. Jesus died on the day of Passover. The apostle Paul even calls Jesus the "Passover Lamb" (1 Cor. 5:7). Similarly, the book of John calls Jesus the "Lamb of God who takes away the sin of the world" (John 1:29), imagery also used in the book of Revelation (e.g., Rev. 5:6).

All these passages indicate that Jesus' death prevents *us* from experiencing God's judgment, just as the blood on the doorposts in Egypt saved the Israelites from the death angel.[8] You can see how closely connected the Christian story is to the Jewish story. The early Christians did not see themselves as part of a new religion but as the true ending to the Jewish story.

The Giving of the Law

Another crucial event in the story of Israel took place just after the Israelites escaped Egypt. On Mt. Sinai God presented Moses with the Law,

> **the covenant:** The solemn agreement between God and Israel. He would bless them if they kept His commandments.

the code of conduct by which the Israelites were to live in order to enjoy the protection and blessing of Yahweh.[9] God and Israel made a solemn agreement, a **covenant**. If Israel would serve Yahweh alone as its God, God would bless Israel with a land of its own and prosper its people.

The Law was at the heart of what it meant to be a Jew. The Ten Commandments are the best-known part of the Law, including such commands as "Thou shalt not kill" and "Thou shalt not steal" (Exod. 20:13, 15 KJV). But the Law was much more than just these commands. Jews often refer to the first five books of the Old Testament—or **Pentateuch**—as the Law.

> **Pentateuch:** The first five books of the Old Testament—Genesis, Exodus, Leviticus, Numbers, and Deuteronomy. According to Jewish tradition, Moses authored all five of these books.

The Law also included a great deal of civil legislation, laws that related to successful living with one another. What would happen if your bull gored someone to death (Exod. 21:28)? Would a man have to pay a "bride-price" to the father of a virgin he seduced (Exod. 22:16)? These legal questions were a part of the Jewish Law.

There was also much concerning the appropriate offering of sacrifices and the proper maintenance of Israel's relationship with God. How were sacrifices to be made (Leviticus 1–7)? In what kind of structure or sanctuary were they to be offered, and what items should the structure contain (Exodus 25–27)? When were sacrifices to be offered, and on what days was Israel to celebrate special religious feasts (Leviticus 23)?

Finally, a great deal of the Law dealt with distinctions that set off Israel as a special people different from other nations; that is, as a people belonging strictly to Yahweh. This category included rules concerning the foods Israel was not allowed to eat (Leviticus 11), as well as some sexual taboos (Leviticus 18). As previously mentioned, circumcision was perhaps the most important practice that distinguished Jewish males from the males of many other races.

Interestingly enough, Jews at the time of Christ had several different views on what the Law meant for them. For example, a group known as the Samaritans had a version of the Pentateuch that differed significantly from the version used by more mainstream Jews. Another group called the Pharisees followed a well-developed oral tradition that extended and supplemented the Law considerably.[10] On the other hand, a group known as the Sadducees had a much more limited understanding of what the Law entailed. They were more conservative in their beliefs and politics than the Pharisees, who taught many things that the Law did not even mention—like the idea of resurrection. We will say more about these groups in chapter 8. Because of the diversity of Jewish views regarding the Law, we will not be surprised to find some diversity in the way the early Christians looked at the Jewish Law as well.

The importance of the Law for Judaism can hardly be underestimated: it is fundamental to what it means to be a Jew. Since Jewish tradition teaches that God delivered the Law through Moses, he is one of the most important figures in the Jewish story, if not the most important. He is known primarily as the lawgiver of Israel, the one through whom God made the covenant. It is no surprise to find that the New Testament compares Jesus to Moses as the giver of a *new* covenant and as one who far surpasses Moses in significance (e.g., Heb. 3:1-6).

Although Moses led the Israelites out of slavery in Egypt, he was not the one who led them into the land God had promised to Abraham—the Promised Land. Only two individuals out of all those who had escaped Egypt lived long enough to enter the land of Canaan. Even though they easily could have completed the trip in under a month, the Israelites spent forty years wandering in the desert between Egypt and Canaan. According to the story, this delay was due to their lack of trust in Yahweh to give them military success against the people that already inhabited the Promised Land. So all but two of the original participants in the exodus died without having reached their goal. Even Moses died just short of entering the Promised Land.[11]

Jews thought of Moses primarily as the great lawgiver, the one through whom God made a covenant with Israel.

Here we see the basic dynamics of Yahweh's relationship with Israel, as the Jews understood that relationship. Yahweh had chosen or "elected" Israel out of all the nations of the world. As a result, Israel was to serve Him exclusively out of all the other gods of the earth. This service primarily consisted of keeping His commands as they were found in the Law. If they kept this covenant arrangement, Yahweh promised to bless them, not least by letting them control their land. Unfortunately, they would fail Yahweh in the years to come.

Things to Think About

1. If you have heard this story before (from Abraham to Moses), did you learn anything new in this chapter, such as a perspective you had never heard before?

2. How do you define yourself? As an individual with certain unique characteristics, likes, and dislikes? Or as a member of various groups: a Christian, a female, an athlete, a Republican?

Key Terms
circumcision
collectivist culture
covenant
exodus
Israel
Passover
Pentateuch
Yahweh

3. Have you ever thought seriously about how central the Law was in the Old Testament and in God's relationship with His people? Put yourself in an ancient Israelite's shoes—would you ever have expected God to "change the rules"?

endnotes

1. I use the term "Palestine" because it is recognizable. However, the Romans promoted the term out of hatred for the Jews after their second revolt (ca. A.D. 135). The defeat of the Jews resulted in their banishment from Jerusalem and the subsequent renaming of the region after the archenemies of ancient Israel—the Philistines.

2. Because of the role God assigned to the tribe of Levi as priests, they did not receive land. Another son, Joseph, received two portions of land by way of his two sons.

3. The fact that circumcision was the most important "boundary marker" between a Jew and a non-Jew indicates how male-oriented the ancient world was.

4. The most important events in this part of the story are found in the book of Exodus, particularly chapters 4–20.

5. An Israelite is a descendant of Israel (Jacob).

6. It is difficult for us today to condone the killing of innocent children, even if they are the children of our enemies. As we have noted, however, the ancient world was a group-oriented culture in which the whole group shared guilt, not just the guilty individual. Therefore, in the eyes of ancient Jews, an "innocent" newborn Egyptian son was guilty of the sins of Egypt simply because he was an Egyptian.

7. The original Hebrew of the Old Testament actually refers to a "Reed Sea" rather than the Red Sea. For whatever reason, the Greek translators of the Old Testament changed it to the "Red Sea," which is how every child who grows up in church learns this famous story.

8. Some modern readers may find the references to blood in the Bible distasteful, but offering sacrifices was a nearly universal practice in the ancient world. It was the way one made peace with the gods. It is thus not surprising that God would reveal himself to the peoples of the Bible in this way.

9. This story is found for the most part in Exodus 19–24.

10. For example, while the Law has some basic comments on what it means to observe the "Sabbath"—the period from sundown Friday to sundown Saturday during which Jews do no work—the Pharisees followed a tradition that provided numerous additional guidelines to specify exactly what was to be considered as "work." One rule even specified how far you could walk from your house before you had "worked."

11. These parts of the story are found in the books of Numbers and Deuteronomy.

CHAPTER 7

The Story Behind the Story: From Promised Land to No Land

Most Jews probably thought of a messiah or son of God in human terms, a political ruler who would defeat the enemies of Israel, particularly Rome.

The Four Pillars

The Law, particularly the Old Testament book of Deuteronomy, presents us with what one scholar has called the "four pillars" of Judaism—four concepts that capture the heart of how many Jews at the time of Christ understood their relationship with God.[1] The passage from Deuteronomy below gives us a glimpse of all four.

The first two pillars that show up in the passage are (1) God's exclusive **election** of Israel and (2) the fact that Israel must serve Yahweh exclusively—**monotheism**. These are two sides of the same coin: it is an exclusive pairing of Yahweh and Israel. Some modern readers, even Christian readers, may find it arrogant or presumptuous of the Jews to believe that God specifically chose them as His people over and against all the other

At a Glance

- The four pillars of Judaism were monotheism, election, covenant, and land.

- King David became the ideal king for the Jews.

- King Solomon built the temple in Jerusalem.

- The New Testament titles "Son of David," "Christ," and "Son of God" are royal titles that originate in the Old Testament.

- Israel was destroyed because it did not keep the covenant.

- The Maccabees led a successful revolt against the Syrians, giving the Jews about one hundred years of freedom (165–63 B.C.).

> "The LORD did not **choose** you and lavish his love on you because you were larger or greater than other nations, for you were the smallest of all nations! It was simply because the LORD loves you, and because he was keeping the oath he had sworn to your ancestors. That is why the LORD rescued you with such amazing power from your slavery under Pharaoh in Egypt. Understand, therefore, **that the LORD your God is indeed God.** He is the faithful God who keeps his **covenant** for a thousand generations and constantly loves those who love him and obey his commands. But he does not hesitate to punish and destroy those who hate him. Therefore, obey all these commands, laws, and regulations I am giving you today. If you listen to these regulations and obey them faithfully . . . he will love you and **bless you and make you into a great nation.**"
>
> **Deuteronomy 7:7-13**

nations of the earth. Yet this is clearly what the Old and New Testaments teach.

Of course, there are parts of the Old Testament that open up the blessings of Yahweh to other peoples as well. In the book of Jonah, for example, Yahweh blesses the Assyrians, one of the archenemies of Israel. It is important to remember that in the days of the Old Testament, people did not decide which gods to worship. Different peoples worshiped different gods. Each nation had its own "patron deity," the god that looked out for the well-being and prosperity of that particular people. When two nations went to war, two gods were also going to war.

The Israelites considered themselves blessed to have the greatest of all gods as their divine patron—Yahweh. Yahweh had chosen them to be His particular people. It was only to be expected that in return they would serve Him only as their God. This relationship was captured in a **covenant** between the two parties, a solemn agreement that if Israel kept the Law, then Yahweh would give the Israelites prosperity.

The focus of this prosperity centered on their **land**. If the Israelites kept the covenant, they would control their land and be free from foreign rule. The reasoning was simple. Yahweh was the most powerful God and could beat the

> "When the Most High assigned lands to the nations, when he divided up the human race, he established the boundaries of the peoples according to the number of angelic beings. For the people of Israel belong to the LORD; Jacob is his special possession."
>
> **Deuteronomy 32:8-9**

god of any other nation. If Israel lost a battle or became enslaved to another nation, the only possible explanation was that the Israelites had broken the covenant. Understanding this way of thinking is key to understanding the background of Christianity.

The Beginnings of a Nation

After Moses died, God used a man named Joshua to lead the Israelites into the Promised Land. Following a series of military victories, the Israelites took possession of Canaan.[2] The next few hundred years brought a tug of war between the tribes of Israel and the surrounding peoples. Israel remained free when it served Yahweh. When the Israelites began to serve other gods, Yahweh enabled their enemies to defeat them. The Old Testament book of Judges is one of the clearest expressions of the four pillars at work in this way. It presents a constantly repeated cycle of freedom to slavery to freedom again, all on the basis of Israel's loyalty or disloyalty to Yahweh.

The Four Pillars of Judaism
- **Monotheism**—Yahweh was the only God Israel could worship.

- **Election**—God chose Israel out of all the nations.

- **Covenant**—an agreement between Yahweh and Israel. If the Israelites followed the Law, God would bless them. If they did not, He would curse them.

- **Land**—what God would give Israel if it followed His commands. The focus of God's presence in the land was the temple in Jerusalem.

> "Hear, O Israel! The LORD is our God, the LORD alone."
>
> **Deuteronomy 6:4**

A little over a thousand years before Christ, Israel made the transition from a loosely connected group of tribes to a nation united under a single king.

Israel's second king, **David**, is very important for our understanding of the New Testament. Not only did David take Jerusalem from its non-Israelite inhabitants and make it the capital of Israel, but he was the first in a dynasty of kings that would ultimately rule for over four hundred years. In keeping with the family orientation of the ancient world, David came to symbolize kingship for

> **David:** The second king of Israel and the first of a long-ruling dynasty. For many Jews at the time of Christ, he symbolized the ideal king.

> **Son of David:** A male descendant of David occupying the throne. In the New Testament, Jesus is referred to as the "Son of David," meaning that He is the king Israel had been awaiting.

many Jews. He was considered the ideal king who had an ideal relationship with Yahweh. At the time of Christ, Israel was without a king. Many looked for another David—a **Son of David**—to come and restore their kingdom to its former glory and boundaries.

David's son **Solomon** also played a significant role in the story behind the New Testament. Before Solomon, Yahweh had been worshiped primarily in a portable tent or "tabernacle." Solomon took on the task of building a permanent temple for Yahweh in Jerusalem. The Old Testament book of Deuteronomy implies that this temple (built on the pattern of the tabernacle) was the only legitimate place to offer sacrifices to Yahweh from that point on.

> **Judah:** After the kingdom of Israel was split into two parts, Judah was the name of the southern kingdom. Since the northern kingdom was obliterated, the Israelites that survived this destruction were largely from Judah. It is thus from this word that the later term "Jew" derives—a descendant of Judah.

The unity of the kingdom disintegrated after the death of Solomon. For the next few hundred years, the Israelites were divided into two different kingdoms. The northern kingdom retained the name "Israel" and constituted the larger nation. The southern kingdom was largely made up of one tribe, **Judah**, from which we actually get the word "Jew." This is the tribe to which David and Solomon had belonged. Thus the "Davidic dynasty" only continued to rule in the southern kingdom. It is in this southern kingdom that the story behind the New Testament continues, for the Assyrians would obliterate the northern kingdom in 722–21 B.C.

Solomon: The third king of Israel. He built the first temple to Yahweh in Jerusalem.

If we are to understand the New Testament, it is important to know a few things about kingship in the Old Testament. Three of the most important "titles" the New Testament uses for Jesus are **Christ, Son of God,** and **Son of David,** all of which are *royal* titles that originate in the Old Testament. If we are unaware of this background, we will probably misunderstand the precise nuances these titles have in the New Testament.

For example, since we refer to Jesus as "Jesus Christ," it would be easy for a modern person to think that Christ was Jesus' last name, like Smith or Jones. But people did not have last names in the ancient world. The word *Christ* actually means "anointed one," a Greek translation of the word *messiah*. In the Old Testament, the phrase "anointed one" referred to someone God had set apart for a special role or purpose, such as a king or high priest.

It is also easy for Christians and even some Jews to believe the word *messiah* always refers to a single individual who brings definitive salvation and judgment to the earth. Christians think of Jesus as that one person who made salvation available to all. Some Jews still believe a messiah will come and usher in a new age.

But the term *anointed one* was used for different kinds of individuals in the Old Testament. In a sense, all of the kings of Judah were *messiahs*—they were "anointed ones" of God (e.g., 1 Sam. 24:10). The book of Isaiah even refers to a pagan king with this term (Cyrus, the Persian), using the exact word Christians would later use of Jesus to mean "Messiah" (Isa. 45:1). The Dead

Sea Scrolls, Jewish literature that was written not long before Jesus was born, expected that a king-messiah would arrive and restore the political kingdom of Israel. But they also looked for the coming of an anointed *priest*, a priest-messiah who would restore a pure temple. Scholars now generally agree that Jews at the time of Christ used the word *messiah* in a number of different ways. Christians to a great extent would create their own unique understanding of this word.

The title *Son of God* is also easily misunderstood. In the Old Testament it is used in several different ways, the most relevant of which is as a title for the kings of Judah.[3] Israel was not unique in considering its kings to be the sons of gods. It was very common to view kings in this way throughout the Near East and the Mediterranean world at that time. With Israel this designation meant the kings had a relationship with Yahweh, that he was the father of the king of Israel (e.g., 2 Sam. 7:14).

> **Son of God:** A term used for the anointed kings of Judah. It indicated that they were in a special relationship with Yahweh, like that of son to father, and that their earthly authority mirrored that of God himself.
>
> "The king proclaims the LORD's decree: 'The LORD said to me, "You are my son. Today I have become your Father. Only ask, and I will give you the nations." ' "
>
> **Psalm 2:7-8**

At one point, the Old Testament even addresses the human king as "God." Psalm 45:6 says of the king, "Your throne, O God, endures forever and ever." Because of this human king's justice and goodness, *the* God "anointed" him as the ruler or "god" of Israel. In the Old Testament, therefore, the title "son of God" shows that the king is in a position of authority that mirrors and represents God himself. It also means the king is in a special relationship with God like that of a son to a father. The king represented God to the people, and he represented the people to God.

Christianity would take these concepts of kingship and develop them well beyond their Old Testament meanings. For example, the Jews were primarily concerned with their own political situation rather than the world at large. Most Jews probably thought of a messiah or son of God in human terms, a political ruler who would defeat the enemies of Israel, particularly Rome. But Christianity would add yet another royal title, **Lord**, to the meaning of Messiah. For Christians, this term meant that Jesus was Son of David, Messiah, and Son of God—

the king par excellence in terms of the nation of Israel. *Lord* also became a cosmic term, one that indicated that Christ was ruler of both heaven and earth, including not only all humans but all spiritual forces as well.

> **Christ/Messiah:** The term translates as "anointed one" and was originally used to refer to someone such as a king or priest who was set apart for a special, divinely appointed role. This person was often installed into office by being "anointed" with oil.

> **Lord:** A term that implied Christ's kingship over heaven and earth and that He is the ruler of all.

A Time of Waiting

In the view of the Hebrew Scriptures, the northern kingdom never served Yahweh appropriately. By setting up shrines in several places in their territory, the people did not worship Yahweh in the correct location. Further, they worshiped gods other than Yahweh. Given the dynamics of the four pillars, it was only a matter of time before God judged them.

In 722–21 B.C., the Assyrians came and obliterated the northern kingdom. Ten of Israel's twelve tribes basically disappeared from the face of the earth, although a group

> **Samaritans:** Those who lived in the region formerly known as the northern kingdom of Israel. They were of ethnically diverse origins, including the race of Israel.

that traced their heritage to Israel would continue to live in the region. These were the **Samaritans**. Even today there are those who claim to be the descendants of this group. Jews at the time of Christ looked down on Samaritans because they were thought to be "half-breeds," tainted by mixture with other races and false beliefs.

Yet the southern kingdom, Judah, did not escape God's judgment either. Judah also failed to keep its covenant with Yahweh. The nation of **Babylon** destroyed Jerusalem and its temple in 586 B.C. The conquering army carried hordes of Israelites back to Babylon as slaves. Unlike the northern kingdom, however, these exiled Israelites managed to keep their identity intact in captivity. After about seventy years, a group or *remnant* returned to Jerusalem.

Babylon: The nation that destroyed Jerusalem and the first temple in 586 B.C., taking many Jews as slaves. Hundreds of years later, Jews and Christians would also use the word "Babylon" to refer to Rome, which destroyed Jerusalem and its second temple in A.D. 70.

But Israel never returned to the former glory and independence it had once enjoyed. For the next few hundred years leading up to New Testament times, the Jews were bounced back and forth from one foreign power to another. The one bright spot in those years was the time of the **Maccabees**, a Jewish family that led a successful revolt against the foreign nation of Syria.

In the last years of the 300s B.C., the Greeks under Alexander the Great conquered all of the Middle East. This included Persia, the nation that controlled the Jews at that time. In its entire

Maccabees: The Jewish family that successfully freed the Jews from Syrian rule, resulting in about a hundred years of freedom.

history, the earth had never been brought together under such an extensive rule and influence. The result would change the face of the world forever. For the first time, a common culture developed that cut across the boundaries of the individual nations. With regard to gods, Greek influence overcame the idea that each nation could only worship its individual gods. This influence helped integrate the nations and created a more unified world, a unity that would later facilitate the spread of Christianity.

In 175 B.C., however, some Jews believed that the Greek influence was threatening to destroy the distinctiveness of Israel and its relationship with Yahweh. For example, some Jews were participating in a Greek "gymnasia" that had been built in Jerusalem. Many underwent an operation to undo their circumcision. The ancient Greeks exercised naked, so one's Jewish identity would have been overwhelmingly obvious in that setting. Those who "erased" the marks of circumcision were thus seen as traitors of the highest degree.[4]

The last straw came when a representative of the Syrian ruler Antiochus Epiphanes IV tried to get the father of the Maccabean family to offer an inappropriate sacrifice.[5] When another Jew went ahead with the sacrifice, the father killed him on the spot, along with all the Syrian emissaries. Several years of guerilla warfare resulted, with the Maccabees surprisingly emerging as the victors. The Jews still celebrate the "Feast of Dedication" every year—**Hanukkah**—to commemorate the resumption of proper worship in the Jerusalem temple. Israel was independent of foreign rulers for about a hundred years under the **Hasmoneans**, the actual family name of the Maccabees.

Hasmoneans: The actual family name of the Maccabees. Israel was self-governing under their rule for about a hundred years.

Hanukkah: The Jewish feast that celebrates the rededication and purification of the temple after the Maccabeans freed the Jews from foreign rule.

Several aspects of this story are important for our understanding of the New Testament. For example, some think that Jews at the time of Christ never felt they had ever really returned from their exile in Babylon.[6] Although a

> "'Comfort, comfort my people,' says your God. 'Speak tenderly to Jerusalem. Tell her that her sad days are gone and that her sins are pardoned . . .' Listen! I hear the voice of someone shouting, 'Make a highway for the LORD through the wilderness. Make a straight, smooth road through the desert . . .'"
>
> **Isaiah 40:1-3**

second temple had been built, it was not as glorious as the previous one. Therefore, it is no surprise that the New Testament describes salvation by using Old Testament imagery about Israel's return from Babylonian captivity. Certain passages in the New Testament even use "Babylon" as a code word for Rome, primarily because the Romans destroyed Jerusalem in A.D. 70, just as the Babylonians had in 586 B.C.

Although we only have hints of what the early Christians thought of the Maccabees, there are at least two places where the New Testament makes an allusion to their successes. The first is in the Gospel of John, where Jesus actually attends the Feast of Hanukkah in Jerusalem, the Feast of Dedication (John 10:22). The other is in Hebrews 11:35. Many scholars believe this is an allusion to a story in which seven brothers chose to die rather than betray the covenant, a story that is set during the Maccabean revolt.[7] However, even more important than actual references to the Maccabees is the tone they set for much of Israel in the days just preceding the New Testament. The following chapter will show how their heritage influenced Jewish thought right up to the time that Jesus walked the earth and the early church was born.

Things to Think About

1. If you have heard this story before (from Promised Land to No Land), did you learn anything new in this chapter, such as a perspective you had never heard before?

2. What do you think about the idea that Israel is/was God's exclusive people over and against any other ethnic group? Does the Old Testament really teach this idea? Do you think modern-day Israel is the same Israel? Do you think Israel's people are still God's people and heir to all these promises?

3. What do you think about the idea that the Jews were not expecting the Messiah to be divine? How do you think they understood the Bible verses the New Testament interprets to be about Jesus? What do you think about the claim that the phrase "Son of God" did not necessarily imply someone was divine in the Old Testament? Can you think of a way to argue against this claim?

Key Terms

Babylon
Christ
David
election (OT)
Four Pillars of Judaism
Hanukkah
Hasmoneans
Judah
Lord
Maccabees
Messiah
monotheism
Samaritans
Solomon
Son of David
Son of God

4. Were you surprised to hear that Jesus might have celebrated Hanukkah? What is your reaction to the claim that the early Christians might have found significance in some of the events and writings mentioned in the Apocrypha? If you have a strong reaction one way or the other, explain why.

endnotes

1. J. D. G. Dunn, *The Partings of the Ways Between Christianity and Judaism and Their Significance for the Character of Christianity* (Philadelphia: Trinity, 1991), 18–36.

2. As the previous chapter mentioned, the obliteration of whole peoples must be read in the light of the understandings of a group culture. The peoples that Israel destroyed worshiped inappropriate deities and practiced things that were detestable to Yahweh. Destroying such peoples was seen as a Holy War, an act of divine judgment.

3. For example, the Old Testament refers to angelic beings as "sons of God" (e.g., Job 1:6) and to the nation of Israel as God's son (e.g., Hos. 11:1).

4. For the story, read 1 Maccabees. This is one of the books found in the Roman Catholic and Orthodox Bibles but not in Protestant Bibles.

5. The term "Maccabeus" probably means "hammer," a name most likely given to one of the Maccabees (Judas) because of his forcefulness in the struggle against the Syrians. The family was thus not called by the name Maccabee until after they had rebelled.

6. For example, N. T. Wright's *The New Testament and the People of God* (Minneapolis: Fortress, 1992) and *Jesus and the Victory of God* (Minneapolis: Fortress, 1996). These are volumes 1 and 2 respectively of the *Christian Origins and the Question of God* series.

7. The story is located in 2 Maccabees 7, a book found in the Apocrypha but not in the Old Testament of most Protestant Bibles.

CHAPTER 8

Jewish Groups at the Time of Christ

Among the known Jewish literature of the period, Paul's language of divine predestination, his view of human sinfulness, and the cosmic scope of salvation all find their closest parallels in the Dead Sea Scrolls.

Most of the Jewish groups important for our understanding of the New Testament trace their stories in one way or another to the period in which the Hasmoneans—the descendants of the Maccabees—ruled. For example, the Sadducees were heirs to the Hasmonean power over the administration of the temple. The Pharisees inherited the Maccabean fervor for the Law, at least as Jewish literature portrays it. The Essenes sharply criticized the way the Hasmoneans ran the temple. Some Essenes even withdrew from society at large to a place called Qumran in the desert. The various revolutionaries who popped up from time to time hoped to follow

At a Glance

- Most Jews in Palestine were just going about their daily lives (people of the land).

- More Jews lived outside Palestine than in Palestine (Diaspora Jews). The majority of these spoke Greek (Hellenistic Jews).

- Samaritan Jews were of mixed race and thus were despised by many other Jews.

- The aristocratic Sadducees ran the temple. They followed only things that were clearly set out in the first five books of the Old Testament.

- Pharisees not only observed the specifics of the Jewish Law carefully, they also followed many oral traditions about how to keep it.

- Essenes kept the highest standards of purity of all. Some of them became like monks in a desert place called Qumran.

- Revolutionaries occasionally tried to oust the Romans by force.

> **priests:** Those from the Israelite tribe of Levi whose role was to administer the Law to the people. Their duties included such things as offering sacrifices in the temple, settling disputes, and declaring individuals ceremonially clean.

the Maccabean example of freeing Israel from foreign rule. All in all, the story of the Maccabeans seems to have had an enormous effect on how Jews in Palestine understood themselves in Jesus' day.

Sadducees and Priests

The Hasmoneans did not descend from David, nor were they in the royal line. Rather, they descended from Israelite **priests**. Some Jews opposed their leadership in part for this reason: they were not "sons of David." Nevertheless, their descendants ruled Israel for well over a hundred years. In 63 B.C., a dispute between two brothers over who should be king led to the intervention of the Roman general Pompey, who defeated Jerusalem and brought Israel under Roman rule.

> **Herod the Great:** The king the Romans appointed to rule Israel just before Jesus' birth. The New Testament tells us that he put all the infants in Bethlehem to death in an attempt to kill Jesus.

Despite the presence of the Romans in Palestine, the Hasmoneans continued as rulers until the infamous **Herod the Great** came to power—the one the New Testament tells us tried to kill the baby Jesus. He put to death almost all the Hasmonean descendants who might have had a claim to the throne. Then from the wealthy class he handpicked a **high priest**, the highest rank of priest in Judaism. Herod was careful to choose someone who would never challenge his rule.

> **high priest:** The highest rank of priest in Judaism. The high priest's most significant religious responsibility was to enter the Most Holy chamber of the temple once a year and offer a sacrifice for the sins of the people. At the time of Christ's death, he was the most powerful Jewish political figure in the land.

Priests took care of the temple in Jerusalem and administered the Jewish Law in general for the people. Ideally, Israelite priests, who lived throughout the nation of Israel, traced their ancestry back to the tribe of Levi, one of the twelve sons of Jacob. The overwhelming majority of priests lived outside Jerusalem, where they often settled local disputes and served as an extension of the temple for the people in the countryside— the **people of the land**. In the time of Christ, there were more priests than any of the other distinct groups we will discuss in this chapter.

> **Sadducees:** A small group of aristocratic Jews who held political power in Jerusalem. They did not believe in a resurrection or any kind of an afterlife in general.

The priests who lived outside Jerusalem were often very poor. In addition to helping people resolve disputes, they provided most of whatever education went on among the common people. Since the temple was the focal point of Israel's land, those who were in control of it held considerable power. Local priests thus derived some authority from their connection with the Jerusalem temple.

Yet there was often a significant difference between the local priests and the Jerusalem priests, both in their status and their thinking. While the local priests were poor, the Jerusalem priests (who largely consisted of a group known as the **Sadducees**) tended to come from the wealthy aristocracy. After Rome took over and Herod the Great renovated the temple on a massive scale, the Sadducees found themselves having to be "buddy-buddy" with the Romans. Since many Jews considered the Romans to be their greatest enemies, no doubt many were suspicious of the Sadducees for this reason alone.

Some believe that the Sadducees only considered the first five books of the Hebrew Scriptures (the Pentateuch) to be authoritative, although this is far from certain. What is certain is that they did not follow the **tradition of the elders**, oral traditions that had developed over the years on how to keep the

> **tradition of the elders:** Oral traditions that arose about how to keep the specifics of the Law. A group called the Pharisees was best known for keeping these traditions.

Law. Groups such as the Pharisees considered these oral traditions to be authoritative in addition to the text of the Old Testament itself. Further, Sadducees did not believe in any sort of afterlife, an idea that only clearly occurs in one or two places in the Old Testament (e.g., Dan. 12:1-3). Acts 23:8 may also imply that Sadducees did not believe in angels.[1]

Sadducees appear several times in the pages of the New Testament. Notably, more than any other group they seem to bring about Jesus' death. As the party in power politically, they tried their best to keep relations good between the Romans and the Jews—after all, they had the most to lose. During times like Passover, when Jerusalem was filled with crowds of people, they watched carefully to keep order. The Romans reacted forcibly against any situation that might turn into a riot. Therefore, when Jesus created conflict in the temple during Passover week, He probably set in motion His eventual arrest and crucifixion (cf. Mark 11:12-19).

> **Qumran:** The location of the Dead Sea community where the Dead Sea Scrolls were discovered. This community was thought to be one branch of a group of Jews known as the Essenes.

> **Essenes:** The Jewish group that followed the highest standard of ceremonial purity—the standard of priests on duty in the temple. They held their possessions in common, and many were celibate.

The Essenes

If the Sadducees inherited the power of the Hasmonean priest-kings, the **Essenes** were a group that opposed and were perhaps even oppressed by that power. Some think that an Essene we know of as the "**Teacher of**

Dead Sea Scrolls: Writings found at Qumran that probably represent a wide variety of Essene communities from the two centuries before Christ. The most distinctive documents probably come from a community that split off from the broader Essene movement.

Teacher of Righteousness: The founder of the particular Essene community that lived at Qumran near the Dead Sea.

apocalyptic: Viewing events on earth as the playing out of spiritual conflicts in the invisible realm, conflicts that will eventually lead to the judgment of the world and the restoration of the righteous.

Righteousness" actually served in the temple until the Hasmoneans forced him out of service, eventually causing him to retreat to a desert location known as **Qumran**. It is here that the **Dead Sea Scrolls** were found in the late 1940s. At Qumran, the Teacher of Righteousness and his followers kept a standard of purity similar to that required of priests on duty in the Jerusalem temple.

The Dead Sea Scrolls have an **apocalyptic** flavor. This means they see Israel's struggles as an invisible battle between spiritual forces in the heavens, a battle that will end with the

One of the caves in which the Dead Sea Scrolls were found.

final judgment of the world. A book quoted in the New Testament, 1 Enoch, was probably considered Scripture by the Essenes, as were other books of a somewhat apocalyptic bent.

A number of interesting parallels exist between the Essenes and the earliest Christians. For example, the New Testament sometimes has an apocalyptic bent similar to that found in the Dead Sea literature. The book of Revelation is a symbolic portrayal of heavenly conflict with similarities to other apocalyptic works found at Qumran. The Gospel of John speaks of Jesus in terms of light (John 1:5; 8:12), and Paul called believers "sons of light" (1 Thess. 5:5)—exactly the kind of language we find in the Dead Sea Scrolls. The picture of the early church in Acts shows a group holding their possessions in common, much as they did at Qumran. Among the known Jewish literature of the period, Paul's language of divine predestination, his view of human sinfulness, and the cosmic scope of salvation all find their closest parallels in the Dead Sea Scrolls.

At this point, however, most scholars do not see any direct relationship between the Scrolls and the early Christians. Rather, the greatest contribution of the Dead Sea literature is the way it helps us better understand the world behind the New Testament. For example, the Scrolls have added greatly to our understanding of what many Jews were expecting the messiah to be. They pictured a political leader who would restore Israel's kingdom and then rule with righteousness and faithfulness to the covenant.

The Pharisees

To us, the **Pharisees** are probably the best-known group of Jews from the time of Christ, not least because the early Christians seem to have had more conflicts with them than with any other Jewish group. Popularly, they are often associated with legalism—a tendency to keep rules just because one likes rules, not because a rule serves any purpose. The English word *Pharisaic* illustrates this fact, since it is used of someone who is self-righteous or hypocritical. This reflects an unfortunate tendency throughout the last two thousand years to equate this view of the Pharisees with Jews in general, sometimes contributing to **anti-Semitism** [or, more accurately, **anti-Judaism**], hatred of Jews.

Yet, this typical view of the Pharisees reflects a great deal of misunderstanding of what they were about. Pharisees made up only a small minority of Jewish individuals at the

> **Pharisees:** A group of Jews known best for their careful keeping of the Jewish Law as it was interpreted in the traditions of the elders. Unlike the Sadducees, Pharisees strongly believed in the resurrection of those who died noble deaths in faithfulness to God's covenant with Israel.
>
> **anti-Semitism/anti-Judaism:** Hatred of Jews.

(24)

time of Christ (about 6,000). And their concern for keeping the Law was based solidly on the four pillars of Judaism we discussed previously in chapter 7 of this text. The Old Testament clearly teaches that Israel was to observe the covenant found in the Jewish Law. But how could Jews be sure they were keeping the covenant? If they truly wanted to serve God, they would no doubt be careful to do everything He wished.

Therefore, when one of the Ten Commandments said not to *work* on Saturday, the Jewish **Sabbath**, the Pharisees wanted to know just how much

effort would constitute "work"? They wanted to make it clear so that the commandment could be kept properly. For example, how much walking could I do on Saturday until I had "worked"?

> **Sabbath:** The period from sundown on Friday to sundown on Saturday during which Jews did not work.

What about an emergency situation that required me to "work" to save someone's life? Could I "work" if it would save someone's life? The Pharisees wanted to spell out exactly what it would take to keep the covenant. The number of rules they came up with is not a proof of their legalism. After all, we have more traffic laws than all their laws put together.

> "It happened also that seven brothers and their mother were arrested and were being compelled by the king . . . to partake of unlawful swine's flesh. One of them . . . said, 'What do you intend to ask and learn from us? For we are ready to die rather than transgress the laws of our fathers.'"
>
> **2 Maccabees 7:1-2 NRSV**
> (often thought to have been written by a Pharisee)

Understanding the way the four pillars worked in the minds of many Jews helps explain their fervor in keeping the Law. The covenant was not just a matter of giving God His due. Israel was promised blessing in their land if they would keep their end of the agreement. Many Pharisees no doubt kept the Law vigorously— and encouraged others to do the same—because they believed that God in return would be faithful and free Israel from the control of the Romans. While not all scholars agree that the Pharisees had such revolutionary aims, the literature clearly indicates that some Pharisees took leading roles during uprisings against the Romans. As the spiritual heirs of the Maccabean fighters mentioned in the last chapter, it would be no surprise if their zeal for the Law followed similar lines.

Revolutionaries

The conflict between Jews and Romans came to a head in A.D. 66, when the Jews revolted against Roman rule. While distinct groups such as the "Zealots" or the "Sicarii" came into existence around that time, the drive to revolution often cut across Israel's other divisions. For example, we know of both Pharisees and Essenes who participated in uprisings. Interestingly enough, one of Jesus' disciples is called

> **Jewish War:** Took place from A.D. 66–73. This attempt of the Jewish people to free themselves from Roman rule resulted in the destruction of Jerusalem and the temple in A.D. 70.

82

"Simon the Zealot" in Luke 6:15. It is indeed possible that some of Jesus' followers came to Him under the expectation that He would be the one to restore Israel's kingdom (cf. Acts 1:6).[2]

The revolutionary attempt to oust the Romans, the **Jewish War**, resulted in the destruction of Jerusalem and the temple in A.D. 70. These events drastically transformed Judaism and detached Christianity even further from its Jewish roots. With the temple gone, the Sadducees disappeared from the scene, as did the Essenes, whom the Romans tracked down and obliterated. Only the Pharisees survived in Palestine. Many think their heirs formed the core of the rabbinic Judaism with which we are familiar today.

"Lord, you chose David to be king over Israel, and swore to him about his descendants forever, that his kingdom should not fail before you.

"But (because of) our sins, sinners rose up against us . . . Lord, raise up for them their king, *the son of David*, to rule over your servant Israel . . .

"Undergird him with the strength to destroy the unrighteous rulers, to purge Jerusalem from gentiles . . . to drive out the sinners from the inheritance . . .

"He will have gentile nations serving him under his yoke . . .

"And he will purge Jerusalem . . .

"And he will be a righteous king over them, taught by God . . .

"He shall be the Lord *Messiah*."

Psalms of Solomon 17:4-5, 21-23, 30, 32

The People of the Land

Most of the Jews in Palestine at the time of Christ did not belong to any of the major parties. They were simply eking out an existence. A large percentage of them worked at farming the land, thus earning the designation "the people of the land" (the *'am ha'arets*). They were not Pharisees, Sadducees, Essenes, or Revolutionaries. They were just common, ordinary people trying to make it from day to day.

"Among themselves [the Jews] they are inflexibly honest and ever ready to show compassion, though they regard the rest of mankind with all the hatred of enemies. They sit apart at meals, they sleep apart, and though, as a nation, they are singularly prone to lust, they abstain from intercourse with foreign women. Among themselves nothing is unlawful. Circumcision was adopted by them as a mark of difference from other men. Those who come over to their religion adopt the practice, and have this lesson first instilled into them—to despise all gods, to disown their country, and set parents, children, and brethren at nothing."

Tacitus (Roman historian)
Histories 5.5

Aramaic: A language that evolved from Hebrew. Most Jews in Palestine spoke this as their first language.

Nevertheless, they were Jews, and this designation alone said something about what they were like—at least in the eyes of the non-Jews of the time. As we learned in chapter 6, there were certain practices that set the Jewish people apart from other nations: circumcision, dietary restrictions, observing the Sabbath, and most significantly, adherence to monotheism.

While many Palestinian Jews spoke some Greek, the majority spoke a language called **Aramaic** that had evolved out of Hebrew, the main language of the Old Testament. Aramaic is the language Jesus spoke to the people of the countryside. Undoubtedly, this "silent majority" was not indifferent to the temple or the political situation. A fair number of them probably made regular trips to Jerusalem each year for one of the many festivals. No doubt many also resented having to pay taxes to the Romans. But most were not involved in any particular political or ideological movement. They were doing what so many of us do today—getting through one day at a time, putting one sandal in front of the other.

Greek-Speaking or "Hellenistic" Jews

Interestingly, more Jews lived outside Palestine than inside at the time of Christ. The word **Diaspora** refers to the dispersion of Jews to all parts of the known world in the centuries preceding the birth of Jesus. Most of these Jews spoke Greek and may not have known any Aramaic, let alone Hebrew. Greek had become the "business language," the *lingua franca* of the ancient world. Just as English speakers can communicate effectively in much of the world today, a Greek-speaker could make it in the ancient Mediterranean. We call Greek-speaking Jews **Hellenistic Jews**, because Hellenistic means "Greek." Since the Hebrew Scriptures were translated into Greek in the third century before Christ (the 200s B.C.), the Bible was available to these Jews in their first language.

Diaspora: The scattering of Jews throughout the Mediterranean world and away from their geographical point of origin.

Hellenistic Jews: Greek-speaking Jews.

Some Diaspora Jews probably did not keep Jewish traditions as scrupulously as many Palestinian Jews. Nevertheless, as noted earlier in this chapter, the Roman historian Tacitus described the Jews in Rome as following the same basic practices as those in Palestine. These included circumcision, Sabbath observance, and dietary laws. Even the most "enlightened" Jews, those who were most influenced by Greek culture and philosophy, showed allegiance to the Jewish temple in Jerusalem.[3]

Not all Greek-speaking Jews lived outside Palestine. Members of the "upper crust" in Jerusalem, the center of Judaism, demonstrated their sophistication by a basic proficiency in Greek. About 40 percent of the tombstones available in Palestine as a whole are written in Greek. The Greek-speaking elite in Jerusalem may have looked down their noses at the poorer, Aramaic-speaking crowds. On the other hand, Aramaic-speaking Jews

Some Jewish Groups at the Time of Christ

Sadducees	Essenes	Pharisees	Diaspora Jews
• name may come from Zadok, priest in days of David	• name may come from word meaning "doers" [of Law]	• name may come from word meaning "separate"	• refers to Jews who did not live in Palestine
• generally upper class and priestly; high priests tended to be Sadducees	• kept the Jewish Law most strictly of all Jewish groups—at level of those on duty in temple	• not only kept the Jewish Law, but also many other oral traditions about how to keep those laws	• such Jews often maintained ties to Jerusalem temple, were circumcised, kept basic food laws, and observed Sabbath days
• may have only kept the Torah; did not keep the oral traditions followed by the Pharisees	• probably looked at some apocalyptic books as Scripture in addition to OT	• the books they considered Scripture may now be our OT	• because of pagan environment, may not have kept purity restrictions/Law as carefully as some Palestinian Jews
• did not believe in resurrection or any kind of afterlife; many would say did not believe in angels	• believed in life after death, but perhaps not in resurrection	• believed in resurrection	
• Josephus claims they believed in free will	• strong sense of predestination and the sinfulness of humanity	• believed it was possible to keep the Law	
• often collaborated with foreign rulers like Romans	• held possessions in common; often celibate	• School of Hillel tended to interpret the Law less strictly, was more fatalistic in its nationalism	
	• some strict Essenes lived at Qumran and compiled the Dead Sea Scrolls	• School of Shammai tended to interpret the Law more strictly, took a more proactive role in revolution	

Revolutionaries: Tended to cross the boundaries of Palestinian groups. We know of individuals from all three main Jewish sects that participated in the Jewish War. Some revolutionary groups that arose in the Jewish War included the *Zealots* and the *Sicarii*.

People of the Land: Most of the Jews who lived in Palestine did not belong to any distinct group. They were just going about the daily business of making a living. Most farmed for their subsistence.

probably were somewhat suspicious about the "purity" of the Greek speakers. Perhaps some Aramaic speakers saw themselves as more faithful to God than the "tainted" Greek speakers.

These kinds of tensions between Greek- and Aramaic-speaking Jews would show up in early Christianity as well. Acts 6 mentions a conflict among early Christians in which Aramaic-speaking Christians failed to provide for Greek-speaking widows while feeding well their own Aramaic-speaking widows. Further, it is possible that some Greek-speaking Christians broke with the Jewish law more radically than Aramaic-speaking Christians did. Indeed, Acts indicates that it was the Greek-speaking Christians more than any other group that first brought Christianity to non-Jews. Understanding the makeup of Jewish groups at the time of Christ enhances our understanding of the dynamics of the early church.

Samaritan Jews

In the previous chapter, we briefly mentioned the Samaritans. Samaritans lived in Samaria, the region between Judea (where Jerusalem was located) and Galilee, where Jesus grew up and carried out most of His ministry. The northern kingdom had occupied this region during the period of the kings. After the Assyrians destroyed the northern kingdom, the remaining Jews intermingled with the other ethnic groups that came to live there. In the minds of many Jews, this mixed ethnicity made Samaritans a "tainted" race. Jesus' Parable of the Good Samaritan was particularly shocking because it took a stereotypical "bad guy" (a Samaritan) and made him the hero of the story. Some Samaritans live in Palestine today. They are the only Jewish group that still offers sacrifices.

Things to Think About

1. Name nine or ten different groups of Jews discussed in this chapter. Describe each group in a sentence or two.

2. What did priests do in Israel at the time of Christ? What did a high priest do?

3. To which of the groups mentioned in this chapter did most Jews belong at the time of Christ? To which group did most Jews living in Palestine belong?

4. In terms of the first century, which Jewish group was most conservative in its approach to the Jewish Law? Which group followed a great number of oral traditions about how to keep the Law? Which group kept the highest standard of purity?

Key Terms

anti-Semitism/anti-Judaism
apocalyptic
Aramaic
Dead Sea Scrolls
Diaspora
Essene
Hellenistic Jews
Herod the Great
high priest
Jewish War
people of the land
Pharisee
priests
Qumran
Revolutionaries
Sabbath
Sadducee
Teacher of Righteousness
tradition of the elders

5. What kind of a "messiah" or king were these groups expecting to come?

6. To which group does Christianity seem most similar? In what way?

endnotes

1. Some think the reference here is not to a general disbelief in angels, but to resurrection in an angelic body.
2. Cf. is an abbreviation for "confer." Acts 1:6 shows that some of Jesus' followers expected Him to restore the kingdom of Israel.
3. For example, a Jewish philosopher named Philo, who lived in Egypt.

CHAPTER 9

Ancient Family Values

*A person was adequately defined in New Testament
times by three basic factors: gender, family, and race.*

Have It Your Way?

A few years ago a fast food jingle proudly proclaimed, "Have it *your* way at Burger King." Only an **individualistic culture** would value giving people a chance to order hamburgers *their* way—with or without pickles, tomato, lettuce, or catsup. We already mentioned in chapter 6 that the people of ancient times were not "wired" to think this way. They saw identity far more as a matter of **groups** than individuals.

In most societies, including those at the time of the New Testament, one's destiny was fairly well determined from birth. One was born male or female, and ancient society had clear-cut ideas about what each gender meant. Vocation was a family matter. If a boy's father farmed the land, the boy would farm the land. If the father were a tentmaker, the son would

At a Glance

- People defined themselves in terms of the groups to which they belonged—particularly their family, their race, and their gender.

- A group's worth was weighed in terms of its honor or shame.

- Men belonged in the public, actively working to bring honor to the family.

- Women directed the home and were the greatest potential source of shame.

- Sons legitimated a woman and served as a mother's ally in the extended family.

- Daughters were a potential source of shame for a father, with whom they might have little contact.

become a tentmaker. The family usually arranged marriage, sometimes even before the child in question was born. Marriage rarely had anything to do with what we think of when we talk about "falling in love." Marriages meant the joining of two families, not two individuals.

How sad, you might think, that so many people throughout history have not had the opportunity to express their individuality. Yet it is important to realize that people in ancient times did not experience these situations in the way *we* would if we were placed in them. For example, women of biblical times did not feel oppressed in the way a modern American woman would if she were transported back in time. By and large they did not experience the limitations of their society as restrictions—as if they were not allowed to have it *their* way. It would not have even occurred to them that they had a "way." They would stand at the Burger King counter in puzzlement: "Have it *my* way? What do you mean, '*my* way'?"

Westerners—individuals of European descent—are raised to think of themselves as individuals from birth. We prize people who think for themselves, and are quick to point out the personality traits that make each one of us special and different from everyone

> " 'The people of Crete are all liars; they are cruel animals and lazy gluttons.' This is true. So rebuke them as sternly as necessary to make them strong in the faith."
> **Titus 1:12-13**

> "I do not allow a woman to teach or hold authority over a man but to be in silence. For Adam was formed first, then Eve. And Adam was not deceived, but the woman, because she was deceived, has come to be in transgression. But they will be saved through childbearing, if they remain in faithfulness and love and holiness with modesty."
> **1 Timothy 2:12, 14 (author's translation)**

Three Key Elements in Ancient Identity
1. **gender** (male or female)
2. **genealogy** (family background)
3. **geography** (race, linked to the land of origin)

else. Dating involves "getting to know" one other and that can take some time, given how many particular quirks and habits we develop as individuals. Does my fiancée squeeze the toothpaste in the middle or roll up the tube from the end? Does she put the toilet paper in the holder so it will roll down the front or does she hang it down from the back? Compatibility on an individual level is very important to us.

> "I have learned how to get along happily whether I have much or little."
> **Philippians 4:11**
>
> *(Paul accepts the lot that God has given him.)*

> **individualistic culture:** A culture in which one's identity is determined on a personal, individual basis.
>
> **group culture:** A culture in which identity is primarily a function of the groups to which an individual belongs—such as one's race, family, or gender.

A person was adequately defined in New Testament times by three basic factors: gender, family, and race.[1] A person did not even need to meet a prospective spouse to know whether or not s/he was compatible. If the gender was right, the race was the same, and the family was of an appropriate social status—the two were compatible. People were not "wired" to ask themselves what made them as individuals different from other individuals. Instead, they asked what made their *gender*, *family*, or *race* different from other genders, families, and races. Someone who thought for him or herself—rather than thinking the same as his or her people, family, or gender—was not prized. That person was considered a misfit, someone who should be looked on with suspicion.

Honor and Shame

One might come across a number of different theories in a psychology or counseling class about what it means to be mature. Abraham Maslow termed

"I am not ashamed of this Good News about Christ."

Romans 1:16

"[Jesus] was willing to die a shameful death on the cross . . ."

Hebrews 12:2

honor/shame cultures: Cultures oriented around the approval or disapproval of your group, rather than around being true to yourself as an individual.

the highest stage of maturity a point of "self-actualization," where each individual forms a way of life regardless of what others say or think.[2] Maslow is not alone. Modern psychology considers the healthiest person to be the one with a strong sense of self-identity, able to resist "peer pressure" to think or live a certain way. The important thing in these theories is being true to yourself and your individual beliefs.

Ironically, many of these theories only relate well with regard to *Western* persons. These conclusions would not ring true to the world in which the Bible was produced—even in the majority of the world's cultures today. In New Testament times, the "healthy" person was the one who accepted the lot that God (or for most ancients, Fate) had dealt him. Such persons did not worry about what *other groups or races* might think. They lived true to their own *group's* beliefs and practices. In other words, their sense of self-worth was based on their group's evaluation of them, not on some individual conscience.

Conscience in such a world was not a matter of an *inner* voice. It was an *outer* voice that did not involve being true to oneself, but being true to one's family and people—those who would let you know when your actions were bringing them **honor** or **shame**. Whereas we are an introspective "guilt culture" made up of people that process blame internally, blame was public and shared in the ancient world. When someone like Jesus was crucified, he was set out in public where everyone could see him and recognize his shame.

Some readers of the Old Testament are puzzled and outraged that a person's entire family could be put to death because of something one family member did. Yet such an action is understandable in

> "Then Joshua and all the Israelites took Achan, the silver, the robe, the bar of gold, his sons, daughters, cattle, donkeys, sheep, tent, and everything he had . . . And all the Israelites stoned Achan . . ."
>
> **Joshua 7:24-25**

a group-oriented world where blame was shared. The apostle Paul argues in Romans 6 that because we are all descendants of the first man, Adam, we all face the consequences of his sin—a difficult idea for an individualist to follow. But it made perfect sense in a world where God was thought to "punish the children for the sins of their parents to the third and fourth generations" (Deut. 5:9).

The ancient world was thus made up of "honor/shame" cultures, including the cultures we see in the Old and New Testaments. Honor related to behavior that embodied the values of the groups to which you belonged. Similarly, shame came from behavior that contradicted your group's values. You might be surprised to know how often honor/shame language occurs in the pages of the Bible. Included are words like *glory*, *honor*, *praiseworthy*, and *shame*. Most Western readers do not even notice such language because honor and shame are not a major part of our world.

Husbands and Wives

A man's place in the ancient world was public. It involved the active pursuit of honor, which was demonstrated by strength, courage, and similar virtues. An honorable death was worthwhile even for those who might not

> "Marketplaces, council halls, law courts, gatherings and meetings where a large number of people are assembled, and life under the open air with discussion and action—all these are appropriate for males in both war and peace.
>
> "But females are best suited for the house and the inside alone, with the virgins in the middle of the house within the innermost doors and already grown women within the outer doors."
>
> Philo, *The Special Laws* 3.169

believe in an afterlife; they would live on honorably in the memory of their people. The ancient world was definitely male-oriented. Sons were far more highly valued than daughters. A father's inheritance was distributed only among his sons; the dowry a father gave to his son-in-law when his daughter married served as her inheritance. It is no coincidence that one of the most controversial subjects in the New Testament—whether non-Jews needed to be circumcised in order to become Christians—completely bypasses women.

In contrast to the men of that time, women belonged to the private domain of the home, where they ruled the roost. Their primary honor was to be found in chaste behavior. A woman who was loose or adulterous brought great shame to her family. A woman's greatest honor came from keeping herself sexually pure. This led to the practice of a double standard: while the sexual exclusiveness of a husband to his wife was not a concern in the ancient world, a wife could never have any sexual partner but her husband.

In fact, one could not technically commit adultery against a woman in the ancient world—adultery was defined as shaming a man by sleeping with his wife. Therefore, a husband did not commit adultery by definition if he slept with a prostitute or an unmarried woman, who in many cases could simply become an additional wife or concubine. A wife, on the other hand, always committed adultery if she had sex with anyone but her husband. In some respects Jesus and the New Testament balance out such double standards with regard to men and women; in other ways they do not. Christians will want to listen carefully to the Holy Spirit and to their fellow Christians when applying these parts of the Bible to today's world!

The kind of intimacy we consider to be ideal between husbands and wives was foreign to the ancient world. Because they did not think as individualists, they had no real individual identity through which to express intimacy. For example, it is highly unlikely that Joseph and Mary, Jesus' parents, had tender conversation in the evenings as they lay beside one another. Not only did husbands and wives seldom sleep together, they often had little contact with one another in general. And there is a good chance that Joseph was substantially older than Mary, who may have been in her early teens when she bore Jesus. We impose our own marital expectations on the Bible if we think the men and women in its pages related to one another in the intimate terms we think ideal.

Look at the quotation from the Jewish philosopher Philo to get a good picture of the respective roles of men and women in the ancient world.

Sons and Daughters

The lack of intimacy that was true of husbands and wives in the ancient world was even more true of parents and children. The picture we have of a cozy family opening Christmas presents as they gather around a fireplace simply did not exist in Bible times. Fathers usually had little interaction with their children, and mothers put their children to hard work at a very young age.

One of the best ways to illustrate how different the parent/child relationship was then in contrast to today is to remember the story of Jesus in Luke 2. His parents traveled a whole day away from Jerusalem before they realized their twelve-year-old son was missing. At this point an American would be ready to call Child Protective Services! How could loving parents travel for an entire day before realizing their child was missing? Joseph and Mary should have been ashamed of themselves, right?

> "A daughter is a secret anxiety to her father, and worry over her robs him of sleep; when she is young, for fear she will not marry, or if married, for fear she will be disliked; while a virgin, for fear she will be seduced and become pregnant in her father's house; or having a husband, for fear she may go astray, or, though married, for fear she may be barren . . .
> "Better is the wickedness of a man than a woman who does good; it is woman who brings shame and disgrace."
>
> **Sirach 42:9-10, 14 NRSV**

One of the problems we have in comprehending this event is that we often think of what is sometimes called the "nuclear family" as the norm: a father, mother, and two kids in the back seat of a car on a road trip. But it was the extended family of one's father that was the core family in New Testament times, including grandparents, aunts, uncles, cousins, etc. The oldest male in this group served as the final authority on any matter.

We should therefore picture Jesus as part of a very large company of individuals. Each wife would form a smaller unit along with her respective children. We can picture Mary assuming Jesus was among the crowd. Indeed, the verse seems to say that He was punished for not staying with the pack (Luke 2:51). In their view, Jesus probably endangered His parents by forcing them to break off from the safety of the larger group,[3] thus shaming His father by giving his other relatives the impression that he was not able to control his children.

Until they reached puberty, sons often had little or no interaction with their fathers. Daughters had even less since they often were married off in their early teens. After joining the household of her husband and moving in with his family, a woman suddenly found herself in an insecure position without any power. Having a son legitimated a woman in her husband's family. Her son could thus become an ally in family matters, a channel for her to increase her power and standing. Thus, sons usually had a special relationship with their mothers.

This short sketch of ancient family life should help you catch a glimpse of how different the world of the New Testament was from our world. It reinforces the importance of reading the Bible in its original context, rather than applying its words blindly to today. For instance, "family values" are a key political issue today, especially among Christians. But we must be very careful about how we use the Bible to address such concerns. We run the risk of mistaking our own ideas for those found in the Bible.

Things to Think About

1. Can you put yourself in the place of someone whose parents decided whom they would marry? They did not see this as an imposition—can you get into their heads?

Key Terms
group culture
honor/shame culture
individualistic culture

2. Are the comments in Titus 1:12-13 prejudiced against people from Crete, or were all "Cretans" really liars, animals, and lazy gluttons?

3. Once we know that such a group dynamic is at work in the Bible, how do we apply it to today? Can we Westerners even make ourselves think like those from group cultures? Does God have a different agenda for us in our culture, or do we need to change our culture at this point to be more like those of ancient times?

4. Where the Bible's teaching supports the values of the ancient world in general (on women? on children?), does this mean that its specific teachings in those areas might not play out the same way for us today?

endnotes

1. Bruce J. Malina and Jerome H. Neyrey, *Portraits of Paul: An Archaeology of Ancient Personality* (Louisville: Westminster John Knox, 1996).
2. Abraham H. Maslow, *Toward a Psychology of Being*, 3d ed. (New York: Wiley, 1998).
3. Travel was often dangerous in the ancient world, not least from the kinds of bandits and thieves pictured in the Parable of the Good Samaritan (Luke 10).

CHAPTER 10

Money and Power in the Ancient World

Almost everything in the ancient world was done on the basis of informal alliances we call patron-client relationships. There was no such thing as love or a friendship without obligation.

The Politics of Ancient Palestine

We have already mentioned some of the more official power structures of ancient Palestine. The Romans took over in 63 B.C. and continued to rule for centuries after the New Testament was written. Not only did they base themselves in the coastal city of Caesarea (see **Map 1**), but they also occupied a fortress in Jerusalem itself that looked down on the temple area. They were thus able to swoop down on any riot or unrest that might arise.

In the early days of Jesus' life, **Judea**—the southernmost region of Palestine where Jerusalem was located—was ruled somewhat independently by kings approved by

At a Glance

- The Romans were the ultimate political power in the Mediterranean world.

- They ruled Palestine by way of "client kings" or Roman governors.

- The Sanhedrin also had a great deal of authority over Jerusalem and its region.

- Society functioned on the basis of informal patron-client relationships: the "haves" took care of the "have nots" in return for the prestige the "haves" received.

- Most individuals preferred to trade goods rather than exchange coins/money for them.

- Ancients operated under the idea of limited good—if one person had more, then someone else must have less.

Judea: The southernmost region of Palestine where Jerusalem and Bethlehem were located.

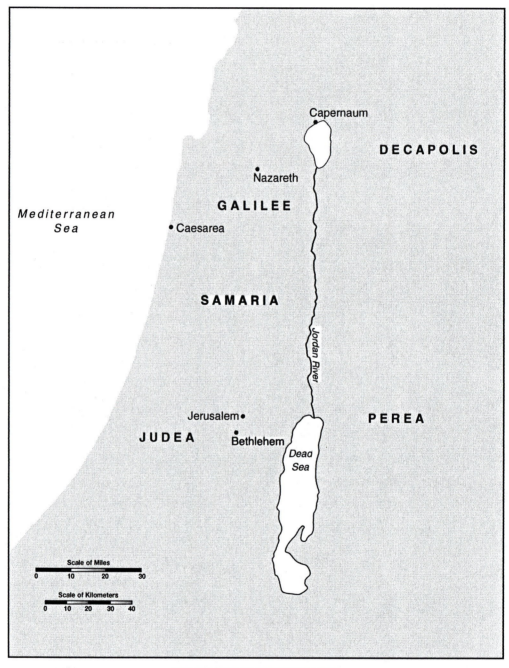

PALESTINE IN CHRIST'S TIME
MAP 1

the Romans. We have already mentioned Herod the Great, who ruled from 37–4 B.C. It was during his reign that Jesus was born.[1] The gospel of Matthew also mentions Herod's son Archelaus, who ruled Judea from 4 B.C. to A.D. 6. Another of Herod's sons, **Herod Antipas**, ruled **Galilee** (4 B.C. to A.D. 39), where Jesus grew up and conducted most of His earthly mission. It was this Herod who beheaded **John the Baptist**, the man whose activities provided a launching point for Jesus' own ministry.

These "client kings" were allowed to run their own kingdoms, raise their own taxes, and maintain their own armies. In return, they paid taxes to Rome, supplied Rome with troops when necessary, and helped maintain the security of the empire's borders. Herod the Great and his family in general were masters of reading the political situation of the Romans. This political savvy not only won them the right to rule as kings, it won a special religious status for the Jewish people among the peoples of the empire. For assisting Julius Caesar in his military ventures, the Jews were exempted from having to offer sacrifices to the Roman emperor and the gods of Rome.

The political situation in Judea occasionally became so volatile that Rome took power away from the descendants of Herod and ruled by way of officials

Herod Antipas: The son of Herod the Great, he ruled the regions of Galilee and Perea from 4 B.C. to A.D. 39. He beheaded John the Baptist; Jesus referred to this Herod as a "fox" (Luke 13:32).

Galilee: The region in which Jesus grew up and conducted much of His earthly ministry. It included **Nazareth**, Jesus' hometown; **Capernaum**, a village in which Jesus may have had a house at one time; and the **Sea of Galilee**, where Jesus "called" some of His first disciples.

John the Baptist: A first-century reformer whose proclamation of coming judgment and restoration provided the launching point for Jesus' own mission.

Sanhedrin: The Jewish ruling council, made up of elders from the Jewish aristocracy.

like Pontius Pilate, the Roman governor who ordered Jesus' crucifixion. It was also during one such period that the Jewish War broke out. But as long as the Jews paid their taxes and kept the peace, the Romans preferred to let them run their own affairs.

The **Sanhedrin** administrated such affairs. This Jewish ruling council was headed by the high priest and made up of seventy-one elders from the Jewish aristocracy. The gospels tell us this group held a preliminary hearing of sorts before Jesus was crucified (Matt. 26:59; Mark 14:55; Luke 22:66). Acts similarly depicts early Christians like Peter, John, and Paul being brought before the Sanhedrin because of their activities (Acts 4 and 23). As the Sanhedrin's discussion in John 11 implies, one of its main concerns was to keep the peace so that the Romans would not take military action themselves. It was probably for this reason as much as any that the high priest had Jesus arrested.

Patron and Client Relationships

We will have to shift our thinking about politics and government significantly—indeed, about relationships in general—if we are to get an accurate picture of the New Testament's meaning. For example, we would like to think that our politicians vote their consciences, that money does not play a role in the decisions they make, and that officials appoint the most qualified individuals rather than their friends and family. We would like to believe the best about our governments, even though they sometimes disappoint us. We would also like to think that those who love us and call themselves our friends do so "unconditionally," although reality sometimes shows us otherwise.

In contrast, almost everything in the ancient world was done on the basis of informal alliances we call **patron-client relationships**. There was no such thing as love or a friendship without obligation. **Patrons**, in this sense, were those who held power, money, and influence and used such resources to benefit others who did not have the same. In return, their **clients** "talked up" their patrons to others—giving them the kind of honor we discussed in the previous chapter. They might also spy for a patron, spread rumors, or do any number of other things to the patron's benefit. For their part, the patron might give clients anything from "their daily bread" to high political office. Sometimes the difference in status between the patron and client was so great that a go-between was needed. We might

patron-client relationships: Ancient networks of informal arrangements between those with money, power, and resources (patrons) and those without (clients). Patrons would provide clients with resources in return for the prestige and influence it brought them. Clients in return did various favors for them and, in general, paid them honor.

patrons: Those with power, influence, and money who were able to assist those with less power.

clients: Those who received such patronage in return for the honor and prestige they gave their patrons.

brokers: Those who served as go-betweens for patrons and clients when the gap between them was significant.

call such a person a power **broker**, someone who mediated power or influence from a person of greater means to someone with fewer resources.

Understanding how these alliances and friendships worked is essential to our understanding of the New Testament. It is in these terms that the early Christians understood their relationships to God and one another. When one form of the Lord's Prayer says, "Forgive us our debts, as we forgive our debtors" (Matt. 6:12), it uses patron-client language. God gives us bread to eat and water to drink; in return we owe Him allegiance and honor. Indeed, the Lord's Prayer begins by praising God's name (Matt. 6:9). The epistle of James tells us that God is the only source of truly good patronage (James 1:17). In contrast, reliance on the rich would be inappropriate (James 2). It is thus unthinkable that any of God's servants would not give Him His due in return—at least not without God breaking off His alliance with them (e.g., Matthew 25).

A proper understanding of patronage is key to several New Testament passages. For example, the apostle Paul told the Corinthian church that he chose to work with his hands rather than rely on patrons, a situation that would have attached strings and inhibited the spread of his message (1 Cor. 9:12). Paul invoked the fact that he was a kind of spiritual patron to Philemon as one reason why Philemon should forgive a runaway slave (Philem. 8–9). And the early Christians undoubtedly viewed Jesus as a "broker" of God's patronage, the one through whom God was mediating a new set of benefits and obligations—a new "covenant" (Heb. 8:6).[2]

Tax collectors and toll collectors in the New Testament provide us with a good example of brokers—"middle men" between patrons and clients. In the days of Christ, the elite placed a number of different kinds of taxes on society. For example, the Romans not only taxed land, crops, and individuals, but they also collected "tolls" from those who shipped goods from one place to another. Matthew, one of the twelve disciples, is pictured as such a toll collector in Matthew 9:9.[3] Further, the temple in Jerusalem collected a tax of its own from the Jewish people, not to mention the "tithe" or tenth of one's harvest that the Law required for the temple. Some scholars believe that such taxes placed heavy burdens on the peasants of Palestine to whom Jesus ministered.[4]

Money in the Ancient World

We can hardly imagine how to carry on the business of life without money. Whether this money is cash, check, or credit card, our lives function on the basis of the exchange of money for goods. Thus, it may be hard for us to appreciate why the New Testament so often is negative about money and wealth. The New Testament has almost nothing good at all to say about money, at one point even noting that the "love of money is at the root of all kinds of evil" (1 Tim. 6:10).

Most people in ancient Palestine were peasants who saw very little coinage at all. Their way of living did not involve giving money for goods; instead, it involved trading goods for goods. It was primarily taxation that required such peasants to use coins at all—and even then coins of lesser value. The elite stored gold coins primarily as a symbol of their prestige. To a lesser extent, silver coins were also the business of those associated with power in one way or another.[5] When Jesus pointed out to a group of elite persons that the silver coin they handed Him belonged to Caesar (Mark 12:13-17), part of His point was probably that coinage and money have nothing to do with God's kingdom—an idea difficult for us to comprehend. However, the peasants to whom He ministered no doubt would have agreed.

Another important difference between our world and that of the New Testament is in the meaning of "getting rich." In our world, many believe that anyone can prosper financially if s/he works hard enough. The fact that my next-door neighbor gets a pay raise usually does not make me worry that my salary will be cut. My prosperity is not necessarily linked to that of anyone else, and no one (at least in theory) is excluded from getting rich.

However, in the ancient world people lived under the assumption that there was a **limited amount of good** to go around. What this implied was that if one person gained, then someone else must have lost. As one Mediterranean proverb from the A.D. 300s says, "Every rich person is a thief or the heir of a

limited good: The idea that there was only a certain amount of wealth, goodness, and value in the world. Therefore, if one person gained, it was assumed that someone else had lost.

rich: Generally thought of as someone who had stolen the goods and possessions of someone else or had descended from someone who had.

poor: Displaced from your inherited place in life, from your possessions, etc.

thief."[6] The assumption was that for anyone to get **rich**, others must have lost their goods and possessions.

Everybody was born into a certain status and location in society. For example, in Palestine you might be born with land that your family had farmed for countless generations. If you were the firstborn son, the expectation was that you also would farm that land all your life. Then after you died, your sons would farm that land. To become **poor** was not primarily about a lack of money or resources. It was about being knocked off track in life, having your inherited position in life taken away.

Therefore, when Jesus said, "It is easier for a camel to go through the eye of a needle than for a rich person to enter the Kingdom of God" (Mark 10:25), it was not so much the rich person's money that was in question. It was the process by which that person became rich. Similarly, when James assumed that "wealthy people will fade away with all of their achievements" (1:11), he was thinking of the person who had oppressed the poor. Keeping some of these basic differences between our society and the one in which the New Testament was written will dramatically increase our understanding of the Bible—and keep us from misappropriating its words today.

Things to Think About

1. If you remember the Four Pillars of Judaism, the Old Testament promises blessing and prosperity to God's people if they obey Him. How does this concept fit together with the prevalent teaching in the New Testament that money is evil and that getting rid of your possessions is extremely honorable?

2. Do you think Americans have more problems with loving their money or with giving too many of their possessions away to the poor?

3. Can you get into the head of someone who believes that when someone else gains something, s/he is taking away from you? How might such views create a climate of envy?

4. Can you imagine living without money, but trading for things instead? Can you picture the conflict an early Christian might have had using a coin with an inscription that said Caesar was a god?

Key Terms

broker
Capernaum
client
Galilee
Herod Antipas
John the Baptist
Judea
limited good
Nazareth
patron-client system
patrons
poor
rich
Sanhedrin
Sea of Galilee

endnotes

1. The individual who created our calendar (in the A.D. 500s) was slightly off on Jesus' birth date. While A.D. 1 was meant to be the year of Jesus' birth, He was actually born at least four years earlier, probably even earlier than that.

2. See Bruce J. Malina, *The Social World of Jesus and the Gospels* (New York: Routledge, 1996), 151–52.

3. For example, Bruce J. Malina and Richard L. Rohrbaugh, *Social-Science Commentary on the Synoptic Gospels* (Minneapolis: Augsburg Fortress, 1992), 81–83.

4. For example, K. C. Hanson and D. E. Oakman, *Palestine in the Time of Jesus:*

Social Structures and Social Conflicts (Minneapolis: Augsburg Fortress, 1998), 114–16.

5. Ibid., 120–25.

6. Bruce J. Malina, *The New Testament World: Insights from Cultural Anthropology*, rev. ed. (Louisville: Westminster John Knox, 1993), 104.

CHAPTER 11

How They Viewed the World

*Recognizing that the Bible expresses itself in the "language" of its original audiences
does not negate the message of the New Testament in any way; it affirms
our belief in a God who wishes to reveal himself to His people.*

Is Heaven Up?

Have you ever tried to explain something really complicated to a child? Where do babies come from? Why do bad things happen to good people? These kinds of questions require you to get down on the child's level and speak in terms the child can understand. If you believe that God inspired the writings of the Bible, then it makes sense to believe that He spoke in this way to those who first received these words—just as He presumably speaks to us today. Indeed, throughout the whole Bible we see language that reflects the way the people of that day viewed the world.

For example, when Jesus ascended to heaven after His resurrection, He went straight up into the clouds (Acts 1:9). Why? Is heaven really straight up? The first

At a Glance

- Many Jews believed in several different heavens (layers of heaven with God himself in the highest heaven).

- Many ancients believed that the earth and its people were inferior in quality to these heavens and the spiritual beings that inhabited them.

- The ancients had a strong sense of fate.

- The Stoics believed the best way to happiness was to accept your fate and live in accordance with divine reason.

- Different groups had different beliefs in an afterlife: some believed in the resurrection of all or of the good; some believed in an impersonal existence after death; some believed in no afterlife at all.

111

person to orbit the earth made fun of Christianity because he did not see God or angels above the clouds. Yet many Jews of Jesus' day certainly thought heaven should be about where the Soviet cosmonaut was looking when he was in orbit. They believed the earth was at the bottom of the universe and that God dwelt straight up above the clouds beyond several layers of sky.

> "And I entered the first heaven, and saw there much water suspended. And again I saw a second heaven much brighter and more lustrous . . . And the angel said to me, ' . . . you will see another heaven more lustrous beyond compare' . . ."
>
> " 'In the uppermost heaven of all dwells the Great Glory in the Holy of Holies superior to all holiness.' "
>
> **The Testament of Levi 2:7-9; 3:4**

Whether you believe Jesus actually left the earth in this way or not, this type of exit was completely appropriate for Jesus' audience. We should not try to impose our own views of the world on the Bible—like the idea that the earth goes around the sun— or be surprised that God would reveal himself in terms to which the Bible's first audiences could relate. Indeed, our great-great-grandchildren will probably have a somewhat different view of the universe than we do.

What the Universe Looked Like

The idea that the earth was a globe did exist in Jesus' day. However, the ordinary person saw the world as basically flat. Heaven was up and earth was down. Under the earth was water and, for some, the mindless spirits of the dead. The glimpses of the world we see on the pages of the Bible do not differ much from this.

For example, Genesis 1 pictures the heavens containing stars, sun, and moon (1:14-19).[1] Above and below these heavens were waters (1:6-8)—if one went "up" from the stars, one would encounter primordial waters. The waters beneath the heavens collected to allow land to appear (1:9). Apparently the same waters pictured "above" the sun, moon, and stars in Genesis 1 came down during the

> "And God said, 'Let there be a space in the middle of the waters, and it will separate the waters from the waters' . . . And God called the space, 'Heavens.'"
>
> **Genesis 1:6, 8 (author's translation)**

Flood, while the waters under the earth came springing up (7:11).[2] Try though we might, this picture is simply not the one we would draw of the universe today. But it was an appropriate way for God to express His creative majesty to the ancient Israelites.

When we get to the New Testament, we are not surprised that Philippians 2:10 divides up the universe similar to the Genesis account—things *in heaven*, things *on earth*, and things *under the earth*. Revelation 5:13 adds the sea to this list: "every creature in heaven and on earth and under the earth and in the sea." Yet there are also some differences between the Old and New Testaments in these regards, just as the view of the world changed a little between the time of Genesis and the time of the New Testament.

For example, the apostle Paul mentions one occasion in which he found himself in the "third" heaven. Interestingly, he was not sure whether he visited this place in or out of his body (2 Cor. 12:2-3). A significant amount of Jewish literature around the time of Christ pictures the sky leading to God as a series of layers of heaven. Even the epistle to the Hebrews pictures Jesus' ascension to heaven as a passage through different heavens (Heb. 4:14; 7:26), with the highest heaven being the place where Jesus now sits next to God's throne (9:24; 10:12).

It is understandable that the ancients would view the heavens as superior to the earth and heavenly beings as superior to earthly beings. The gods and angels had far more power than human beings. In some respects the gods were a way for people to express the mysterious aspects of their world that were beyond their control. As nature was unpredictable and fickle, so the Greeks and Romans pictured their gods as forces whose whims and fancies were to be feared. What was certain was that no human should ever boast of being in complete control of his own life or destiny. To do so was almost a challenge for the gods to exert their power over such a person. We will say more about the **fatalism** of the ancient world later on in this chapter.

However, for some, heaven was purer than its portrayal in certain Greek myths. For Jews and Christians, heaven was the purest place of all and God was predictably as faithful as could be. The Greek philosopher **Plato**, although he did not really picture gods in heaven, similarly saw the heavenly world as more perfect than the earthly world. For him, the earthly realm was simply a copy, a shadow of the heavenly realm.[3] For example, a horse you might see running around on earth was an imperfect copy of the perfect idea of a horse that existed in heaven—a world we only have access to through our minds.

> **fatalism:** The sense that nothing happens by chance, that everything that takes place is determined by forces beyond human control.

This sense that heaven and earth contained two different kinds of things, one perfect and the other imperfect, was also fairly common in Jesus' day, both for Jews and non-Jews. It plays itself out in the epistle to the Hebrews, where one of the reasons Christ's death is such an effective sacrifice is because it is offered *in heaven* in the true sanctuary and not in an *earthly* temple made with human hands (9:11). Whether it came by way of Greek influence or not, Jewish apocalyptic literature similarly divided the world into the earthly, visible world we see, and the hidden, spiritual realm where spiritual forces battle. This is the world of Matthew, Revelation, and Jude.

Recognizing that the Bible expresses itself in the "language" of its original audiences does not negate the message of the New Testament in any way;

it affirms our belief in a God who wishes to reveal himself to His people. It also presents us with a strong warning in relating the Bible's words to modern science or psychology. We should not mistake the envelope in which God's message came to His people for the message itself.

What Is a Human Being?

The idea that the earthly was inferior to the heavenly played itself out in the way the ancients viewed human beings. For Plato, a person was made up of two parts, a body and a soul. The soul was a part of your mind; it was here that you could reach heaven and think about truth. Your body was only a hindrance to reason. While he did not consider the body evil as the Gnostics later would,[4] Plato believed that it was an obstacle to perfection. This belief was common at the time of Christ.

We see traces of this way of thinking in the New Testament. While the apostle Paul did not think of a soul in the same way Plato did, he made interesting distinctions between flesh and *spirit*. The physical body, one's flesh, is the foothold of sin's power over humanity. On the

"Now if he were on earth, he would not be a priest at all, since there are priests who offer gifts according to the law. They offer worship in a sanctuary that is a sketch and shadow of the heavenly one."

Hebrews 8:4-5 NRSV

"Therefore, since we have a great high priest who has gone through the heavens, Jesus the Son of God, let us hold firmly to the faith we profess."

Hebrews 4:14 NIV

"Such a high priest meets our need—one who is holy, blameless, pure, set apart from sinners, exalted above the heavens."

Hebrews 7:26 NIV

"The point of what we are saying is this: We do have such a high priest, who sat down at the right hand of the throne of the Majesty in heaven, and who serves in the sanctuary, the true tabernacle set up by the Lord, not by man."

Hebrews 8:1-2 NIV

> "I am of the **flesh**, sold into slavery under sin . . . I know that nothing good dwells in me, that is, **in my flesh** . . . Who will rescue me from this **body** of death . . ."
>
> **Romans 7:14, 18, 24 NRSV**

other hand, God's *Spirit* frees a person from that power. The epistle to the Hebrews similarly sees the body as the place where Satan holds sway over humans. Because human beings share flesh and blood, as Hebrews tells us, Christ also partook of them so He could destroy the devil's power (2:14). God prepared a body for Christ to enable Him to accomplish His mission (10:5). What we see here is that at least Greek-speaking Christians used some of the psychological "lingo" of the day to express truths about what God was doing in their lives.

> "In the beginning was the Logos, and the Logos was with God, and the Logos was God . . . And the Logos became flesh, and made his tent with us."
>
> **John 1:1, 14 (author's translation)**

> "The reasoning of mortals is worthless and our designs are likely to fail, for a **perishable body** weighs down the soul, and this earthy tent burdens the thoughtful mind."
>
> **Wisdom of Solomon 9:14-15 NRSV**

Perhaps the most significant philosophy in the world at the time of Christ was that of **Stoicism**. Unlike Plato, the Stoics emphasized the *similarity* between the heavenly and earthly rather than the *difference*. They believed that everything that happened in the world happened for a reason, and that the world operated according to a divine Mind that governed everything. While they could talk about this Mind as if it were like God, they really did not think of it as a person. It was Reason itself or a divine "Word" relating to the creation. The Greek word that meant all these things was *logos*.

With this in mind, it is interesting that we find *logos* language in the New Testament in reference to Christ. When the Gospel of John states that the "*Logos* became flesh" in the person of Jesus, for example, the author may have meant that the whole purpose of God for the world is to be found in Christ. It was common in the Jewish literature of Jesus' day to consider this *Logos* to be the image or copy of God's goodness and perfection—a kind of mixture of Stoic and Platonic thought. Therefore, it is no surprise that the New Testament uses exactly this type of language to refer to Christ.

Since the Stoics believed the *Logos* governed the world without any possible opposition, it was pointless to fight against it. Indeed, the ancient world in general was very fatalistic; they

"The law of the Spirit of life in Christ Jesus has set you free from the law of sin and of death. For God has done what the law, weakened by the flesh, could not do . . . so that the just requirement of the law might be fulfilled in us, who walk not according to the flesh but according to the Spirit."

Romans 8:2-4 NRSV

"[Christ] is the **image** of the invisible God, the firstborn of all creation; for in him all things in heaven and on earth were created."

Colossians 1:15 NRSV

"[Christ] is the **reflection** of God's glory and the **exact imprint** of God's very being, and he sustains all things by his powerful word."

Hebrews 1:3 NRSV

believed that Fate was in control of the world. Even the gods submitted to its will. Everyone was "predestined" to a certain fate. Resistance was futile.

The Stoics believed that there was a divine fragment of the *Logos* in everyone, namely, the human spirit. It was a little *logos* seed in every person. The key to happiness was listening to this seed. The Stoic life meant living according to reason and learning to love one's fate. People should not care about their hardships or pain; they should accept the lot that the *Logos* assigned them.

In general, the New Testament and especially the letters of Paul often echo this way of thinking. Paul frequently made statements that sound "deterministic," which means the things that happen are determined; everything that happens is a part of God's plan. For example, Paul pointed out that God selected him "from [his] mother's womb" as the one who would bring Christianity to non-Jews (Gal. 1:15). Paul often referred to Christians as people whom God has called (e.g., Rom. 1:7), and his discussion of "predestination" in Romans 9–11 is a notorious point of contention between many denominations. Many Christians believe that God has already chosen who will go to heaven—we are unable to choose God unless He has selected us.[5] Any discussion of the subject should take into account the fact that this way of talking was a common feature of the ancient world.

> "I have learned how to get along happily whether I have much or little. I know how to live on almost nothing or with everything. I have learned the secret of living in every situation, whether it is with a full stomach or empty, with plenty or little."
>
> **Philippians 4:11-12**

Once you understand the deterministic aspect of ancient thinking, you will have to decide how you think it relates to the New Testament. For many ancients, some personal force or agent was behind everything that happened. A rock did not just happen to fall on someone—a spiritual being caused it to fall. So as you read the gospels, you will have to decide whether the demons described were real beings or an ancient cultural expression of physical or psychological illness. The gospels certainly do make a distinction between Jesus' healings and His exorcisms.

> "[Paul] also had a debate with some of the Epicurean and Stoic philosophers . . . When they heard Paul speak of the resurrection of a person who had been dead, some laughed, but others said, 'We want to hear more about this later.' "
>
> **Paul in Athens, Acts 17:18, 32**

The Afterlife

Plato believed that the soul had always existed and was placed into a body at birth. When that person died, the soul continued to exist and would eventually migrate to another newborn. While Plato believed in an afterlife, he did not see that afterlife as personal, one where one kept memories and individual identity.[6]

The **Stoics**, who came several years after Plato, also believed in an afterlife. The *logos* seed in a person—the spirit—returned to the heavens at death and reunited with the *Logos* of the world. Again, this was not a personal afterlife in which a person retained individuality after death.

However, many in the ancient world did not believe in life after death at all. The **Epicureans** believed that existence completely came to an end at death. By the time of Christ, they believed you should "feast and get drunk, for tomorrow we die" (1 Cor. 15:32).[7]

They did believe we had souls. It is important for us to realize the

---

"Not all of us will die, but we will all be transformed. It will happen in a moment, in the blinking of an eye, when the last trumpet is blown. For when the trumpet sounds, the Christians who have died will be raised with transformed bodies."

1 Corinthians 15:51-52

Relevant Philosophies at the Time of Christ

Platonists: Platonists believed that earthly things were simply copies, images, and shadows of heavenly realities and that the only way to access these truths was through the mind. They believed in a soul that survived death only to migrate to another body.

Stoics: Stoics believed that the Logos, the divine Reason that was in all things, directed and ordered the world. Since we could not possibly overcome its direction, we should accept our fate and not be concerned with pain or emotion. We should listen to the small seed of logos that is the human spirit. This seed returns to the Logos of the world at death.

Epicureans: They did not believe in an afterlife; a person's soul atoms disintegrated at death just like the body. By the time of Christ, they believed that one should "eat, drink, and be merry, for tomorrow we die."

idea of a soul not made out of matter is a fairly recent idea. The ancients believed that spirits and souls were made out of "stuff" just like our bodies were; it was just heavenly stuff, "ethereal" matter. Angels were thought of in terms like "winds" and "flames" (Heb. 1:7), just as the Holy Spirit was compared to wind (John 3:8).

Therefore, when Paul thought of resurrection, he was thinking of us as having a spiritual body. A spiritual body has a different kind of "glory" from other bodies, such as our physical bodies or the "bodies" of the sun and stars (1 Cor. 15:40-41). But he thought of them all as being made up of matter.

Also of importance is realizing that the New Testament says very little about humans having immortal souls, as most Christians think. We tend to think we go immediately to heaven or hell at death, our souls detaching from our bodies. Yet this idea is not primarily what the New Testament teaches.

resurrection of the dead: The dead brought back to life when Christ returns. At that time God will provide the dead with "spiritual" bodies.

Early Christianity based its thought on the **resurrection of bodies** rather than on the immortality of souls. The continuation of our existence after death centered on that point in the future when God would reconstitute a body for us.

What would happen in the meantime? Passages in the New Testament do seem to indicate that human existence continues between death and the resurrection, a future time when Christ returns to earth. Jesus tells the thief on the cross that he will be with Jesus in Paradise on that very day, implying that both of their spirits would continue to exist after death. However, the focus of the afterlife for early Christianity was in the future when God would put the world back in order.

~

Things to Think About

1. Many Christians have strong beliefs about things like evolution or the existence of a detachable soul. Many look to the Bible for a "biblical" perspective on psychology and countless other topics of modern concern. If God revealed himself within the worldviews of those to whom He was originally speaking, however, to what extent is the Bible really the place to go for answers to questions like these today?

Key Terms

Epicureanism

fatalism

Platonism/Plato

resurrection of the dead

Stoicism/Stoics

2. Some would say that beneath the cultural skin of the Bible—the points where it relates to the worldviews and practices of its day—is a core that is timeless. Others resist the notion that there is anything "cultural" in the Bible at all; they might suggest that those who start to "peel away" at the Bible will find themselves with an onion that disappears completely. How would you enter into this debate? Can we get away from the idea that ancient worldviews are part of the Bible?

3. When the Bible is read in context, is there such a thing as a "biblical worldview" at all, or are numerous perspectives recorded in the Bible, all of which are related to the worlds to which God was speaking at the time? Does the Bible give us a timeless, absolute worldview? How do we find it? Is such a viewpoint even attainable for a human being? Is it possible to mistake our own cultural perspective for God's absolute perspective?

endnotes

1. The original languages of the Bible do not distinguish between "heaven" and sky"—it is the same word. While some modern translations make Genesis 1 recognizable for us by using the word sky, the word heaven is equally appropriate.

2. One should not think of this depiction as an "error," for Genesis presents its picture from the perspective of someone standing on the earth. The purpose of the chapter is not to give us a scientific description of creation. To think it in error, therefore, is to fault it for something completely alien to its purpose.

3. Many translations of Hebrews 8:5 and 9:24 say that the earthly sanctuary of the Israelites was a "copy" and "shadow" of a heavenly original, making Hebrews' argument sound really Platonic. Indeed, this language may have some Platonic overtones. Nevertheless, "sketch" is closer than "copy" to what the word originally meant.

4. See chapters 28 and 52 of this text.

5. See chapters 38 and 40 of this text.

6. Remember, the ancients did not think in terms of individual identity, anyway.

7. The original Epicureans did not teach this way of life, however.

CHAPTER 12

Religious Thinking at the Time of Christ

*Religion in the ancient world revolved around satisfying
the gods in order to keep life in this world from becoming miserable.*

A Different Mind-Set

For many Americans, religion is just one aspect of their total life concerns. The "separation of church and state" is a theme we often hear aimed at keeping religious matters out of anything relating to American government. A popular cliché warns that "you don't discuss religion or politics" unless you want to get into an argument.

The ancients did not compartmentalize their lives in this way. Serving the gods appropriately exemplified good citizenship; willingness to sacrifice to them was a sign of patriotism. The Romans praised the gods for military victories, and Roman politicians were often priests. The gods were involved in every arena of one's life, not just at a temple. Failure to serve the gods could be a crime punishable by the state. For Jews, as well,

At a Glance

- In ancient times, no clear dividing line existed between the "religious" or the "political."

- The Greeks and Romans worshiped many gods.

- Mystery religions involved secret rituals and secret knowledge for those who were members.

- Many Jews at the time of Christ believed in a host of angelic and demonic powers.

- The ancients generally believed some personal force or agent was behind everything that happened.

- Some Roman emperors demanded worship.

the worship of Yahweh involved the whole of their life—not just one day a week or a few hours here and there.

Important Differences

However, there were some important differences between how **pagan** religions functioned—those that involved the worship of many gods—and how Judaism and Christianity operated. For example, most religions of Jesus' day had little to do with what people believed or how they lived their lives. Instead, religion involved offering prayers and sacrifices to gods and being involved in certain ritual ceremonies.

pagan: Worshiping many gods (polytheistic) as opposed to one god (monotheistic).

Belief in the gods did not matter as much as the prayers and rituals. Evidently some Christians who held public office in the city of Corinth saw no problem with eating at pagan temples. In their minds, eating there did not necessarily equate to belief in that particular god. Non-Christians would hardly favor a person who did not take part in the ritual meals.

Nor was there any expectation that a person honored the gods by living a certain way. The philosophers taught those kinds of things. Perhaps this understanding of religion partially explains why some Christians at Corinth were not alarmed that one of their people was sleeping with his stepmother; they were not used to connecting religion with a code of conduct.

Religion in the ancient world revolved around satisfying the gods in order to keep life in this world from becoming miserable. It was not about having a good afterlife or going to heaven. Most of the ancients either did not believe in an afterlife or thought of it as a shadowy existence in the underworld. Among other things, they served the gods to prevent disease and sickness, to enable their crops to grow, or to protect themselves from their enemies. In other words, religion helped a person in *this* life. Again, perhaps this mindset helps us better understand how the Thessalonian church could have such fundamental questions about the fate of the dead, while some of those in Corinth evidently did not believe in a future resurrection.

Finally, Judaism and Christianity differed from the other religions of that day in the number of gods they worshiped. Many ancients looked down on the Jews and considered them immoral because they worshiped only one God—Yahweh. The rest of the world had countless gods to serve. People often considered the gods of other nations to be the same gods they worshiped under different names. So Isis of Egypt was Demeter of Greece or Ceres of Rome.

Because Christians and Jews only worshiped one God, many people considered them to be atheists. They thought it best to respect all the gods to keep disaster away. On the other hand, it was also illegal to invent new gods. In Acts 17, the men of Athens brought Paul to a kind of hearing to investigate what he was teaching. "He seems to be a proclaimer of foreign divinities" (Acts 17:18 NRSV), they said. All these dynamics are quite foreign to the way we think of religion.

> "According to some people, there are many so-called gods and many lords, both in heaven and on earth. But we know that there is only one God, the Father, who created everything, and we exist for him. And there is only one Lord, Jesus Christ, through whom God made everything and through whom we have been given life."
>
> **1 Corinthians 8:5-6**

> "When the listening crowd saw what Paul had done, they shouted in their local dialect, 'These men are gods in human bodies!' They decided that Barnabas was the Greek god Zeus and that Paul, because he was the chief speaker, was Hermes. The temple of Zeus was located on the outskirts of the city. The priest of the temple and the crowd brought oxen and wreaths of flowers, and they prepared to sacrifice to the apostles at the city gates."
>
> **Acts 14:11-13**

Perhaps you have heard of the Greek and Roman gods. The planets bear some of their names–Mercury, Venus, Mars, Jupiter, Saturn, Neptune, and Pluto. Their Greek counterparts are Hermes, Aphrodite, Ares, Zeus, Cronus, Poseidon, and Hades. Of these, Zeus was the chief and most powerful god. Temples to these and other gods could be found anywhere in the ancient Mediterranean world. As Christianity spread across the world, it increasingly came into conflict with the worship of these gods.

For example, the city of Corinth contained a major temple to Aphrodite, the goddess of love. Some suggest that Paul's comments on prostitutes in 1 Corinthians 6, perhaps even what he had to say about homosexual activity in Romans 1 and 1 Corinthians 6:9 carry overtones of the temple prostitutes involved in the rituals of such temples. Similarly, regarding 1 Timothy's harsh-sounding words about women in the church, some scholars relate this to the practice of giving women prominent roles of leadership in the temple of Artemis in Ephesus.

Acts mentions a tremendous uproar in Ephesus when the growth of Christianity began to affect those who sold statuettes or **idols** of Artemis. A riot burst out at the amphitheater there with the crowds shouting, "Great is Artemis of the Ephesians!" For some it may be hard to imagine such strong feelings over things like statues and figurines. We must realize that their feelings on such issues ran as deeply as ours might over our religious or political views today.

idol: A physical representation of a god, such as a statue or figurine, that is used to worship the god.

Mystery Religions

Some of the most popular forms of religion at the time of Christ were called **mystery religions**. Participants underwent secret rituals to overcome the chaos of life and to secure a happy afterlife in the underworld. The secret rituals and the mysteries were kept so secret that we still do not know much about them. We know they usually were associated with the death of a god. They sometimes involved ritual washings and special communal meals. The "initiate," or person entering the religion, received secret knowledge and, in some cases, "salvation" at the hands of a particular god or goddess, who transformed the initiate and kept him or her safe from the whims of chance.

> **mystery religions:** Religions that involved secret rituals relating to the death of a god, secret knowledge, and the guarantee of a happy afterlife.

> "And if I have prophetic powers, and understand all **mysteries** and all knowledge . . . but do not have love, I am nothing."
>
> **1 Corinthians 13:2 NRSV**

Does this description sound familiar? If you know much about Christianity, it should sound very much like some of what Christians believe about Jesus Christ. Indeed, at one time some scholars thought that many Christian beliefs about Christ did not exist until Christianity came into contact with the mystery religions of the Greco-Roman world.[1] However, the great majority of scholars no longer hold to this idea.

Some superficial similarities exist in the New Testament—particularly in Paul's writings—between language about coming to Christ and the language of the mystery religions. It seems likely that some new Christians understood their newfound religion in terms similar to their previous experiences with mystery religions. When Paul mentioned "mysteries" in 1 Corinthians 13:2, some in his audience no doubt thought of the mysteries of Isis at Corinth and Demeter at Eleusis. It is not a stretch to suggest that part of the Corinthian Christians' problem was that they *did* understand Christianity as a new mystery religion in which they had received secret wisdom. They thus had become "superior" in their knowledge—even to other Christians in the community.

It is when Paul talked about **conversion** to Christianity—the process of becoming a Christian—that his language sounded most similar to the "salvation" of the mystery religions. One account of initiation into the mysteries of Isis in Corinth, for example, involved both a descent into the realm of the dead and an ascent into the heavens above—a kind of symbolic death and rebirth. When Paul spoke of conversion, he similarly talked about being buried into death with Christ and rising with Him in His resurrection. We cannot know for sure if Paul was deliberately imitating the language of the mysteries when he spoke in these terms. He did say at one point that he always presented himself and his message in ways that would help win converts to Christ. Perhaps he did this when he was dealing with people who had participated in the mystery religions.

conversion: The process of changing from one religion to another; the process of becoming a Christian.

Spiritual Forces

Non-Jews at the time of Christ believed in numerous divine forces with less power than gods like Zeus or Isis, but with far more power than human beings. This group not only included lesser gods and spirits—the gods of rivers, for example, or the gods of your particular family—but also human beings who had reached divine status, like Hercules or the emperors of Rome. Many non-Jews who heard the Christian story no doubt first thought of Jesus as a hero like Hercules, who was given a place among the gods because of his good deeds for humanity.

The Jews also believed in a host of

"The high priest said, 'Both the gates of death and the guardianship of life were in the goddess's hands, and the act of initiation was performed in the manner of voluntary death and salvation obtained by favour . . .'"

Apuleius, *The Golden Ass* 11.21

spiritual beings like angels and demons that inhabited the heavenly regions between God and humanity. For example, the apostle Paul did not deny the spiritual forces behind the temples of the Greek and Roman gods. He just considered them to be demonic beings (1 Cor. 10:20). The power behind the temple of Aphrodite in Corinth existed, but it was a demon. Paul told the Corinthian church that Christians would judge such angels on the Day of Judgment (1 Cor. 6:3).[2] It was probably to these kinds of spiritual forces that he referred when he said that God was bringing to nothing the "rulers of this world" that killed Jesus (1 Cor. 2:6-8).

> "Don't you know that all of us who were baptized into Christ Jesus were baptized into his death? We were therefore buried with him through baptism into death in order that, just as Christ was raised from the dead . . . we too may live a new life."
> **Romans 6:3-4 NIV**

> "Therefore, if anyone is in Christ, he is a new creation; the old has gone, the new has come!"
> **2 Corinthians 5:17 NIV**

Good angels also appear in the pages of the New Testament. For example, Gabriel, the messenger angel, brought Mary the message that she was about to give birth to Jesus (Luke 1:26). The warrior angel Michael appears in Jude 9, where he argues with Satan about the body of Moses. Countless other good angels appear in such books as Revelation and Hebrews.[3]

Satan, or the devil, is of course the most evil of the spiritual forces that inhabit the space between God and humanity. He is Beelzebul, the prince of demons (Mark 3:20-30). Until the time Jesus walked the earth, Satan dominated the earthly realm. The primary significance of Jesus' exorcisms—casting demons out of people—was to end Satan's rule on earth. As Jesus said when the disciples told Him they had cast out demons, "I saw Satan falling from heaven as a flash of lightning" (Luke 10:18). Jesus' mission foreshadowed the end of Satan's power.

Concern about such demonic or "unclean spirits" was common to both

> "I am convinced that nothing can ever separate us from his love. Death can't, and life can't. The angels can't, and the demons can't . . . even the powers of hell can't keep God's love away. Whether we are high above the sky or in the deepest ocean, nothing in all creation will ever be able to separate us from the love of God that is revealed in Christ Jesus our Lord."
>
> **Romans 8:38-39**

Ruins of Domitian's temple at Ephesus

Jew and non-Jew at the time of Christ. Jesus was not the only human of that day said to heal people and cast out demons. As we mentioned in the last chapter, the general assumption was that nothing happened without someone causing it, whether that someone was a human, spirit, or god. Disease and misfortune were often interpreted as the acts of a demon or spirit. The common person often resorted to magic to try to be rid of such spirits, although this practice could also backfire.[4] Others turned to the mystery religions for the protection of a god. No doubt some also turned to Christianity to escape these kinds of forces. One of the eeriest things Paul told the Corinthian church to do was to turn out one of its own into the world—away from the spiritual protection of the church into the domain of Satan (1 Cor. 5:5). The hope was that while his body—the foothold of the devil—would be destroyed, his spirit might be reclaimed.

Emperor Worship

It may seem strange to us that the Romans and other ancient peoples worshiped their rulers as gods. Part of this stems from the way we look at

130

emperor worship: The practice in the Roman empire of venerating the emperors as gods, usually after their deaths. In many places, however, they were worshiped prior to their deaths (e.g., Asia Minor), and a few emperors actually demanded worship (e.g., Caligula and Domitian). Such worship at the very least involved offering sacrifices to them as gods.

human beings. We believe a person to be a body made up of chemicals like carbon, oxygen, and nitrogen. We also have a well-developed sense of who a person is individually. In a sense, we look at people from the inside out. How then would we view a human as divine? Would the chemical makeup of the human-divine body be different? What kind of thoughts or personality would such a person have?

Divinity in the ancient world was more about power and honor than about makeup. It was more about having a particular status and role than existing as a specific kind of being. It might mean that such a person had the authority to act upon a world to which most people could only submit. In short, the ancients viewed divine individuals more from the outside looking in than from the inside looking out.

"Herod [Agrippa I] put on his royal robes, sat on his throne, and made a speech to them. The people gave him a great ovation, shouting, 'It is the voice of a god, not of a man.'"

Acts 12:21-22

Even then, most ancient rulers were not afforded divine status until after their deaths. It is only around the first century A.D. that some Roman emperors demanded worship while they were still living. Participating in such worship was

"This woman you saw in your vision represents the great city that rules over the kings of the earth."

Revelation 17:18

an act of patriotism as much as anything else. It is no surprise that in the second century, a Roman official named Pliny would test Christians by demanding they offer sacrifices to the emperor. If they refused, they were put to death.

Some of the imagery of Revelation may relate to the **emperor worship** that was particularly strong in the area where this book was written (Rev. 13:4, 12). Other scholars suggest that the "abomination" predicted in Mark 13:14 refers to the emperor Caligula's attempt to set up his own statue in the Jewish temple. Terms like "Savior," "Lord," and "Son of God" were all applied to the Roman emperors. It was thus inevitable that Christians would come into conflict with Roman authorities—the language they used set Jesus in direct conflict with the emperor as the ruler and authority of this world.

Things to Think About

Key Terms
conversion
emperor worship
idol
mystery religions
pagan

1. Would you say that religion is simply one *part* of your life or does it connect to all the aspects of your life in general?

2. Can you get into the head of someone for whom religion is not about the afterlife but about this life?

3. How far are you willing to take the idea that the ancients interpreted natural phenomena as the product of spiritual forces? Do you believe that demons, angels, or Satan exist today? Do you think any of the demon-possessed people Jesus healed actually had something like epilepsy, or is this going too far?

4. Can you get into the head of people who considered their emperors to be gods? Put yourself into a situation where an inscription on American currency would declare our ex-presidents to be gods—would you spend this money? Using the model of ancient emperor worship, what would it mean to say that an American president was a god?

endnotes

1. That is, the Greek-Roman world. The two became so blended at the time of Christ that they basically made up one culture and worldview (although distinctions can be made).
2. The apostle Paul did not restrict the word angel to good beings only; he also used it in reference to fallen angels.
3. For example, Hebrews 1 shows how much greater Christ is than angels. Hebrews 12:22 shows angels celebrating in heaven.
4. In *The Golden Ass*, a second-century novel by Apuleius, Lucius accidentally becomes a donkey when someone untrained in magic tries to work its art on him.

For Further Study

Introductions to the Old Testament

- Arnold, Bill T. and Bryan E. Beyer. *Encountering the Old Testament: A Christian Survey*. Grand Rapids: Baker, 1999.

- Harris, Stephen L. *Understanding the Bible*. 5th ed. Mountain View, CA: Mayfield, 2000.

- Hill, Andrew E. and John H. Walton. *A Survey of the Old Testament*. Grand Rapids: Zondervan, 1991.

Judaism Before Christ

- Boccaccini, Gabriele. *Beyond the Essene Hypothesis: The Parting of the Ways between Qumran and Enochic Judaism*. Grand Rapids: Eerdmans, 1998.

- Saldarini, Anthony J. *Pharisees, Scribes, and Sadducees in Palestinian Society: A Sociological Approach* (Biblical Resource Series). Grand Rapids: Eerdmans, 2001.

- Sanders, E. P. *Judaism: Practice and Belief 63BCE–66CE*. Valley Forge, PA: Trinity, 1992.

- VanderKam, James C. *The Dead Sea Scrolls Today*. Grand Rapids: Eerdmans, 1994.

- _____. *An Introduction to Early Judaism*. Grand Rapids: Eerdmans, 2001.

New Testament Background

- Barrett, C. K. *The New Testament Background: Writings from Ancient Greece and the Roman Empire That Illuminate Christian Origins*. Rev. ed. San Francisco: HarperCollins, 1987.

• Bell, Albert A., Jr. *Exploring the New Testament World: An Illustrated Guide to the World of Jesus and the First Christians*. Nashville: Thomas Nelson, 1998.

• Ferguson, Everett. *Backgrounds of Early Christianity*. Grand Rapids: Eerdmans, 1987.

• Hanson, K. C. and Douglas E. Oakman. *Palestine in the Time of Jesus: Social Structures and Social Conflicts.* Minneapolis: Fortress, 1998.

• Malina, Bruce J. *The New Testament World: Insights from Cultural Anthropology*. Rev. ed. Louisville: Westminster John Knox, 1993.

• _____. *The Social World of Jesus and the Gospels*. New York: Routledge, 1996.

Unit 3:
Gospels

Chapters 13–28

CHAPTER 13

What Is a Gospel?

Ancient biographies focused primarily on an individual's character. Biographers told their audiences about events they thought would present that person's character effectively.

Good News

You may have heard the word *gospel* before, especially if you are someone who goes to church every once in a while. Perhaps you have even heard someone say that the word *gospel* basically means "good news." This definition provides a good place to start. In fact, some Bibles translate the word in this way.

But the word **gospel** did not refer to just any old good news. The Romans and Greeks reserved this word for good news of an extraordinary sort, such as an important military victory or the birth of a future emperor. In the Old Testament, Isaiah 52:7 proclaims the "good news" that Israel has been freed from its captivity in Babylon—

At a Glance

- In general, the word gospel refers to good news of an extraordinary sort.

- The first meaning of gospel for the New Testament is the "good news" that Jesus brought to Israel—the restoration of God's people and the reestablishment of God as their King.

- The second meaning is the "good news" that God accomplished this salvation through Jesus himself.

- When the word gospel refers to a type of writing, it is referring to literature whose broad aim is to present the good news of Jesus Christ.

- With the possible exception of Luke, the gospels resemble ancient biography more closely than any other ancient genre.

- Ancient biographies focused on the character of an individual, who was assumed to fit a certain type.

incredibly good news indeed! What this particular good news indicates for Isaiah is that "God reigns"; He really is the ultimate King who brings victory to His people when they serve

> **gospel:** Good news of an extraordinary sort, such as an important military victory or the birth of a future emperor.

Him. Thus, this verse in Isaiah is an announcement of the "kingship of God"—that God rules.

> "How beautiful on the mountains are the feet of those who bring **good news** of peace and salvation, the news that the God of Israel **reigns!**"
>
> **Isaiah 52:7**

> " 'At last the time has come!' he announced. 'The Kingdom of God is near! Turn from your sins and believe this Good News!' "
>
> **Mark 1:15**

> "Augustus . . . a benefactor among men . . . a Savior for us and those who come after us, to make war to cease, to create order everywhere . . . ; the birthday of the god [Augustus] was the beginning for the world of the good news that has come to men through him."
>
> **An inscription from Asia Minor**

> **kingdom of God:** The reign or rule of God, on earth as it is in heaven.

A lot of this may sound familiar. When we were telling the "story behind the story," we mentioned that many Jews at the time of Christ felt Israel was still in captivity and that an anointed king (a messiah) would come to free them. The good news that Jesus proclaimed was freedom from this captivity. If you know a little about Jesus' teaching, you may also know that His preaching centered on the kingdom of God. He had come to announce the good news that God was taking control of the world.

The first meaning of "gospel" for the New Testament, therefore, was the "good news" that Jesus proclaimed to the Jews of the countryside. He proclaimed the **kingdom of God**; that is, that God reigned. God was in control of their situation and was about to bring peace and freedom to His people once again. Jesus' central message was: "The time is fulfilled, and the **kingdom of God** is at hand; repent, and believe in the **gospel**" (Mark 1:15 RSV). The "gospel of Jesus Christ" was Jesus' teaching that God was about to restore His people Israel, renew His covenant with them, and reestablish himself as their King.

> **sin:** In general, any wrongdoing. For Jews it meant breaking the Old Testament Law.
>
> **salvation:** Escaping God's wrath, which is the consequence of our sins; being "saved" from our sins.

However, a further meaning of the word *gospel* arises because the early Christians believed that Jesus himself made this restoration possible. The New Testament does not restrict the restoration of God's people to the realm of politics. While many believe that the early Christians did believe Israel would be restored as a political nation, the New Testament teaches that God used Jesus to bring **salvation** to the whole world. That is, God not only can bring freedom from political slavery, He can free people from the "slavery" that comes from whatever wrong things they might do in this life—their **sins**. The New Testament focuses primarily on this meaning of *gospel*: *the gospel of Jesus Christ is the good news that God has used Christ to "save" us from the consequences of our sins.*

> **Gospel:** A type of literature whose aim is to present the gospel of Jesus Christ.

When we talk about the "**Gospel** of Matthew," however, we are using the word *gospel* in yet another way. The Gospel of Mark begins by saying that it is the "gospel of Jesus Christ" (Mark 1:1 RSV), which probably means that the book as a whole presents the good news that God is saving His people. Eventually, however, the whole book of Mark came to be called a "gospel." A new genre or kind of literature was born.[1] In this sense, a gospel is a type of literature which presents the good news of Jesus Christ. Although there are only four such gospels in our New Testament, a number of others also exist.

The Ancient Genre(s) of the Gospels

The gospels in our New Testament were written before "gospel" became a recognizable type of literature in its own right. So what kind of literature did the authors of these documents think they were writing? What other kinds of books would the ancient audiences have thought of as they listened to Matthew, Mark, Luke, and John? Some think this is not an important question. They believe God inspired these authors to write something unique, something different from anything that had been written before.

What *would* make this question important, however, is if the authors and audiences of these books had significantly different expectations than we do. Even today we have certain unspoken expectations of texts like these as we read them. While some read the gospels like they might read novels, others read them as if they were histories. Reading a gospel as a modern history, the reader would expect to learn things as if s/he were following Jesus around with a video camera or microphone. History and fiction are two basic genres (categories of literature or writing) that we have in our heads today; biography is another.

What about the ancient authors and readers? Did ancient authors write histories and biographies like today's history books and documentaries? Did they write what we call "historical fiction," stories in which the essential content is historical but some of the characters and events are fictitious? Or, will we simply have to learn a whole new set of rules for dealing with the gospels? These kinds of questions are very important in determining how to read the gospels.

The ancient genre that seems to come closest to most of the gospels is that of **biography**. Ancient biographies focused primarily on the *character* of the person in question. With that in mind, biographers then told their audiences about events they thought would present that person's character effectively. However, the ancients understood a person's character somewhat differently than biographers do today.

On the one hand, since the ancients often had a strong sense of destiny, they generally believed a person's character remained the same over the course of his or her life. If you turned out to be a great person, you must have always been great and probably even showed signs of greatness from birth. Similarly, a person did not become evil as a result of various events in his or her life; s/he was evil from birth. Modern biography does not presume that a person is born a certain way. It looks

> **biography (ancient):** In the ancient world, a genre of literature presenting a person primarily in terms of that person's character. This was made evident in the circumstances of the individual's birth, what others said about him or her, and the person's own actions and statements.

> "My subject in this book is the life of Alexander . . . I am writing biography, not history . . . When a portrait painter sets out to create a likeness, he relies above all on the face and the expression of the eyes and pays less attention to the other parts of the body: In the same way it is my task to dwell upon those actions which illuminate the workings of the soul."
>
> **Plutarch's *Life of Alexander*, 1**

for specific events that have impacted a person, causing him or her to develop specific character traits. Especially important are the turning points in a person's life, defining moments that bring about decisive direction in one's life.

A second aspect of ancient biography derives from the fact that the ancients were group oriented rather than individualistic in their focus. While modern biography emphasizes the individuality and uniqueness of an individual, ancient biography looked more to the typical—how an individual either conformed to or violated the biographer's values. Ancient characterization tended to be predictable, what we sometimes call "flat," rather than dynamic or "round." Biography relied more on stereotype than particularity.

Did ancient biographers stick closely to what actually happened? Did they check up on their sources? This varied from author to author. We live in a world that gives us amazing access to an incredible amount of information. We have cameras on the scene for any important event. In general, the ancients did not have the means to validate every detail, nor were they especially concerned with precision in their history writing. If a story about someone fit the "type" of character a biographer was portraying, that biographer would probably include it, whether or not he could confirm that the event actually happened.

We should keep in mind these aspects of ancient biography when we read the gospels. A careful study of the gospels reveals that they also focused on various aspects of Jesus' character. The gospels presented Jesus in terms of various themes. Matthew presents Jesus as a person like Moses, both a king and the supreme teacher/interpreter of the Jewish law. Mark presents Him as a king who shows His kingship most powerfully when He dies for His people. John presents Him as God come down from heaven to bring eternal life to those who believe in Him. In each case, the events each gospel writer shares and the way he tells those events fit his overall portrait. It is important to read each gospel as an individual entity in order to learn the aspect of Jesus' character on which that particular gospel is focusing. When we prematurely mix the different portrayals together, we do not really hear them.

Scholars debate whether the Gospel of Luke is more like ancient history or biography. Luke is actually the first of two volumes, the second of which is the book of Acts. Taken as a whole, these two books focus on several different individuals rather than one. In fact, the author of Luke tells us that he is presenting us with a "narrative" (Luke 1:1). Acts does not look much like a continuation of Jesus' biography either. It begins with Luke describing his "first book" (Luke) as a presentation of the things that Jesus began *to do* and to teach (Acts 1:1). We will discuss the ancient genre of history further when we get to the book of Acts.

Things to Think About

Key Terms
biography (ancient)
gospel
Gospel
kingdom of God
salvation
sin

1. How are each of the meanings of the word *gospel* "good news" to those using it?

2. Do you think the gospel writers wrote these books in terms of the conventions of their day, or are the four gospels unique in genre? Should we read them with the expectations an ancient might have had toward a biography or history? With the expectations we have of a modern biography or history? With what other expectations might we read them?

3. Would the gospels be less "inspired" or "authoritative" if they did not give us the precise words Jesus said or exactly what He did (e.g., if some of the events were told out of order)? Would they be less inspired or authoritative if Jesus did not say or do all the things the gospels portray Him as saying and doing?

endnote
---
1. See chapter 3 of this text.

CHAPTER 14

The Life and Teachings of Jesus: An Overview

The keynote of Jesus' preaching was the "kingdom of God" or the rule of God that was coming to the earth.

Framing the Story of Jesus

The New Testament gives us four different presentations of Jesus' earthly mission. Each gospel records slightly different events and sayings, sometimes in a different order. Because of this variety, it is tempting to try to combine the four into one story of Jesus—one gospel. As early as the late A.D. 100s, a Christian named Tatian spliced the four portraits together into one "harmony" of the gospels, as such combinations are called.[1] Our Christmas and Easter pageants do similar things on a much more limited scale, combining the various accounts of Christ's birth, crucifixion, or Resurrection into a single story.

At a Glance

- John the Baptist baptized people to symbolize the forgiveness of their sins in preparation for God's coming judgment.

- Jesus' early ministry as seen in Mark was overwhelmingly positive and optimistic, including healings, exorcisms, teaching, and miracles.

- Jesus preached the coming reign of God, with judgment for the wicked and salvation for the righteous.

- Jesus appointed twelve men as His key followers or disciples.

- In Mark, from the time of Peter's acknowledgment that Jesus is Messiah, Jesus focused on His coming death.

- Jesus' crucifixion paid the price for the wrongdoing of God's people.

- God raised Jesus from the dead.

baptism: A dipping in water that symbolized the washing away of one's sins.

repentance: Changing decisively from one attitude or way of life to another.

The wisdom of combining the four gospels into one story is questionable. Inevitably, what you end up with is a "fifth" gospel of your own making that is no longer true to any of the original four. Since biographies in the ancient world were primarily concerned with capturing the *character* of a person, they arranged events and paraphrased words so that the person's character came through "loud and clear." In a similar way, each gospel has framed the story of Jesus to bring out the particular emphases and themes that would speak most powerfully to its intended audience. Thus, combining the details of the gospel accounts is a little like trying to fit the pieces of four different puzzles together—even though the four puzzles all picture the same scene.

However, history is the backdrop of the gospels. Since the portraits of Matthew, Mark, and Luke in particular are much the same, it is still helpful to get the big picture of Jesus' earthly mission before we go on to look at each gospel in detail. For this reason, this chapter presents an overview of Jesus' life and teachings, relying mostly on Mark, but dabbling in Matthew and Luke as well.[2] John's portrait is significantly different from those of the other gospels, so we will wait until later to look at it.

The Events of Jesus' Mission

Any story has three basic elements: what takes place (events), where those things take place (settings), and those involved in what takes place (characters). In Mark, for example, Jesus' earthly ministry takes place between two events: it starts when He is **baptized** by John the Baptist and essentially ends when He is crucified (although Mark certainly indicates that Jesus rose from the dead). These two events frame Mark's presentation.

These two events also tell us who Jesus is and explain the significance of His ministry. John the Baptist's mission was to "prepare the way" for the coming king and for God's coming judgment. John preached that the people needed to **repent** or turn from their sins in order to escape God's judgment. By dipping people in the waters of the river Jordan— baptizing them—he symbolized the washing away of their sins and their turning toward God. In other words, John the Baptist urged his fellow Jews to renew their commitment to the Jewish covenant in preparation for God's

> **virgin birth:** Jesus' miraculous birth; His mother Mary gave birth to Him, even though she had never slept with a man.
>
> **the Resurrection:** Jesus' miraculous return from the dead.
>
> **the Transfiguration:** Jesus, along with Moses and Elijah, was transformed into a heavenly state in front of three disciples—Peter, James, and John.

> "So Jesus healed great numbers of sick people who had many different kinds of diseases, and he ordered many demons to come out of their victims."
> **Mark 1:34**

coming judgment and the renewal of His people.[3] Jesus was also baptized, which at the very least shows that He agreed with John's message.

According to the gospels, Jesus was that king or "Messiah" for whom John was preparing the Jewish people. Ironically, the Gospel of Mark most powerfully affirms that Jesus is the Messiah at the most unlikely moment of the story—His crucifixion. Jesus' death frees His people from their sins and thus from God's judgment. He takes the punishment for their wrongdoing so that they will not have to pay the price themselves. For Mark, this act captures Jesus' kingship more meaningfully than anything else He did on earth.

Of course, some incredibly important events in the Christian story occurred both before and after these two pivotal events of baptism and crucifixion. We learn more details of these events in the other gospels. The

Resurrection, for example, is an extremely important event in the New Testament. Jesus rising from the dead signals Christ's victory over death and God's approval of Jesus' entire mission on earth. For many New Testament authors, the Resurrection is an even more significant event than Jesus' death for sin. Matthew, Luke, and John present several occasions in which Jesus' followers see Him alive after His death.

> "I have not come to call the righteous, but sinners."
>
> **Mark 2:17 NIV**

Matthew and Luke also present the story of Jesus' miraculous birth—the **virgin birth**. They tell how a young woman named Mary gave birth to Jesus, even though she had never had sex with a man. Rather, the "Holy Spirit"—God's Spirit— supernaturally brought about her pregnancy.

Another event in Mark divides Jesus' earthly mission into two parts, although Matthew and Luke do not present the story in quite the same way. In Mark, the first half of the gospel presents Jesus' public ministry in overwhelmingly positive and optimistic terms. He has a wide following and is busy helping and healing, announcing the coming reign of God.

Then, in the middle of Mark, Jesus reveals His identity as Messiah to His closest followers. One of the leaders, Peter, acknowledges or "confesses" for the first time that Jesus is the Messiah. From this point on, Mark portrays Jesus as focused on His upcoming death, and the gospel concentrates on Jesus' interaction with His twelve main followers. It is in this part of the gospel that Jesus discusses the coming judgment. Peter's confession of Jesus as Messiah or "Christ" is thus an important turning point in the story of Jesus as Mark presents it.[4]

We should probably mention one other event before we move on—the **Transfiguration** of Jesus, in which three of Jesus' disciples see Him transformed into a heavenly form (Mark 9:2-10). Along with Moses (who represents the Old Testament Law) and Elijah (who represents a part of the Old

Testament known as the "Prophets"), Jesus turns spectacularly white. God affirms from heaven that Jesus is the Son of God, just as He had at Jesus' baptism (Mark 1:11). It is as if Peter, James, and John are allowed to see Jesus' true identity as He momentarily takes on a heavenly appearance. This event takes place in the story just after Peter has confessed that Jesus is the Christ—perhaps demonstrating a little of what this means.

The Kinds of Things Jesus Did

In the first half of Mark, Jesus is involved in several *kinds* of activities that indicate the reign of God indeed has begun. For example, Jesus heals the sick and casts out demons. As we mentioned earlier in chapter 12, Jesus' **exorcisms**—when He caused evil spirits to leave the bodies of various individuals—indicates that God is "cleaning house" in the earthly realm that Satan and his evil spirits had taken over. Every demon Jesus casts out demonstrates that God is in fact King and that the Kingdom of God is on its way; in some respects, it was already here.

Jesus' ministry focused on the physical needs of the Jewish people, as well as on their spiritual needs. In fact, the ancients would have had difficulty separating the two. The Gospel of Luke in particular emphasizes Jesus' ministry to the poor and needy. Jesus also performed miraculous deeds that

> **exorcism:** Causing an evil spirit(s) to leave the body of someone it was controlling.
>
> **disciple:** A follower of Jesus, someone who attached him or herself to Jesus in order to learn from and become like Him.

showed God's approval of Him. He walked on water (Mark 6:47-52), for example, and turned a few fish into a meal for several thousand people on more than one occasion (Mark 6:30-44; 8:1-10).

"He used many such stories and illustrations to teach the people as much as they were able to understand. In fact, in his public teaching he taught only with parables, but afterward when he was alone with his disciples, he explained the meaning to them."

Mark 4:33-34

Another activity in which Jesus engages in the gospels is *teaching*. Closely related to this teaching is the appointment of twelve particular **disciples**. A disciple was a "follower" or a "learner" who, like an apprentice, followed a carpenter or a blacksmith around in order to learn those trades. Jesus taught many disciples in the countryside of Galilee, the region where the gospels say much of His ministry took place. But He also picked out twelve special disciples from the crowds that followed Him.

It is extremely significant that Jesus chose *twelve* disciples to stay with Him, for this was the number of the tribes of Israel. It highlights the fact that

"After that, no one dared to ask him any more questions."

Mark 12:34

at least part of the good news Jesus preached was the restoration of Israel. What is more significant is that He did not include himself among those twelve. In other words, He saw himself in another category. Jesus saw himself as the king, the ruler, not as one of the subjects. It is no coincidence that He was crucified with the sign "King of the Jews" above His head.

The keynote of Jesus' preaching was the "kingdom of God" or the rule of God that was coming to the earth. Jesus' power over evil spirits was an important sign that to some extent God's rule had already arrived. This reign of God meant "good news" to the people of Israel, particularly those who were like "lost sheep" that had strayed from the flock (Luke 15:1-7). According to the gospels, Jesus did not target those who were trying to keep the Jewish covenant, like the Pharisees. Rather, He proclaimed good news to those who were spiritually off track—tax collectors, prostitutes, and "sinners" (Matt. 21:31-32). He also aimed at those who were simply in need—like the poor, widows, and orphans (Luke 4:18-19).

Jesus' primary method of teaching was by telling stories called **parables** or "riddles." While we often think that such stories make Jesus' message clearer, the Gospel of Mark indicates that Jesus himself told these stories to confuse those whose hearts were not in the right place (Mark 4:11-12). One of Jesus' parables, sometimes known as the "Parable of the Prodigal Son," captures the different ways Jesus' audiences reacted to His message (Luke 15:11-32).

> "For even I, the Son of Man, came here not to be served but to serve others, and to give my life as a ransom for many."
> **Mark 10:45**

> **parable:** A rather wide category of figurative speech that included such types as riddles, similes (x is like y), and even allegories (where several elements in a story are given symbolic meanings).

Those who had strayed from faithfulness to God were like a son who had disgraced and shamed his father, treating him like he was dead. Astonishingly, the father (God) gave the son another chance when he repented of what he had done. Even more shocking is that the son who had been faithful all along rejected his father in the end. Those who heard this parable would have known what Jesus was saying: God was taking back the sinners of Israel and forgiving them. The "righteous" of Israel, on the other hand—those like the Pharisees who had tried to keep the covenant—were now rejecting God and would face His judgment.

> **faith:** Primarily trust in something. It also involves belief in that something and faithfulness or commitment to it.

Of interest is that in the Gospels of Matthew, Mark, and Luke, Jesus teaches little about the need to believe in *Him*, although at times He hints at the importance of His role in the coming of the

Characters in the Story

God: Although Jesus is the focus of the gospel, God is behind the scenes as the one who is ultimately causing the action to move forward.

Jesus: The main character. He is the promised king, the Messiah, the Son of God, and Son of Man. He works miracles, showing that God approves of Him. He casts out demons, showing His goodness and power over evil. He is the authoritative teacher and interpreter of the Jewish Law. Most of all, He dies to pay for the sins of His people. He indicates that He will return in the future to judge Israel and the world.

the disciples: The followers of Jesus who learn from Him. Jesus chooses to train twelve in particular. Some of the most important in the gospels are Peter, James, and John—not to mention Judas Iscariot, the one who hands Jesus over to the religious leaders.

Satan and demonic forces: The spiritual opponents of Jesus and His ministry.

the religious leaders: Human opponents of Jesus and His ministry, like the Pharisees and Sadducees.

the crowds: At times the crowds follow Jesus, but at other times they work against Him. They include toll collectors, prostitutes, and sinners who receive Jesus' message. The crowds also cry for Jesus' crucifixion.

kingdom. Instead, the Gospel of John and the rest of the New Testament highlight the importance of **faith** in Christ in order to be saved from God's wrath. In Matthew, Mark, and Luke, Jesus proclaims the good news of God's reign without highlighting His own role in that kingdom. The rest of the New Testament, on the other hand, proclaims Jesus as the one through whom God's reign comes about.

In the gospels, Jesus also participates in debates. Throughout His ministry, He got into controversies with various religious leaders. Such events were honor challenges, like chess matches, to determine the most worthy teacher and leader. Jesus won every such challenge. In the pages of the gospels, Jesus encounters scribes, Pharisees, Sadducees, and other Jewish

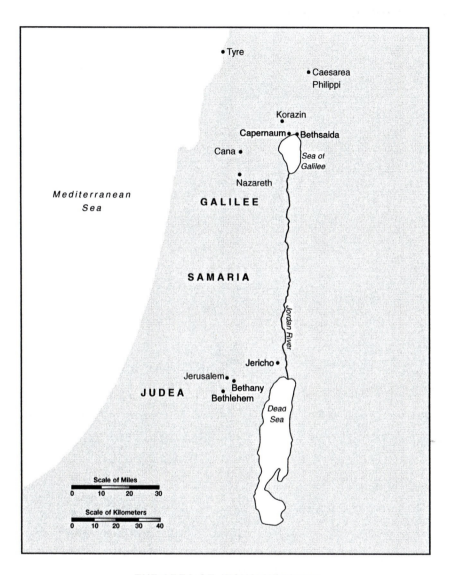

**THE AREA OF JESUS' MINISTRY
MAP 2**

leaders who pose difficult questions. In every case the gospels present Him as the supreme teacher, one who speaks with unchallenged authority.

The Settings of the Story

The Timing

The gospels give us slightly different impressions regarding the time frame during which Jesus' ministry took place. For example, if all we had were Matthew, Mark, and Luke, we would have the impression that Jesus' mission took place largely over the course of one year, although they do not specifically say how long Jesus' ministry lasted. The Gospel of John, on the other hand, clearly presents Jesus' ministry as lasting two to three years.

The Lay of the Land

You can get a sense of the land in which Jesus ministered from **Map 2**. According to Matthew and Luke, Jesus was born in the village of *Bethlehem*, just southwest of *Jerusalem*, the "capital city" of Judaism.[5] Both of these cities were located in the region of *Judea*, which was the size of an average American county. The large sea to the west of Palestine is the *Mediterranean Sea*. It spans the distance from Israel to Greece, Italy, and finally to Spain. The North African coast follows its southern coastline. To the east of Jerusalem is the *Jordan River*, which runs from the *Sea of Galilee* in the north into the *Dead Sea* in the south.

John the Baptist baptized the Jews of the countryside and Jesus himself in the Jordan River. However, Jesus grew up in *Nazareth*, in the region to the north of Judea known as *Galilee*. The events recorded in Matthew, Mark, and Luke for the most part take place here. Jesus may actually have had a home at one time in the small village of ***Capernaum*** on the north shores of the Sea of Galilee (Mark 2:1). It was near this place, apparently, that Jesus performed most of His miracles (Matthew 11:20-21).

Samaria is the region between Galilee and Judea. Some Jews seem to have avoided this region, although according to John, Jesus traveled through it. John 4 presents a shocking conversation between Jesus and a disreputable Samaritan woman. The well-known "Parable of the Good Samaritan" (Luke 10) also shows how open Jesus was toward Samaritan Jews.

Also according to the Gospel of John, Jesus spent much more time in Judea and Jerusalem than the other gospels record. In Matthew, Mark, and Luke, we only see Jesus in Jerusalem at the end of His earthly ministry. It was during this time that He encountered conflicts with the religious rulers, created a disturbance in the temple, and was finally arrested and crucified. He seemed to stay just outside the city in a little village called ***Bethany***. As recorded in John, however, Jesus made regular trips to Jerusalem from Galilee to observe the various Jewish festivals. John's presentation thus gives us the impression that a significant part of Jesus' earthly mission took place in the city of Jerusalem.

Keep the events, characters, and settings mentioned in this chapter in mind as you go through the individual gospels. Note how each gospel presents a slightly different emphasis than Mark, which we have used as the starting point for this overview. What you may find is that some of the other gospels also used Mark's presentation as the starting point for framing their own portraits of Jesus and His mission.

Things to Think About

Key Terms

baptism

disciple

exorcism

faith

parable

repentance

Resurrection

Transfiguration

virgin birth

1. What are the main settings of Jesus' ministry? How do the settings differ slightly in the Gospel of John?

2. What are the key events of Jesus' earthly life and ministry? Which ones are most important for the salvation of humanity? Why?

3. Who are the main characters in the gospel story? In what ways do these individuals provide good examples for us to imitate? In what ways should we avoid their example?

4. What are the dangers of "splicing" the four gospels together into a single account?

endnotes

1. This work was called the "Diatessaron," meaning "through four." It was the gospel for some Christians in the Eastern part of the Mediterranean world for almost three hundred years.

2. There are several reasons to focus on Mark at this point. It is the shortest gospel, giving us mostly events and thus the basic outline of Jesus' mission. Matthew and Luke largely follow Mark's structure; in fact, only thirty-one verses of Mark are not also found in Matthew and Luke.

3. See chapter 6 of this text for more about God's covenant with Israel.

4. "Christ" is the Greek translation of "Messiah," which is a Hebrew term meaning "anointed one."

5. We should not think of Jerusalem as a capital in the sense of modern nations. It was the ethnic and political focal point of all things Jewish. The temple was in Jerusalem, and those with the most political power lived in Jerusalem. But the modern idea of a nation with police able to enforce the laws in every city of the nation differs from the ancient world in which travel involved so much more time. People in one place were in many ways isolated from those in other places. It could take months to muster an army to enforce a "nation's" laws somewhere in that nation's general "territory."

CHAPTER 15

The Gospel of Matthew:
Jesus, the Son of David

The Gospel of Matthew presents Jesus not just as a teacher of God's wisdom, but as God's Wisdom itself.

The Character of Jesus in Matthew

If the main point of ancient biography was to capture the character of a person, the Gospel of Matthew gives us several insights into who Jesus was. The primary identifying feature is that Jesus is the Jewish Messiah, the King of the Jews. The gospel begins with the **genealogy** or "family tree" of Jesus,

> **genealogy:** A family tree. In Matthew, the genealogy starts with Abraham and moves forward to Jesus.

tracing His father's line back through David and the kings of Judah to Abraham. By beginning his gospel in this way, Matthew wanted his audience to know in no uncertain terms that Jesus was the Son of David.

At a Glance

- Matthew presents Jesus:
  a) As the Jewish Messiah, the Son of David.
  b) As a new Moses, the authoritative interpreter of the Law for God's people.

- Matthew emphasizes the continuity between Jesus and the Hebrew Scriptures by portraying events in Jesus' life:
  a) As the "fulfillment" of various Old Testament Scriptures.
  b) By showing that His earthly mission was focused on the Jews.
  c) By implying that the Jewish Law continues to be authoritative for Israel when it is understood appropriately.

But Jesus was not just an ordinary king to Matthew. Like King David's son, Solomon, who was known for his wisdom, Jesus, the "Son of David," was also the supreme teacher of God's wisdom.[1] In fact, merely to call Him a teacher or a rabbi did not capture how significant Matthew believed Jesus to be. Throughout the gospel, Matthew portrays Jesus as the greatest teacher of God's wisdom that ever walked the earth—even greater than Moses. In fact, some scholars would say that the Gospel of Matthew presents Jesus not just as a *teacher* of God's wisdom, but as God's *Wisdom itself.*

Jesus, the Son of David

The Gospel of Matthew begins with a genealogy whose main point is that Jesus is the Son of David, the expected king of Israel, the Messiah. A genealogy

> "Where is the newborn king of the Jews? We have seen his star as it arose, and we have come to worship him."
>
> **Matthew 2:2**

is a kind of family tree that traces your parentage back in time. For Matthew, the most meaningful place from which to trace Jesus' lineage was Abraham, the ultimate starting point for the Jewish race. But even more important, Matthew divided the list of names in such a way that each part pointed to David, the ideal king of Israel.[2] Matthew's arrangement of Jesus' genealogy emphatically shouts: "Jesus is King of the Jews, Jesus is King of the Jews, Jesus is King of the Jews!"[3]

Matthew's unique gospel brings out Jesus' kingship elsewhere. When Jesus is born, for example, "wise men," who are interpreters of the stars, recognize that a king of incredible importance has been born. They travel to Bethlehem and bow before the world's new king (Matt. 2:11). On the other hand, Herod the Great, the ruler of Judea at that time, treats Jesus as a rival king and attempts to have Him killed. In either case, both recognize that Jesus is a king.

Jesus, a New Moses

Although the Gospel of Matthew does not explicitly compare Jesus to Moses, its presentation would have made a Jewish audience think of Jesus as a leader like Moses. For example, Matthew's birth account reminds us of the story of Moses in the Old Testament. Just as Moses lived in Egypt and later led Israel out of that land, so Jesus lives in Egypt for a time as an infant and then is led out by God (Matt. 2:13-22). Just as the child Moses escaped the hand of an evil ruler who killed the children of Israel, so Jesus escapes Bethlehem as the evil ruler Herod the Great puts to death the children of that city. The Gospel of Luke includes none of these elements in its presentation of Jesus' birth. The Gospel of Matthew includes them at least in part because Matthew wished to make known that Jesus was a *new* Moses, the one through whom God was making a new covenant with His people.

One of the most striking features of Matthew is the way this gospel presents Jesus as the supreme teacher of the Law. Just as God gave the Old Testament Law to Moses on Mount Sinai, Jesus also delivers the heart of His message on a mountain. In this "Sermon on the Mount" (Matthew 5–7), Jesus repeatedly gives authoritative interpretations of the Jewish Law, at times correcting the way other religious leaders interpreted it (e.g., Matt. 5:43-48).

Of all the gospels, Matthew includes Jesus' strongest rebukes of religious leaders like the Pharisees (e.g., Matthew 23). Some scholars have suggested that the gospel was written in the years after the destruction of Jerusalem (A.D. 70), when the Pharisees were the dominant force in Judaism. According to this hypothesis, the Christian writer of Matthew wished to show his fellow Jews that Jesus' interpretation of the Law was more authoritative than the interpretations of the Pharisees. As Matthew 7:28-29 says, "After Jesus finished speaking, the crowds were amazed at his teaching, for he taught as one who had real authority—quite unlike the teachers of religious law."

You can even read Matthew as five sections like the Jewish Law, with a major block of teaching by Jesus in each part. Each section ends with exactly the same words, "And it came about when Jesus finished . . ." (7:28; 11:1; 13:53; 19:1; 26:1, author's translation). Some scholars suggest that Matthew arranged Jesus' ministry into five blocks of teaching and miracles because the Jewish Law is made up of the five books of Genesis, Exodus, Leviticus, Numbers, and Deuteronomy. In other words, as the Jews thought Moses had written the five books of the Law, Matthew presented Jesus' teaching in five blocks to show that Jesus was an authoritative teacher like Moses, presenting God's Law to His people.

The Continuity of Jesus with the Hebrew Scriptures

Jesus, the Fulfillment of Scripture

Another feature of Matthew is the way it presents events in the life of Jesus as the fulfillment of Old Testament Scripture. For example, after Herod the Great finds out that Jesus has been born, he tries to kill Him by having all the children in Bethlehem under two years of age killed. Matthew's conclusion is that this event "fulfilled" the words of the Old Testament **prophet** Jeremiah: "A cry of anguish is heard in Ramah—weeping and mourning unrestrained. Rachel weeps for her children, refusing to be comforted—for they are dead" (Matt. 2:18).

prophet: Someone through whom God speaks messages of challenge and hope to human beings. A prophet's messages usually addressed contemporary situations rather than the distant future.

Time after time in the birth story and in other places in this gospel, Matthew points out events in Jesus' life and ministry that fulfill various things the prophets of the Old Testament had foretold. Even in His teachings, Jesus tells the crowds that He has not come to abolish the Jewish Law and the Prophets—the Old Testament. Instead, Jesus says that He has come to "fulfill them" (Matt. 5:17).

What is important to realize, however, is that what Matthew meant by "fulfill" is not what you might think at first. He was using Jewish methods for extracting meaning out of the Old Testament—methods that did not read Scripture so much for its original meaning, but for what its words might mean if applied to what was going on in Matthew's day. As was perfectly acceptable at the time, Matthew read the Old Testament "spiritually" rather than in terms of what it actually meant when it was originally written.

For example, if you turn to Jeremiah 31:15 (the Scripture Matthew says is fulfilled when Herod kills the infants of Bethlehem), you will see that it is not a prediction that some day in the future a king will kill babies. It actually refers to the fact that most of Israel at that time had been destroyed by the nation of Assyria. God went on to tell the prophet Jeremiah that this group of people "will come back to you from the distant land of the enemy" (Jer. 31:16). The "children" Jeremiah was talking about, therefore, were grown people. Unlike the children of Bethlehem, God promised that these would return. This event in the life of Jesus thus "fulfills" the Old Testament in that it gives a "fuller" meaning to Jeremiah's words. It is not a straightforward prediction that came true. This was Matthew's standard way of interpreting the Old Testament.

The Jewish Law is Still Valid

Another important feature of Matthew is the way in which it affirms the ongoing validity of the Jewish Law. Jesus tells the crowds that He did not come to abolish the Law or the Prophets. Further, He tells them that anyone who disobeys the *least* commandment in the Law is in the wrong (Matt. 5:19). This statement makes us think of commands like Leviticus 19:19, where the Israelites are forbidden to wear clothing made out of two different kinds of material.

In fact, Jesus even tells the crowds to do the things that the Pharisees were telling them to do (Matt. 23:3) and affirms the Pharisees' attention to detail in keeping the Law (23:23). His critique of them is not because of the energy they expend in keeping the minute details of the Law, but because they miss its most important points—like mercy and justice (23:23).

Matthew probably wrote to Jewish Christians, not Gentile (non-Jewish) Christians. The rest of the New Testament makes it clear that few Jews abandoned their observance of the Jewish Law in the early days of Christianity. Some Jewish Christians even refused to eat with Gentile Christians for fear they would become ceremonially unclean (see Galatians 2:11-12).

Matthew is a Jewish gospel, and it emphasizes throughout that Jesus' earthly mission was directed toward the Jews, not the Gentiles. Whereas Luke highlights Jesus' interaction with non-Jews, Matthew emphasizes that Jews were the focus of Jesus' ministry while He was on earth. When Jesus commissions His disciples in Matthew 10:6, He tells them *not* to preach to the Gentiles or the Samaritans. His earthly ministry focuses on the lost sheep *of Israel*. It is only after He has risen from the dead that He commands His followers to "go and make disciples of all the nations" (Matt. 28:19).

The Who's and When's of Matthew

The Gospel of Matthew is technically anonymous. Although we do not know of a time when Christians thought the author was anyone other than the tax collector Matthew (mentioned in 9:9), the book itself never names him as author.[4] The titles of the New Testament books were not part of the original documents. They were added more than a hundred years after the books first appeared. As with many questions we have about the Bible, we will not know for certain who wrote the Gospel of Matthew while we are on this earth.

"Matthew arranged the sayings in the Aramaic language, and everyone translated them as well as he could."

Papias, around A.D. 140

The earliest mention that Matthew wrote something about Jesus appears around the year A.D. 140 in the writings of a Christian named Papias. He told us that "Matthew arranged the sayings in the Aramaic language, and everyone translated them as well as he could."[5] There are some significant differences between the writing to which this comment refers and the Gospel of Matthew as we now have it. First of all, Papias said that Matthew wrote in a language called Aramaic.[6] However, the first gospel in our New Testament is written in Greek. Some of this Greek *does* seem to be a translation from Aramaic, particularly some of Jesus' sayings. However, most of our Gospel of Matthew was originally composed in Greek.

Another possible difference between our Gospel of Matthew and the writing Papias referred to is that Papias said it contained the *sayings* of Jesus. The Gospel of Matthew contains much more than just quotations of Jesus, which appear in red print in many Bibles. What Papias mentioned sounds a little like some of the collections of sayings we have found from the same time period.[7] For example, the Gospel of Thomas, which is not in our Bible, is basically a collection of sayings attributed to Jesus, although many of them may not be genuine.[8] The Dead Sea Scrolls also contain fragments of documents that are collections of verses on a single theme.

What these differences mean is that while there may be some relationship between what Papias said Matthew wrote and the actual Gospel of Matthew in our New Testament, the differences probably outweigh the similarities. Some have suggested that one of the main sources behind the Gospel of Matthew in our New Testament is the Apostle Matthew's own collection of sayings. But this suggestion is only an educated guess. We cannot know for sure.

What we can do, however, is form some general impressions of what kind of person put together the gospel of Matthew and what kind of audience he had in mind. We have already made some educated guesses along these lines. We can feel fairly confident that the author was a Jew who was fluent in Greek and who wrote to Greek-speaking Jews. Not only is Matthew written in fairly fluent Greek, but this gospel is the most Jewish of the four in our New Testament.[9]

For example, Matthew consistently uses the phrase "kingdom of heaven" (e.g., Matt. 4:17), whereas Mark and Luke use the phrase "kingdom of God" (Mark 1:14). It was common for Jews like the scribes and Pharisees to show reverence for God by not saying His name directly but by using indirect ways to refer to Him. They might refer to the place where God lives or to His glory instead of stating His name.

scribe: One whose function was to copy documents—primarily the Jewish Law. Scribes were thus closely associated with the Pharisees.

Using "kingdom of heaven" instead of "kingdom of God" is just one hint indicating the author of the Gospel of Matthew was a reverent Jew, perhaps even a converted **scribe** whose job was to copy the Law and other documents. While the author of the Gospel of Mark explained Jewish practices (Mark 7:3-4), Matthew evidently did not need to, for his audience was Jewish (Matt. 15:1-3). Matthew's method of interpreting the Old Testament also reminds us of the methods used in the Dead Sea Scrolls and by the later rabbis—very Jewish ways of arguing from Scripture. These are just a few indications that the author and audience of the first gospel were Jews.

Things to Think About

1. How do the events that Matthew presents and the way this gospel arranges the story of Jesus' ministry work together to emphasize certain aspects of Jesus' character?

2. Do you think that Jewish Christians today are still obligated to keep the Jewish Law? How would you fit the claim that Jesus did *not* abolish the Law (Matt. 5:17) with Paul's claim that Jesus *did* abolish the Law (Eph. 2:15)?

3. Would it change your faith in the Bible if you learned that the disciple of Jesus named Matthew actually did not write the Gospel of Matthew?

Key Terms
genealogy
prophet
scribe

endnotes

1. See chapter 7 of this text.

2. In Hebrew, the letters of the alphabet were not just used to make words. They were used for numbers as well. If you treat the letters in David's Hebrew name as if they are numbers instead of parts of a word, you get the number fourteen. Matthew divided Jesus' lineage into three groups of fourteen, emphasizing that Jesus was indeed the expected king, the Son of David. The use of this technique is a strong indication that the author of Matthew was a Jew.

3. Another interesting thing about Matthew's genealogy is the mention of several women in Jesus' background, all of whom had something "suspicious" in their past. Rahab, for example, had been a prostitute, and Tamar bore her father-in-law's child. Ruth was a Moabitess by race, and the Moabites were enemies of the Jews. King David had an affair with Bathsheba and then arranged for her husband's death. Perhaps Matthew wanted to show that even though the circumstances of Mary's pregnancy might look suspicious, God often had worked in such ways to bring about His plans.

4. Given the way of the ancient world, it is not likely that a woman wrote Matthew. I will thus refer to the author as a "he" because it is most probable. Even though

the author is anonymous, I will continue to refer to the author as "Matthew" for convenience.

5. Quoted by the early church historian, Eusebius, *History of the Church* 3.39.16.

6. Technically, Papias said that Matthew wrote in the "Hebrew language," but he probably meant Aramaic, which was the "Hebrew" spoken in Palestine at the time of Christ (cf. Acts 22:2).

7. However, Papias could have referred to a whole gospel by the word *sayings*, since he apparently used the same word in reference to the whole Gospel of Mark.

8. See chapter 28 of this text.

9. A close look at the Greek of the New Testament reveals that each author had his own style and perspective. Matthew's Greek style, for example, is smoother than Mark's. And a comparison of Luke and Acts with the "writing manuals" of that day makes us think that this author probably had some advanced training in "rhetoric," something like an advanced degree in writing. All these observations indicate that God inspired the writing of these books by way of the personalities and styles of the individual authors, rather than simply dictating to them the exact words to write down.

CHAPTER 16

The Sermon on the Mount

The Sermon on the Mount encapsulates the heart of Jesus' message in Matthew.

Unconventional

The "Sermon on the Mount" in the Gospel of Matthew contains some of Jesus' best-known teachings (Matthew 5–7). In fact, Matthew likely meant this sermon to encapsulate the heart of Jesus' message. Sayings like "turn the other cheek," "the wise man built his house on the rock," as well as the Lord's Prayer and the Golden Rule, are all in this sermon.

In keeping with Matthew's implicit comparison of Jesus to Moses, Jesus delivers this sermon from a mountain, just as God delivered the Jewish Law to Moses on Mt. Sinai. Indeed, much of the sermon deals with the question of how Jesus' teaching relates to the Jewish Law and how to live on earth as we await the

At a Glance

• The Sermon on the Mount encapsulates the heart of Jesus' teaching on how to live on earth while waiting for the kingdom.

• The Beatitudes are blessings Jesus proclaims on individuals who normally would not receive honor on earth.

• Jesus emphasizes that His teaching "fulfills" the Jewish Law.

• Jesus teaches that God rewards the person who orients himself or herself around heavenly rather than earthly reward, the person who trusts in God rather than in money or possessions.

• Jesus teaches the Lord's Prayer (6:9-13), the Golden Rule (7:12), and "love your enemies" (5:44).

kingdom of heaven. Throughout the sermon, Jesus shockingly overturns conventional ways of thinking and presents a radical shift of human and religious priorities.

The Beatitudes

The sermon begins with a revolutionary perspective on what is honorable. Sorrow and persecution are not usually things to celebrate. But the **Beatitudes** or "blessings" that begin the sermon indicate that those who find themselves in such situations are "blessed." They will have great honor in God's coming kingdom. While some versions translate the word blessed as "happy," it means much more than a good feeling or even joy.

Beatitudes: The blessings Jesus pronounces on the poor in spirit, mourners, the meek, and others in Matthew 5:3-10.

Since the ancient world thought in terms of honor and shame, to be blessed meant to receive high honor in God's estimation. God honors the "poor in spirit," for example, because they recognize their utter dependence on Him. Those who mourn are

"Don't misunderstand why I have come. I did not come to abolish the law of Moses or the writings of the prophets. No, I came to fulfill them . . . So if you break the smallest commandment and teach others to do the same, you will be the least in the Kingdom of Heaven."

Words of Jesus, Matthew 5:17, 19

blessed, as are the humble and those who hunger for righteousness. They may not be in the greatest of situations now, but God will give them places of high honor when His kingdom fully arrives. Blessed are the merciful, the peacemakers, the pure in heart. We often do not honor such people in this world. The world more often stampedes right over them. In God's coming kingdom, however, they will fully recoup their losses.

The Beatitudes set the tone for the whole Sermon on the Mount because they tell us the correct priorities of God's kingdom. When we truly serve God as king, we look to Him for our glory, not to those around us. We do not seek human honor, nor do we worry about the necessities of life like food and clothing. Rather, we seek the high estimation of God and depend on Him—He is our true "patron," the one upon whom we should rely for our needs.[1] We keep the heart and spirit of the Law, not just the part that those around us can see.

Jesus Fulfills the Jewish Law

One of the main things we see from the Sermon on the Mount is that Jesus is an authoritative interpreter of the Jewish Law. He is a figure like Moses. Matthew points out the crowds' reaction to Jesus as a teacher: "The crowds were amazed at his teaching, for he taught as one who had real authority—quite unlike the teachers of religious law" (Matt. 7:28-29).

One key idea of the sermon is that Jesus, far from taking away from the Jewish Law, has come to "fulfill" it. The impression we get from Matthew 5:19 is that Jesus did not wish to cancel even the smallest of Jewish laws.[2]

Nevertheless, the Gospel of Matthew records some very strong criticisms about the way the scribes and Pharisees interpreted and kept the Law. In a scathing remark, Jesus states, "But I warn you—unless you obey God better than the teachers of religious law and the Pharisees do, you can't enter the Kingdom of Heaven at all!"(5:20). While they were good at keeping those aspects of the Law that others could see, they often violated the spirit of the Law, the most integral part about which God cares.

Jesus contrasts His interpretation of the Law with that of oral tradition on six different topics: murder, adultery, divorce, making oaths, retribution, and one's enemies. In each case, Jesus starts with what His audience "has heard." He then goes on to give the correct understanding: "But *I* say . . ." The Greek of these sayings is presented in such a way as to emphasize contrast. So while his audience had certainly heard "Do not murder" (Matt. 5:21), for example, Jesus teaches that even someone who hates has broken the Law. The man who plots in his mind to commit adultery with another man's wife has already committed adultery in his heart (5:27-30).

It is important to realize that some of Jesus' "fulfilled" interpretations of the Old Testament are *real changes* from what the Scripture originally meant. Jesus may have been getting at the heart of the Law, but in doing so He nullifies some of its previous instruction. For example, the Old Testament Law *did* permit a man to divorce his wife (Deut. 24:1). One of the Ten Commandments *demands* that one keep any oath made in God's name.[3] The Law *did* set up a law of retribution that, at least on paper, encouraged "an eye for an eye and a tooth for a tooth" (e.g., Deut. 19:21): if someone put out someone else's eye, the punishment was for his or her eye to be put out. The Old Testament at various points *does* seem to condone the hatred of Israel's enemies (e.g., Ps. 137:9).

> "'Teacher, which is the most important commandment in the law of Moses?'
>
> "Jesus replied, 'You must love the Lord your God with all your heart, all your soul, and all your mind.' This is the first and greatest commandment. A second is equally important: 'Love your neighbor as yourself.' All the other commandments and all the demands of the prophets are based on these two commandments.'"
>
> **Matthew 22:36-40**

In the gospels, however, the essence of the Law for Jesus comes down to two commandments: (1) loving God, and (2) loving one's neighbor—and one's enemies (Matt. 22:34-40). The permission God gave concerning divorce in the Old Testament is not God's preference, Jesus says. God allowed it because Israel was hard-hearted and unreceptive to Him (Matt. 19:8-9). Although divorce was a part of Scripture, Jesus severely restricts it, probably because it was out of keeping with love for one's neighbor. In Matthew, only sexual infidelity is an acceptable basis for a man to divorce his wife (5:32; 19:9).[4]

Jesus also preaches against hating one's enemies because it does not measure up to God's love for all. "If you love only those who love you," Jesus says, "what good is that? Even corrupt tax collectors do that much. If you are kind only to your friends, how are you different from anyone else? Even pagans do that. But you are to be perfect, even as your Father in heaven is perfect" (Matt. 5:46-47). The fulfillment of the Law that Jesus proclaims, therefore, is a heartfelt keeping of its basic essence: love of God and love of neighbor. It is not really about keeping all the smallest commandments in all their details, even though this is the impression we get from Matthew 5:17-20. Jesus seems to have often spoken in "hyperbole" or exaggerated language to drive His point home.[5]

For Christians who try to base their lifestyles on the Bible, there are some important warnings to take from Jesus' use of the Old Testament in Matthew. First of all, He did not take God's commands as arbitrary rules; He believed in some basic principles in determining how to keep them. For example, God's command on divorce in the Old Testament had everything to do with Israel's situation at that time. Both Jesus and Paul were concerned about the spirit of God's commands, not with the "letter of the Law" (Rom. 2:27-29; 2 Cor. 3:6). Neither took the commands as absolutes to be followed, especially when doing so violated love of God, one's neighbor, or one's enemies. Jesus' actions in the gospels reflect a great deal of "common sense" when it comes to the Law, always keeping in mind that loving God and loving one's neighbor are the bottom line (e.g., Mark 2:23-28).[6]

Seeking Honor from God, not People

The Beatitudes emphasize that our honor comes from God, not from the world around us. The "kingdom values" of heaven are different from the values of earth. Persecution for Christ's sake is not enjoyable on earth, but it means we are on track for blessing in the coming kingdom. Similarly, the Pharisees kept the Law in its externals (what you could see on earth), but they missed what God was really after.

The next part of the Sermon on the Mount talks about the appropriate way to do good deeds. The key, Jesus implies, is to do them for God to see and honor, rather than for those around you to see and honor. Do not give to the needy, pray, or deliberately go without food (i.e., "fast") in such a way as to draw human attention to yourself (6:1-24). Look to God for your reward.

> **"This, then, is how you should pray:**
>
> 'Our Father in heaven,
> hallowed be Your name,
> Your kingdom come,
> Your will be done,
> on earth as it is in heaven.
> Give us today our daily bread.
> Forgive us our debts,
> as we also have forgiven our debtors.
> And lead us not into temptation,
> but deliver us from the evil one.' "
>
> **Matthew 6:9-13 NIV**

We are beginning to see that this sermon is really about what it means to live on earth while being a part of the kingdom of heaven. It is about God's will being done "on earth as it is in heaven" (6:10). It is about storing up treasures in heaven rather than on earth (6:19) and serving God as our master rather than serving money or worldly possessions (6:24). It is about seeking first God's kingdom and what is honorable in His view (6:33). He will then make sure we have the food and clothing we need.

As far as dealing with others in the world, Jesus summarizes with the Golden Rule: "Do to others what you would have them do to you, for this sums up the Law and the Prophets" (Matt. 7:12 NIV). The Golden Rule is simply another expression of Jesus' belief that loving your neighbor is the essence of the Jewish Law. When you love everyone, you do not hypocritically judge others (7:1-5).

> "But seek first his kingdom and his righteousness, and all these things will be given to you as well."
>
> **Matthew 6:33 NIV**

Finally, the Sermon on the Mount has elements that may be surprising to some. For example, the sermon teaches that there will be rewards of various degrees in the kingdom of heaven. It also implies that more people are headed for destruction than for eternal life (7:13-14). Another statement even suggests that God will reject some that prophesy, drive out demons, and perform miracles in Jesus' name, claiming to be Christians (7:15-23). The conclusion is a warning to all of Matthew's audience, past, present, and future. Some build their houses on sand, like the Pharisees. Such persons will encounter great distress when the kingdom of heaven arrives and their houses come tumbling down. Rather, Jesus urges people to build their houses on a rock that will stand the storm.

Things to Think About

1. In what ways does the Sermon on the Mount reverse the way we normally think about what it means to be blessed and honored?

> **Key Term**
> Beatitudes

2. In what ways do Jesus' interpretations of the Jewish Law "fulfill" it? What is the ultimate way to fulfill the Law?

3. Could it ever be appropriate for a Christian to hate someone: a mass murderer, a homosexual, someone of another color or race?

4. Does Jesus' idea of turning the other cheek fit with the idea of civil disobedience or nonviolent resistance? Does Jesus advocate submission to oppressors?

5. What do you make of Jesus' statements about different levels of reward in heaven? What of His indications that not all those in the church will make it into the kingdom—even some of those who prophesy?

endnotes

1. See chapter 10 of this text for a discussion of the patron-client arrangements of the ancient Mediterranean world. The sense of God as our true patron is just one of several interesting similarities between the Sermon on the Mount and the Epistle of James.

2. The previous chapter notes that Matthew probably wrote for Jewish Christians. As such, he seemed to assume that Jews must still obey the Jewish Law even after they became Christians, although not as the Pharisees interpreted the Law.

3. Exodus 20:7: "Thou shalt not take the name of the LORD thy God in vain" (KJV). The importance of keeping oaths made in God's name was so great that Jephthah sacrificed his daughter because of a foolish oath he had made before battle (Judg. 11:29-40).

4. Matthew does not even mention the possibility of a woman divorcing her husband. Mark's version of this teaching does not record any exception in Jesus' prohibition of divorce, not even sexual infidelity (Mark 10:11-12).

5. Some examples of hyperbole in Jesus' teaching are his statement that if someone slaps you on one cheek, you should offer the other (Matt. 5:39) and the claim that it is easier for a camel to get through the eye of a needle than for a rich person to get into God's kingdom (19:24).

6. In fairness to the ancient rabbis, not all Pharisees were as legalistic and hypocritical as we sometimes think. We can find statements by the rabbis of this general period that parallel Jesus' teaching regarding love as the essence of the Law, placing a proper emphasis on justice and mercy.

CHAPTER 17

Being a Follower of Christ

In Matthew, Jesus teaches that following Him is more important than life itself.

How to Fish

Although all four gospels have instructions for those who wish to be followers of Jesus, Matthew records what some Christians call **the Great Commission**, the command to make disciples from the peoples of every nation. It probably best describes what the early Christians thought it meant to be a Christian, a follower of Jesus.

As we saw in chapter 14, the word disciple in Greek actually means "a learner." But because of the way the ancients learned, we will probably better understand disciples if we think of them as followers. If you wanted to learn in the ancient world, you attached yourself to someone whose specialty was the thing you wanted to learn. Perhaps you wanted to learn philosophy.

At a Glance

- A disciple is someone who follows a teacher in order to learn from and model that teacher.

- What Jesus' disciples learn is to "fish for people" for God's kingdom.

- To be a disciple requires absolute allegiance to Jesus and the cause of God's kingdom.

- The Sermon on the Mount teaches Jesus' followers how to live.

- Matthew's mission speech tells them how to preach the gospel to Israel.

- Matthew ends with the Great Commission, the command to make disciples for Jesus from all nations.

The Great Commission: Jesus' command to make disciples from the peoples of every nation; found in Matthew 28:18-20.

If so, you would join a group that followed a particular philosopher, basically living with that person and learning by association.

So what trade was Jesus teaching? Jesus was teaching His disciples how to fish for people—how to go about bringing people into God's kingdom. When Jesus found Peter and Andrew fishing at the Sea of Galilee, He called out to them, "Come, be my disciples, and I will show you how to fish for people!" (Matt. 4:19). That is exactly what we see Jesus doing when He instructed the disciples about their mission to the "lost sheep of Israel" (10:6). After His Resurrection, when He had finished His instruction, He then sent His disciples into the whole world.

What a Disciple Looks Like

Matthew records that after Jesus rises from the dead, He commands His followers to go out and make other disciples. He tells them to do two things: (1) to baptize these new followers in the name of the Father, the Son, and the Holy Spirit, and (2) to teach them to obey the commands Jesus gave them (Matt. 28:19-20). None of the gospels ever mention that the original disciples were baptized in this way. It is quite possible, though, that everyone in the New Testament who became a Christian after the Resurrection was baptized.

> "Do to others what you would like them to do for you. This is a summary of all that is taught in the law and the prophets."
>
> **The Golden Rule, Matthew 7:12**

Jesus has a number of things to say about the attitude one must have in order to get into the kingdom of heaven. "Unless you turn from your sins and become as little children, you will never get into the Kingdom of Heaven" (Matt. 18:3). What is it about children that Jesus has in mind? Like the poor in spirit, the children in ancient times had a sense of utter dependency and submission to their parents. Absolute

178

obedience was required. To be in the kingdom of heaven was to submit utterly to God's rule.

What commands are new Christians to keep? Matthew no doubt wished his audience to remember such teachings as the Sermon on the Mount (Matthew 5–7) and Jesus' discussion with the Pharisees about the most important commandment in the Law (Matt. 22:34-40). In these examples, Jesus teaches that keeping the Golden Rule and loving God with one's complete being are the essence of what God's Law requires.

Jesus' interaction with His disciples and others demonstrates just how big a commitment it was to be His follower. Perhaps the most startling example is when a potential disciple wants to wait until his father dies before following Jesus. "Follow me now!" Jesus says. "Let those who are spiritually dead care for their own dead" (Matt 8:22). Given the incredible importance ancient Jews placed on honoring their parents and families, Jesus' statement is truly shocking. Jesus implies that following Him is a higher priority than what most considered the most important earthly loyalty (cf. Matt. 12:46-50).

Jesus also teaches that following Him is more important than life itself. He says, "If anyone acknowledges me publicly here on earth, I will openly acknowledge that person before my Father in heaven. But if anyone denies me here on earth, I will deny that person before my Father in heaven" (Matt. 10:32-33). Some would die because they followed Jesus, but Jesus says, "Whoever loses his life for my sake will find it" (10:39 NIV). In short, to follow Jesus meant to make Him and His cause the ultimate priority of one's life above every other value. "If you love your father or mother more than you love me, you are not worthy of being mine; or if you love your son or daughter more than me, you are not worthy of being mine. If you refuse to take up your cross and follow me, you are not worthy of being mine" (10:37-38).

The Missions to Israel and the World

Matthew 10 presents us with Jesus' "mission speech" to His twelve disciples. Here Jesus instructs His disciples to go on a mission to Israel *only*. They were not to go to any of the Gentiles or to any of the villages of the Samaritans (Matt. 10:5), only to the lost sheep of Israel who were not keeping God's covenant. These were the prostitutes and toll (or tax) collectors that Jesus targeted in His own ministry (9:9-13). As we saw earlier, the fact that Jesus chose twelve disciples was important. Since Israel originally had twelve tribes, the twelve disciples probably symbolized the restoration of Israel.

It is easy for Christians today to forget that the Jewish people and the Jewish nation were Jesus' audience while He was on earth. Matthew 10 emphasizes this fact when it portrays Jesus telling His disciples to go exclusively to Israel and not to the Gentiles and Samaritans. This changes at the end of Matthew, of course, when Jesus sends His disciples to the whole world and every nation (28:19). While He was on earth, however, He specifically targeted the "lost sheep" of Israel.

Mark and Luke also tell of Jesus sending His disciples out while He was still on earth (Mark 6:6-13; Luke 9:1-6). They record some of the same instructions found in Matthew 10, such as Jesus' command not to take bread, money, or a beggar's purse. Instead, Jesus tells His disciples to depend completely on the hospitality of the villages they visit (Mark 6:8-11; Luke 10:4-12).[1]

Because Matthew 10 also talks about Jesus' later return to earth (v. 23), it is clear that this chapter also has instructions that apply to His disciples in the time after His Resurrection. For example, Matthew 10 has a sense of foreboding, as if persecution awaits the disciples throughout the rest of their lives. They will be flogged in the Jewish synagogues (10:17); they will be brought before Gentiles (10:18). "Brother will betray brother to death, fathers will betray their own children, and children will rise against their parents and cause them to be killed. And everyone will hate you because of your allegiance to me" (10:21-22). Far from offering material prosperity to those who would follow Him, Jesus promised His followers hardship and persecution in this life.

The Gospel of Matthew includes a significant amount of teaching relating to Jesus' followers for the time after His Resurrection. Matthew 16, for example, mentions that Jesus gives Peter the "keys to the kingdom," so that whatever he would "lock and unlock" on earth would be guaranteed by heaven's authority (16:13-20).[2] Roman Catholics believe that by giving such authority to Peter, Jesus was establishing the office of the pope as the supreme authority for the church. Such an interpretation, of course, goes well beyond what Matthew actually says. It is likely, however, that Matthew believed Peter to have been the most foundational figure in the church after Jesus' Resurrection. In fact, Matthew's gospel in general features Peter more prominently than any of the other gospels do.[3]

Matthew also gives a great deal of authority to the church in general, to the collective group of those who are followers of Jesus.[4] Christians together hold the authority to make decisions regarding what should be allowed or prohibited (Matt. 18:18). If only two or three agree on something for which they are asking, "My Father in heaven will do it for you" (18:19). To be sure, these statements do not mean the church can do whatever it wants, but they place an incredible responsibility on Christians with regard to the course we take in the future. Matthew invites Christians to take on the awesome task of shaping what Christianity looks like in every time and place.

Matthew alone records the Parable of the Weeds, which tells what the church will look like in the period between the Resurrection and Christ's return (Matt. 13:24-30, 36-43). Apparently, until Judgment Day, the church not only will have legitimate followers of Jesus—"seeds"—in its fellowship, but also "weeds" who are not true followers of Christ. Such weeds will face judgment and be cast into hell at Christ's second coming. Matthew implies that visible churches will always have both true and false followers of Jesus while we are still on earth.

Jesus also says in the Sermon on the Mount, "Many will say to me on that day, 'Lord, Lord, did we not prophesy in your name, and in your name drive out demons and perform many miracles?' Then I will tell them plainly, 'I never knew you. Away from me, you evildoers!'" (Matt. 7:22-23 NIV). In this startling statement, Matthew implies that one could even perform miracles in the name of Christ and still not be a true follower.

Of the four gospels, Matthew presents the most "apocalyptic" picture of Jesus' return to earth. Apocalyptic here means a strong sense of the interaction between spiritual beings in the heavenly world and those on the earth, often with cataclysmic results. Take, for example, what Jesus says after He has interpreted the Parable of the Weeds: "I, the Son of Man, will send my angels, and they will remove from my Kingdom everything that causes sin and all who do evil, and they will throw them into the furnace and burn them. There will be weeping and gnashing of teeth. Then the godly will shine like the sun in their Father's Kingdom" (Matt. 13:41-43).

> "I have been given complete authority in heaven and earth. Therefore, go and make disciples of all the nations, baptizing them in the name of the Father and the Son and the Holy Spirit. Teach these new disciples to obey all the commands I have given you. And be sure of this: I am with you always, even to the end of the age."
>
> **Matthew 28:18-20**
> **The Great Commission**

Elsewhere in Matthew Jesus says, "Then the King will turn to those on the left and say, 'Away with you, you cursed ones, into the eternal fire prepared for the Devil and his demons! For I was hungry, and you didn't feed me. I was thirsty, and you didn't give me anything to drink. I was a stranger, and you didn't invite me into your home. I was naked, and you gave me no clothing.

I was sick and in prison, and you didn't visit me' . . . And they will go away into eternal punishment, but the righteous will go into eternal life" (Matt. 25:41-43, 46).

The Gospel of Matthew ends with the Great Commission, Jesus' command to the eleven to go to the whole world and preach to every nation. Some Christians believe that the only reason Christ has not yet returned is because this task is not completed, although some early Christians probably believed the gospel had reached the whole world by the end of the first century (e.g., Col. 1:23; 1 Clement 5:7). However, this commission remains a "standing rule" for Christians who are true followers of Jesus. His instruction is to continue to fish for people to become a part of His coming kingdom.

Things to Think About

1. In Matthew, Jesus asks His disciples to follow Him even if it means death. Do you think you could be that committed to a cause?

Key Term
The Great Commission

2. Do you agree that Jesus almost exclusively targeted marginal Jews while He was on earth? If you are not Jewish, do you feel that this idea would take away from His relevance to you? Would this conclusion lead us to read Jesus' words more carefully, since they were originally directed at Jews and not at Christians or non-Jews?

endnotes

1. Why did Jesus forbid money or a beggar's purse? Perhaps God was testing the hospitality of His people. Or perhaps Jesus did not want His disciples to be confused with Cynic philosophers, who carried a beggar's purse. Some scholars recently have argued that Jesus modeled himself after such Cynics. In the end, this suggestion is unlikely, not only because Jesus' instructions distinguish His disciples from Cynics, but also because there is no evidence of any Cynics in Palestine at this time.

2. The fact that Matthew used the singular word for "you" means that it was specifically to Peter that Jesus was giving these keys in this passage, although Jesus gave this authority to all His disciples in other places in the gospel (Matt. 18:18; 28:18).

3. One example of this fact is the mention of Peter trying to walk on water (Matt. 14:28-31). Of course, John has almost the opposite favoritism for the "disciple Jesus loved," traditionally taken to be John.

4. Matthew was not referring to a particular organization, like our churches today, but to what we might call the "invisible" church—the group of all those who are true followers of Christ.

CHAPTER 18

The Gospel of Mark:
Jesus, the Suffering Messiah

Mark shockingly proclaims that Jesus is king because He dies!

The Gospel of Mark, like the Gospel of Matthew, presents Jesus as a king. But while Matthew presents Jesus as the kind of king we would expect—someone who rules and leads—Mark shockingly proclaims that Jesus is king because He dies! For Mark, Jesus' "kingship" becomes most evident when the Romans put Him to death—because Jesus died for the sins of His people (Mark 10:45). This unexpected twist is just one example of the way Mark presents the gospel as something that only those with true faith will understand. To everyone else, the meaning of the gospel is hidden.

At a Glance

• Mark presents Jesus as the Messiah, Son of David and Son of God, but emphasizes that Jesus is king most meaningfully at His death.

• Mark highlights the secrecy with which Jesus tried to conduct His mission, forbidding those who knew His identity to tell others.

• Mark portrays the disciples more negatively than the other gospels do.

• Mark was probably written around the time of the destruction of Jerusalem (A.D. 70).

• Mark's audience was probably non-Jewish.

The "Messianic Secret"

A noticeable trait of Mark's gospel is Jesus' consistent effort to keep His identity and activities a secret. For example, He commands those He has healed not to tell anyone who healed them. In Mark 1:43-45, Jesus tells a man healed of leprosy, "Don't tell this to anyone. But go, show yourself to the priest and offer the sacrifices that Moses commanded for your cleansing" (NIV). Interestingly, none of those Jesus heals obey Him—soon He finds the crowds around Him so great that He cannot enter a town openly without being mobbed (Mark 1:45).[1]

Yet the "hidden" feel to Mark's gospel goes well beyond this attempt at secrecy. In Mark, Jesus also keeps His identity as the Messiah very secret. From the very beginning of the gospel, for example, the demons recognize that Jesus is the "Holy One of God"—a title that may imply that Jesus is a heavenly being as well as an earthly king. But Jesus commands the demons to be silent about His identity, a command they have no choice but to keep.[2]

> "And whenever those possessed by evil spirits caught sight of him, they would fall down in front of him shrieking, 'You are the Son of God.' But Jesus strictly warned them not to say who he was."
>
> **Mark 3:11-12**

Two other places in Mark also give us hints that Jesus is not of this earth. One is when He is "transfigured" and becomes "dazzling white" (Mark 9:2-10), as if His heavenly identity is finally coming out into the open. As with the demons, the disciples who see this event are commanded not to tell anyone what they have seen until after Jesus rises from the dead (v. 9).

Jesus also hints at His heavenly origin when He stumps the religious leaders on the nature of the Messiah. Jesus points out that King David called the Messiah "Lord." If that is the case, Jesus asks them, how then could the Messiah be David's son? Jesus may imply here that the Messiah is much more than human—He is a heavenly being that existed before David and has come down to earth. Yet in all these cases where Mark hints that Jesus is not an ordinary human being, an air of secrecy and hiddenness prevails.

Matthew, who may have based his gospel presentation on Mark, incorporated many of these elements into his gospel as well. But they are not nearly as noticeable in Matthew. The clandestine feel of Mark, on the other hand, permeates his entire gospel.

Whereas Matthew and Luke mention one sign that Jesus provides for the Jewish people, Mark quotes Jesus emphatically stating that "no sign will be given to this generation" (Mark 8:12 NRSV)—no exceptions are mentioned.[3] Clearly, Jesus' purpose in using parables is so that those who stand against Him will *not* understand His message (Mark 4:10-13). Mark does not tell us of Jesus' spectacular birth, as Matthew and Luke do. Even more surprisingly, Mark ends without the news getting out that Jesus is no longer dead.[4] While a "young man" tells the women who visit Jesus' tomb that He is alive again, "They said nothing to anyone, because they were afraid" (Mark 16:8 NIV).

Perhaps the most significant example of Jesus commanding secrecy occurs near the end of His earthly life when Peter finally acknowledges that Jesus is the Messiah, the Christ. Jesus accepts this designation, but then warns His disciples not to tell anyone (Mark 8:30). Because Jesus consistently commands this silence about His identity in Mark, some scholars have called this aspect of His presentation the "messianic secret."

The hidden, secretive feel to Mark seems too consistent to be a coincidence. The other gospels tell the same events without the same degree of secrecy. There is a message in the way Mark presents these things. A scholar named William Wrede suggested Mark invented Jesus' claim to be Messiah. Wrede believed that no one actually thought of Jesus as Messiah while He was on earth, so Mark made up the idea that Jesus had kept it a secret.[5]

However, there is good reason to believe not only that Jesus' disciples thought of Him as the Messiah while He was on earth, but that Jesus also viewed himself in these terms. As we saw in a previous chapter on Matthew, when Jesus appointed twelve disciples, He implied that the nation of Israel was being restored, for there were twelve tribes in Israel. But Jesus did not include himself among the twelve, implying that He placed himself in a different category. The most likely role He would have had in mind was that of king over Israel.[6] The way He entered Jerusalem resembled the procession of a king. Jesus was also crucified with the sign "King of the Jews" hanging above His head. Thus, there is good historical evidence that both Jesus and His followers understood His role in messianic terms.

The Messiah Must Die

On the other hand, the popular Jewish idea of what a Messiah would look like and the reality of what Jesus actually looked like were quite different. No Jew expected the royal Messiah to die. Messiahs did not lose—that would prove they were false messiahs. No, the true Messiah would win when He came. He would drive out the Romans from the land of Israel and reestablish the kingdom as it used to be.

However, Mark teaches that Jesus' kingship was demonstrated most emphatically when He died for the sins of His people. When the Roman soldier at the cross sees how Jesus dies, he exclaims, "Truly this man was God's son" (Mark 15:39, author's translation). After Peter acknowledges that Jesus is the Messiah, Jesus immediately begins to tell the disciples about His coming death (Mark 8:31). In other words, Jesus' death defines what it means to be the Messiah in the Gospel of Mark.

Jesus tells His disciples two more times on the way to Jerusalem that He is going to die (Mark 9:31; 10:32-34). Interestingly, in each of these three times that Jesus predicts His coming death, the disciples misunderstand His kingship. The very first time Jesus speaks of His death, Peter rebukes Him for what He is saying. After all, the Messiah cannot lose! But Jesus rebukes Peter: "Get away from me, Satan!"

Mark has framed this episode in such a way as to show that while Peter correctly believes Jesus to be the coming king, he misunderstands what being a king is all about. Mark wanted his audience to know that the hallmark of the Messiah was His death for sins, not His military victory—at least in this phase of Jesus' mission. While Mark teaches that Jesus will return as the "Son of Man" to judge the world in power (Mark 13:26; 14:62), that was not the order of the day while Jesus was on earth.

After Jesus predicts His death again in Mark 9:31, the disciples similarly demonstrate a lack of understanding about Jesus' kingship. This time they argue over who will be the greatest in the new Israel. After the final incident in which Jesus announces His coming death, the disciples James and John ask Him if they can have places of authority in the coming *political* kingdom. The culmination of Jesus' response is His statement that He came to give His life "as a ransom for many" (Mark 10:45). He came to pay the penalty for the sins of God's people.

In Mark's presentation of Jesus, therefore, the heart of Jesus' identity as Messiah comes with His death on the cross for the sins of God's people. This claim radically contradicted the traditional Jewish views of what a messiah would do. Thus, it made sense for Jesus to be somewhat ambiguous and secretive about who He was. To proclaim himself as Messiah certainly would have created a different set of expectations. For most Jews, the claim to be a messiah was a call to arms, not a signal of self-sacrifice.

The Failure of the Disciples

It is important to connect the so-called "messianic secret" of Mark with the failure of Jesus' disciples to understand Him as Messiah. Historically, it was perhaps not so much that they lacked faith in Jesus as that they had the wrong expectations of Him. They seemed prepared to go into battle with a political messiah, but they were caught completely off guard by a suffering messiah. From Mark's perspective, on the other hand, they misunderstood who Jesus was from the very beginning.

Mark's presentation of the disciples is the harshest of all the gospels. As we have already mentioned, each time Jesus announces His coming death, one or more of the disciples display a blatant lack of understanding. First, Peter rebukes Jesus, earning him the response, "Get away from me, Satan!" Next, the disciples argue over who is the greatest among them. Finally, James and John want positions of high honor in the coming kingdom. When the moment of truth comes, they all scatter. Peter denies that he even knows Jesus, and Judas betrays Him, turning Him over to the religious leaders.

But these examples of the disciples' lack of understanding (indeed, their lack of faith) are not the first recorded in Mark. For example, although both Matthew and Luke record the Parable of the Seeds (Matthew 13; Luke 8), neither of them expresses Jesus' shock at the disciples' lack of understanding. In Matthew, when the disciples ask Jesus what the parable means, Jesus says, "Blessed are your eyes because *they see*; and your ears, because *they hear*" (Matt. 13:16).

But Jesus' reaction is much different in Mark: "Don't you understand this parable? How then will you understand any parable?" (4:13 NIV). Jesus is shocked because the disciples do not understand a riddle whose meaning can only be understood by those who have faith. The implication is startling— could it be true that the disciples do not have faith? Only Mark records this reaction on Jesus' part.

In three boat scenes, the disciples also demonstrate a lack of faith (Mark 4:40; 6:51-52; and 8:17-18). In each case, Mark's presentation is harsher on the disciples than Matthew's or Luke's. In the first instance, for example, Mark's Jesus asks the disciples, "Do you still have no faith?" (Mark 4:40 NIV). Matthew's Jesus points out that they have *little* faith, rather than no faith at all (Matt. 14:31), and Luke's Jesus just asks them where their faith is (Luke 8:25). Mark's Jesus, on the other hand, speaks bluntly of a complete absence of faith.

Mark 6:52 boldly states that the hearts of the disciples were "hardened" (KJV, RSV), unreceptive to Him, and that this was the reason they did not believe Jesus could walk on water. Matthew does not draw this conclusion—in fact, Peter tries to walk out to Jesus (Matt. 14:28-31).

Finally, one of Mark's harshest conversations between Jesus and the disciples occurs after He has miraculously fed a great crowd for a second time. Jesus asks the disciples once again if their hearts are *still* hardened, if they have eyes but cannot see, ears but cannot hear (Mark 8:17-18). While Mark's Jesus ends this scene by asking the question again—"Do you still not understand?"—Matthew ends this story by saying the disciples finally *did* understand what He was saying (Matt. 16:12).

Mark's gospel thus is more critical of the disciples and their lack of faith than the other gospels. A number of different explanations can be offered. Some think that Mark's gospel reflects the actual regrets of the early disciples and their own sense of failure. Others think Mark's presentation is meant to inspire its audience to succeed where the original disciples failed. Whatever the explanation, the theme of the disciples' failure to understand contributes to the hidden feel of Mark's gospel.

The Who's and When's of Mark

As with the Gospel of Matthew, the earliest reference to the Gospel of Mark comes from the first half of the second century in the writings of the early Christian Papias.[7] In his works, Papias indicated that someone named Mark wrote down stories about the ministry of Jesus, stories he had heard from the apostle Peter. However, Papias noted that Mark did not write down these events in the order in which they happened. Further, he indicated that Peter "adapted his teaching to the situation," which may mean that he told these stories in different ways to serve different audiences.

While Papias claimed to have received his information from a follower of Jesus named John, we are not sure how much of his information came from John and how much was his own thinking. Perhaps he was trying to defend the Gospel of Mark against those who thought it was disorganized or out of synch with the Gospel of John, which may have been the favorite where Papias lived. Mark's gospel does indeed jump from one event to another without much continuity. It is the shortest gospel of the four and includes the least amount of teaching. It tells us nothing of Jesus before John the Baptist and does not record any of Jesus' Resurrection appearances. One could understand why Papias saw Mark as a somewhat random collection of short stories about Jesus.

> "Mark, who became Peter's interpreter, wrote accurately whatever he remembered—certainly not in order. He wrote the things that had either been spoken or done by the Lord. For he had neither heard nor followed the Lord. Later he had followed Peter, who adapted his teaching to the situation but did not arrange the Lord's sayings. So Mark did no wrong when he wrote down some things as he remembered them. For his single purpose was to leave out nothing he had heard without saying anything false about them."
>
> **Papias, ca. A.D. 140**

From the oldest evidence we have available, the church has believed that the author of this gospel was John Mark, the same Mark who in Acts traveled briefly with Paul and who also seems to have become a traveling companion of Peter. This tradition about Mark traces all the way back to a man who had actually known Jesus, a man named "John." Since the gospel is technically anonymous, however, we should probably be careful not to superimpose our idea of its authorship into its words.

As with Matthew, a few things about the situation in which the gospel was written can be gleaned from clues scattered here and there in Mark. For example, when some Pharisees ask Jesus why His disciples do not wash their hands before they eat, Mark explains that "the Jews, especially the Pharisees, do not eat until they have poured water over their cupped hands, as required by their ancient traditions. Similarly, they eat nothing from the market unless they have immersed their hands in water. This is but one of many traditions they have clung to . . ." (Mark 7:3-4). While Matthew also recorded this event, he did not feel the need to explain Jewish practice. After all, Matthew's gospel was written to Jews who would know such things. Mark's explanation, therefore, probably means that his gospel was written to non-Jews or Gentiles.[8]

There is another parenthetical comment in Mark that might clue us in on when the gospel was written. In Mark 13 Jesus responds to a question from His disciples concerning when God will destroy the Jerusalem temple in judgment, an event that took place in A.D. 70. Jesus warns of something He calls the "abomination of desolation." Whatever this horrible thing was, it would be placed somewhere it should not be (Mark 13:14). At this point in Jesus' speech, the author of Mark interrupts with a warning: "Reader, pay attention!" The author may have wanted those who heard the gospel to realize that the events about which Jesus spoke were in the process of taking place.

Many of the events in Mark 13 did take place in the years surrounding the Jewish War (A.D. 66–73). Roman soldiers sacrificed to some of their gods within the confines of the Jewish temple, desecrating it. Jerusalem and the temple were destroyed. An old tradition holds that the Christians of Jerusalem fled from Jerusalem just before it was destroyed (Mark 13:14-18). Indeed, Luke's version is worded in such a way that one can visualize the Roman armies surrounding the city of Jerusalem (Luke 21:20-24). While we cannot be absolutely certain, it seems quite possible that Mark was written some time in the early part of the Jewish War, A.D. 66–70.

Things to Think About

1. In what way was Jesus' death on a cross a victory for God's people?

2. Why do you think Jesus would want to keep His identity as Messiah a secret from the crowds?

endnotes

1. See also Mark 5:43; 7:36; and 8:26.
2. Examples of Jesus commanding the demons to be silent concerning His identity include 1:25, 34 and 3:11-12.
3. In Matthew and Luke this sign is the sign of Jonah. But while the sign of Jonah in Matthew is the Resurrection (Matt. 12:39-40), in Luke the sign of Jonah is the repentance that followed Jesus' preaching (Luke 11:29-30). In John, of course, Jesus performs countless signs—so many, in fact, that the whole world could not contain the list (John 21:25).
4. As we saw in chapter 5 of this text, the overwhelming majority of scholars believe the Gospel of Mark originally ended at 16:8 and that the verses that follow in some Bibles were later added to Mark.
5. William Wrede (1859–1906) wrote his revolutionary *Messianic Secret in the Gospels* in 1901.
6. See E. P. Sanders, *The Historical Figure of Jesus* (New York: Penguin, 1993), 120, 238–48.

7. Eusebius, *Hist.* 3.39.14–15.

8. It is also interesting that Matthew does not include Mark's statement that Jesus' teaching on this occasion meant that a Christian could now eat things the Old Testament forbade the Jews to eat (Mark 7:19). As the book of Acts indicates, the church struggled for many years to decide whether Gentiles needed to follow the Old Testament dietary laws or not. If this was the implication of what Jesus taught, therefore, it took the church many years to realize it. Similarly, one wonders whether Matthew believed that Jewish Christians were truly "off the hook" as far as keeping the Old Testament dietary laws. Perhaps all foods were clean for Gentile Christians, but for Jewish Christians this was quite a different matter.

CHAPTER 19

The Gospel of Luke:
The Beginnings of Jesus' Mission

*Luke and Acts defend the claim that as a part of His plan,
God has now brought salvation to the whole world through Jesus.*

The Certainty of Things

Even though the Gospel of John falls between them, Luke and Acts are two parts of the same work. Acts begins where the Gospel of Luke leaves off. Both books have the same author, audience, themes, and general perspective. While Luke presents the things Jesus "began to do and teach until the day he ascended to heaven" (Acts 1:1-2), Acts presents the things Jesus continued to do through His Spirit-empowered disciples. For this reason, scholars often refer to them both as a single work: Luke-Acts.

Many believe that taken together, these two books fit best in the ancient genre of historical writing. They may even be classified as general history, a special kind of history that traces the origins of a race or people. Others think that regardless of Acts, Luke itself still comes closest in genre to ancient biography.

At a Glance

- The Gospel of Luke is the first volume of a two-volume history written to demonstrate the certainty of Christianity.

- Luke teaches that the salvation Jesus brings is for all peoples and that God always planned to bring salvation in this way.

- Luke emphasizes Jesus' ministry to the poor, to women, and to the oppressed.

- Luke highlights the role of prayer and the Holy Spirit in Jesus' ministry.

- Luke was probably written several years after the Romans destroyed Jerusalem.

Luke actually gives us a general sense of its purpose: "It seemed good also to me to write an orderly account for you . . . *so that you may know the certainty of the things you have been taught*" (Luke 1:3-4 NIV). In a way, Luke and Acts together are a defense of Christianity. What exactly do they defend? They defend the claim that as a part of His plan, God has now brought **salvation** to the whole world through Jesus.

For Israel, this salvation seems to include its restoration as a nation, with deliverance from its political enemies (Luke 1:68-75; Acts 1:6). It also means bringing back into the fold those in Israel who have not been keeping the covenant, like prostitutes and toll (or tax) collectors (e.g., Luke 15). God also gives full place to society's downtrodden, like the poor, women, and widows (Luke 8:3; Acts 6:1-6). Finally, God restores those who are physically impaired, like the blind and the lame (Luke 14:13; Acts 3:1-10), as well as those who spiritually are under the control of Satan. All these aspects of salvation are God's doing, leaving a strong warning to anyone who might oppose Jesus' followers: "If it is of God, you will not be able to stop them. You may even find yourselves fighting against God" (Acts 5:39).

---

salvation: In Luke, it can imply freedom from Israel's enemies or from demonic forces, freedom from the enslavement and consequences of sins, or physical liberation from disease and sickness.

"Lord, now lettest thou thy servant depart in peace, according to thy word:

For mine eyes have seen thy salvation,

Which thou hast prepared before the face of all people;

To be a light to lighten the Gentiles, and to be the glory of thy people Israel."

Luke 2:29-32
from the *Book of Common Prayer*
These verses are read every evening in many churches.

Salvation for the Whole World

In Luke's account, after Jesus is born, His parents bring Him to the Jerusalem temple to present Him to the Lord.[1] While they are there, a man named Simeon blesses the baby Jesus and joyfully expresses what has come to be known as "Simeon's Song." Several statements in this "hymn" reflect key themes in Luke-Acts. For one, Simeon's Song emphasizes that Jesus brings salvation to the whole world. For Israel, this salvation seems to mean an escape from its political enemies (e.g., Luke 1:71). After Jesus rises from the dead, His disciples ask if He will now restore the kingdom to Israel. Interestingly, His answer is not that the disciples have misunderstood His mission; rather His answer is more like a "not yet" (Acts 1:6-7).[2]

This salvation is a unifying salvation. For Israel, it means bringing back into the fold many who have been like lost sheep. In the well-known Parable of the Prodigal Son in Luke 15, Jesus compares the toll collectors, prostitutes, and other notorious "sinners" of His day to a son who abandons and shames his father, treating him as if he were dead. When this son returns to his father and begs forgiveness, the father welcomes him back. So God was now recklessly welcoming back into Israel those who had lost their way.

But an older brother finds God's forgiveness extremely unfair, since he has stayed and worked faithfully for the father his whole life. This brother represents the Pharisees and those in Israel who had actually tried to keep the covenant. Ironically, they also ended up shaming their heavenly Father by rejecting His plan and desires. By the end of Jesus' mission, many of those outside the kingdom had come back in, while many that were trying to keep the Law lost out.

Simeon's Song affirms that salvation is universal; it is for everyone. Jesus is a "light to lighten the Gentiles." The Gospel of Luke does not give us the impression that Jesus focused exclusively on Israel during His earthly mission. Luke does not tell the story of Jesus calling a foreign woman a dog, and His hesitating to heal her daughter because she was not an Israelite (Matt. 15:21-28; Mark 7:24-30). On the contrary, in addition to the mission of the twelve disciples to Israel, Luke includes a mission of seventy-two individuals, a number that symbolized all the nations of the world.[3] Luke includes positive material about Samaritans (Luke 10:25-37) and shows Jesus trying to minister to Samaritans (9:51-56; 17:11-19), unlike the impression we get in Matthew 10:5. Also unlike Matthew, Luke presents Jesus' genealogy all the way back to Adam, the father of all people (Luke 3:23-38). Matthew starts with Abraham, the father of the Jewish race (Matt. 1:1-17).

In keeping with the universal focus of Luke, the message of Acts verifies that the gospel is for everyone. The key verse of Acts says that the disciples will be witnesses to Jesus' Resurrection all over the world (Acts 1:8). While Jewish Christians continued to keep the Jewish Law to a great degree (e.g., Acts 21:24), Acts makes it clear that Gentile Christians were in no way inferior to them. God had put no distinction between the two because He had given the Holy Spirit to both equally (Acts 15:9).

A final aspect of Simeon's Song that reflects Luke's perspective is the belief that God had planned this salvation from the very beginning. Luke has a strong sense that God is in control of the world and that the events that happen are all a part of His plan. In the sermons of Acts especially, the disciples make it clear that Jesus' death was not a victory for His earthly opponents. Rather, God himself was bringing about things He had promised in the Old Testament.

Some have suggested that Luke paints a more human picture of Jesus than some of the other gospels. For example, several times Luke calls Jesus a prophet (e.g., Luke 7:16; Acts 7:37) and even describes Him as a "*man accredited by God* to you by miracles, wonders, and signs" (Acts 2:22 NIV). Interestingly, while Luke's gospel tells us that Jesus was born of Mary while she was still a virgin (Luke 1:34), Luke gives us little indication that Jesus had existed before His birth. Acts claims that Jesus became Lord and Messiah most meaningfully after He rose from the dead (Acts 2:36; 13:33). This aspect of Luke reminds us why the church believes that Jesus not only is fully God, but fully man, as well.

Good News for the Poor and the Oppressed

Luke's presentation of Jesus' ministry begins in His hometown of Nazareth. Luke uses an event there to set the tone for the rest of Jesus' ministry, as if His words in His home synagogue were a kind of inaugural address. Picking up the scroll of Isaiah, Jesus reads this Scripture:

> "The Spirit of the Lord is upon me, for he has anointed me to preach Good News to the poor. He has sent me to proclaim that captives will be released, that the blind will see, that the downtrodden will be freed from their oppressors, and that the time of the Lord's favor has come."
>
> **Luke 4:18-19, quoting Isaiah 61:1-2**

Jesus' ministry to the poor and those on the edges of society is one of the main emphases of Luke-Acts. When John the Baptist sends his disciples to Jesus to confirm that He is the Messiah, Jesus proves that He is by pointing out these same things: He is giving sight to the blind, preaching good news to the poor, and raising the dead (Luke 7:18-23). Jesus' salvation brings a wholeness to those who are physically, spiritually, and socially broken.

As we saw earlier in chapter 10 of this book, there are significant differences between what it meant to be poor in the ancient world and what it means today. Basically, poverty in an agrarian society like ancient Israel was not so much about a lack of money as about being knocked off track from one's inherited place in society. If you lost the land on which your ancestors had lived for generations, if you had to sell yourself into slavery to pay debts, if you were dependent on others for the basic resources of living—this was being poor. Being poor was not necessarily about losing money, since the exchange of goods (trade) was more typical of buying and selling than the exchange of coins.

Since poverty involved a lack of goods, many thought of rich people as thieves or the descendants of thieves. After all, the rich were the ones who received these goods from those who lost them. Today we generally do not connect one person's prosperity with another's loss; however, the ancient world had a sense of "limited good." In a world with only so many apples to go around, the only way to get more was to take someone else's apples.

The New Testament in general has almost nothing positive to say about money and the rich, but Luke's presentation of Jesus is especially negative toward the rich. While Matthew's version of the Beatitudes says, "Blessed are the poor *in spirit*"—those who have an *attitude* of dependence on God (Matt. 5:3 NIV)—Luke states bluntly, "Blessed are you who are poor" (Luke 6:20 NIV). And in Luke, Jesus goes on to say, "Woe to you who are rich" (Luke 6:24 NIV). It is Luke that tells the parable of a rich man and a poor beggar named Lazarus (Luke 16:19-31).[4] In this story the rich man dies and wakes up in a place of fiery torment, while God greatly rewards Lazarus in Paradise. When Acts describes the earliest Christians, it says, "There was no poverty among them, because people who owned land or houses sold them and brought the money to the apostles to give to others in need" (Acts 4:34-35). In other words, they were the exact opposite of the rich, who *took* land and houses from others, making them poor.

In some of the passages we have just mentioned, Luke mentions the physically impaired, such as the blind or the lame, along with the poor. He associated both kinds of individuals in his mind. Luke joins the other gospels in presenting Jesus as a healer of such people. As in the other gospels, Jesus also casts out demons. In Acts, the early Christians continue Jesus' ministry along these same lines. Through the power of the Holy Spirit, they also heal the impaired and cast out demons.

We have already mentioned how Jesus welcomes the disenfranchised of Israel back into the fold in Luke. Luke also has an emphasis on others that ancient Jewish society often neglected, people like Samaritans and women. Women are so noticeably present in Luke's gospel that some scholars have wondered if the author of Luke-Acts were actually a woman.

Luke is the only gospel, for example, that mentions the women who support Jesus' ministry from their own means, including a woman who manages the household of Herod Antipas (Luke 8:1-3). Acts also mentions women of high status, like Lydia, a seller of expensive purple cloth (Acts 16:14) and the "prominent women" of Berea (Acts 17:12). Luke tells us about Jesus' stay in the home of two women, Mary and Martha (Luke 10:38-42), and Luke's presentation of Jesus' birth is oriented around His mother, Mary.[5]

The Samaritans were another Jewish group on the edge of society in the first century. In Luke, Jesus is seen rebuking James and John for wanting to pray down fire on a Samaritan village (Luke 9:54). Luke gives us the impression that many of the seventy-two disciples Jesus sends out actually go to the villages of Samaria. And Luke alone among the gospels gives us the Parable of the Good Samaritan. All these aspects of Luke's presentation emphasize that the salvation Jesus brings is truly for all.

The Power of Prayer and the Holy Spirit

A final feature of Luke-Acts is the emphasis on prayer and the power of the Holy Spirit in the lives of Jesus and the apostles. For example, Luke is the only gospel that tells us Jesus is praying when the Holy Spirit descends on Him at the Jordan River (Luke 3:21). While the other gospels record this event, they do not mention the prayer. The same is true of Jesus' Transfiguration; only Luke mentions that Jesus goes up the mountain *to pray* and is transformed while He is praying (Luke 9:28-29).

Luke also includes unique teaching on prayer that is missing from the other gospels. Luke is the only gospel to tell the Parable of the Persistent Widow, the story of a widow who keeps bothering a judge until he finally provides her with justice (Luke 18:1-8). In the same way, Luke says God will answer the continuing Israelite prayer for justice. And only Luke tells the Parable of the Pharisee and the Toll Collector (18:9-14). The Pharisee prays boastfully to be seen and heard by others; the toll collector is truly repentant and does not even lift his eyes.[6]

In Acts especially, the Holy Spirit is the power behind everything the apostles do. But the Holy Spirit similarly empowers Jesus to do miracles in Luke (Acts 10:38). As in the other gospels, Jesus' ministry really does not start until after the Spirit descends on Him at His baptism (Matt. 3:16; Mark 1:10; Luke 3:22). But Luke is the one that points out He was "full of the Holy Spirit" (Luke 4:1 NIV) and "in the power of the Spirit" (4:14 NIV) as a result. These glimpses of the Holy Spirit in Luke will take main stage in Acts.

The Who's and When's of Luke-Acts

As with Matthew and Mark, the Gospel of Luke is technically anonymous. However, Christianity has never associated this gospel with any other author but Luke, a physician who sometimes accompanied Paul (cf. Col. 4:14; 2 Tim. 4:11). Certain passages from Acts give the impression that its author traveled with Paul (e.g., Acts 16:10; 20:6), and Luke's name must rank high on the list of possibilities. Nonetheless, various scholars have also suggested that at these points of the story the author of Luke-Acts was relying on someone else's travel diary or even that Acts is a novel not meant to be taken historically.

Both Luke and Acts are addressed to someone named Theophilus. This name is so uncommon in the ancient world that some have suggested it does not refer to a real person. The name Theophilus means "lover of God," which could suggest that Luke was writing to all who love God.[7] However, the way the author of Luke-Acts refers to Theophilus is also similar to the way ancient authors dedicated their writings to the patron who sponsored and funded their work. If Theophilus was a real person, therefore, he was probably the one who funded the writing of Luke-Acts.

The church has traditionally believed that Luke was a Gentile; in fact, the only non-Jewish writer in the New Testament (cf. Col. 4:11-14). If the author was not Luke, however, he writes nothing that a Greek-speaking Jew could not also have written. Luke-Acts is striking in its implications that Jewish Christians must continue to keep the Jewish Law (cf. Luke 1:6; Acts 13:39; 21:21-24), as well as the central role it gives to the Jerusalem temple. The intended audience was probably a mixture of both Jews and Gentiles, although the focus on Gentiles in the gospel and Acts might suggest that it was primarily Gentile. Also noticeable in Luke is the use of the term *Savior* (e.g., Luke 2:11). Greeks and Romans, rather than Jews, tended to use this Greek term.

We can say with great probability that Luke-Acts was written *after* the destruction of the Jerusalem temple in A.D. 70. Some have argued that the author wrote Acts (and therefore Luke) in about A.D. 62 because Acts ends in Rome without telling us the outcome of Paul's trial before Nero. If Luke wrote Acts so much later, the argument goes, why did he stop so abruptly? But while *we* are curious about the outcome of Paul's trial, Luke's audience likely knew such information already. (For further discussion on how Luke's basic themes and goals fit the ending of Acts, see chapter 34 of this book.)

The strongest evidence that Luke-Acts was written after the destruction of the temple comes from a comparison of the way Luke presents Jesus' prediction of Jerusalem's destruction to Matthew's and Mark's predictions. For example, Mark warns: "When you see the desolating sacrilege set up where it ought not to be (let the reader understand), then those in Judea must flee to the mountains" (Mark 13:14 NRSV). Perhaps written during the Jewish War of A.D. 66–73, this statement is somewhat cryptic.

Luke's version of this prophecy, however, is worded vividly: "When you see Jerusalem surrounded by armies, then know that its desolation has come near" (Luke 21:20 NRSV). Given that Luke probably drew from Mark, it is difficult to explain why Luke is so clear and Mark so vague, unless Luke wrote after the events had taken place. He took an indistinct prophecy and gave it the depth of hindsight (cf. the similar drama of Luke 19:43-44).[8]

Things to Think About

Key Term
salvation

1. What kind of person would you today classify as a Samaritan—someone you would find the hardest to love as your neighbor? Someone of a different race? A homosexual? A serial killer? Reread the Parable of the Good Samaritan with this type of person in mind.

2. Some Christians oppose the idea of helping today's poor, even though our poor are often in far more dire straits than even the poor of the first century. What do you think Jesus would say about the attitude of modern churches toward our society's marginal people?

3. How does Luke's presentation of Jesus in relation to Samaritans and Gentiles compare to Matthew's? Can you explain the difference in orientation on the basis of author and audience?

endnotes

1. One interesting feature of Luke-Acts is its focus on Jerusalem. For example, while Matthew and Mark tell us Jesus appeared to His disciples in Galilee after He rose from the dead, Luke does not mention such a trip at all. All of Jesus' Resurrection appearances in Luke take place in or around Jerusalem.

2. It is important to notice this fact about Luke-Acts because some scholars wrongly believe that Acts discards the Jews as God's people. Acts does end with a strong note of criticism toward Jewish opponents to Christianity (Acts 28:25-28). On the other hand, Luke-Acts maintains a conservative stance toward keeping the Jewish Law (e.g., Luke 1:6; Acts 13:39; 21:21-24), as well as toward the Jerusalem temple. Luke simply believed that God's turning toward the Gentiles was part of His plan for this phase of history: "the times of the Gentiles" (Luke 21:24).

3. For example, the Greek translation of Genesis 10 gives seventy-two as the number of all the nations of the world.

4. The fact that this story begins with the same basic wording as some of the other parables in Luke makes it very likely that this story is also a parable. Luke gives us no reason to think that Lazarus here is the same Lazarus Jesus raises from the dead in John 11.

5. Matthew, on the other hand, focuses on Joseph.

6. Repentance is also a significant emphasis in Luke-Acts.

7. As with Matthew and Mark, I have chosen to refer to the author of Luke-Acts as "Luke" for convenience.

8. A further argument that Luke was written after A.D. 70 comes from the fact that it probably drew on Mark itself as a source. Mark is often dated to the late A.D. 60s, perhaps in the early part of the Jewish War.

CHAPTER 20

The Synoptic Question: How Do Matthew, Mark, and Luke Fit Together?

Matthew, Mark, and Luke are so close in their wording, order, and content that they must either have relied on common sources or on each other in some way.

A Look at the Synoptics

Even a casual reader of the gospels will notice a similarity in the stories found in Matthew, Mark, and Luke. In fact, the majority of the stories and events in the first three gospels are the same. Ninety percent of Mark's account also appears in Matthew, while all but thirty-one verses of Mark can be found somewhere in either Matthew or Luke. In contrast, the Gospel of John tells few of the same stories about Jesus. When we consider how much Jesus did in the period these gospels cover (cf. John 21:25), it is remarkable indeed that Matthew, Mark, and Luke all present the same basic events.

At a Glance:

• Matthew, Mark, and Luke are called the synoptic gospels because their portraits of Jesus are so similar to one another.

• The synoptic "problem" is the question of how the content, wording, and order have come to be so similar.

• The most likely answer is that Matthew and Luke both drew from Mark when creating their gospels.

• If Mark is the main source for Matthew and Luke, there must have been a second source consisting mostly of Jesus' sayings. Scholars call this second source "Q" from the German word for "source."

Matthew, Mark, and Luke are often called the **synoptic gospels** because they are so similar in their presentation and content. "Synoptic" means these gospels look at Jesus in a similar way (cf. "optic").

synoptic gospels: Matthew, Mark, and Luke, so called because they present similar portraits of Jesus.

synoptic problem: The question of how the synoptic gospels came to be so similar in content, wording, and arrangement.

John, on the other hand, differs significantly both in its content and perspective.[1] The question of how Matthew, Mark, and Luke came to be so similar in content, wording, and arrangement is called the **synoptic problem**. Over the course of the last one hundred fifty years or so, scholars have suggested almost every imaginable scenario to explain this problem.

Take the following example of an occasion when a man with leprosy approaches Jesus. Here is what the man says to Jesus in Matthew, Mark, and Luke:

Matthew 8:2-4
"Lord, if you will, you are able to cleanse me."

Mark 1:40-44
"If you will, you are able to cleanse me."

Luke 5:12b-14
"Lord, if you will, you are able to cleanse me."

Example 1

With the exception of whether he addresses Jesus as "Lord" or not, what the man says to Jesus is exactly the same, word for word in the Greek of all three gospels.[2] This observation leads naturally to the first possible explanation for the similarities between Matthew, Mark, and Luke.

Option 1: The synoptics are so similar because the Holy Spirit inspired the disciples to remember the exact words Jesus and other people spoke on each occasion.

While God certainly had the power to inspire the gospel writers to remember the exact words Jesus spoke on each occasion, this option simply does not work as an explanation for the similarity between Matthew, Mark, and Luke's wording.[3] First of all, Jesus spoke Aramaic, not Greek, so the gospels do not record the actual words Jesus spoke.[4] At best, they give us translations of Jesus' original words.

As the variety of English Bibles indicates, there is always more than one way to translate a sentence from one language to another. The fact that Matthew, Mark, and Luke frequently have the exact Greek wording implies that they have some common source (even if that source is the Holy Spirit). This similarity in wording happens so often that they could not have translated Jesus' words in exactly the same way by coincidence.

Further, it is not just what Jesus and others *say* that frequently is worded exactly the same. Often, the *telling of the story* also is worded exactly the same in these three gospels. Look at how Matthew, Mark, and Luke describe the way Jesus heals the man:

Matthew 8:3
"And having stretched out the hand he touched him saying, 'I will; be cleansed.' "

Mark 1:41
"And having had compassion, having stretched out his hand he touched and says to him 'I will; be cleansed.' "

Luke 5:13
"And having stretched out the hand he touched him saying, 'I will; be cleansed.' "

Example 2

Not only are Jesus' words the same in these three gospels—"I will; be cleansed"—but there is a remarkable similarity in the wording of the action itself—the way Jesus stretches out His hand and touches the man. Matthew and Luke in this instance have *exactly* the same wording! Because it is a similarity *in storytelling* in addition to what is said, it cannot come from someone's memory of the event. We have to conclude that these three gospel writers used a common source or sources when writing their gospels.

Option 2: God inspired the gospel writers to tell the story with exactly the same wording.

The problem with this suggestion is that while the synoptic gospels often *do* have a remarkable similarity in wording and arrangement, they also often *do not*. Take the following example:

Matthew 8:16

"When evening came, they brought to him many who were demon possessed."

Mark 1:32

"When evening came, when the sun was setting they were bringing to him all those sick and demon possessed."

Luke 4:40

"When the sun had set, all who had people sick with various diseases led them to him."

Example 3

Once again, the wording of these three sentences is very similar. What is interesting is that this sentence is not an event in the story but a *summary* of Jesus' activities. All three gospels make this summary at roughly the same point in their stories. It is highly unlikely that three storytellers would summarize Jesus' activities at the same point in their stories just by complete coincidence. The best explanation is that they were relying on a common source or sources.

However, the inspiration of the Holy Spirit is not the best explanation for the similarity in wording and placement. Certainly God *could* have inspired the

> Matthew, Mark, and Luke used a common source or sources when writing their gospels.

gospels to be written exactly the same or in any way He wished. Indeed, if the wording was *always* exactly the same, as in **Example 1**, it might make sense to say it was the Holy Spirit. But what reason would God have to inspire the gospels to be exactly the same sometimes, *mostly the same* at many other times, and then sometimes significantly different at still other times? Why, for example, would God inspire: (1) Matthew to write, *"when evening came,"* (2) Luke to write, *"when the sun had set,"* and (3) Mark to write *both*? It is hard to imagine why God would inspire the writers in this way if He were dictating to them word for word.

Inspiration becomes a very strange and haphazard thing if one uses it to explain these similarities. And what about John? Did God just decide to do something completely different after inspiring such incredible similarities in the synoptic gospels? Any close examination of the New Testament reveals that God allowed the personalities and worldviews of the writers to have an effect on the particular words they wrote. These observations mean that the similarities almost certainly go beyond the Holy Spirit to common sources of some kind.

The idea of using sources does not contradict the Bible's inspiration in any way. For example, Joshua 10:13 quotes from the *Book of Jashar*. First and Second Kings seem to draw material from books called the *Annals of the Kings of Judah* and the *Annals of the Kings of Israel* (e.g., 1 Kings 14:29; 2 Kings

13:8). To say that Matthew, Mark, and Luke relied on sources does not diminish their authority or inspiration in any way.

Option 3: The similarities come from oral tradition–Matthew, Mark, and Luke are recording the traditions they have heard passed down.

Some have suggested that the similarity in wording between the synoptics has resulted from the fact that these stories were so well known. Because the early Christians told and retold them so often, they often had them memorized word for word. This option has the strength of explaining not only the similarities but also the minor differences in the way Matthew, Mark, and Luke word events.

On the other hand, some have dismissed this option because it seems incredible that people completely independent of one another would remember the exact words. How could Matthew, Mark, and Luke in different parts of the world remember the exact wording of the story of the leper's healing? However, in recent years we have begun to regain a sense of how *oral* the ancient world was. The overwhelming majority of the ancients could not read—theirs was not a literary world like ours. For this reason, we should not picture the early Christians *reading* the New Testament; we should picture them *hearing* it read to them. We should speak of the *audiences* of the New Testament books rather than their *readership*.

> The overwhelming majority of the ancients could not read. For this reason, we should not picture the early Christians *reading* the New Testament but *hearing* it. We should speak of the *audiences* of the New Testament books, not their *readership*.

One typical aspect of oral cultures is their ability to remember far more than literate cultures. It is perhaps surprising to learn that the stereotypical poet of ancient Greece *was blind* and yet could recite the entire *Iliad* or *Odyssey*. Plato even argues in one of his "dialogues" (!) that writing is bad because it makes the memory weak.[5]

The fact that these stories circulated orally goes a long way toward explaining why the synoptic gospels can be so similar and yet not exactly the same in many cases. In and of itself, this is probably not the only element in the equation. It is not just the individual stories that reveal these similarities, but also the overall *order* in which the stories are arranged (see **Figure 1**). Add to this the fact that the same basic stories in the ministry of Jesus appear in Matthew, Mark, and Luke—out of the thousands of

---

The Order of a Few Selected Events in the Synoptics

Matthew

1. Stories of Jesus' birth
2. Jesus' baptism
3. Jesus recruits His first disciples
4. The Sermon on the Mount
5. Jesus heals a leper
6. Jesus heals Peter's mother-in-law

Mark

1. Jesus' baptism
2. Jesus recruits His first disciples
3. Jesus heals Peter's mother-in-law
4. Jesus heals a leper

Luke

1. Stories of Jesus' birth
2. Jesus' baptism
3. Jesus heals Peter's mother-in-law
4. Jesus recruits His first disciples
5. Jesus heals a leper
6. The Sermon on the Plain

Figure 1

---

things Jesus did during this period—and we become increasingly convinced that the gospels had some written source or sources in common.

It is not sufficient just to say that these stories were told so often that most people had *each one of them* memorized *individually* word for word. They would have needed to memorize practically verbatim a whole gospel, perhaps the Gospel of Mark. While this is possible, it becomes increasingly likely that the authors of Matthew, Mark, and Luke used a common *written* source to create their gospels.

You may not find it surprising to learn that the synoptic gospels present the events of Jesus' ministry in almost exactly the same order. After all, they describe the same Jesus, and Jesus did things in a certain order. Why would the gospels *not* present the events of His ministry in the same order? But as you can see from the brief comparison above, the synoptic gospels *do* differ slightly in the order in which they present things. For example, Luke puts Jesus' recruitment of the first disciples later than Matthew and Mark do. Matthew and Mark place the healing of the man with leprosy and the healing of Peter's mother-in-law in the opposite order. The most obvious conclusion is that the gospels do not always present events in the exact order in which they happened.

For many of you, it will not matter much whether the gospels differ from one another on such a small scale. Others, however, find this observation very troubling. It is tempting for some to say that Jesus healed *two* men with leprosy—one before Peter's mother-in-law got sick and one afterward. We often approach the gospels by "harmonizing" them, finding ways to fit the precise order and details of the gospels together without any discrepancies.

But there are good reasons not to approach the stories of the gospels in this way. First of all, the wording of the leper's healing is so similar in Matthew, Mark, and Luke (see **Examples 1** and **2**) that it becomes extremely likely these all refer to the same event. In other words, harmonizing the order of Matthew and Mark at this point requires us to ignore what the text seems to be telling us—it requires us to twist Scripture rather than listen to it. And ancient history and biography simply were not as precise as modern history and biography are. The boundaries were different on what was acceptable, and the ancients were allowed to be more creative in their presentations than we are today. For this reason, it would be wrong to call such minor differences "errors."

Secondly, harmonizing does not really show respect to the text of the

Bible as a text—it often requires us to *reject* the way the story actually appears *in any one gospel* so that we can create a hypothetical gospel of our own. In other words, it rejects the individual gospel presentations in order to create some fifth gospel that fits *our* preconceptions. While those who harmonize are extremely sincere and devout, they ironically show less respect to the actual text of the Bible than those who allow the gospels to "be themselves."

Thus, the similarities between the first three gospels probably do not derive from the fact that the early Christians told the same stories in the same way. It is much more likely that these authors used a source that was very nearly a complete gospel in itself. It seems very likely that these three gospels have a *literary* relationship to one another. That is, they have taken most of their material either from one another or from a common *written* source.

Option 4: Matthew was written first; in compiling their gospels, Mark and Luke in some way have taken material from Matthew.

This option has been the favorite of the church since a man named Augustine suggested it back in the A.D. 300s. Because the Gospel of Matthew was the favorite gospel of the church, and since the disciple Matthew was an eyewitness of the gospel events, it made sense to suggest that he had written first and that the non-eyewitnesses, Mark and Luke, had copied from him.

Augustine believed that Mark was a shortened version of Matthew, since the two were so incredibly similar in wording at so many points. In the late 1700s, a man named **Griesbach** suggested that Matthew was written first, Luke second, and that Mark

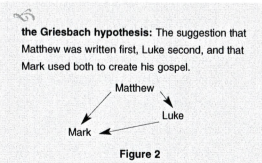

the Griesbach hypothesis: The suggestion that Matthew was written first, Luke second, and that Mark used both to create his gospel.

Figure 2

Matthew 8:3

"And having stretched out the hand he touched him saying, 'I will; be cleansed.' "

Mark 1:41

"And *having had compassion* having stretched out his hand he touched and says to him 'I will; be cleansed.' "

Luke 5:13

"And having stretched out the hand he touched him saying, 'I will; be cleansed.' "

Example 2

created a much shorter version using both of these (see **Figure 2**). A respectable minority of scholars continues to hold this position today.

The strongest arguments in favor of this explanation refer to the few situations such as those previously explained in **Example 2**. In this instance, Matthew and Luke have exactly the same wording, but Mark has something slightly different. Modern proponents of the Griesbach hypothesis would say that Luke copied Matthew's account of this incident word for word, while Mark reworded it a little. These "minor agreements" of Matthew and Luke against the wording of Mark are the strongest arguments in favor of the Griesbach hypothesis.

The problem is that this example is the exception rather than the rule. Most of the time when there is a disagreement over wording, Matthew and Luke *dis*agree with one another and Mark agrees with one or the other. In other words, Mark agrees with the wording of Matthew against Luke, or Mark and Luke agree against Matthew's wording. It is only on very rare occasions that Matthew and Luke agree together against Mark's wording.

With regard to the order of events, Matthew and Luke never agree over and against Mark. When Matthew and Luke disagree with one another on the order of things, one of them always agrees with Mark's order. These observations make it more likely that Mark was written first and that Matthew and Luke both created their gospels from Mark's account.

A number of other factors also point to Mark as the original from which Matthew and Luke copied. For example, Mark's Greek style is "rougher" than Matthew's or Luke's. This is obvious in **Example 2**. Here is another example:

Matthew 3:11

"The one who comes *after me* is stronger than me, whose sandals I am not worthy to carry."

Mark 1:7

"One comes who is stronger than me after me, the straps of whose sandal I am not worthy, bending over, to untie."

Luke 3:16

"*One comes* who is stronger than me, *the straps of* whose sandals I am not worthy to untie."

Example 4

(Items in italics are where Matthew or Luke agree with Mark but disagree with one another.)

As you can see, Luke has exactly the same words as Mark, except that Luke has taken out two somewhat awkward phrases.[6] Matthew also follows Mark exactly at some points, but has smoothed the Greek out a little. Because Mark's Greek is consistently "rougher" than Matthew's and Luke's, it makes more sense to say Matthew and Luke copied from Mark than the other way around. We can understand why Matthew would "comb Mark's hair." It is much more difficult to explain why Mark would have consistently "mussed up" Matthew's and Luke's.

We can say similar things about the thinking of Matthew and Luke—they have dotted Mark's *i*'s and crossed his *t*'s. Mark did not make an effort to answer questions that might arise from various things Jesus said and did. For example, since John the Baptist was baptizing people so that their sins could be forgiven, someone might wonder why Jesus was baptized. Did Jesus have sins? While Mark simply tells us Jesus was baptized, Matthew's presentation makes it clear that Jesus did not *need* to be baptized (Matt. 3:14-15). Matthew thus "combed" Mark's presentation to make sure no one got the wrong idea.

Matthew does the same thing with regard to Jesus' disciples. The Parable of the Seeds teaches that only His true followers will be able to understand His parables (Mark 4:11-12). But Jesus' disciples did not understand this parable! Mark leaves us wondering about the disciples: "If you can't understand this story, how will you understand all the others I am going to tell?" (Mark 4:13). Matthew could not leave us wondering like that. Matthew made sure we knew this: "Blessed are your [the disciples'] eyes, because they *see*; and your ears, because they *hear*" (Matt. 13:16). Matthew thus combed Mark's hair again.

Mark also has a number of Aramaic phrases that do not appear in Matthew and Luke. These could mean that Mark comes earlier than Matthew and Luke, although this is not a definitive argument. When Jesus raises a young girl from the dead, Mark quotes and translates the Aramaic, "Talitha cum" ("Get up, little girl!") (Mark 5:41). When Jesus heals a deaf man, Mark writes, "Ephphatha," ("Be opened!") (7:34). When Jesus prays in the Garden of Gethsemane, he calls God "Abba" ("Father") (14:36). These Aramaic words give Mark an earlier feel, since he alone quotes them. All these factors taken together lead to the next option, the one most scholars favor.

Option 5: Mark or some version of Mark was written first; Matthew and Luke have used it as the basis for their gospel presentations.

The majority of scholars have come to the conclusion that Mark, or some version of Mark, was written first and that Matthew and Luke used it as the basis for their own presentations. As we said at the beginning of the chapter, all but about thirty-one verses of Mark can be found in Matthew or Luke, and approximately 90 percent of Mark can be found in Matthew alone. Those few instances where Matthew and Luke agree over and against Mark's wording can be explained if they followed oral traditions—the way other Christians were telling the story—or an earlier version of Mark (an oral one?).

The problem with this suggestion is that Matthew and Luke have a lot of material in common that is not found in Mark—primarily Jesus' teachings (e.g., the Sermon on the Mount). If Mark was written first, then there must have been another source for Matthew and Luke's common teaching material. Since German scholars really developed this line of thought, scholars refer to this hypothetical source as **Q**, after the German word for source, *Quelle*.[7]

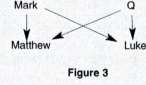

the two-source hypothesis: The idea that Matthew and Luke based their presentations on Mark and a collection of some of Jesus' sayings, called **Q**.

Figure 3

The most common answer to the synoptic question is thus the **two-source hypothesis** (see **Figure 3**). This hypothesis says that Mark was written first, and that Matthew/Luke used it to provide the basic storyline of Jesus' ministry. They also used a collection of Jesus' teachings, **Q**, to supplement Mark's story with the various things Jesus taught. If this reconstruction is correct, then Matthew has reorganized the sayings into sermons, something perfectly acceptable within the limits of ancient biography and history writing. Luke then probably provides us with the more original order of the sayings, although we find them scattered throughout his gospel.

Things to Think About

1. Would it take away from the authority and inspiration of the gospels if the two-source hypothesis were correct?

Key Terms
Griesbach hypothesis
synoptic problem
synoptic gospels
two-source hypothesis

2. Of the five options discussed in this chapter, which option do you find most convincing? Can you solve or address the problems associated with that option? How would you understand the Bible differently knowing that its first audiences were largely illiterate and *heard* it rather than *read* it?

3. Would it take away from the authority and inspiration of the gospels if we could not completely reconcile their wording and order on a historical level?

endnotes

1. See chapter 25 of this text.

2. In order to bring out the exact similarities and differences among the synoptics, all translations in this chapter are the author's.

3. Of course, even if we accept the traditional authorship of Matthew, Mark, and Luke, only Matthew would have been an eyewitness to Jesus' ministry. Mark and Luke were not firsthand disciples of Jesus. In other words, they had no memories of Jesus' words because they were not present to hear them.

4. Although they occasionally do record some Aramaic phrases Jesus used (especially Mark).

5. Cf. *Phaedrus* 274c–277a: "If men learn this, it will implant forgetfulness in their souls; they will cease to exercise memory because they rely on that which is written, calling things to remembrance no longer from within themselves, but by means of external marks" (275a); translation taken from *Plato: The Collected Dialogues*, E. Hamilton and H. Cairns, eds. (Princeton: Princeton University, 1961), 476–525.

6. In most cases, Matthew follows Mark's wording more closely than Luke does. This particular verse is an exception. The Gospels of Matthew and Mark overall are closest to one another in wording and order.

7. We have other examples of collections of sayings from the ancient world. For example, the Gospel of Thomas is a collection of Jesus' sayings that resembles what we suppose Q to have looked like. Although they are slightly different, two documents found at Qumran are also collections of quotes ("4QTestimonium" and "4QFlorilegium"). It is interesting that Papias called the original Aramaic Matthew a collection of Jesus' "sayings." While it is highly speculative, one wonders if the Gospel of Matthew was so called because it was based on Matthew's own collection of sayings—the collection scholars today call Q.

CHAPTER 21

Jesus and the Downtrodden

Throughout Luke, Jesus' approach to the notorious sinners of Israel is not a stern word of repentance, but an optimistic welcome home to those who have gone astray or been left behind.

A Picture of Grace

While all four gospels tell of Jesus' ministry to the outcasts of Palestinian society, the Gospel of Luke in particular emphasizes Jesus' desire to bring back into Israel many of those society had abandoned. Included in this group were the poor, those who were physically challenged, like the blind and the lame, as well as the spiritually impaired. Prostitutes, tax collectors, the demon possessed—Jesus offered a second chance to them all.[1]

> **At a Glance**
>
> • Luke focuses on the good news Jesus' mission brought to the disenfranchised and downtrodden of Israel.
>
> • Jesus offered good news to the poor and oppressed of society.
>
> • Jesus welcomed women and Samaritans into the restored kingdom of Israel.
>
> • Jesus cast out demons and healed the sick, making them whole members of Israel.

The books of Luke and Acts emphasize that Jesus and the early Christians were concerned about what we would consider the physical and social dimensions of a person rather than just the "spiritual" aspect. While today we tend to put such things into separate compartments, Jesus' audience would have interconnected the spiritual, social, and physical aspects of a person. A person with a physical problem probably had a "spiritual" problem that led to the sickness or handicap. Unfaithfulness to God was often the reason a person was placed on the margins of Jewish society.

It is easy for us to think Jesus' openness to tax collectors and prostitutes was a kind of unconditional love, an affirmation of these people for what they were. But Jesus did not expect such individuals to continue in prostitution or to continue unjust practices with regard to the collection of taxes (cf. Luke 3:10-14). The idea of "unconditional love"—in which God accepts a person despite his/her behavior—was quite foreign to the ancient world. God welcomes all to Himself, no matter the nature of their pasts; but God's **grace**, His willingness to be a source of life and goodness to us, came with the expectation that we honor and obey Him.[2] In Jesus, God was offering a second chance to those who had not kept the covenant, a chance to return to God. But unless such individuals turned from their sins, they could not continue in His favor.

grace: God's willingness to serve as the supplier of our needs, our divine patron. In return, He expects honor and obedience.

For the Gospel of Luke, the most important aspect of Jesus' earthly mission was the restoration He was bringing to God's people. As we mentioned in chapter 13, Luke introduces Jesus' ministry with an event in His hometown of Nazareth. Reading from the scroll of Isaiah, Jesus says: "The Spirit of the Lord is upon me, for he has anointed me to preach Good News to the poor. He has sent me to proclaim that captives will be released, that the blind will see, that the downtrodden will be freed from their oppressors, and that the time of the Lord's favor has come" (Luke 4:18-19, quoting Isaiah 61:1-2). After He sits down, Jesus tells his audience that He is the fulfillment of this prophecy.

Because Luke introduces Jesus' ministry with this event, he hints that these words from Isaiah are the key to understanding Jesus' mission—a mission to the poor, the oppressed, and the physically impaired. When John the Baptist sends his followers to Jesus to verify that He is the Christ, Jesus' response in Luke is a recap of this passage in Isaiah, confirming that its good news is the essence of His ministry. Throughout Luke, Jesus' approach to the notorious sinners of Israel is not a stern word of repentance, but an optimistic welcome home to those who have gone astray or been left behind.

The Poor and Oppressed

The first hints that Luke in particular was focusing on Jesus' ministry to the disenfranchised of Israel come even before Jesus is born. The angel of the Lord tells Zechariah, the father of John the Baptist, that his son will "bring back to the Lord their God" many of the people of Israel (Luke 1:16 NIV). While Matthew relates the royal story of Jesus' birth through the eyes of Joseph, Luke chooses Mary's perspective. This choice fits in with the greater role Luke gives to women in the story of Jesus and the early church. Mary praises God for what He is doing, because "He has taken princes from their thrones and exalted the lowly. He has satisfied the hungry with good things and sent the rich away with empty hands" (1:52-53).

Rather than focus on the prestigious wise men of Matthew, Luke presents Jesus' birth through the eyes of shepherds, who certainly did not enjoy a high place in ancient society. Both an elderly man and an elderly woman in the temple acknowledge that Jesus' birth is significant in terms of the "rescue" of Israel (2:25) and the deliverance of Jerusalem from its captivity (2:38). These comments indicate that Jesus would play an important role in unifying and restoring Israel as a people.

As we saw in chapter 19, Luke's Jesus has a special place for the poor and the oppressed in His mission. Luke is the only gospel writer to tell the Parable of the Rich Man and Lazarus, in which God rewards a poor beggar after he dies, while a rich man goes to the place of the dead and suffers (Luke 16:19-31). Luke alone gives us the Parable of the Rich Fool (12:13-21), the Parable of the Persistent Widow (18:1-8), the Parable of the Pharisee and the tax collector (18:9-14), and the story of Zacchaeus, the Tax Collector (19:1-9). While Matthew's Sermon on the Mount states, "Blessed are the poor in spirit" (Matt. 5:3 NIV), Luke's Sermon on the Plain states flatly, "Blessed are you who are poor" (Luke 6:20 NIV). He also adds, "Woe to you who are rich" (6:24 NIV). In short, Luke has much more to say about God's desire to include and restore the downtrodden and lost of Israel than the other gospels. It is no coincidence that Luke is also the only gospel to tell the Parable of the Prodigal Son (15:11-32).

Women and Samaritans also existed on the margins of Jewish society. While we will mention Luke's concern for women later in this chapter, let us first look at Luke's concern for Samaritans—and his hints that the good news of Jesus was for Samaritans. Jesus refuses to call down fire in judgment of certain Samaritan villages, even though they have rejected His disciples (9:51-55). Luke's Jesus also tells a parable that places a Samaritan in a very positive light (10:30-37, the Parable of the Good Samaritan). Luke tells these parts of the story in the context of a mission that includes certain Samaritan villages. Further in this book, our study of Acts 8 will tell us that some of the early Christians later preached the gospel in Samaria with some success, a fact that some think the Gospel of John also reflects.[3]

The Sick and Demon Possessed

Luke retains the stories told also in Matthew and Mark in which Jesus casts out demons and heals the sick. In all three synoptic gospels, this power demonstrates that Jesus has defeated Satan and the evil forces that have been in control of the earthly realm. Luke 10 portrays the amazement of some of Jesus' followers after they successfully cast out demons. Jesus responds, saying that He has seen Satan fall from heaven like lightning (10:18). This refers to the fact that His power over the demonic forces in control of the present world signals the end of Satan's power in this age.

Women in Luke-Acts

We have already hinted that Luke pays more attention to women in his presentation of Jesus' ministry than the other gospels do. We mentioned, for example, that Luke features Mary rather than Joseph in the story of Jesus' birth. He also describes Elizabeth, the mother of John the Baptist. And only Luke tells us about the prophetess Anna at the temple, who recognized the baby Jesus and "spoke about the child to all who were looking forward to the redemption of Jerusalem" (2:38). The well-known Mary and Martha seem to be two women who opened their home to Jesus (10:38-42). One of the women who supported Jesus was even part of Herod Antipas' administration, the Herod who beheaded John the Baptist (Luke 8:3)!

Some of the unique stories and parables in Luke seem to reflect this emphasis on women. We have already mentioned the Parable of the Persistent Widow (Luke 18:1-8), found only in Luke. Luke also is the sole one to mention that Jesus cast seven demons out of Mary Magdalene (8:2). Luke alone tells of the healing of a crippled woman on the Jewish Sabbath, and how Jesus points out to His opponents that she too is "a daughter of Abraham" (13:16 NIV).

This attention to the role of women in the gospel does not end with the Gospel of Luke but continues in Acts, Luke's story of the early church. When God's Spirit arrives on earth after Jesus has gone to heaven, Luke explains what is taking place by quoting the Old Testament prophet Joel. Joel not only declared that men would prophesy in the days when the Spirit came, but that women would, too (Acts 2:17-18). In fact, we do see that women prophesy later on in Acts (21:9).

Both men and women are featured prominently in the expansion of Christianity. On more than one occasion, Christians meet in the houses of women. Among these are the house of Mary in Jerusalem (Acts 12:12) and Lydia in Philippi (16:15, 40). Acts makes a special effort to point out when prominent women become Christians, implying that women continued to serve as patrons to the early Christian communities (17:4, 12, 34). Perhaps most striking of all is the mention of Priscilla's name before the name of her husband, Aquila (18:26), something Paul also did (Rom. 16:3). Such references may imply that her role in the Christian mission at least equaled, if not exceeded, that of her husband.

Things to Think About

1. Decide if the following statement is true, false, or a little of both: "In the Gospel of Luke, Jesus never associates His gospel with personal salvation. Instead, He repeatedly emphasizes that the gospel is good news for the poor, the oppressed, and the downtrodden."

Key Term
grace

2. Is God's grace unconditional? In other words, is it possible that God would withdraw His favor from me if I did not return to Him the appropriate honor He deserves?

endnotes

1. Only Matthew 21:31-32 explicitly mentions Jesus' inclusion of prostitutes among those whom God is reclaiming, although the sinful woman of Luke 7:36-50 may very well have been such a person.

2. See chapter 10. The ancient world was oriented on the basis of "patron-client" relationships. This was a system in which "patrons" provided the means of living (such as food) to those who did not have such means ("clients") in return for the honor and prestige such clients returned to them. "Grace" is the willingness of God to serve as our patron, but we must give Him the appropriate honor in return in order to continue receiving His patronage. The idea of patronage without an accompanying obligation simply did not exist in the ancient world.

3. Namely, in Jesus' interaction with a Samaritan woman in John 4.

CHAPTER 22

The Parables: Stories Jesus Told

The kingdom of God is about God ruling on earth—in the hearts of His people today, in the person of His Christ tomorrow.

Ears to Hear

The primary method Jesus used to teach the crowds in the countryside was storytelling. In particular, He taught in parables, a word that can also be rendered "riddles." An older definition of a parable is "an earthly story with a heavenly meaning"—in other words, a story told in terms of everyday life in order to teach something about God, heaven, or something of a spiritual nature. Some have even taken Jesus' use of stories as a model for how to preach. The assumption is that Jesus taught in stories so that the crowds could better understand His message.

We can imagine that this comprises one aspect of Jesus' storytelling, but the synoptic gospels of Matthew, Mark, and Luke highlight a much different reason for Jesus to speak in parables.[1] The synoptic gospels present Jesus'

At a Glance

- A parable is much more like a riddle than a teaching tool to make the message clearer.

- At least in part, Jesus taught in parables to screen the understanding of His audience.

- Some of Jesus' parables relate to the varying reactions in Israel to His message. Some who were on the outskirts of Israel were reclaimed; others who had kept the Law now found themselves out of God's favor.

- Several parables, notably in Matthew, deal with the judgment of all, especially followers of Jesus who are unworthy.

- Several parables in Luke deal with topics like prayer and money.

Parable of the Seeds as the key to understanding all of His parables (Matt. 13:3-9; Mark 4:3-8; Luke 8:5-8). In this story, Jesus tells how a farmer's seed lands on four different kinds of soil. Some seed falls on the path and is eaten by birds. Some falls on rocky ground and is scorched by the sun. Some falls among thorns and is choked. Only a portion of the seed falls on soil good enough for the seed to grow and produce a harvest.

This parable illustrates the fact that not everyone will accept Jesus' message about the kingdom of God. In fact, only those who "have ears to hear" will even understand it. Jesus goes on to tell His disciples why He speaks in parables, or "riddles," a possible meaning of the Hebrew equivalent to the word *parable*: "You are permitted to understand the secret about the Kingdom of God. But I am using these stories to conceal everything about it from outsiders, so that the Scriptures might be fulfilled: 'They see what I do, but they don't perceive its meaning. They hear my words, but they don't understand'" (Mark 4:11-12).

The synoptic gospels make the astonishing claim that the reason Jesus spoke in parables was not to make His message clearer—at least not to most of His audience. He spoke in riddles to obscure His message to those whose hearts were not truly oriented to the kingdom. No wonder Jesus is astonished that His own disciples do not understand the Parable of the Seeds. "How then will you understand any parable?" He asks them (Mark 4:13 NIV). In keeping with the "hidden" feel of Mark's presentation, he notes that Jesus "did not say anything to them [the crowds] without using a parable" (Mark 4:34).

The Kingdom of God

Jesus' parables provide teaching on many different topics. Several of Matthew's parables deal with God's judgment of humanity. A number of

Luke's are about issues such as prayer and money. Still others tell what the **kingdom of God** is like.

Mark 1:15 tells us that Jesus' primary message to Israel was about the "kingdom of God." Scholars have debated for years what Jesus meant by this phrase. Was He talking about something still to come in the future, or was the kingdom of God something that arrived while Jesus was on earth, something still with us today? Was Jesus referring to a spiritual kingdom among Christians here on earth now, or did He mean a kingdom in heaven that awaits us when we die? Still others think Jesus referred to the political restoration of Israel or the kingdom He would set up after He returned to earth in apocalyptic glory.

The thing that makes the issue so complicated is that almost every one of these positions can find support from one passage or another in the gospels. While Jesus looked forward to God's kingdom in many respects, in other respects He saw himself as inaugurating that kingdom on earth. Perhaps the Lord's Prayer captures it best when it says in reference to God, "Your kingdom come, your will be done on earth as it is in heaven" (Matt. 6:10 NIV). The kingdom of God is about God ruling on earth—today in the hearts of His people, tomorrow in the person of His Christ.

One of the parables that best captures this understanding of the kingdom is the **Parable of the Mustard Seed** (Matt. 13:31-32; Mark 4:30-32; Luke 13:18-19). In this parable, Jesus compares the kingdom of God to a mustard seed, one of the smallest of seeds. While the mustard seed starts out small, it grows to be a disproportionately large plant. So, Jesus implies, the kingdom of God starts small, almost imperceptibly, but in the end will manifest itself throughout the entire world.

Parables of Israel

It is easy for Bible readers today to lose sight of the fact that Jesus was a Jew and that He directed his message to ancient Israel. This audience stands behind a number of stories often taken out of context by modern readers.

In the short *Parable of the Two Sons* (Matt. 21:28-32), Jesus compares those in His audience to two sons whose father tells them to go work in his vineyard. One son says he will, but does not. The other, although he initially says he will not work, changes his mind.

These two sons were like those in Israel who heard Jesus' message. The tax collectors and prostitutes were like those who said they would not keep Israel's covenant with Yahweh. But then they accepted Jesus' message and repented. While they initially said they would not "work" in God's vineyard, in the end they did. On the other hand, the chief priests and elders who were questioning Jesus, along with the Pharisees, were like those who said they would work but then did not. While such individuals had previously made an effort to keep the Jewish covenant, they rejected what God was doing through Jesus.

Several variations of this basic message can be found in other parables. In the *Parable of the Lost (Prodigal) Son* (Luke 15:11-32), for example, the one son prematurely asks for his inheritance, treating his father as if he were dead.[2] Then he turns his back on Israel and his home, living it up in a foreign land. But after he reaches rock bottom and returns to his father, he is wholeheartedly welcomed back.

Meanwhile, an elder brother who has remained faithful his whole life resents the almost shameful forgiveness his father shows toward his younger brother. This brother, like the son who said he would work but did not, ends up shaming his father when he refuses to join in the celebration over the lost son's return. Like the Pharisees who had tried to remain faithful to God's covenant, the elder brother loses out in the end because he does not honor his father's wishes.

In the *Parable of the Day Laborers* (Matt. 20:1-16), a landowner agrees to pay workers a denarius to work for a day. At various stages throughout the day, the landowner hires more workers, each time promising the same wage. At the end of the day, those who have worked all day grumble because they receive the same pay as those who have only worked for an hour. So God welcomes the sinners of Israel back into his covenant alongside those like the Pharisees who never stopped keeping the Law.

Two very similar parables about a banquet occur in Matthew and Luke: The *Parable of the Wedding Banquet* (Matt. 22:1-14) and the *Parable of the Great Banquet* (Luke 14:15-24). In both parables, a certain person throws a banquet. In both stories, those who were initially invited do not come. In both cases, less likely individuals are given an invitation. In keeping with Luke's emphasis on the poor and downtrodden of Israel, the "poor, the crippled, the lame, and the blind" are invited (Luke 14:21). In keeping with Matthew's understanding of the church as a mixture of both true and false followers of Jesus, the servants of the king bring both good and bad individuals to the banquet (Matt. 22:10). Those who are not properly "dressed" are cast out into the darkness (Matt. 22:11-13). Once again, those initially invited were probably those in Israel who were trying to keep the Jewish Law, God's covenant with Israel. Since they refused God's invitation through Jesus, however, God instead turned to less likely guests like the disenfranchised of Israel.

The *Parable of the Tenants* (Matt. 21:33-46; Mark 12:1-12; Luke 20:9-19) makes a good transition to the next group of parables. In this parable, a landowner goes away for some time and leaves his land in the hands of some farmers. But when the landowner sends for some of the crop, his servants only meet opposition, even death. Finally, the landowner sends his own son, hoping they will listen to him. Instead, they kill him because he is the heir.

The landowner's anger is understandable under such circumstances, and the gospels liken such a situation to the way in which the Jewish religious authorities rejected and then killed Jesus, God's Son. As such, God would judge Israel for its rejection of Jesus, a judgment that came most significantly in A.D. 70 when the Romans destroyed Jerusalem and its temple.

Parables of Judgment

Jesus' parables of judgment both echo the message Jesus took over from John the Baptist and spell out the fate of those that reject His message. Matthew in particular has a number of parables about the final judgment of the whole world, not just the judgment of Israel. Most of these parables are oriented around the time between Christ's Resurrection and His final return.

In the *Parable of the Weeds* (Matt. 13:24-30; 36-43), a farmer finds that both good seed and weeds are growing together in his field, much as servants of the king in the Parable of the Wedding Feast had invited both good and bad to the feast. The farmer instructs his servants to wait until the harvest, at which time God's angels will "weed out" the kingdom of heaven and throw the unworthy into hell. The implication would seem to be that the church includes both genuine and false followers of Jesus. On the Day of Judgment, God will show who are truly His and who are not.

The *Parable of the Sheep and the Goats* (Matt. 25:31-46) has the same basic message, although the focus is more on the whole world than the church.[3] On the Day of Judgment, God will separate the sheep from the goats, largely on the basis of how each has treated those who are downtrodden in life—those without food, water, and clothing.

Two other parables focus on readiness for Christ's return and on what we are doing in the meantime. The *Parable of the Ten Virgins* (Matt. 25:1-13) contrasts two groups of bridesmaids: those who keep enough oil in their lamps in order to see the bridegroom when he arrives, and those who do not. This parable again relates best to Jesus' followers. While all followers of Jesus appear to await His coming, some evidently will be rejected when He comes.

The *Parable of the Talents/Ten Minas* (Matt. 25:14-30; Luke 19:11-27) tells about a king that goes on a trip, leaving three of his servants with varying amounts of money.[4] The first two servants use the king's money to make more money for him. The third is so scared of the king that he buries it (Matthew) or hides it in a cloth (Luke). The king is very angry with the servant who has done nothing with the money he gave him. So the king decides to give the money in his charge to the servant who gained the most interest for his master. The implication would seem to be that God expects His servants to have made gains for His kingdom (converts?) by the time He returns.

Parables of Kingdom Values

A final category of Jesus' parables deals with various aspects of living. Whom am I supposed to love in this world? How should I pray? What should my attitude be toward wealth and poverty? The Gospel of Luke especially presents us with parables on such topics.

The *Parable of the Good Samaritan* in Luke 10 (verses 25-37) deals with the question of whom we are to love and how. In context, Jesus notes that the whole of the Jewish Law can be summarized as, "Love God and love your neighbor." This statement leads to the question, "Who is my neighbor?" Jesus answers with this parable.

A traveler was mugged on his way from Jerusalem to the village of Jericho. As he lay there, both a priest and a Levite (someone of priestly descent) passed by but did nothing to help the traveler. Finally, a Samaritan helped the man and took him to a place of shelter.

Since many Jews at this time looked down on Samaritans as "half-breeds" and did not include them in Israel, Jesus' answer would seem to be: "Everyone is my neighbor, including those I despise. I am to love everyone."

In keeping with Luke's interest in prayer, it is not surprising that he gives us some parables on how to pray. In the *Parable of the Pharisee and the Tax Collector* (Luke 18:9-14), we learn that one needs to pray with a humble attitude in order to be heard. A toll (tax) collector who prays with an attitude of dependence on God finds favor, while a Pharisee who boasts about how he has kept the Law finds God's rejection.

In the *Parable of the Persistent Widow* (Luke 18:1-8), Luke teaches that persistence in prayer pays off, like a widow who bugged a judge so much that he finally gave her justice. It is possible that this parable also originally had political connotations.

Other parables fit in with Luke's focus on the poor and his correspondingly negative attitude toward money and wealth. In the *Parable of the Rich Fool* (Luke 12:13-21), Jesus tells of a foolhardy man who makes a lot of plans to use his wealth and then dies before he can carry them out. Jesus encourages us to live in submission to what *He* has planned for our lives rather than what *we* might plan.

In the *Parable of the Rich Man and Lazarus* (Luke 16:19-31), Luke contrasts a beggar with a rich man.[5] While the rich man enjoyed his time on earth, he finds himself in reversed circumstances after death. The implication is that those who enjoy their money in this life (while allowing the poor to continue in abject need) will suffer in the afterlife.

Finally, one of the parables most difficult to understand is also about money, the *Parable of the Shrewd Manager* (Luke 16:1-13). In this story a certain rich man's manager has misused his master's possessions. As he faces the loss of his master's patronage, he shrewdly does favors for the people who owe his master money. If their debt is a certain amount of oil, he makes the

The Parables of Jesus

The Parable about Parables
The Parable of the Seeds (Matt. 13:3-9; Mark 4:3-8; Luke 8:5-8)

Parables of the Kingdom
The Parable of the Mustard Seed (Matt. 13:31-32; Mark 4:30-32; Luke 13:18-19)
The Parable of the Yeast (Matt. 13:33; Luke 13:20-21)
The Parable of the Growing Seed (Mark 4:26-29)
The Parable of the Treasure (Matt. 13:44)
The Parable of the Pearl (Matt. 13:45-46)

Parables of Israel
The Parable of the Lost Sheep (Matt. 18:12-14; Luke 15:3-7)
The Parable of the Lost Coin (Luke 15:8-10)
The Parable of the Lost Son (Luke 15:11-32)
The Parable of the Unforgiving Servant (Matt. 18:21-35)
The Parable of the Day Laborers (Matt. 20:1-16)
The Parable of the Two Sons (Matt. 21:28-32)
The Parable of the Tenants (Matt. 21:33-46; Mark 12:1-12; Luke 20:9-19)
The Parable of the Wedding Banquet/Great Banquet (Matt. 22:1-14; Luke 14:15-24)

Parables of Judgment
The Parable of the Weeds (Matt. 13:24-30)
The Parable of the Net (Matt. 13:47-51)
The Parable of the Ten Virgins (Matt. 25:1-13)
The Parable of the Talents/Ten Minas (Matt. 25:14-30; Luke 19:11-27)
The Parable of the Sheep and the Goats (Matt. 25:31-46)

Parables of Kingdom Values
The Parable of the Good Samaritan (who is my neighbor; Luke 10:25-37)
The Parable of the Persistent Widow (prayer; Luke 18:1-8)
The Parable of the Rich Fool (money; Luke 12:13-21)
The Parable of the Pharisee and the Tax Collector (prayer; Luke 18:9-14)
The Parable of the Shrewd Manager (money; Luke 16:1-13)
The Parable of the Rich Man and Lazarus (money; Luke 16:19-31)

debt half as much. The rich man then salutes his manager for his cleverness. Jesus concludes that his followers should also "use your worldly resources to benefit others and make friends" (Luke 16:9).

While to us Jesus may seem to applaud this servant for his dishonesty and stealing, the parable probably reflects Luke's sense that money in and of itself is morally negative and that the appropriate thing to do with money is to give it away.[6] In fact, the key to the parable may be Luke's implication that the rich will be judged by how they use their wealth (Luke 16:11). To pass the test, you must give the resources in your control to those who are in need.

Things to Think About

1. Do you think that Jesus' parables made His message clearer or more difficult to understand? To whom did they make His message clearer and to whom did they make it harder to understand? Why would Jesus want to make His message hard for some individuals to understand?

2. If the kingdom of God was about God's rule returning to the earth, is the kingdom already here? If so, in what way? Is the kingdom still to come? If so, in what way? Is the kingdom both here and yet to come? If so, in what ways?

3. What can we learn of Israel's restoration from Jesus' message? Was its restoration fulfilled in 1948 when Israel became a nation again? Did God reject Israel as a nation forever because of its failure to accept Jesus and the early Christians? Can you find a spiritual meaning in Jesus' message to Israel?

4. Many Christians believe that God's sense of justice demands that someone must pay the penalty for every human wrongdoing, as well as pay back every debt. Can you find this picture of God in these parables? Does God ever just forgive without demanding someone pay a debt or incur a punishment? In the parables, do some individuals have more for God to forgive than others—is the amount of God's grace equal toward all individuals?

endnotes

1. The Gospel of John records no parables, although it is filled with metaphors. See chapter 25 of this text.

2. Very similar to the Parable of the Lost Son are the parables of the Lost Sheep and the Lost Coin, both in Luke 15 (the Parable of the Lost Sheep is also in Matt. 18:12-14). In Matthew, the Parable of the Unforgiving Servant (18:21-35) is in the same chapter as the Parable of the Lost Sheep. This parable is about a servant who refuses to forgive someone who owes him a small amount, even though he himself was once forgiven an immense debt he had owed his king. This story may originally have targeted those who refused to welcome the "sinners" of Israel whom Jesus was welcoming into God's kingdom.

3. Interestingly, while many of Matthew's parables of judgment are designed to be about the whole world, their content seems to have its greatest meaning for the church.

4. Some have suggested that the larger amount that Matthew uses in his version of the parable (it would take a lifetime for most workers to earn a talent) reflects that the community for which Matthew writes is more affluent than that of Luke (or Mark).

5. As we have pointed out previously, the words that introduce this story are the same as those that introduce the Parable of the Lost Son and the Parable of the Shrewd Manager. It is very likely, therefore, that this story is also a parable and not a historical event. Neither Luke nor John give us any reason to think that this is the Lazarus Jesus raises from the dead in John 11.

6. See chapter 10 of this text.

CHAPTER 23

The Gospels and Judgment Day

In the gospels, Jesus predicts two events of future judgment: the destruction of Jerusalem (that would take place in A.D. 70) and the final judgment of the world, which is still to come.

Sobering Words

Jesus is often associated with the idea of love and forgiveness. Christians value Him as the One who has made salvation possible, which we often associate with going to heaven. However, it is important to realize that if Jesus "saves" us, He must save us from something—hell, for example. Paul's writings teach that Jesus' death enables us to escape God's wrath on the coming day of judgment.

The gospels present Jesus' earthly teaching in very positive

At a Glance

• In all three synoptic gospels, Jesus predicts God's judgment of Israel and the destruction of Jerusalem.

• Matthew and Mark teach that Jesus will return one day with angels to judge the world.

• These two images of judgment are often mixed, particularly in Matthew and Mark.

• According to Luke, there are both good and bad destinations in the afterlife.

• In all four gospels, Jesus teaches that the dead will one day become alive again, especially those God will reward. Luke and John also teach a resurrection that will follow judgment.

terms: He came to offer restoration to the lost of Israel; He healed the sick and those possessed by evil spirits; He rose from the dead. But the gospels also present some very sobering words for those who do not accept Jesus' message and do not repent of their wrongdoings. Some argue that the historical Jesus did not really teach such things.[1] However, all the gospels indicate that Jesus not only offered incredible hope to the downcast and oppressed, He also offered stern warnings to those who did not accept the message He preached from God.

In particular, we can distinguish two main images of judgment as we look at the gospels, both of which are often mixed together in the gospels themselves. One is the coming destruction of Jerusalem, an event that actually took place in A.D. 70. In both Matthew and Luke, Jesus mourns the fact that Israel so often had not served God faithfully, a fact that Jesus predicts will result in its judgment (Matt. 23:37-39; Luke 13:34-35).

But the picture of Judgment Day with which we might be more familiar is that of Jesus coming with His angels to judge the world. In Matthew and Mark, the focus of this picture is Jesus coming to judge those alive on the earth. In Luke and John, on the other hand, the focus is on a judgment that comes after God has brought all the dead back to life—some so they can live forever and others so they can be punished.

"Those will be days of greater horror than at any time since God created the world. And it will never happen again. In fact, unless the Lord shortens that time of calamity, the entire human race will be destroyed."

Mark 13:19-20

The Judgment of Israel

Some Christians think of judgment strictly in terms of what happens after you die: You die and go to heaven, or you die and go to hell. In addition, some Christian traditions such as that of the Roman Catholic Church also believe in purgatory. This is a kind of "halfway house" for those who will eventually end up in heaven, but who are not pure enough to go there immediately when they die.

But the early Christians did not think of God's judgment primarily as something you experience in the afterlife. The Apostle's Creed, a famous statement of belief from the first few centuries of Christianity, states that Jesus will come again from heaven down to earth "to judge the living and the dead." This event is popularly called Christ's "second coming" or the **parousia**, which is the Greek word for "arrival."

> **parousia:** The arrival of Jesus on earth a second time, this time to judge the earth.

> **Son of Man:** One of the main ways in which Jesus referred to himself. The phrase can be taken in several different ways. One is simply as "a human being." It also was used of a king God would send from heaven to judge the nations and rule Israel.

Among some Christians today, there is a great deal of interest in the "end times"—the events that will happen before Jesus comes back to judge the earth. Jesus predicts in Mark 13, "Nations and kingdoms will proclaim war against each other, and there will be earthquakes and famines in many parts of the world. But all this will be only the beginning of the horrors to come" (13:8). Some Christians think that these kinds of things are taking place right now around the world.

The chapter goes on to tell of persecution (13:9-13) and an evil presence being somewhere it is not supposed to be (13:14). There is talk of flight from destruction and days of incredible distress. The sun will be darkened and the moon will turn blood red as "stars" fall from the sky (13:24-25). Mark 13 continues, "Then everyone will see the Son of Man arrive on the clouds with great power and glory. And he will send forth his angels to gather together his chosen ones from all over the world" (13:26-27).

When the title **Son of Man** is used in this way, its meaning comes from the book of Daniel in the Old Testament. Daniel 7:13-14 pictures "one like a son of man," a human being, coming on the clouds of heaven to the "Ancient of Days"—God. God grants authority to this person to be king over all the peoples of the earth and the enemies of Israel. Matthew, Mark, and Luke unanimously present Jesus as this Son of Man, a role that Jesus will fulfill most meaningfully when He returns to earth to judge the nations of the world.

It is easy to see why many Christians read Mark 13 as a blueprint for the end of time, a time when Jesus will return to earth. After all, Jesus has not yet returned to earth in the way this chapter seems to say He will. Many of the predictions in Mark 13 simply have not yet taken place, such as "stars" falling from the sky (13:25) or a time of horror greater than any since God created the world (13:19). Matthew's version of this sermon notes, "The Good News about the Kingdom will be preached throughout the whole world, so that all nations will hear it; and then, finally, the end will come" (Matt. 24:14).   Many Christians eagerly support "missionaries" who take Christianity to various parts of the world in the hope of finally achieving the goal described in this verse.

Yet those who read Mark 13 and Matthew 24 in this way only miss a very important aspect of these chapters. The beginning of each chapter makes it clear that these events will take place *around the time that the Jewish temple is destroyed*. Jesus tells His disciples that not one stone of the temple will be left on top of another in the days to come (Mark 13:2). The disciples ask, "When will all this take place? And will there be any sign ahead of time to show us when all this will be fulfilled?" (Mark 13:4). In other words, we would expect this chapter to be about the destruction of the Jerusalem temple. These chapters even end with Jesus saying that "this generation will not pass from the scene until all these events have taken place" (Mark 13:30)— something that is true in regard to the destruction of Jerusalem, but not regarding the end of time.

We would not be the first ones to understand this chapter in terms of the destruction of Jerusalem. The Gospel of Luke, evidently written after A.D. 70

and after Matthew and Mark had been written, seems to have understood Jesus' teaching in this way. When Luke presents what Matthew and Mark call the "abomination that causes desolation"—an evil presence placed somewhere it is not supposed to be—he words it in this way: "When you see Jerusalem surrounded by armies, then know that its desolation has come near" (Luke 21:20 NRSV). In other words, he interprets the evil presence or "abomination" to be the presence of the Roman armies around Jerusalem in A.D. 70. The "desolation" is the destruction of Jerusalem those armies brought. Luke also omits the statement that this time will be the worst period of distress the world will ever see. Most likely Luke presented this teaching so clearly because he wrote after these events had already taken place.

But what of the imagery that has not yet taken place? There are several ways of solving this dilemma. First of all, there are those who would say that when Jesus spoke of the coming of the Son of Man or of the sun darkening and the moon turning to blood, He was speaking metaphorically and not literally.[2] When we talk about an "earth-shattering" event, for example, we do not mean that the earth actually broke apart. Some would say Luke believed the sun darkened and the moon turned to blood metaphorically on the Day of Pentecost, when God gave power to His disciples to spread Christianity throughout the world (Acts 2:16, 20).

And what do we make of Jesus' statement to His disciples in Matthew 10:23? "You will not have gone through all the towns of Israel before the Son of Man comes" (NRSV). The disciples have been dead a long time, but the Son of Man has not yet literally returned to earth. These are some reasons one might believe the Son of Man came figuratively in judgment in A.D. 70 when Jerusalem was destroyed, and that the entirety of these chapters has already been fulfilled.

Another possibility is that Matthew and Mark mix two different times of judgment together: the judgment on Israel in A.D. 70 and the final judgment when Jesus literally comes back with His angels. Luke presents those elements that relate to the destruction of Jerusalem, while Matthew and Mark blur the two, probably believing that all such judgment would take place in the very near future.

Paul seemed to think Christ would return within his lifetime. He probably advocated celibacy in part for this reason (1 Cor. 7:29). Jesus seems to imply the same timetable in Mark 9:1: "I assure you that some of you standing here right now will not die before you see the Kingdom of God arrive in great power!" It is very likely that most of what the early Christians taught had more to do with the near future than with the end of time.

The Judgment of the World

The Gospel of Matthew has a number of unique images relating to the judgment of the entire world, as well as to the meantime while we await for Christ's second coming. In the Parable of the Weeds (Matthew 13), for example, Matthew compares our current period of history as a time when both wheat and weeds are growing together in a field. At the time of harvest, the weeds will be burned. So now the church has both true "wheat" in it, along with weeds that are not true followers of Christ. Matthew says Jesus will disown these individuals on the Day of Judgment (Matt. 7:22-23). Matthew's picture of that final judgment is foreboding: "I, the Son of Man, will send my angels, and they will remove from my Kingdom everything that causes sin and all who do evil, and they will throw them into the furnace and burn them. There will be weeping and gnashing of teeth. Then the godly will shine like the sun in their Father's Kingdom" (Matt. 13:41-43).

Another striking picture of judgment unique to Matthew is that of the separation of the sheep from the goats (Matt. 25:31-46). The Son of Man comes in His glory to the earth and sits on a throne in heavenly glory.[3] Then the nations gather together and the Son of Man separates everyone into two categories (sheep and goats). Those who have fed the hungry, given drink to the thirsty, clothed the naked, and given shelter to the homeless will go on to eternal life. Those who have not will go off "into the eternal fire prepared for the Devil and his demons" (Matt. 25:41).

> **Valley of Hinnom:** A valley outside Jerusalem where Jews burned their trash.
>
> **Gehenna:** The Aramaic way of referring to the Valley of Hinnom, although it became a metaphor for hell.

Matthew contains quite a bit of fiery imagery relating to judgment. The image of **Gehenna**, for example, is more frequent in Matthew than in any other gospel. Originally, Gehenna referred to the **Valley of Hinnom** where the Jews burned the trash of Jerusalem. The fire smoldered continuously. This image became the one many Jews associated with hell. Jesus referred to this image regarding the day when God would judge the living: "So if your eye—even if it is your good eye—causes you to lust, gouge it out and throw it away. It is better for you to lose one part of your body than for your whole body to be thrown into hell [Gehenna]" (Matt. 5:29).

Luke is the only gospel that tells us what happens to people who die before Jesus returns to judge the earth. Much of Jesus' prophecy in Luke concerns the destruction of Jerusalem. Since Jesus' return to earth might not happen for some time, the question naturally arose, "What happens to people who die in the meantime?" The New Testament only alludes to this topic a few times, two of which are found in Luke.

Luke gives us two strong images of what happens. The first comes in the Parable of the Rich Man and Lazarus. Immediately at death, the rich man experiences torment and Lazarus finds himself comforted in a place called "Abraham's Bosom" (Luke 16:19-31). The implication is that even though we are ultimately waiting for the resurrection of everyone in the future, we experience immediate reward at death. Jesus confirmed this thought on the cross when He promised one of the thieves that he would be with him that very day in "Paradise" (Luke 23:43).

Finally, the gospels teach a resurrection of both the righteous and the wicked one day, a day when all will be judged. Jesus says, "The people of Nineveh . . . will rise up against this generation on judgment day and condemn it, because they repented at the preaching of Jonah" (Luke 11:32). These righteous individuals will be brought back to life to condemn the wicked. Similarly, Jesus curses certain villages that did not receive Him, even though He performed miracles there: "Even wicked Sodom will be better off than such a town on the judgment day" (Luke 10:12). Here Jesus indicates that the wicked will also rise on the Day of Judgment so that they can be judged.

Things to Think About

1. Why do you think Jesus referred to himself as the "Son of Man," if the term is so ambiguous in meaning?

2. How much of Jesus' prophecy would you say was about the events of A.D. 70 and how much about events at the end of time?

3. Did Jesus think of Gehenna as a literal place somewhere? Did He really believe that sinners would spend eternity in literal fires?

Key Terms
Gehenna
parousia
Son of Man
Valley of Hinnom

endnotes

1. See chapter 28 of this text.
2. See N. T. Wright, *The Original Jesus: The Life and Vision of a Revolutionary* (Grand Rapids: Eerdmans, 1996), 115–119.
3. This description has some interesting similarities to a book called 1 Enoch, a Jewish writing whose various parts were composed over the period from 200 B.C. to the first century after Christ. In the latest parts of this book, the "Son of Man" also judges the nations from a throne (1 Enoch 61–62; 69:29).

CHAPTER 24

Stories of Jesus' Birth

The two versions of Jesus' birth emphasize certain themes and proclaim certain messages. By mixing the two stories together, we lose the distinctive message each one has to give us.

A Christmas Play

Most of us have seen a Christmas play at some point in our lives and could come up with the standard cast of characters fairly easily. We know of Mary and Joseph, wise men and shepherds. And most of us can picture in our minds the typical manger scene with all these figures standing around the baby Jesus—as well as donkeys, cows, sheep, and camels. It is one of the most familiar Bible stories, and it presents one of the most strongly held beliefs in all Christianity: the virgin birth.[1] From the early centuries of Christianity, one of the most important Christian claims has been that Jesus was "born of the virgin Mary"—that she did not become pregnant by having sex with someone.

A typical Christmas play might begin in a little village in Galilee called Nazareth where Mary is engaged to Joseph, a carpenter. The angel Gabriel appears to Mary and announces that she will give birth to the Savior of the

At a Glance

- Matthew and Luke are the two gospels that present the story of Jesus' birth.

- Both agree that Jesus was born to Mary before she had sex with any man (the virgin birth) and that Jesus was born in Bethlehem.

- Matthew presents Jesus' birth from the standpoint of His royalty and portrays Him as a new Moses.

- Luke presents Jesus' birth with a view to His identification with the lowly and the downtrodden.

world. This announcement puzzles her—she has never been intimate with a man. But the Holy Spirit comes upon her and she miraculously becomes pregnant. Joseph, naturally thinking that she has cheated on him, is about to call off the marriage when God tells him in a dream what is going on.

About this time, the emperor Augustus calls for a census and Joseph is required to travel to the place of his family's origin, Bethlehem. The typical Christmas play pictures the couple finding shelter in a stable after failing to find an available room. Angels appear to shepherds in the countryside to announce the child's birth, and wise men from the East are led to Bethlehem by a star.

While our Christmas play might end here, a knowledgeable Bible reader might continue with the story. Jesus is circumcised on the eighth day of His life. Then a little over a month later, Jesus' parents take Him to the temple to be dedicated, where two elderly people recognize Him as the Messiah, the king for whom they have been waiting. When King Herod the Great realizes that the wise men—or **Magi**—have not returned with the precise location of the baby Jesus, he slaughters all the male children under the age of two in Bethlehem. Warned in a dream, Joseph escapes to Egypt, where he lives with Mary and Jesus until Herod dies. On the family's return to Palestine, they go back to Nazareth rather than to Bethlehem, fearing Herod's son Archelaus, who has succeeded his father.

Magi: "Wise men," often thought to be astrologers or star watchers. The similarity of the Greek word to "magician" is obvious.

What is interesting about our Nativity story is that it is a mixture of Matthew and Luke's accounts, the only two gospels to record the story of Jesus' birth.[2] These two accounts are strikingly different, although they also share important common ground. They both agree that Jesus was born in Bethlehem and raised in Nazareth, for example. More significantly for

Christian belief, they both teach that Jesus was born of Mary while she was still a virgin.

Matthew: Jesus, a Leader like Moses

If all we had were Matthew's version, we would not think the story started out in Nazareth.[3] We would think that Joseph and Mary lived in Bethlehem and would have continued to live there if not for Archelaus. We would not know of shepherds or mangers, nor would we know of the angel's appearance to Mary. In fact, if we read Matthew carefully, we would have to correct parts of our Christmas play as well.

Matthew does not give us the number of wise men—this gospel does not say there were three. Matthew actually says all Jerusalem was troubled at the arrival of the Magi, probably indicating a large company rather than a small group (Matt. 2:3). Matthew also does not say they arrived the night of Jesus' birth. Since Herod killed the babies under two years of age, we should probably picture the Magi bowing before Jesus as a toddler rather than as a newborn (Matt. 2:16).

These matters are somewhat trivial, however. We potentially miss a much more significant aspect of the birth stories when we mix them together. The two versions of Jesus' birth emphasize certain themes and proclaim certain messages. By mixing the two stories together, we lose the particular message each one has to give us.

Matthew, for example, presents the birth of Jesus in a way that would have *reminded his audience of Moses* (Exod. 1:8–2:10). Like Moses, a king threatens the life of the baby Jesus. In the case of Moses, *Pharaoh* orders all the Israelite males to be put to death at birth. Moses' parents hide the baby Moses so he will not be killed. For Jesus, it is *Herod the Great* who is after Him. Herod also orders the slaughter of Jewish males, and Jesus also escapes by way of His godly parents.

Matthew is also unique in saying that Jesus spent some of His earliest days in Egypt, just as Moses did. But what is of most importance for Matthew is Jesus' exit from Egypt. This exit, Matthew 2:15 says, fulfills Hosea 11:1: "Out of Egypt I have called my son." Chapter 15 of this book discusses how Matthew highlights parallels between the life of Jesus and the words of the Old Testament. As that chapter shows, the gospel writer Matthew read those words "spiritually" rather than for what they meant originally. Hosea 11:1 is a good example of this fact. The full verse reads, "When *Israel* was a child . . . I called my son out of Egypt." In other words, this verse was not a prediction of a future event; it was a comment on the exodus—an event that had taken place hundreds of years before Hosea's time and over a thousand years before Jesus was born.

Matthew did not do this by mistake, and it would be entirely inappropriate to find fault with him. That would be to impose our way of doing things on him; it would reflect a lack of awareness of the glasses we are wearing. This method of interpretation was perfectly legitimate in the Jewish circles of

Just as Moses led the children of Israel out of slavery in Egypt, Jesus would "save his people from their sins" (Matt. 1:21).

Matthew's day. Particularly in this case, Matthew did not choose this verse because he was unaware that it was about the exodus—he chose it *precisely because he did* realize this fact. He was implying a connection between Jesus and the exodus, as well as between Jesus and Moses. Just as Moses led the children of Israel out of slavery in Egypt, Jesus would "save his people from their sins" (Matt. 1:21).

Further events in the first chapters of Matthew might also have reminded his audience of Moses. For example, many Jews at the time of Christ believed Pharaoh was trying to put the Israelite infants to death because of information given him from "wise men." While Moses was leading Israel, a "wise man" named Balaam prophesied that a *star* and *scepter* would rise from Israel to be king (Num. 24:17)—and Balaam was from the East. The Dead Sea Scrolls show that some Jews at the time of Christ thought this star was the Messiah.[4]

After starting with these overtones, Jesus' baptism might have reminded Matthew's audience of the crossing of the Red Sea. And His testing in the desert for forty days is like the testing of Israel in the wilderness for forty years. With so many similarities, it is quite possible that Matthew's audience would have thought of Moses giving the Law on Mt. Sinai when they read the Sermon on the Mount. After all, the Sermon on the Mount presents Jesus as the authoritative interpreter and fulfiller of the Law's meaning (cf. Matt. 5:17).

However, even more important than the overtones of Moses is the way Matthew's birth story continues the theme of *Jesus as king*. Earlier, chapter 15 of this text showed how the genealogy of Matthew 1 opens the gospel with the idea that Jesus is the Son of David, the promised king of the Jews. Matthew's birth story will continue to show that Jesus is king.

We mentioned a couple of paragraphs ago that many Jews associated the star and scepter of Numbers 24:17 with the Messiah, the coming king. It fits with the theme of Jesus as king, therefore, for a star to announce His birth. The Magi from the East asked Herod, "Where is the newborn king of the Jews?" (Matt. 2:2). They understood that Jesus was king. When they found Him, they bowed before Him as king, which is the sense of the word *worship* in Matthew 2:11. In fact, many Jews at the time of Christ thought of Moses as a kingly figure and believed that the Messiah, the coming king, would be a "prophet like Moses" (Deut. 18:18). The pictures of Jesus as a king and as a figure like Moses thus fit together.

Luke: Jesus, Savior of the Downtrodden

While Matthew's presentation of Jesus' birth emphasizes that He is a king, Luke's highlights such things as God's favor toward the humble and downtrodden. As with Matthew, Luke's birth story hits on many themes that appear later in the gospel (and Acts). In addition to the attention Luke gives to the poor and downtrodden, Luke's birth story also highlights the role of women in Jesus' birth, includes several prayers, shows that God's people are honorable, and proclaims that the gospel is for everyone.

As with Matthew, we would tell the story of Jesus' birth somewhat differently if Luke's presentation were all we had to go on. If we went by Luke's account, for example, we would not know about the wise men or of Herod's persecution. We would think Joseph and Mary went back to Nazareth as soon as Mary's forty days of purification were over (Luke 2:22, 39). We also would know almost nothing about Joseph's role in Jesus' birth, particularly his impulse to call off the marriage. Interestingly, however, Luke probably provides more material for the typical Christmas play than Matthew does.

With the coming of Jesus, God has "satisfied the hungry with good things and sent the rich away with empty hands" (Luke 1:53).

In keeping with the attention Luke gives to women elsewhere in Luke and Acts, the birth story of Luke focuses heavily on the role of Mary in Jesus' birth. While in Matthew it is Joseph who receives a revelation from God in a dream,[5] Luke focuses on the revelation given to Mary through the angel Gabriel. Gabriel's greeting to Mary is well known in Roman Catholic circles as the "Hail Mary," since the angel says this to her as he appears, telling her she is highly favored among women. Luke also tells us of Mary's interaction with the mother of John the Baptist. It is in the course of this exchange that Luke records the "Magnificat" (Luke 1:46-55), a poetic "hymn" that along with the Song of Simeon in 2:29-32, has been an element of morning and evening prayer for Christians since the early centuries of Christianity.[6]

Here we see some of the other unique features of Luke's birth narrative. Luke has no fewer than three "hymns" in this section, all of which Christians have used in worship throughout the history of the church.[7] Luke also is the only gospel to present the circumstances behind the birth of John the Baptist in addition to those behind the birth of Christ. Uniquely, Luke alone tells us that Jesus and John the Baptist were related. As we have said, most of the special themes Luke emphasizes elsewhere, themes that are unique to his gospel, show up in these first two chapters.

In chapter 20 of this text, we saw that Luke highlights Jesus' ministry to the poor and downtrodden. We are not surprised, therefore, that Mary considers her pregnancy as God's blessing on someone of humble birth (Luke 1:48). With the coming of Jesus, God has "satisfied the hungry with good things and sent the rich away with empty hands" (Luke 1:53). Luke is interested in humble—perhaps even sinful—shepherds rather than rich wise men, and it is no surprise that in Luke, Jesus is born in the presence of animals rather than in guest accommodations (2:7).

The situation of John the Baptist's parents points to another kind of ancient poverty—the inability to have children. Like Sarah in the Old Testament, John's mother Elizabeth lived with the shame of barrenness, a particularly difficult situation for a Mediterranean woman in ancient times.[8] Ancient society judged a woman's worth largely on her ability to bear children (cf. 1 Tim. 2:15), particularly male children. God removes Elizabeth's disgrace, as he did Sarah's in the Old Testament, by giving her a child (Luke 1:25). Like Sarah, Zechariah also gets in trouble for his doubts—in this case, with the angel Gabriel. He loses his ability to speak until John is born.

The widow Anna in Luke 2:36-38 gives us yet another example of God's favor on the "poor," this time through a godly woman in her eighties whose husband had died after only seven years of marriage. Widows were in a potentially vulnerable state in the ancient world, as is shown by their need for material support in Acts 6:1-2. First Timothy 5:3-16 deals with the remarriage of widows and reflects the fact that widows often remarried for the sake of security. Anna had great honor because of her reliance on God for perhaps over sixty years as a widow, without the benefit of remarriage. In keeping with Luke's attention to women elsewhere who are involved in ministry (e.g., Luke 8:3; Acts 2:17-18; 21:9), he notes that Anna is a prophetess.

Another special theme of Luke that appears in the birth narrative is the universality of the gospel, the fact that the good news is for the whole world. An old man named Simeon proclaims this truth at the temple as Jesus' parents bring Him to be dedicated. This child, Simeon says, will be a "light to reveal God to the nations" (Luke 2:32). The word "nation" here can also be translated "Gentile." We will see Simeon's prophecy come true in Acts when the gospel spreads to the ends of the earth.

One noticeable "Gentile" element in Luke's birth story is his use of the word *Savior* in reference to Jesus (Luke 1:47; 2:11). While the idea of salvation from enemies was a common enough Jewish idea, the word *Savior* carried interesting

> From the beginning of the Gospel of Luke to near the end of Acts, Luke clearly considers the Jerusalem temple a legitimate place of worship and orients both books around Jerusalem.

connotations in the non-Jewish world. For this, among other reasons, many scholars believe Luke's audience was primarily Gentile. The word *Savior* had overtones of one who brought mundane benefits like health, safety, and material blessings. The use of this word thus fits with Luke's emphasis on Jesus' favor toward the poor and oppressed, not to mention his startling emphasis on the restoration of Israel.

Many Christian readers might be surprised at just how much Luke emphasizes the restoration of the nation Israel, along with stressing the importance of the temple in Jerusalem and the keeping of the Jewish Law. Some of this emphasis probably relates to Luke's desire to portray Christians as respectable people who were law abiding and not troublemakers.[9] Luke makes it clear that John the Baptist's parents kept God's commandments blamelessly (Luke 1:6). Mary and Joseph follow the letter of the Jewish Law when they present Jesus in the temple (2:22). They do not leave town until everything required by the Jewish Law is done, including Mary's forty days of purification (2:22-24, 27, 39). Simeon and Anna, whom they meet at the temple, are both godly individuals who pray and fast to show their commitment to God (2:25, 37). Luke tells us that Jesus' parents are faithful to go to the Passover every year (2:41).

But Luke's interest in Jesus' Jewish heritage goes beyond respectability. From the beginning of the Gospel of Luke to near the end of Acts, Luke clearly considers the Jerusalem temple a legitimate place of worship and orients both books around Jerusalem.[10] The birth story clearly teaches the restoration of Israel as a political entity, just as Acts 1:6-7 does even after Jesus has risen from the dead. Simeon was not looking for God's abandonment of Israel, but for its consolation (Luke 2:25). Anna similarly expected the eventual redemption of Jerusalem, not its destruction (2:38). Zechariah, John the Baptist's father, saw in Jesus the salvation of Israel from its political enemies (1:71, 74) and the prospect of peace (1:79). Within Israel, both John the Baptist and Jesus would bring the people back to the Lord their God by preaching repentance (1:16, 77; 2:34).

We learn elsewhere that Luke considered this current period of history to be the "age of the Gentiles" (Luke 21:24). Perhaps he believed Israel would finally be restored after this time, much as Paul claims in Romans 11:26 that "all Israel will be saved" eventually. In any case, Luke's birth story brilliantly captures the "good news" God has brought to both Jew and Gentile through Christ. It is good news to the poor and oppressed, as well as to the downtrodden like widows and the barren. It is a message about a Savior who brings peace and blessing to His people.

What Do We Do with the Christmas Stories?

While we will continue to enjoy our Christmas plays, we can have a new appreciation of what each birth story has to offer when read on its own. We will see the Jewish Messiah in Matthew 1–2, hearing overtones of Jesus' royalty and of His authority as a new Moses. We will see God's favor on all humanity in Luke 1–2 and remember Jesus' identification with the lowly and downtrodden. Both birth narratives did the job an ancient audience expected them to do in a biography. They showed that Jesus' birth fit hand in glove with who He was as an adult. The elements of His later glory and greatness were there in a nutshell in His birth.

Things to Think About

Key Term
Magi

1. What is the significance of the virgin birth for Christian faith? Is it so that Jesus can be seen as divine (remember that Christians do not believe Jesus is half-God and half-man)? Is it so that He can be perceived as sinless? Is it because sex is bad? Is it to signify Jesus' greatness?

2. What role does the virgin birth play in the thinking of the New Testament as a whole?

3. Is it important for our faith and for the authority of Scripture to fit the two birth accounts together historically? Do we lose anything when we combine them into one story?

endnotes

1. Or, more accurately, the virginal conception. Many Roman Catholics also believe that Mary did not "open the womb" at birth (thus, virgin birth) and that she remained a virgin her entire life (her "perpetual virginity").

2. The New Testament makes almost no mention of Jesus' birth anywhere else (cf. Rom. 1:3; Gal. 4:4) and makes no mention at all of the virgin birth elsewhere.

3. As in previous chapters, I will refer to the authors of Matthew and Luke as "Matthew" and "Luke," even though these gospels are technically anonymous.

4. For example, in a document called the "Covenant of Damascus" (7:19) in the Dead Sea Scrolls.

5. Which may imply he was old—cf. Acts 2:17. In a typical ancient Mediterranean marriage, the man generally was significantly older than the girl, who might be in her early teens.

6. "Magnificat" is the Latin for the first word of the hymn, "let it [my soul] glorify . . ." Simeon's Song is known as the "Nunc Dimittis" for the same reason, meaning "now you dismiss."

7. In addition to the Magnificat and the Nunc Dimittis (see the previous footnote), Luke also includes the "Benedictus," meaning "blessed" (1:68-79; Zechariah, the father of John the Baptist, sings this hymn). Some think the "Gloria" of Luke 2:14 is also part of an early Christian hymn.

8. Although Mary is not in quite the same situation as Elizabeth, her song has a lot of similarities to the song of another famous barren woman from the Old Testament: Hannah, the mother of the prophet Samuel (1 Sam. 2:1-10).

9. See chapter 8 of this text.

10. The Gospel of Luke both begins and ends in Jerusalem and omits all reference to Jesus' Resurrection appearances in Galilee. Acts begins in Jerusalem and returns there near the end (Acts 21), although it is important for the author to show that Paul reached the ends of the earth (Rome) at the closing of the book.

CHAPTER 25

John: Jesus, the Way

John wishes us to know that when we are looking at Jesus, we are seeing nothing less than God's presence among us.

The Gospel of John differs strikingly from Matthew, Mark, and Luke in some ways. For example, it has no parables, no exorcisms, no commands of silence concerning Jesus' identity, and little mention of the kingdom of God—all things that feature prominently in the synoptic gospels. Many of the stories in John do not appear in Matthew, Mark, and Luke. In fact, even when John does present events that appear in the synoptics, he usually tells them in a substantially different way. For this reason, some early Christians considered John to be a "spiritual" gospel that was more a picture of Jesus' spiritual significance than a presentation of how He would have appeared to those who first saw and heard Him.

At a Glance

- The Gospel of John records no exorcisms, no parables, no commands of silence concerning Jesus' identity, and differs in many other ways from the synoptic gospels.

- The purpose of John is to lead its audience to faith in who Jesus is and what He has done. It emphasizes that believing only in Jesus frees you from condemnation.

- John presents Jesus as one who came down from heaven, God's Word in human form.

- John is filled with "I am" statements that point out Jesus' spiritual significance.

- John, the son of Zebedee, is the traditional author, although a certain "John the elder" has some claim as well. The gospel is technically anonymous.

Differences Between John and the Synoptics

We have already mentioned some of the ways John differs from Matthew, Mark, and Luke. For example, while Mark 4:34 says that Jesus "did not say anything to them without using a parable" (NIV), Jesus tells no parables in John.[1] While the casting out of demons portrayed in Matthew, Mark, and Luke signals the fact that the kingdom of God is arriving on earth (e.g., Luke 11:20), Jesus performs no exorcisms in John and scarcely mentions the kingdom of God. The synoptics, on the other hand, indicate that the kingdom of God is the essence of what Jesus preached (Matt. 4:23; Mark 1:14-15; Luke 4:43).

Another difference between John and the other gospels is how open Jesus is about His identity. In the synoptics, Jesus commands the demons and His disciples to be silent about the fact that He is the Messiah (e.g., Mark 1:34; 8:30). In John, Jesus not only proclaims openly that He is the Messiah, *He publicly claims to be from heaven*, someone who existed in heaven before He was born (e.g., John 8:23-24, 58; 10:22-39). Matthew, Mark, and Luke give only the barest hints that Jesus is a heavenly being. And while Jesus flatly says in Mark that He will give *no* signs to the people of that day (Mark 8:12), the Gospel of John is filled with the signs Jesus provides. In fact, John states that Jesus did "many other miraculous signs in the presence of His disciples, which are not recorded in this book" (John 20:30 NIV).

"Now my soul is deeply troubled. Should I pray, 'Father, save me from what lies ahead'? But that is the very reason why I came!"

John 12:27

Jesus appears much less "human" in John than He does in the synoptics. John presents little of Jesus' human struggles and tends to avoid anything that might make Jesus appear weak or less than "superhuman" in any way. In Luke, for example, Jesus sweats drops of blood under the pressure of His coming death (Luke 22:44). In Mark, He asks God if it is possible for Him to avoid death (Mark 14:35-36)—He would rather not "drink the cup" that has been given to Him. In John, on the other hand, Jesus says He will *not* ask to escape His coming death (John 12:27; 18:11). When they come to arrest Him, the soldiers fall to the ground at the power of Jesus' presence (John 18:6).

In the synoptics, the words Jesus says on the cross differ distinctly from what Jesus says in John. Matthew and Mark record Jesus crying out in anguish, "My God, my God, why have you abandoned me?" (Matt. 27:46; Mark 15:34, author's translation). In John, however, Jesus victoriously says, "It is finished" (John 19:30), and then "hands over" His spirit to God. More than any of the other gospels, John emphasizes that Jesus is in control of everything that is going on during His trial and crucifixion.

What do we make of these differences? Even if we believe John's presentation can be fit together with that of Matthew, Mark, and Luke in some way historically, John still has a much different "feel" to it than the others. Some have completely rejected the Gospel of John as unhistorical for this reason. Others try to account for the differences by supposing that John simply did not want to paint the same picture of Jesus all over again, but instead wanted to record events omitted from the other gospels. Indeed, the church has long believed that the Gospel of John was written last, perhaps even long after the other gospels had appeared. Whichever position one takes, John gives us a picture of Christ the way Christians eventually came to see Him—a presentation of Jesus in hindsight as He really was, even if some did not fully recognize Him at the time.

Why John Was Written

The Gospel of John helpfully states why it was written. Although Jesus provided countless "signs" that showed who He truly was, the ones in John were written "**so that you may believe** that Jesus is the Messiah, the Son of

God, and that by believing in Him you will have life" (John 20:31). There are only small hints in Matthew, Mark, and Luke that believing in Jesus himself is important for escaping God's coming judgment. The focus is rather on God's coming rule of the earth and on obtaining His forgiveness through repentance for your wrongdoings. Christ *is* someone to be imitated (Matt. 10:38) and His death pays the price for sins (Mark 10:45), but the synoptics do not clearly state that one must believe in Jesus to be saved from judgment.

John, however, like much of the rest of the New Testament, teaches repeatedly that one must believe or *have faith* in Jesus in order to escape eternal death. Perhaps the verse best known to present this theme in the entire New Testament is John 3:16. Jesus came from heaven to earth. Whoever believes in His true identity will live forever; anyone who does not will perish. Jesus tells the crowds these things numerous times. After He miraculously feeds five thousand people, they ask Him what God wants them to do. "This is what God wants you to do," Jesus replies. "Believe in the one He has sent" (John 6:29). At another point Jesus compares himself to manna—food that fell from heaven to feed the Israelites when they were wandering in the desert. He calls himself the bread of life and encourages the crowds to "feed" on Him so that they can live forever: "I assure you, anyone who believes in me already has eternal life" (John 6:47). This theme of *faith* in Jesus is thus one of the distinctive features of the Gospel of John. One of Jesus' many "I am" statements sums it up well: "I am the way, the truth, and the life. No one can come to the Father except through me" (John 14:6).

> "God so loved the world that he gave his only Son, so that everyone who believes in him will not perish but have eternal life."
>
> **John 3:16**

More than any of the gospels, John connects the truth about Jesus' identity with His miraculous "signs." The first part of John's gospel presents seven of these "signs" that in one way or another reveal His true identity.[2] This divine power provides the single most convincing indication that He is who He says He is in John. While Jesus also performs miracles in Matthew, Mark, and Luke, these gospels do not call His miracles "signs." In the synoptics, a **sign** is something like a miracle on demand, such as when Jesus' opponents ask Him to give them a "sign" to prove that He is the Messiah. He flatly refuses to give them any such signs.

The Gospel of John, however, was written to a group of Christians in the late first century—its presentation is geared more to its audience than to Jesus' original situation. The author wanted his audience to

> **sign:** An indication of something. In John, signs indicate that Jesus came down from heaven. In the synoptics, Jesus refuses to give in to the demand for "signs" as proof that He is the Messiah, although He performs many miracles.

know with certainty that Jesus' deeds showed who He truly was, regardless of whether His first audiences understood them to be signs. Thus, while Jesus himself may have avoided calling His miracles "signs," the Gospel of John in hindsight recognizes His powerful deeds for what they really were— indications and *signs* that Jesus was divine.

Jesus is God's Word for the World

Matthew and Luke both begin their gospels with the story of Jesus' birth, as was appropriate for ancient biographies. Mark's introduction noticeably lacks a birth story. John's introduction is even more striking. While John does start at the beginning, the beginning for John is not Jesus' birth. John starts before the creation of the world.

"In the beginning," he says in the first sentence, "the Word already existed" (John 1:1).[3] This Word was with God, John explains; in fact, it was a divine Word. John goes on to say that God made everything through this "Word." It was thus a Word that brought life, a creative Word. God's Word brought light out of darkness, and His Word can also bring hope to humanity (John 1:3-5). In John 1:14 we find out what this "Word" of God to humanity was/is: "the Word became human and lived here on earth among us." This Word, John makes clear, was Jesus.

One of the distinctive features of John's gospel is the claim that *Jesus came from heaven.* While there are hints in the synoptics that Jesus has a heavenly identity (e.g., the Transfiguration), John is the only gospel that explicitly teaches that God sent Jesus from heaven down to earth. In what is sometimes called Jesus' "high priestly prayer" (where He prays for all those who would later believe in Him), Jesus prays to God, "And now, Father, bring me into the glory we shared before the world began" (John 17:5). In John 6:38, Jesus says, "I have come down from heaven to do the will of God who sent me," just as in John 8:23 He says to the Pharisees, "You are from below; I am from above."

Telling his opponents that Abraham looked forward to the day He would come is perhaps the most startling thing that Jesus says in John. His opponents scoff at the boldness of such a claim and point out that He is not even fifty years old. The New Living Translation brings out part of the meaning of Jesus' response well: "The truth is, I existed before Abraham was even born!" (John 8:58). More exactly, Jesus says, "Before Abraham was, I AM" (my translation). In so many words, "I AM" is the name God used to introduce himself to Moses at the burning bush in Exodus 3:14. Jesus' opponents recognize by Jesus' statement that He is claiming to be divine.

To return to the opening of the Gospel of John, we can see that it also indicates Jesus came down from heaven. What you may not realize, however, is what John meant by calling Jesus the "**Word**"—the "**Logos**" in Greek. *Logos* is a Greek word that had been around for a long while before the Gospel of John was written. It was a way for Jews to refer to the fact that God's commands, His "Word," always came to pass. For example, "God *said*, 'Let there be light,' and there was light" (Gen. 1:3). Isaiah 55:11 says this of God's word: "I send it out, and it always produces fruit. It will accomplish all I want it to."

> **Word/Logos:** Many Jews at the time of Christ talked about God's actions in the world by speaking of His word doing things. The world was created through His word, for example. His word represented His will and purpose for His creation.

Some Jews around the time of Christ viewed these verses through the glasses of a philosophy known as Stoicism.[4] The Stoics believed that the world had a certain order, an order that they also called the Logos or Word. For them, the Logos gave order and purpose to the world. Therefore, when John says the Word became human, it probably implies that Jesus embodies God's purpose for the world.

Further, when John says that the human Word "lived here on earth among us" (John 1:14), it uses a word that basically means "to set up a tent" among us—like the tent where God met the Israelites while they were traveling in the desert. John wishes us to know, therefore, that when we are looking at

> **incarnation:** The idea that Jesus was God made flesh, that He came from heaven and became human.

Jesus, we are seeing nothing less than God's presence among us. Jesus' opponents in John understand these claims and repeatedly pick up stones in order to kill Him. "You, a mere man," they say, "have made yourself God" (John 10:33). The Gospel of John is unique in presenting Jesus in such high, exalted language.

The idea that Jesus was—and still is—God in human form is one of the most important teachings of Christianity.[5] The central part of the most important Christian creed states that in order to save us, Jesus "came down from heaven and was incarnate by the Holy Spirit from the Virgin Mary, and was made man."[6] The word **incarnation** means Jesus was put "in-flesh." This Christian teaching comes primarily from the Gospel of John (see also Phil. 2:6-7).

Pictures of Who Jesus Is

Chapter 26 of this text discusses some of the unique features of John's story of Jesus' ministry. We should at least mention some of them in this overview of John. In particular, John presents a number of events that define Jesus' spiritual significance, usually "I am" statements in which Jesus tells the audience who He is.

In most cases, these "I am" statements relate to a particular situation Jesus confronts at the time. Before Jesus raises Lazarus from the dead, for example, He tells Lazarus' sister, "I am the resurrection and the life. Those who believe in me, even though they die like everyone else, will live again" (John 11:25). Not long after Jesus has miraculously fed well over five thousand people from five loaves of bread and two fish, He tells a crowd, "I am the bread of life. No one who comes to me will ever be hungry again" (6:35). John provides a number of these pictures of Jesus' true identity, such as John the Baptist's statement that Jesus is the Lamb of God (1:29) or Jesus' description of himself as the good shepherd (10:11). The next chapter will discuss these in more detail.

The Who's and When's of John

One of the unique features of the Gospel of John is its references to the "disciple Jesus loved." This disciple is first mentioned in John 13 after Jesus has arrived in Jerusalem for the last time (John 13:23). He then appears occasionally throughout the rest of the gospel. Interestingly, though, the gospel never tells us his name. John 21:24 tells us that he "is that disciple who saw these events and recorded them here. And we all know that his account of these things is accurate." But nowhere does the gospel tell us who he was.

> "Peter turned around and saw the disciple Jesus loved following them . . . Peter asked Jesus, 'What about him, Lord?' Jesus replied, 'If I want him to remain alive until I return, what is that to you? You follow me.' So the rumor spread among the community of believers that that disciple wouldn't die."
>
> **John 21:22-23**

Since the late A.D. 100s, the church has more often than not believed that this disciple was John, the son of Zebedee, one of the core disciples mentioned in the synoptics (e.g., Mark 9:2). The reasons are easy enough to see. The beloved disciple was present at the last dinner Jesus had with His disciples, so it seems likely he was one of the twelve core followers of Jesus (Matt. 10:1-5; Mark 3:13-19; Luke 6:12-16; Acts 1:13). Indeed, the disciples closest to Jesus in the synoptics are Peter and the sons of Zebedee (James and John). These are the ones who seem closest to Jesus both at the Transfiguration (Mark 9:2) and in the Garden of Gethsemane (Mark 14:33). A title like the "beloved disciple" surely would apply most appropriately to one of these three.

Of these three it cannot be Peter, since the gospel distinguishes Peter from the beloved disciple on every occasion when the beloved disciple is mentioned.[7] It is unlikely that it would be James, the son of Zebedee, since Herod Agrippa I killed him in the early A.D. 40s. No one argues that the gospel was written this early. John thus seems the most likely candidate among the core group of disciples mentioned in Matthew, Mark, and Luke. Interestingly, while the Gospel of John mentions Peter, Andrew, Nathaniel, Philip, Thomas, and Judas Iscariot by name, it does not explicitly mention John. Some think such an omission would be appropriate if John were the actual author.

The idea that John, the son of Zebedee, was the author is not without its complications, however. For one thing, although the disciple Jesus loved is the ultimate source of the gospel's information, he was not likely the person that wrote down the gospel exactly as we now have it. Would this disciple have written of himself, "And we all know that *his* account of these things is accurate" (John 21:24)? The story is never in any place told in the first person:[8] "I saw these things" or "We went to Jerusalem." In fact, John 21:2 uses the *third* person when stating that the sons of Zebedee (including John) were by the Sea of Galilee. The author does not say, "I was there by the Sea of Galilee," let alone that one of these sons of Zebedee was the beloved disciple. In other words, the present form of the Gospel of John most likely comes from the people who were associated with that person, rather than from the disciple himself.[9]

One of the strongest arguments against John, the son of Zebedee, being the author comes from Mark 10:35-40, in which James and John ask Jesus for high positions of honor in the kingdom of God. Jesus asks them if they can "drink from the cup" he is about to drink—in other words, whether they are prepared to die for their faith. After they claim that they are prepared, Jesus indicates that they would indeed drink from that cup of martyrdom. As we just mentioned, Herod Agrippa I put James to death in the early 40s. The Gospel of Mark leads us to believe that John was martyred as well. In fact, many think Mark hints that John was already dead by the late A.D. 60s when Mark was probably written. If the author of the fourth gospel was not martyred, as church tradition has long held, then John, the son of Zebedee, was not likely its author.

At this point we should probably mention that some early Christians were aware of another John whose life and ministry may have paralleled that of John, the son of Zebedee—a man called John the elder. The church father Papias, writing about A.D. 140, mentioned him as a second-level disciple—not one of the twelve, but a disciple nonetheless.[10] Dionysius of Alexandria recognized early on (A.D. 200s) that the style, language, and thought of the Gospel of John is strikingly different from that of the book of Revelation. The church historian Eusebius, writing in the early 300s, suggested accordingly that John the elder must have written one of these two books and John, the son of Zebedee, the other.[11] In this light it is extremely interesting to see that some of the books associated with the Gospel of John (namely, 2 and 3 John) were both written by someone who called himself "the elder." Some take this fact to indicate that John "the elder" stands behind the fourth gospel rather than John, the son of Zebedee.

At least on the surface, a fair case can be made that a rather unknown disciple, John the elder, stands behind the fourth gospel, a man who was not one of the twelve. Interestingly, the Gospel of John makes almost no mention of there being *twelve* core disciples (only John 6:67-71). In contrast to the synoptics, John downplays the significance of Peter and highlights disciples like Philip, Thomas, and Nathaniel, who either are not mentioned at all or play no significant role in the synoptics. These individuals, as indeed the Gospel of John itself did, came to play important roles in one of the earliest Christian heresies—Gnosticism. It is quite possible that some of the early members of this Gnostic Christianity had originally been a part of John's community (cf. 1 John 2:19).

If John the elder was the man behind the gospel, he was probably from the area of Judea, which would explain why he is not mentioned until Jesus arrives in Jerusalem for the last time. It would also explain why the Gospel of John highlights Jesus' visits to Jerusalem more than the other gospels. This man was known to the high priest (John 18:15) and was present at the crucifixion (19:35). Whoever the author was, tradition holds that he eventually made his way to Ephesus in Asia Minor. In this context, perhaps in the last decade of the first century, the community of this "beloved disciple" edited and passed on to the church this magnificent gospel that is the favorite of so many.

Things to Think About

Key Terms
incarnation
Logos/Word
sign

1. In what way does Jesus provide us with the meaning and purpose of the universe?

2. Jesus never explicitly tells His followers to have faith in Him in the synoptic gospels, yet this idea is central to Jesus' message in John. How would you explain this difference?

3. John is the only gospel to clearly tell its audience that Jesus existed before He came to earth. What is the significance of Jesus' preexistence? In what state did He preexist?

4. Who do you think wrote the Gospel of John?

endnotes

1. John does have quite a number of metaphors: "I am the bread of life" (John 6:35); "A shepherd enters through the gate. The gate keeper opens the gate for him, and the sheep hear his voice and come to him" (John 10:2-3). But these are not the parables of the synoptics, which are self-contained stories.

2. For this reason, a number of scholars have called the first part of John the "Book of Signs" (John 1:19–12:50) and even thought it was originally a document that existed apart from the rest of John. In contrast, the second half of John has sometimes been called the "Book of Glory" (13:1–20:31). The epilogue is John 21.

3. The words, "In the beginning was the Word" (NIV), remind us of another opening verse—the first verse in the Bible. Genesis 1:1 states, "In the beginning God created the heavens and the earth."

4. See chapter 11 of this text.

5. Christianity teaches that Jesus is still both God and human. However, His humanness is no longer in flesh. The Apostle Paul indicated that Jesus' body was transformed into a spiritual body at the point of His Resurrection, just as Paul believed our bodies will be in the future (1 Cor. 15:20, 42, 48).

6. From the Nicene Creed. The church affirmed these truths even before it agreed on what books should be in the New Testament (A.D. 325 at the Council of Nicea). The creed reached its current form at the Council of Constantinople in A.D. 381.

7. In fact, every time the gospel mentions the beloved disciple, it contrasts him to Peter—with the beloved disciple coming out superior in every case. For this reason, many scholars believe that the community behind the Gospel of John saw themselves in competition in some way with more mainstream, "Petrine" Christianity, such as is represented by the Gospel of Matthew.

8. To speak in the "first person" is to say that "I" or "we" did something. "You" is the second person. "He," "she," "it," or "they" are ways of speaking in the third person.

9. John 21:24 mentions that the beloved disciple had written down his testimony, so some or most of the gospel may come from a source written by this disciple.

10. Quoted in Eusebius, *Hist.* 3.39.4.

11. *Hist.* 3.39.4.

The Story of Jesus in John

Of all the gospels, John paints the most exalted portrait of Christ,
equating Him most clearly with God.

The previous chapter explained how strikingly different the Gospel of John is in some ways from the synoptic gospels. It also set out some of its special features. The purpose of this chapter is to highlight some of the stories unique to John, as well as to look at John's unique perspective regarding the events his gospel has in common with Matthew, Mark, and Luke. The previous chapter has already mentioned that John begins with the "incarnation," the fact that Jesus is God's Word in human form (John 1:1-18). Many divide up the rest of the gospel into two main parts, with John 21 as a kind of "epilogue" or wrap-up of the book. We will focus on these two main parts in this chapter.

At a Glance

- In John, Jesus' earthly ministry takes place over a period of two to three years and includes a number of trips to Jerusalem.

- The Gospel of John has two basic parts. The first presents Jesus' public ministry, while the second focuses on His disciples.

- John includes seven signs that demonstrate Jesus' messianic identity.

- John places great significance on the festivals Jesus attends, aligning their Old Testament symbolism with Jesus himself.

- John links several statements of Jesus' spiritual identity ("I am" statements) to the situations in which He finds himself.

- In contrast to the synoptics, John presents Jesus giving long speeches to His disciples (almost philosophical discourses).

The "Book of Signs" (1:19–12:50)

Jesus and John the Baptist

One of the interesting features of John is the way it seems to downplay the significance of John the Baptist in relation to Jesus. For example, the Gospel of John alone tells us that Jesus began His ministry *before* John the Baptist was arrested (John 3:22-24; 4:3; cf. Mark 1:14). We see John the Baptist sending his followers to Jesus while John is *still* baptizing (John 1:37) and Jesus' disciples are baptizing people during the same time.

The effect of this presentation is to reduce the significance of John's mission from what it is in the synoptics. The synoptics give the impression that Jesus waited until after John was imprisoned to begin His mission. However, as soon as Jesus arrives on the scene in John, the Baptist's mission is really over. Now that Jesus has come, the implication is that John's followers should follow Jesus.[1] Interestingly, the Gospel of John does not actually record Jesus being baptized by John the Baptist![2]

Why would the gospel present John the Baptist's ministry in this way? It is perhaps no coincidence that the Gospel of John is associated with Ephesus. The book of Acts mentions at least two incidents in Ephesus involving followers of John the Baptist (Acts 18:24–19:7). In both cases, we find individuals who had accepted John's teaching but had no knowledge of Jesus. For this reason, many scholars believe that Ephesus was home to a group of John the Baptist's followers. According to this theory, the Gospel of John was written in such a place, a place where some people had rejected Jesus, yet had accepted the ministry of John. This kind of situation would explain why the gospel consistently downplays John's significance over and against Jesus.

Seven Signs

For various reasons, many scholars believe that the Gospel of John has drawn on more than one source in order to create its spiritual presentation of Jesus. Perhaps the most frequent suggestion is that John's community had in its possession an account of seven "signs" that Jesus had performed. You will notice as you read through the Gospel of John that the first two signs are numbered: (1) Jesus turns water into wine in a little village called Cana in Galilee (John 2:11), and (2) Jesus heals the son of a royal official (4:54). Accordingly, some suggest that this "Signs Source" recorded seven signs in order to prove that Jesus was the Messiah.[3] Whether or not we accept this theory, these seven signs help us get acquainted with some of the stories in John.

The Seven Signs in John
1. Turning water into wine (John 2:1-11)
2. Healing the royal official's son (4:43-54)
3. Healing the lame man at the pool (5:1-15)
4. Feeding the five thousand (6:1-15)
5. Walking on water (6:16-24)
6. Healing the blind man (9:1-12)
7. Raising Lazarus from the dead (11:38-44)

Several of these signs are unique to the Gospel of John. For example, the first miracle recorded in John is the changing of water into wine mentioned above. This miracle appears nowhere else in the New Testament. Also, while the other gospels record Jesus healing the blind and the lame, the particular healings mentioned in John are found only in John. Even the stunning sign that climaxes this section of John's gospel, the raising of Lazarus from the dead, is unique to John. If these stories do originate from a separate source, it surely had a missionary purpose and was meant to convince the doubtful that Jesus truly was the Messiah—which is also the purpose these signs serve in John as we now have it.

Several of these signs connect with another special feature of John, namely, the "I am" statements Jesus makes at various points in His ministry. John usually associates such statements with the immediate situation in which Jesus finds himself. It is after He feeds the five thousand, for example, that Jesus says, "I am the bread of life" (John 6:35). The Gospel of John thus powerfully uses the signs Jesus performs in order to teach who Jesus is. The literal event teaches us about Jesus' symbolic identity.

It is probably no coincidence that Jesus says, "I am the light of the world" (John 8:12), and then heals a blind man in the next chapter (9:1-12). Both illustrate a greater truth, namely, that Jesus brings understanding while the Jewish leaders perpetuate blindness. In the following chapter of John, Jesus goes on to say, "I am the good shepherd," contrasting himself with the Pharisees as thieves and robbers (10:7-11). Jesus' statement, "I am the resurrection and the life," (John 11:25) also fits this pattern, since He says it just before raising Lazarus from the dead.

Some of Jesus' "I am" Statements
- "I am the bread of life" (John 6:35, 51).
- "I am the light of the world" (8:12).
- "Before Abraham was, I AM!" (8:58).
- "I am the good shepherd" (10:11, 14).
- "I am the resurrection and the life" (11:25).
- "I am the way, the truth, and the life" (14:6).
- "I am the true vine" (15:1).

We mentioned the most startling "I am" statement of all in the last chapter—when Jesus says that He existed before Abraham: "Before Abraham was born, I am!" (8:58 NIV). The way He words this statement implies that He is divine, since God basically names himself "I AM" when He appears to Moses at the burning bush (Exod. 3:14).[4] Thus, of all the gospels, John paints the most exalted portrait of Christ.

Jesus, the Way to Life

Another unique feature of Jesus' public ministry as expressed in the Gospel of John is seen in His frequent trips to Jerusalem. If all we had were Matthew, Mark, and Luke, we might think that Jesus' public ministry was limited mostly to Galilee and took place within the space of about a year. In the synoptics, Jesus only visits Jerusalem at the very end of His ministry. However, in John Jesus regularly attends the festivals in Jerusalem, as well as such feasts as Passover, Tabernacles, and even the Feast of Dedication (Hanukkah). Jesus attends three Passovers in John, and since Passover comes only once a year, the Gospel of John implies that Jesus' earthly ministry lasted two to three years.

The Gospel of John may use Jesus' attendance at these festivals, along with the things He says, to underscore Jesus' spiritual significance in relation to the practices of Old Testament Judaism. For example, in John 1:19–6:71 John seems to present us with events and teaching that show us Jesus as the only way to eternal life. As Jesus says later in John 14:6: "I am the way and the truth and the life. No one can come to the Father except through me."

One of the ways John presents this truth is through the idea that Jesus is the Lamb of God. At the first Passover Jesus attends, He overturns the tables of those who exchange money and sell animals for sacrifices, proclaiming that He will destroy the temple and raise it up again in three days (John 2:19). What He means is that His sacrifice as the "Lamb of God" replaces the need for an earthly temple with its animal sacrifices and blood (cf. 2:21; 4:23). He is now the way to God.

Many scholars believe that John has powerfully arranged and presented the events of Jesus' life to bring out this message. Of all the gospels, John uniquely teaches that *Jesus is the Lamb of God*. Only in John does John the Baptist proclaim, "Look! There is the Lamb of God who takes away the sin of the world!" (John 1:29). To emphasize this point, John's gospel alone seems to time Jesus' death just *as the Passover lambs are being slaughtered*, a fact that powerfully parallels His designation as the Lamb of God.[5]

Further, while Matthew, Mark, and Luke indicate that Jesus threw the money changers out of the temple in the last week of His life, John places this

Eucharist: Often called "**communion**," it literally means "thanksgiving." It is a celebration in memory of Jesus' atoning death on the cross. Bread represents His body, while wine represents His blood.

event right after Jesus turns water into wine at Cana, in the first year of Jesus' ministry. Since John probably thought of this wine as a symbol of Jesus' blood, it may have made sense to him to place the temple incident—which showed that Jesus' body would replace the temple—right next to it.[6] Here we have both the body and blood of Jesus, a symbolic reference to the **Eucharist** or Christian **communion**. John probably wanted his audience to know that Jesus' body and blood have taken the place of the Jewish sacrificial system as the way to life.

John seems to allude to the Christian celebration of communion several times in his gospel. As we just mentioned, both the miracle at Cana and Jesus' actions in the temple have overtones of this celebration of Jesus' death as a sacrifice for sins. The feeding of the five thousand may also carry these overtones. After feeding the crowds, Jesus tells them that He is the bread of life and explains what He means: "Unless you eat the flesh of the Son of Man and drink his blood, you cannot have eternal life within you" (John 6:53). This comment was very difficult for the crowds to accept, and many of His disciples stopped following Him at that point (6:66). At the very least, John was saying that salvation from God's condemnation comes only through Jesus' death.[7]

Another image that Jesus uses to explain what He means by the designation *bread of life* comes from Israel's distant past. During the time that the Israelites wandered in the desert, God sent down food called manna to keep them alive. Jesus compares himself to that same manna, saying He provides spiritual food that gives life (John 6:31-33). This statement reminds us of something Jesus tells a Samaritan woman in John 4, another incident unique to John. Jesus meets a Samaritan woman at a well and asks her for a drink.

In the course of their conversation, Jesus reveals not only that He knows everything about her, but also that He is the giver of living water: "Whoever drinks the water I give him will never thirst" (John 4:14 NIV). Both as living water and as the bread of life, Jesus gives eternal life to those who feed on Him.

John 3 gives us some of the clearest teaching on how to receive eternal life. This chapter tells of a man named Nicodemus who comes to Jesus secretly, believing Him to be a great teacher with answers to his questions. Jesus gets right to the point: unless a person is "born from above" or "born again," s/he cannot be a part of the kingdom of God (John 3:3). What Jesus means is that one must receive the Holy Spirit in order to be a part of God's kingdom, a teaching John shares with most of the New Testament.

Jesus also alludes to the importance of Christian baptism in this chapter: one must be born *of water* as well as of the Spirit (3:5). John's most important verses appear in the middle of Jesus' conversation with Nicodemus: "For God so loved the world that He gave His only Son, so that everyone who believes in Him will not perish but have eternal life. God did not send His Son into the world to condemn it, but to save it" (3:16-17). These verses emphasize the theme that in so many different ways appears throughout the first six chapters of John: Jesus is the only way to eternal life.

Jesus and Jewish Opposition

After Jesus' radical statement about the need to feed on His body and drink His blood, He loses many followers. John 7–12 details the steadily increasing opposition to Jesus. In these chapters, the theme turns to Jesus as the good shepherd, an image that contrasts to the Jewish leaders who help perpetuate blindness. It is probably no coincidence that in this section Jesus heals a blind man, attends Hanukkah, the Feast of Lights (John 10), and attends the Jewish Feast of Tabernacles, a festival also involving lights and water. Jesus proclaims on that occasion that He is a provider of living water (John 7:37-38), echoing the same image He used with the Samaritan woman (John 4).

Here we see again John's penchant for revealing Jesus as the replacement of the Old Testament festivals. We indicated this earlier in the image of Jesus as the Lamb of God, thus replacing the temple and Passover. These passages thus imply that He is the true symbolic replacement of Tabernacles and Hanukkah as well. John also pictures Jesus replacing Sabbath observance. In contrast to the Jewish observance of the Sabbath, for example, Jesus is always working like God His Father (5:17).

The climax of the first half of John comes in John 12 with the Jews' rejection of Jesus' message. The Gospel of John is distinct in having Jesus refer to His enemies as "the Jews." This feature is striking because, after all, Jesus and His loyal followers were also Jews. Because of this wording, the Gospel of John has unfortunately played into the hands of anti-Semitism, even though the gospel probably was not racist in its original context. However, many scholars have suggested that the members of the community behind this gospel had, like the blind man of John 9, been cast out of the synagogues of Ephesus because of their faith in Christ (cf. 9:22, 34).

The "Book of Glory" (13:1–20:31)

Scholars have often called the second half of John the "Book of Glory" because of the way it presents Jesus' death and Resurrection as His achievement of glory (e.g., John 13:31-32). Whereas the events highlighted in the first half of John are conducted in public, these last chapters focus on Jesus' teaching to His disciples. In fact, five consecutive chapters (John 13–17) all describe events that take place at the last dinner Jesus has with the disciples who have remained with Him. Jesus demonstrates His love to the very end, noticeably when He washes their feet, another event recorded only in John (13:2-12).

Jesus makes a long speech to His disciples in this part of John. Some of the main themes are Jesus' oneness with God, His imminent departure from earth, and His promise to send a helper back from heaven— the Holy Spirit. The Holy Spirit, Jesus says, will lead the disciples to understand things like what constitutes truth (John 14:17, 26), sin, and right living (16:8-9). Here we have some of the clearest references in the New Testament to the Holy Spirit as a person.

Jesus and the Jewish Festivals

• Sabbath—Like God, Jesus is always working, even on the Sabbath (John 5:17).

• Passover—Jesus is the Lamb of God; His body replaces the temple (1:29; 2:21).

• Tabernacles—Jesus is God "tabernacling" with humanity (1:14); He provides living water (7:37-38) and is the light of the world (9:5).

• Dedication (Hanukkah)—Jesus is the light of the world (9:5) and the new temple (2:21).

In John 17, John presents what is sometimes called Jesus' high priestly prayer; included in that prayer are those of us who would believe many years later. Jesus' main thrust is that we would be one, just as Jesus was one with God. This message may have had special meaning for John's original audience, since some of its members had probably left the church at some point (see 1 John 2:19).

John's presentation of Jesus' death is extremely victorious in tone. Jesus tells Judas when to leave to betray Him (John 13:27). John does not record Jesus' anguish in the Garden of Gethsemane (cf. 12:27; 18:1-2). The soldiers who arrest Jesus fall all over themselves at the mere mention of His name (18:6). John makes it very clear that Jesus is in complete control of His trial and crucifixion. Jesus tells Pilate that the only reason He has any authority over Him is because it is God's will (19:11). On the cross, He gives instruction to the beloved disciple to watch over His mother (19:26-27). He then appears to die by an act of will after He fulfills a final prophecy by saying, "It is finished" (19:28-30).

The Gospel of John ends with a number of Resurrection appearances that the other gospels do not record. The best known of these is Jesus' appearance to "doubting Thomas," a disciple who doubts whether Jesus has really risen from the dead. Skeptically, he says he will not believe until he touches the scars from Jesus' crucifixion. Only when Jesus suddenly appears and offers Thomas that opportunity does Thomas believe, calling Jesus "my Lord and my God" (John 20:28). Jesus' concluding statement to Thomas aptly fits John's purpose in this gospel: "Blessed are those who haven't seen me and believe anyway" (20:29).

Epilogue (John 21)

John 21 comes almost as a surprise—the last two verses of John 20 sound somewhat like an ending in their own right. For this reason, some have suggested that John 21 was added after the gospel had already been completed. In any case, this chapter presents us with an interesting encounter between the resurrected Jesus and Peter.

The main players in this encounter are Jesus, Peter, and the beloved disciple. Jesus asks Peter three times if he loves Him, perhaps echoing Peter's three denials after Jesus had been arrested. Peter responds each time that he does, after which Jesus commands him to take care of the church. Jesus then prophesies that Peter will die by crucifixion.

Peter, interested in the fate of the beloved disciple, asks what his end will be. Jesus refuses to answer, but allows for the possibility that he might live until the second coming. The editor of John then implies that many in his day believed John would live until Christ's return. This editor then tells us that this beloved disciple was the basis for the gospel—a gospel whose testimony is true.

What Do We Do with John?

For some Christians, the symbolic meanings many scholars find in John are exciting and give life to the text beyond what they might have imagined. For many others, however, the suggestion that John presents a spiritual message more than a blow-by-blow historical presentation is highly suspect. If God inspired John to speak truth in this way, of course, then God surely was not in error—nor is John. It just requires us to read this gospel with the right expectations. Whether you see it as highly symbolic or as a straightforward historical account, John remains one of the most meaningful books in the New Testament.

Things to Think About

Key Term
Eucharist or communion

1. What are some of the "I am" statements in John and what do they tell us about the character of Jesus?

2. What do you think the "seven signs" signify at the beginning of John?

3. Do you think John was deliberately comparing Jesus to Jewish festivals and Sabbaths?

4. What would you make of the claim that John gives us more of a symbolic than a historical portrait of Jesus?

endnotes

1. We might also note that while Matthew 11:14; 17:10-13 and Luke 1:17 indicate that John the Baptist was "Elijah" in terms of the prophecy in Malachi 4:5, the Gospel of John only mentions the Baptist's denial when asked if he was Elijah (John 1:21). The fourth gospel elevates Jesus in relation to the Baptist, while at the same time reducing John's significance.

2. Matthew realized what someone might say about the fact that Jesus submitted to baptism by John the Baptist. John baptized those that repented of their sins and wanted God's forgiveness. Matthew, therefore, records a conversation in which John and Jesus both acknowledge that Jesus does not need to be baptized (Matt. 3:14-15). Jesus allows it to show agreement with John's message. The Gospel of John goes even further than Matthew by not mentioning that Jesus was actually baptized, only that He came to where John was baptizing.

3. One argument for such a source notes that while John 4:54 calls the healing of the royal official's son the second sign, John 2:23 indicates that Jesus had already performed far more than two signs by this point of His ministry (cf. 2:11). This kind of minor inconsistency often reveals a "seam" where a source has been edited and incorporated into a larger work.

4. The name of God, Yahweh, seems to come in some way from the Hebrew word *hayah,* which means "he is."

5. In Matthew, Mark, and Luke, the "Last Supper" is the Passover meal (e.g., Mark 14:12). John, however, seems to want to emphasize that Jesus is the Lamb of God by showing His death the morning before the Passover meal is eaten. On the morning of Jesus' death, the Jews who take Jesus to Pilate do not enter the palace because they wish to eat the Passover that night (John 18:28; cf. 19:31). If this is the case, it is another indication of the highly symbolic nature of John's gospel.

6. The miracle at Cana gives several hints that it symbolizes Jesus' blood on the cross, as well as communion. For example, Jesus tells His mother that it is somewhat inappropriate for Him to turn the water into wine because His hour has not come yet—a reference to His death (John 2:4). Also, the jars contain water used for purification (2:6).

7. For Christians from the Roman Catholic and Orthodox traditions, these verses give strong support to the doctrine of transubstantiation—the idea that communion bread and wine literally become Jesus' flesh and blood.

CHAPTER 27

What Would Jesus Do?

While Mark and John may not disagree when understood in the proper context,
they do present significantly different pictures of Jesus.

"What would Jesus do?" This question originated from a sermon by Charles Sheldon one Sunday morning in the late 1800s. His book, *In His Steps*, soon became classic Christian literature. Viewing Jesus as the greatest moral example, Sheldon's book encouraged people everywhere to pattern their attitudes after Jesus' way of thinking. Sheldon believed a person would know the right thing to do in any situation by asking, "What would Jesus do?" Recent years have seen a resurgence of this slogan in Christian circles, resulting in everything from wristbands to CDs inscribed with the initials "WWJD."

At a Glance

- The quest for the historical Jesus is the attempt to use historical methods to determine who Jesus was, what He did, and what He said.

- From a historical perspective, the actual existence of Jesus is not in question.

- Eschatological portraits of Jesus hold that He preached the coming end to the current period of history, perhaps even the end of the world.

- Ethical or non-eschatological portraits see Him simply as a wise teacher or a social reformer.

The interesting and predictable thing about this question is that people answer it differently. If you were hiding Jews and a Nazi officer asked if there were any Jews in your house, would you lie? What would Jesus do? Some Christians would answer emphatically that Jesus would lie and that it would be

The Quest for the Historical Jesus:
The attempt to determine as much as
possible about the life, teachings, and
aims of Jesus of Nazareth—the one
from whom Christianity originated.

immoral *not* to lie in this situation. Others would just as surely assert that Jesus would never lie under any circumstance. Just as people read into the Bible various and varying messages, so too most people see in Jesus what they already think about right and wrong. Your answer to the question usually affirms more about the values you already hold than what Jesus actually would have done two thousand years ago.

So what did the "historical Jesus" do and teach—the real Jesus who walked this earth two thousand years ago? Surprisingly, as you survey those who know the most about the gospels and ancient Palestine, you will find significant disagreements about who Jesus thought He was, what He actually did, and what He really said. Answers to these questions range from those who think the gospels give us accurate pictures of Jesus to those who do not even think Jesus really existed.

The question of what Jesus really did and taught is called the **Quest for the Historical Jesus**; various scholars have addressed the issue for several hundred years. For some, the answer is obvious—look at the gospels and you will know exactly what Jesus did and taught. For others, the historical Jesus looked quite different from the pictures in our gospels. Still others do not think we have enough evidence to know for sure. Some scholars do not even think it is important to know who Jesus really was. To them, what is important is the *idea* of Jesus—the "Christ of faith" and not the "Jesus of history." In some respects, this way of thinking is not too different from those who use the *idea* of Jesus to express the values they already hold.

Is It a Legitimate Quest?

Many Christians no doubt will find this whole discussion unnecessary, even illegitimate, since they think it questions the validity of the Bible. Those who do not think we can know who Jesus really was might also object to the question, especially if they do not think it is relevant to being a good Christian. Nevertheless, the sheer number of books written on this subject in the last few years makes it important enough to at least mention.

> Even if you believe that Mark and John fit together historically, when read individually they give us quite contrasting impressions of Jesus' identity and earthly mission.

On the one hand, the majority of historians—even atheist historians—now agrees that there is enough "data" about the historical Jesus to form intelligent hypotheses about His defining activities and teachings. Such an agreement was not always the case. For a thirty-year period or so, the subject was taboo among scholars. Yet we certainly have as much material about Jesus as we have for many other figures about which scholars feel relatively confident making hypotheses. For example, Socrates wrote down none of his teachings. All we know of him has come to us through his followers, which is also the case with Jesus.

On the other hand, we have seen from our study of the gospels thus far that each has a particular perspective on Jesus that influences the way He is presented. One can believe that Mark and John do not really disagree when they are understood in the proper context, yet it is undeniable that they present significantly different pictures of Jesus. If we had only John's gospel to go by, we would think that Jesus consistently proclaimed His divine origins and that He clearly taught the need to believe in Him in order to attain eternal life. If we had only Mark's gospel, on the other hand, we would think that Jesus consistently hid the fact that He was the Messiah, and we would have the barest outline of the need to believe *in Jesus* in order to escape God's wrath.

Even if one believes both these pictures to be completely compatible, it is legitimate to ask how their portraits fit together historically.

As we have also seen from our study of the synoptic question, the gospels do not present us with the exact words of Jesus—the gospels were written in Greek and Jesus spoke Aramaic. At best we have *translations* of Jesus' words. Indeed, many of the sayings of Jesus do seem to be translations of Aramaic sentences. On the other hand, many of the sayings attributed to Jesus in the gospels do not seem to come from Aramaic. Recent studies of oral tradition argue that while the core of a story often gets passed on word for word, oral tradition tends to be very flexible about the surrounding details. All these things indicate that it is at least legitimate to ask what Jesus actually said and did, even if we expect to end up basically where we started.

Most reconstructions of the historical Jesus fall into two basic categories: those that believe Jesus preached about world-changing events that were going to happen in the near future and those that believe Jesus was more of a social reformer or moral teacher. For example, the traditional understanding of Jesus is that He proclaimed the coming judgment of the world and the resurrection of the dead. This is an **eschatological** portrait of **Jesus**, a Jesus who taught that the current period of history was coming to an end—perhaps even that the end of the world was near.

eschatological Jesus: Oriented around the end of the current period of history, perhaps even of the world.

ethical Jesus: Oriented around how to live in the present time.

On the other hand, many current portraits of Jesus picture Him simply as a wise teacher who basically taught wise things. Proponents of this view might claim that Jesus was merely a social reformer who addressed the social injustices of His day. We call this the **ethical Jesus**, a Jesus who taught people how to live but who did not think history was nearing a major turning point.

While traditional Christianity accepts that such teaching was a part of Jesus' ministry, it has always held that Jesus was much more than just a good teacher or a social reformer.

Did Jesus Really Exist?

Before we sketch the two basic portraits of Jesus, we should address those few individuals who have claimed that Jesus never existed. Occasionally you will come across people who believe Jesus is a fictional, mythical character. Frankly, it is difficult to take this viewpoint seriously. Not only does it seem incomprehensible for the Christian movement to have survived in a hostile environment without some historical validation,[1] but the historical evidence itself presents us with no basis for arguing against Jesus' existence. The overwhelming consensus of scholars—even atheist scholars—is that Jesus did in fact exist.

First, even if you do not believe the Bible to be inspired, it cannot be dismissed as evidence for the existence of Jesus. Some scholars of the past argued that Paul knew almost nothing about the historical Jesus and was the actual founder of Christianity.[2] Groups such as the Jesus Seminar that we will discuss below make a strong distinction between the earliest followers of Jesus, sometimes called the **Jesus movement**, and the later church that Paul would develop throughout the Mediterranean world.

In our opinion, these scholars are largely irresponsible in their conclusions. Paul's and Peter's ministries overlapped too much for Paul to have "invented" Christianity in the way some suggest. Two of the most important cases in point are Paul's personal knowledge of Peter (Galatians 2) and Paul's discussion of the Resurrection in 1 Corinthians 15. In Galatians, we

Jesus movement: A way of referring to the earliest followers of Jesus both before and after His crucifixion.

realize that Paul personally knew Peter, John, and James, the brother of Jesus. These individuals on all accounts had been a part of Jesus' ministry and were a part of Christianity from its earliest beginnings. In 1 Corinthians 15, Paul passed on traditions about Peter and James that the Corinthians could verify— some of them apparently knew quite a bit about Peter and his ministry (e.g., 1 Cor. 1:12; 9:5-6).

The burden of proof lies squarely on anyone who would say that Paul's comments in these instances are a complete fabrication—there is not a single reason to disbelieve the essence of what Paul says. After all, the Galatians and Corinthians knew about Peter and James independently of Paul. In some instances, they were getting their information from Christians who did not like Paul and who disagreed with him on a number of points. You do not bluff people who are already questioning you and who are likely to check up on your sources. "Anything is possible," as the saying goes, but many things are highly improbable. Those who question the existence of Jesus do so because they *want* to question His existence, not because a single shred of evidence supports their cause.

Second, a number of non-Christian historians from this period of early church history mention Jesus. Two of these are the Jewish historian Josephus and the Roman historian Tacitus. Josephus' statement is not without its problems. It appears that some early Christian "doctored" it somewhat to exalt Jesus more highly than Josephus originally did. After all, Josephus was no Christian. For this reason, some reject the quote entirely as something a Christian inserted into the text of Josephus' history of the Jews.

Nevertheless, it is unlikely that the entire quote was invented. It seems more likely that Josephus mentioned a few things about Jesus that were only "spiced up" later. A scholar by the name of John Meier has suggested that the original quotation read in this way:[3]

"At this time there appeared Jesus, a wise man. For he was a doer of startling deeds, a teacher of people who receive the truth with pleasure. And he gained a following both among many Jews and among many of Greek origin. And when Pilate, because of an accusation made by the leading men among us, condemned him to the cross, those who had loved him previously did not cease to do so. And up until this very day the tribe of Christians (named after him) has not died out."

Josephus, *Antiquities* 18.3.3

There is nothing about Meier's reconstruction that seems incompatible with a non-Christian Jewish historian.

Tacitus had no particular liking for Christians either, but he did not question that a person named Jesus had actually existed.

"Christus, from whom the name [Christian] had its origin, suffered the extreme penalty during the reign of Tiberius at the hands of one of our procurators, Pontius Pilatus, and a most mischievous superstition thus checked for the moment, again broke out not only in Judaea, the first source of the evil, but even in Rome, where all things hideous and shameful from every part of the world find their center and become popular."

Tacitus, *Annals* 15.44

The overwhelming weight of the evidence thus indicates unambiguously that Jesus was a person who actually existed, ministered, and was crucified around the year A.D. 30. While someone might sincerely question whether the gospels are historical in all their details, the evidence gives us no plausible basis on which to doubt that Jesus was a real person.

The "Ethical" Jesus

It has become very popular to identify Jesus as a social reformer and general "do-gooder." Many people think of Jesus simply as someone who taught His followers to love everyone and to help those in need. He helped the poor and spoke frankly to those in authority who were unjust and oppressive. He despised legalism and those who hid their hate behind their religion. He preached forgiveness, no matter how bad your sins were, and taught His followers not to judge anyone.

It is likely that Jesus taught some of these things, and these teachings are extremely attractive to us today. The paragraph above embodies some of the best values of modern Western culture. Thus, it is no surprise that some of today's most popular reconstructions of the historical Jesus focus on this kind of teaching, while denying that Jesus preached anything about judgment or eternal damnation. In the minds of some, Jesus was strictly a social reformer and a teacher of wisdom.

The **Jesus Seminar** is typical of those who do not think Jesus believed He was the Messiah or that He saw Himself as important in the course of history. They picture Jesus much like a hippie from the sixties, flaunting the establishment and teaching that the kingdom of God was inside each person, having nothing to do with history or coming events. Many in the Jesus Seminar believe the teachings of Christianity today are a corruption of what Jesus himself really taught. They might say that Christianity was invented by the church but had little to do with Jesus himself.

Jesus Seminar: A group of scholars who voted to decide what they thought Jesus really said. In general, they eliminated all of Jesus' sayings in which He viewed himself as a part of world-changing events or in which He preached the coming of God's judgment on Israel or the world.

It is no surprise that scholars who look at the historical Jesus in this way tend to downplay the historical significance of the gospels in the New Testament. They often rely more on books that are not in the Bible, like the Gospel of Thomas or the Gospel of Peter, both discussed in the following chapter. Such scholars also look to Q—the hypothetical source of sayings behind Matthew and Luke—to reconstruct their picture of Jesus.

While we should not minimize the intelligence and knowledge of those who hold such positions, we can raise a number of questions about their conclusions. First, surely there is something suspicious about theories that end up making Jesus look exactly like modern culture might want Him to look, eliminating the elements of the gospels' portraits that might make a modern person uncomfortable. That seems a little too convenient.

Second, it also seems suspicious that this theory relies so heavily on a *hypothetical* text like Q and on gospels that were written later than any of the gospels in the New Testament. While reconstructing Q or hypothesizing about early forms of the Gospel of Thomas are perfectly legitimate scholarly activities, surely it is all too tempting to reconstruct these texts so that they say exactly what one wants them to say.

Finally, given what we know of first-century Judaism and Jesus' original context, an eschatological Jesus who talked about the end of that period of history is far more plausible than one who was simply a social reformer or do-gooder. Almost no one would question that Jesus' ministry launched from that of John the Baptist, and John the Baptist preached a coming judgment. The Christians who wrote the books of the New Testament also preached that God's judgment would soon come to the earth. Since Jesus' ministry is the historical link between John the Baptist and these early Christians, it is difficult not to conclude that Jesus also taught in the expectation that God was coming to judge the earth.

The Jesus of Restoration and Judgment

As we just mentioned, a number of historical factors make it more likely that Jesus believed He was doing something far more significant in history than just reforming the society of His day. Eschatological reconstructions of Jesus emphasize that He believed something of tremendous significance was happening and that He was a major player in it. What we know of John the Baptist, for example, both from the New Testament and from other sources, indicates that he preached God's coming judgment of Israel. Since Jesus submitted to John's baptism, it is highly likely that He agreed.

John also preached the forgiveness of sins for those who repented. In fact, he baptized in the same spot where the priests had stood as the Israelites crossed the Jordan River to begin their conquest of the Promised Land. Here is a message of restoration to Israel. Jesus' appointment of *twelve* disciples echoes this message of restoration, for Israel had twelve tribes when it was whole. The fact that Jesus did not include himself among the twelve placed Him in a different category—that of king or Messiah. As we saw earlier, it is probably no coincidence that He was crucified with the title "King of the Jews" over His head.

Jesus' ethical message belongs in the context of *both* God's forgiveness and judgment. Jesus preached the restoration of all, especially the "sheep" who had lost their way, such as the tax collectors and sinners who were not trying to keep God's covenant with Israel. While Jesus preached forgiveness for all, He did so in the context of changed lives. He did not expect the tax collector to continue defrauding his brothers or the prostitute to continue her trade. The forgiveness He offered did not seem to be unconditional or irrevocable.

We should agree with Matthew 10:5-6 that the focus of Jesus' earthly ministry was on Israel, not on Gentiles. He focused on the restoration of *Israel* while He was on earth. It is worth repeating that the Parable of the Two Sons in Matthew 21:28-32 seems to sum up the two basic reactions of Israel to Jesus: A father asks two sons to go work in the field. One says he will but then later does not; the other initially says he will not, but in the end does. The son who said he would but then does not is like the Pharisees and religious leaders of Israel who were trying to keep the Jewish Law—you would expect them to obey God. In the end, however, the prodigals and sinners of Israel accept Jesus instead, the ones who were not even trying to obey God's word.

Jesus' healings and exorcisms add a further important dimension to Jesus' ministry. By healing and casting out demons, He indicated that God was also reclaiming the spiritual landscape of the earth. This fact meant that the repercussions of Jesus' ministry were not limited to Israel. With the demonic powers of the earth removed, the entire world would return to God's sovereignty and all the nations would be blessed through God's chosen people.

Jesus thus proclaimed the arrival of the kingdom of God on earth as it is in heaven (cf. Matt. 6:10). This kingdom involved much more than simply the restoration of the nation of Israel. It meant taking Satan's power from the earth and returning the earth to the way it had been before Satan took over. In our opinion, this reconstruction of Jesus is much more plausible from a historical standpoint than any offered by the Jesus Seminar or other non-eschatological portraits of Jesus.

For some, this Jesus may seem foreign and strange. Decades ago, Albert Schweitzer took another view in these poignant words: "He comes to us as One unknown, without a name, as of old, by the lake-side, He came to those men who knew Him not. He speaks to us the same word: 'Follow thou me!'"[4]

Things to Think About

1. "What would Jesus do?" When we ask this question, do we ask it because we really want to know what Jesus would do, or do we simply use the question to reinforce what we already believe?

Key Terms
eschatological Jesus
ethical Jesus
Jesus movement
Jesus Seminar
Quest for the
    historical Jesus

2. To what extent would you say that the "quest for the historical Jesus" is legitimate? Does even raising the issue indicate a lack of faith in God's word?

3. Which portrait of Jesus do you think comes closer to the truth: (1) the "eschatological" Jesus, (2) the "ethical" Jesus, or (3) a combination of the two?

4. Could a person be a Christian "in good standing" and believe that material in the gospels is not historical?

endnotes

1. I would go further and argue that we cannot really explain the survival of the Christian movement unless the earliest disciples were extremely convinced that Jesus had risen from the dead.

2. This idea sometimes rears its ugly head today—the notion that the Christianity of the New Testament is in sharp discontinuity with the earliest followers of Jesus like Peter. Examples are A. N. Wilson's *Jesus* (London: Sinclair-Stevenson, 1992) and, more recently, his *Paul: The Mind of the Apostle* (London: Norton, 1997). Far from being new ideas, Wilson's popular claims are "more of the same"—ideas with a little truth but largely way off.

3. John Meier, *A Marginal Jew: Rethinking the Historical Jesus* (New York: Doubleday, 1991), 61.

4. Albert Schweitzer, *The Quest for the Historical Jesus: A Critical Study of Its Progress from Reimarus to Wrede*, trans. W. Montgomery (New York: Collier, 1968 [1906]), 403.

CHAPTER 28

Other Gospels Not in Our Bible

A number of "gospels" have survived from the early church that are not included in the New Testament.

The Gospel of Luke mentions that "many" written accounts of Jesus' earthly ministry were circulating at the time Luke was written, giving us the impression that there were many more gospels around in the first century than we have in our New Testament. In the last century or so, fragments and even some complete manuscripts of still more gospels have been uncovered, although it is not at all certain that any of these were the ones to which Luke refers. One group of scholars thinks that some of these give an earlier or more accurate picture of the historical Jesus than the "canonical gospels"—the gospels in the Christian New Testament.

The purpose of this chapter is to provide some exposure to a few of these gospels. Certain members of the Jesus Seminar have given a lot of attention to the Gospel of Thomas and the Gospel of Peter. They feel that when discussing the historical Jesus, these two gospels are equal in importance to the canonical gospels.[1] The Protoevangelium of James gives us some of the first examples of Catholic beliefs like the "immaculate conception" and Mary's "perpetual virginity." Gospels such as those to the Hebrews, Ebionites, and Nazarenes give us

Some Non-Canonical Gospels
- Gospel of Thomas
- Gospel of Peter
- Infancy Gospel of Thomas
- Protoevangelium of James
- Gospel of the Hebrews
- Gospel of the Ebionites
- Gospel of the Nazarenes

insight into the diversity of early Christianity, particularly Jewish Christian groups outside the "mainstream" of Christianity.

The Gospel of Thomas

More than any of the other "extra-canonical" gospels (the ones not in our canon), the Gospel of Thomas has received the most attention—primarily as a document that might preserve traditions about Jesus that are more original than the gospels in our Bible. Along with a host of other "Gnostic" writings, this gospel was found in 1945 at an Egyptian site called Nag Hammadi.

Gnosticism was a second-century movement that believed matter was evil and that our bodies were prisons for our spirits. "Salvation" was about getting free of our physical prison cells. This was accomplished by way of secret knowledge that allowed our spirits to soar in the spirit world, in spite of our bodies. The Gospel of Thomas reflects these ideas, thus seriously calling into question its validity as a reference to the historical Jesus. It is not likely that a first-century, Aramaic-speaking Jew from the Galilean countryside would have espoused a second-century doctrine with these kinds of overtones.

Gnosticism: A movement—both Christian and Jewish—that believed the salvation of our spirits from our physical bodies came from hidden knowledge.

However, it is possible for the Gnostic elements to be "peeled back" or removed in some cases in order to find authentic traditions from the historical Jesus. In the first place, the Gospel of Thomas is comprised of individual *sayings* reputed to have come from Jesus. In other words, the Gospel of Thomas is not a story; it is a set of 114 individual statements reputedly made by Jesus and largely presented without any context. It thus looks a bit like what "Q"—the hypothetical source of sayings used by Matthew and Luke—would have looked like, although scholars do not equate the two. It is possible that some of these sayings do go back to Jesus, even though they are not recorded in our gospels.

The Gospel of Peter

John Dominic Crossan has claimed that Matthew, Mark, and Luke used the Gospel of Peter as a source for their presentations of the last week of Jesus' life.[2] Very few agree with him. It is possible that the Gospel of Peter gives us a window to the oral traditions that are unique to Matthew. When the Gospel of Peter refers to events also found in Mark, though, it seems to be using Mark as its source rather than vice versa. It was probably written in the A.D. 100s.

The Infancy Gospels

Some early Christians were understandably curious about the childhood of Jesus. Only the gospel of Luke records anything about Jesus as a child, and only Matthew and Luke even record Jesus' birth. The Infancy Gospel of Thomas and the Protoevangelium of James were two attempts to fill in such gaps. These two "infancy gospels" were probably written in the 100s.

> "The kingdom is inside of you, and it is outside of you. When you come to know yourselves, then you will become known, and you will realize that it is you who are sons of the living Father."
>
> **Gospel of Thomas, 3**

The Infancy Gospel of Thomas emphasizes Jesus' miraculous powers as a child. In one interesting incident, Jesus is caught making pigeons out of clay on the Sabbath. To escape punishment, He transforms the clay pigeons into real ones. However, this picture of the child Jesus is very harsh; He even kills some of His childhood teachers.

The Protoevangelium of James is more significant because it presents us with the earliest evidence of some key Roman Catholic beliefs, namely, the **immaculate conception** and **Mary's perpetual virginity**. It is the belief of the Roman Catholic and Orthodox traditions that not only was *Jesus* conceived without sin, but that *Mary herself* was also conceived "immaculately." These traditions hold that Mary did not have sex for the rest of her life. Therefore, the brothers and sisters of Jesus are thought to be children of Joseph by a former marriage or perhaps cousins. The impetus for such beliefs may have been connected with an increasingly negative view of sex as an expression of passion in this period of history.

Jewish Christian Gospels

The Gospel of the Hebrews and the Gospel of the Ebionites were probably editions of Matthew's gospel made to suit certain Jewish Christian groups outside mainstream Christianity. For example, we know that the Ebionites believed Jesus to have been "adopted" as Christ by God at the time of His baptism. They did not believe in the virgin birth, that He had preexisted His earthly life, or that He was divine before His baptism. The Gospel of the Nazarenes was probably also a version of Matthew, although the group using this was more "orthodox." More mainstream Christians accepted this group, even though their distinctively Jewish flavor separated them socially from other Christians.

immaculate conception: The Roman Catholic belief that not only was Jesus free of original sin, but Mary was as well.

Mary's perpetual virginity: Also a belief among many Roman Catholics that Mary remained anatomically intact throughout childbirth and then remained a virgin her entire life.

Things to Think About

1. Do you think that any of the traditions in these other gospels actually go back to Jesus—particularly the sayings and stories not found in the New Testament?

Key Terms

Gnosticism

immaculate conception

Mary's perpetual virginity

endnotes

1. See chapter 27 of this text.
2. For example, see John Dominic Crossan, *Four Other Gospels* (Minneapolis: Winston Press, 1985).

For Further Study

Introduction to the Gospels/Synoptic Gospels
- Malina, Bruce J. and Richard L. Rohrbaugh. *Social-Science Commentary on the Synoptic Gospels.* Minneapolis: Fortress, 1992.

- McKnight, Scot. *Interpreting the Synoptic Gospels.* Grand Rapids: Baker, 1988.

- Powell, Mark A. *Fortress Introduction to the Four Gospels.* Minneapolis: Fortress, 1998.

Gospel of Matthew
- Kingsbury, Jack D. *Matthew As Story.* 2d ed. Philadelphia: Fortress, 1988.

Gospel of Mark
- Matera, Frank J. *What Are They Saying About Mark?* New York: Paulist, 1987.

- Rhoads, David and Donald Michie. *Mark As Story: An Introduction to the Narrative of a Gospel.* Philadelphia: Fortress, 1982.

Gospel of Luke
- Powell, Mark A. *What Are They Saying About Luke?* New York: Paulist, 1989.

Synoptic Problem
- Black, David A. and David R. Beck, eds. *Rethinking the Synoptic Problem.* Grand Rapids: Baker, 2001.

- Dungan, David L. *A History of the Synoptic Problem: The Canon, the Text, the Composition, and the Interpretation of the Gospels.* New York: Doubleday, 1999.

• Goodacre, Mark. *The Case Against Q: Studies in Markan Priority and the Synoptic Problem.* Harrisburg, PA: Trinity, 2002.

Parables
• Blomberg, Craig. *Interpreting the Parables.* Downers Grove, IL: InterVarsity, 1990.

• Drury, John. *The Parables in the Gospels: History and Allegory.* Philadelphia: Fortress, 1989.

Birth Stories
• Brown, Raymond E. *The Birth of the Messiah.* New York: Doubleday, 1977.

Gospel of John
• Burge, Gary M. *Interpreting the Gospel of John.* Grand Rapids: Baker, 1992.

• Culpepper, R. Alan. *The Anatomy of the Fourth Gospel: A Study in Literary Design.* Philadelphia: Fortress, 1983.

• Malina, Bruce J. and Richard L. Rohrbaugh. *Social-Science Commentary on the Gospel of John.* Minneapolis: Fortress, 1998.

Historical Jesus
• Witherington, Ben III. *The Jesus Quest: The Third Search for the Jew of Nazareth.* Downers Grove, IL: InterVarsity, 1995.

Non-Canonical Gospels
• Koester, Helmut. *Ancient Christian Gospels: Their History and Development.* Harrisburg, PA: Trinity, 1990.

.

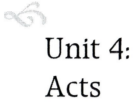

Unit 4:
Acts

Chapters 29–35

CHAPTER 29

Acts: Luke's Sequel

Acts is the sequel to Luke, picking up the story right where it left off.

"Acts of the Holy Spirit"

Acts, the fifth book in the New Testament, begins with a reference to a previous book the author had written to the same person. "Dear Theophilus," it begins, "In my first book I told you about everything Jesus began to do and teach" (Acts 1:1). The mention of the name Theophilus tells us that this previous book is none other than the Gospel of Luke. Acts is thus the sequel to Luke, picking up the story right where it left off. Although our Bibles separate these two books by putting the Gospel of John in between, they really should be read together. They originally worked together toward a common purpose. Having them separated, as is the case in our Bibles today, actually hinders us from appreciating their full meaning.

At a Glance

- Acts is the sequel of Luke, written by the same author.

- Acts emphasizes the same themes as the Gospel of Luke, such as the significance of women and concern for the poor and downtrodden.

- Even more than Luke, Acts emphasizes the fact that the gospel is for all people. It points out that Christians are not troublemakers or seditious individuals, and highlights the importance of prayer and the Holy Spirit.

- The genre of Acts is probably that of history, which in ancient times allowed for more creativity on the part of an author than modern histories do.

- Acts, like Luke, is technically anonymous and was likely written after A.D. 70.

The Gospel of Luke, the author tells us, was about all the things that Jesus *began* to do and teach. The implication is that Jesus *continues* to do and teach in Acts as well. However, in Acts Jesus works through the Holy Spirit, who brings Jesus' continued presence to His disciples. Therefore, some have suggested that rather than call the book the "Acts of the Apostles," a more accurate name for the book would be the "Acts of the Holy Spirit."

Special Emphases of Acts

Since Luke and Acts are really a single work in two volumes, it is no surprise to find that they share the same basic themes. If the Gospel of Luke brings out the universal implications of Jesus' mission more than the other gospels, the book of Acts shows even more emphatically that the gospel is for everyone. Acts shares Luke's concern for the poor and oppressed, and also highlights the role of women in the spread of the gospel. Acts emphasizes even more the importance of prayer in the life of the early Christians and the centrality of the Holy Spirit. Finally, Acts more than the Gospel of Luke demonstrates the unified and peace-loving nature of Jesus and His followers, indicating that the opponents of Christianity were those who stirred up trouble rather than the Christians themselves.

"When the Holy Spirit has come upon you, you will receive power and will tell people about me everywhere—in Jerusalem, throughout Judea, in Samaria, and to the ends of the earth."

Acts 1:8

The Gospel Is for the Whole World

Acts may start in the city of Jerusalem, but it ends with the gospel being preached in Rome. In the interim the word spreads not only throughout

Palestine but also throughout Greece and what we now call Turkey. The book summarizes this expansion in the very first chapter: "When the Holy Spirit has come upon you, you will receive power and will tell people about me everywhere—in Jerusalem, throughout Judea, in Samaria, and to the ends of the earth" (Acts 1:8). The next chapter of this text gives further details about how the good news spreads to all these different places, starting with the incredible growth that takes place among the Jews in Jerusalem and ending with the spread of the gospel throughout the Mediterranean.

More important than the geography of this expansion is the way Christianity goes from being exclusively Jewish to a movement that includes people from countless other races and cultures. The Gospel of Luke more than any other gospel pictures the interaction and concern of Jesus for people of all races. Even when Jesus is born, a man named Simeon foretells that Jesus will be a "light for revelation to the Gentiles and for glory to your people Israel" (Luke 2:32 NIV). The book of Acts shows the fulfillment of his prediction.

Acts' presentation leaves no doubt about the possibility for non-Jews to escape God's wrath. For example, it is Peter—the most significant disciple for Luke—who first brings the gospel to the Gentiles (Acts 10). Acts shows the Holy Spirit filling these Gentiles before they had even been baptized (10:44); by "converting" them himself, God leaves no room for debate. James, Jesus' brother and apparently the leader of the Jerusalem church, agrees that they can become Christians without converting to Judaism first (15:13-21). Finally, more than half of Acts narrates Paul's mission to the Gentiles and clearly indicates that God is the one who commands him to go to them (e.g., 22:21). Acts thus not only *tells* us that the gospel is for everyone, but it also *shows* us this truth on almost every page.

However, Acts differs from Luke in one very important respect with regard to the gospel—it defines the "good news" more precisely than the Gospel of Luke does. The gospel that Jesus preaches in Luke is good news for the poor, the oppressed, the blind, and the downtrodden in general (e.g., Luke 4:18-19). Of course, the gospel is good news to these individuals in Acts as well. But after God raises Jesus from the dead, *the Resurrection becomes the central feature of Christian good news*, the most important element in the gospel in Acts. Acts thus gives us the "rest of the story." It shows us that it is through Jesus' victorious Resurrection that all of the promises of the gospel can actually come true.

Good News for Women, the Poor, and the Oppressed

As the Gospel of Luke features the role of women in Jesus' ministry and His concern for the poor more prominently than the other gospels, so Acts features these things as important elements in the ministry of the early church. From the very birth of the church on the Day of Pentecost,[1] Acts makes it clear that both men *and women* receive the Holy Spirit equally and thus both receive revelations from God to proclaim to the church (Acts 2:17-18; cf. 21:9). Acts mentions numerous women of status in the early church, many of whom open their homes for the worship of the early Christians.

For example, Peter goes to the house of a woman named Mary after an angel frees him from prison. Christians were evidently accustomed to gathering there to pray (Acts 12:12). Both the men and the women of the church at Philippi seem to meet in the house of a wealthy Christian woman named Lydia (16:15, 40). And Acts

> "And all the believers met together constantly and shared everything they had. They sold their possessions and shared the proceeds with those in need. They worshiped together at the Temple each day, met in homes for the Lord's Supper, and shared their meals with great joy and generosity–all the while praising God and enjoying the goodwill of all the people. And each day the Lord added to their group those who were being saved."
>
> **Acts 2:44-47**

typically mentions a wife named Priscilla first when it speaks of a husband-wife team who ministered with Paul (18:18, 19, 26). This woman evidently played an important role in teaching a man named Apollos the basics of the Christian faith (18:26). Apollos would go on to become an important Christian preacher at the famous city of Corinth. In short, the book of Acts not only wants us to see that both men and women can be saved, it also shows us that women played an important role in early Christian ministry (cf. 8:12; 17:4, 12, 34).

> The Resurrection is the most important part of the gospel message in Acts.

Acts also continues Luke's concern for the poor and downtrodden. As Acts 4:32-35 summarizes the early church, it notes that the earliest Christians "felt that what they owned was not their own; they shared everything they had . . . There was no poverty among them, because people who owned land or houses sold them and brought the money to the apostles to give to others in need." Acts indicates that the early church distributed food to widows (6:1) and sent help to one another in times of famine (11:27-30).

Jesus' ministry of healing also continues in Acts. In fact, Acts seems to want us to notice a similarity between Jesus' healing ministry and that of early Christians like Peter and Paul. As Jesus healed a crippled man (Luke 5:25), so do Peter (Acts 3:7) and Paul (14:10). As Jesus raised the dead (Luke 7:15), so do Peter (Acts 9:40) and Paul (20:12). These events demonstrate that the early Christians preached the same gospel that Jesus preached and shared the power of the same Spirit of God.

The Centrality of Prayer and the Holy Spirit

Just as Luke highlights the role of prayer in Jesus' earthly ministry, so Acts features prayer as the key to obtaining power and direction from God. The believers of Acts seem to pray constantly (e.g., Acts 1:14; 2:42), especially when a special need arises. For example, the early Christians pray when they are facing strong opposition. When the Jewish ruling council, the Sanhedrin, opposes them, they pray (4:23-31). When Stephen is being stoned to death, he prays (7:59). When Peter is in prison facing execution, Christians pray (12:5, 12), just as Paul and Silas do when they are imprisoned at Philippi (16:25). In many instances, God miraculously delivers the person for whom they pray.

In Acts, the Holy Spirit often comes during prayer. After they pray about the opposition of the Sanhedrin, the apostles get a "refill" of the Holy Spirit to give them the power to be bold in the face of attack (Acts 4:31). The apostles Peter and John lay hands on believers in Samaria who have been baptized so that they will receive the Holy Spirit (8:15-17). Although Acts 6:6 does not specifically mention the Holy Spirit, we can imagine that the apostles lay hands on these seven men so that they will be filled with the power necessary to minister appropriately.

The Holy Spirit is truly the power behind everything good that happens in the book of Acts. In fact, *receiving the Holy Spirit is the key ingredient in becoming a Christian in Acts*, as chapter 32 of this text discusses later. When some Samaritans are baptized and yet have not received the Spirit, the apostles come to them to help them receive the Spirit, so that they can become Christians fully. God ends all debate over whether Gentiles can be Christians by sending them the Holy Spirit and thus fully "converting" them. In fact, Acts 15:9 shows that it is the Holy Spirit that cleanses a person of his or her sins after s/he repents and turns to God.

The main consequence of having the Holy Spirit is power (cf. Acts 1:8). This power shows up sometimes as boldness to proclaim the gospel (e.g., 4:31). On three occasions, believers speak in "tongues," languages they have never learned (e.g., 2:4; 10:46; 19:6), when they receive the Holy Spirit.[2] At other times the Holy Spirit enables the apostles to perform miracles (e.g., Acts 3) or provides them with direction. He reveals the future to early Christians through prophets (e.g., 21:11) and tells them what to do when they need directions (e.g., 16:7).

Christians Are Not Troublemakers

Even more than Luke, Acts is careful to show the unity of the early church. Acts portrays the conflict that sometimes accompanies early Christianity as something that comes from those who oppose it rather than as a result of Christians themselves. Acts 28:22 indicates the reputation the author of Acts was up against: "the only thing we know about these Christians is that they are denounced everywhere." It appears that Acts is carefully presented in such a way as to show that Christians are orderly and peace-loving individuals.

> Receiving the Holy Spirit is the key ingredient to becoming a Christian in Acts. The main consequence of having the Holy Spirit in Acts is power.

The early chapters of Acts give us a church that is "of one heart and mind" (Acts 4:32). They "met together constantly and shared everything they had" (2:44); they regularly share "in the Lord's Supper and in prayer" (2:42). When problems and conflicts arise, they resolve them in an orderly manner with clearly drawn lines of authority. The apostles and James, for example, give the final ruling on matters of controversy (e.g., 6:1-6; 15:6-35). The church then submits to the decisions that those in authority make under the direction of the Holy Spirit (e.g., 6:5; 15:31).

From what we know of church conflicts from Paul's writings, we can see that Acts is putting the church's best foot forward. For example, Acts does not mention an important argument between Peter and Paul at a city called Antioch (Gal. 2:11-14). Even Barnabas, a traveling companion of Paul, sided against Paul on that occasion regarding the issue of whether Jewish and Gentile

Christians should eat together. Interestingly, Acts only tells us that Paul and Barnabas argued over whether Barnabas' cousin should travel with them (Acts 15:36-41). Acts may omit this other argument because it reflects one of the most precarious moments in the early church, jeopardizing not only the unity of the church but its mission to the world as well. As a result, the next phase of Paul's ministry seems to have taken place without the clear blessing of the leaders of the Christian movement.

On the other hand, Acts wants us to see the fundamental continuity and unity between the missions of Peter and Paul. We have already mentioned how Acts shows Peter and Paul *both* doing the same kinds of things that Jesus himself did while on earth. Yet Acts also hints at the fact that many Jewish Christians had misgivings about Paul's mission: "Our Jewish Christians here at Jerusalem have been told that you are teaching all the Jews living in the Gentile world to turn their backs on the laws of Moses" (Acts 21:21). Acts wants its audience to know that these claims are untrue—Paul still observes the Jewish Law. Acts has thus given us a somewhat "Gentile-friendly" picture of Peter and a "Jew-friendly" picture of Paul.

Similarly, Acts provides us with a fairly simplistic picture of the opposition Christians faced around the world. Acts regularly blames Jewish opposition to Christianity as the culprit for the riots and controversy that sometimes followed the early Christians. Local authorities, on the other hand, regularly either affirm the innocence of Christians or consider the charges against them as irrelevant in a legal setting.

Just as someone going for a job interview puts his or her best foot forward, so Acts emphasizes the peaceful nature of Christianity and downplays events that might have confirmed the reputation Christians seem to have had as troublemakers. In the process, Acts presents us with a somewhat idealistic picture of the early church. In reality, the early church had most of the same warts and struggles that churches have today.

The Genre of Acts

A quick look through Acts suggests almost immediately that it is a history of the early church, although some scholars creatively have suggested that it is a novel. However, the opening of Luke makes it clear that the author of Luke-Acts wants us to think of these two works as a record of things that actually happened, rather than as a fictional portrayal of Jesus and the early Christians (Luke 1:1-4). Many think that Acts fits best into an ancient genre called **general history**, a kind of history writing that presented the history of a nation or people from its origins down to contemporary times. Luke and Acts would fit this pattern since they present the origins of the race known as "Christians" from their "birth" on the day of Pentecost to the time near the deaths of the first apostles.

> **general history:** An ancient genre of history writing that presented the story of a nation or people from its origins to contemporary times.

The question for us as readers is how ancient history writing might have differed from modern history writing. In other words, should I expect from Acts the same things I would expect of a modern history book, or are there some differences? When we compare the ending of Luke and the beginning of Acts, we may catch a glimpse of one such difference.

If all we had were the ending of the Gospel of Luke, we would probably conclude that Jesus not only rose from the dead on Easter Sunday, but also made all His appearances to the disciples and ascended to heaven on that same day—all in and around the city of Jerusalem. Luke 24:13 says that Jesus appears to two men on their way to the village of Emmaus "that same day" that He rose from the dead. That same evening Jesus has supper with them and reveals himself to them (Luke 24:29-31). Once they realize Jesus is alive, they return "within the hour" to Jerusalem (24:33). While they are telling the disciples what happened, Jesus appears to the disciples as well (24:36). After He finishes explaining things to them, He takes them out near the village of

Bethany and is taken up to heaven (24:50-51). The Gospel of Luke gives us the impression that Jesus rose, appeared, and ascended all on Easter Sunday.

Thus, you might be surprised to turn to Acts 1:3 and read that Jesus was with His disciples in Jerusalem for *forty* days—or turn to Matthew or Luke where Jesus never appears to His disciples in Jerusalem at all but *in Galilee* instead (Matt. 28:7, 16; Mark 16:7). At this point, a skeptic might cry foul! But to accuse Luke of error is to misunderstand the genre in which he was writing. Since Luke and Acts both have the same author and the same audience, it seems highly unlikely that Luke was just hoping Theophilus would miss the apparent difference in timing.[3] The genres of ancient biography and history writing allowed for some artistry in presentation.

"I have found it difficult to remember the precise words used in the speeches that I listened to myself and my various informants have experienced the same difficulty. My method, therefore, has been to make the speaker say what, in my opinion, was called for by each occasion, while keeping as closely as possible to the general sense of the words that were actually used."

Thucydides, Greek historian
The Peloponnesian War **1.22**

This conclusion may apply to the sermons of Acts as well. In Acts 20:9, Paul preaches so long that a young man dozes and falls out a third-story window, yet you could read any one of the sermons of Acts in less than five minutes. At the very least, the sermons of Acts are shortened versions of what was actually said. Further, one of the most respected ancient historians tells us that he sometimes composed speeches when he did not have access to eyewitnesses. While you will have to decide whether you think Luke has composed any of the sermons in Acts, Thucydides makes it clear that doing so was acceptable within the ancient genre of history writing.

The Who's, When's, and Why's of Acts

Chapter 19 of this text has already discussed some of the general background of Luke (and, thus, of Acts), since they both have the same author and audience in mind. Acts, like Luke, is technically anonymous, although the only name tradition has ever suggested for the author is that of Luke, the physician, occasionally a traveling companion of the apostle Paul. Chapter 19 also presented the basic argument that Luke and Acts were written after the destruction of the temple in Jerusalem in A.D. 70. The primary evidence is the clarity with which Luke portrays the destruction of the temple by the Romans in Luke 21:20—Matthew and Mark's picture is much more ambiguous (Matt. 24:15; Mark 13:14). The fact that Luke probably used Mark as a reference also makes a date after A.D. 70 likely.

Like the Gospel of Luke, Acts is a tool of the gospel message. Like Luke, it reassures Theophilus that the things he has been taught are true (cf. Luke 1:4). The main truth is of course the Resurrection of Jesus, the central message of the sermons in Acts. In the process, Luke confirms that Christians are honorable and that Christianity is a movement whose bad reputation is completely undeserved. While both he and his audience already knew the dark chapter that soon followed in Rome—the deaths of Peter and Paul at the hands of Nero, along with many other Christians—he ends the story on an appropriately high note. Just as Jesus predicted that the gospel would go everywhere, Acts ends with the gospel reaching Rome, the end of the civilized world. The time of the Gentiles was in full season (Luke 21:24). Christians were waiting for a day when the Jews too would accept Christ, and God would restore the kingdom of Israel (Acts 1:6).

Things to Think About

1. What themes does Acts most noticeably share
   with the Gospel of Luke?

Key Term

general history

2. How does the content of the "good news" change
   after Jesus has risen from the dead?

3. How close to a documentary do you think Acts is? How much freedom do
   you think Acts takes in its presentation? At what point, if any, would such
   creative license negate the authority or inspiration of Acts?

endnotes

1. See the next two chapters.
2. It is not clear whether these are the same tongues as described in 1 Corinthians 14,
   particularly regarding Acts 2, since unbelievers seem to hear them as human languages. See chapter 42 of this text.
3. Some are also quick to find fault with the apparent contradiction between two of
   the accounts of Paul's vision of Christ. One says his companions heard a voice
   but saw no one (Acts 9:7). The other says they saw a light but did not hear the
   voice (22:9). If this is a contradiction, it is not an error in terms of the general
   parameters of ancient history writing. Oral retellings often varied in their details
   as they were retold, while the core details remained the same.

CHAPTER 30

The Story of the Church in Acts, Part 1: Jerusalem, Judea, Samaria

The message and miracles of the apostles had two basic results: expansion and persecution.

The Overall Plot

Acts 1:8 is this book's key verse. Jesus tells His disciples, "When the Holy Spirit has come upon you, you will receive power and will tell people about me everywhere—in Jerusalem, throughout Judea, in Samaria, and to the ends of the earth." This verse basically gives us an outline of the story in Acts. The first seven chapters are set in and around Jerusalem. Chapters 8 through 12 take place in the broader area of Palestine; that is, in the regions of Judea and Samaria (see **Map 3**). The last sixteen chapters present the ministry of Paul as the gospel reaches the "ends of the earth." In that day and for all intents and purposes, this meant

At a Glance

- The story of Acts has three parts: the spread of Christianity in Jerusalem (Acts 1–7), its spread throughout the regions of Judea and Samaria (Acts 8–12), and its spread throughout the broader Mediterranean world (Acts 13–28).

- The main character is the Holy Spirit, who brings the power behind everything good that happens in the story.

- The Day of Pentecost is the birthday of the church and Christianity.

- Peter's ministry to the Jews dominates the first part of the story in Jerusalem (Acts 1–7), while Paul's ministry to the Gentiles dominates the last part (Acts 14–28).

- The church at the "Council of Jerusalem" (Acts 15) recognizes that Gentiles can be Christians without first becoming Jews.

- Acts ends with Paul in Rome, where he awaits trial before the emperor Nero.

Rome (see **Map 4** in chapter 31).[1]

The main character in the story of Acts is the **Holy Spirit**, who stands behind everything good that happens in the story. If the Gospel of Luke is about the things Jesus *began* to do and teach (Acts 1:1), then Acts shows us what the Spirit of Jesus *continues* to do in the church through His followers (e.g., 16:7). Whenever the Spirit comes, the followers of Jesus receive power. This power not only gives them boldness to proclaim Jesus' Resurrection, but it also enables them to perform miracles and sometimes speak in languages they have never learned.

Holy Spirit: Primarily a way of referring to God's (or Jesus') presence and action in the world. However, the New Testament often speaks of the Holy Spirit as a distinct person from Jesus and God the Father. The church spelled out His identity more clearly in the years following the writing of the New Testament.

Beside the Holy Spirit, *Peter* and *Paul* are the next two most prominent characters in the story. Peter's ministry to the Jews dominates the first part of the story in Jerusalem (Acts 1–7), while Paul's ministry to the Gentiles dominates the last part, as the gospel reaches the ends of the earth (Acts 14–28). We might almost think of the first half of Acts as the "Peter half" and the second as the "Paul half." Since Luke viewed the period of history in which he lived as the "age of the Gentiles" (Luke 21:24), it is no coincidence that the story of Acts shows a gradual shift of Christianity from Jews to Gentiles. While Acts begins in Jerusalem with Jewish Christians, it ends in Rome with Paul turning decisively to the Gentiles (Acts 28:28).[2]

In Jerusalem

Both the Gospel of Luke and the book of Acts demonstrate a greater interest in Jerusalem and its temple than Matthew and Mark do. In the Gospel of Luke, this interest shows up primarily in the events surrounding Jesus' birth and after He rises from the dead. For example, the birth story in Luke tells of events at the Jerusalem temple that the other gospels do not include (Luke 1 and

Day of Pentecost: Also known as the Feast of Weeks and the Feast of First Fruits, Pentecost celebrated the end of the grain harvest, fifty days after Passover. For Christians, it represents the birthday of the church.

2). Even after Jesus' Resurrection, only Luke tells us about Jesus' appearances around Jerusalem (e.g., Luke 24:13, 36), as well as His ascension nearby.[3] Matthew and Mark, on the other hand, mention nothing about Jesus appearing to His followers in Jerusalem. They only tell about His appearances in Galilee (Matt. 28:7; Mark 16:7), where Jesus gives the "Great Commission" (Matt. 28:18-20).

In Acts, Jerusalem features as the center of Christianity, the place where the highest authority of the church resides. It is in Jerusalem that Acts depicts the birth of the church on the **Day of Pentecost**, the Jewish festival on which the Jews celebrated the first fruits of the grain harvest. From that day on, the disciples are called apostles, individuals who have been sent on a mission as ambassadors, in this case for God. At least in theory, Jerusalem remains the center of the church throughout the book of Acts. Even while the church is under persecution, the apostles remain there (Acts 8:1). When the church makes important decisions in Acts, it makes them in Jerusalem (Acts 15). Even Paul returns to Jerusalem near the end of his ministry and near the end of the story of Acts (Acts 21).

In Jerusalem, the temple plays an important role in the lives of the early Christians. Acts 2:46 mentions that they meet daily in the temple courts, and it is while they are there to pray that Peter and John heal a lame man (3:1). What is a little surprising is the implication that they also continue to participate to some extent in the temple's sacrificial system. For example, Acts depicts Paul near the end of his ministry offering a sacrifice at the temple—paying for certain Christian men to finish a vow they had made (21:24-27). The book of Hebrews implies that *all* earthly sacrifices are now inappropriate, since Christ's death definitively accomplished everything they symbolized (e.g., Heb. 7:12; 9:9-10; 10:1). Therefore, either Luke and Hebrews have slightly different theologies, or we conclude that it was a long process for the early Christians to figure out all the implications of Christ's death—a process we can witness as we read through the pages of the New Testament.[4]

the Ascension: Jesus' passage up to heaven forty days after his Resurrection; narrated in Acts 1.

martyr: Someone who dies for what s/he believes.

The first seven chapters of Acts begin with the **Ascension** of Jesus to heaven and end with the stoning of a man named Stephen, who becomes the first Christian **martyr**. A martyr is someone who dies because of what s/he believes. In the meantime, the Holy Spirit comes, the church is born, the gospel is preached, miracles and judgment take place, and the Christians face their first conflicts and opposition. This period of beginnings probably covers about the first three to five years after Jesus' Resurrection (ca. A.D. 30–33).

Since according to Acts a person cannot really be considered a Christian until s/he has received the Holy Spirit, there are technically no Christians until the Day of Pentecost, which for Acts is the birthday of the church and Christianity.[5] Not even the original disciples were technically Christians until that day. After forty days of teaching, Jesus tells the disciples to wait in Jerusalem until the Holy Spirit comes and fills them with power (Acts 1:8). This power is one of the main results of receiving the Spirit in Acts. While the disciples are waiting, they decide to name a replacement for Judas, the disciple who betrayed Jesus into the hands of the Jewish authorities. To do this, they "cast lots," which was something like throwing dice, and trust as a result that God has chosen a man by the name of Matthias to replace Judas (Acts 1:15-26).[6]

Once the Spirit comes, a typical chain reaction occurs. The Holy Spirit emboldens the apostles to proclaim the message of Jesus' Resurrection (e.g., Acts 2:14; 4:31). On the Day of Pentecost, He miraculously enables the disciples to speak in languages they have never learned so that the crowds can understand the good news (2:4). The Spirit also brings the power to perform miracles. One example of this takes place when Peter and John heal a crippled man (Acts 3). Beyond boldness and miraculous power, the Spirit also brings unity to the church (4:32).

The message and miracles of the apostles elicit two basic responses. On the one hand, the church experiences phenomenal growth as, first, three thousand received the message (Acts 2:41), then five thousand (4:4), then "more and more people believed and were brought to the Lord—crowds of both men and women" (5:14). Acts mentions not only Pharisees who came to believe (15:5), but also a large number of priests (6:7). By the end of the book, people everywhere have heard about Christianity (28:22).

On the other hand, the Jewish leaders who put Christ to death have a different reaction to the message—they become increasingly hostile to the

> **Key Events in Acts 1–7**
> • Jesus ascends to heaven (Acts 1:9).
>
> • The disciples replace Judas with Matthias (1:26).
>
> • The church is born as the Holy Spirit comes on the Day of Pentecost (Acts 2).
>
> • Peter and John heal a lame man at the temple (Acts 3).
>
> • They face opposition from the Sanhedrin (Acts 4).
>
> • God judges Ananias and Sapphira for lying to the Holy Spirit (Acts 5).
>
> • The Jerusalem Christians have a conflict over the feeding of Greek-speaking widows. They appoint seven men for this task (Acts 6).
>
> • Stephen becomes the first Christian martyr (Acts 7).

early Christians. After Peter and John heal a lame man, these religious leaders bring them in and interrogate them. They bring the apostles in a second time when they do not stop preaching. The climax of their opposition in these chapters takes place when they put Stephen to death, the first Christian to die because of his commitment to Christ (Acts 7:60).

In the meantime, the church experiences its first inner conflicts as well. In Acts 5, we hear a story about a couple named Ananias and Sapphira. While the early Christians were not required to sell all their possessions, Acts tells us that many did sell their houses and land in order to take care of the needy among them (Acts 4:34).[7] Barnabas, who will show up again later in the story, provides us with a good example, selling a field and giving the money from the sale to the apostles (4:36-37). Ananias, on the other hand, lies to Peter about how much he had made on the sale of his land. For his attempt to gain honor from this falsehood, the Holy Spirit causes him and his wife to die (5:1-11).

In Acts 6 we read about a very significant conflict in the early church, one that involved the social division between Jews that spoke Aramaic, the language of Palestine, and Jews that spoke Greek, the language of the broader world. Evidently, those who distributed food to the widows of the community were showing favoritism to the Aramaic-speaking widows (Acts 6:1). What is significant about this event is that it probably indicates a bigger problem, namely, that the church was not ministering effectively to the non-Aramaic-speaking Jews of Jerusalem.

The appointment of seven Greek-speaking men in Acts 6:3-6 prepares us for the second part of Acts, in which the gospel spreads beyond Jerusalem to the broader regions of Judea and Samaria. Philip, one of the seven, is a key player in that expansion. The story of Acts 6 also introduces us to Stephen, who is one of the seven. The first part of Acts' story ends in chapter 7 with his death. Stephen is so zealous—and perhaps so much more controversial in his preaching than the apostles—that the Sanhedrin has him stoned.

Throughout Judea and Samaria

Acts 8–12 are transitional chapters in some ways. To a great degree they prepare us for the last section of Acts, in which Paul carries the gospel throughout the Mediterranean world. However, we should not think of them as unimportant chapters—quite the opposite is true. Stephen's death pushes the gospel out of Jerusalem and the focus of the mission turns increasingly to Greek speakers, a process that we see expand throughout the rest of Acts.

These transitional chapters (Acts 8–12) include some significant events. The gospel first comes to the Gentiles when Peter preaches to a centurion named Cornelius (Acts 10). Paul (or Saul, as Acts calls him at this point) has a vision of the risen Jesus and joins the Christian movement (Acts 9). The church at Antioch in Syria is founded and begins to flourish. It is from this city that Paul will launch all the missionary journeys recorded in Acts. These chapters roughly cover a space of ten to fourteen years (A.D. 33–46?), some of the most crucial years in the development of Christianity.

Events of Acts 8–12

- Philip takes the gospel to Samaria and the broader area of Palestine (Acts 8).

- Saul (Paul) joins the Christian movement (Acts 9).

- Peter ministers outside Jerusalem (9:32-43); takes the gospel to the Gentiles (Acts 10).

- The church at Antioch in Syria begins to thrive (11:19-30).

- Herod Agrippa I beheads James the apostle (12:2). When Herod tries to kill Peter, God delivers him (12:3-19).

- The angel of the Lord kills Herod (12:20-23).

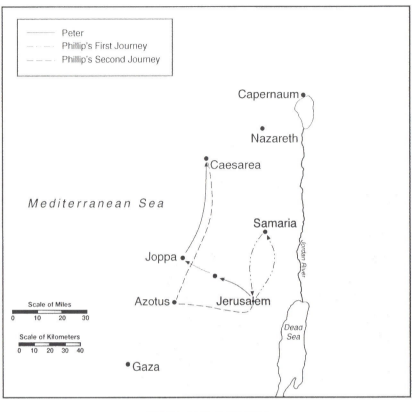

**JUDEA AND SAMARIA
MAP 3**

The Ministry of Philip

In Acts 8 Philip, "the evangelist," one of seven men appointed to take care of the Greek-speaking community, takes the gospel to the region of Samaria, initiating its spread beyond Palestine. Interestingly, the converts he baptizes do not receive the Holy Spirit, and Peter and John have to come up from Jerusalem. One of those who hears Philip in Samaria is a man named Simon, "the wise man."[8] Some later Christians considered Simon to be the father of all heresy. According to tradition, Philip starts a chain of events that eventually brings the gospel to Ethiopia. God leads him to an Ethiopian "eunuch," someone who manages a king's affairs. Eunuchs were castrated as a symbol of loyalty and in order to prevent adultery in the management of the king's wives.

Saul/Paul Becomes a Christian

Acts 9 presents us with the story of how one of the most important figures in the history of Christianity came to join the Christian movement.[9] Most people know him by his Roman name, Paul, but Acts begins his story with his Jewish name, Saul. This use of names in Acts subtly tells a story in and of itself. By starting with Paul's Jewish name, Acts highlights the fact that Paul was a Jew—in fact, a very militant Pharisee who persecuted Christians before he had a life-changing vision of Jesus. Acts then uses the shift in names from Saul to Paul to illustrate the shift in Paul's mission from Jew to Gentile. His Roman name also hints that he was a person of some status in the Roman world, since he was both a Roman citizen and a Hellenistic Jew.[10]

Acts tells us that he came from one of the largest cities in the ancient world, *Tarsus*, which was located in the southeast corner of what is now modern-day Turkey (Acts 9:11). But Acts also tells us that he was raised in Jerusalem and received his education "at the feet of" a famous and highly respected Pharisee named Gamaliel (22:3). An important earlier reference to Gamaliel is found in Acts 5.

We should not think of this event as Paul's "conversion" to Christianity, as if he changed from one religion to another.[11] For Paul, Christianity was nothing other than true Judaism. What does happen on this occasion, however, is a call to the truth. Jesus appears to Paul while he travels to the city of *Damascus* in order to persecute Christians. Paul was convinced that he was serving God by putting a stop to this group. On the way, Jesus gives him a "wake-up" call, validating that the Christians are correct about what God is doing in history. Not only does God tell Paul to preach the good news of

Christ's Resurrection, but Acts 22:21 and 26:17-18 also depict this experience as a call to go to the Gentiles. God leads Paul to a man named Ananias, where he is baptized and receives the Holy Spirit.

The Ministry of Peter, the Opposition of Herod

The last part of Acts 9 through Acts 12 largely focuses on the ministry of Peter in Judea and Samaria. Peter heals a bedridden man named Aeneas and raises a woman named Dorcas from the dead. In one of the most significant events in the book of Acts, Peter brings the gospel to a Gentile named Cornelius, the first Gentile to become a Christian in Acts (Acts 10). While Peter is preaching, God sends the Holy Spirit to Cornelius and the Gentiles with him, demonstrating that Gentiles can be Christians just like Jews.

The book of Acts makes it clear that the possibility of salvation for non-Jews is anything but a foregone conclusion, even after Christ rises from the dead. Not only does Peter himself resist this idea at first, but Acts 11 also relates how the Jewish Christians in Jerusalem question Peter when he returns. They even object to the fact that Peter had entered a Gentile's home. However, when they hear about the vision God had given Peter and what the Holy Spirit had done, they accept this unexpected turn as the way God has chosen to deal with the world.

In Acts 12, we hear largely about the exploits of Herod Agrippa I, the grandson of the Herod who put the babies to death (Matthew 2). He was also a nephew of Herod Antipas, the one who beheaded John the Baptist (Matthew 14). Herod Agrippa I puts the apostle James to death and tries to do the same to Peter. However, as an answer to prayer, God miraculously delivers Peter from prison. Herod finally meets his end when the angel of the Lord causes worms to eat him. Because Herod had accepted worship from his people, God causes him to die.

Things to Think About

1. How would you describe the Holy Spirit in Acts?

2. Why do you think Luke focuses on Jerusalem to such a degree in his presentation?

3. How did the martyrdom of Stephen help the spread of the gospel?

4. Do you agree with the claim that Paul would not have interpreted his vision of Christ as a call or conversion to a new religion?

Key Terms
the Ascension
Day of Pentecost
Holy Spirit
martyr

endnotes

1. Writing in the late first century, a Christian named Clement noted that Paul "reached the limits of the West" (1 Clement 5:7; see the text box in the next chapter). While many think Paul did make it to Spain (cf. Rom. 15:24), it is possible that Clement was actually referring to Rome, since it was the westernmost part of what the people of that time thought of as the truly civilized world.

2. Even though Acts is technically anonymous, I will refer to the author as "Luke" for convenience.

3. The other significant events before Jesus' death concern His mourning over the future of Jerusalem (Luke 19:41-44; 23:28-31).

4. Here is another reason why we must be careful about using one book of the New Testament to help us interpret another—different books may have slightly different theologies or may represent different stages of early Christian understanding. See chapter 2 of this text.

5. Chapters 31 and 32 of this text discuss in further detail the significance of the Day of Pentecost. Those in the Wesleyan tradition may find statements like this one of concern, since the Wesleyan tradition generally relates the Day of Pentecost to the experience of entire sanctification. This book does, however, affirm the possibility of victory over sin through the power of the Holy Spirit. See the first three pages of chapter 38.

6. This practice comes from Old Testament times and should not be connected with gambling. It is rather a reflection of the fatalism of the ancient world—it was presumed that God would cause the lots to point to the appropriate person to replace Judas.

7. This picture of the early church reminds us of what we can reconstruct about Essene practice. At Qumran, for example, a new entrant surrendered his possessions when he entered the community, and the community then shared possessions in common ("Community Rule" 6.18-23; cf. Josephus, *Jewish War* 2.122). From hints elsewhere in the "Community Rule" of Qumran, however, it seems that the members of the community still had some possessions. In other words, it was not completely communistic. See J. C. VanderKam, *The Dead Sea Scrolls Today* (Grand Rapids: Eerdmans, 1994), 82–84.

8. The word magus used of Simon is the same word used of the wise men in Matthew.

9. The story is also told with minor variations in Acts 22:3-21 and 26:4-23.

10. A Hellenistic Jew was a Greek-speaking Jew, usually from the Diaspora—the Jews dispersed outside of Palestine. See chapter 8 of this text.

11. For an overview of Paul's mission and message, see chapter 37 of this text.

CHAPTER 31

The Story of the Church in Acts, Part II: To the Ends of the Earth

The last sixteen chapters of the book of Acts (13–28) cover the missionary activities of Paul throughout the Mediterranean world.

The last sixteen chapters of the book of Acts (13–28) cover the missionary activities of Paul throughout the Mediterranean world. We traditionally speak of Paul's *three* missionary journeys, although Acts itself does not number them. In fact, Acts fails to record a number of Paul's trips.[1] Acts even runs together what we call his second and third journeys. Nevertheless, we will continue to refer to "three" journeys for convenience.

Paul's First Missionary Journey (Acts 13:1–14:28)

All three of the missionary journeys in Acts begin in the city of **Antioch** in the region of Syria, in the northernmost part of Palestine. This city had an immense impact on the history of the church. Although Acts portrays

---

Events of Acts 13-28

- Paul's First Missionary Journey (Cyprus, Pamphylia, Pisidia, Lycaonia).

- The "Jerusalem Council."

- Paul's Second Missionary Journey (Turkey, Macedonia, Greece, mostly in Corinth).

- Paul's Third Missionary Journey (Turkey, Macedonia, Greece, mostly in Ephesus).

- Paul is arrested in Jerusalem, imprisoned for two years at Caesarea.

- On his way to Rome to appear before Caesar Nero, Paul is shipwrecked. He remains under house arrest in Rome for two years.

Jerusalem as the center of early Christianity, the church at Antioch is the one Christians today might find most appealing. For example, the Christians here did not let racial boundaries get in the way of their fellowship with one another—Jew and Gentile intermingled and ate together (Acts 11:20; Gal. 2:12).[2] According to Acts, this church both submitted to those in authority above them (e.g., Acts 15:2) and freely gave to their fellow churches when they were in need (e.g., 11:29-30). Most notable of all, of course, is this city's role in sending out missionaries like Paul to spread the good news of salvation from God's coming wrath. Somehow it seems appropriate that the followers of Jesus were first called "Christians" in the city of Antioch (11:26). The book of Acts indicates that the more usual term for Christians at that time was "followers of **the Way**."[3]

the Way: The term Christians seem to have used to refer to themselves as a group in the first century A.D.

The so-called first missionary journey took place roughly in the years A.D. 46–48 and covered the island of ***Cyprus*** and the southeast part of what is now modern-day Turkey, then called ***Asia Minor***. "Saul," Barnabas, and Barnabas' cousin John Mark start out from Antioch in Syria on the mission, but only "Paul" and Barnabas finish it.[4] After arriving on the mainland of Asia Minor (in a region called Pamphylia), Mark goes back home.

Why did he leave them in the middle of their missionary journey? Acts gives us the impression of a lack of commitment on Mark's part (cf. Acts 15:37-38). A colleague of mine who was traveling in this area once expressed sympathy for Mark when he looked north toward the incredibly huge mountains Mark would have seen when he landed in Asia Minor![5] Perhaps Mark was just tired of the woes of travel. Perhaps he and Paul just did not get along.

However, Acts and Galatians give us hints that there was more to it than just Mark's weariness and lack of commitment. The later argument between Paul and Barnabas over Mark probably had a lot to do with the way Paul was relating to Gentiles in his ministry (cf. Gal. 2:13). It is probably no coincidence that Acts begins to call Paul by his Roman name at this point in the story—he increasingly focuses on the Gentiles.   Nor undoubtedly is it a

> **elders:** A group of individuals, probably older men, who oversaw the direction of individual churches.

coincidence that it is shortly after Paul, Barnabas, and John Mark depart from Cyprus—Barnabas' homeland—that Mark leaves them and returns to Jerusalem. What started out as a mission to Jews—perhaps with Mark's cousin Barnabas in charge—had become a mission primarily to Gentiles under the direction of Paul (13:13)!

A number of interesting things happen on this journey in Acts. Paul strikes a sorcerer blind on the island of Cyprus. In the village of Lystra, the villagers not only acclaim Paul and Barnabas as gods—they also end up stoning Paul! Acts gives us a small peek at the way some early churches were organized when it mentions that Paul and Barnabas "appointed **elders**" in each

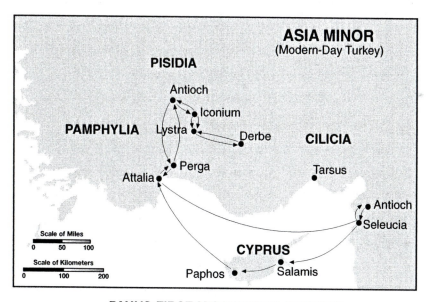

PAUL'S FIRST MISSIONARY JOURNEY
MAP 4

church to oversee them (Acts 14:23). The implication seems to be that a group of individuals, probably older men in each particular congregation, directed these churches.

The "Jerusalem Council" (Acts 15:1-35)

Chapter 35 of this text goes into more detail on the significance of an event often referred to as the "**Jerusalem Council**," which probably took place in about the year A.D. 49. While Acts itself does not call this meeting a "council," this significant meeting looks somewhat like the Christian councils of the 300s and 400s—which decided issues like the Trinity and the nature of Christ. Chapter 35 of this text also discusses the possible contrast between how Paul viewed this meeting and the more official way Acts presents it.

Jerusalem Council: The name often given to the meeting in which it was decided that Gentiles could become Christians without being circumcised.

In Acts, the basic issue under discussion in the Jerusalem Council is whether Gentile men need to be circumcised in order to escape God's judgment. In other words, could they be Christians without having to become Jews first? Some Jewish Christians who were also Pharisees insisted the Gentiles must become Jews first and fully observe the Jewish Law (Acts 15:5). Paul and Peter argue that God accepted them as they were, giving them the Holy Spirit while they were still uncircumcised (15:8, 12). James seems to strike a middle position, one that probably would allow Jewish and Gentile Christians to eat together. His judgment is that the Gentiles can remain uncircumcised, but they are to abstain from four things: meat offered to idols, meat from animals that have been strangled, blood, and sexual immorality (15:20).

Paul's Second (Acts 15:36–18:22) and Third Missionary Journeys (Acts 18:23–21:16)

Paul's second and third missionary journeys in Acts cover roughly the same territory. Both begin in Antioch of Syria (Acts 15:35; 18:23). Both traverse the length of Asia Minor (modern-day Turkey; e.g., 15:41; 18:23). Both involve missions in **Greece** and **Macedonia**, the region just north of Greece (e.g., Acts 16-18; 20:1-5). Both involve a trip to Jerusalem at the end of each journey (18:22; 21:17), although the second journey continues on from Jerusalem back to Antioch (18:22).

These two journeys in Acts also feature some of the same traveling companions Paul had taken on the first. However, before the second journey begins, Paul and Barnabas have an argument about whether Mark is suitable to go with them (Acts 15:36-39), with the result that they each go their separate ways. A man named Silas goes with Paul instead. On their way through Asia Minor, Paul also picks up a young man named Timothy to accompany them. Although his mother is Jewish, his father is not, so Paul circumcises Timothy in keeping with the

The theater at Ephesus mentioned in Acts 19:29.

Jewish Law. Interestingly, another person that seems to accompany Paul during parts of these two trips is the author of Acts himself, traditionally a physician named Luke (cf. Col. 4:14).[6]

The main difference between the two journeys is the location in which

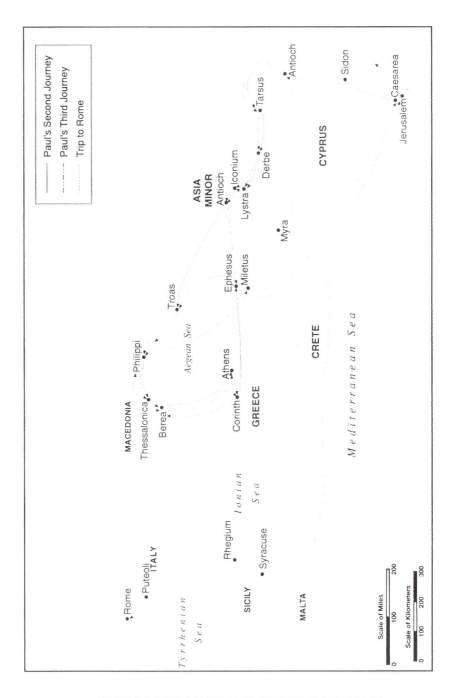

PAUL'S LAST JOURNEYS AND TRIP TO ROME
MAP 5

Paul concentrates his missionary efforts. On his second missionary journey, Acts indicates Paul spends about a year and a half in the city of **Corinth** in Greece (18:11). On his third, he spends about two and a quarter years in the city of **Ephesus** on the east coast of Asia Minor (19:8, 10). Since the ancients rounded their numbers up, we can say that Paul spent two years in Corinth on his seond missionary journey and three years in Ephesus on his third (cf. Acts 20:31).

The second missionary journey (ca. A.D. 50–52) is significant in that Paul leaves the East and crosses over into what is now Europe. After revisiting the churches he and Barnabas had founded on the first missionary journey, he goes northwest across Asia Minor until he comes to Troas, near the site of the famous ancient city of Troy.[7] After Paul has a vision, he crosses into Macedonia, the region just north of Greece. There he follows a famous Roman road called the Egnatian Way, founding churches at the cities of **Philippi, Thessalonica**, and **Berea**. He would later write letters to the first two of these cities.

Acts tells us about a number of interesting events in Philippi, a Roman colony whose official language was Latin.[8] It is in Philippi that we meet Lydia, a wealthy Jewish woman who sells purple, a very expensive dye (Acts 16:13-15). In Philippi Paul and Silas are arrested and put in jail. But their chains fall off in a miraculous earthquake at midnight while they are praying and singing hymns (16:25-26). In the end, the jailer and his whole family become Christians (16:33). At Paul's release, we find out for the first time that he and Silas are Roman citizens—and thus that they have been beaten illegally (16:37). Paul insists that the city officials personally escort them out of jail (16:38-39).

In Thessalonica and Berea, we see a pattern that shows up regularly during Paul's mission in Acts. He founds a church and then is forced to leave town because of Jewish opposition to his message (Acts 17:5-9, 13). After he is forced to leave Berea, Acts tells us he moves south to **Athens** in Greece, leaving Silas and Timothy behind to work further with the church (17:14-15). This famous center of ancient philosophy does not receive Paul's message well, although Acts 17 presents us with a brilliant sermon Paul preaches there in defense of the gospel. Paul moves on again to Corinth, another Roman colony, where he spends a year and a half (18:1).

At Corinth we first meet Priscilla and Aquila, a wife-husband team that plays a prominent role in the spread of Christianity (Acts 18:2). They arrive in Corinth because the emperor Claudius has expelled all Jews from Rome, perhaps over the controversy Christianity is bringing to the Jewish community there. These two individuals appear several times in the pages of the New Testament. For example, they accompany Paul to his next stop, **Ephesus**, on the east coast of Asia Minor (18:18). There a church

"Since the Jews constantly made disturbances at the instigation of Chrestus, he [the Roman emperor Claudius] expelled them from Rome."

Suetonius, *Claudius 25*,
a Roman history

meets in their house (1 Cor. 16:19), and there they convince a man named Apollos that Christians have the correct understanding of the Jewish Scriptures (Acts 18:24-26). This man goes on to work with the church at Corinth (e.g., 1 Cor. 1:12). At some point, Priscilla and Aquila move back to Rome, where another church meets in their house (Rom. 16:3-5).

Acts tells us that Paul becomes acquainted with Priscilla and Aquila because they are tentmakers "just as he was" (Acts 18:3). This fact gives us a peek into one way Paul probably found opportunities to share the good news with new people. While Acts indicates he went to the synagogues to speak with Jews, we can imagine that his tentmaking spot in the marketplace was an important place for him to speak to Gentiles. Whenever he came to a new city, he probably sought out the part of the city where those in the tentmaking trade stayed. Given the likelihood that Paul was a person of some means, he may have "lowered" himself somewhat by actually using his hands to make tents (cf. 1 Cor. 4:12; 2 Cor. 11:7)—of course, he originally might have been the one in charge!

The so-called third missionary journey (ca. A.D. 53-58) covers much of the same ground as the second, but with a different focus. According to Acts, Paul spends more time in the city of Ephesus than he does in any other individual city. From there he writes several letters to Corinth—two of which apparently have not survived to today (1 Cor. 5:9; 2 Cor. 2:3-4)—and perhaps one to Galatia as well. Paul was also imprisoned in Ephesus, although Acts does not tell us about it (1 Cor. 15:32). It is therefore quite possible that he wrote his letters to Philippi and to Philemon while he was under guard.

> "Paul . . . a herald both in the East and West, received the noble glory of his faith. After he had taught the whole world righteousness, come to the limit of the West, and witnessed before the rulers, he left the world and was taken up to the holy place."
>
> **1 Clement 5:6-7, ca. A.D. 96**

Acts does tell us about other events at Ephesus, however. Paul convinces some followers of John the Baptist that Jesus is the Messiah (Acts 19:1-7). Some scholars think that Ephesus may have been home to a community of individuals who believed John's message, but who were not Christians.[9] We hear of incredible miracles that take place in Ephesus; people are healed just by touching handkerchiefs and aprons that had touched Paul (19:11-12). Acts 19:19 implies that Ephesus experienced a sharp decrease in the use of magic, a common practice among the lower classes of the empire. Acts also indicates that the idol-making trade was affected enough for a silversmith named Demetrius to stir up a riot (19:23-41).

Paul's Arrest and Trip to Rome (Acts 21:17–28:31)

The book of Acts takes on a tone of foreboding after Paul leaves Ephesus. As he completes the third missionary journey, we increasingly are made to feel that something bad is about to happen and that Paul's ministry is nearing its end. Paul is determined to get to Jerusalem by the feast of Pentecost (Acts 20:16; cf. Rom. 15:25), so he stays only a day in Troas. He talks so long that night a young man named Eutychus falls out the third-floor window of the room where Paul is speaking. Paul miraculously revives him.

Paul bypasses the city of Ephesus so he will not be delayed. Instead, the elders of Ephesus meet him in Miletus, a city to the south. In his farewell speech, he prophesies that he will never see them again (Acts 20:25). Rather, "the Holy Spirit has told me in city after city that jail and suffering lie ahead" (20:23). When Paul reaches Palestine, a prophet named Agabus binds his own hands and feet with Paul's belt, implying that Paul himself would be imprisoned if he went on to Jerusalem (21:11). So it is no surprise that despite Paul's efforts to please the Jewish Christians in Jerusalem, a riot ensues and the Romans arrest him (21:17-36).

The last chapters of Acts cover the roughly four or five years during which Paul was imprisoned in Palestine, taken to Rome under guard, and put under house arrest in Rome (ca. A.D. 58–63). Roman soldiers rescue Paul from the riot in Jerusalem, and he is kept in the Roman fortress there until after he has appeared before the Sanhedrin (Acts 21:30-33; 22:30–23:11). When informed by Paul's nephew of a plot by the Jews to kill him, the soldiers transport Paul to the coastal city of *Caesarea*, the headquarters of Roman rule over Judea and Samaria at that time.

Paul spends the next two years or so imprisoned there, first under the Roman governor Felix (who governed between A.D. 52-60), who would have released Paul for a bribe, and then for a short time under Festus (A.D. 60-62). Neither these two nor Herod Agrippa II, the son of Herod Agrippa I, find any fault in Paul after hearing him. Because Festus attempts to have Paul transported back to Jerusalem, however, Paul invokes his right as a Roman citizen to appeal to the emperor and is transported to Rome to stand trial.

The trip is not without its perils. The soldiers do not listen to Paul's advice and attempt to continue sailing too late in the year, when the Mediterranean Sea was particularly hazardous to travel. Ships in the ancient world typically wintered at a suitable port. Because they disregard Paul's advice, the ship wrecks, but miraculously all those aboard survive. Ashore, Paul is bitten by a poisonous snake but remains unaffected. The people of the island of Malta think Paul is a god. Three months later, the ship's survivors leave Malta and sail for Rome.

Paul spends two years in Rome, where Acts leaves him in the last chapter (ca. A.D. 61–63). During that time he rents a house where he is able to see any who come to him. Acts ends with a decisive turn away from the Jews and toward the Gentiles (Acts 28:28). Not that Luke thought God had abandoned the Jews, but perhaps he was foreshadowing the Jewish War that would start less than five years later, ending with the destruction of Jerusalem and the temple in A.D. 70.

What happened to Paul next is uncertain. Many scholars suggest that Paul was freed after his first appearance before Nero. This would accommodate information we get from the letters of First and Second Timothy and Titus. In this reconstruction, Paul may not have died in the persecution of A.D. 64, but perhaps as late as A.D. 67. Other scholars note Paul's statement to the Ephesians that he would never see them again (Acts 20:25). Many of these suppose that Acts leads right up to the point of Paul's death.

Things to Think About

1. Why do you think John Mark left Paul and
   Barnabas and returned home?

2. Why do you think Acts ends where it does?

Key Terms

elders

Jerusalem Council

the Way

endnotes

1. We know, for example, that he made a trip to Corinth that Acts does not mention (2 Cor. 12:14), and Paul tells us in Romans 15:19 that he had gone as far as Illyricum, a region in between Greece and Italy. Some suggest that Paul even went to Spain in the years after those the book of Acts covers (cf. Rom. 15:24).

2. Although Galatians 2 does tell us about a period of confrontation and discord. Interestingly, mentioned among the prophets at Antioch are two men named Simeon and Lucius, who may very well have been persons of color.

3. The book of Acts indicates that the early Christians did not call themselves "Christians" or their faith "Christianity." Rather, they called the movement of which they were a part "the Way" (cf. Acts 9:2; 19:9, 23; 22:4; 24:14, 22). It would capture the original flavor of the "Jesus movement," therefore, to refer to the early Christians as "followers of the Way" (e.g., 22:4; 24:14) rather than as "Christians." This term may have come from Isaiah 40:3: "Prepare the way for the LORD" (NIV), the verse used of John the Baptist (e.g., Mark 1:3; cf. John 14:6). Interestingly, this verse seems to have formed an important part of the Essene self-understanding at Qumran as well (cf. "Community Rule" VIII, 14).

4. Colossians 4:10 tells us that Barnabas and Mark were cousins. The prayer meeting for Peter in Acts 12:12 took place in Mark's mother's house. Mark traditionally is known as the author of the Gospel of Mark and is thought to have been a traveling companion of Peter (cf. 1 Pet. 5:13).

5. Professor Keith Drury of Indiana Wesleyan University.

6. In several places Acts shifts from talking about "them"—Paul, Silas, and Timothy—to talking about "us," implying that the author is along with Paul. Generally, the author seems to have joined Paul at Troas on the second missionary

journey (Acts 16:11) and accompanied him as far as Philippi (16:16, 40). The author then rejoins them in Philippi near the end of the third missionary journey (20:4-6) and accompanies Paul all the way to Rome (28:16).

7. Troy had of course been destroyed over a thousand years before Christ. It was probably at this point of Paul's second missionary journey that he founded the church in Galatia. He most likely wrote the letter of Galatians on his third missionary journey, while he was in the area of Ephesus. Others think Galatians was written to the churches Paul and Barnabas founded on his first missionary journey in southern Asia Minor. Thus, he would have written Galatians from Antioch before the Council of Jerusalem. See chapter 45 of this text.

8. While Rome governed the whole Mediterranean world, some special cities were Roman colonies, meaning that they were not under regional control and were granted the same rights as cities located in Italy. As a colony, Philippi would have been a likely city for the descendants of retired Roman troops to inhabit.

9. Some suggest this idea in order to explain why the Gospel of John, which may have originated in the area of Ephesus, downplays the significance of John the Baptist.

CHAPTER 32

The Basic Christian Message

The Resurrection is the central feature of the Christian good news in Acts and the most important element in the gospel.

The Heart of the Gospel

The sermons of Acts are among its most notable features. Acts gives us a consistent picture of the earliest Christian preaching in a number of sermons, mostly given by Peter and Paul as they spread the good news that Jesus had risen from the dead. These sermons provide us with some important insights into the early Christian message or **kerygma**, as it is sometimes called. Not least, they show us what some early Christians believed was necessary to join the Christian movement and thus escape God's coming judgment of the world.

The first sermon in Acts comes in chapter 2 on the day the church was born, the Day of Pentecost. It

At a Glance

- The sermons of Acts provide a consistent picture of the earliest Christian preaching.

- These sermons claim that God is in control of history and that His plan is revealed in the Old Testament.

- Most importantly, this plan involves Jesus of Nazareth, whom God raised from the dead, an event the apostles witnessed.

- God exalted Jesus to His right hand and sent the Holy Spirit as the beginning of a period of renewal.

- The appropriate human response to the message is repentance and baptism, after which one receives the Holy Spirit.

- Miraculous power and unity will follow.

kerygma: The basic Christian message.

provides us with a good summary of what Luke understood the early Christian message to be.[1] For Luke, the heart of the gospel, the good news, was the fact that God had raised Jesus from the dead. If you "repented" and were baptized in water for the forgiveness of your sins, you would receive the Holy Spirit. The fact that God raised Christ was what made this "baptism by the Holy Spirit" possible.

The Day of Pentecost

The Jewish Day of Pentecost was a one-day feast that celebrated the end of the grain harvest with an offering of its "first fruits" to God. It is no coincidence that Acts depicts the birth of the church on this day. It is on this day that the promised Holy Spirit comes and that Christianity gains its first converts. In a very real sense, there were no Christians until then. According to Acts, a person is not fully a "Christian" until s/he has received the Holy Spirit (e.g., Acts 19:1-6).[2] In this sense, even the twelve disciples technically were not Christians until the Day of Pentecost, for none of them received the Spirit until that day.

"A voice came out of the middle of the fire streaming from heaven as the flame became understandable in a dialect familiar to the hearers."
Philo, *Decalogue* 46
(Jewish philosopher, referring to the giving of the Law at Mt. Sinai)

Given the importance of this event, it is no surprise that Peter's sermon on the Day of Pentecost provides us with the clearest expression of the kerygma in Acts. Luke presents the essence of the Christian message via Peter. The violent wind and tongues of fire that Acts describes on that day are similar to what some Jewish writings say happened when God gave the Old Testament Law to Moses at Mt. Sinai. Since many Jews associated the Day of Pentecost with the first covenant God made with Israel, we should probably see the coming of the Spirit at Pentecost as the beginning of a "new covenant," a new way for God to deal with His people.

Peter's sermon has several key elements, all of which resurface in the other speeches of Acts. First of all, these sermons make it clear that all the events taking place are a part of God's plan, foretold by the Old Testament prophets (Acts 3:24). These events are the restoration of Israel and the salvation of the whole earth, accompanied by the judgment of the wicked (3:20-21). God was bringing

> "Do not leave Jerusalem until the Father sends you what he promised . . . John baptized with water, but in just a few days you will be baptized with the Holy Spirit."
>
> **Acts 1:4-5**

these things about by way of Jesus of Nazareth, a man toward whom God showed His approval by empowering Him to do miracles (2:22). Put to death by the ill will of the Jews of Jerusalem, God raised Him from the dead and exalted Him to heaven—an event to which the apostles gave witness (3:15). Jesus now held the royal titles of "Lord," "Christ," "Son of God," and "Savior" (2:36; 5:31; 13:33), and God had sent the Holy Spirit back to earth to begin a new and refreshing period of history (2:32-33). Through repentance, a true turning toward God and away from sin, along with baptism in water, one could receive this Holy Spirit, accompanied by miraculous power (2:38). Acts presents this as the process by which one could escape God's coming judgment.

Peter's sermon in Acts includes all these elements. Peter gives this speech in order to explain the miraculous sign the crowds were seeing on the Day of Pentecost—the fact that unlearned Galilean men like himself were miraculously preaching in languages they had never studied (2:4-12). While the crowd thought they were drunk, Luke makes it clear that these things were happening because the Holy Spirit had come to earth with power.

All a Part of God's Plan

In Acts 2, Peter quotes the prophet Joel to explain to the crowd what has just happened, namely, that God has begun to pour out his Spirit on all people, both men and women (Acts 2:17-18). Throughout Peter's sermon in Acts 2, as well as in the other sermons of Acts, Luke frequently quotes from the Old Testament to show that things like Christ's death and Resurrection were all a part of God's plan for the world. The opponents of Jesus did not win, and Jesus' death was not a sign of defeat. Rather, these were all things God had intended to happen exactly as they did. In Acts 2, Peter especially makes it clear that the prophets had written about the Day of Pentecost centuries earlier (2:17-21, 25-28, 34-35).

> "You followed God's prearranged plan. With the help of lawless Gentiles, you nailed him to the cross and murdered him."
>
> **Acts 2:23**

By Luke's time, the expectation that God would eventually restore Israel and judge its enemies had been around for a long time. As Acts 7 details, this expectation flowed neatly from the Old Testament, which taught that God had chosen Israel as His special people and promised to bless them if they kept the Jewish Law. Many Jews at the time of Christ were expecting a human political leader to come as Messiah and help restore Israel as a free nation. Acts echoes these expectations (e.g., Acts 1:6), even if it gives them a particularly Christian twist.

> "Starting with Samuel, every prophet spoke about what is happening today."
>
> **Acts 3:24**

More important for Acts, however, is its claim that it was God's plan for the Messiah to suffer death and be raised from the dead. No Jew thought of the Messiah in this way prior to Christianity. Emphasizing that Christ's death was a part of God's plan all along and could be found in the Old Testament Scriptures is one of Acts' key concerns.

As chapter 15 of this text shows with regard to the Gospel of Matthew, the early Christians typically read the Old Testament with "spiritual" rather than historical glasses; that is, they looked for deeper meanings in the words than what these words meant in context. The biblical writers were not "wired" to look for the original meaning of a passage. Using ancient methods of interpretation, the early Christians found a number of texts in the Old Testament whose words reminded them of Jesus' suffering, death, and Resurrection.[3]

> "As was Paul's custom, he went to the synagogue service, and for three Sabbaths in a row he interpreted the Scriptures to the people. He was explaining and proving the prophecies about the sufferings of the Messiah and his rising from the dead."
>
> **Acts 17:2-3**

> "[Apollos] refuted all the Jews with powerful arguments in public debate. Using the Scriptures, he explained to them, 'The Messiah you are looking for is Jesus.'"
>
> **Acts 18:28**

Christ, the Way of Salvation

In his further explanation of Pentecost, Peter goes on to discuss Jesus of Nazareth, "a man accredited by God to you by miracles, wonders and signs" (2:22 NIV), yet put to death by wicked men (e.g., 2:23; 3:13; 4:10; 5:28). In what is an extremely familiar statement in Acts, the author notes victoriously that "God raised him from the dead" (2:24 NIV). The apostles serve as witnesses to this event (e.g., 3:15; 4:33; 10:39-41; 13:31). As we saw earlier in explaining the elements of Acts' sermons, Jesus was then exalted to the right hand of God as king and given royal titles like "Lord" and "Christ" (2:36), "Prince" and "Savior" (5:31), and "Son of God" (13:33).

For Luke, Christ's Resurrection signifies the beginning of restoration for Israel and indeed the whole world, as well as the judgment of the wicked. This

"And he [God] ordered us to preach everywhere and to testify that Jesus is ordained of God to be the judge of all—the living and the dead."

Acts 10:42

two-fold purpose of God in history is seen in the quotation from Joel, who prophesied about what would happen in "the last days" (2:17). On the one hand, this quote mentions the coming "Day of the Lord," which the Jews understood to be the judgment of their enemies, as well as Israel's own unfaithful. On the other hand, not everybody would perish, for "anyone who calls on the name of the Lord will be saved" from the coming wrath (2:21).[4]

Christ's Resurrection is the focal point of almost every sermon in Acts. Its sermons state repeatedly, "God raised him [Christ] from the dead" (NIV; e.g., 3:15; 4:2, 10; 5:30; 10:40; 13:30, 33, 37; 17:3, 18, 31; 23:6; 24:15; 26:23). Christ's return from the grave is the first example of what will eventually happen to all the dead (26:23). It is the beginning of the restoration and eventual judgment of the world. After God exalted Christ to heaven, God sent the Holy Spirit back to earth: "Now he [Christ] sits on the throne of highest honor in heaven, at God's right hand. And the Father, as he had promised, gave him the Holy Spirit to pour out upon us, just as you see and hear today" (Acts 2:33). At one point, Acts even calls this Spirit "the Spirit of Jesus" (16:7).

Here is another indication that the Holy Spirit could not have come in this way until Christ's Resurrection. The Spirit is a taste of the refreshing times that are coming. As Hebrews puts it, to receive the Holy Spirit is to taste the "power of the age to come" (Heb. 6:5). Meanwhile, Jesus waits in heaven until the time comes to restore everything (3:21) and to judge the living and the dead (10:42).

Christ thus plays the key role in God's coming restoration and judgment. This restoration does seem to involve the nation of Israel. After Jesus has risen from the dead, the disciples ask Him if He will restore the kingdom to Israel.

While we might think His answer would be, "You do not understand," He basically answers, "Not now" (Acts 1:6-7). In other words, Luke seemed to believe that the actual nation of Israel not only would eventually be restored to God, but would have its land restored as well.[5] Peter tells the Sanhedrin that Christ has been exalted as Prince and Savior "that He might give repentance and forgiveness of sins to Israel" (5:31 NIV). Peter encourages the Jews of Jerusalem to repent so that "wonderful times of refreshment" might come (3:20).

> "This is the promise our twelve tribes are hoping to see fulfilled."
>
> **Acts 26:7 NIV**

However, Acts also indicates that the Jews of that day largely rejected this message. This is reflected in the climax of the book, Acts 28. Paul rebukes the Jews of Rome for rejecting the gospel and says, "I want you to realize that this salvation from God is also available to the Gentiles, and they will accept it" (28:28). Therefore, while God hopes to reclaim Israel in the future, the books of Luke and Acts consider the current period of history to be the "age of the Gentiles" (Luke 21:24).

But no matter what race or culture you belong to, the message of Acts teaches that the only way to be saved from God's judgment is through Jesus. For Gentiles: "God overlooked people's former ignorance about these things, but now He commands everyone everywhere to turn away from idols and turn to Him" (Acts 17:30). For Jews: "Everyone who believes is justified from everything you could not be justified from by the law of Moses" (Acts 13:39 NIV). The bottom line is, "There is salvation in no one else! There is no other name in all of heaven for people to call on to save them" (Acts 4:12).

The Appropriate Response to the Message

After Peter has presented this message of salvation to the crowd on the Day of Pentecost, they realize the incredible seriousness of what he is saying, particularly since they participated in Jesus' crucifixion. They ask him what they need to do. His response sums up for us even today how to become a Christian and escape God's future judgment:

> "Peter replied, 'Each of you must turn from your sins [i.e., repent] and turn to God, and be baptized in the name of Jesus Christ for the forgiveness of your sins. Then you will receive the gift of the Holy Spirit.' "
>
> **Acts 2:38**

The first step in becoming a Christian is thus repentance, what the NLT means when it says to "turn from your sins." Given the nature of ancient personality, repentance was not a private matter of introspective feeling or regret—"feeling sorry," as we might put it. Repentance *was* a matter of attitude, but it was more a matter of choice than of feeling. It was a public admission that you had done wrong, along with a public decision to live differently.

When John the Baptist preached to his Jewish audience that they needed to repent, he meant that they needed to acknowledge their unfaithfulness in keeping God's laws and then make a choice to start keeping them. The members of Peter's audience needed to repent for their involvement in Christ's death (Acts 3:17-19) and then choose to trust in Him. Gentiles needed to repent for their worship of idols (17:29-30), as well as other "typically" Gentile sins like sexual immorality (e.g., 15:20).

Faith is closely related to repentance.[6] If repentance represents a change in orientation and commitment, faith is a positive commitment toward that new direction. On several occasions, Acts implies that faith in Christ is what results in the forgiveness of sins (10:43; 13:39; 16:31; 20:21; 26:18). In the group culture of ancient times, faith was not an individual or private matter. Nor was it simply a question of what one thought. It involved a public commitment to Christianity and its way of life.

The way that you publicly demonstrated your repentance and faith was through baptism. Since repentance and faith in a group culture are public matters rather than private, it was important to have some ritual act to signify repentance and conversion. Baptism, with its symbolic connotation of washing, was just such an appropriate ritual. Jews at the time often baptized themselves in conjunction with various ceremonies for purification.[7] *Mikvaot*, or immersion pools, have been found in a number of places in Palestine, including Masada and Qumran. Those converting to Judaism especially needed to baptize themselves as a part of becoming a clean individual.

John the Baptist's baptism was unique because he did the baptizing *for* others rather than having them do it to themselves. He implied that the baptism he performed signified an especially important change and beginning for the people he baptized—it had to do with escaping

> "The School of Shammai says: 'If a man became a proselyte on the day before Passover, he may immerse himself and consume his Passover in the evening.'"
>
> ***Mishnah Eduyot* 5.2**
> (collection of Jewish oral traditions on how to keep the Law, ca. A.D. 200)

God's wrath on Judgment Day. Christians understood an even greater significance to their baptism. John's baptism symbolized cleansing, but it did not actually cleanse. Christian baptism entailed not only a baptism of one's body, but also a baptism by the Holy Spirit that would follow the baptism in water. It was this spiritual baptism more than anything else that assured one a place in God's kingdom.

While water baptism thus symbolized *outwardly* the washing away or forgiveness of one's sins (2:38), receiving the Holy Spirit did this *inwardly*. When he sees that the Gentiles have received the Spirit, Peter notes that God "made no distinction between us and them, for he purified their hearts by faith" (15:9 NIV). The Holy Spirit becomes the basis for your identity as a Christian—not your race.

359

Throughout Acts, baptism, repentance, and the reception of the Holy Spirit go hand in hand. All three are essential to becoming a Christian. Three incidents emphasize this fact. The first is when believers in Samaria have been baptized, yet have not received the Holy Spirit. This anomaly results in Peter and John going to Samaria so that these believers can receive the Spirit (Acts 8:14-17). The opposite situation holds true for the Gentile Cornelius. In his case, the Gentiles receive the Holy Spirit *before* they have been baptized (10:44). Peter's response is one of amazement: "Can anyone object to their being baptized, now that they have received the Holy Spirit just as we did?" (10:47). We can infer from these two events that both water baptism and receiving the Holy Spirit were essential elements of the conversion process.

"Believe [i.e., have faith] on the Lord Jesus and you will be saved, along with your entire household."

Acts 16:31

As we noted earlier, a final incident related to this occurs when Paul comes upon some Jews who have been baptized by John the Baptist, but not in the name of Christ. Paul requires that they be baptized in the name of Jesus, after which they also receive the Holy Spirit (19:1-7). This incident shows us once again that it was only after Christ rose from the dead that Christian baptism and the coming of the Holy Spirit could take place.

About three thousand individuals respond favorably to the message on the Day of Pentecost and are baptized (Acts 2:41). Such a response frequently follows the proclamation of the Christian message in Acts. "A deep sense of awe came over them all, and the apostles performed many miraculous signs and wonders" (2:43).

Things to Think About

1. Does Christ's Resurrection from the dead hold any significance for your life? If so, what?

2. Do you believe that a time of judgment and restoration is still to come on the earth?

3. Do you think God has a plan for your life?

Key Term

kerygma

endnotes

1. Acts, like Luke, is technically anonymous, but I will refer to the author as "Luke" for convenience.

2. Acts does not use the word Christian in quite this way, but it clearly teaches that you cannot escape God's coming judgment unless you have received the Holy Spirit. For those in the Wesleyan tradition who find these claims to be of concern, see endnote 5 of chapter 30.

3. One example is Acts 2:25-28, which quotes Psalm 16:8-11. In its original context, the statement "you will not abandon me to the grave" (NIV) related to a premature death—not to a resurrection. It meant that God would keep David (or the psalmist) from dying in his current situation, not that once dead he would be raised again.

4. Interestingly, while the Lord to whom this verse refers is Christ, the Lord to whom Joel referred was Yahweh—the personal name of God himself in the Hebrew of the Old Testament. The book of Acts thus refers to the exalted Christ in language the Old Testament uses of God.

5. From the standpoint of Acts, the return of the current nation of Israel to Palestine could not be the fulfillment of the New Testament's expectation here and in Romans 11:26. Luke and Paul connected any expectation they might have had regarding the future of Israel to a turn to Christianity. Modern-day Israel is certainly not Christian (in fact, it is illegal to try to convert Jews to Christianity there). Only a small percentage of modern Israel's citizens are even practicing Jews.

6. Interestingly, it is Paul's sermons in Acts that talk the most about faith. Luke par-

tially reflects the fact that Paul's writings focus overwhelmingly on faith and very little on repentance (see chapter 37 of this text). For Luke, on the other hand, repentance is the more important category.

7. The quote from the relevant text box is from *The Mishnah*, translated by H. Danby (Oxford: Oxford University, 1933). *The Mishnah* is a collection of "rabbinic" sayings made about the year A.D. 200. At least in part, these rabbis were the heirs of the Pharisees of Jesus' time. The quote in question indicates that baptism was enough to permit a proselyte to celebrate the Passover, even though he had not yet had time to be circumcised. The School of Hillel, the other Pharisaic school, believed circumcision was more essential.

CHAPTER 33

Baptism with the Holy Spirit

In Acts, baptism with the Holy Spirit results in two basic things:
purity and power.

What is "Baptism with the Holy Spirit"?

The idea of being baptized "with the Holy Spirit and with fire" (Luke 3:16) is important to a number of different Christian denominations. However, most of these bring different "dictionaries" to the words of Acts and thus predictably vary in their interpretations of what happened on the Day of Pentecost. For most "Pentecostal" groups, the evidence of the Holy Spirit is the gift of speaking in **tongues**, which in their "dictionary" refers to an ecstatic, unknown prayer language

At a Glance

• "Baptism with the Holy Spirit" basically refers to the inner "cleansing" of one's sins that takes place when that person becomes a Christian.

• Along with repentance and baptism, Acts depicts baptism of the Holy Spirit as an essential element in becoming a Christian.

• In Acts, receiving the Spirit results in power, which translates into preaching the gospel boldly, performing miraculous deeds, and maintaining the astounding unity of the early church.

• The demonstration of this power often leads not only to Christianity's expansion, but also to strong opposition by its enemies.

such as that discussed in 1 Corinthians 14. Some groups do not believe you have truly become a Christian until you "speak in tongues." The difficulty with this position is that Acts 2 portrays these "tongues" as human languages that were understood by persons of assorted nationalities rather than as angelic prayer languages (cf. Acts 2:4-11). Further, even when Paul talked about such ecstatic languages, he indicated that only some Christians had such a "gift" (1 Cor. 12:30).

Other groups, particularly in the Methodist tradition, understand "being filled with the Spirit" as what the eighteenth-century reformer John Wesley called "Christian perfection," although Wesley

tongues: Languages. In Acts 2 they are human languages, while 1 Corinthians 14 seems to refer to an angelic language some Christians can speak.

himself did not connect his teaching with the book of Acts. Using this "dictionary," being filled with the Spirit is something that happens apart from becoming a Christian—a *second*, later experience of God that enables you to stop sinning completely and to love one another fully. In this understanding, the disciples were Christians *before* the Day of Pentecost; thus, the Day of Pentecost is not considered to be the birthday of the church, but the time when the disciples received this second experience.

The majority of New Testament scholars do not read Acts in this way. While a person can be "filled" with the Holy Spirit more than once (e.g., Acts 4:31), and while the New Testament does teach that a person can be victorious over sin (e.g., Rom 8:4; 1 John 3:9), receiving the Spirit in Acts—as in Paul's writings—is the most important step in becoming a Christian, not something that happens later on. Acts and the writings of Paul make it clear that a person is not

baptism with the Holy Spirit: The inner cleansing of your heart when your sins are forgiven and you become a Christian. It corresponds to the outer cleansing of baptism in water.

a Christian unless s/he "receives the Holy Spirit" (e.g., Acts 2:38), is "baptized with the Holy Spirit" (e.g., 1:5), or is "filled with the Holy Spirit" (e.g., 2:4), all of which are different ways of saying the same thing in the book of Acts.

So what *does* it mean to be **baptized with the Holy Spirit**? On the one hand, it means that one's sins are forgiven or "cleansed," to use the imagery of baptism. When Peter argues that Gentiles can become Christians without becoming Jews, he defends his position by telling how the Holy Spirit came on a group of Gentiles, even though they had not even been baptized in water. What did this mean? To Peter it meant that God had "cleansed their hearts through faith" (Acts 15:9) and thus forgiven their sins. By sending them the Holy Spirit, in effect, God had made them Christians, even though they were uncircumcised and thus non-Jews.

On the other hand, receiving the Spirit means power. This is the primary manifestation of the Spirit in Acts. Jesus himself predicts this fact when He says to the disciples, "When the Holy Spirit has come upon you, you will receive power" (Acts 1:8). In part, this power demonstrates itself as boldness in proclaiming Christ's Resurrection, the gospel message (e.g., 4:31). At other times it shows itself as the power to perform miracles, such as when Peter and John heal a lame man (3:7; 5:12). And Luke no doubt saw the Spirit as the reason why the early church enjoyed such a high level of unity (4:32).

The Spirit and Becoming a Christian

Because baptism with the Holy Spirit is what really "cleanses" a person of the "stain" of his or her sins, it is clear that it is necessary to have the Spirit in order to be a Christian. Paul confirms this idea when he writes,

> "If anyone is in Christ, he is a new creation; the old has gone, the new has come!"
>
> **2 Corinthians 5:17 NIV**

"Those who do not have the Spirit of Christ living in them are not Christians at all" (Rom. 8:9). In another place Paul writes that the Spirit is God's "seal of ownership . . . a deposit guaranteeing what is to come" (2 Cor. 1:22 NIV;

see also 5:5). Paul uses a word in this verse that is similar to what we call "earnest" money—money that is put down on a house, not only to *guarantee*

that the owner will not sell it to someone else, but also to act as a *down payment* toward the actual purchase of the house. Receiving the Spirit, therefore, doesn't just guarantee us salvation from God's wrath. The Spirit is also a "little taste of heaven" and a "foretaste of glory divine" (Heb. 6:4-5).[1]

> "Repent and be baptized, every one of you, in the name of Jesus Christ for the forgiveness of your sins. And you will receive the Holy Spirit."
>
> **Acts 2:38 NIV**

The ancients thought of spirit as the breath inside a person. According to Genesis 2:7, when God made Adam, he made dust from the earth (=body) come alive by *breathing* into it the breath of life (=spirit). *While the New Testament also speaks of the Holy Spirit in personal terms, we might think of the Holy Spirit as the Breath of God that fills and empowers believers.* Having the Holy Spirit is thus having God inside of us.

> While the New Testament speaks of the Holy Spirit in personal terms, we also might think of the Holy Spirit as the Breath of God that fills and empowers believers.

In Jeremiah 31:33 God says, "This is the new covenant I will make . . . I will put my laws in their minds, and I will write them on their hearts." Paul believed that this verse referred to the Holy Spirit living inside Christians (2 Cor. 3:6; cf. Heb. 8:7-13). Becoming a Christian, therefore, was being "born" of the Spirit (cf. John 3:6), becoming a "new creation" (2 Cor. 5:17). When Christ returns to earth someday, Paul believed our physical bodies would actually become spirit bodies (1 Cor. 15:44, 50-54). Paul apparently believed that we were already in the process of becoming spirit beings, even while we still had flesh and blood (2 Cor. 3:18).

While we should not presume that Luke thought of these things in exactly the same way as Paul, John, or the author of Hebrews, Luke's "dictionary" does seem to be much the same as theirs with regard to the Holy Spirit and the process of becoming a Christian. The story of the early church in Acts depicts receiving the Spirit as an essential element of "conversion."[2] Acts 2:38 gives the process: "Repent and be baptized, every one of you, in the name of Jesus Christ for the forgiveness of your sins. And you will receive the Holy Spirit" (NIV). The first sentence tells us our part—repentance and water baptism; the second is God's response—baptizing us with the Holy Spirit.

> "Our evil consciences have been sprinkled with Christ's blood to make us clean, and our bodies have been washed with pure water."
>
> **Hebrews 10:22,**
> (probably alluding to the two baptisms—in water and in the Spirit)

Two unique events in the story of Acts highlight the importance of both water baptism and Spirit baptism in the process of becoming a Christian. The first takes place in Samaria. On this occasion, a number of individuals have repented, believed, and been baptized in water, but they have not received the Holy Spirit (Acts 8:14-17). Acts treats this situation as a problem—they should have received the Holy Spirit at the time of their baptism. The apostles Peter and John go up to Samaria and lay hands on them so they can receive the Spirit.[3]

The second event occurs when Peter brings the gospel to Cornelius and the company of Gentiles with him. On this occasion, the Holy Spirit comes *before* they are baptized (Acts 10:44-48). The significance of this fact is that it ends the debate about whether Gentiles can become Christians without being circumcised and becoming Jews first—God ends the debate before it even starts (see the later discussion in Acts 15)! These unique situations underline

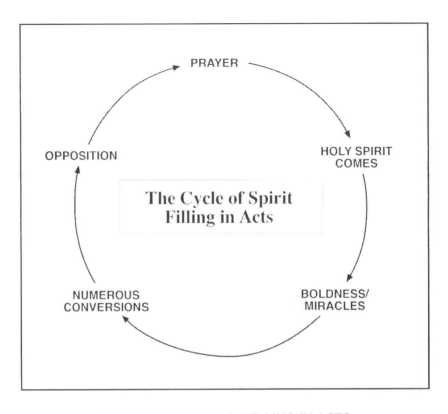

THE CYCLE OF SPIRIT FILLING IN ACTS
Figure 4

the fact that Luke viewed baptism in water and baptism in Spirit as two sides of the same coin; both were essential in the normal process of becoming a Christian. The two baptisms regularly appear side by side throughout Acts (e.g., 2:38; 9:17-18; 19:5-6; cf. Heb. 6:2).

The Spirit and Power

We have mentioned several times the chain of events that typically accompanies the coming of the Holy Spirit in Acts. Sometimes the Holy Spirit comes when Christians are praying about some pressing situation (e.g., Acts

4:31). Sometimes the Holy Spirit comes when an apostle lays hands on a new believer (e.g., 8:17). But no matter what the particular situation, when the Holy Spirit comes, believers receive power. This power reveals itself in various ways, sometimes as boldness, sometimes as the ability to work miracles. Sometimes believers speak in languages they have never learned; always they have unity.

Two further consequences follow in Acts. Some hear and accept the good news—the number of Christians inevitably grows. Others oppose God's work and try to stop the Christians. Both situations often require more power, and so the cycle continues (see **Figure 4**).

Boldness

In Acts, when a person is filled with the Holy Spirit s/he receives boldness. When they receive the Spirit on the Day of Pentecost, the first thing the disciples do is to preach. In fact, the Spirit gives them the power to preach in "tongues," which in Acts 2 seem to be human languages the disciples have never learned (Acts 2:4, 8). Acts 4:8 notes that Peter is "filled with the Holy Spirit" when he speaks to the Sanhedrin. Consequently, "the members of the council were amazed when they saw the boldness of Peter and John, for they could see that they were ordinary men who had had no special training. They also recognized them as men who had been with Jesus" (4:13).

Believers consistently proclaim Christ's Resurrection with boldness when they are filled with the Holy Spirit. Stephen is full of the Holy Spirit as he boldly proclaims the gospel in the Greek-speaking synagogues of Jerusalem (Acts 6:8-10). He faces his death with a similar courage because he is "full of the Holy Spirit" (7:55). A great number of people become Christians under the ministry of Barnabas because he is full of the Holy Spirit (11:23-24). Paul preaches the kingdom of God with boldness wherever he goes, no doubt also through the power of the Holy Spirit (19:8; 28:31).

Miraculous Power

Another manifestation of the Holy Spirit in Acts is the power to work miracles. After Pentecost, Acts tells us that the apostles were enabled to perform miraculous signs (Acts 2:43). The chapter that follows gives one example: the healing of a lame man who had sat for years at one of the gates of the Jerusalem temple. Paul is also full of the Holy Spirit when he strikes a sorcerer named Elymas blind on the island of Cyprus (13:11). In Ephesus, just touching handkerchiefs and aprons that have made contact with Paul brings healing (19:11-12). God sends miraculous signs like these along with boldness to confirm that the message these men proclaim is true (e.g., 14:3).

Unity and Direction

Although Acts does not explicitly connect the Holy Spirit with the unity of the early Christians (e.g., Acts 4:32), it does associate the Spirit with their encouragement (9:31) and joy (13:52). We can connect the dots and conclude that the unparalleled unity the Christians enjoy in Acts comes from the fact that they all share the Holy Spirit. The apostle Paul certainly believed this and said so explicitly in passages like 1 Corinthians 12.

Acts also makes it clear that the Holy Spirit is the main source of the church's direction. Not only does the Spirit make it possible for various individuals to prophesy and predict impending events (e.g., Acts 19:6; 21:11), but the Holy Spirit also tells men like Philip, Paul, and Barnabas where they are to take the gospel. The Holy Spirit directs Philip to preach to the Ethiopian eunuch (8:29). The Spirit directs Paul to start his missionary journeys (13:2), tells him which way to turn in the middle of his mission (e.g., 16:6-7), and leads him to Jerusalem near the end (20:22). Interestingly, the same Spirit even tries to lead to truth those who do not accept Him, although they stubbornly resist Him (e.g., 7:51; cf. John 16:13).

Expansion and Opposition

Both the boldness of the apostles and the miracles God works to confirm their message lead to a rapid and phenomenal growth of the Christian movement. The early chapters of Acts enumerate three thousand who join the Christian movement after the Day of Pentecost (Acts 2:41). This number grows to five thousand (4:4) and then to "more and more" (5:14). As we also noted earlier, a large number of priests believe (6:7), as well as Pharisees (15:5).

The success of the gospel also brings opposition. In Jerusalem, the Sanhedrin interrogates the apostles more than once and has Stephen put to death (e.g., Acts 4:3; 5:18; 6:12, 57-58). Throughout the Mediterranean world, Paul's Jewish opponents consistently stir up trouble for him, once even resulting in his stoning (e.g., 14:19; 17:5, 13; 18:12). At other times, Christians get into trouble because of demons they have cast out (e.g., 16:18-24, in Philippi) or because they are hurting the idol-making business (e.g., 19:23-29, in Ephesus). These times of persecution call for prayer, which inevitably brings the Spirit of God back to fill the apostles with power and boldness (e.g., 4:31). Then the cycle begins all over again!

Things to Think About

1. Do you still need to have the Holy Spirit today in order to be a Christian? If so, what happens when a person is "baptized with the Spirit"?

Key Terms

baptism with the Holy Spirit

tongues

2. Do Christians today still have access to the power of the Holy Spirit, or was this power just something God provided back then?

3. Do growth and opposition indicate that a church has the Spirit today? Unity? Boldness?

endnotes

1. The writer of the hymn "Blessed Assurance" may very well have taken these words of the song from this verse in Hebrews.

2. As we saw earlier, the word conversion is often misleading, for Jewish Christians did not think of themselves as changing religions. They saw Christianity as nothing other than true Judaism.

3. "Laying hands" on a person seems to have been the early Christian ritual used to symbolize receiving the Holy Spirit (cf. Acts 8:17; 9:17; 19:5-6; Heb. 6:2).

CHAPTER 34

Christians and Troublemakers
in Luke-Acts

Acts presents the early church in a way that emphasizes its unity and orderliness.

Best Foot Forward

Christians did not always have a good reputation in the Mediterranean world of the first century A.D. In fact, the Roman historian Tacitus called them "criminals" and Christianity a "deadly superstition."[1] The emperor Nero took advantage of this bad reputation and blamed them for the devastating fire of Rome in A.D. 64. He set Christians on fire and used them to provide light for his gardens. In the 100s, rumors circulated that Christians carried on shameless orgies and ate human flesh. Acts 28:22 illustrates the reputation the author of Acts was up against: "The only thing we know about these Christians is that they are denounced everywhere."

Some have suggested that Luke wrote Acts in part to defend Christianity against such denunciations. At the very least, he presents the early church in a way that emphasizes its unity and orderliness. Other parts of the New Testament, particularly Paul's writings, make it clear that Acts puts the

At a Glance

- Acts tells the story of the first Christians in a way that shows they were not troublemakers, although their opponents often stirred up trouble.

- Luke emphasizes the unity of the early church and downplays conflicts among early Christians.

- Luke depicts the resolution of the conflicts that did occur as an extremely orderly and harmonious process.

- Luke points out the innocence of those Christians who were arrested on various occasions.

373

"Nothing the emperor did—neither gifts to the crowds nor sacrifices to the gods—could overcome the popular belief that he had ordered the fire to be set. To squelch the rumor, he accused a class of people called Christians, who were despised by the people for their crimes, and inflicted the most elaborate tortures on them. Christus, the origin of the name, was crucified by the procurator Pontius Pilate during the reign of Tiberius. Though checked for a time, this deadly superstition erupted again not only in Judea, where the evil originated, but even in Rome, where everything hideous and shameful flows together and is relished. First those who pleaded guilty were arrested. Then, on their testimony, a huge crowd of people was convicted, not so much of arson as of hatred of humanity. Disgrace was heaped on their deaths. Covered in the pelts of wild animals, they were torn by dogs, or were crucified, or were set on fire as torches when the daylight had faded . . . However people began to feel sympathy for them, even though they were criminals deserving extreme punishment as an example. It seemed they were being destroyed not for the public good but to satisfy one man's cruelty."

Tacitus, ***Annals*** **15.44**
Roman historian

church's "best foot forward" with regard to the peacefulness and law-abiding nature of the early Christians. Some have even suggested that Acts was written to defend Paul when he came to trial before Nero in Rome, although this suggestion is unlikely.[2] For whatever reason it was written, the picture of the church in Acts is a good model for Christians today, illustrating how to get along and how to resolve conflicts in a peaceful way.

The Unity and Orderliness of the Church

The picture of the church in the earliest chapters of Acts is of a group of people who were extremely harmonious and unified. The basis for this unity was, of course, the fact that they were all full of the Holy Spirit. Acts presents us with an ideal church that prayed constantly, obeyed God's direction consistently, and shared its possessions. We often hear the word **koinonia** used to describe how Christians should get along with one another.

We know from hints in Acts itself and from other writings in the New Testament that the church was not always as unified as portrayed in the first chapters of Acts. Perhaps we should think of Acts as showing us what the church *ought to have been* more than what it often was. Like a person interviewing for a job, Luke puts the church's best foot forward, casting controversies in the best light possible and omitting some of the less flattering incidents.

> "All the believers were of one heart and mind, and they felt that what they owned was not their own; they shared everything they had. And the apostles gave powerful witness to the resurrection of the Lord Jesus, and God's great favor was upon them all. There was no poverty among them, because people who owned land or houses sold them and brought the money to the apostles to give to others in need."
>
> **Acts 4:32-35**

> **koinonia:** The Greek word for "fellowship," often used to indicate how Christians should get along with one another.

The Controversy over the Widows

Acts 6 tells us of one event in the life of the early church that probably involved more disunity and disorder than is revealed. This incident involved those who were distributing food to the church's widows; some complained that the Greek-speaking widows were being neglected. Acts tells us only about the problem of food distribution, and it presents the resolution to the problem by way of a very orderly "town meeting," in which a committee of seven is appointed. Many churches today have "deacons" whose roles are modeled on this "committee of non-ministers" chosen to administrate the everyday aspects of church life.

If we dig a little deeper, we see that these seven individuals did not perform roles anything like modern-day deacons. First, the names of these seven are all Greek—one is not even a Jew by birth (Acts 6:5). Thus, it is highly doubtful that they served the *whole* church, as if they had been chosen strictly for an administrative role. It is more likely that they worked only with the aggrieved part of the church, namely the Greek-speaking Christians, a part of the church to which the apostles were not ministering effectively. In other words, this event reinforced social boundaries instead of bringing the church closer together.

Second, we never see a single one of these individuals administrating the mundane aspects of the church's business. Instead, we see them preaching the gospel to Greek-speaking audiences and others who were not being reached by the other apostles (Acts 6:9; 8:5, 27). Philip, one of the seven, was not a "lay person" or non-minister. He was a prophet whose only role in the book of Acts is that of a preacher (e.g., 8:5-40; 21:8-9). Acts 21:8 calls him an "evangelist," a word sometimes used today for individuals who travel to numerous locations to preach.

> "Paul and Barnabas were sent to Jerusalem . . . to talk to the apostles and elders about this question . . . [They] were welcomed by the whole church, including the apostles and elders. They reported on what God had been doing through their ministry."
>
> **Acts 15:2, 4**

> "I went there because God revealed to me that I should go. While I was there I talked privately with the leaders of the church."
>
> **Galatians 2:2**

Thus, this controversy involved far more than administration. It involved a major segment of the Christian population to whom the apostles were not adequately ministering. In keeping with the overall purposes of Acts, Luke shows us that these seven men were under the authority of the Jerusalem church. In practice, however, they probably functioned more like "free agents" who went where they believed the Spirit was leading them.[3] While we are not certain about Acts' intended audience, a Roman audience might not have found such prophetic individuals attractive. It would be understandable, then, for Luke to present them in the most orderly way possible.

The Controversy over Circumcision

We see Acts' tendency to present Christian conflict in a harmonious light even more clearly in what is often called the "Jerusalem Council" of Acts 15.[4] Most scholars view Galatians 2:1-10 as Paul's version of this same event, although the differences between the two presentations are significant enough for some to question whether they describe the same event. These differences are interesting because each author's version fits so well with the particular points he is trying to get across.

For example, Paul's letter emphasizes to the Galatians that his authority derives from God, not from Peter or the Jerusalem church. Understandably, he downplays the significance of his private meeting with Peter and James about whether non-Jewish Christians need to be circumcised. He calls into question the special status of Peter, James, and John, arguing that God does not show favoritism (Gal. 2:6, 9). He emphasizes that he went to Jerusalem not because he was called but because God told him to go (2:2). James and Peter in no way contribute to his message (2:6). Paul calls those who oppose him "false brothers" (2:4 NIV), "so-called Christians" (NLT).

On the other hand, Luke gives us a picture that fits well with his special concerns. Acts 15 refers to Paul's opponents as *believers* who belong to the party of the Pharisees (15:5), not false Christians. As described in Acts 15, the church at Antioch in the north *appoints* Paul and sends him with Barnabas to Jerusalem as official representatives of the Antioch church (15:2-3). Once in Jerusalem, the apostles and elders meet *publicly* (15:6). By turn individuals present their cases for discussion while the others remain silent (15:7-12). Finally, James, apparently the leader of the church by this time, makes a final decision (15:13). This account gives us a different perspective than Paul's version; Paul speaks only of a *private* meeting in which Peter and James merely confirm what he already thinks and practices.

If this is the same event as Galatians 2, it is clear that Acts presents it in a much more official and orderly matter than Paul does. Everything is done by way of a chain of command with everyone respectfully going through the proper channels. A Roman official would probably have found this portrait of the church highly appealing. It would imply that far from being rabble-rousers who were always stirring up crowds, Christians were unified, peace-loving individuals whose reputation for troublemaking was undeserved.

The Argument at Antioch

One glaring omission in Acts' presentation of the early church is the argument between Peter and Paul at Antioch, related by Paul in Galatians 2:11-14. As chapter 46 of this text argues later, this event may have taken place after the Jerusalem Council. The church had already decided that Gentiles could escape God's wrath without being circumcised. What was at stake at Antioch was something different: whether Jewish and Gentile Christians could eat together. Because of Jewish purity laws, eating with a Gentile would typically make a Jew ceremonially unclean for one reason or another.[5]

What may be surprising to some is to realize that both Peter and Barnabas side against Paul in the argument. Peter and Barnabas had stopped eating with Gentile Christians so they would not become unclean. Paul then publicly confrontes Peter and calls him a hypocrite. Interestingly, Paul does not tell us in Galatians that Peter admitted he was wrong—something Paul almost certainly would have done given the nature of what he was arguing in that letter. The implication is that for at least a short time Paul was "on the outs" to some degree with the Jerusalem church, and that they did not fully approve of the way he related to Gentile Christians.[6]

Therefore, it is surely no coincidence that Acts fails to record this event. Since Luke wanted to show that the gospel was for everyone and that Jesus was a "light for the Gentiles," it would have been counterproductive to go into detail about events where church leadership was moving in the wrong direction.[7] Luke also wanted to counteract the reputation Paul had as someone who taught "the Jews living in the Gentile world to turn their backs on the laws of Moses"; that is, that they need not circumcise their children or follow other Jewish practices (Acts 21:21).[8] Recounting this event would have worked against both purposes.

One way Acts demonstrates the unity of the early church is by showing continuity and similarity between the ministries of Peter and Paul. Like Jesus, both Peter and Paul heal crippled men (Luke 5:25; Acts 3:7; 14:10). Like Jesus, both Peter and Paul raise someone from the dead (Luke 7:15; Acts 9:40; 20:12). Peter, far from opposing a mission to the Gentiles, is the one by whom the gospel first comes to them (Acts 10). Paul, far from opposing the traditions of Judaism, always starts in the synagogues of a new city (e.g., 17:2); his message to Jews includes keeping the Jewish Law as a part of being acceptable to God

> "Their disagreement over this was so sharp that they separated. Barnabas took John Mark with him and sailed for Cyprus. Paul chose Silas, and the believers sent them off, entrusting them to the Lord's grace."
>
> **Acts 15:39-40**

(13:39).[9] Acts 21:24 even implies that Paul himself keeps the Jewish Law. In short, Acts gives us a somewhat "Gentile-friendly" picture of Peter and "Jew-friendly" picture of Paul, more than you might have concluded if you had actually known and heard them.

While Acts does not tell us about this argument between Peter and Paul, it *does* tell us about an argument between Paul and Barnabas at about the same time. But Acts only tells us that they argue over whether Barnabas' cousin, Mark, should travel with them (Acts 15:36-41). The disagreement results in Paul and Barnabas going their separate ways on the next missionary journey. The two arguments seem too close in both time and result to be two unrelated events. Acts thus tells us the side of the event that best shows the unity and order of the church.

The Innocence of Accused Christians

Another way Acts demonstrates most clearly that Christians are not troublemakers is its portrayal of the interaction between Christians and those in authority. In the book of Acts, as in the Gospel of Luke, those accused are never legitimately found guilty of any charge brought against them. Rather, those who oppose Christianity are the ones to consistently stir up trouble.

Acts details a number of situations in which Christians are wrongly punished, just as Luke strongly emphasizes the innocence of Jesus (Luke 23:4, 14-15, 22, 47). For example, the Sanhedrin brings false witnesses against Stephen (Acts 6:13), despite the fact that the godly Gamaliel had told them not to interfere with the Christians (5:34-39). The godliness of Stephen's death would only have confirmed his innocence in the mind of a first-century listener (7:59-60).[10]

When the Sanhedrin condemns Peter and John for their disobedience, Peter echoes the words of Socrates when he was on trial: "Do you think God wants us to obey you rather than Him?" (Acts 4:19).[11] Such an echo is probably not coincidental. Luke wanted his audience to know that the apostles were following a higher law, even though in this case they were disobeying the authorities. To the audience of Acts, Socrates was probably an impeccable example to follow.

Herod Agrippa I has James, the brother of John, put to death. He tries to put Peter to death, as well, but Acts makes it clear that he does so only because it will make him popular with Christianity's opponents (Acts 12:3). God's miraculous deliverance of Peter proves his innocence. In Acts 16:22-23, Paul is illegally beaten because of greed—a mistake so great on the officials' part that they have to come in person to escort him from the city (16:37-39).

Roman officials consistently find Paul innocent of the charges against him or dismiss them as irrelevant matters of Jewish Law. In Corinth, Gallio becomes irritated with Paul's Jewish opponents for troubling him with scruples that have nothing to do with Roman law (Acts 18:14-16). The magistrate in Ephesus similarly indicts the crowd for rioting, telling them that if they really had some legal complaint, they could press charges. He disbands the mob. Even though Paul is imprisoned for two years in Palestine, none of the Roman officials who hear his case find him guilty of anything. The governor Festus, like Gallio, says that it is a matter of Jewish religion, not Roman law (25:19, 25). Herod Agrippa II thinks it a pity that Paul has appealed to Caesar, since he obviously has done nothing illegal (26:31-32).

Acts consistently points to the trouble that follows Paul as coming from Jewish opponents to Christianity. Starting in Damascus after Paul first comes to Christ, the Jews seek to take his life (Acts 9:23, 29). They are behind his stoning in Lystra (14:19). Their jealousy leads to a riot and his expulsion from Thessalonica (17:5, 10). They follow him to Berea (17:13). [And everywhere that Paul went, the Jews were sure to go.]

In every case, the source of the "trouble all over the world" (Acts 17:6 NIV) is not truly Paul, but his Jewish opponents.[12] Of course, we know from Paul's own writings that he did occasionally face opposition from Gentile officials as well. For example, Paul tells us it was the *governor of Damascus* who was after him there (2 Cor. 11:32-33), a fact that Acts does not mention. Perhaps Luke omits mentioning the governor's opposition because he wants to emphasize that Christians are godly, peaceful, and unified individuals.

It is probably no coincidence that Acts ends as it does. If it was written after A.D. 70, as is likely, the author already knew that Paul had died at the hands of Nero. However, ending the book with Paul's death would not have fit very well with Luke's desire to emphasize the general innocence of the early Christians.[13] Besides, the original audiences of Acts would already have known what happened to Paul. Since Acts started with Jesus' prediction that the gospel would reach the ends of the earth (Acts 1:8)—i.e., Rome, for all intents and purposes—it was appropriate to end the book with Paul's arrival in Rome.

Things to Think About

1. This chapter argues that Acts gives only one side of the history of the early church. Does the author make his case? Do you agree with his conclusion? How would you feel if another history of the early church were found, one that depicts much more controversy and division than Acts does?

Key Term
koinonia

2. With this fact in mind, to what extent should we try to pattern ourselves after the portrait of the early church in Acts?

3. Should we aim at becoming just like the early Christians, or does God have a unique plan for each generation?

endnotes

1. *Annals* 15.44.

2. It is unlikely that Acts was written as a way to defend Paul before Nero because of the likelihood that Luke-Acts was written after A.D. 70, several years after Paul's death. See chapters 19 and 29 of this text.

3. Luke shows us the subordination of these seven to the twelve apostles with two examples. First, in the commissioning ceremony, the apostles lay hands on the seven men (Acts 6:6)—a clear statement of subordination. Second, Peter and John must "help" Philip's ministry because he has been unable to convey the Holy Spirit to the Samaritans (8:14-17). Certainly, most of those who became Christians did not have the luxury of an apostle to lay hands on them, so it makes sense to think Luke included this incident to make clear that the progression of the church took place along very orderly lines. Luke did not want to give the impression of disorder, which typified some congregations and false prophets (e.g., Matt. 7:15-23; 1 Cor. 14:26, 29-33; 1 John 4:1-3; see also the early Christian writing, *The Didache*, which speaks of traveling prophets as late as A.D.100).

4. See chapter 31 of this text.

5. For example, Gentiles might eat meat that had not been drained of its blood or meat that had been sacrificed to an idol. It was generally assumed that Gentiles were sexually immoral. In short, a Gentile might do any number of things that would "contaminate" the eating event, since uncleanness was "contagious."

6. In this light it is also significant that Paul did not mention the "Jerusalem Council" to the Corinthians when he was discussing the issue of meat offered to idols (1 Corinthians 8–10). Yet this is one issue that Acts 15 explicitly deals with, presumably so that Jewish and Gentile Christians could eat together (Acts 15:20, 29). Perhaps Acts 15 has summarized to some degree the long process of figuring out how Jews and Gentiles were to get along in the church.

7. Perhaps for the same reason, Acts emphasizes that Peter was the one who initiated the mission to the Gentiles (Acts 15:7-10). Ironically, Acts almost ascribes to Peter the role for which Paul himself was so proud: apostle to the Gentiles (Gal. 2:7-8).

8. Accordingly, Acts makes sure to tell us that Paul had Timothy circumcised (Acts 16:3) and shows Paul joining in the purification rites of four men at the temple (21:23-26). Like James in Acts 21, Luke wants us to know that Paul himself was living in obedience to the Law and that rumors to the contrary were false (21:24).

9. Acts 13:39 says that "by this Jesus everyone who believes is set free from all those sins from which you could not be freed by the law of Moses" (NRSV). In one interpretation, this verse implies that the law of Moses could free you from some sins, just not all sins.

10. Luke portrays Stephen's trial and death in such a way as to echo Jesus' death, a fact that also underscores Stephen's innocence.

11. See Plato's *Apology* 29D: "I will obey god rather than you."

12. We should not think of Luke as anti-Jewish. After all, in some ways he was more conservative than Paul in detailing how closely a Christian needed to keep the Jewish Law. He also placed special emphasis on Jerusalem and the temple, and he seemed to indicate that eventually the nation of Israel would be restored. However, he did believe that the current period of history was oriented around the Gentiles. If Acts was written after Jerusalem was destroyed, surely the Jews' rejection of the Christian message (e.g., Acts 28) was an implicit explanation for God's judgment and a call for Jews to turn back to Christ.

13. Not that the Romans thought of Nero as a particularly impartial judge, as the earlier quote from Tacitus illustrates.

CHAPTER 35

Did the Early Church Have Denominations?

While the early church did not have politically organized denominations like today's church, it did have distinct groups that sharply disagreed with one another.

Differences in Belief

A "denomination" is a religious group with a common name and organizational structure, usually with its own set of particular beliefs and practices. Examples of denominations today include names like the United Methodist Church, the Presbyterian Church P.C.A., the Southern Baptist Church, and countless others. Of course, no denominations of this sort existed in the early church. The earliest Christians did not have such well-developed, "politically organized" groups with official statements of faith and common practices. The early church was much more like a loosely connected movement than a political body with distinct boundaries.

At a Glance

- Acts does not tell us much about the diversity of the early church.

- Judaizers believed all Christians should continue to keep the Jewish Law in its entirety.

- Antinomians believed the Law was not binding on any Christian.

- Some Hellenistic Jewish Christians (Greek speakers) saw a greater need for breaking with the Law than other Jewish Christians did.

- Paul believed that keeping the Law would not save anyone, but he continued to observe most of the Law, insisting that its essence remained valid.

- Although James agreed that Gentiles could become Christians, he did not think Jews should eat with them, unless the Gentiles kept certain dietary aspects of the Jewish Law.

On the other hand, distinct groups in the early church did disagree sharply with one another. Because Acts emphasizes the unity of the early church, it can give the impression that the early Christians rarely disagreed with one another and that when they did, they reached unanimity with minimal effort. Acts gives us a picture of the ideal church, one that has little division of any significant kind. Some Christians look at the book of Acts and long for today's church to be what the church seemed to be then, a church in which "all the believers were of one heart and mind" (Acts 4:32). Many think the church has only gone downhill since the time of Acts.

Four Positions in the Early Church

1. **Judaizers:** Gentiles must become Jews and follow the Law of Moses.
2. **James:** Gentiles do not need to become Jews, but should observe a core of prohibitions.
3. **Paul:** If Gentiles become Jews, they have rejected Christ.
4. **Antinomians:** "I am allowed to do anything."

The text box above is just a small indication of the diversity among the early Christians, although it is no doubt quite an oversimplification.[1] On one side, the most "conservative" Christians believed that Gentiles could not escape God's wrath unless they became circumcised and followed the Jewish Law. We might call them the "**Judaizers**." On the other end of the spectrum, some Christians did not seem to think that any part of the Law was still in force for them, including its teaching on what was sexually appropriate. We might call them "**Antinomians**" because they were "anti-Law" (*nomos* is Greek for law).

The mainstream church seems to have functioned somewhere between these two positions. James, the brother of Jesus and leader of the Jerusalem church, believed an uncircumcised Gentile could be saved. Paul believed that the sexual prohibitions of Leviticus 18 were still binding on a Christian. These leaders of the church thus avoided the extremes of some other early Christian groups.

However, James and Peter were stricter in their adherence to the Jewish Law than Paul. For example, while he believed Gentiles could become Christians, James would not eat with Gentiles unless they followed certain dietary guidelines. Paul

> "Then some of the believers who belonged to the party of the Pharisees stood up and said, 'The Gentiles must be circumcised and required to obey the law of Moses.' "
>
> **Acts 15:5 NIV**

believed such behavior was hypocrisy. The remainder of this chapter spells out how these differences in belief played themselves out in the conflicts of the early church.

The Judaizers

It may surprise you to learn that some early Jewish Christians saw no contradiction between Christianity and Pharisaism. Acts 15:5 implies that some Christians remained Pharisees, even after accepting that Jesus was the Messiah and that God had raised Him from the dead. After all, Christians believed in resurrection; Pharisees also believed in resurrection (cf. Acts 23:6-10, *where Paul calls himself a Pharisee in the present tense*!). As we will see, the overwhelming majority of Jewish Christians in Jerusalem believed that the Jewish Law was still valid, and they continued to meet and worship in the Jerusalem temple (e.g., Acts 21:17-26). In the dispute of Acts 15, these believers argue strongly that Gentile converts needed to be circumcised, after which they would have to observe the Jewish Law. Because they insist that Gentile converts become Jews, we can call this group the "Judaizers." While Acts disagrees with their position, it treats them as legitimate Christians.

Acts 15 might give you the impression that the "Jerusalem Council" in A.D. 49 settled this issue once and for all. As we saw earlier, this council ruled that salvation was available to Gentiles by faith, but that they should abstain from: (1) meat offered to idols, (2) meat from strangled animals, (3) blood, and (4) sexual immorality (Acts 15:20). You might think that Christians everywhere immediately adopted the "official" position of James and Peter. While Acts 21:20 implies that thousands of Jewish Christians in Jerusalem were militant in keeping the Jewish Law, surely they all agreed with James that Gentiles could still escape God's judgment without circumcision.

> "It is actually reported that there is sexual immorality among you, and of a kind that is not found even among pagans; for a man is living with his father's wife. And you are arrogant! Should you not rather have mourned, so that he who has done this would have been removed from among you?"
>
> **1 Corinthians 5:1-2 NRSV**

Unfortunately, many among these thousands probably did *not* agree with James and Peter. We should refrain from thinking that Paul's opponents in places like Galatia were *non-Christian* Jews who opposed Christianity. Rather, Paul's principal opposition came from Jewish *Christians* who opposed the way he conducted his mission to the Gentiles.

Paul calls them "false brothers" (Gal. 2:4 NIV) who had sneaked into the Christian movement to spy on its freedom. In Philippians 3:2 he calls them "dogs"—ironically, the very term Jews sometimes used for Gentiles because they were uncircumcised. Paul implies that these Judaizers, whom he calls "mutilators of the flesh" (NIV) because they insist that Gentile converts be circumcised, are truly the ones who are uncircumcised as far as God is concerned. Paul leaves no doubt about what he thinks of them: "I only wish that those troublemakers who want to mutilate you by circumcision would mutilate themselves" (Gal. 5:12).

It might also surprise you to know that Judaizers in one form or another managed to convince a good number of Gentile Christians to observe the Jewish Law. For example, Paul's letter to the Galatians was written to *Gentile* converts *who had been convinced that they needed to become circumcised* (cf. Gal. 1:6-7; 6:12). Similarly, Colossians was written to Gentiles who were under pressure to keep Jewish dietary laws and to observe Jewish festivals (Col. 2:16-23). Many in the audience of Hebrews also may have been Gentiles, yet they were tempted in some way to rely on Old Testament sacrifices for their peace with God (cf. Heb. 7:12; 13:9). In the second century, some from this stream of Jewish Christianity may very well have become a group known as the **Ebionites**, Jewish Christians who did not believe that Jesus was divine.

Antinomians

Acts understandably does not directly mention any Christians who had stopped keeping the Jewish Law altogether. Part of Acts' "best foot forward" approach even highlights Paul's keeping of the Jewish Law (e.g., Acts 21:24), so it would have worked against its interests to go into detail about Christians who had completely abandoned the Law. Yet the text box verses from 1 Corinthians 5 clearly indicate that some Christians were actually proud of the fact that they were no longer under the Jewish Law.

First Corinthians 6:12 and 10:23 repeat one of their slogans: "I am allowed to do anything." These Christians had perhaps interpreted Paul's claim that "you are not under

Ebionites: Jewish Christians of the second century who continued to observe the Jewish Law, but did not view Jesus as divine.

Docetism: A form of Gnosticism that believed Jesus only had seemed to be human when He was on earth. He was really a spirit being.

Cynics: They believed that the rules of society had no basis in reality and that one should live life without worrying about possessions or human rules. Some scholars have dubiously suggested that Cynic thought influenced Jesus' teaching.

law, but under grace" (Rom. 6:14 NIV; cf. 1 Cor. 9:20) to mean that Christianity had no moral boundaries at all. Their position reminds us a little of ancient Cynic philosophy, which taught that the rules of society were artificial and man-made. The founders of this philosophy were called "**Cynics**" because they acted like dogs in public (*cynic* means "dog" in Greek), doing things civilized society only did in private. Some of the Corinthians in Corinth were also proud of their freedom from the "earthly" laws of Moses; they were actually proud of a man who lived in blatant violation of Leviticus 18:8 by having sexual relations with his stepmother (1 Cor. 5:1-2).

Some Christians of this stripe became the Gnostics of the second century. This group saw a strong break between things earthly and things heavenly. Accordingly, some thought that what you did with your body was irrelevant to what you did with your spirit. Your spirit could know God no matter what your body did. Others in this group found it increasingly hard to believe that Jesus had actually become human because His soul would then have become tainted with human flesh. Some who said that Jesus only *seemed* to become human were called **Docetists** (from the Greek word "to seem"). First John 2:19 may allude to such a group of Christians who split off from John's church.[2]

While Acts does not tell us about any "hard core" Antinomian Christians, it does tell us about a group of Jewish Christians who perhaps went a little further than Paul in their break with the Jewish Law. We might call this group the "Hellenists" (e.g., Acts 6:1, 9, 13). This group consisted of certain Greek-speaking Jewish Christians like Stephen who saw much less of a role for the temple and the Law in Christianity than the leaders of the church did. It is this group that may have believed what Paul himself was falsely accused of teaching; namely, for "all the Jews who live among the Gentiles to turn away from Moses, telling them not to circumcise their children or live according to our customs" (21:21 NIV).

Hellenistic Jews in general were not necessarily any less committed to

Jewish ideals than Aramaic-speaking Jews. Both were circumcised, both had a general reverence for the temple, and both kept basic dietary laws. On the other hand, pound for pound we would not be surprised if Hellenistic Jews as a whole were looser in keeping the Jewish Law than the Aramaic-speaking Jews of Jerusalem. We should also not be surprised if some Aramaic-speaking Jews in Jerusalem looked down on Greek speakers as religiously inferior. It is thus understandable why Paul speaks Aramaic to the crowd in Jerusalem in Acts 21:40–22:2. Only then does the crowd stop rioting and listen to him.

Acts hints that some Greek-speaking Jewish Christians were also looser in keeping the Law than other Jewish Christians were. For example, it is interesting that while the Christians scatter in the persecution after Stephen's death (Acts 8:1)—Paul travels an incredibly long way to arrest Christians in Damascus (9:2)—*the twelve foundational apostles were able to remain unharmed and untouched in Jerusalem.* When Peter is actually the target of persecution in Acts 12, he does not even take the time to tell James he has escaped prison—he leaves the city immediately (12:17). The clear implication is that the apostles were not actually the targets of Paul's persecution. Rather, his targets were the more radical Greek-speaking Jewish Christians like Stephen and Philip.

So how did Christians like Peter and James manage to remain active in ministry in Jerusalem while the Hellenists did not? The best answer is that the message and activities of the Hellenists were just a little more controversial than those of the apostles. In particular, their remarks about the temple seem to have been more revolutionary.

The charges brought against Stephen were not that different from those brought against Jesus—"This man is always speaking against the Temple and against the law of Moses. We have heard him say that this Jesus of Nazareth will destroy the Temple and change the customs Moses handed down to us" (Acts 6:13-14). The false accusers may have been wrong on some details and on the spirit of Stephen's preaching, but Stephen probably agreed with their basic claims. He probably *did* believe that Jesus would return to destroy the temple. He may even have thought that Solomon made a mistake to build it in the first place (Acts 7:47-48)! It is interesting that the Sanhedrin felt it had enough authority to have Stephen put to death, whereas they sought out the Romans for Jesus' death. Some have suggested that the only basis on which the Sanhedrin had such authority was if an individual made seditious comments about the temple.

Various writings in the New Testament seem to underscore similarly strong positions against keeping the Jewish Law. For example, Ephesians says that God "ended the whole system of Jewish law" for both Jews and Gentiles (Eph. 2:15). Colossians even associates the Law with evil spiritual powers (Col. 2:15). These comments are not only more radical than what we see Paul doing in Acts (cf. Acts 21:24), but they seem even more radical than some of Paul's own writings (e.g., Rom. 4:31; cf. 1 Tim. 1:8). As chapters 46 and 47 of this text discuss, the actual wording of Ephesians and Colossians may come more from Paul's "cowriters" than from Paul himself.[3] Certainly the author of Matthew would not have talked about the Law in this way (cf. Matt. 5:17-19).

We can probably consider the author of Hebrews as a Hellenist of this sort as well. He wrote to a group of Christians who were tempted to continue to rely on the Jewish sacrificial system in some way, much as Acts 21 pictures the Jerusalem church continuing to use the temple. Scholars have long pointed out the strong similarities between Stephen's speech in Acts 7 and the argument Hebrews makes.[4] Acts thus gives us hints about a group of early Christians who were somewhat more "liberal" in their attitude toward the Jewish Law than the original apostles or even Paul. The mainstream church would eventually absorb their view, which is the one most Christians today basically have toward the Jewish Law.

The Teaching of James and Peter

We can easily distinguish the views of James and Peter from those of Judaizers, Hellenists, and Antinomians. On the one hand, James and Peter clearly were more open to Gentiles than the "Judaizers," although the New Testament gives us the impression that James and even Peter ministered almost exclusively to Jewish Christians (e.g., Gal. 2:7). Hellenistic Jewish Christians took the gospel primarily to Gentiles (cf. Acts 11:20).

Yet James believed that Gentile Christians would escape God's wrath on Judgment Day, even if they remained uncircumcised. When Paul took an uncircumcised convert named Titus to Jerusalem, neither James nor Peter thought he needed to be circumcised (Gal. 2:3). We also know that at least on some occasions Peter even ate with Gentile Christians (Gal. 2:12). While the Christianity of James and Peter was very Jewish in flavor, it was easily distinguishable from that of the Judaizers. It is no surprise to find James mediating between Paul's Christianity and Jerusalem's Christianity in Acts 21.

On the other hand, it is highly doubtful that James would have said that God had "ended the whole system of Jewish law" (Eph. 2:15). Rather, we can see James affirming Matthew 5:17-19: "I did not come to abolish the law of Moses or the writings of the prophets. . . if you break the smallest commandment and teach others to do the same, you will be the least in the Kingdom of Heaven." In this respect, James would have differed dramatically with the Hellenists we have mentioned.

Indeed, it is interesting that the Gospel of Matthew is missing one of Mark's conclusions about a disagreement between Jesus and the Pharisees over the Law. Mark interpreted Jesus' position to mean that "every kind of food is acceptable" (Mark 7:19). Matthew, on the other hand, even though he was probably copying Mark at this point, did not repeat this comment (Matt. 15:10-11). The best way to process these details is to conclude that James—and Matthew—saw an important distinction between how Jewish and Gentile

> James: "Then everyone will know that the rumors are all false and that you
> [Paul] yourself observe the Jewish laws. As for the Gentile Christians, all we
> ask of them is what we already told them in a letter: They should not eat
> food offered to idols, nor consume blood, nor eat meat from strangled
> animals, and they should stay away from all sexual immorality."
>
> **Acts 21:24-25**

Christians were to keep the Jewish Law. For James and Matthew, *Jewish* Christians needed to continue to keep the Law in its entirety (cf. Matt. 23:2-3, 23). *Gentile* Christians, on the other hand, largely did not.[5] The differences between Matthew and Ephesians thus come primarily from their target audiences: Matthew was written to Jewish Christians and Ephesians was written to Gentiles.

James' belief that Jewish Christians must continue to keep the *entirety* of the Jewish Law held important implications for fellowship between Jewish and Gentile Christians. As we will see below in our discussion of Paul, James at least at one point must not have believed that Jewish and Gentile Christians should eat together (Gal. 2:12). This was probably because Gentiles would normally have eaten unclean things or otherwise come into contact with things that would have made Jewish Christians unclean. In a famous incident at Antioch, Paul sided against Peter and Barnabas with regard to such segregation, arguing that it was nothing short of hypocrisy on Peter's part.

We might say that James had a "separate-but-equal" policy with regard to Gentile Christians. They would escape God's wrath and have a place in His kingdom; thus, they were "equal" as far as salvation was concerned. But because Jews still needed to keep the entirety of the Jewish Law, the separation between Jew and Gentile that existed previously also needed to continue. Acts 11 gives us an accurate sense of the general separation between Gentile

Christians and the church in Jerusalem—the church was shocked when Peter went into the home of a Gentile.

Acts 15 may hint at the solution to the problem of Jewish and Gentile Christians eating together. As we have discussed, Acts indicates four things which James required Gentile converts to avoid: (1) meat offered to idols, (2) meat from strangled animals, (3) blood, and (4) sexual immorality (Acts 15:20). It is probably no coincidence that most of these prohibitions are about what to eat. They may in fact provide us with James' solution to the problem of "table fellowship." If a Gentile would follow these basic rules, then Jewish and Gentile Christians could eat together.[6]

Although second-century Christianity would largely adopt the position of the Hellenists with regard to the Law, it is possible that much of what we might call "Catholic" Christianity had its roots in the Jerusalem church and the Christianity of James and Peter. The church at Rome, even though it was predominantly Gentile, seemed to have had more of a Jewish flavor than some other churches in the Mediterranean, like those at Corinth or Ephesus. It is perhaps no surprise that even today, many Roman Catholic practices have more direct models in the Old Testament than in the New.[7]

Paul's Teaching

So where does Paul fit into the diversity of the early church? On the one hand, Paul's position on the matter of Gentiles and circumcision is clear: Gentiles emphatically did *not* need to be circumcised (e.g., Gal. 5:6). In fact, Paul believed that reliance on such things for salvation "set aside the grace of God" (Gal. 2:21 NIV) and was a slap in Christ's face! He wrote in Galatians, "If you let yourselves be circumcised, Christ will be of no value to you at all" (5:2 NIV). We can thus distinguish Paul's beliefs and mission from that of the Judaizers, who were some of Paul's main opponents.

We can also distinguish Paul from the Hellenists and particularly from Antinomians. As 1 Corinthians 9:20-22 indicates, Paul believed in right and wrong ways to live. For example, his affirmation of the Jewish Law did not change in any way with regard to sexual immorality, whether it be homosexuality (e.g., 1 Cor. 6:9) or sleeping with your stepmother (1 Cor. 5). In theory he could agree with the Corinthians when they said, "I am allowed to do anything" (1 Cor. 6:12; 10:23), but he did not agree at all with them when it came to practice.

> "To the Jews I became like a Jew, to win the Jews. To those under the law I became like one under the law (though I myself am not under the law), so as to win those under the law. To those not having the law I became like one not having the law (though I am not free from God's law but am under Christ's law), so as to win those not having the law . . . I have become all things to all men so that by all possible means I might save some."
>
> **1 Corinthians 9:20-22 NIV**

However, Paul as a Jew also had more of a place in his own life for the Jewish Law than we sometimes think, since we tend to hone in on passages like Ephesians 2:15 and Colossians 2:14. Acts certainly portrays Paul as a much more ardent Law-keeper than most people think (e.g., Acts 21:24). But at times even Paul described himself this way: "Do we then overthrow the law by this faith? By no means! On the contrary, we uphold the law" (Rom. 3:31 NRSV). Paul affirmed that "the law is holy, and the commandment is holy, righteous and good" (Rom. 7:12 NIV). In fact, he believed that it was possible through the Holy Spirit that "the righteous requirements of the law might be fully met in us" (Rom. 8:4 NIV). These comments indicate that Paul had a positive view of the Jewish Law, even if he did not think it offered a way to escape God's judgment.

Yet when Paul spoke of upholding the Law and keeping its requirements through the power of the Spirit, he did not mean exactly the same thing as James might have meant. For Paul, what primarily continued to be valid regarding the Law was its essence: the need to love God and one's neighbor. While I suspect Paul continued in general to observe the Jewish Sabbath and follow some basic dietary regulations, his mission to the Gentiles required him to "fudge" a little on the details.

In the argument at Antioch, Paul was furious at any kind of "separate-but-equal" policy for table fellowship. No one was acceptable to God on the basis of the Jewish Law, he insisted. We can infer that he did not care whether Gentiles had inadvertently eaten blood with their food because they happened to strangle the goat rather than cut its throat. And Paul never mentioned James' position on meat offered to idols when the subject came up in Corinth (1 Cor.

> The picture of the early church that emerges from our study is not so unlike the diverse forms of Christianity we see today.

8-10). Paul could eat with someone who in faith had eaten such meat. The one Paul would *not* eat with was a believer who was sexually immoral, or greedy, or verbally abusive, or a drunkard, or a swindler, or who worshiped idols (1 Cor. 5:11).

Paul was thus representative of a group of Jewish Christians who continued to observe the Jewish Law in general, but abandoned its practices when these practices would cause difficulty for fellowshipping with Gentile Christians. His letters imply clearly that Gentiles need not keep those aspects of the Law that most obviously separated Jew and Gentile, things like circumcision, dietary laws, and Sabbath observance (Rom. 14:5-6; Gal. 4:10; 5:2). Yet Paul did not completely abandon the Law. Circumcising Timothy, who was Jewish, was an example of how Paul honored the Law "in deference to the Jews" (Acts 16:1-3).

Obviously Christians disagreed over theology in the early church, and there were groups that "un-Christianized" other groups for one reason or another. We see these same things today. Most of the groups we have discussed in this chapter are represented elsewhere in the New Testament. Thus, the New Testament is a microcosm of the church.

Things to Think About

Key Terms
Antinomians
Cynics
Docetism
Ebionites
Judaizers

1. Do you believe that this much diversity actually existed in the early church?

2. Which of these groups do you think were *really* Christians? Which would Paul consider to be true Christians? Which would Acts consider to be true Christians? The Gospel of Matthew?

3. Could the New Testament still be authoritative and inspired if its books reflected the diversity discussed in this chapter?

endnotes

1. I have borrowed the basic concept from R. Brown and J. Meier, *Antioch and Rome: New Testament Cradles of Catholic Christianity* (New York: Paulist, 1983).

2. A split with Docetists would explain, for example, why 1 John argues so strongly about the importance of believing Jesus came "in the flesh" (e.g., 1 John 4:2; cf. John 1:14).

3. Colossians, for example, mentions Timothy as a cowriter (Col. 1:1), someone whose outlook on the Law might have been slightly more radical than Paul's. Further, we will discuss the issue of pseudonymity—writing under the authority of someone else's name—in chapter 47 of this text.

4. For example, both speak of the Law coming at the hands of angels (Acts 7:53; Heb. 2:2). Both refer to the wilderness tabernacle rather than the temple (Acts 7:44; Heb. 8:5). Both imply that the earthly sanctuary is not the place of God's true presence (Acts 7:48; Heb. 8:2). Both give the sense that no place on earth is truly home for the Christian (e.g., Acts 7:3; Heb 11:13).

5. It is possible to see the division between Judaizing Christians and the James/Matthew/ Peter-type Christians in Matthew's strong criticism of the Pharisees. The Gospel of Matthew is harsher toward the Pharisees than any other gospel.

6. J. D. G. Dunn has made the intriguing suggestion that Luke has taken two different decisions—an earlier one concerning Gentiles and circumcision, and a later one concerning the matter of Jews and Gentiles eating together—and combined them into what he records as the Jerusalem Council of Acts 15 *(Jesus, Paul, and the Law: Studies in Mark and Galatians* [Louisville: Westminster John Knox, 1990 {1980}], 160). It would have been within the scope of ancient history writing to economize and simplify the story in this way, especially since Luke was emphasizing the orderly nature of early Christianity.

7. Examples include the concept of priests as intermediaries to God, the way a church is set up with certain areas accessible only to priests, the comparison of communion to a sacrifice offered by the priest, etc.

For Further Study

Acts in General
- Powell, Mark A. *What Are They Saying About Acts?* New York: Paulist, 1991.

History of the Early Church
- Witherington, Ben III. *New Testament History: A Narrative Account.* Grand Rapids: Baker, 2001.

Baptism in the Holy Spirit
- Dunn, James D. G. *Baptism in the Holy Spirit.* Philadelphia: Westminster, 1970.

Diversity in the Early Church
- Brown, Raymond and John Meier. *Antioch and Rome: New Testament Cradles of Catholic Christianity.* New York: Paulist, 1983.

- Dunn, James D. G. *Unity and Diversity in the New Testament: An Inquiry into the Character of Earliest Christianity.* 2d ed. Philadelphia: Trinity, 1990.

Unit 5:
Paul's Letters

Chapters 36–50

CHAPTER 36

The Life and Writings of Paul

*During the time Paul was a Pharisee, he thought he kept the
Jewish Law blamelessly.*

Next to Jesus himself, the Apostle Paul features most prominently in the New Testament. Some have considered him to be Christianity's true founder—even more so than Jesus—although this claim is highly debatable. Paul probably started his mission on the margins of Christianity, but seems to have been the single most important person behind its spread to the Gentile world. Since Gentile Christians soon overshadowed the original Jewish Christians in number and authority, Paul's writings eventually moved from the margins to the mainstream of the Christian movement.

At a Glance

- Paul (Saul) was a Jew from Tarsus who was a Pharisee before he became a Christian.

- Paul's ministry was primarily directed at Gentiles rather than Jews.

- Paul took at least three missionary journeys, during which he ministered primarily to urban centers of the Mediterranean.

- Thirteen letters in the New Testament bear his name: Romans, 1 and 2 Corinthians, Galatians, **Ephesians**, Philippians, **Colossians**, 1 and **2 Thessalonians**, **1 and 2 Timothy**, **Titus**, and Philemon.

- Scholars argue about whether the six letters in bold font above are pseudonymous.

- According to tradition, Paul died in Rome around A.D. 64.

Paul (Saul) Before Christianity

If you had known Paul in his early years, you would not have picked him as a very likely candidate to become a Christian, let alone someone who would associate freely with Gentiles. After all, this man was one of the most vigorous opponents of Christianity, a person who traveled long distances just to arrest Christians (Gal. 1:13; cf. Acts 9). Paul describes himself in his pre-Christian days as: (1) an Israelite from the tribe of Benjamin, (2) a Pharisee who kept the Jewish Law blamelessly, and (3) someone who persecuted Christians (Phil. 3:5-6).

Chapter 9 of this text discusses the way ancient people tended to think of themselves. It mentions three key factors in ancient identity, all of which had to do with the groups to which one belonged. Basically, you could know a person if you knew his/her: (1) gender, (2) geography or race, and (3) genealogy or family background.[1] In this light, the things Paul mentions in Philippians 3 go a long way toward telling us who Paul was, given the way people in his day thought about themselves.

"For I was circumcised when I was eight days old, having been born into a pure-blooded Jewish family that is a branch of the tribe of Benjamin. So I am a real Jew if there ever was one! What's more, I was a member of the Pharisees, who demand the strictest obedience to the Jewish law."

Philippians 3:5

First of all, Paul was a Jew, which pinpointed the most important aspect of his "geography." No matter where he might be in the world, people would think of him as someone from the land of Israel. He was also from the tribe of Benjamin, which gives some indication of his family background. Another group to which he belonged was that of the Pharisees. As a Pharisee, he would have been fully committed to the Jewish Law, as well as to the oral traditions about how to keep the Law, the tradition of the elders.

Interestingly, Paul does not mention in his own writings that he was born in Tarsus, a city in southeast Asia Minor where Greek was the primary language. We have to turn to Acts for this information (9:30). Perhaps he thought that mentioning his birth outside Palestine would have worked against his argument that "I am a real Jew if there ever was one!" (Phil. 3:5). Paul even seems to have used a different name in his pre-Christian days, the Jewish name, Saul. However, as his mission turned more and more toward the Gentiles, he increasingly seems to have used his Roman name, Paul (cf. Acts 13:9).

Paul persecuted the church before he joined it. We can make a good argument that Paul targeted Greek-speaking Christians like Stephen, rather than the main apostles. The Jewish leaders probably saw more potential for trouble from these people than they did from the apostles, whose teaching seems to have been more "conservative."[2] Thus, Paul did not seem to go after the Aramaic-speaking Christians of Jerusalem (Acts 8:1), among whom Acts tells us were a number of Pharisee converts (15:5).

Perhaps the most interesting comment Paul makes was that he had been *blameless* with regard to "righteousness under the Law" (Phil. 3:6 NRSV).[3] Some interpreters of Paul think he struggled heavily with a guilty conscience before he turned to Christianity. But Philippians 3 and Paul's other writings give us little reason to think he felt inadequate in any way about how he kept the Jewish Law before he came to believe the gospel.[4] The Pharisees believed that one *could* keep the Law adequately enough to be accepted before God.[5] In fact, the reason they had so many different rules was due to their desire to spell out clearly and *concretely* what one needed to do so that the Law could be kept. Paul evidently considered himself to have done so before he turned to Christianity.

Paul also seems to have had strong ties to the Hellenistic world. Acts tells us that he was a Roman citizen (Acts 16:37)—a privilege very few enjoyed in that world. This is just one of the reasons why many believe Paul came from a family of some wealth. His parents probably owned the tent-making business, rather than being the ones who actually made the tents! Paul may very well have been lowering himself when he worked with his hands (1 Cor. 9:12). Not only does Acts tell us he was educated "at the feet" of the most prominent Pharisee of his day, Gamaliel (Acts 22:3), many scholars now believe Paul may have had some Greek education as well.

Paul's Early Days as a Christian

Paul seems to have joined the Christian movement somewhere between A.D. 32–36, although it is impossible to date most of the events in his life with absolute certainty. The drastic turning point came while he was traveling to a city called Damascus, which was north of Jerusalem approximately 150 miles by foot. He left Jerusalem an ardent opponent of Christians; when he arrived in Damascus, he was one of them. Along the way he had seen a vision of the risen Jesus, drastically changing his outlook on Christianity. After spending some time to process what had happened, he emerged a different person. He was no longer Saul/Paul, the persecutor of Christ; now he was Paul, the preacher of Christ (Gal. 2:18).

The turnaround in his life was so dramatic that within three years he found himself fleeing Damascus for his own life (2 Cor. 11:32). Suddenly he was being pursued for the same reason he had pursued others. Since people in Paul's day generally did not view such significant changes in direction in a positive light, it was important for Paul to see his new life as his destiny and calling. Accordingly, Paul believed that God had chosen him from birth as the main person to bring the gospel to the Gentiles (Gal. 1:15).[6]

Paul's activities over the next ten years are sketchy, but we know that he briefly met Peter and James after he left Damascus and that he spent some time in his home country (Gal. 1:18-24). Knowing Paul, he probably preached his newly found faith vigorously there in Tarsus. Acts tells us that Barnabas, another important early Christian, went to Paul and brought him to Antioch, a city about three hundred miles north of Jerusalem (Acts 11:25-26). This city was to become the center of Greek-speaking Jewish Christianity—indeed, the most important center of Christianity at this time outside Jerusalem. It is here that believers in Christ were first called "Christians" (Acts 11:26).

Paul's Three Journeys

When people speak of Paul's three missionary journeys, they refer to the three trips described in Acts. Each of these Paul initiated from Antioch on his mission to spread the gospel. From things Paul says in his letters, we know that Acts gives us the "boiled down"

"But then something happened! For it pleased God in his kindness to choose me and call me, even before I was born! What undeserved mercy!"

Galatians 1:25

version of his missionary work. In reality, he moved around a lot more than Acts tells us. For example, 2 Corinthians 13:1 implies a visit to Corinth that goes unmentioned in Acts; Romans 15:19 tells us that Paul preached in a place west of Macedonia, well outside the boundaries Acts gives us.

Paul took his first "missionary" trip (ca. A.D. 46–48) with Barnabas. This trip seems to have covered the island of Cyprus and a limited portion of Asia Minor.[7] The second and third journeys were more expansive and included Greece. According to Acts, Paul spent about two years in Corinth on his second journey and three years in Ephesus on his third. He was then arrested in Jerusalem after his third journey and eventually taken to Rome.

An inscription—words carved in stone—has helped us immensely to date Paul's mission to Greece. This inscription from the ruins of ancient Corinth names a man also mentioned in Acts 18:12, a man who held office in Corinth around the years A.D. 51–52.[8] This "fixed point" allows us to date Paul's second missionary journey in the early years of the fifties (ca. A.D. 50–52). The first journey thus would have taken place in the last few years of the forties (ca. A.D. 46–48) and the third journey in the mid-fifties (ca. A.D. 53–58).

Most if not all of Paul's letters were written during his second and third journeys. First Thessalonians, for example, was written from Corinth during Paul's second missionary journey—probably the first book of the New Testament to have been written. Paul wrote several letters to Corinth from Ephesus during his third journey. He probably wrote Galatians at this time as well, and perhaps even Philippians and Philemon. He wrote 2 Corinthians after he had left Ephesus while traveling through Macedonia to the north of Greece. Finally, he wrote Romans from Corinth near the end of the third journey.

We can imagine that Paul arrived as a prisoner in Rome about the year A.D. 61, where Acts says he remained under house arrest for the next two years. Tradition holds that Paul wrote his "Prison Epistles" from this site, although we certainly know of other places where he was imprisoned. Some would say that he was freed after his first trial before Nero and even went on to Spain. Traditionally, the "Pastoral Epistles" were his last, written soon before he died. We cannot know for certain, but Nero probably had him put to death. He may have been among the Christians Nero blamed for the fire of Rome (A.D. 64). Others place his death at Nero's hands a few years later, perhaps A.D. 67.

Paul's Writings

The New Testament does not arrange Paul's letters in the order in which he actually wrote them. Rather, the early collectors of Paul's writings arranged them roughly from longest to shortest. It is thus no coincidence that Romans is first and Philemon is last. We will follow this conventional order as we discuss each of these letters in subsequent chapters.

The order in which you study Paul's letters does not make much difference *given the way most Christians read them.* Chapter 2 of this text discusses how Christians often have taken the Bible's words slightly out of context in order to make its message more directly relevant to today. For example, many people today read Romans as a "how-to" book on becoming a Christian in general. While this prevalent interpretation is not completely wrong, it does not give us the most accurate understanding of what Paul was trying to do when he wrote the letter.

Although it is not bad to read Paul's letters in the order in which they appear in our Bibles, reading them in the order in which Paul actually wrote them has greater advantages. It helps us gain a better sense of the context of his teaching and the flow of his ministry. It helps us to keep a balanced understanding of the various things Paul preached, particularly as he wrote to different audiences. It even allows us to see some changes in his emphases and approach over the course of his mission.

The following chapters allow you to approach Paul's letters in whichever way you prefer. Except for Philemon, the order of the chapters themselves follows the order in which they appear in your Bible. On the other hand, if you wish to read them in the order in which Paul probably wrote them, follow the numbers in the upper right-hand section of the first page of each chapter. Note the following suggestion for the order in which Paul wrote his letters, although scholars disagree on where to place some letters:

• 1 and 2 Thessalonians (ca. A.D. 51):

Most scholars think that of all his letters Paul wrote 1 Thessalonians first. While some do not think Paul wrote 2 Thessalonians, those who believe he was the author date it close to the writing of 1 Thessalonians.

Both letters deal with significant issues involving Jesus' return to earth. They show us that Paul's earliest preaching focused heavily on Christ's "second coming," not on "justification by faith" or heaven and hell.

• [Possibly Philippians, Philemon (ca. A.D. 52)]:

Although tradition holds that Paul wrote these letters at the end of his ministry while he was imprisoned in Rome, it is possible that he wrote them while he was imprisoned in Ephesus on his third missionary journey (cf. 1 Cor. 15:32). Those who argue for Ephesus note that Ephesus was closer geographically than Rome to Philippi and Colossae, to which he sent the letters of Philippians and Philemon.[9] Note also Paul's optimism and confidence that he would not be put to death (e.g., Phil. 1:25-26).

• 1 Corinthians (ca. A.D. 53–54):

First Corinthians was probably the second letter Paul sent to Corinth from Ephesus on his third missionary journey (1 Cor. 5:9), but the first one did not survive to today. The Corinthian church was plagued with disunity, and this letter addresses a number of the issues over which the Corinthians were arguing. We are truly blessed by their problems, though, for this letter is a gold mine of information about what made the earliest Christians tick!

• Galatians (ca. A.D. 54–57?):

Scholars also disagree about when Paul wrote the letter to the Galatians. Some think it was written to the churches Paul founded on his first missionary journey; thus, it was the first of his letters and was written about A.D. 48–49. Chapter 45 of this text, on the other hand, gives the reasons why most scholars place it later. One argument we should mention here is the way Galatians fits with what Paul says in 2 Corinthians 10–13 and Romans. All three letters reflect an incredible crisis in Paul's ministry over his authority and the legitimacy of his mission to the Gentiles.[10]

• 2 Corinthians (ca. A.D. 56–57):

Just as Paul wrote a letter to Corinth preceding 1 Corinthians, he wrote another letter between 1 and 2 Corinthians that we do not have today (2 Cor. 2:4-11), although some think that the last chapters of 2 Corinthians are actually the missing letter. These individuals believe that 2 Corinthians is actually comprised of two letters that have been spliced together; chapters 10–13 make up one letter, and chapters 1–9 are a second, later letter.

Paul wrote 2 Corinthians after he had left Ephesus for Greece near the end of his third missionary journey. He thus wrote it while he was on the road, making his rounds through Macedonia, the region north of Greece. Chapters 1–9 are warm and friendly—they reflect the end of a fierce struggle over Paul's authority in the Corinthian church. By the time Paul wrote these chapters, he had reestablished his legitimacy.

In this light, chapters 10–13 are surprising, for Paul suddenly starts to defend his authority again in some of the strongest language he has used in any of his letters. For this reason, some think these chapters reflect the situation *before* Paul wrote the first nine chapters. Others think the sudden change in tone resulted from new information he had received from the church after writing the first nine chapters. After hearing that some were still resisting his authority, he finishes 2 Corinthians with yet another vigorous defense of his apostleship.

• Romans (ca. A.D. 57–58):

Paul wrote Romans from Corinth at the end of his third missionary journey. He wrote this letter just before he left for Jerusalem, where he would be arrested and eventually sent to Rome under guard (cf. Rom.

15:23-33). Because Paul had never visited Rome and because the church there probably had strong connections with the Jerusalem church, Paul wrote Romans as a basic defense of his mission and message to the Gentiles. He sent the letter to prepare the church at Rome for his upcoming visit and to secure their support for a mission to Spain.

• Ephesians, Philippians, Colossians, Philemon
(traditionally, ca. A.D. 61–63):

We refer to these four letters as Paul's **Prison Epistles**, since they all indicate Paul was in prison when he wrote them. Tradition has it that he wrote them from Rome while he was under house arrest (cf. Acts 28:30). However, a good number of scholars think he wrote Philippians and Philemon from Ephesus almost ten years earlier. Further, a significant number of scholars think Colossians and especially Ephesians are pseudonymous; that is, written under the authority of Paul's name but not by Paul himself. Conservative scholars, on the other hand, strongly tend to support Paul as the author of all the writings bearing his name in the New Testament.

Prison Epistles: The letters of Ephesians, Philippians, Colossians, and Philemon. According to tradition, Paul wrote these letters while under house arrest in Rome.

Chapter 47 of this book deals with the issue of pseudonymity in general, a not uncommon first-century practice that we probably should not equate with forgery. It was an ancient genre that simply does not exist today. One potential solution to some of the difficulties, particularly with regard to Colossians, is to note that Timothy's name also appears on the letter as an author. It is possible that some of the differences in style and thought between Colossians and Paul's other letters result from Timothy taking a more active role than Paul in its authorship.

412

• 1 & 2 Timothy, Titus (traditionally, A.D. 64–67):

We call these three letters the **Pastoral Epistles** because they reflect how Paul mentored and trained Timothy and Titus for ministry. As with Ephesians, a solid majority of scholars believe that these writings are pseudonymous, meant to give Paul a "pastoral" voice many years after he had passed from the scene. Once again, conservative scholars strongly tend to argue that we are reading the words of Paul himself, suggesting that the differences in style and thought reflect the personal nature of these letters, as well as Paul's maturity at the end of his life.

First Timothy and Titus deal primarily with matters of how to run the church. We not only find instructions concerning the overseers and "deacons" of the church (1 Tim. 3:1-13; Titus 1:5-9), but also guidelines for women, slaves, and worship (1 Tim. 2:1-15; 5:1–6:2; Titus

> **Pastoral Epistles:** 1 & 2 Timothy and Titus, so called because they give instructions to two "pastors" on how to shepherd their "flocks." Timothy and Titus were two of Paul's most trusted "trainees."

2:1-15). Second Timothy is a majestic farewell letter reflecting Paul's strong love for Timothy as a Christian "son" (e.g., 2 Tim. 1:2; 2:1), as well as his confidence in the face of his approaching death. Despite the fact that many had abandoned him (e.g., 2 Tim. 4:9-18), Paul victoriously looked to the completion of his "race" (2 Tim. 4:7).

Things to Think About

1. What were the three key factors in determining ancient identity? Using them, how did the pre-Christian Paul identify himself?

Key Terms
Pastoral Epistles
Prison Epistles

2. How adequately did Paul think he kept the Jewish Law according to Philippians 3? How did this compare to the way the Pharisees assessed their "righteousness" in general?

3. What is the traditional number of Paul's missionary journeys? Overall, what regions did Paul visit on his journeys?

4. Do Paul's writings appear in the order in which they were written? If not, how have they been arranged? Which letter do most scholars think was written first? Do we have all the letters Paul wrote to these churches? Over which ones is there debate about pseudonymity?

endnotes

1. See B. J. Malina and J. H. Neyrey, *Portraits of Paul: An Archaeology of Ancient Personality* (Louisville: Westminster John Knox, 1996), 3.
2. See chapter 35 of this text. In particular, Stephen seems more hostile toward the Jerusalem temple than the other apostles in Acts.
3. The NIV's translation "legalistic righteousness" gives the false impression that Paul was discussing "rule-following" in general. When Paul wrote of "Law," however, he almost always had the Old Testament Law in the back of his mind, not some abstract law of nature.
4. One of the most important articles ever written about Paul shows the degree to which Paul has been misunderstood in this way over the years: K. Stendahl's "The Apostle Paul and the Introspective Conscience of the West," *Harvard Theological Review* 56 (1963): 199–215.
5. Luke 18:10-12 probably gives us a more accurate picture of the pre-Christian Paul.

These verses picture a Pharisee who is quite confident about his own righteousness in the sight of God.

6. For more information, see Malina and Neyrey, *Portraits*, 40–41.

7. For maps and further information, see chapter 31 of this text.

8. Namely, Gallio, who was proconsul of the southern part of Greece at this time.

9. Philemon deals with a runaway slave who probably sought out Paul as a go-between with his master in Colossae, something more likely to happen in Ephesus than in Rome.

10. The fact that Philippians also alludes to Paul's conflict with Judaizers (e.g., Phil. 3:2) makes it fit with these years in Ephesus as well.

CHAPTER 37

Paul's Mission and Message

Paul saw the Law and Christ as two distinct approaches to God:
only Christ worked.

Paul's letters typically begin not only with his name—the usual beginning for an ancient letter—but also with a description of himself. While he sometimes calls himself a servant[1] or prisoner[2] of Jesus Christ, he almost always refers to himself in his greetings as an *apostle*—that is, as an ambassador from Christ to the world.[3] This one word, *apostle*, holds the key not only to understanding who Paul thought he was, but also to understanding the nature of his message.

More than anything else, Paul saw himself as the "apostle to the Gentiles," the principal person God had chosen to bring the good news of Jesus Christ to those who were not Jews. His message was in many

At a Glance

- Paul saw himself as the primary person God had chosen to bring the good news of Jesus Christ to the Gentiles.

- As a Pharisee, Paul was confident that he had kept the Law well enough for God to accept him.

- After he saw the risen Christ, he concluded that the power of sin was so extensive in the world that no one could escape God's wrath.

- A person could only be justified and found innocent in God's sight by faith or trust in Christ's death and victorious Resurrection.

- Christians thus are not "under the Law." No one is judged by how well he or she keeps it.

- Nevertheless, the Holy Spirit enables victory over the power of sin and provides the basis of unity for those in the body of Christ.

417

respects the same as that of most Christians: Jesus' death had now made it possible to escape God's coming wrath. But Paul believed God had a special role for him to play in the spreading of that message.

As most Jews did, Paul divided the world into two groups, Jew and Gentile. He believed that God had chosen one primary apostle to reach each group. While Peter was the apostle to Jews, Paul believed God had chosen *him* as the ambassador to everyone else (Gal. 2:7). His special mission was to bring the gospel of Jesus Christ to the Gentiles of the world. Because this mission would come into conflict with the way Christians before him had done things, he would find before he was through that his message, as well as his mission, had become unique.

Paul's "Calling"

The ancient world in general was fatalistic—people tended to think nothing happened by chance and that the world was under the power of divine forces beyond human control.[4] Similarly, they generally did not think that people could change (like the contemporary proverb that says a "leopard can't change its spots"). They expected a great person to be born under spectacular circumstances and to show signs of greatness even in childhood. On the other hand, people did not suddenly make bad choices; bad people had always been bad, even if it did not show up in public for a while.

Using this same idea of destiny, Paul explains his sudden change from persecutor of the church to preacher of the gospel: "It pleased God in his kindness to choose me and call me, even before I was born!" (Gal. 1:15). Paul believed that God had chosen him even before birth for a special role in the divine plan. After Jesus had risen from the dead and appeared to all the other apostles, God singled out Paul in particular and appeared to him "long after the others, as though I had been born at the wrong time" (1 Cor. 15:8). It was this appearance that Paul considered to be his commissioning as an apostle (1 Cor. 9:1). The success of his ministry among the Gentiles proved that he had understood Jesus correctly—God had truly sent him as His emissary, because people accepted his message (1 Cor. 9:2).

The ministry that God entrusted to him was one of reconciliation. Not only Israel, but all humanity was separated and alienated from God because of sin. Before he became a Christian, Paul thought he *could* be acceptable to God by keeping the Jewish Law adequately. After all, he had been a Pharisee who had followed the Law and the traditions of the elders scrupulously (cf. Phil. 3:6).

Despite what many might think, Paul gives us no reason to believe he struggled with a guilty conscience before he believed in Christ. He did not feel like a failure at keeping the Jewish Law. As we mentioned earlier, we should probably think of the pre-Christian Paul as someone more like the Pharisee in the parable about prayer in Luke 18:9-14. As this Pharisee prayed to God, he expressed incredible confidence in his own **righteousness**, his acceptability and innocence before God. He not only thought he was perfectly adequate to escape God's condemnation, he actually thought his goodness was commendable.[5]

> **righteousness:** In a legal context, one's innocence or acceptability in the eyes of the law; in a Christian context, acceptability before God, the righteous judge.

But Paul's vision of Christ required him to rethink everything. If the Christian message was legitimate, then he evidently was not as acceptable to God as he once thought. He needed something more and didn't even know it. Paul eventually came to believe that the power and presence of sin in the world was more extensive and untreatable than he ever had imagined in his days as a Pharisee. Without Christ, no amount of Law observance could eliminate the stain.

Paul came to understand himself as a special ambassador from God to the Gentiles with this message of hope. Certainly Paul believed that neither Jew nor Gentile could escape God's judgment without trusting in Christ's death and Resurrection. But he especially saw Christ as an open door *for the Gentiles*, a door that previously had been shut. If it was only Christ's death that made someone acceptable to God, then the Gentiles did not need to keep the Jewish Law in order to be saved. God thus removed the biggest obstacle standing between the Gentiles and himself.

Paul and His Jewish-Christian Opposition

Someone who expects all of Paul's comments throughout his letters to fit together easily and in a straightforward manner may be in for some disappointment. Although we believe that the Bible is inspired by God, the varying styles and emphases of its writings show that the personalities and worldviews of the authors exerted a strong influence over what they wrote. It would not contradict the notion of inspiration to find that Paul's understanding developed or that his emphases changed over the course of his letters.

"You and I are Jews by birth, not 'sinners' like the Gentiles."

Galatians 2:15

A lively debate has continued for years over the best way to describe Paul's thought; this has resulted in some general agreement. But we still find a great deal of controversy over the real heart of his message, even though we have so many of his writings from which to choose. Some people have even thrown their hands up and concluded that Paul was simply a bad thinker, a man of perpetual contradiction.

We can get around much of this confusion if we realize from the start that many of Paul's arguments have as much to do with the practical situations he faced as they do with logic or reason. In other words, what really mattered to Paul were the implications of his arguments, not so much the arguments themselves. Like a good ancient rabbi, he might use different arguments on different occasions to reach the right conclusion. Perhaps those arguments would even contradict each other if you placed them side by side. The most important thing was where the argument led him, not so much the path of reasoning he used to argue a point.

> "Some of his [Paul's] comments are hard to understand, and those who are ignorant and unstable have twisted his letters around to mean something quite different from what he meant."
>
> **2 Peter 3:16**

Thus, one of the best ways to get a grip on Paul's thought is to follow the path of his life and the practical situations he encountered in the course of his ministry. We have already noted that Paul the Pharisee believed himself to be blameless in his observance of the

> "Since we know that no one is accepted [by God] on the basis of their keeping of the Jewish Law—unless by way of what Jesus Christ faithfully did—we also have put our faith in Christ Jesus.
>
> **Galatians 2:16**
> **(author's translation)**

Jewish Law (Phil. 3:6). He likely felt "righteous" in God's eyes and had no fear of God's judgment. But when he saw the risen Christ, he was forced to rethink his whole understanding.

Galatians 2:15-21 provides us with a good sense of how his thinking changed after he saw Christ, particularly as he came into conflict with various other Jewish Christians. In the course of these verses, we can almost see the birth of Paul's message as he moved from what he believed before he saw Christ to the teachings for which he is best known today. For example, he started off with the basic stereotype almost every Jew accepted: Gentiles are sinners; Jews are acceptable to God (2:15).[6]

Although scholars do not fully agree on all the exact nuances of Galatians 2:16, the translation in the text box may help us get a sense of how Paul moved past what the Jewish Christians before him had thought. Christians like James certainly believed that Christ's death was essential in order to be **justified** by God—*to be accepted or found innocent* when He came to judge the world. James also agreed with Paul that keeping the Jewish Law in and of itself was insufficient to bring **salvation**—escape from God's wrath. Unless you put your faith or *trust* in what Christ's death had done, God would destroy you on Judgment Day.

Many early Christians thought of Christ's death as a kind of sacrifice, somewhat like the sacrifices they offered in the temple. To them, trusting in Christ's death probably meant trusting that His sacrificial death had **atoned** for their sins; that is, brought them back on good terms with God. In general, the ancients offered sacrifices to stay on good terms with the gods. They often thought of the gods as unpredictable characters who needed to be kept happy and honored with constant sacrifices. Sacrifices prevented them from getting angry and helped appease them if they were already angry. While the early Christians may not have thought of God

"But if, in our effort to be justified in Christ, we ourselves have been found to be sinners, is Christ then a servant of sin?"

Galatians 2:17 NRSV

as unpredictable and unloving, they did think of Christ's sacrifice in part as something that took away His anger toward human sin.

We should not be surprised that God revealed himself to the people in the Bible through this same category that they understood so well. For example, Romans 3:25 refers to Christ's death as a "sacrifice of atonement" (NIV). The New Living Translation does a good job with the same verse, showing us what it would mean for Christ's death to be such a sacrifice: "God sent Jesus to take the punishment for our sins and to satisfy God's anger against us."

James certainly believed that only trusting in Christ's sacrificial death ultimately could save one from God's judgment. But for him, that had nothing to do with whether a Jew should keep the Law; a Jew must still maintain his or her acceptability to God by staying true to the covenant God had made with Israel. At this point, Paul moved one step beyond the thinking of Jewish Christians like James and Peter.

justification: Legally considered innocent; declared "not guilty"; for it to be "just as if I'd never sinned."

justification by faith: The idea that the only way to be found "not guilty" by God is through trusting in what Jesus Christ has done for you on the cross.

atonement: The process of getting on good terms with God ("at-one-ment") by offering Him something.

salvation: In Paul's writings, escape from God's wrath on the Day of Judgment.

Paul had not viewed himself as a sinner before he saw the risen Christ. He felt quite confident in how well he had kept the Law. But if he had not been acceptable to God as a Pharisee—that is, if *even he* had been a sinner, then sin must be something more extensive and untreatable than he had imagined. It must be something that no human effort could overcome or defeat. In short, it must be something cosmic in its proportions. Paul came to the important conclusion that not just Gentiles but also Jews were sinners. In fact, "all have sinned and fall short of the glory of God" (Rom. 3:23 NIV), both Jew and Gentile.

Paul concluded that Christ was an entirely new way of being right with God, a new system of righteousness, if you will. He saw the Law and Christ as two distinct approaches to God. Only Christ worked, however. A person who tried to rely on the Jewish Law to be acceptable to God brought him or herself under the curse of failure (e.g., Gal. 3:10). A Christian who turned to this approach fell from God's grace and was in danger of judgment (Gal. 5:4).

Paul's argument in Galatians 2:15-21 is not always easy to follow, but it seems understandable enough. The problem is that it is only one of the ways

Paul pictures the Law. In these verses, Paul thinks of the Law as a standard no one can attain. First, the Law tells me what is right; then it shows me that I do not have the power to keep it (e.g., Rom. 7:7). In fact, Paul indicates that the Law is a tool in the hands of sin's power: "Sin took advantage of this law and aroused all kinds of forbidden desires within me! If there were no law, sin would not have that power" (Rom. 7:8). Because no one can keep the Law perfectly, Paul teaches that the person relying on Christ is not "under the Law" (e.g., Rom. 6:14; 1 Cor. 9:20), meaning that this person is no longer judged on the basis of its standard. It is like a child's guardian that provides boundaries for the child until he or she comes of age (e.g., Gal. 3:24-25).

What makes Paul's thought so complicated is the fact that in the end he did *not* throw out the Jewish Law entirely. For example, Paul believes that Gentiles needed to keep the sexual prohibitions of the Jewish Law (e.g., 1 Cor. 5). At some points he even teaches that a person must *keep* the Law's requirement (Rom. 3:31; 8:4, 8; 1 Cor. 7:19) and that through the power of the Holy Spirit a person *can* actually do it (Rom. 8:4). As far as Jewish Christians were concerned, Paul does *not* encourage them to stop circumcising their children, to stop observing the Jewish Sabbath on Saturday, or to start eating foods that Leviticus prohibited—in other words, he supports their continued observance of much of the Jewish Law (e.g., 1 Cor. 7:17). Seemingly contradictory teachings such as these have brought about such incredible disagreement over what Paul actually thought about the Jewish Law.

> "I make myself guilty if I rebuild the old system I already tore down. For when I tried to keep the law, I realized I could never earn God's approval. So I died to the law so that I might live for God."
>
> **Galatians 2:18-19**

The secret to getting a handle on Paul is to realize that all this "theory" was really about how he believed Christians needed to live in the world. Paul was not trying to throw out the Jewish Law regarding circumcision or food.

He probably did not want Jews to stop observing these practices, but saw Christ as an opportunity for Gentiles to find salvation from God's wrath without having to observe them. On the other hand, some Jewish practices regarding purity interfered with Jewish and Gentile Christians eating together and having full fellowship. Paul had no problem telling Jews that they should avoid wrangling over aspects of the Jewish Law when they were among Gentile Christians. But he had distinct boundaries, of course. For Paul, it was unthinkable for a Christian to sleep with his stepmother or practice homosexuality. And he never would have taught that murder was permitted because Christians were not "under the Law." He kept some parts of the Law and threw out others, never really stopping to explain how it all fit together.

Later Christians would work out these two aspects of Paul's teaching by speaking of two parts in the Jewish Law: the "moral" part and the "ceremonial" part. Paul kept the first and taught the removal of the second for Gentiles. While a Jew never would have divided the Law in this way, it is a fair means of capturing Paul's teaching for us. The essence of the Jewish Law for him was the command to love our neighbor (e.g., Rom. 13:9; Gal. 5:14). This is the "Law of Christ" (1 Cor. 9:21) that the Spirit enables the Christian to keep (e.g., Gal. 5:22)—what we might call the "moral" part of the Law. The key is realizing that Paul expressed all his arguments because of how he believed Christians should live among one another in the world. To focus exclusively on any one aspect of his "theory" is to get him out of focus.

Paul's Understanding of Salvation for All

It was primarily when Paul was debating with his Jewish-Christian opponents that he got into the issues we have just discussed—issues like justification and the role of the Jewish Law for the believer. However, we sometimes miss the richness of his message when we focus on those issues.

Paul refers to the fact that we are "in Christ" far more frequently than he talks about the fact that we are "**justified by faith**."

For Paul, it was not just that salvation was bigger than the Jewish Law. Sin was bigger than the Jewish Law as well. It goes back to the first human being: Adam, the father of the human race. In the story of Genesis 2—3, God gives Adam the incredible honor of ruling over the earth. In return God commands only one thing of Adam—he is not allowed to eat from a particular tree. According to Paul, when Adam broke this command he lost the *glory* he was supposed to have on the earth (cf. Rom. 3:23). Instead of humanity ruling the earth, the earth became enslaved to demonic powers, **Satan** in particular.

Because our human flesh is a part of this earthly realm where Satan rules, a person begins life enslaved to the power of sin.[7] The result is that no one is able to keep the Law. "No one is good—not even one" (Rom. 3:10). "In Christ," however, God has given us another power, one that frees us from the power of sin. This power is the Holy Spirit. The person "enslaved" to the Spirit is freed from the power of sin (e.g., Rom. 6:7, 22) and thus able to keep the essence of the Law— namely, love (Rom. 8:4; Gal. 5:16, 22).

Satan: The prince of demons, leader of demonic forces, and the epitome of evil; also known as Belial, Beelzebub, and the devil.

By sending the Spirit, God has established the beachhead of His invasion of the earth so that His kingdom will come "on earth as it is in heaven" (Matt. 6:10 NIV). Indeed, Paul's understanding of the Holy Spirit is similar to Jesus' phrasing in Luke 10:18: "I saw Satan falling from heaven as a flash of lightning!" The rule of the demonic was at an end, and the Spirit signaled the return of glory to humanity. Christians are in the process of a continuous inner spiritual transformation (2 Cor. 3:18) that will culminate at the resurrection, a time when we will actually receive new bodies made of spirit (1 Cor. 15:44, 50).[8]

We will miss one of the most fundamental aspects of Paul's thought if we think of the Holy Spirit as something that only individual Christians receive. The "body" that God's Spirit inhabits is not the body of an individual Christian. God's Spirit inhabits the "body of Christ"; that is, all Christians taken together, the church (1 Cor. 12:12-13). Thus, for Paul, it is the fact that we all share the same Spirit that unifies us. No one Christian is better than another. "There is no longer Jew or Gentile, slave or free, male or female. For you are all Christians—you are one in Christ Jesus" (Gal. 3:28).[9]

Because we all make up the body of Christ, we are all "in Christ." In some mystical way, the Spirit of Christ in us makes us one with Christ. While we as sinners could not possibly merit salvation, Christ could. When we are joined to Him, *we* stop existing. In a sense, we are crucified with Christ (Gal. 2:19-20). "Our old sinful selves were crucified with Christ so that sin might lose its power in our lives" (Rom. 6:6). In a sense, we become a "new creation" (2 Cor. 5:17 NIV). Best of all, "Since we have been united with him in his death, we will also be raised as he was" (Rom. 6:5). The Spirit is our guarantee and down payment (2 Cor. 1:22; 5:5; Heb. 6:4-5) of the spiritual glory we will experience when God resurrects us from the dead.

Things to Think About

1. What is the key element to how Paul understood himself and his mission? Into what two groups did Jews divide the world?

2. Which is more accurate: to speak of Paul's "conversion" or to speak of his "calling"?

3. How does Paul's way of explaining his coming to Christ fit well with the general approach to life shared by the ancient world?

Key Terms
atonement
justification
justification by faith
righteousness
salvation
Satan

4. React to and evaluate this comment: "The most important thing was where [Paul's] argument led him, not so much the path of reasoning he used to argue it."

5. How "righteous" had Paul probably thought himself before he saw the risen Christ? What conclusion did he eventually reach regarding his earlier righteousness? What did Paul eventually come to see as the sole factor bringing about our justification?

6. What are some of the varying images of the Jewish Law and its function as described in Paul's writings? Did Paul reject the Law entirely? If he did not, in what ways did he retain it? How did his view of the Jewish Law probably differ from that of James and Peter? How would some later Christians work out which parts of the Law Paul "kept" and which he believed were no longer in force?

7. Do we possess the Holy Spirit more individually or as a community of Christians? How does the Holy Spirit relate to unity? With whom are we in "mystical union"? Into what aspects of His experience do we join in baptism? Into what aspects of His experience will we join after death?

endnotes

1. For example, Rom. 1:1; Phil. 1:1.
2. Philemon 1.
3. Rom. 1:1; 1 Cor. 1:1; 2 Cor. 1:1; Gal. 1:1; Eph. 1:1; Col. 1:1; 1 Tim. 1:1; 2 Tim. 1:1; Titus 1:1. Even if you do not think Paul himself wrote Ephesians, Colossians, or the Pastoral Epistles, the fact that these letters still refer to him as an apostle shows that this was a crucial aspect of his identity.
4. See chapter 11 of this text.
5. It is notable, therefore, that unlike Luke, repentance is not a major category of Paul's thinking—even after he joined the Christian movement, he did not struggle with the inadequacy of his lifestyle. In fact, he frequently told the churches to which he ministered to model their behavior on his, scarcely something someone who felt like a constant moral failure would say (e.g., 1 Cor. 4:16; Phil. 3:17; 4:9; 1 Thess. 1:6).

6. In all honesty, calling the Gentiles "sinners" was not really a stereotype. Sin from the standpoint of the Old Testament was violating the Law God revealed as a part of His covenant with Israel. The word "sinners" in this verse thus should not be in quotation marks. Gentiles by definition did not keep the Jewish Law; therefore, they were sinners in reality, not just in stereotype.

7. Being married to a Christian apparently provides some protection from Satanic power (cf. 1 Cor. 7:14).

8. See chapter 43 of this text.

9. In fact, our spiritual bodies may all be the same, neither male nor female.

CHAPTER 38

Paul's Letter to Rome:
Is God Really Faithful?

Romans boldly proclaims the righteousness of God. God did not divorce Israel or break His covenant. Rather, He found a way not only to save Israel, but to save the whole world as well!

Clear and Systematic

Paul's letter to the Romans is both his best-known writing and the one that has had the greatest impact on Christianity. This book played a major role in the lives of a number of individuals who went on to shape the thinking of millions of other Christians. While not everyone may recognize the name Augustine, Christianity would be substantially different if he had not converted while reading Romans.[1] Martin Luther, the father of Protestantism, drastically changed the course of Christianity in the 1500s after he came to have a new understanding of the book of Romans.[2] And as he left a

At a Glance

- Paul wrote Romans in preparation for his visit to Rome, in part as a defense of his mission and message to the Gentiles.

- Paul's basic concern is to show that his message does not contradict God's faithfulness to His covenant with Israel.

- Paul insists that all humans—both Jews and Gentiles—can only be accepted by God on the Day of Judgment through their trust in Christ.

- Adam, the first human, brought the power of sin into the world. Christ brought the power of the Spirit into the world—potential victory over sin's power over us.

- Paul asserts that God has not abandoned Israel—Israel has rejected Him. In the end, however, all Israel will be saved.

- In the last chapters of Romans, Paul emphasizes the need for love, unity, and peace among Christians.

Bible study on Romans, the heart of John Wesley was "strangely warmed," eventually resulting in a movement we know today as Methodism—a movement whose influence may very well have helped save England from the bloody revolution its French neighbors experienced.

> "I am not ashamed of the gospel; it is the power of God for salvation to everyone who has faith, to the Jew first and also to the Greek. For in it the righteousness of God is revealed through faith for faith; as it is written: 'The one who is righteous will live by faith.' "
>
> **Romans 1:16-17 NRSV**

Romans presents us with Paul's most systematic thinking, although it is far from a philosophy or theology textbook. Christians often read it slightly out of context, taking arguments that had much to do with the relationship between Jew and Gentile and making them into abstract debates over issues like whether a person can earn his or her salvation. Only in recent years have we begun to regain a sense of how the book tied into Paul's ongoing defense of his mission to the Gentiles.

Romans is Paul's clearest and most systematic argument for how God has brought salvation to *all* people, especially in light of God's special relationship with the Jews. Paul wrote this letter near the end of his third missionary journey, just before he departed from the city of Corinth for Jerusalem. He was hoping to travel to Rome in the near future, something he managed to accomplish—even if it turned out to be under Roman guard. We can thus read

righteousness of God: The fact that God is not only faithful to His covenant with Israel, but is in general a merciful God who wishes to save all people.

Romans as a letter to prepare the already existing church at Rome for his arrival, a letter that implicitly defended his mission and message to the Gentiles. If the past was any indication, Paul knew he would face opposition after he arrived.

Romans: How God Has Shown His Righteousness

Romans is about the **righteousness of God**, the fact that God not only is faithful to His people Israel, but that He in general is a merciful God whose desire is to save people of all kinds.[3] As other chapters of this book have mentioned, Paul believed that God had chosen him as an ambassador to the Gentiles.[4] The message he preached was that the only way anyone could escape God's wrath was by trusting in the death and Resurrection of Jesus. Gentiles did not need to convert to Judaism or become circumcised. Further, even Jews could become acceptable only through faith or trust in what Christ had done *for* them.

ROME, THE CENTER OF THE ROMAN EMPIRE
MAP 6

While Paul affirmed the continuing validity of the Law's essence—love—he taught that God did not accept either Jew or Gentile on the basis of the Law.

Many Jewish Christians found Paul and his Gentile mission alarming, if not infuriating. The heart of Jewish religion was the Law: Genesis, Exodus, Leviticus, Numbers, and Deuteronomy. These books contained God's covenant with Israel, the solemn arrangement to which Yahweh and Israel had agreed over a thousand years previously. God's promise was that if Israel

Different Views of the "Righteousness of God" in Romans 1:17

A young German monk by the name of Martin Luther once struggled deeply with Romans 1:17: "the righteousness of God is revealed" in the gospel. He did not feel like such a gospel was "good news" for him, because he did not think he was good enough for God to accept him. Rather, he expected God to condemn him on the Day of Judgment. When Luther saw the words "the righteousness of God," he understood them to mean the "justice of God." The gospel revealed a God who would justly condemn him for his sins. To him, God was an exacting judge who one day would severely punish those who did not measure up to perfection. Luther only feared such a day.

Then it occurred to him that the phrase "righteousness of God" in this verse could be taken in another way. What if it did not refer to God's righteousness—God's justice or rightness? What if the verse was talking about human righteousness—the possibility for humans to become right in the eyes of God? What if this verse was about how righteousness came from God by way of the gospel, about God making it possible for humans to be declared innocent of their sins? When Luther read the verse this way, the gospel truly became good news: what is revealed in the gospel is the acquittal of God, a way to be forgiven for our sins.

A load lifted from Luther's mind. Yes, he thought—in the courtroom of God's judgment, the "righteousness" in this verse is my "not guilty" verdict. God finds me innocent of all charges, and I am not held accountable for my sins—not that I actually am innocent. Luther believed a Christian at all times is "both righteous and a sinner, as long as they are always repenting." The beauty of it all for Luther was that God finds me "not guilty" even though he knows I am "guilty as sin." He only declares me righteous—acquitted in the court of heaven—even though I am really guilty.

God does this for me because of my faith or trust in Jesus Christ. I am "justified," declared innocent or not guilty, because I trust in what Christ has done. Jesus' "righteousness" counts as my "righteousness." "Justification by faith" thus became the center of Luther's message, just as Luther thought it had been the center of Paul's. We might call this "imputed" righteousness.

Some two hundred years after Luther, another man by the name of John Wesley took Luther's line of thought one step further. He believed that this right standing we get from God was not just a "legal fiction"—something that was true in the eyes of the law but was not really true in reality. Wesley believed that God could actually make us righteous so that we did not sin all the time. For him, the "righteousness" God gave us became a reality, not just a legal decision—it was "imparted" righteousness. The righteousness revealed from God is the possibility of truly becoming righteous, a goodness from God that He actually makes possible for His people. For Wesley, God actually imparted righteousness to the Christian; He did not just impute it. Wesley believed that the Spirit of God gave the believer the power actually to do the right thing, truly to become righteous.

While all these positions have an element of truth to them, none of them precisely captures what Paul himself meant when he said that the righteousness of God was revealed in the gospel. In the light of the Old Testament (e.g., Isa. 42:6), as well as the Dead Sea Scrolls, the phrase "righteousness of God" in Romans 1:17 almost certainly refers to God's righteousness and not to ours. Thus, while the conclusions of Luther and Wesley were largely true, they have viewed Romans slightly out of focus.

would keep the Law, He would make them prosperous and free from foreign rule.[5]

Many Jewish Christians saw no contradiction between the importance of Christ's death and the continuing validity of the Jewish Law (e.g., Acts 21:20). They thought that Christ's death provided essential "atonement"—the means of getting/keeping one on good terms with God. But they also believed that keeping God's covenant with Israel, the Law, was essential.[6] As Acts 13:39 puts it, "Through Him [Christ] everyone who believes is justified from everything you could not be justified from by the law of Moses" (NIV). The implication is that the Law of Moses *did* "justify" or make you right with God to some extent, just not completely.

Paul's teaching, however, takes the significance of Christ's death one step further than some of his fellow Jewish Christians take it.[7] For him, the Jewish Law plays *no role for anyone* to become acceptable to God—not even Jews. Rather, becoming acceptable to God is *entirely* a matter of trusting in what Christ has done *for us*. This fact makes it possible for the Gentiles to fully become Christians without keeping the Jewish Law, and it enables Jewish Christians to have full fellowship with Gentiles, even though such fellowship requires them to violate some of the Law's rules of purity.

"I am bringing *my righteousness* near, it is not far away; And *my salvation* will not be delayed."

Isaiah 46:13 NIV

"You atone for sin and cle[anse man] of his fault through your justice [or righteousness]."

1QH 4.37 (Dead Sea Scrolls)

These ideas and practices raised all kinds of questions for many of Paul's fellow Jewish Christians. Was Paul throwing the Jewish Scriptures out the window, teaching his followers not to observe Genesis, Exodus, Leviticus, Numbers, and Deuteronomy? Was Paul implying that being a Jew did not put you on any special terms with God? Whatever happened to God choosing Israel, His election of them as His special people (cf. Deut. 7:6; 32:9)? Paul seems to be saying that God had suddenly thrown out His marriage vows with Israel, divorcing them for another woman, the Gentiles. And how was it fair that after so many years of the Jews keeping the Law, the Gentiles suddenly

"You have shown me your wondrous
   mysteries . . .
What is flesh compared to this?
What creature of clay can do wonders?
He is in sin from his maternal womb,
and in guilty iniquity right to old age."

1QH 4.27, 29-30 (Dead Sea Scrolls)

"No one is good—not even one.
No one has real understanding; no one
is seeking God."

Romans 3:10-11, quoting Psalm 51

could be right with God without putting in all that effort (cf. the Parable of the Day Laborers in Matt. 20:1-15)? It is easy to see why Paul's opponents might have said, "If you're right, Paul, then God is not righteous. If you're right, God is unfaithful to His promises and to His covenant with Israel."

It is against this backdrop that we should read Romans. Paul was indeed explaining the process by which anyone could get right with God. But he was doing it in the light of the Jew-Gentile issue he had been debating for so long in his ministry.

Romans boldly proclaims the righteousness of God. God did not divorce Israel or break His covenant. Rather, He found a way not only to save Israel, but to save the whole world as well! Such a God deserves no blame, and thus Paul's message does not contradict the character of God or His covenant with Israel. Paul's message affirms these things in the strongest of terms.

All—Both Jew and Gentile—Have Sinned

In roughly the first three chapters of Romans (1:18–3:20), Paul establishes the first point of his argument; namely, that the Law does not put anyone into a right relationship with God. Rather, if God were to judge anyone on the basis of the Law, whether Jew or Gentile, no one

> "All have sinned and lack the glory of God."
>
> **Romans 3:23 (author's translation)**

would escape the Day of Judgment. The claim that Paul was undercutting the validity of the Law was thus mistaken. For Paul, the goodness of the Law was not disputed (e.g., Rom. 3:31; 7:12) and the faithfulness of God was not in question (e.g., 3:3-4). The problem was with all humanity—the Jews had not kept the Law perfectly any more than the Gentiles had.

Romans 1:18-32 establishes a point with which none of Paul's Jewish opponents would disagree: God was angry with some of the sinning that was going on out there. In a sense, these verses set a trap for those who disagree with him. He picks out some typically "Gentile" sins—idolatry and sexual immorality—and then talks about how those who practice and affirm such things are worthy of death (1:32).

In Romans 2 he triggers the trap. Merely to agree that such things are bad does not let you off the hook as far as judgment is concerned: "It is not merely knowing the law that brings God's approval. Those who obey the law will be declared right in God's sight" (2:13). Paul's point is that simply being a Jew does not help one escape judgment any more than being a Gentile automatically means you will not escape. The bottom line is that only someone who keeps the Law is considered innocent, regardless of race.

In Romans Paul arrives at his conclusion. Because no one keeps the Jewish Law perfectly, everyone—both Jew and Gentile—stand under God's wrath. "No one is good—not even one" (3:10). Whether one is Jewish or Gentile, "all have sinned" (3:23). Therefore, God is not unrighteous to find us guilty. As the NLT vividly puts it, "He will win his case in court" (3:4). Thus, the advantage of being a Jew does not lie in acceptability before God but in the privilege the Jews have of receiving God's word directly.

Christ-Faith, God's Solution

Since no one kept the Jewish Law well enough to escape God's wrath, God found another way to show His commitment to Israel and the world. Jesus was so faithful to God that He was willing to die on a cross (cf. Phil. 2:8);[8] the consequence was that His blood became a sacrificial offering for sins (Rom. 3:25). Through the atonement provided by Christ's death, God passes over the sins of anyone who has faith (3:25). Thus, God not only has proved that He is righteous, but He has provided a way for us to be found innocent on the Day of Judgment as well (3:26).

The middle chapters of Romans discuss the dynamics of how our faith in what Christ did makes salvation from God's wrath possible. Romans 4 discusses how Abraham was considered acceptable to God because of the way he trusted God, not because he was circumcised (cf. Gen. 15:6). Here is a strong argument that a person could be accepted by God even though he was uncircumcised (i.e., a Gentile). Romans 5 and 6 discuss at various points how Christ's work undoes the problems created by the sin of Adam, the first human. While Adam's sin brought death, condemnation, and the power of sin to the whole world (e.g., 5:12), Christ brought life, acquittal, and the power of the Spirit (e.g., 5:16).

Romans 6 and 7 also discuss what role the Jewish Law plays in the life of the believer. On the most basic level, the Law informs a person of God's standard and expectation (Rom. 7:7). On a darker level, the power of sin uses the Law to make us fall to temptation (5:20; 7:8). The power of sin is such that a person wanting to keep the Law could not

> **flesh:** On the most basic level, skin. By extension, the part of a human being that is under the power of Satan because it is a part of the earth; the "carnal nature."

successfully keep it—s/he could not do the good things s/he wanted to do (7:15-24). What a dreadful state to be under the power of sin! Paul exclaims, "Oh what a miserable person I am! Who will free me from this life that is dominated by sin?" (8:24).

Paul's answer is Jesus Christ, God's solution to the problem of sin. If Christ's death provides atonement, Christ's Spirit frees a believer from the power of sin (Rom. 8:2). A person with the Holy Spirit is a person who is not controlled by his or her "**flesh**," the earthly part of a person that belongs to the domain of Satan (e.g., 8:8). With the Spirit inside, we are potentially immune to the power of sin and thus able to keep the essence of the Jewish Law—love (8:4; 13:8-10). Eventually, even our flesh will be transformed into spirit, along with the rest of the created realm, which "anticipates the day when it will join God's children in glorious freedom from death and decay" (8:21).

We become a part of these incredible promises by uniting with Christ and what He has done. Symbolically, this union takes place when we are baptized.

"We died and were buried with Christ by baptism. And just as Christ was raised from the dead by the glorious power of the Father, now we also may live new lives . . . Our old sinful selves were crucified with Christ so that sin might lose its power in our lives. We are no longer slaves to sin" (Rom 6:4, 6).

What About Israel As God's Chosen People?

When you read Romans as a blueprint for how to "get saved," chapters 9–11 seem somewhat out of place. It seems like Paul suddenly stops talking about how to become a Christian and then goes off on a tangent about Israel and the Gentiles. However, as we now know, these chapters are anything but a tangent. They are the climax of the subject Paul is really talking about in the first eight chapters; namely, the fact that the gospel as Paul preached it confirms God's righteousness and faithfulness.

Even back in Romans 3 Paul had anticipated how a Jew might respond to his teaching. If salvation had nothing to do with keeping the Jewish Law, then what was the advantage of being a Jew (Rom. 3:1)? Had God just thrown away His special relationship with the Jews all of a sudden, as if He had divorced His older wife for a younger woman? What happened to the fact that God had elected or chosen Israel out of all the people of the earth (e.g., Deut. 7:6)? What about His promises to bless them if they kept the Jewish Law (e.g., Deuteronomy 28)? By saying that God saved both Jew and Gentile in the same way, how could anyone really consider God to be righteous?

Romans 9–11 deals with this issue. Paul gives two basic answers: (1) God can do whatever He wants and, (2) God has *not* abandoned Israel as His chosen people. The second point is the most important in Paul's argument, for it is the one that defends God's faithfulness to Israel. Paul does not believe that God has done away with Israel as His special people, even though the Jewish Law could not make them acceptable to Him.

In fact, Paul says exactly the opposite: "The Jews are still His chosen people because of His promises to Abraham, Isaac, and Jacob. For God's gifts and His call can never be withdrawn" (Rom. 11:28-29). Paul even thinks that Israel will eventually come to accept Christ. He says, "And so all Israel will be saved" (11:26). At present, however, "not everyone born into a Jewish family is truly a Jew! Just the fact that they are descendants of Abraham doesn't make them truly Abraham's children" (9:6-7). Currently God had chosen only a select group of Jews to accept the message.

The idea that God chooses some and not others occurs frequently in these three chapters. This fact has led some denominations to teach the idea of **predestination**—the notion that God has predetermined who will believe and who will be saved. In this way of thinking, no person is really free to decide to have faith: either God has already programmed

> **predestination:** The idea that God has already decided who will believe and be saved.

you to believe or He has not. If He has not, you will not believe. In particular, Romans 9 certainly sounds like it teaches this idea. Paul says, "God shows mercy to some just because He wants to, and He chooses to make some people refuse to listen" (Rom. 9:18).

However, it is important to read Paul's words in context. In general, he is not talking about which *individuals* God had chosen to save and which He had not. He is talking primarily about Jews and Gentiles, particularly the Jews who had rejected Christ. He is thus thinking far more about *groups* of people rather than about individuals. Paul argues that God can do whatever He wants. If He wants to open the door of salvation to the Gentiles by making the Jews reject Christ, God can do that—He's God (Rom. 9:16; 11:15).

Many of Paul's comments in these chapters emphasize the absolute authority of God as the creator of all, but in the process the picture of God can seem cold and unfeeling (Rom. 9:20-23). It is thus very important to keep these comments in proper perspective. Paul ultimately holds out hope for the very ones he said God had currently *not* chosen—the Jews. "Did God's people stumble and fall beyond recovery? Of course not! His purpose was to make his salvation available to the Gentiles, and then the Jews would be jealous and want it for themselves" (11:11). In other words, *Paul holds out hope for the very people God had currently hardened!*

This shows that Paul is not primarily talking about the predestination of individuals. He is talking about the people of Israel. We should be careful not to construct a wholesale doctrine of predestination when Paul himself held out hope to anyone who confessed Christ (e.g., Rom. 10:9). In the end, Paul's arguments aim to explain or describe what happened to Israel. Paul was not formulating a philosophy concerning how individuals come to be saved in general.

Paul's Instructions in Romans 12–15

Most of the instructions Paul gives in these chapters concern the need for Christians to show love, to be unified, and to live at peace with everyone—instructions that fit well with Paul's belief that Jew and Gentile are one in Christ. In Romans 12, for example, Paul explains how all Christians are part of the same body, the body of Christ (Rom. 12:5). He urges Christians to have sincere love (12:9) and to live at peace with everyone, letting God take care of judgment (12:18-19). In Romans 13, Paul explicitly points to love as the essence of the Jewish Law (13:10), and he encourages Christians to submit to those in authority over them (13:1). They should even pay their taxes (13:6-7)!

Chapter 14 deals with another way Christians should show love—by acting in a way that does not hinder the faith of a fellow Christian. In particular, most of the things he mentions could apply to how Gentile

Christians should behave around conservative Jewish Christians. For example, someone sensitive to another's beliefs might eat only vegetables, probably to avoid eating meat offered to idols (14:2). Others might observe the Jewish Sabbath (14:5). Paul indicates that both those who observe these aspects of the Jewish Law and those who do not are acceptable to God as long as they act out of faith (14:23). The one should not look down on the other (14:3).

A Letter of Commendation (Romans 16)

Romans ends with what appears to be a letter of commendation from Paul to the Roman Christians on behalf of a woman named Phoebe. She appears to have been a "patron" or supporter (*diakonos*) of the church that met in the port village of Corinth, a village called Cenchrea. She is likely the one who took the letter of Romans to Rome.

amanuensis: A scribe, someone who actually wrote an author's words on paper.

The chapter is mostly taken up with greetings both from Paul to various Christians in Rome and from various individuals in the Corinthian church. We learn that Priscilla and Aquila, a wife-husband ministry team, had returned to Rome and were hosting a church meeting in their house (Rom. 16:3-5). We learn of another husband-wife team, Andronicus and Junias, who probably were eyewitnesses of Jesus while He was on earth. Paul calls them both apostles, including the wife (16:7).

Paul mentions a man named Gaius, who must have been a rather wealthy member of the Corinthian church, for all the house churches of Corinth were able to meet in his house (16:23). Paul also mentions a man in Corinth named Erastus, whose name has been discovered on an inscription from Corinth. He was the city treasurer (16:23). Finally, Paul's **amanuensis**, the one who actually wrote down the words of the letter, gives his greeting. His name was Tertius (16:22).

Things to Think About

1. What are some of the ways that Christians have interpreted the phrase "the righteousness of God"? Which one do you think is correct?

Key Terms

amanuensis

flesh

predestination

righteousness of God

2. In which part of a human being does Paul locate the power of sin? Who holds control over the domain in which that part of a person exists? Whose sin handed power over this domain to an evil power? What is God's antidote to the power of sin?

3. Do you agree with this chapter's approach to the meaning of Romans? Is Paul's main concern the question of salvation for Gentiles in the light of God's prior covenant with Israel?

endnotes

1. Augustine lived from A.D. 350–430.

2. Luther was known for teaching the doctrine of "justification by faith" from Romans, the idea that we can become acceptable to God only by trusting in Christ, not by any effort of our own.

3. See the text box on the next page for some interpretations of the phrase "the righteousness of God" in Romans 1:17.

4. See chapters 36 and 37 of this text.

5. See chapters 6 and 7 of this text.

6. See the previous chapter, chapter 37, for more detailed discussion of terms like atonement and justification.

7. Here is a slight difference between Acts' presentation of Paul and what we know of him from his own writings. Acts 13:39 pictures Paul talking about the Law as if it plays some role in justification. Paul himself insisted that it played no role in justification.

8. Along with a number of others, I believe that some of Paul's references to faith in Romans 3 and Galatians 2 are to the faith of Jesus Christ and not exclusively to our faith in Christ. Take, for example, the following translation of Rom. 3:21-22, calculated to bring out its meaning: "But now God has shown his righteousness apart from the Jewish Law—even though the Law and the Prophets witness to it. This is God's willingness to save through the faithfulness of Jesus Christ, a salvation He has provided for all those who trust in Christ."

CHAPTER 39

How Do You Get to Heaven?

Salvation for Paul was about escaping God's wrath when God comes to judge the world, something Paul himself probably believed would take place in his near future.

In many Christian traditions, the way to become a Christian is quite clear. You go through a series of classes in which you learn the basics of Christian faith (**catechism** or **confirmation** classes); you commit to those basics; and you are baptized. Faith in Christ *is* important in these traditions, even if it has been placed ritually at the end of a process that extends a number of weeks or even months. While a person might escape hell if he or she died before completing the process, certainly these churches believe that the rituals are extremely important to becoming a Christian.

At a Glance

• Conversion is to change to a new religion.

• The Roman Road provides a good overview of why and how to become a Christian (Rom. 3:23; 6:23; 5:8; 10:9).

• Paul's teaching is oriented around Christ's second coming rather than heaven and hell.

• Sin for Paul is more than just the wrong acts an individual might commit; it is a power that rules over earth and flesh.

• For Paul, Christ's death was a sacrifice that satisfied God's anger and justice.

• We appropriate the benefit of Christ's death through faith in His victorious Resurrection. We are joined to Christ's death and Resurrection through baptism.

• The down payment and guarantee of future salvation is the Holy Spirit within us.

altar: In some Christian denominations, a kneeling board at the front of the church where a person can pray.

catechism: Basic instruction in the teachings of Christianity.

confirmation: For churches that baptize infants, the process of personally affirming or "confirming" the faith your parents affirmed for you when you were a child.

However, some Christian traditions or denominations have reacted strongly against the highly ritualistic dimension of conversion (becoming a Christian) in such churches. Chiefly, they are troubled at the possibility of going through such a ritual process without having a *personal* experience or encounter with God. For them, becoming a Christian is a highly personal matter. It is thus no coincidence that these churches also tend to reject the baptism of infants. They generally believe baptism should only take place if you are mature enough to understand what you are doing when you are baptized.

Ironically, such churches also have rituals for becoming a Christian. In some, you come forward and pray at an **altar**—a kneeling board at the front of the church. In others, you meet with the minister after the service in a back room and pray. Either way, prayer is the most important element in the process of becoming a Christian for such churches.[1] It ultimately does not matter where you are or what circumstances lead up to the prayer, as long as you admit to God that you have done wrong and ask Him to forgive you. Because this prayer involves an admission that you have done wrong or sinned, it is sometimes called the "**sinner's prayer**." Some churches urge baptism as soon as possible thereafter.

evangelism: The practice of telling others about the need and the possibility of salvation from God's wrath.

plan of salvation: A brief explanation of why and how you become a Christian.

Interestingly, conversion in these churches also involves a kind of

catechism—instructions on what becoming a Christian is all about. Because they emphasize the personal or spiritual dimension of conversion, however, such instruction often takes place *after* you have already committed your life to Christianity by praying the sinner's prayer. In churches that urge immediate baptism, such instruction even takes place after baptism.[2]

Nevertheless, a highly shortened "catechism" is considered important

> **sinner's prayer:** A prayer in which you admit that you are a sinner in need of God's forgiveness.
>
> **salvation:** In general, escape from God's wrath when He judges the world. For many churches it has become a shorthand way of referring to becoming a Christian—"getting saved."

for a person before praying the sinner's prayer. Because for such churches **salvation**—escaping God's wrath—is a personal matter, you must understand what you are doing when you pray the prayer. A shortened **plan of salvation**—an explanation of why and how one becomes a Christian—is necessary *before* the prayer if the prayer is to be meaningful.

Groups of this sort often emphasize **evangelism**, the practice of telling others about the need to be "saved" (from hell) as well as the possibility of salvation. Sometimes this evangelism takes place with total strangers. You might talk to someone next to you on an airplane about Christianity. A typical lead question asks, "Do you know where you would go if you were to die suddenly?" If the stranger is interested in converting, a short catechism becomes crucial so s/he can pray the sinner's prayer with understanding.

Although several such "catechisms" exist, one of the better known is called the **Roman Road**, taking its name from the book of Romans. It provides the basic rationale and mechanism for becoming a Christian by way of four verses from the book of Romans. The first, Romans 3:23 states, "All have sinned and fall short of the glory of God" (NIV). A person thus needs to recognize that s/he is a sinner before that person can be forgiven for his/her sins.

The second verse is Romans 6:23: "The wages of sin is death, but the free gift of God is eternal life through Christ Jesus our Lord."

These two verses present us with the problem for which Christianity has the solution. Not only are we sinners, but we face the prospect of death as a consequence. Usually, those who **witness** (tell others about the Christian message) by way of the Roman Road interpret death in this verse to be a *spiritual* death more than a physical one. In other words, because we are all sinners, we all face the prospect of spending **eternity**—forever—in the burning fires of hell.

Roman Road: A series of four verses from Romans (3:23; 6:23; 5:8; 10:9) that explain the "plan of salvation"—the basic reasons for becoming a Christian and how to do so.

to "witness": To tell others about the possibility of salvation; to "evangelize"; to share the "gospel."

eternity: Forever.

However, Romans 6:23 also holds out hope when it mentions a gift that Jesus has provided. This gift is spelled out in the next verse on the "Roman Road," Romans 5:8: "God showed His great love for us by sending Christ to die for us while we were still sinners." Here is the solution to the problem of humanity—Christ's death for us. A person sharing the gospel (good news about the possibility of salvation) might say that Christ "took our place" on the cross. By such a statement, he would mean that although we deserved death for our wrongdoings, Jesus—someone who had never sinned—died instead. While *we* deserved death, Christ took our punishment for us.

The final verse of the Roman Road tells us how to "sign up" for such salvation from judgment. Romans 10:9 says, "If you confess with your mouth that Jesus is Lord and believe in your heart that God raised Him from the dead, you will be saved." Those who witness often teach that it is only through faith or trust in what Jesus has done that we can be saved. Such a Christian often will draw a strong distinction between "justification by faith" (getting right with God by trusting in Christ) and trying to "earn" your salvation through **good works** (doing good things, being a fairly good person). In Romans 10:9, it is through faith or belief in one's heart that salvation becomes possible. You can never be good enough to earn salvation, just as Romans 3:23 is often interpreted: "all have sinned and fall short of God's glorious standard."[3]

> **good works:** Good deeds; doing good things.

The Roman Road is not a bad way of summarizing what Paul thought about the why's and how's of becoming a Christian. Nevertheless, Paul himself presented the gospel message a bit differently, and Christians regularly take his words slightly out of context. While the Roman Road is not completely wrong, the rest of this chapter gives us a more precise understanding of how Paul himself presented the prospect of salvation.

God's Approaching Wrath

We just mentioned the opening line of one approach to evangelism: "If you were to die tonight, would you have the assurance of going to heaven?" In fact, the title of this chapter is "How Do You Get to Heaven?" I chose this specifically because it echoes what many Christians think about "getting saved." For many, Christianity is about going to heaven when you die and having an existence that goes beyond death. The other option, of course, is to go to **hell**, usually thought of as a place of eternal torment in fire.

When Paul thought about salvation, however, he did *not* think of it primarily in terms of heaven and hell. For example, Paul does not mention hell a single time in all of his writings. He gives us only some vague comments that might indicate that Christians will go to heaven at some point in the future.[4] So what is salvation about for Paul? It centers not on God's judgment of the *dead*, but on His judgment of those *living* on earth when Jesus returns.

hell: The place of eternal torment for the damned.

resurrection: Coming back to life from the dead.

second coming: Christ's return to earth on the Day of Judgment.

Thus, salvation for Paul is about escaping God's wrath when He comes to judge the world, something Paul himself probably believed would take place in his near future (cf. 1 Cor. 7:26; Phil. 4:5). If you die before that judgment comes, salvation also involves **resurrection**—becoming alive again after dying. The first letter Paul wrote to the city of Thessalonica confirms that his preaching focused on Christ's **second coming**, His return to earth on the Day of Judgment—rather than on where people go when they die. Paul spent at least several weeks in this city, probably several months (Phil. 4:16). Even though he fully presented the gospel to them, apparently in all that time he never addressed the question of what happens to people after they die. He had to write the Thessalonians a letter about this issue *after he had left the city*!

For Paul, God's coming wrath would not only visit the humans of the earth, but sinful angels as well. In fact, Paul teaches that Christians will participate in the judgment of the world (e.g., 1 Cor. 6:2). Thus, when 1 Thessalonians 4:17 says that Christians will meet Christ in the air, it is probably not to go off to heaven immediately. It is probably an assembly for battle.

One helpful insight we gain from Paul is that the most literal sense of salvation deals with the future. On the one hand, it is true that Christ's death has *already* made salvation a "done deal"—the check is paid and it will not bounce. Also, we can be assured *today* that we are right with God, justified in His court and, therefore, that we will experience salvation from God's wrath when He comes to judge the earth in the future. When Christians say they "are" saved or "have been saved," they are thinking of salvation in these ways.

On the other hand, the most literal sense of salvation is future. I only literally escape God's wrath on the Day of Judgment. Technically, therefore, no one has been saved yet, for no one will be literally saved until the "Day of Christ" (1 Cor. 5:5).[5] Viewing salvation from this perspective will help us gain important insights into issues like whether one can "lose" his or her salvation. In a literal sense, no one has it fully to lose yet.

The Cosmic Power of Sin

Paul did believe that all individuals except for Jesus (e.g., 2 Cor. 5:21) had sinned at some point in their lives, and he did believe that death was the main consequence of sin. However, the typical ways many Christians today think of sin and death are somewhat different from Paul's understanding. For example, when Paul says, "all have sinned" (Rom. 3:23), he is focusing on all *groups*—both Jew *and* Gentile—rather than on all individuals. Paul's writings are not about whether doing good works in general will get you to heaven or not. Rather, Paul's writings discuss the question of whether a Jew can be acceptable to God on the basis of keeping the Jewish Law.

Further, Paul's idea of sin goes beyond "something I do" or "something inside of me." Sin for Paul seems to be a power that rules on the earth—the earth of which our human flesh is a part. Apparently, after **Adam** sinned, God allowed the creation to become subject to demonic powers (cf. Eph. 2:2-3). Not just humanity,

> **Adam:** The first human being; described in Genesis 1-3. Paul indicates that his moral failure resulted in the power of sin over the world.

but the whole creation became enslaved to the power of sin and its corruption (Rom. 8:20). On our own, we are powerless to do the good dictated in the Jewish Law. Even if we would want to keep the Law, the power of sin consistently foils us (Rom. 7:14-17).

Our flesh, the earthly part of a human being, is a part of the creation and is thus a foothold of sin's power. It is no coincidence that a person's "flesh" is the part of us that is susceptible to death, the consequence of sin. Paul even goes so far as to say that "nothing good dwells within me, that is, *in my flesh*" (Rom. 7:18 NRSV) and that "those who are in the flesh cannot please God" (8:8 NRSV). In this last verse, flesh has become more than just skin; it has become skin as it is enslaved to the power of sin over the earth.[6]

Christ Died for Us

It is common for Christians to speak of Christ "taking our place" on the cross. In other words, Christ stood in as a *substitute* for us: we deserved death, but He died instead. Paul certainly says things along these lines, but we must read very carefully. Paul never says that Christ took *my* specific place on the cross. Indeed, Paul talks about us *joining* Christ on the cross (Gal. 2:19-20). When we say that Christ took our *punishment* for us, we come closer to what Paul actually says, but Paul still did not think of Christ as taking my *individual* punishment. Rather, he thought of Christ paying for the atonement of the sins of the whole world in general.

Paul inherited from Christians before him the sense that Christ's death had been a kind of "sacrifice" that *satisfied* God's anger toward the sins of the world. God's justice and anger demanded satisfaction, meaning that some price needed to be paid for sin (Rom. 1:18). God's solution—offering Christ as a sacrificial offering (Rom. 3:25)—showed that God was even more righteous than if He had slaughtered us all. God showed himself righteous with regard to us by placing the sin of the world on Christ (2 Cor. 5:21). He satisfied His anger and was faithful to save Israel in a single act—the offering of Christ on the cross for sin. By uniting with Christ's death through baptism, we will escape God's wrath when He comes to judge the earth (Rom. 6:3-4).

Therefore, while it is true that Christ died *for us*, Paul is not saying that He died *in my specific place*. More often than not, Paul uses this phrase to mean that He died *for our benefit*. He threw himself on the grenade of sin and saved us from certain death. He satisfied God's wrath and defeated the powers of sin. Even so, Paul never connects the dots to say that Christ *substituted* for *our punishment*. Indeed, if hell were our eternal destiny, Christ would have needed to endure eternal torment if He were truly to take our place.

A number of scholars have recently suggested another interesting difference between Paul's thinking and how we often think about salvation; namely, that the faith *of Jesus himself* played an important role in making this salvation possible. At a few key points in Paul's arguments, he uses a phrase that is usually translated "faith *in* Christ" (e.g., Rom. 3:22; Gal. 2:16). However, an equally if not more valid translation of the phrase is "the faith *of* Jesus Christ."[7] While faith *in* Christ is certainly important for Paul, many scholars now suggest that the *faithfulness* of Christ—a possible meaning for the word *faith*—was even more crucial for our salvation. If they are correct, then it is not even so much *my* faith that makes me right with God. Rather, it is my trust in the faithfulness *of Christ*. My faith is powerless apart from the *faithful death* of Jesus.

Finally, Christ's death is not the only event that has saving significance in Paul's teaching. Christ's Resurrection and His exaltation to the right hand of God are also important for salvation. Christ's Resurrection implies His victory over death—something in which we can also participate (Rom. 6:4). Christ's seating at God's right hand in heaven was the "crowning moment" of salvation, when Jesus most literally came into His kingship. Once Jesus arrived at God's right hand, He began to intercede for our salvation (Rom. 8:34).

Faith in Christ

Although *Christ's* faithful death certainly is the most important element in salvation, *we* must also trust or have faith in Christ in order to receive its benefit. We take advantage of the salvation Christ has made possible by trusting in Him. Romans 10:9 puts it well:

> "If you confess with your mouth that Jesus is Lord and believe in your heart that God raised him from the dead, you will be saved."
>
> **Romans 10:9**

Paul saw that we could ensure our future salvation by trusting in the victorious Resurrection of Jesus from the dead. We come to believe that *Christ's* victory over death entails *our* victory over death. And Christ is not done with His saving activities. When the early Christians confessed, "Jesus is Lord," they meant not only that He had risen victoriously from the dead, but also that God had enthroned Him as king in the heavens. As king He would return again to save His people from God's wrath and rule the earth. Therefore, trusting in Christ as Lord also implies that we trust Him to save us on Judgment Day because we have committed to His kingship.

One debate has often followed the church in the last five hundred years or so. It is the question of whether we escape God's judgment through our faith in Christ alone or by our good deeds as well. In the classic debate of the 1500s, Martin Luther insisted that it was by faith alone that we are "justified" and found acceptable to God. His Roman Catholic opponents, on the other hand, insisted that both faith and works were essential for our salvation. Luther drew his arguments primarily from Paul's writings, while the strongest support for the Roman Catholic position came from James.

Look at the two verses below:

> "For it is by grace you have been saved, through faith—and this not from yourselves, it is the gift of God—not by works, so that no one can boast."
>
> **Ephesians 2:8 NIV**
>
> "So you see, we are made right with God by what we do, not by faith alone."
>
> **James 2:24**

The first one is a classic text for those who believe you cannot *earn* salvation in any way. For Luther, we could only become right with God on the basis of faith alone (*sola fide*). Indeed, for many of the first Protestants—particularly a man named John Calvin—even our faith was completely a gift from God. No one could decide on his or her own to have faith. God had chosen those individuals who would be saved even before He had created the world. Accordingly, He predestined them to have faith. We can admire this position in that it keeps the act of faith from being the "work" of the person who comes to Christ—God even does the faith part for you.

On the other hand, the quote from James sounds quite different from the position of most Protestants. While Paul never explicitly says that faith *alone* makes us right with God—Paul never uses the word *alone* in this way—James *does* explicitly say that faith alone will *not* make us right with God. For this reason, Martin Luther was very hesitant even to translate James into German, considering it an "epistle of straw" in its thinking about Christ.

We can eliminate most of the apparent contradiction between Paul and James, as well as Protestants and Catholics, if we break down the issue of "faith versus works" into some clearer questions.

When are we truly saved? We are most literally saved on the Day of Christ, His second coming (Rom. 5:9; 1 Thess. 5:9). How is it that we come to be saved—by being a good person? Paul emphatically teaches that no one

"Therefore, since we have been justified through faith, we have peace with God through our Lord Jesus Christ, through whom we have gained access by faith into this grace in which we now stand."

Romans 5:1-2 NIV

"If anyone is in Christ, he is a new creation; the old has gone, the new has come! All this is from God, who reconciled us to himself through Christ . . ."

2 Corinthians 5:17-18 NIV

keeps the Jewish Law perfectly enough to merit salvation (Rom. 3:10, 23; Gal. 3:10-11).[8] Faith in Christ is also significant for James (e.g., James 2:1), although James barely even mentions Christ in his letter (only 1:1 and 2:1). Clearly James and Paul each emphasize this differently, but it is reasonable to believe that both see faith in Christ as an essential element in salvation.

Did both Paul and James believe that how you lived after you became a Christian was important? They most certainly did! Both Paul and James had definite expectations about how a Christian should live. James focuses on social matters like the poor, widows, and the fatherless (James 1:27)—concerns Paul also shares (Gal. 2:10). Paul seems especially troubled by those who violate the sexual prohibitions of Leviticus 18 (e.g., 1 Cor. 5; Romans 1). Both Paul and James consider certain "works" to be important and others prohibited in the Christian equation, even if they do not believe anyone can *earn* salvation. Therefore, we can see that on the fundamental issues not only Paul and James agree, but even Protestant and Catholic.

New Spiritual Creation

Salvation for Paul was not simply a matter of a court decision in our favor. God did not simply declare us innocent and leave it at that until the future when Christ would return to earth. In Paul's eyes, God started the process of transforming us into creatures of heaven from the moment of our justification. God made us a "new creation" through His Holy Spirit.

It was common in Paul's day to think of spirit as the substance of heaven. A philosophical group known as the Stoics, for example, believed that the human spirit was just a little bit of the substance of heaven and of God. It may be helpful for you to follow what Paul and the early Christians had to say about the Holy Spirit by thinking of Him as God's breath inside us, empowering us to live the way God wants us to live and to do what God wants us to do.[9]

According to Paul, a person could not even be considered a Christian if s/he did not have the Holy Spirit inside him or her (e.g., Rom. 8:9). Paul thought of the Holy Spirit inside us as our heavenly reservation, our guarantee of a heavenly body at the resurrection and the seal of God's ownership of us (2 Cor. 1:22; 5:5). But the Spirit is more than just God's brand on us—the Spirit is a "little bit of heaven" inside us. The Spirit is a "foretaste of glory divine" (cf. Heb. 6:4-5), a "deposit" of what is to come (2 Cor. 1:22; 5:5). At the resurrection, we will receive bodies that are completely spiritual, without any flesh or blood to them (1 Cor. 15:44, 50). In the meantime, we are in a continual process of spiritual transformation (2 Cor. 3:18; 4:16).

Things to Think About

1. How does Paul's understanding of sin, salvation, and judgment differ from how Christians today tend to think about these concepts (e.g., the Roman Road)?

2. Reflect on these two questions:
   a) How much do Christians *read into* the text of the Bible?
   b) How many of their ideas actually come *from the text*?

3. Do your observations imply that Christian tradition tends to be equally or more important than the Bible itself in terms of what Christians believe? Notice how many contemporary Christian terms in the "Key Terms" section do not actually come from the Bible!

4. After reading this chapter, what would you say to someone who wanted to become a Christian? How would you tell this person to go about this process?

Key Terms

Adam

altar

catechism

confirmation

eternity

evangelism

good works

hell

plan of salvation

resurrection

Roman Road

salvation (in general)

second coming

sinner's prayer

to witness

endnotes

1. Prayer is, of course, a part of the ritual of becoming a Christian in the "mainline" churches as well—churches with sufficient history, numbers, and prominence to be widely known by the general populace (e.g., Roman Catholic, Lutheran, Methodist, etc.).

2. Some denominations so emphasize the spiritual nature of conversion that baptism becomes significantly less important or even unimportant in the process of becoming a Christian. While the Church of Christ and Baptist churches urge immediate baptism after praying the sinner's prayer, Quakers and the Salvation Army do not baptize at all. The Wesleyan Church allows baptisms of all kinds—infant or adult; by immersion, pouring, or sprinkling; soon, later, or never after conversion—chiefly because it does not think the ritual act is what saves a person.

3. You might note that I used the NIV when I quoted Romans 3:23 earlier. I did this because the verse almost certainly does not refer to our falling short of a glory that God has, but to our falling short of a glory God intended for us to have. The NLT has thus slightly changed the meaning of the verse.

4. Perhaps 1 Thessalonians 4:17; Philippians 1:23; 3:20. Paul, however, also speaks of the transformation of the heavens and earth, perhaps implying that our future

existence will be on a transformed earth (Rom. 8:21).

5. Paul, of course, could speak of salvation in the past tense (e.g., Rom. 8:24). But he was not being fully literal when he wrote in this way. The most literal sense of salvation is found in verses like Romans 5:9-10.

6. The NIV and NLT often translate the Greek word for *flesh* with "sinful nature." However, this term makes us lose sight of the connection between *skin* and *sin* that certainly stands at the root of Paul's use of this word.

7. The phrase is actually ambiguous—it can legitimately mean "faith in Christ" or "faith of Christ." The English word *faith* often gets in our way here, since we are not used to speaking of Christ having faith.

8. A major difference between the Protestant-Catholic debate and Paul's own debate is the way we think of the word *works*. Paul was always thinking of works of *Jewish Law* when he talked about works. Protestants and Catholics argue about good deeds in general.

9. Of course, early Christians would increasingly understand the Holy Spirit to be a person in His own right, which is still the belief of Christians today. For Christians, God is three persons but only one God. However, we must allow that it took the church hundreds of years (presumably also under the influence of the Holy Spirit) to figure out these things fully—long after all the New Testament writings had been written.

CHAPTER 40

Contemporary Issues in Romans

The Bible often does not directly address the issues about which we are
most concerned today.

Matters of Debate

The book of Romans touches on a
number of issues that are of interest to
Christians today. While the New
Testament does not always directly
address our concerns, Christians have
always selected their favorite passages
from which to argue specific points.
Sometimes they debate over **theological**
issues—issues that relate to what we
should believe. At other times they use
the New Testament to address practical
issues—issues of how to live.

Frequently the New Testament's
verses support more than one position,
even opposing positions. One reason this
happens is because the New Testament
addresses a world two thousand years
removed from our world. As we have
seen, sometimes their categories are

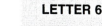

Contemporary Issues and Romans

• Can a person practice homosexuality
  and be a Christian (Rom. 1:24-27)?

• Do we become right with God by faith
  or by works (Romans 3–4)?

• Can a Christian stop sinning
  (Romans 7–8)?

• Does God decide who will be saved
  (Romans 9–11)?

• Once a person is made right with
  God, can s/he still fail to be saved in
  the end (Rom. 8:35-39)?

• Should a Christian obey the Law
  (Rom. 13:1-7)?

theological: Pertaining to our beliefs
about God and related issues.

simply different from ours. As we have also seen, the early Christians themselves sometimes differed in their perspectives. Often a person's denomination or culture has a big influence on which verses s/he ends up favoring.

The purpose of this chapter is to discuss some of the passages Christians debate in the book of Romans. We will lay out some of the basic positions people take. Certain aspects of ancient culture may be relevant, and in such cases we will try to mention factors that might significantly alter our perspective on an issue. What we may find is that sometimes we are not asking the text questions that it wants to answer. The Bible often does not directly address the issues about which we are most concerned today.

Homosexuality

Romans provides us with the most extensive mention of homosexual practice in the New Testament, although it is mentioned in at least two other places (1 Cor. 6:9; 1 Tim. 1:10). In addition, Romans 1 is the only passage in the whole Bible that seems to allude to the practice of lesbianism (Rom. 1:26). Romans 1:24-27 implies that homosexual practice is unacceptable to God.

Anyone who uses the Bible to justify hatred is using the Bible incorrectly.

While some have argued that these verses referred exclusively to male temple prostitution or homosexual rape, this interpretation is unlikely.

After we have concluded that Paul is opposed to homosexual practice, it is important that we do not misread other aspects of what Paul is saying. First, there is a distinction between homosexual acts and what we call a homosexual orientation. The idea of orientation is a modern one that would have been foreign to Paul. In Paul's mind, homosexuals were people who regularly had homosexual sex—not people who were "wired" to find the same sex attractive. The New Testament does not condemn people who struggle with one kind of lust any more than it condemns those who struggle with another. As such, the church might prayerfully consider how it could minister to "celibate homosexuals."

Second, Paul does not single out homosexual sin as a sin worse than all others. Those who think the chapter gives us a spiral to greater and greater perversity must reckon with the fact that the final sins mentioned are things like slandering, arrogance, and boastfulness (Rom. 1:30). In fact, it is not clear that Paul's comment—that some sinners are worthy of death—is even about practicing homosexuals (1:32). This comment comes at the end of the chapter after he has listed other vices, such as the ones just mentioned.

Paul's comments on homosexual sex are logically placed in his argument as a way to set up his audience. He picks some typically Gentile sins that Jews loved to talk about, namely, the fact that Gentiles served nonexistent gods and were sexually immoral. He does this, however, to set up the Jews in his audience for what he would say in Romans 2 and 3. His point is that no matter how immoral the Gentiles (who did not have the Jewish Law) might be, Jews were not off the hook because they did not keep the Law perfectly either. His conclusion is that all—both Gentile *and* Jew—have sinned and fallen short of the glory God intended humanity to have.

What these observations mean is that we cannot use Paul's comments in Romans 1 as an excuse to hate homosexuals, which seems to be the way some Christians use verses like these. The guiding principle for applying any Scripture must always be that of love. Not only does Scripture affirm that God is love (1 John 4:8), but Jesus tells us that all of God's requirements for humanity can be summed up in the need to love God and to love our neighbor (Matt. 22:34-40). Anyone who uses the Bible to justify hatred is using the Bible incorrectly.

Saved by Faith or Works?

The previous chapter touched on a familiar debate between Protestants and Catholics over whether a person gets right with God by way of his or her trust in Christ or by way of how s/he acts. Look in the text box at the following verses from various places in the New Testament.

These three passages almost seem to say different things. The first talks about getting right with God as a matter of our faith, saying nothing about how we might keep the Jewish Law. The third seems to say that doing the right things is just as important for getting right with God as our faith is. The second goes beyond talk of getting right with God to the matter of our salvation from God's judgment. Not only are we made right with God through our faith, but we escape God's wrath as well.

> "We become right with God, not by doing what the law commands, but by faith in Jesus Christ."
>
> **Galatians 2:16**

> "God saved you by his special favor when you believed. And you can't take credit for this; it is a gift from God. Salvation is not a reward for the good things we have done, so none of us can boast about it."
>
> **Ephesians 2:8-9**

> "So you see, we are made right with God by what we do, not by faith alone."
>
> **James 2:24**

Christians mix these ideas together in several different ways. We can find Christians on the extremes: (1) those who believe that what we do is completely irrelevant to our salvation, or (2) those who believe we must fully earn our salvation. Most people, however, probably fall somewhere in the middle.

Most Protestants believe that it is our faith alone that gets us in good standing with God, but that the Holy Spirit causes us to live better lives as a result—that we bear "fruit" from the fact that we are saved (e.g., Gal. 5:22-23). While "works" do not save us, they are important for the Christian.

Most Catholics, on the other hand, believe that salvation is a cooperative effort between our faith and our deeds. The practical result between these two emphases in how we are to live may not come out too differently in the end.

One important thing to consider in this debate is the question of when salvation occurs and what is necessary for it to occur. Very few would contest that trust in what Christ has done for us is the key to escaping God's judgment. However, some Christians believe that it is possible to be right with God initially and yet not be saved in the end if one goes astray. For such individuals, some element of "doing" becomes a part of the equation for salvation, as it is in James. There comes a point at which we are mincing words over whether it is faith or works that saves us—both play a role as we "work out our salvation" (Phil. 2:12 NIV).

Can a Christian Stop Sinning?

The majority of Christians probably view sin as a constant element of human life—try though we might, no human on earth can help but sin while s/he is on earth. While 1 John 1:8 often plays a feature role in this idea, Romans 7 also is a key passage used to support this perspective. Paul's comments are taken to reflect his continual experience of life: "I really want

> "Those who have been born into God's family do not sin, because God's life is in them. So they can't keep on sinning, because they have been born of God."
>
> **1 John 3:9**

to do what is right, but I don't do it. Instead, I do the very thing I hate" (Rom. 7:15). Interpretation stops with 7:24, "Oh, what a miserable person I am! Who will free me from this life that is dominated by sin?"

There are important reasons to reconsider this prevalent interpretation, not least because it seems to skew most of what the New Testament actually says

> "I know perfectly well that what I am doing is wrong, and my bad conscience shows that I agree that the law is good. But I can't help myself, because it is sin inside me that makes me do these evil things."
>
> **Romans 7:16-17**

about sin. One of the main purposes of 1 John, for example, is actually *to prevent sin* (1 John 2:1), not to argue for its continual existence in the life of the believer. On the contrary, 1 John 3:9 insists that sin is *incompatible* with someone who has been born of God. The standard interpretation of Romans 7 is also a misinterpretation of large proportions, leading us in exactly the opposite direction that Paul actually was going with his argument.

When we read Romans 7 in context, we see that Paul is dealing with the role of the Jewish Law in the process of getting right with God. Throughout the book he emphasizes that no one can become acceptable to God on the basis of keeping the Law (Rom. 3:20). Rather, the Law prepares me for Christ by showing me that I have sin (3:20) and, in some strange way, leads me to sin even more than I would have if I did not know the Law (5:20; 7:5, 8, 13). Perhaps because he had learned his lesson in Corinth (cf. 1 Cor. 5:1-2; 6:12; 10:23), Paul also emphasizes that freedom from the Law does not give one an excuse to sin (Rom. 3:31; 6:1, 15).

Therefore, we read Romans 7:14-25 drastically out of context if we do not connect it to the person who is "under the Law"—that is, to a person who has not yet become a Christian and received the Holy Spirit. Indeed, the chapter begins with the claim that a person who dies is freed from the Law. Romans 7:5-6 puts it this way, "While we were living in the flesh, our sinful passions, *aroused by the law*, were at work in our members to bear fruit for death. But now *we are discharged from the law*, dead to that which held us captive, so that we are slaves not under the old written code but in the new life of the Spirit"

(NRSV). The rest of this chapter as well as the next expand upon this statement.

Romans 7:7-13 plays out in more detail the situation of a person under the Law. As Romans 3:20 states, Romans 7:7 notes again that the Law provides me with a knowledge of sin. As in Romans 5:20 and 7:5, Romans 7:8-13 notes again that the "sinful passions" of the person living "in the flesh" actually grow *because of* the Law. It is in this context that the famous verses of Romans 7:14-25 appear. While Paul uses the word *I* in these verses and while he uses the present tense, the context demands that we read these words in terms of a person who is still under the Law. In other words, Paul is speaking hypothetically, placing himself in the shoes of such a person.[1] His conclusion is that a person under the Law has no power to overcome sin.

We seriously skew what Paul is saying, therefore, if we do not move beyond Romans 7 into Romans 8, where Paul stops talking about the person who is a slave "under the old written code" and resumes his consideration of those who are

> "For God has done what the law, weakened by the flesh, could not do . . . he condemned sin in the flesh, so that the just requirement of the law might be fulfilled in us, who walk not according to the flesh but according to the Spirit."
>
> **Romans 8:3-4 NRSV**

"slaves of righteousness" (cf. Rom. 6:18). The shift in the discussion from a non-Christian under the Law to a Christian under grace is signaled in 8:1-2 where Paul announces, "So now there is no condemnation for those who belong to Christ Jesus. For the power of the life-giving Spirit has freed you through Christ Jesus from the power of sin that leads to death."

While the Law is putty in the hands of the power of sin, enslaving us to a life of unstoppable sinning, the Spirit empowers us actually to fulfill the "just requirement of the law" (Rom. 8:4 NRSV), a requirement Paul later indicates as love (13:8). This person is no longer "in the flesh" (8:8 NRSV) or "walking" according to the flesh (8:4). This person is walking "in the Spirit." Obviously, Paul is not suggesting that we throw away our bodies, our "flesh."

Rather, flesh has become a way of talking about that part of a human being that is susceptible to the power of sin: the so-called **sinful nature**, as many translations put it.

sinful nature: The way that some Bibles translate the Greek word for *flesh*. It refers to that part of a human being (i.e., the physical part) that is subject to the power of sin if a person does not have the Holy Spirit within.

The argument of Romans is difficult to follow because Paul "flies by" the same basic idea over and over again. Galatians 5:16 gives us a compressed and much clearer version of what Paul is saying in Romans: "Live by the Spirit, I say, and do not gratify the desires of the flesh" (NRSV). As in Romans, we have a contrast between living "in the Spirit" and living "in the flesh." Paul is talking about how *you* live—he is not talking about some legal fiction of how God just *considers* you good when you are not. And Paul not only affirms the possibility of victory over the flesh through the Spirit—he commands it! In other words, a Christian can live victoriously over sin in this life.

Predestination

One issue over which Christians sometimes disagree is that of whether God has already handpicked who will be saved in the end. The idea is that before He created the world, God decided or predestined those who would be saved. In this way of thinking, since only those whom God has chosen can make it, those He has *not* chosen obviously will not be saved.[2] Romans 9–11 provides some of the strongest arguments for this view.

It is undeniable that the New Testament uses language of predestination extensively. Take the verses on the next page, for example. These verses seem to say that "even before he made the world," God "chose" or **elected** those who would become Christians, as well as those who would disobey. God planned these things according to His **foreknowledge**—the fact that He knew ahead of time.

Those who do not believe God literally chooses who will be saved sometimes use the idea of foreknowledge to argue that this language does not mean God actually *determines* who will be saved. Rather, they argue that God just plans things according to His knowledge of the free choice a person would have made anyway. On the other hand, those who take this language literally think that what God is "foreknowing" is the existence of all the people who will live. The one interpretation says God foreknows what our **free will** choice will be; the other says God foreknows who will exist and then chooses among those.

> "God knew his people in advance, and he chose them to become like his Son . . . And having chosen them, he called them to come to him."
>
> **Romans 8:29-30**

> "Long ago, even before he made the world, God loved us and chose us in Christ to be holy and without fault in his eyes . . . He chose us from the beginning, and all things happen just as he decided long ago."
>
> **Ephesians 1:4, 11**

> "To God's elect . . . who have been chosen according to the foreknowledge of God . . ."
>
> **1 Peter 1:1, 2 NIV**

> "They stumble because they do not listen to God's word or obey it, and so they meet the fate that has been planned for them."
>
> **1 Peter 2:8b**

Romans 9–11 certainly *sounds* like it supports the idea of predestination. Take the verses on the next page, for example. Many will find these verses shocking. Did Paul really say that God makes some people for trash?[3]

The implications of the idea that God arbitrarily decides who will be saved and who will be damned seem staggering. First Timothy 2:4, for example, says that God "wants everyone to be saved and to understand the truth." But this would not be the case if salvation were strictly a matter of God's choice—if God predestines those who will be saved and if God wants everyone to be saved, then everyone would be saved. However, the New Testament does not teach that all will be saved. From the standpoint of human logic, we would either conclude that God does not want everyone to be saved or that God does not arbitrarily determine who will be saved.

> "God shows mercy to some just because he wants to, and he chooses to make some people refuse to listen.
>
> "Well then, you might say, 'Why does God blame people for not listening? Haven't they simply done what he made them do?'
>
> "No, don't say that. Who are you, a mere human being, to criticize God? Should the thing that was created say to the one who made it, 'Why have you made me like this?' When a potter makes jars out of clay, doesn't he have the right to use the same lump of clay to make one jar for decoration and another to throw garbage into?"
>
> **Romans 9:18-21**

You will have to decide which way to go, but a few considerations are in order. First of all, it is important to realize that Romans 9–11 is not really about the predestination *of individuals*, although these chapters may have implications for individual predestination. As we noted earlier in chapter 38 of this book, these chapters come at the climax of Paul's defense of God's righteousness, particularly in light of the fact that God had now welcomed the Gentiles. Paul insists that being a Jew and keeping the Jewish Law does not in any way assure a person of salvation. Rather, God has chosen to make the world right with Him through Christ.

This fact raises the question of God's relationship with the Jews. What about His covenant with Israel? Has God divorced His people? How could God just change his mind and plans when He had chosen (elected) Israel to be His special people? How could He adopt the Gentiles without forcing them to live under the Jewish Law?

It is in this context that Paul discusses election in Romans 9–11. He affirms that "God's gifts and his call can never be withdrawn" (Rom. 11:29). He believes that "all Israel will be saved" (11:26), by which he means all *true* Israel—those that will trust in Christ (9:6-7). When he talks about God making some jars for destruction (9:22), he is talking about the fact that Israel had, for the most part, rejected Christ. God has every right, Paul says, to bring the Gentiles to salvation without requiring them to keep the Law. In short, God is God and He can do whatever He wants.

foreknowledge: Knowledge of something before it happens.

election (New Testament): The idea that God chooses who will be saved.

free will: The idea that God has allowed humans freedom to some extent to make choices and that God has not already decided who will be saved.

sovereign: Having absolute control.

deterministic: Holding that everything that happens is predetermined.

While Paul's discussion of God's predestination deals primarily with groups—Jew and Gentile—it has obvious implications for individuals. For example, it certainly sounds as if God has decided which Jews will be true Israel and which He has made for judgment. The question is how much Paul would want us to connect the dots beyond his basic argument. After all, Paul had been known to go to some extremes to argue a point.

If we are to keep the whole New Testament in balance, it seems we have to live with paradox regarding the idea of predestination and God's desire for all to be saved. Paul's language of determinism never seems to impact his thoughts on how to live. While he seems in some places to affirm predestination in the strongest of terms, he conducts his mission to the world as if anyone has a chance. The language of predestination, it seems, talks about the world in order to affirm the fact that God is **sovereign**—in control— yet does not affect how we are to live or conduct ourselves. It is "after the fact" language—you know what God has predestined after it has happened. You do not let it affect what you do.

This is a good time to remember that the ancient Mediterranean world in general tended to be fatalistic. As the saying goes, "Que sera, sera"—"What will be, will be." Most of those at the time of Christ believed that they were pawns in a divine chess game. Nowhere is this clearer than in the non-biblical story of Oedipus. His father received a prophecy that he would have a son who would kill him, after which the child would marry his own mother. Oedipus' father thus tried to kill his son when he was born.

Unknown to him, however, he did not succeed. Another man raised Oedipus in a different city, never telling Oedipus he was not his real son. When Oedipus later received the same prophecy, he left town, not wanting to kill his father or marry his mother. By fate, he came across his real father in his travels, got into a dispute, and killed him. He then settled in a city where, as you have probably guessed by now, he married his mother without realizing it. This story illustrates so well the paradox between free will and determinism in the ancient Mediterranean mind. Although we live out our lives with the impression that we are acting freely, the end result always turns out just as it was fated to turn out.

Second Peter 1:10 lends support to this interpretation of the New Testament's language of predestination. This verse says that Christians should "be all the more eager to make your calling and election sure. For if you do these things, you will never fall" (NIV). Obviously, if election were exclusively a matter of God's choice, no human action would be required in order to make it "sure." Further, the most obvious sense of the verse implies that one can become a Christian, yet not be saved in the end. This verse is a strong indication that whatever God's predestination is, it is not simply a one-way street. His choice of us seems contingent on our response.

Judaism also had its **deterministic** elements—groups that believed nothing happened by chance. For example, the Essenes near the Dead Sea had an extremely deterministic view of those who were good and those who were evil. God had chosen who would be part of the "sons of light" and who would be "sons of darkness." Other groups were more open to the possibility that humans could make choices and actually affect their world (e.g., the Sadducees and some groups of Pharisees). All in all, the fact that the Essenes said things similar to Paul on predestination at least makes us take his language seriously—it was one of the options on his cultural plate.

Once Saved, Always Saved?

In our discussion of predestination, we have mentioned that, logically, we cannot believe both that God chooses who will be saved and that God wants everyone to be saved. Follow the logic: (1) God's choice of some implies that He did not choose others, (2) Christ only died for some, and (3) those whom God chose will certainly make it to heaven in the end. Some Christians, generally known as **Calvinists**, after a man named John Calvin (1509-1564), accept one or more of these ideas. We might oversimplify this approach by thinking of the letters in the word **TULIP**.

The **T** stands for "total depravity," by which Calvinists mean that a human being has no power in him or herself to choose God at all. A human being is completely and utterly sinful and has no true desire to choose God on his or her

> "You have made us fall into the lot of light . . . From of old you appointed the Prince of light to assist us . . . and all the spirits of truth are under his dominion. You created Belial for the pit . . ."
>
> **1QM 13.9-11**

own. The **U** stands for "unconditional election." This is the interpretation of predestination language that believes God arbitrarily chooses who will be saved and, thus, at least by implication, those who will not. The **L** stands for "limited atonement." If God only chooses some, then Christ's atonement does not apply to everyone but only to those whom God has chosen. The I then stands for "irresistible grace," meaning that if God has chosen you, you cannot resist His desire to save you. Finally, **P** stands for the "perseverance of the saints," the idea that if God has truly chosen you, you will certainly make it.

Calvinism: A theological view that typically believes in individual predestination and "eternal security."

eternal security: The belief that once a person has become right with God, s/he cannot fail to be saved on the Day of Judgment.

TULIP: An acronym for remembering the basic beliefs of Calvinism; namely, **T**otal depravity, **U**nconditional election, **L**imited atonement, **I**rresistible grace, and **P**erseverance of the saints.

This system is certainly logical, but does it actually match what Paul taught? Does it make sense with our heads but actually violate the greater revelation of God's character as love? For example, this approach must give God *direct* responsibility for all the evil of the world.[4] Thus, God makes Hitlers and bin Ladens so that He can show His power as He destroys them. It is hard to know what meaning the statement "God is love" really has in this system. It gives us a good sense that God is in control, but not that He really cares.

While not all Calvinists today accept the whole system, all Calvinists would accept the idea of the "perseverance of the saints." As we have just mentioned, this phrase means that those whom God has chosen will, of course, make it to the end—they will certainly be saved on the Day of Judgment. The original Calvinists, like the Puritans of the 1600s and 1700s, did not believe a person could know in this life whether he or she were predestined for salvation. In John Bunyon's famous classic, *Pilgrim's Progress*, for example, Christian does not know if he will make it to the Celestial City until he has actually made it there.

However, much of modern Calvinism has followed other Christian traditions in believing you can know in this life whether you are saved. Mixing this idea with the notion of predestination, we get a belief known as **eternal security**. Those who believe this idea believe that once you know you have become right with God, you cannot fail to be saved in the end: "once saved, always saved."

As you can see, we have defined and explained this belief without mentioning a single Scripture. It is clearly a very logical belief, given the other beliefs out of which it is built. The question is, does the New Testament actually teach it?

On the one hand, the Gospel and letters of John do seem to imply such things. Take the following two verses:

"My sheep recognize my voice; I know them, and they follow me. I give them eternal life, and they will never perish. No one will snatch them away from me, for my Father has given them to me, and he is more powerful than anyone else."

John 10:27-29

"These people left our churches because they never really belonged with us; otherwise they would have stayed with us. When they left us, it proved that they do not belong with us."

1 John 2:19

It is probably correct to see a connection between a sense of predestination and 1 John's claim that if these individuals had really been Christians, they would not have left. The verses from the Gospel of John similarly give us a strong sense that once someone is "in the sheepfold," s/he is there to stay.

The question is how far do we take this language? Is it really the case that no matter what a person does, s/he will make it? When some in John's community did not stay, he simply said they were never "in" in the first place—a typically fatalistic view of things. But to what extent is this true?

When we try to take this approach and connect it to other parts of the New Testament—particularly Paul's teaching that we can become right with God now—we run into problems. Take the verses in the adjacent text box. Paul himself, whom no one can doubt was really a Christian, indicates it is possible that *even he* might not make it to the end—you could be in the race and yet not finish the race. Hebrews is even more emphatic on this point, indicating that a person who has "lost" his or her salvation cannot get it back. And while it is possible that John was talking about literal death in 1 John 5:16-17, he may also have been saying that there is a sin that brings spiritual death—a sin like those who had left his community had committed.

If you can "lose it," how many sins does it take? Hebrews 10:26 simply says that if we "deliberately continue sinning," Christ's sacrifice is no longer in force for us. We see clearly that the kind of sin to which we are referring is not accidental wrongdoing, but deliberate, willful sinning.

"Remember that in a race everyone runs, but only one person gets a prize. You also must run in such a way that you will win . . . I discipline my body like an athlete, training it to do what it should. Otherwise, I fear that after preaching to others I myself might be disqualified."

1 Corinthians 9:24, 27

"It is impossible to restore to repentance those who were once enlightened . . . and who then turn away from God. It is impossible to bring such people to repentance again because they are nailing the Son of God to the cross again by rejecting him, holding him up to public shame."

Hebrews 6:4, 6

"If you see a Christian brother or sister sinning in a way that does not lead to death, you should pray, and God will give that person life. But there is a sin that leads to death, and I am not saying you should pray for those who commit it. Every wrong is sin, but not all sin leads to death."

1 John 5:16-17

But what about the man Paul "hands over" to Satan in 1 Corinthians 5:5? Because this man had had sex with his stepmother, Paul was throwing him out of the church and delivering him over to Satan. But

> One of the main reasons there are so many denominations is the fact that it is hard for us to discipline ourselves not to fill in the blanks with our logic.

even though Paul turned him over to Satan "for the destruction of the flesh" (5:5 NRSV), Paul's purpose in doing so was "so that his spirit may be saved in the day of the Lord" (NRSV). This man seemed to be on the brink of destruction, but had his sins pushed him over even at this point?

How do we fit all these verses together, if they can fit together? You will have to decide. The fact of the matter is that the Bible does not give us nice little theological packages in which to wrap our ideas. The Bible is full of figurative language and arguments that use hyperbole to emphasize their points. One of the main reasons there are so many denominations is the fact that it is hard for us to discipline ourselves not to fill in the blanks with our logic.

It is as if the Bible has left us with a number of puzzle pieces, with perhaps even a majority of the pieces stuck back in the first century A.D. We fit the pieces we have together in ways that match our "artistic" sense, but more than one picture can be created from our pieces. Then, lo and behold, it turns out that we actually have the pieces to more than one puzzle—a John puzzle, a Paul puzzle, etc. Most denominations can find words in the New Testament to at least match the pictures their traditions have drawn.

> "I am convinced that nothing can ever separate us from his love. Death can't, and life can't. The angels can't, and the demons can't. Our fears for today, our worries about tomorrow, and even the powers of hell can't keep God's love away. Whether we are high above the sky or in the deepest ocean, nothing in all creation will ever be able to separate us from the love of God that is revealed in Christ Jesus our Lord."
>
> **Romans 8:38-39**

We should close our brief remarks on eternal security with a favorite of those who support the idea—the verses in Romans that initiated our discussion in this chapter. While these verses probably are not about whether Christians can lose their salvation, they do bring out the most important truth in the doctrine of eternal security: God loves us and has every desire for us to be with Him. In the context of such love, it is truly surprising that anyone would ever turn away from Him!

Christians and the Law

A final issue that Romans touches on is the matter of obedience to governments and the law. Paul says, "Obey the government, for God is the one who put it there. All governments have been placed in power by God. So those who refuse to obey the laws of the land are refusing to obey God, and punishment will follow" (Rom. 13:1-2). These comments are similar to ones we also find in 1 Peter: "For the Lord's sake, accept all authority—the king as head of state, and the officials he has appointed. For the king has sent them to punish all who do wrong and to honor those who do right" (1 Pet. 2:13-14).

civil disobedience: Disobeying the law of the land because you disagree with it on principle.

In the case of 1 Peter in particular, we are to endure suffering at the hands of rulers, even if they are unjust (e.g., 1 Pet. 4:14, 16, 19). These comments seem to imply that revolution and **civil disobedience** are inappropriate for a Christian, even if they are for just causes. Was it wrong for the American colonists to revolt against England or for the civil rights movement of the 60s to take place? For that matter, was it wrong for some to establish an underground railroad in the mid-1800s to help slaves escape to freedom? In this sense, parts of the New Testament seem to teach the opposite of what many of us think Jesus would do if He were here today.

The New Testament regularly adopts what we might call a "defensive" stance toward the world and its oppression—grin and bear it because our day is coming. But what if "our day" could come sooner? With regard to slavery, for example, we did not simply endure it as a part of a sinful world—the stance the New Testament generally takes toward slavery—*we did away with it!* Arguably we moved the world—whether it liked it or not—a little closer to what it will be like in heaven. To some extent, we did this because our democratic world allowed us to do it. Can we do the same with the relationships of wives and husbands?

On a final note, we should be clear that we are not to obey the government or the law when it contradicts essential Christian matters. For example, the book of Revelation does not encourage anyone to take the "mark of the beast" (Rev. 13:17). The disciples disobeyed the Sanhedrin when it commanded them to stop preaching (Acts 4:19). Clearly, there are some real limits on what a Christian can obey.

Things to Think About

1. In what ways is the modern issue of homosexuality different from Paul's discussion of homosexual sex in the culture of his time? In what ways is the issue the same? Is the sin of homosexual sex a greater sin than cheating on your income taxes?

2. Do we "get right" with God by way of our trust in Christ (faith) or by being a good person (works)? Will we escape God's wrath at the judgment (i.e., are we saved?) without having to change some sinful aspect of our life, something we did before coming to Christ?

Key Terms
Calvinism
civil disobedience
deterministic
election (NT)
eternal security
foreknowledge
free will
sinful nature
sovereign
theological
TULIP

Once a person is a Christian, is s/he eternally secure; in other words, no matter what s/he might do afterwards, will s/he make it into heaven?

3. Is Romans 9–11 about God's predestination of individuals for salvation or condemnation, or is it really about Israel and the Gentiles? Does it have implications for both? How would you personally reconcile that God elects and chooses His people, yet prefers for all to choose Him?

4. Is it possible through the power of the Holy Spirit for a Christian to live without frequently and deliberately sinning? Have Christians "copped out" with what the New Testament actually has to say about sin because of our own sense of personal and corporate failure?

5. Was the American wrong from a Christian perspective? Does the New Testament give us any basis for civil disobedience when the law of the land is not directly in conflict with God's law? Would "taxation without representation" count?

endnotes

1. We have already noted in chapter 37 of this text that Paul had not experienced life in this way before he became a Christian. Rather, he felt very good about his ability to keep the Law (cf. Phil. 3:6). Even in Romans 7, Paul places the blame for sin not on the person wanting to keep the Law, but on the power of sin at work in a person still under the Law (7:20).
2. Some dispute this point, but it follows all too logically from the former claim.
3. The Greek does not actually say "to throw garbage into." The NLT has taken the original phrase "for ordinary use" and concluded that the ordinary use for a piece of pottery would have been as a trash can.
4. Those who believe in free will must still accept that God created the possibility of evil, even if a person's free will is directly responsible for bringing it. From a purely Calvinist perspective, however, God must be the planner of evil.

CHAPTER 41

The Corinthian Letters: Unity Problems

Like many churches today, the various Christians in Corinth did not always get along as well as they should have.

House Churches and Division

When you hear about the church at Corinth, you might picture a building like the ones we have today. Maybe you think of a large structure where lots of people can meet or perhaps a smaller church with a steeple on top. In reality, the earliest Christians did not have church buildings like we do. Such structures did not exist until the A.D. 300s—after the Romans stopped putting Christians to death. Instead, the churches to which Paul ministered met primarily in the homes of people in the community. Thus, when he referred to **churches** he did not

At a Glance

- The churches at Corinth had serious unity problems, mostly along social lines—some had a higher social standing than others.

- Some questioned Paul's authority in favor of other early Christian leaders like Apollos.

- Some thought they had superior knowledge and wisdom to that of other, weaker Christians.

- Some did not believe in a resurrection.

- Some thought that sexual freedom demonstrated spiritual power; others thought Christians should stop having sex altogether.

- Some boasted about the spiritual gifts God had given them, thinking themselves superior to others for this reason.

- Paul's solution to all this disunity was love, which he praised in 1 Corinthians 13.

refer to buildings but to "assemblies" or groups of Christians joining together in worship.

A city like Corinth probably had more than one **house church**—a fact that might have contributed to the divisions among Christians in the city. When Paul mentions the household of a woman named Chloe (1 Cor. 1:11) or of a man named Stephanus (1 Cor. 1:16; 16:15), it is possible that he is referring to various house churches in Corinth. Nevertheless, the main meeting place for the churches at Corinth was the house of a man named Gaius (Rom. 16:23). This man must have had a fairly large house to accommodate the whole church in this city, probably indicating that he was a person of some means.[1]

church: A group of believers who assemble together (church means "assembly" in Greek).

house church: A group of believers who meet together in the house of a particular person.

Like many churches today, the various Christians in Corinth did not always get along as well as they should have. But their problems have worked to our advantage, for now we are able to study Paul's responses to their situations. The two letters called 1 and 2 Corinthians are full of information we simply would not have if Corinth had not been such a divided church. The next few chapters will deal in more detail with the various issues the Corinthian church faced.

The Situation in Corinth

We have more information about Paul's dealings with the church at Corinth than with any other single church to which Paul ministered. Acts tells us he made two visits to the city, and we have two letters that he wrote to the Christians there. We know further from Paul's own writings that he wrote at least two more letters that have not survived to today. He also visited Corinth an additional time that Acts does not mention.

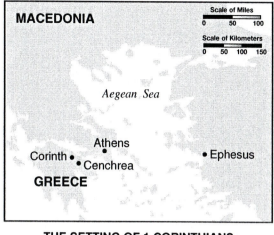

THE SETTING OF 1 CORINTHIANS
MAP 7

Acts tells us that Paul spent a year and a half in Corinth when he founded the church (ca. A.D. 50–52). He then continued to watch its progress carefully from Ephesus, a city about 250 miles east across the Aegean Sea (see **Map 7**). First Corinthians is actually the second letter Paul wrote to Corinth from Ephesus, and 2 Corinthians is Paul's fourth, written while he was en route there.[2] At the time he wrote 2 Corinthians, he was traveling through the region of Macedonia, just to the north of Greece.

Paul wrote 1 Corinthians for at least two reasons. First of all, he had heard reports that the Christians in Corinth were divided and did not get along with one another. Some even questioned his authority and the validity of his message. The fundamental problem at Corinth, therefore, was disunity. It is no coincidence that 1 Corinthians 13, the "love chapter" of the New Testament, is in this book, for a lack of love was the heart of the Corinthians' problem.

Paul also wrote for a second reason. He was answering some questions that the Corinthian church had written to him. Many of these questions related to matters that were causing division in the Corinthian church—things like whether they should speak in angelic "tongues," whether or not there is a resurrection, and whether they should eat meat that had been sacrificed to an idol—a statue of a god. Paul used the second half of 1 Corinthians to address these issues.

Social Divisions at Corinth

First Corinthians 11 gives us one snapshot of the division in the Corinthian church. The last part of this chapter deals with what had been happening when the church partook of the **Lord's Supper**—the weekly meal early Christians had on Sunday to remember Christ's death. Although today we celebrate communion or the Eucharist as a small part of a church worship service, originally the Christians had a meal together—much as Jesus did with His disciples at his **Last Supper**, the prototype of Christian communion.[3] This was the Passover meal, so it involved a whole meal.

The Lord's Supper: Also called communion or the Eucharist (meaning "thanksgiving"), this was the weekly meal early Christians had on Sundays to remember the significance of Christ's death. It mirrored the **Last Supper** Jesus had with His disciples, the Passover meal.

table fellowship: The matter of who was appropriate to eat with.

"If three have eaten at one table and have not spoken over it words of the Law, it is as though they had eaten of the sacrifices of the dead."

Mishnah Aboth 3.3
(collection of Jewish oral traditions ca. A.D. 200)

Eating together in the ancient world was a very significant thing. Generally you only ate with people of your own sort, and having a meal often was calculated to increase your prestige according to who shared the meal with you. For Jews, eating was a highly religious event and a time when ceremonial purity was a chief concern. The issue of **table fellowship**, whom you should eat with, was thus a major issue that showed up time and again in Paul's writings.

In Corinth, the way Christians were eating together reflected their disunity. The wealthier individuals of the church ate sumptuously. They did not share their food with the less fortunate, nor did they wait for them (1 Cor. 11:21). At the end of such meals, some of the wealthy would even be drunk from the amount of wine they had consumed, while others in the church went home hungry. It also seems likely that the wealthier group ate meat on such occasions—something most people could not afford. The likelihood that such meat came from one of the nearby pagan temples created yet another issue over which the church was divided.

This state of events was an atrocity to Paul. A meal that was meant to show the oneness and unity of Christians had become a matter of division and privilege. If you are going to do it that way, Paul writes, eat at home (1 Cor. 11:34).

In 1 Corinthians 1:26 Paul notes that the majority of the Corinthian church were not born with worldly power and influence. But he implies that some were. We know from Romans 16:23 that Erastus, a member of the church, was the city treasurer. Archaeologists have actually unearthed a stone indicating that a man with this name paid for a building in the city. This may very well be the same person. We have already mentioned that Gaius also must have been well off, since his house apparently was big enough for the whole church to assemble inside.

While Paul probably was not on bad terms with Gaius and Erastus, a great deal of Paul's opposition probably came from this more powerful element in the Corinthian church. These are the ones likely to have favored the educated Apollos over Paul. These are the ones likely to have scoffed at the notion of physical resurrection and to have favored eating meat that had been offered to an idol. And surely the man who was sleeping with his stepmother was from this group or else he would not have been able to get by with it.

Questioning Paul's Leadership

Acts tells us that Paul was not the only Christian leader to spend time ministering to the church of Corinth. A man named Apollos also ministered there in the period after Paul founded the church (Acts 18:27-28). In time, some in the community, probably from the social elite, used Apollos as a way to undermine Paul's authority, proclaiming him more educated and a greater intellect than Paul. Acts tells us that Apollos was from Alexandria, a place where Jews were known for their knowledge of Greek philosophy (Acts 18:24-26). It is quite possible that he really did differ from Paul in his approach to some issues.

First Corinthians 1:12 describes the situation that resulted in the church: "Some of you are saying, 'I am a follower of Paul.' Others are saying, 'I follow Apollos,' or 'I follow Peter,' or 'I follow only Christ.'" If some used Apollos' supposed "wisdom" to undermine Paul's instructions, others pointed to Peter as a "real" apostle, in contrast to Paul. Indeed, it is quite possible that Paul did not have the wholehearted support of Peter and the church in Jerusalem at the time he wrote 1 Corinthians.[4] Paul's opponents in Corinth probably used this fact to their advantage.

In what was a fairly common situation, Paul found himself needing to defend his authority to the Corinthians. He argues in 1 Corinthians 9 that he deserves just as much material support as Peter, although he does not take advantage of this right. In 2 Corinthians 10–13 he later defends his apostleship even more vigorously, providing a kind of apostolic "resume" to the unconvinced in Corinth.

Paul also has some things to say to those who thought him an inferior speaker and thinker. He takes the first four chapters of 1 Corinthians to argue that *human* wisdom—such as that his opponents claim to have—has nothing to do with *God's* wisdom. God's wisdom, Paul writes, was to send the Messiah to die on a cross—something the Greeks would consider ridiculous and something the Jews viewed as offensive.

The heart of the Corinthian problem, Paul writes, is that they are oriented around their "flesh," the part of their person most susceptible to the power of sin and Satan (1 Cor. 3:1-4). They are thinking with their human, fleshly minds and not with the mind of the Spirit. When we are spiritual, we realize that all of us taken together make up the body of Christ and that no part of that body is unimportant (12:22-23). It is *together* that we are the temple of the Lord in which the Holy Spirit lives (3:16; 6:19).

Superior Wisdom and Knowledge

Paul's opponents in Corinth claimed to have superior wisdom and knowledge. Paul describes their attitude:

> "You think you already have everything you need! You are already rich! Without us you have become kings! I wish you really were on your thrones already, for then we would be reigning with you . . . Our dedication to Christ makes us look like fools, but you are so wise! We are weak but you are so powerful! You are well thought of, but we are laughed at."
>
> **1 Corinthians 4:8, 10**

This attitude probably stood behind a number of issues about which the Corinthian church had questions. The bottom line for Paul was that "the foolishness of God is wiser than man's wisdom, and the weakness of God is stronger than man's strength" (1 Cor. 1:25 NIV).

One person in the community seems to have had "superior" wisdom on a sexual matter. Perhaps using Paul's teaching that Christians were not "under the Law" (e.g., 1 Cor. 9:20), some at Corinth were proud because one in their number was living with his stepmother in open violation of the Jewish Law (cf. Lev. 18:8). Paul says to such individuals: "And you are so proud of yourselves! Why aren't you mourning in sorrow and shame?" (1 Cor. 5:2). Instead they were flaunting the slogan, "I am allowed to do anything" (6:12; 10:23).[5]

The place of judgment (or court) where Paul was accused by the Jews in Acts 18:12. In the background is the Acrocorinth, upon which the temple of Aphrodite once stood.

One of the big questions Paul addresses in 1 Corinthians is the matter of meat that had been sacrificed to idols (1 Cor. 8–10). This issue was somewhat complex and involved a number of factors. First, there was the social issue, the fact that only the wealthy would have meat at all. Second, there was the fact that much of the meat available at the marketplace would have come from nearby temples. Third, we must also consider the possibility that Apollos' teaching on this matter might have differed from Paul's.

All of these factors made the issue of meat offered to idols a divisive one. The "wise" at Corinth saw eating meat that had been sacrificed to a pagan god as an indication of their strong conscience. After all, they knew that "an idol is not really a god and that there is only one God and no other" (1 Cor. 8:4). They could eat such meat with full confidence that the gods or goddesses to which it had been offered did not really exist. It was just meat.

Paul does not completely contradict them, at least not initially. His tactic was not to deny the strength of their conscience but to remind them that the well-being of their brothers and sisters was far more important than their individual rights. He steers them toward an attitude of love: "If what I eat is going to make another Christian sin, I will never eat meat again as long as I live" (1 Cor. 8:13).

A final matter about which this group may have viewed themselves superior is in their view of the afterlife. Evidently some in the Corinthian church did not believe in a resurrection (e.g., 1 Cor. 15:12). It is hard to know exactly what they were saying, but one strong possibility is that they rejected the notion of a *physical* resurrection—a very strange idea for the Greek world. It is possible they believed that our *spirits* survived death, perhaps even that we were already reigning spiritually with Christ (cf. 4:8). However, Christianity taught resurrection, not the immortality of the soul. Paul's response is a combination of both: a spiritual resurrection; a body is involved, but it is a different kind of body. "Flesh and blood cannot inherit the Kingdom of God" (15:50).

Divisions over Spiritual Gifts

Another point of division in the Corinthian church derived from their exercise of "spiritual gifts," special abilities God had given them through the power of the Holy Spirit. The two most prominently discussed in 1 Corinthians are the **gift of prophecy** (the ability to present messages from God about the community and its future) and the **gift of tongues** (the ability to speak in angelic languages). While it is hard to know for sure how this division related to those who claimed superior wisdom, it is possible that these same people were some of the ones speaking in tongues. They would thus feel that they had a special channel to God. If this is the case, it would explain how they thought they were already reigning with Christ spiritually. Paul does not forbid speaking in tongues, but he puts limits on its use in the Christian worship assembly (1 Cor. 14:27-28).

gift of prophecy: The ability to present messages from God about the church and its future.

gift of tongues: The ability to speak in angelic languages.

The exercise of prophecy in the church could bring disruptions as well, although Paul encourages it in worship (1 Cor. 14:1-3). Like tongues, Paul limits the use of prophecy to two or three individuals per service (14:29). He insists that women who pray and prophesy in such a setting have their heads veiled out of respect for their husbands (11:5), perhaps a reflection of ancient concerns for modesty. The worship of men and women together in such close quarters (a house church), with women taking prominent roles like praying or prophesying, probably created a somewhat awkward social situation.[6] The veiling of the women probably helped ease such tensions.

Things to Think About

1. Do you know of any contemporary churches that remind you of the Corinthian church? How often do churches today have cliques and divisions? What are some of the issues behind the cliques and divisions; e.g., different church leaders, matters of social status or wealth?

2. Are Christians today ever tempted to think themselves superior to other Christians? Do some denominations think they have more "knowledge" than others or that they are "purer"? Have you ever known a Christian to think s/he had a superior "spiritual gift" to another Christian?

Key Terms

church
gift of prophecy
gift of tongues
house church
table fellowship
the Last Supper
the Lord's Supper

endnotes

1. The church at Cenchrea, the port village of Corinth, probably met in the house of a woman named Phoebe (cf. Rom. 16:1).

2. In 1 Corinthians 5:9 Paul alludes to a letter written before 1 Corinthians itself. Second Corinthians 2:4 mentions a letter Paul wrote in great distress and anguish—a letter that does not seem to be 1 Corinthians.

3. We now would distinguish between communion and the "love feast" mentioned in Jude 12, but Jude probably was referring to the celebration of communion—it was more like a meal. The clear abuses we see taking place in 1 Corinthians and Jude probably led to its becoming a distinct ceremony, so that it was different from a meal.

4. See Galatians 2.

5. Paul took a jab at these "wise" individuals in 1 Corinthians 6:5 as he addressed those who were taking other members of the church to court (both parties were from the upper end of the social ladder): "Isn't there anyone in all the church who is wise enough to decide these arguments?"

6. Paul's comment about angels in this verse is difficult (1 Cor. 11:10). Perhaps it was also awkward for women to prophesy unveiled with evil angels around (cf. 1 Cor. 6:3). Others think the angels were a concern because of their role as guardians of proper worship.

CHAPTER 42

Contemporary Issues in 1 Corinthians

If our interpretation of Scripture would ever lead us to contradict an authentic love of our neighbor, then we must not follow through with our interpretation!

Applying Scripture Today

In Chapter 40 we discussed various passages in Romans that relate to issues Christians sometimes debate today. First Corinthians also covers a number of topics that connect with contemporary Christian debate. While many of the issues in Romans are more "theological" in nature—what a Christian should believe—the issues of 1 Corinthians have more to do with Christian practice—how a Christian should live. While it was unfortunate that the Corinthian church had so much division, we have definitely benefited from hearing how Paul addressed their problems!

As always when applying Scripture to today, a word of caution is in order. The New Testament warns several times about making "rules" an end in themselves. Jesus gave us a very helpful principle when He said, "The

Contemporary Issues and 1 Corinthians

- Should a Christian have sex? With a stepmother (1 Corinthians 5)? With a prostitute (1 Corinthians 6)? With a wife (1 Corinthians 7)?

- Should a Christian marry (1 Corinthians 7)? Should a virgin marry? Should a divorced person remarry?

- Should Christians take each other to court (1 Corinthians 6)?

- What do we do when Christians disagree on how we should live (1 Corinthians 8, 10; Romans 14)?

- Is it appropriate for a Christian to speak in tongues (1 Corinthians 12–14)?

495

Sabbath was made to benefit people, and not people to benefit the Sabbath" (Mark 2:27). The implication is that God's laws are never meant to enslave or entangle but to free and benefit us.

Whenever we are in doubt, the heart of what God expects is laid out clearly in His commands to love Him and to love our neighbor (cf. Matt. 22:34-40). The New Testament repeatedly emphasizes that everything God requires connects to these two basic commands (e.g., Rom. 13:10; James 2:8; 1 John 3:23). In fact, 1 John powerfully states that "God is love" (1 John 4:8), relating God's requirements to His own character. *If our interpretation of Scripture would ever lead us to contradict an authentic love of our neighbor, then we must **not** follow through with our interpretation!*

Christians, Sex, and Marriage

Although several of Paul's letters emphasize that Christians are not "under the Law" (e.g., Rom. 6:14; 1 Cor. 9:20; Gal. 5:18), Paul clearly did not believe a person could now do anything s/he wanted. Nowhere does he make this fact clearer than when it comes to sexual issues. In 1 Corinthians alone Paul indicates a Christian must not have sex with a stepmother (1 Cor. 5:1), visit a prostitute (6:15), commit adultery (6:9), or have homosexual sex (6:9). Thus, when Paul says Gentiles are not obligated to keep the Jewish Law, he clearly does not mean they are exempted from the sexual prohibitions of Leviticus 18.[1]

Sex with a Prostitute

Christians today do not disagree much on the issue of whether they should be visiting prostitutes. When Paul asks, "Should a man take his body, which belongs to Christ, and join it to a prostitute?" the answer that comes to mind is the same that Paul gives: "Never!" (1 Cor. 6:15). This is simply not an issue that Christians really debate today.

On the other hand, we may miss some of the nuances of Paul's argument because we do not wear the same glasses he did. For example, all the things Paul mentions in 1 Corinthians 5 and 6 relate in some

> **body of Christ:** A metaphor Paul uses for all Christians. Each of us has a different function, and the Holy Spirit dwells in the whole body.

way to protecting the **body of Christ** from Satanic violation.[2] The person who visits a prostitute allows Satan to violate the body of Christ—he sins "against his own body" (1 Cor. 6:18 NIV). In a way that we cannot really see in English, Paul makes no distinction between my individual physical body and the body of Christ made up of all Christians. The person who visits a prostitute allows Satan to defile the Christian community.

It is perhaps also significant that Corinth was famous for its temple prostitution, particularly that associated with the goddess Aphrodite. If Paul had this particular temple in mind, his comment that we are the temple of the Holy Spirit would be extremely relevant (1 Cor. 3:16; 6:19). To have sex with prostitutes at a pagan temple would especially pollute the body of Christ.

Sex with a Stepmother

Prostitution was not the only kind of sex Paul thought polluted the body of Christ. He had a particularly strong reaction to the news that someone in the Corinthian church was "having" his stepmother (1 Cor. 5:1). Ironically, some in the Corinthian church seemed proud of this extreme example of freedom (5:2). Paul, on the other hand, saw sex of this kind as an entryway for Satanic invasion of Christ's body. He reprimands them by using a familiar experience: "Don't you know that a little yeast works through the whole batch of dough?" (5:6 NIV).

It is easy for us to understand this comment as a matter of influence—this person might have a bad influence on the church. However, Paul had much more than merely human influence in mind. The presence of this man in the church meant spiritual pollution, a concept we find hard to understand. This passage is one of many examples of how we **demythologize** the New Testament message, removing elements that seem foreign to our current worldview. Because we do not think of acts like this in terms of pollution, we read this aspect out of the text.

demythologize: To remove aspects of the New Testament that seem foreign to our current worldview.

Paul deals with this man as a potential source of spiritual infection in the church. "Hand this man over to Satan for the destruction of the flesh," Paul demands, "so that his spirit may be saved in the day of the Lord" (1 Cor. 5:5 NRSV). If Satan was in control of the earthly realm and the church was the only place where Christians could find protection from his control, then individuals like this person were compromising the security and insulation of the body from Satan.[3]

We will talk a little more about what this passage might mean for the church today in the section on whether Christians should take one another to court. Should we really not even eat with Christians involved in sexual immorality? Do we need to kick out of our fellowship sinners in our churches to avoid spiritual corruption today?

Homosexual Sex

Chapter 40 has already mentioned the issue of homosexuality in the New Testament. First Corinthians does not discuss the matter in any detail, but it may provide us with some insights on how Paul and other Jews viewed such practices. In particular, Paul uses two words in 1 Corinthians 6 that seem to relate to homosexual sex, words rendered by the NIV as "male prostitutes" and "homosexual offenders" (1 Cor. 6:9).

Some have suggested that Paul only had male temple prostitution and homosexual rape in view in this verse, but this seems unlikely. In fact, it seems likely that Paul or other Jews created the word "homosexual offenders" out of two words in the Greek translation of Leviticus 18:22. Although Paul modified the Jewish Law in many respects, he did not see a need for any change in its sexual taboos.

Sex Outside of Marriage

It is unclear whether Paul directly addresses the question of sex before marriage (perhaps 1 Cor. 7:8), but we can be fairly certain of what his answer would be.[4] His entire argument about female virgins in 1 Corinthians 7:25-38

> "Yes, it is good to live a celibate life. But because there is so much sexual immorality, each man should have his own wife, and each woman should have her own husband."
>
> **1 Corinthians 7:1-2**

presumes that a woman would indeed be a virgin when she married for the first time. With regard to men, Paul forbids all the other avenues in which a man might have sex outside of marriage. He could not have sex with a prostitute (6:15) nor could he commit adultery (6:9). To have sex with a virgin violated her need to remain a virgin when she married. Paul does not give any special freedoms to widows either (e.g., 1 Cor. 7:8).

It is Paul's desire to channel sex in an appropriate direction that leads him to encourage marriage for those who do not have the self-control to remain celibate (1 Cor. 7:2). Far from the romantic notion you often hear today, Paul's view of sex and marriage is much more pragmatic. Paul never directly says that God designed sex for marriage; he just excludes it from anywhere else.

Sex Within Marriage

The idea that married people have sex seems overwhelmingly obvious to us today. We tend to have this "healthy view" of sex in our culture. This has not always been the case, however. Throughout much of the history of the church, Christians have thought of celibacy as the ideal. The Roman Catholic Church, for example, still does not allow its priests to marry. As early as 1 Timothy, there were those who did not believe Christians should marry (1 Tim. 4:3).

Because we have such a positive view of sex in our culture, 1 Corinthians 7 often takes us a little by surprise. The NRSV translation of 1 Corinthians 7:1 reads, "Now concerning the matters about which you wrote: 'It is well for a man not to touch a woman.'"[5] Is Paul really saying that life without sex is the ideal? Apparently so, for he goes on to talk about how husbands and wives should nevertheless have regular sex so that they are not tempted to go elsewhere to satisfy their sexual needs (7:3-7). The ideal, he indicates, is to go without sex completely (7:7).

We should probably remember that Paul believed Christ would return to earth very soon (e.g., 1 Cor. 7:26, 29-31). This fact made celibacy the ideal for at least two reasons. On the one hand, the gospel needed to be preached to as many as possible before the Day of Judgment. Marriage created responsibilities that hindered a person from doing as much for the Lord as s/he otherwise might have been able to do (e.g., 7:32-35). On the other hand, there would be no sex or marrying in the kingdom of God (cf. Mark 12:25). Some may have thought they could begin what would eventually be the case in the kingdom.[6]

Divorce and Remarriage

In the middle of his discussion on sex, Paul offers some comments on divorce and remarriage. Many Christians today face this issue and the number of contrasting views about it. For example, some teach that a Christian must never initiate a divorce, even if a spouse is physically abusive. In such cases they might allow for a separation, but insist that a person can never remarry—even if a divorced spouse does. Others do not place specific restrictions on divorce or remarriage, accepting it as a reality that often happens even if it is not the ideal.

With this issue great care is necessary, for it is far from a matter of classroom discussion. Even after we have clarified what the New Testament has to say, we will still need the body of Christ and the Holy Spirit to understand how the principle "God is love" might play out in the lives and circumstances of real people today. We will leave that decision to you and those whose counsel you respect, although we will try to clarify what 1 Corinthians 7 says.

First, we must consider whether the comments Jesus and Paul make on divorce are absolute, timeless rules. Both Jesus and Paul seem to speak their words in the context of real people. Their commands are meant to free and build up, not constrict or enslave. Jesus' words, for example, were directed at men who could throw their wives away for no reason, taking the woman's honor and her family away (e.g., Mark 10:1-12). Except in the case of the wealthy, a woman without a man in the culture of that day was a woman without any support or means of living. Jesus' restriction of divorce to cases of sexual immorality was meant to protect women, not enslave them to abusive husbands (Matt. 5:32).

First Corinthians 7 also gives us hints that Paul's commands on divorce had a lot to do with the structure of society in his day. On the one hand, he bluntly gives us Jesus' teachings on women—they were not to divorce their husbands or remarry if they did divorce them (1 Cor. 7:10-11).[7] When it came to men, on the other hand, they were not to divorce their wives either (7:11), *but remarriage was allowed!* The Greek of 1 Corinthians 7:27-28 reads, "If you have been bound to a wife, do not seek a loosing. If you have been loosed from a wife, do not seek a wife. But if you marry, you have not sinned, and if the virgin marries, she has not sinned." Paul seems to teach a double standard on remarriage—it was forbidden for a woman but allowed for a divorced man.

Divorce often led to feuding and war, since it dealt shame to the family that had given the wife in marriage. Although a woman apparently could not divorce a husband in Palestine, it would have been particularly insulting for a woman to divorce a man anywhere. We can imagine the kind of conflict her remarriage might have brought to a second husband. Is it possible that the social implications of divorce and remarriage were the driving forces behind Jesus and Paul's commands? If so, then we must be careful how we apply their words to a different social context with different social implications.

Going to Court

Apparently, some in the Corinthian church were taking other Christians to court in Corinth to settle their disputes. Paul is horrified: "Don't you know that someday we Christians are going to judge the world? . . . Don't you realize that we Christians will judge angels?" (1 Cor. 6:2-3). How ironic that those who were destined to judge the world would need to turn to the world to make judgments for them!

We should see this problem as part of the broader divisions at Corinth. On the one hand, it was unlikely that the rich would take the poor to court—what would they gain? Evidently, these were conflicts among the upper crust and leadership of the church, perhaps a way for the "Apollos" group to gain power over the "Paul" group. Indeed, it was Paul's opponents, those who thought themselves wise (cf. 1 Cor. 1:17, 26; 2:1, 4-5; 3:18), who were taking others to court. Paul insults them: "Isn't there anyone in all the church who is *wise* enough to decide these arguments?" (6:5).

> Like these other situations, those Christians who were taking their cases before pagan courts were tampering with the boundaries of the body of Christ and thus exposing the church to Satan's domain.

Although it might not be obvious to us, Paul's comments about going to court fit in well with what he said previously about the man sleeping with his stepmother (5:1-13) and what he would say later on about visiting prostitutes (6:15-20). Like these other situations, those Christians who were taking their cases before pagan courts were tampering with the boundaries of the body of Christ and thus exposing the church to Satan's domain. In all these situations, Paul paints a picture of Christianity as something like a bubble of Spirit in a sea of Satan. You could not get out of the sea just yet (e.g., 1 Cor. 5:9-10), but it was essential that you maintain the bubble in airtight condition and keep all Satanic water out.

Some of Paul's comments are good reflections of the ancient group culture in contrast to our modern individualistic perspectives. Those who were in the group must maintain the values of the group. Those who did not maintain the group's values became the focus of a shaming process, sometimes so the shamed individual would repent and conform. On the other hand, the honor of the group to outsiders was also of immense importance. You will have to decide whether the differences between Paul's culture and ours would lead us to use different tactics to reclaim those who do not follow the rules.

Disputable Matters

Perhaps the main issue on which Paul's opponents claimed superior wisdom was in the matter of meat sacrificed in pagan temples (1 Corinthians 8–10). Much of the meat available in a city like Corinth came from its temples. When a person offered a sacrifice to a god, the bulk of the meat was not used up but was later eaten by the temple priests and those who brought the sacrifice. In a sense, therefore, going to a temple was like going to a restaurant, except you brought the meat.

Those at Corinth claimed to have a superior understanding of what was going on with such sacrifices. "All of us possess knowledge" (8:1 NRSV), they claimed. These Gentile Christians had come to believe that "no idol in the world really exists" and, like the Jews, that "there is no God but one" (8:4 NRSV).[8] Therefore, they boldly ate meat that had been sacrificed to pagan gods without fear or a bad conscience—after all, the god did not really exist.

Paul does not completely disagree with them. Perhaps these were things Apollos had taught, and Paul was being particularly careful not to contradict him. Only in 1 Corinthians 10:20 do his true feelings seem to show for just a moment: "What I am saying is that these sacrifices are offered to demons, not to God. And I don't want any of you to be partners with demons."

The bulk of Paul's discussion, however, focuses on relationships between Christians. His fundamental point is that love must always trump my "rights" as an individual. The real issue for Paul—at least as he discusses it—is the effect your freedom has on others. If your freedom and superior knowledge might cause a brother or sister to fall into spiritual trouble, you must not act on your freedom. First Corinthians 9 shows how Paul himself surrendered his rights as an apostle so that he could preach Christ more effectively.

> The real issue for Paul—at least as he discusses it—is the effect your freedom has on others. If your freedom and superior knowledge might cause a brother or sister to fall into spiritual trouble, you must not act on your freedom.

Paul's conclusion on the matter is basically, "Don't ask." Buy meat at the market without asking if it comes from a nearby temple (1 Cor. 10:25). If an unbeliever places meat before you at his house, you are not to ask him where he bought it (10:27). If you find out it has been sacrificed to an idol, you are not to eat it so that you will not give him the impression such gods are legitimate (10:28). Certainly Paul's discussion rules out the possibility that you would actually participate in a meal at a pagan temple (8:10).

Similarly, Paul warns about the effect such a "wise" individual might have on a "weaker" brother or sister. Your conscience might be okay, Paul says, but what if this weaker Christian eats the meat and then experiences it as sin before

504

God? It could destroy his or her relationship with God. "We don't miss out on anything if we don't eat it, and we don't gain anything if we do" (1 Cor. 8:8). Paul's conclusion is that "if what I eat is going to make another Christian sin, I will never eat meat again as long as I live" (8:13).

As we saw in chapter 40 of this text, the problem over meat sacrificed to idols was related to the overall division at Corinth. The upper crust of the church had an arrogant attitude toward those of lower social status, not only because they thought they possessed a superior understanding of things, but also because of their superior social status. One undercurrent of the whole debate was the fact that meat in and of itself was a delicacy—the majority of people rarely had any opportunity to eat meat. Therefore, the whole issue was somewhat "in your face" to those in the Christian community of lower status. It was another example of the attitude that was also showing itself at Corinth during the communion meal—some in the church were getting drunk while others left hungry.

First Corinthians 8–10 and the more general discussion in Romans 14 give us some good insights on how to resolve disputable matters in the church. The vast number of different denominations and churches indicates that we are stuck with differences in belief over things that the New Testament does not directly address. Paul's conclusion in Romans 14 is that "each one should be fully convinced in his own mind" (Rom. 14:5 NIV).

Such conviction does not necessarily mean that your conclusion is right or just as good as anyone else's, however. Paul blesses the person who "does not condemn himself by what he approves" (14:22 NIV)—it is possible to be wrong even though you are fully convinced. The important thing is that you have true faith that what you are doing is acceptable to God, that you are doing it with an attitude of love toward fellow Christians, and that you are sending a good message to those who do not yet believe. God will sort out the rest on the Day of Judgment.

Paul presents us with an interesting warning as we relate to one another as Christians. Take the issue of whether Christian children should celebrate Halloween. One argument says that Halloween is the stuff of demons—its imagery is principally drawn from categories that the Bible abhors, things like magic and witchcraft (e.g., Deut. 18:10-12; Gal. 5:19-20). If Paul were alive today, he might very well think that an evil pollution was attached to the practices of Halloween, even though most celebrate it innocently.

On the other hand, Paul does not treat the issue of meat offered to idols as if the meat itself was contaminated with an evil presence. In Romans 14:14 he says, "I am fully convinced that no food is unclean in itself. But if anyone regards something as unclean, then for him it is unclean" (NIV). In the final analysis, Paul does not make his decisions on the basis of a Satanic presence in the meat, but on the basis of the faith of the individual Christian. The bottom line then and now is that "everything that does not come from faith is sin" (Rom. 14:23).

Tongues

One issue that has frequently proved to be extremely divisive among Christians is that of "speaking in tongues." Tongues, simply stated, are languages. One issue in 1 Corinthians 14 is whether the tongues to which Paul refers are human languages or angelic prayer languages that God inspires certain individuals to speak. While some do contend that Paul was only talking about human languages, most readers of 1 Corinthians understand tongues as languages of a nonhuman nature, probably the "angelic languages" to which Paul alludes in 1 Corinthians 13:1.

Christians take a wide variety of positions on this issue, ranging from those who think you cannot be a Christian unless you have the gift of tongues, to those who believe tongues speakers to be demon possessed. Both of these extremes fail to measure up to the text of 1 Corinthians. On the one hand, Paul is very straightforward about the fact that not all Christians have the "gift" of tongues (1 Cor. 12:30). On the other hand, Paul treats tongues as a legitimate gift that should not be forbidden (14:39).

Where Christians more legitimately disagree is on the tone of 1 Corinthians 14 toward tongues. Is this chapter basically discouraging the use of tongues in Christian worship, or does it simply give guidelines for how it should be practiced in worship? Those who think Paul was discouraging its use note that Paul starts the chapter by pushing the Corinthians toward prophecy in contrast to tongues (1 Cor. 14:1-2). Those who think he encourages its use point to Paul's claim to speak in tongues more than the Corinthians themselves (14:18).

Certainly Paul does provide guidelines for the use of tongues in worship. As with prophecy, Paul insists that only two or three speak in tongues in the course of any one worship setting. These are to speak one at a time and then only if someone has the gift of interpretation (1 Cor. 14:27-28). You will have to decide what role you think tongues might play in your life.

Things to Think About

Key Terms
body of Christ
demythologize

1. Does it surprise you that some Christians would question whether sex was appropriate *at all*, let alone just within the context of marriage?

2. Does Paul prefer marriage or complete celibacy? Does the context in which Paul writes shed any light on Paul's reasoning? Does Paul think of marriage as an intimate context God designed for the beauty of sex or as a "safe haven" for individuals to channel their sexual energies? In other words, have contemporary Christians romanticized Paul's teaching on sex?

3. Should contemporary Christians take each other to court? Should churches take Christian individuals to court and vice versa?

4. Some verses in 1 Corinthians sound like evil is contagious (e.g., casting out the sexually immoral individual of 1 Corinthians 5), while others seem to imply that it is your individual attitude that makes something unclean or evil (e.g., 1 Corinthians 8 on the issue of meat offered to idols). Which is it? Is participation in Halloween wrong regardless of your attitude toward it, or is it all a matter of your attitude? In what circumstances should a "sinner" be ousted from a congregation to save it from contamination?

5. Do you think Paul was encouraging the use of tongues in worship or discouraging it? What would your policy be on tongues in a local church?

endnotes

1. The overlap between Leviticus 18 and Paul's prohibitions on sex is fairly significant. For this reason, we should probably refer to this chapter to know what Paul meant by the term "sexual immorality."

2. For a fascinating exploration of this idea in 1 Corinthians, see Dale B. Martin, *The Corinthian Body* (New Haven: Yale University, 1995).

3. This line of thinking may explain what Paul means in 1 Corinthians 7:14 when he says an unbelieving spouse is "made holy" by a believing one. This comment does not seem to imply salvation from God's wrath (e.g., 7:16), but some degree of spiritual protection.

4. Those who use the King James Version sometimes have taken the word fornication to refer to sex before marriage. However, that word refers to any kind of sexual immorality, as most modern translations have recognized.

5. The idea that sex is good was evidently so strong in the mind of the NIV translators of this verse that they rendered it, "It is good for a man not to marry."

6. It is possible that some in Corinth had overreacted to the others among them who were sexually promiscuous. Perhaps they began to teach that a person should not have sex even if s/he was married.

7. Paul's wording is very interesting—he says she was not to divorce her husband, but if she did she was to remain unmarried. The fact that he moves beyond the

ideal to a "second best" indicates that he is giving us the way it should be, yet accepting that reality does not always match up to the ideal. Divorce does not seem to have been possible for women to initiate in Palestine, making Jesus' words puzzling—why would He give such a command if it were not possible to carry it out? Some think Paul and Mark at these points were expanding Jesus' words (originally directed only at men), in order to fit a context in the Roman world where women of privilege were able to divorce their husbands.

8. The statements in quotation marks seem to be slogans that some in Corinth were saying. The last statement is of course the Shema of Deuteronomy 6:4, the fundamental cornerstone of Judaism.

CHAPTER 43

Is Death the End?

Christ's Resurrection from the dead was not a unique event in history for Paul – he believed Christ was only the firstborn from the dead. Christians who die before Christ's return will also rise.

Resurrection and Immortality

One of the last issues that Paul deals with in 1 Corinthians is the question of resurrection. Paul had the impression that some in the Corinthian church did not believe there would be a time when the dead would come back to life. Unfortunately, since we do not know exactly what position they took, we cannot fully appreciate some of what Paul says in this chapter. For example, it is not clear if they believed in any afterlife at all. It very well may be they disbelieved the idea of resurrection in particular.

Most Christians today probably are not aware of the difference between the idea that we have an immortal soul and the Christian belief in the resurrection of your body. But it was primarily the Greek philosopher Plato who taught the immortality of the soul. By this Plato meant that there is a part of us, the soul, which has always existed and will continue to exist forever. This soul is obviously detachable

At a Glance

• Some of those in Corinth evidently did not believe in a future resurrection of dead bodies.

• In 1 Corinthians 15, Paul argues that Christ rose from the dead.

• Paul argues that Christ's Resurrection is of the same kind as our resurrection. If there is no such thing as resurrection, then Christ has not risen either.

• Paul answers questions about the kind of body you will have when you are resurrected. It is a spiritual body.

from our bodies; in fact, our bodies only weigh our souls down and encumber them. Many Christians believe that your soul goes immediately to heaven or hell when you die.

However, the idea of resurrection is distinct from that of immortality. It is resurrection that has always been the fundamentally Christian view of the afterlife. The phrase "the resurrection of the dead" actually refers to bringing dead bodies back to life.[1] In some Jewish teaching this did not mean that you continued to exist after death, at least not until God gave your body back to you. And some Pharisees taught that not all the dead would come back to life—only those who did not get what was coming to them in this life, whether it was reward or punishment.

Paul's writings give us the impression that however we continue to exist at death, it is like sleeping until Christ returns to earth (1 Thess. 4:13-16; 1 Cor. 15:18, 20). He also says that to be away from our bodies is to be present with Christ (2 Cor. 5:8-9). But if this comment means anything other than the sleep that Paul mentions in his earlier letters, then it represents a change or development in Paul's understanding. Further, he only refers to the resurrection of those *in Christ* in his letters. Paul nowhere discusses the fate of the wicked when they die.

Luke and Acts were written several decades after Paul wrote his letters to the Corinthians and the Thessalonians, plenty of time for Christians to reflect further on the question of what happens to you when you die. Luke tells us a parable about a rich man and a beggar, both of whom die and immediately go to a place of either reward or torment (Luke 16:19-31). In Luke 23:43, Jesus tells one of the thieves on the cross that he will go to Paradise that very day after he dies. Similarly, in Acts Paul tells a Roman governor that he believes in the resurrection of both the good *and the wicked* (Acts 24:15).[2]

We have already mentioned in several previous chapters that Paul's message was focused on God's impending judgment of those living on earth, not of the dead. Knowing this fact helps us understand how the Corinthians could have faith (1 Cor. 15:17), could become Christians, and yet could not believe in the idea of resurrection.

The Key: Christ's Resurrection

The key to Paul's argument in favor of resurrection is the Resurrection of Christ from the dead, for Christ is only the first of the crop to be harvested (1 Cor. 15:20). Adam, the first human being, sinned and suffered death as a punishment. The entire human race has descended from him, and thus all humans are a part of Adam's family. Paul argues that all those in Adam's family will die. Those who become a part of Christ's household, on the other hand, will all come back to life again

> "And if we have hope in Christ only for this life, we are the most miserable people in the world."
>
> **1 Corinthians 15:19**

(15:22). But if there is no such thing as resurrection, Paul declares, then not even Christ has come back to life.

First Corinthians 15 includes a list of those who at one time or another had seen Jesus after He died. These are the people Paul considers to be apostles, witnesses of the Resurrection (cf. 1 Cor. 9:1). Starting with Peter and the twelve disciples, Paul states that over five hundred people saw Him at the same

> **creed:** A statement of basic belief.

time (15:5-6). He then mentions James, Jesus' brother, and other apostles, probably including men like Barnabas (15:7). Finally, Paul mentions that Jesus had appeared to him as well (15:8). Some of what Paul was passing on to the Corinthians here was probably from a **creed**, a statement of basic beliefs that Christians taught (e.g., 15:3-4). Since Paul had contact with men like

Peter (cf. Gal. 1:18), it becomes very difficult to deny that all these men truly were convinced that they really had seen Jesus after He had died on the cross.

For Paul, as seen in this chapter, it was either resurrection or no conscious afterlife at all. If there is no resurrection, those Christians who had died were simply "lost," Paul says (1 Cor. 15:18 NIV). He does not imply that they could be off somewhere being rewarded at that moment—resurrection was the point of reward for him. If the dead are not raised, then the suffering he had undergone was worthless (15:32). He might as well live as some Epicureans of his day suggested: "Let's feast and get drunk, for tomorrow we die" (15:32). And what of Christians who evidently were baptizing themselves so that some who had died could receive the benefit of Christ (15:29)?[3] There is no reward at all, Paul teaches, unless there is a resurrection.

Given some of the things Paul says elsewhere in 1 Corinthians, it is also possible that some of the community thought that Christ enabled them to rule spiritually now while they were still on earth. As Paul says somewhat cynically in 1 Corinthians 4:8, "You are already rich! Without us you have become kings! I wish you really were on your thrones already, for then we would be reigning with you!" Perhaps it is no coincidence that Paul discusses the Resurrection of Christ and the resurrection of the dead just after he has addressed spiritual gifts like speaking in tongues and prophecy. While some in the community believed they were experiencing the full benefits of Christ right then, Paul's sufferings told him that our primary reward as Christians is something yet to come, something that will take place after Christ returns to earth a second time.

What Kind of Body Will We Have?

For most Jews, a person was not a person without a body. The word *soul* in the Old Testament refers to the whole person, not a detachable part of a person. In the creation of man as recorded in Genesis 2, God took some dust for Adam's body; He breathed spirit in (breath = spirit in Hebrew and Greek) and Adam became a living *soul* (soul = the whole person). The idea of life without a body was thus foreign to the Old Testament, although some Jews at the time of Christ did believe that your spirit continued to live on at death.[4]

However, the idea of the resurrection of corpses definitely involves your body, for it is your body that is brought back to life.[5] Paul imagines those who disagree with him as asking what kind of a body a resurrected person would have (1 Cor. 15:35). Here Paul disagrees with some Pharisees who believed the righteous came back from the dead with exactly the same body they had when they died. The Pharisaic book called 2 Maccabees tells the story of a man named Razis who tried to kill himself before his enemies could. After a couple of failed attempts, he was mortally wounded. He grabbed some of his intestines and threw them at the crowd, "calling on the One who rules life and spirit to give them back to him

last Adam: An image Paul uses of Christ as the counterpart to Adam. Adam sinned, brought death, and prevented his family from ruling the earth. Christ brings life to those "in Him" and enables them to attain to the glory God originally meant humanity to have.

"But let me tell you a wonderful secret God has revealed to us. Not all of us will die, but we will all be transformed. It will happen in a moment, in the blinking of an eye, when the last trumpet is blown. For when the trumpet sounds, the Christians who have died will be raised with transformed bodies. And then we who are living will be transformed so that we will never die. For our perishable earthly bodies must be transformed into heavenly bodies that will never die.

"When this happens—when our perishable earthly bodies have been transformed into heavenly bodies that will never die—then at last the Scriptures will come true:

'Death is swallowed up in victory. O death, where is your victory? O death, where is your sting?' "

1 Corinthians 15:51-55

again" (2 Macc. 14:46). For the author of 2 Maccabees, resurrection was a reconstitution of one's *physical* body.

For Paul, one comes back to life with a *spiritual* body. God created Adam a living soul, which Paul interprets to include a body; but God had made Jesus, the **last Adam**, into a life-giving *spirit* (1 Cor. 15:45). Flesh and blood, Paul says, cannot enter the kingdom of God (15:50). Both earthly and heavenly bodies have different levels of "glory" (15:40). The bodies we will have when we are raised from the dead will be heavenly bodies of a spiritual rather than a physical nature.

For early Christians like Paul, God created humanity to rule the earth in a position of highest honor. But because of Adam's sin, death came instead; humans do not rule at present. Christ, however, is the "last Adam," whose choices potentially have exactly the opposite effect that Adam's choices had. Christ rose from the dead and now rules until death is finally defeated and all Christians rise from the dead (1 Cor. 15:25-26).

Things to Think About

1. Have you ever realized the connection between Christ's Resurrection and yours? What is the connection?

Key Terms

creed

Last Adam

2. What is the difference between the immortality of the soul and the resurrection of the body? Which did Paul teach?

3. What do you think happens to a Christian in the time between his or her death and the resurrection that is still to come?

4. Do you think we will have male and female bodies in heaven? What do you think spiritual bodies are like?

endnotes

1. The word dead here in Greek refers to corpses.

2. Depending on how you understand the Bible, you can see these examples from Luke in two ways. They may fill in blanks for us that Paul does not make clear, but that originate with Jesus. Or they may represent a different or more developed understanding than the one Paul has.

3. Scholars highly debate what such people thought they were doing. I suggest that they were trying to include dead relatives and friends within the benefit of Christ's death. Perhaps these are relatives who died before the gospel reached Corinth. Some may have seen such actions as ensuring these individuals a happy life in the underworld rather than guaranteeing them a resurrection.

4. Chiefly the Essenes and some philosophically oriented Jews like Philo of Alexandria.

5. The idea that Christ was resurrected from the dead, therefore, involves Christ's dead body. It implies that Paul, Peter, and the other apostles believed in an empty tomb.

CHAPTER 44

2 Corinthians: Healing Relationships

Paul writes 2 Corinthians after a period of significant tension.
With the tension largely resolved, Paul writes some of the most uplifting
words in the entire New Testament.

A Touchy Situation

As we mentioned earlier, 1 and 2 Corinthians are not the only letters that Paul wrote to the Corinthian church. In fact, *First* Corinthians is actually the *second* letter Paul wrote to Corinth (see 1 Cor. 5:9), and what we call *Second* Corinthians is probably the *fourth* letter he sent them (2 Cor. 2:4). Knowing these things helps us realize that our New Testaments just give us the tip of the iceberg. We really know very little of the many things that took place in the first century of Christianity.

When reading through the first nine chapters of 2 Corinthians, it is clear that there had been a crisis in the Corinthian church and in Paul's relationship with that church. Paul had written a previous letter shaming the

At a Glance

• Paul wrote more letters to Corinth than we have today, and he visited the city at least one time more than Acts tells us.

• It is possible that 2 Corinthians consists of two of Paul's letters to Corinth that have been put together (chapters 10–13 would then be from a letter Paul wrote before he wrote chapters 1–9).

• Second Corinthians 1–9 reflects that Paul and the Corinthians had been reconciled to one another. Paul rejoiced that because of a harsh letter he had sent, someone had repented of his sins.

• Second Corinthians 10–13 is a vigorous defense of Paul's authority. Some think these chapters are an excerpt from the harsh letter just mentioned.

Corinthians, in part because they had not dealt properly with someone in the church who had wronged another Christian in the community (2 Cor. 7:12). Paul had evidently defended his authority in that previous letter (3:1) and had informed the church that he was coming himself to straighten things out. In the end, he had sent Titus instead (1:23–2:4, 13). Given a touchy situation, some of the leaders of the community perhaps felt that Paul had left them holding the bag and that he had talked out of both sides of his mouth. He said he would come but then did not follow through (1:17-18).

Against this background, the first nine chapters of 2 Corinthians give us the rest of the story. The church had risen to the occasion and had taken appropriate action with regard to the wrongdoer (2 Cor. 2:6-7). More importantly for Paul, they had reaffirmed their submission to his authority (2:9; 7:12). Paul was delighted when he met up with Titus and found out that the church was back on track (7:6-7). Second Corinthians 1–9 presents us with a comforting tale of reconciliation between Paul and the house churches at Corinth.

Given the warm and conciliatory tone of the first nine chapters of 2 Corinthians, the reader is immediately struck when s/he gets to 2 Corinthians 10. All of a sudden, Paul is seen to be back on the defensive again, vigorously defending that he is an apostle. In 3:1 and 5:12 he leads us to believe he is not going to do that again. In fact, the content of 2 Corinthians 10–13 has much in common with what Paul implies was in the harsh letter he had previously written them. He mentions coming to visit them to straighten things out regarding sexual immorality (12:21). He is uncertain about their loyalty and goes to great lengths to demonstrate his authority. These are the things the first part of 2 Corinthians assumes have been sufficiently resolved.

For this reason, some scholars argue that 2 Corinthians 10–13 is an excerpt from the harsh letter Paul mentions in the first nine chapters. In this theory, the excerpt had been appended to the conciliatory letter as Paul's writings were being collected and passed around, perhaps as a point of reference for the other chapters. It is important to note that this view would not affect the Bible's inspiration, nor does it attribute error to the Scriptures in any way. We already know that the Bible's "packaging" as one book has nothing to do with the way these books were written or the order in which they first appeared.[1] It would thus be quite a mistake to think that the Bible's

> "We are pressed on every side by troubles, but we are not crushed and broken. We are perplexed, but we don't give up and quit. We are hunted down, but God never abandons us. We get knocked down, but we get up again and keep going. Through suffering, these bodies of ours constantly share in the death of Jesus so that the life of Jesus may also be seen in our bodies."
>
> **2 Corinthians 4:8-10**

authority is somehow connected with how its packaging appears *to me*. And, of course, it *is* possible that these chapters were originally part of the same letter anyway. Perhaps they were aimed at those in the Corinthian church who had not yet come around to accepting Paul's authority.

Getting Back Together: Chapters 1–9

The key idea in these chapters is comfort or encouragement, a Greek word Paul uses in one way or another over twenty times in these first nine chapters. Paul writes to encourage the Corinthians after a period when significant tension had existed between them. With the tension largely resolved, Paul writes some of the most uplifting words in the entire New Testament.

We have already mentioned the basic circumstances of the discomfort. Someone in the Corinthian church had wronged someone else in the church. Perhaps it was the man from 1 Corinthians 5 who was sleeping with

> "God was in Christ, reconciling the world to himself, no longer counting people's sins against them. This is the wonderful message he has given us to tell others."
>
> **2 Corinthians 5:19**

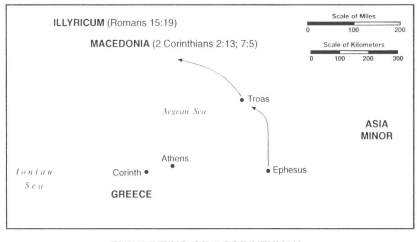

ILLYRICUM (Romans 15:19)

MACEDONIA (2 Corinthians 2:13; 7:5)

Scale of Miles
0   100   200

Scale of Kilometers
0   100   200   300

Troas

Aegean Sea

ASIA
MINOR

Athens

*Ionian
Sea*

Corinth •

• Ephesus

GREECE

**THE WRITING OF 2 CORINTHIANS
MAP 8**

his father's wife, although we cannot know one way or another for certain. Some among the house churches of Corinth did not accept Paul's authority on the matter. Rather, they favored those whom Paul called in 2 Corinthians 11:5 "super apostles."

As Paul travels around the Aegean Sea from Ephesus to Troas to Macedonia (see **Map 8**), he meets up with Titus, who was going around in the opposite direction. Titus reassures Paul that the church is still loyal to his authority and that the sinner has been dealt with. In the middle of telling the story of this meeting with Titus, Paul sidetracks for about five chapters to speak comforting words to the Corinthians. While things are not always going well on the outside, he says, we are inwardly being prepared for heavenly things to come.

Chapters 3–6 in particular are filled with the contrast between how things look on the outside and what is really happening on the inside. "Though outwardly we are wasting away, yet inwardly we are being renewed day by day" (2 Cor. 4:16 NIV). The glory that Christians have in them comes from the Holy Spirit (3:18), and it is encased in a "jar of clay" (4:7). The jar is very breakable, but inside there is a transformation going on. The "earthly tent" we live in, our bodies, will eventually be destroyed, but God has another house for us that He will give us at the resurrection (5:1-5), the spiritual body of which Paul spoke in 1 Corinthians 15. Until then, the Holy Spirit in us is a guarantee of that body, as well as a down payment of that glory yet to come (1:22; 5:5). Paul even notes that we are already becoming "more and more like him and reflect his glory even more" (3:18). Even from the moment we become a part of Christ, we become a "new creation" (5:17).

The bottom line of what his ministry is about, Paul tells the Corinthians, is getting humanity back together with God: reconciliation. Paul sees his job as that of an ambassador from God to people like the Corinthians. Ultimately, God is using to bring Christ humanity back to himself. He had Christ take on the sins of the world, so that Paul and ambassadors like him could bring an invitation to all people. Paul gives them the message plain and simple: "Be reconciled to God!" (5:20).

The final two chapters of this section deal with an offering Paul and the churches he founded have been patiently collecting so that they can bring it to the church in Jerusalem. Paul holds up to the Corinthians the model of Christ: "Though he was very rich, yet for your sakes he became poor, so that by his poverty he could make you rich" (8:9). This offering was certainly "for the poor among the saints in Jerusalem" (Rom. 15:26 NIV), but it also may have been a peace offering between Paul and a part of the church with which he himself was at odds. As such he may have seen it as part of his own reconciliation to the church.

A Vigorous Defense: Chapters 10–13

Even if 2 Corinthians 10–13 was originally a part of the same letter as the first nine chapters, we can imagine that it was similar to the harsh letter Paul had sent previously. Paul tells them that he is coming for a third visit, during which he will settle some matter in dispute. He had warned them on his second visit. When he returns, he warns, "I will not spare those who sinned earlier or any of the others, since you are demanding proof that Christ is speaking through me" (2 Cor. 13:2-3 NIV).[2] They had accused him of being "timid" when face to face with them but "bold" when he was communicating with them by letter (10:1, 10; 13:3).

He felt compelled to boast about his qualifications as a minister. The better part of 2 Corinthians 11–12 presents excerpts from his "resume." He illustrates in 2 Corinthians 11 the significance of his service to God by the many troubles he has faced. He has been thrown in prison, flogged, beaten, stoned, and shipwrecked. He has endured the dangers of travel by land and sea, and has faced the opposition of both Jews and Gentiles. When the governor of Damascus had the city gates guarded in order to arrest him, Paul escaped by being lowered in a basket from a window in the city wall (11:32-33).

In 2 Corinthians 12, Paul verifies his spiritual qualifications in terms of the visions and revelations he has experienced. He tells how he had gone up to the third heaven, "caught up into Paradise," where he had heard inexpressible things (12:2, 4). His experiences were so tremendous, Paul states, that God had to give him a physical problem just to keep him from becoming conceited (12:7).

His conclusion is that while he might not have the standing of some of the "super apostles" so valued by his opponents in Corinth, he is in no way inferior to them (11:5-6; 12:11). "The things that mark an apostle—signs, wonders and miracles," Paul does among them patiently (12:13 NIV). His warning to them is very serious indeed: "Examine yourselves to see whether you are in the faith; test yourselves. Do you not realize that Christ Jesus is in you—unless, of course, you fail the test?" (13:5 NIV).

Things to Think About

1. Which model(s) of Christ's death is (are) most meaningful to you: (1) His death as a sacrifice for sins and to satisfy God's anger, (2) His death in your place, taking your punishment, (3) Christ's defeat over evil powers that enslave humanity, (4) Christ as an ambassador from God to humanity to reconcile us to one another?

2. How angry is Paul in 2 Corinthians 10–13? Is he modeling an appropriate Christian response to his situation?

3. Would it affect the authority or inspiration of 2 Corinthians if it were actually two of Paul's letters that someone had joined together?

4. If someone were to find Paul's other letters to the Corinthians, should we put them into the Bible? Did God and the church already set the boundaries for the canon? What qualifies a book as Scripture?

endnotes

1. Psalms gives us many good examples of this fact. For example, Psalm 137 was written some 500 years after Psalms 138-145, if David wrote these last psalms.
2. This statement does not fit well with 2 Corinthians 2:7 if both comments were originally part of the same letter. Second Corinthians 2:7 says the community should comfort the one who had sinned and repented, while 13:2 says that when Paul comes he will not spare those who have previously sinned.

CHAPTER 45

Galatians: Paul on the Defense

Some Jewish Christians had taught the Galatians that they would not escape God's judgment unless they were circumcised and kept the Jewish Law.

A Slap in Christ's Face

Although there is some disagreement about when Galatians was written and about what group it addressed, one solid suggestion is that Paul wrote it in the same general time period that he wrote 2 Corinthians and Romans. During his so-called second missionary journey, some crisis—perhaps a physical problem with his eyes (cf. 2 Cor. 12:7)—forced Paul to spend some time with the non-Jewish Galatians (Gal. 4:13-15). Although they became Christians, he did not circumcise them. He had come to believe that Gentiles did not need to be circumcised in order to escape God's coming wrath. Christ's death alone atoned for their sins.

Not long after Paul had departed, some Jewish Christians came in and

At a Glance

- Paul probably wrote Galatians near the end of his mission to Asia Minor and Greece (A.D. 53–57), not long before he wrote Romans. Others think it was the first letter he wrote (ca. A.D. 48–49).

- Paul wrote because some group was exerting pressure on the Galatians to be circumcised and to follow the Jewish Law.

- Paul formulates a different way for Gentiles to be acceptable to God: by faith rather than by keeping the Old Testament covenant.

- It is Christ's faithfulness and their faith in Christ that gives them a "not guilty" verdict in God's court.

- The result of this faith was incorporation into Christ, the presence of the Holy Spirit, and the resulting fruit (especially love).

taught the Galatians that they would not escape God's judgment simply because they had been baptized and trusted in Christ's death to atone for their sins. They told the Galatians that unless they also followed the Jewish Law by being circumcised, observing the Sabbath, and keeping the Old Testament covenant in general, they would still be found guilty in God's eyes when He judged the world. What is worse, the Galatians were buying it! Paul saw this teaching as a slap in Christ's face and a horrible perversion of the Christian message.

Galatians was Paul's response. From some of his comments, we can tell that Paul was rather angry when he wrote this letter (e.g., Gal. 5:12). It is also the only one of Paul's letters without the standard introduction in which Paul gives thanks to God for those to whom he is writing. Instead, he gets right down to business after his greeting: "I am shocked that you are turning away so soon from God, who in his love and mercy called you to share the eternal life he gives through Christ" (Gal. 1:6).

Background

In the first two chapters of Galatians, Paul recounts for his audience some of the key events in his ministry, with a focus on the disagreement of which they now find themselves a part. Paul begins by letting them know how strongly he believes God chose him specifically to bring Christianity to non-Jews or Gentiles. From his mother's womb, God had chosen him for this mission (Gal. 1:15-16). His call to Christianity came by way of a direct revelation from God, after which Paul explains that he immediately went to Arabia. Only after three years did he then travel to Jerusalem to meet Peter and James. He makes it clear that he has never been under their authority.

His next visit to Jerusalem was fourteen years later. During this trip, which may very well be Paul's version of the Jerusalem Council of Acts 15,

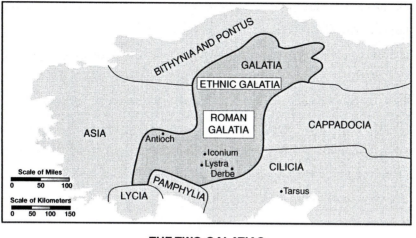

THE TWO GALATIAS
MAP 9

Paul presented the message he gave to Gentiles. The Jerusalem Council, as you recall, decided the issue of whether Gentiles needed to be circumcised in order to escape God's wrath. But neither Peter, John, nor the Lord's brother, James, opposed his mission or the fact that he did not circumcise Gentiles. The uncircumcised Titus, Paul's helper, remained uncircumcised. The only thing the Jerusalem leaders added was concern for the poor, something Paul had already included in his ministry.

We might think that the Jew-Gentile matter was solved at this point. The church had agreed that Gentiles could escape God's coming wrath on earth without being circumcised. Some readers might be surprised, then, to see what happened next. Peter, Barnabas, and Paul were in the city of Antioch, where Jewish and Gentile Christians were eating together in fellowship. But when certain men came from James in Jerusalem, both Peter and Barnabas separated themselves and would not eat with the Gentiles anymore. Paul considered this to be hypocrisy, which at that time was understood to be a failure to discern God's will appropriately. In front of everyone, he corrected Peter.

It would be hard to underestimate the significance of this one event for Christianity. In the short term, this argument probably was part of why Paul and Barnabas went their separate ways on their "second" missionary journeys.[1] But more important is the fact that Paul seems to have lost this argument. Knowing how Paul reacted on other occasions, he almost certainly would have told us if Peter had come to agree with him on this occasion. The implication is that Paul suddenly found himself outside the mainstream of Christianity, out of favor with the apostles and leaders of the church. Now he would have to justify his authority in places like Galatia and Corinth.[2] He had a long road ahead of him.

Ironically, this conflict may have been the catalyst for bringing the gospel in force to Greece and Rome, since it probably pushed Paul away from Palestine and its nearby regions. It may also have been the speck of dirt that resulted in the pearl Christians call "justification by faith." This event may have led Paul to formulate teachings that would eventually become some of the most significant doctrines in the history of the modern church.

Why did Peter and Barnabas stop eating with the Gentile Christians if they already believed the uncircumcised could be saved in the judgment? They probably stopped because they felt God still expected them to keep the Jewish laws regarding purity and what foods to eat. The Gentiles might not die when God came to judge the earth, but this fact did not make them clean in the eyes of the Jewish Christians, nor did it place them on the same level of acceptability as the Jews before God. If the Gentile Christians were to eat with Jewish Christians, they would have to be clean in accordance with the Old Testament codes regarding holiness.

Justification by Faith

One reason Paul considered Peter's actions hypocritical is because Peter himself did not keep the Law perfectly. As Paul also says of the ones troubling the Galatians, "Even those who advocate circumcision don't really keep the whole law. They only want you to be circumcised so they can brag about it and claim you as their disciples" (Gal. 6:13). In fact, Paul did not believe anyone could keep the Law perfectly. Therefore, anyone relying on the Jewish Law in order to be accepted by God at the judgment was doomed: "Cursed is everyone who does not observe and obey *all* these commands that are written in God's Book of the Law" (3:10).

After Paul had done so well at keeping the Law as a Pharisee, the meager efforts of the Galilean Peter and the Jerusalem Christians to enforce the Law must have seemed almost ridiculous to him. As Paul says to Peter, "You are a Jew, yet you live like a Gentile and not like a Jew. How is it, then, that you force Gentiles to follow Jewish customs?" (2:14 NIV).

The Day of Judgment will be a day when the living come before the greatest Judge of all, God. Everyone will be on trial, and everyone will either receive a verdict of "guilty" or "not guilty." Any Jew who depended on keeping the Jewish Law to escape a guilty verdict, Paul says, is doomed. Rather, the only way to be justified, to be found "not-guilty" and innocent, to be acquitted of all charges and declared righteous—the only way for that to happen is by trusting or having faith in Christ's death. This idea is called justification by faith, a concept we explored in chapter 37.

A number of scholars think that Paul refers in Galatians not only to our faith in Christ but also to Christ's own faithfulness. For example, Philippians 2:8 talks about how Jesus obeyed God to the point of dying. Those who think that Galatians and Romans focus on Christ's faithfulness argue that it is not even so much our faith that saves us as the fact that we put our trust in the faith Christ showed when He died for our sins and trusted God to raise Him from the dead (cf. Heb. 5:7).

Here is how Galatians 2:16 looks when interpreted in this way:

"Since we knew that no one is considered 'not guilty' by keeping the Jewish Law unless declared innocent through the faith of Jesus Christ, we also had faith in Christ Jesus so that we might be declared innocent on the basis of Christ-faith and not by keeping the Law. By keeping the Law, no one will be found 'not guilty.' "

Galatians 2:16 (author's translation)

The great thing about this interpretation is that it focuses on Christ rather than on the individual believer. It holds true to the fact that for Paul, it is being *in* Christ that saves us, the fact that we are part of the body of Christ. It also fits with the idea that all Christians share the same Spirit of Christ.

A balanced understanding of what Paul understands as justification by faith avoids some of the arguments different denominations have had over the years. For one thing, Paul is not exactly talking about whether we are saved by faith or by good deeds. Roman Catholics believe that God accepts us in part by the good deeds we do, while most Protestants vigorously argue that it is faith *alone* that saves us. Protestants and Catholics alike understand the "faith versus works" debate as a matter of "faith only" versus "good deeds" saving us.

In these passages, Paul is not really talking about good works in general. Instead, he is talking about whether Jews are saved because of the way they keep the Old Testament Law, the Jewish Law. Paul is thinking mostly about the issue of circumcision facing the Galatians and the fact that they were observing the Sabbaths and festivals of the Old Testament (Gal. 4:10). The debate was not faith versus works in general; it was trust in Christ's death versus keeping the old covenant.

For Paul, therefore, faith includes some works. As he writes, "In Christ Jesus neither circumcision nor uncircumcision has any value. The only thing that counts is faith *expressing itself through love*" (5:6 NIV). Paul would thus agree with James 2:17 that faith without works is dead.

Living by the Spirit

The way we get into Christ's body is for God to get into us. Just as we are "in Christ," the Spirit of God is in us. In Paul's mind, to be a Christian was to have God's Spirit in our hearts (cf. Rom. 8:9). Paul expresses some of his thinking in Galatians and Romans by talking about two parts of a human being: body and spirit. When he is talking about how sin can have control of our bodies, he refers to our flesh, a word translated as our "sinful nature" by the New International Version. Our **spirit**, on the other hand, is the part of us that most directly receives God's power by way of God's Holy Spirit. When God's Spirit is in us, it is as if God has put a little bit of heaven in us, even though we are still on earth in our fleshly bodies.

Paul clearly believes that sin and evil spiritual forces have virtually uncontained power over our flesh before we come to Christ (e.g., Rom. 7:18; Gal. 4:8-9). As he sees it, the Jewish Law is oriented around our physical existence on earth and constantly reminds us of our slavery to powers beyond our control. Freedom from these forces and the power to love come from God's Spirit (Gal. 5:1, 13-14, 16). After the Galatians had started out with the Spirit, Paul could not comprehend why they would subject themselves all over again to the power

spirit: The heavenly part of our nature that God's Holy Spirit can enter.

fruit of the Spirit: The natural result of having God's Spirit within—love, joy, peace, patience, kindness, goodness, faithfulness, gentleness, and self-control.

sin had over the flesh (3:3). They had freed themselves from the spiritual forces that rule this earthly realm (4:9). The earthly Jerusalem, enslaved to Rome, was no longer their "mother." Now they were the children of the heavenly Jerusalem.

Paul encourages the Galatians to live by the Spirit, not to return to their days in the flesh. Relying on their flesh, they would simply find themselves doing things that would not gain them entrance into God's kingdom, things like sexual immorality, hatred, envy, drunkenness, and the like (Gal. 5:19-21). But under the power of the Spirit, they would yield the **fruit of the Spirit**: love, joy, peace, patience, kindness, goodness, faithfulness, gentleness, and self-control (5:22-23).

The Who's and When's of Galatians

Two different regions have emerged as possible destinations for the book of Galatians (see **Map 9**). One was located in north central Asia Minor and was called "Galatia" because of the Gauls who settled there. Scholars refer to this region as "ethnic" Galatia. However, at the time of Paul, the Roman province of Galatia also included the area to the south of ethnic Galatia, an area that included a number of cities Acts tells us Paul visited. To which one of these two did Paul write the Epistle to the Galatians?

Some scholars favor the south part of the Roman province of Galatia because Acts tells us Paul planted churches there. Those who argue for this destination usually date the writing of Galatians early among Paul's letters, often as the first New Testament letter he wrote (ca. A.D. 48–49). Some of the motivation for such an early date is to better fit events in Galatians with the way Acts presents Paul's life. In particular, Galatians 2 differs enough from Acts 15 for some to consider them two different events. If they were two different events, the meeting in Galatians 2 would need to have happened before the Jerusalem Council of A.D. 49. Nor do some think Peter and Paul would have argued over eating with Gentiles after the Jerusalem Council.

However, we know that Paul passed through the area of northern Galatia, and we know that he did many things that were not recorded in Acts. Further, Galatians 2:1-10 may very well be Paul's version of the Jerusalem Council. In fact, most scholars equate the two. Those who argue for northern Galatia as the destination go with a later date like A.D. 53–57, placing the writing of Galatians at about the time Paul was writing books like 2 Corinthians and Romans. Indeed, those three books share many of the same themes. Finally, we have no reason to believe Paul founded the churches in southern, Roman Galatia because of some physical illness (Gal. 4:13-15). On the other hand, we could easily picture such a providential "layover" in ethnic Galatia while Paul was on his way through during his second missionary journey.

Things to Think About

1. What do you make of Paul's attitude in Galatians? Does it indicate that it is okay for a Christian to get angry?

Key Terms
fruit of the Spirit
spirit

2. Do you find it surprising that some early Christians believed you needed to continue to keep the Jewish Law after you became a Christian?

3. Does Paul indicate that a Christian's behavior changes after the Spirit is in his or her life? According to Paul, will a Christian give in to the desires of the "flesh" when s/he is walking in the Spirit?

endnotes

1. Acts omits this event, perhaps because it would have worked against Luke's desire to demonstrate the unity of the early Christians.
2. See chapter 41 of this text.

CHAPTER 46

Ephesians, Philippians, Colossians, Philemon: Letters from Prison

Traditionally, Paul wrote the Prison Epistles (Ephesians, Philippians, Colossians, Philemon) during his (first?) imprisonment in Rome.

The four short letters to the Ephesians, Philippians, Colossians, and to the slave owner Philemon are often called the "Prison Epistles." They are so called because in each letter Paul mentions that he is in chains as he writes (Eph. 6:20; Phil. 1:13; Col. 4:18; Philemon 13). Tradition has it that Rome was the place from which Paul wrote these letters, but Paul was also imprisoned in the cities of Ephesus and Caesarea, leading others to suggest one of these as the point of origin. Some also argue that Colossians and Ephesians are pseudonymous, written under the authority of Paul's name but not by Paul himself.[1]

At a Glance

- Ephesians, Philippians, Colossians, and Philemon are Paul's "Prison Epistles."

- Traditionally, Paul is thought to have written them from Rome while imprisoned there.

- Ephesians celebrates the unity of the church, particularly between Jew and Gentile.

- Philippians is a letter of thanks to Philippi after the church sent support to Paul.

- Colossians warns Christians at Colossae about a false teaching involving the Jewish Law.

- Philemon is a letter asking a slave owner to receive back his slave, Onesimus, who apparently had run away.

- Some think Colossians and Ephesians are pseudonymous—written under the authority of Paul's name, not literally by Paul himself.

537

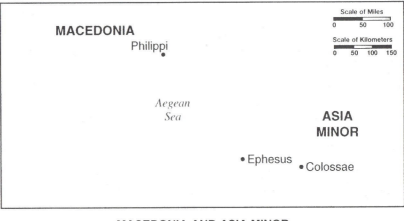

MACEDONIA AND ASIA MINOR
MAP 10

Ephesians

To a great degree, Ephesians is a *celebration of* the unity of the church as well as an *argument for* its unity. Obviously written to a Gentile audience (e.g., Eph. 1:13; 2:11, 19; 4:17), Ephesians takes Colossians' comments on the cancellation of the Jewish Law and incorporates them into a grand statement on how God has "abolished" the dividing wall of hostility between Jew and Gentile (Col. 2:14; Eph. 2:14-18).[2] Ephesians builds on the imagery of Colossians regarding the mystery of how God has brought Jew and Gentile together through Christ, a plan that "God did not reveal . . . to previous generations" (Eph. 3:5). The letter gives a tone of certainty to this plan by its strong language of election and predestination (Eph. 1:4-13), language that should be read as God's favor toward the Gentiles rather than as individual predestination.[3]

> "We are all one body, we have the same Spirit, and we have all been called to the same glorious future. There is only one Lord, one faith, one baptism, and there is only one God and Father."
>
> **Ephesians 4:46**

Shifts Between Paul's Earlier Writings and Ephesians

Earlier Writings	Ephesians
1. all things not yet under Christ's feet (1 Cor. 15:27, 28; cf. Heb. 10:13)	all things already under Christ's feet (1:22)
2. *will be* raised with Christ (Rom. 6:5; 8:11)	already raised with Christ; seated with Christ (2:6)
3. have been *justified*; will be *saved* (Rom. 5:9)	have been *saved* (2:8)
4. works of *Jewish Law* (Gal. 2:16)	works (2:9)
5. least of apostles (1 Cor. 15:9)	less than the least of all the saints (3:8)
6. body of *Christ* (1 Cor. 12:27)	body of *church*; Christ as head of body (1:22-23), but also body of Christ (4:12)
7. *not* abolish the Law; uphold it (Rom. 3:31)	abolished the Law (2:15)
8. foundation is Christ (1 Cor. 3:11)	apostles and Christian prophets are foundation; Christ is cornerstone (2:20)
9. Satan (1 Cor. 5:5)	Devil (6:11)
10. *church* refers primarily to specific congregations	*church* refers consistently to all Christians everywhere

In continuity with Paul's earlier writings, Ephesians mentions that the unified church is the body of Christ (Eph. 1:23; cf. 1 Cor. 12), a holy building and temple (Eph. 2:21; cf. 1 Cor. 3:10, 16).[4] In a magnificent passage, Ephesians notes, "We are all one body, we have the same Spirit, and we have all been called to the same glorious future. There is only one Lord, one faith, one baptism, and there is only one God and Father" (4:4-6). Within the unity of the church there are various roles to play: some apostles, some prophets, some evangelists, some pastors and teachers (4:11). Even the household has its proper order: wives are to submit to their husbands (5:22); husbands are to love their wives (5:25); children are to obey their parents (6:1); and slaves are to obey their masters (6:5). You are to "keep yourselves united in the Holy Spirit, and bind yourselves together with peace" (4:3).

Ephesians closes with a familiar encouragement to put on the armor of God, to be prepared for spiritual battle. In keeping with Colossians' heightened sense of evil spiritual powers, Ephesians notes that "we are not fighting against people made of flesh and blood, but against the evil rulers and authorities of the unseen world, against those mighty powers of darkness who rule this world, and against wicked spirits in the heavenly realms (6:12).[5] To combat such forces, Ephesians encourages us to arm ourselves with the virtues represented by a "belt" of truth, a "breastplate" of righteousness, "shoes" of readiness to preach, a "shield" of faith, a "helmet" of salvation, and a "sword" of the Spirit (6:14-17). This kind of armor will enable the believer to stand firm against the devil's temptations (6:13).[6]

A quick comparison of Ephesians and Colossians shows that the two are very similar indeed. In fact, at one point they have exactly the same wording for over twenty-five words (Eph. 6:21-22; Col 4:7-8). This paragraph is only the tip of the iceberg, however, for they share many other verses in common and have many common themes, although they do not always discuss those themes in the same way.

For those who believe Paul wrote both of these letters, the similarity is usually explained by the fact that they are both written at about the same time to two different churches. Many traveling preachers preach the same basic message in different locations. Since the earliest manuscripts of Ephesians leave out the words "to Ephesus," some scholars have suggested that this letter was actually the letter of Laodicea mentioned in Colossians 4:16.[7]

Ephesians does not explicitly address a specific problem or situation. For this reason some have suggested it was written to circulate widely without having a specific destination in view—a "circular letter." One scholar even suggested it was a cover letter written as a kind of preface for all of Paul's writings as they began to be collected.[8] Whatever we decide on such issues, Ephesians does have a different feel and tone than Paul's other letters and, like Colossians, its imagery differs as well. It even seems to be built out of the letter to the Colossians, although it has a much grander style and artfully fills out what are sometimes very "bare bones" statements in Colossians.[9]

Philippians

Paul wrote Philippians partially in response to aid he had recently received from the church at Philippi. This aid was sent to him by way of a man named Epaphroditus (Phil. 4:18). The letter presents a Paul who is in prison, yet at peace with his sufferings. If Paul was in Rome as he wrote this letter, it appears that near the end of his ministry he achieved a certain peace about those who opposed him personally. He no longer seemed to be bothered that some preached Christ "out of jealousy and rivalry" rather than with "pure motives" (1:15). He was just pleased that Christ was being preached (1:18). Rejoicing is a key theme in the epistle, even in the face of suffering.

Paul's reflections on his sufferings indicate someone who is prepared to die. If he lives, he has a job to do in spreading the gospel. But to die, he says,

Christ Jesus...

Who being in the form of God,

Did not consider equality with God something to plunder;

But he emptied himself,

Taking the form of a servant.

Having become in the likeness of men,

And having been found in form as a man,

He humbled himself,

Having become obedient to death . . .

Therefore God highly exalted him,

And gave him a name above all names

That at the name of Jesus every knee should bow . . .

And every tongue confess that Jesus Christ is Lord . . .

Philippians 2:6-11 (author's translation)

is better (Phil. 1:21). To be with Christ is something he finds very desirable, but he also feels that he still has some work to do on earth.[10] For this reason he believes that God will set him free from his chains.[11] In either case, he has learned to be content in whatever situation he finds himself (4:11-12)—an attitude he has in common with the Stoics of his day. He is trusting in God to supply his every need (4:19).

Philippians reflects traces of themes found in some of his other letters. He warns the Philippians about the "dogs," an ironic way of referring to those Jewish Christians who insisted Gentile converts to Christianity become circumcised (3:2). The reason this is ironic is because many Jews referred to *non-Jews* as dogs specifically because they were *un*circumcised. Paul, on the other hand, gave up his earthly Jewish credentials for Christ, although he formerly was a Hebrew of Hebrews and a strict Pharisee who kept the Law blamelessly (3:5-6). Philippians 3:9 echoes Paul's teaching elsewhere on the fact that acceptability with God comes on the basis of faith and not by keeping the Jewish Law.

If the recent gift of the Philippians provides Paul with a reason to write this letter, Paul takes the opportunity to address some of his concerns about the Philippians, concerns like the "Judaizers" we mentioned in the preceding paragraph. Paul also wishes to encourage the Philippians to be joyful in the persecution they evidently were undergoing (Phil. 1:25, 29). He urges them to imitate his attitude toward suffering (3:17–4:1) and to rely on God for their needs (4:19). In the process, he encourages them to remain unified—an indication that those who opposed them would be destroyed in the end (1:28). He encourages them to press on and make their way together toward their eventual salvation on the Day of Christ (2:12; 3:12-16).

syncretism: A mixture of religions.

mysticism: Practices and beliefs that relate to achieving a oneness of one kind or another with the divine realm.

asceticism: Involved extreme self-discipline or even the abuse of one's body.

Paul sums up the appropriate attitude of a Christian in what seems to be an early Christian hymn about Jesus (Phil. 2:6-11). Unlike those who are selfishly oriented, this hymn tells how Christ did not take advantage of His royal identity but instead played the role of a servant, emptying himself of His divine prerogatives. He obeyed God and suffered death as a result, but God consequently exalted Him as Lord of the universe. Here is some of the most exalted language of the New Testament regarding Christ, as well as one of the clearest indications in the New Testament that Christ existed before He became a human being.

Colossians

Paul and Timothy seem to have written the letter to the Colossians to warn those at Colossae about a "philosophy" (Col. 2:8) they believed might potentially threaten their faith. Indeed, it seems likely that some in the audience had already accepted its claims (cf. 2:19-20). While scholars disagree significantly over the nature of this "philosophy," it clearly had Jewish components. As was the case with the Galatians, the Colossians might have felt pressure to keep aspects of the Jewish Law. The philosophy insisted on the observance of Jewish festivals and Sabbaths (2:16) and adherence to the Old Testament food laws (2:21). The Colossian males might also have felt pressure to become circumcised (3:11).[12]

Yet the situations in Galatia and Colossae differed significantly from one another. Paul's opponents in Galatia were Jewish *Christians* compelling the Gentile Galatians to fully become Jews as a part of their conversion to Christianity. In Colossae, on the other hand, the philosophy in question did not seem to be Christian at all. In fact, many suggest it was not really Jewish either, but a highly **syncretistic** movement—a mixture of Judaism with the pagan religions of the region, the Lycus valley.

"You shall be like an angel of the face in the holy residence for the glory of the God of the Hosts . . . You shall be around, serving in the temple of the kingdom, sharing the lot with the angels of the face . . ."

Rule of the Blessings 4.25-26
Dead Sea Scrolls

If we take the "worship of angels" mentioned in Colossians 2:18 to indicate that the followers of this philosophy literally worshiped angels, then the philosophy stood squarely outside what the overwhelming majority of Jews would have found acceptable. After all, the cornerstone of Jewish religion is monotheism— the worship of Yahweh to the exclusion of all other gods. For some scholars, the incredible strangeness of such a mixture of ideas makes them wonder if the phrase "the worship of angels" is an exaggeration of this philosophy; i.e., angels simply played an extremely important role in the philosophy in question, but no one actually worshiped them.

A better suggestion is that the phrase "the worship of angels" was not about worshiping angels at all, but about *angels worshiping*. In other words, the philosophy in question was a form of **mystical** Judaism that highly valued visions of the heavenly realm. One who had such a vision mystically entered into the divine world and participated in heavenly worship. Several worship texts from the Dead Sea Scrolls indicate that the Essenes desired to participate with the angels in the heavenly worship of God. Another mystical movement within Judaism called "Merkabah mysticism" also aimed at participation in the worship of heaven around the divine throne of God. Some have argued that Paul's vision of the third heaven in 2 Corinthians 12:2 and his claim to speak in (angelic?) tongues more than all the Corinthians (1 Cor. 14:18) indicate that he too was acquainted with such mystical practices.

If this philosophy were a form of Jewish mysticism, it would go a long way toward explaining some of the differences between Colossians and Paul's earlier letters. For example, while Paul's opponents in Galatia disagreed with him over how to escape God's wrath *in the future*, those in Colossae may not have even anticipated a coming judgment at all. For them, the issue seemed to be about how to attain spiritual wisdom by entering into the angelic realm.[13] They believed that keeping the Jewish Law and certain **ascetic** practices—matters of extreme self-discipline (e.g., Col. 2:18, 23)— qualified you for access to the heavenly realm alongside the angels, thus providing true wisdom (e.g., 2:18).

Paul's response is highly appropriate. First, he connects both the Jewish Law and the spiritual forces admired in this philosophy with the created realm rather than with heaven and God's presence. This move was natural because the Jews believed that angels had delivered the Jewish Law to the earth (e.g., Acts 7:38, 53; Gal. 3:19; Heb. 2:2) and that they functioned as God's ambassadors to the creation (e.g., Heb 1:5, 14).[14] By associating the Jewish Law and angelic powers with the created realm, Paul locates the elements of

Christ

Who is the image of . . . God,	**Who is** the beginning,
The firstborn of all creation.	**The firstborn** from the dead . . .
Because in him were	**Because in him** [God] desired
created all things . . .	the fullness to dwell
All things through him and for him	And **through him** to reconcile
were created.	**all things** to him.
And he is **before all things**,	[That He might become
And all things in him	**supreme in all things**,]
became united . . .	**Making peace** through the
	blood of his cross.

Colossians 1:15-20
(author's translation)

this Jewish philosophy in exactly the opposite position in which its proponents place it. While they claim their practices will lead to heaven and spiritual wisdom, Paul argues that their practices are wholly associated with the earthly.

In contrast, Paul locates Christ and Christians squarely in the heavenly realm. Paul's normal orientation around *coming* salvation and the *coming* kingdom have shifted somewhat to focus on the *current* participation in heaven and its kingdom. That is, while his earlier writings are largely "horizontal" in orientation—focused on the future in relation to the present, Colossians is more "vertically" oriented—focused on the heavenly in relation to the earthly. Thus Paul says that we have *already* been raised with Christ (3:1),[15] and he speaks of us *already* being in the kingdom of the Son (Col. 1:13).[16]

Further, he makes it clear that angels and other spiritual forces are not the highest authorities in the creation, nor are they the means by which atonement takes place. In a majestic "hymn" that many think existed even before Colossians was written (1:15-20), Paul clearly gives Christ the supreme place over the creation. "By him all things were created: things in heaven and on earth, visible and invisible, whether thrones or powers or rulers or authorities; all things were created by him and for him. He is before all things . . ." (1:16-17 NIV). In Christ "lie hidden all the treasures of wisdom and knowledge" (2:3), unlike those who try to attain wisdom by their heavenly visions. And while the Essenes may have believed that angels offered the true sacrifices of atonement in a heavenly temple,[17] Colossians clearly notes that it is through Christ that "God has purchased our freedom with his blood and has forgiven all our sins" (1:14).

Like the hymn in Philippians, the Colossian hymn also presents Christ in some of the most exalted language of the New Testament.[18] The first half of the hymn is the most likely part to have existed at some time before the writing of Colossians and sounds extremely similar to something a Jew might have said about God's wisdom or Word. It is probably no coincidence that the Gospel of John begins by calling Jesus God's "Word," just as other parts of the New Testament also indicate that Jesus is God's wisdom.[19]

If the first half refers to Christ as the supreme wisdom of God for the creation, the second half similarly presents Christ as the supreme Savior of all things. The second half may also have existed before Paul wrote Colossians. If the world came together through God's wisdom, so in Christ all things also have come together and have become reconciled to God. The hymn thus powerfully brings out the close relationship between creation and salvation. As Paul says in 2 Corinthians 5:17, our reconciliation to God makes us a "new creation."

As we mentioned in our discussion of Ephesians above, Colossians and Ephesians have a great deal of material in common, leading some scholars to believe they were both written at about the same time. Those who believe Paul wrote them usually think he was in Rome at the time.[20] Those who believe Ephesians to be pseudonymous usually argue that Colossians was written first.

One reason is that while Colossians addresses a specific problem in Colossae, Ephesians does not seem to have a particular situation in view.

A good number of scholars believe Colossians to be pseudonymous as well, although fewer scholars suggest this for Ephesians. The vocabulary and style of Colossians differ from what Paul uses elsewhere. He also applies some of his typical imagery from earlier letters differently in Colossians. For example, while Paul talks of all Christians together making up the body *of Christ*—some are eyes, some are ears (e.g., 1 Cor. 12:16-17)—Colossians talks of the body *of the church*, with Christ as the head. Christ is thus no longer the *whole* body, but a *part* of it.

Since Timothy is also one of the authors of Colossians (1:1), others have suggested that he is the primary author of the letter. Paul thus would have known what Timothy wrote and agreed with it, but its style and imagery would represent Timothy's way of thinking more than his own. In this scenario, Timothy would be somewhat of a "ghostwriter" for Colossians—he wrote the words but its *autho*rity came primarily from Paul.[21] Many conservatives find this suggestion attractive because it preserves Paul's authorship while also explaining the differences between Colossians and Paul's earlier letters.

Philemon

One of the shortest books in the New Testament, Philemon is a letter Paul sent to a slave owner named Philemon. One of Philemon's slaves, a man named Onesimus, had somehow become alienated from his owner. Perhaps his owner had sent him somewhere on business, and he had run off with his owner's money or property. Whatever the cause of the separation, Onesimus seems to have sought out Paul in prison in the hope of being reconciled to his master. In the process, he became a Christian and a help to Paul.

Paul wrote Philemon so that Philemon would receive Onesimus back, forgiving him for running away as well as for whatever other wrongs he might have done. "If he has harmed you in any way or stolen anything from you, charge me for it" (verse 18). While receiving back a runaway slave without serious penalty was not unheard of in the ancient world, Paul was asking a rather large thing of Philemon. To support this desire, Paul "leans" on Philemon by calling in the "spiritual" debt Philemon owes Paul—"I won't mention that you owe me your very soul!"(19). Further, while the issue was a private matter between Onesimus and Philemon, Paul wrote to the entire church (2), putting Philemon on the spot. The whole church would see how he responded to Paul's authority!

Interestingly, Paul never tells Philemon to free Onesimus, although Christians often presume that this is what the letter is about. Rather, Paul only tells Philemon to "give him the same welcome you would give me if I were coming" (17). Indeed, Colossians, which Paul may have sent at the same time as the letter to Philemon, says nothing about freeing slaves, even though it mentions master/slave relations and even Onesimus himself (Col. 3:22–4:1; 4:9). It only commands slaves to obey their masters in everything they do (3:22).

Philemon seems to have lived in Colossae, since the letter shares almost all the names found in Colossians. Indeed, Colossians indicates that Epaphras and Onesimus were from Colossae, both major players in the letter to Philemon (Philem. 10, 23). While Paul may not have commanded Philemon to set Onesimus free, it is interesting that a man named Onesimus became the bishop of Ephesus in the years that followed.[22] If this is the same man, then it seems Philemon finally did release him from slavery. Paul hints in Philemon that he would prefer to keep Onesimus with him rather than send him back (13). Perhaps Philemon set Onesimus free so he could return to help Paul.

Things to Think About

1. Identify one major theme from each of the Prison Epistles by which to remember them. What aspect of each one stands out the most to you?

Key Terms

asceticism

mysticism

syncretism

2. How might Christians today model the unity celebrated in Ephesians?

3. How would you explain the unique shifts in Paul's imagery in Ephesians, especially since they do not appear in letters reputedly written at the same time or afterward?

4. What can we learn from Philippians about how to suffer? What attitude did Paul have toward life and death?

5. Christians often revere the Ten Commandments as a part of the Jewish Law still in force today. What does Colossians have to say about Gentiles and keeping the Sabbath?

6. Does Paul hint in Philemon that Philemon should set the slave free, or is this idea simply what we want to hear Paul say?

endnotes

1. See chapter 47 of this text.
2. In typical fashion, Colossians' statement is terse and relates directly to the false teaching it addresses. Ephesians is grandiose and nonargumentative. These are reasons to believe Colossians was written first, with Ephesians using it as its basis. Interestingly, Paul's claim in Ephesians 2:15 that Christ "abolished" the Law is the same Greek word he uses in Romans 3:31 to say that we do not abolish the Law because of faith.
3. See chapter 40 of this text.

4. Like Colossians, however, Ephesians differs from Paul's earlier writings in the way it shifts from talking about Christians (as a whole) being the body of Christ to an emphasis on Christ as the head of the body. This shift also fits with the fact that Ephesians refers to the *church* as all Christians everywhere (e.g., Eph. 1:22). In his earlier writings, Paul primarily uses the word church to refer to individual congregations. Ephesians also takes a different tact from Paul's earlier writings in expanding the foundation of Christianity. Whereas Paul restricts the foundation of Christianity to Jesus Christ Himself ("no one can lay any other foundation than the one we already have—Jesus Christ" [1 Cor. 3:11]), Ephesians now adds apostles and prophets to the foundation of the church, with Christ as the cornerstone (Eph. 2:20). Such a statement differs from Paul's orientation in his earlier letters—letters in which he bases his message on direct revelation from God (Gal. 1:12; 2:2)— and contrasts his apostleship with that of the other "so-called pillars" of the church (Gal. 2:9). In his earlier letters he largely views his own authority as sufficient for the churches under his care (e.g., 1 Cor. 4:15). If Paul wrote Ephesians, he seems to have undergone somewhat of a change in perspective toward the "structure" of the church as a whole, although such a change is not reflected in his other "last letters" (e.g., Phil. 3:17). On the whole, Ephesians lacks the concrete personality of Paul we see so well in his earlier letters. This letter is somewhat of an abstract theological presentation that lacks Paul's usual dialogical, question/answer style of argument. Those opposed to pseudonymity might argue that Paul gave his amanuensis extensive freedom in composing this letter, or that the situation behind the epistle led Paul to use a whole different approach to these topics.

5. Ephesians also differs from Paul's earlier writings in its frequent use of the phrase "in the heavenlies" (e.g., Eph. 1:3, 20; 2:6; 3:10; 6:12), a phrase that appears nowhere else in any of Paul's writings. Ephesians is also lacking in Paul's usual sense of the imminence of Christ's return. Instead, Ephesians is oriented around the Christian's current participation in the heavenly realm, what is sometimes called "realized" eschatology (e.g., 2:6). Indeed, while 1 Corinthians 15:25 indicates that Christ does not yet have all His enemies under His feet, Ephesians 1:22 implies that everything is already under His feet. And while in 1 Corinthians 4:8 Paul longs for the day when he will rule, the perspective of Ephesians 2:6 is that we are already seated at God's right hand in the heavenlies. Finally, the orientation of salvation has shifted from a future event in the life of a believer (e.g., Rom. 5:9) to a largely finished one (Eph. 2:8). If Paul wrote Ephesians, we must conclude once again that he adopted a significantly different perspective in Ephesians than he took in his earlier (and contemporaneous) writings.

6. Paul's earlier epistles typically use the word *Satan* rather than *Devil* (e.g., Eph. 4:27; 6:11). Only the Pastoral Epistles use the word *Devil*. Paul's other writings

consistently refer to Satan (e.g., Rom. 16:20; 1 Cor. 5:5; 7:5; 2 Cor. 2:11; 11:14; 12:7; 1 Thess. 2:18; 2 Thess. 2:9).

7. There are other good reasons for thinking that this letter was not originally sent to Ephesus, not simply because the oldest manuscripts and witnesses lack the words "to Ephesus." The strongest reason comes from the comments in Ephesians 1:15 and 3:2, which give the clear impression that Paul has never met the audience of the letter. Paul could hardly say this of the Ephesians, since he spent over two years there. For these reasons, some scholars argue that Ephesians was not sent to a specific destination but was meant to circulate widely (i.e., that it was a "circular" letter).

8. E. Goodspeed, *The Key to Ephesians* (Chicago: University of Chicago, 1956), 1-75.

9. The "household codes"—which spell out the basic expectations for various roles in a household—give us a good sense of how Ephesians and Colossians relate to one another. While Colossians' advice is terse and mostly literal (covering nine verses), Ephesians' treatment is more polished (covering twenty-one verses), gives theological reasons for each piece of instruction, and moves beyond the literal to expound on the mystery of the church.

10. Philippians 1:23 gives us one of the few indications that Paul believed our existence continued in some way between death and our future resurrection. Another possible instance is 2 Corinthians 5:2-3, 6-8.

11. If Philippians were written from Rome, it probably represents a significant shift in the direction of Paul's mission. When he wrote Romans 15:23, Paul was looking to move beyond Rome to Spain. He felt that he had finished his work in the regions of Greece, Macedonia, and Asia. Acts 20:25 presents a similar picture of a Paul who never expected to minister again in these areas. However, in Philemon 22 and possibly Philippians 1:25, 27, it is evident that Paul planned to visit Asia and Macedonia. Here is one argument for Ephesus as the place from which Paul sent these letters.

12. Here is a major shift in focus from Paul's opponents in Galatia—they primarily urged circumcision. The Colossian philosophy seems more to involve the observance of Jewish festivals and food laws.

13. The components of the Colossian philosophy have reminded many of a movement of the second century known as Gnosticism, a philosophy that saw "salvation" as a matter of rising above the earthly to the heavenly by way of knowledge. As we argue, the philosophy is more likely a form of Jewish mysticism involving visions of the heavenly realm and its worship of God.

14. Paul's earlier writings also associate the earthly and fleshly with the power of sin and with the Law as a tool in the hand of that power (Rom. 7:11; 1 Cor. 15:56). Further, they also use the word angel for both good and bad spiritual forces (e.g.,

1 Cor. 6:3). Colossians moves beyond sin as an abstract force to focus on demonic forces.

15. In his earlier writings, Paul associates resurrection primarily with a future event (e.g., Rom. 6:5; 8:11), although he does speak of us walking in newness of life as a kind of current resurrection (Rom. 6:4). This newness of life is still different from the kind of spiritual resurrection Colossians 3:1 seems to entail.

16. In his earlier writings, his kingdom language is usually focused on the future (e.g., 1 Cor. 6:9-10; 15:24, 50; Gal. 5:21), although see Romans 14:17; 1 Corinthians 4:20.

17. Dead Sea Scrolls: *Songs of Sabbath Sacrifice* 1.16; also *Testament of Levi* 3.5-6, perhaps a document of broader Essenism—those from whom the Qumran community split off.

18. Numerous reconstructions have been suggested, not one of which seems completely satisfactory. One possibility is that the first half was originally a hymn to the Logos/Word and that Colossians created the second half roughly parallel to the original, but not exactly in the same order.

19. For example, 1 Corinthians 1:24. Both Hebrews 1:3 and Matthew 23:34 imply that Jesus is God's wisdom when you realize what they are quoting. Hebrews 1:3 alludes to the book of Wisdom 7:26, which uses similar language to refer to God's wisdom. Matthew 23:34 is probably based on a verse in Q found in its more original form in Luke 11:49—"the wisdom of God says . . ." Matthew renders Jesus simply as saying, "I say . . ."

20. Usually this reconstruction of events has Paul being imprisoned twice in Rome. After the first, he was released to return to the East. After the second, he was beheaded. The Prison Epistles are usually connected to the first imprisonment and the Pastoral Epistles to the second.

21. See chapter 47 of this text.

22. Mentioned in the letter from Ignatius, *To the Ephesians*, 1:3.

CHAPTER 47

Ghostwriting in the New Testament?

Most conservative scholars make a direct equation between
pseudonymity and forgery.

Introduction

The overwhelming majority of those who lived at the time of Christ were illiterate. It is even possible that most of Jesus' twelve disciples could not read (cf. Acts 4:13). As such, the ancient world was oriented far more around hearing than reading—it was an *oral* culture rather than a literary one. People of that day relied far more on their memories to tell stories than we do.

In keeping with the fact that ancient culture was oral in nature, the ancient Mediterraneans valued traditions passed on by word of mouth more than we do. In order for traditions to have real significance for us, they need to be

At a Glance

• The ancient world was an oral culture—oriented around hearing rather than reading.

• A **pseudonymous** writing is one that is written under the authority of a dead figure from the past to address a contemporary situation.

• Paul and the ancients in general used *amanuenses* or "secretaries" to put their words down on paper.

• Some writings in the New Testament may have been "ghostwritten"—composed by coauthors and then approved by those we think of as the primary authors (e.g., Paul or Peter).

• Many scholars argue that writings like Ephesians, 1 Timothy, Titus, and 2 Peter are pseudonymous, and that they were written after the deaths of both Paul and Peter.

written down so that they will not change. It is when things are written down that real interaction with ideas takes place. For the ancients, however, the core of an oral tradition was carefully preserved in its retelling and potentially had just as much authority as anything written down.

One reason why the earliest manuscripts of the New Testament vary more than those copied after the A.D. 300s is probably because the New Testament originally retained a strongly oral character. Those who used the New Testament writings sometimes modified or expanded upon the original text to make it clearer. The text the church later came to use—the text behind the King James—is thus a cleaner and slightly more theologically sensitive text than the originals were. In a sense, Matthew and Luke also seem to have done this in their use of Mark. They often seem to have expanded upon Jesus' words in Mark, both to bring out their particular points more forcefully and to guard against inappropriate conclusions.

Given this background, authorship in the ancient world was more about the *author*ity behind a document—the origin of a tradition—than about the actual person who put pen to paper or who actually formulated the words of a text. You can see this connection even in the two words *author* and *author*ity. The question is whether the ancients could consider someone the "author" of a written piece even if s/he were already

pseudonymity: The practice of writing under the authority of someone else's name, usually an authoritative figure from the past who has long since died.

dead. Did the ancients consider it legitimate to "give voice" to an authority figure from the past by writing under his or her name, his or her *author*ity?

Whether it was legitimate or not, we have many examples of writings like this, writings that used the authority of a dead individual in order to address contemporary situations. The practice is called **pseudonymity**. For example, we have three books labeled with Enoch's name, although it is extremely unlikely that Enoch himself wrote them. The Jewish *Letter of Aristeas* and the Christian *Epistle of Barnabas* similarly were not actually written by these persons. Rather, individuals from a later time presented messages that they believed related in some way to these figures from the past.

When we come to the New Testament, the question becomes much more sensitive. No one contests the existence of pseudonymous writings in both the ancient Jewish and Greco-Roman world. But given our modern presuppositions, it is easy for us to view such documents as forgeries, intended to deceive their audiences. Accordingly, the majority of conservative scholars strongly oppose the notion that any New Testament writing is pseudonymous. On the other hand, the majority of scholars in general—perhaps even 80 to 90 percent—have concluded that books like 2 Peter and 1 Timothy were not written by Peter or Paul themselves.[1] This chapter deals with the issues related to pseudonymity and asks whether a pseudonymous writing could ever be considered authoritative or inspired.

Amanuenses

We can infer from a number of comments throughout Paul's writings that he used a scribe or an amanuensis to do the actual writing of his letters. For example, a man named Tertius actually put the words of Romans on a scroll (Rom. 16:22). In Galatians and 2 Thessalonians, Paul did not write down most of the letter, but he did write his name at the end to show that the letter was truly from him (Gal. 6:11; 2 Thess. 3:17). To what degree did a person like Paul allow such an amanuensis to alter and improve his style or clarify his thoughts? We can at least assume that, as would be the case today, some gave their secretaries more freedom than others.

"Ghostwriting"

The president of the United States rarely composes an entire speech from scratch. Nor do many prominent figures do most of the actual work of writing the books that have their names on them. Rather, they often have **"ghostwriters"** write the first drafts of such books, saying the kinds of things they know the person in question would say. This work is submitted to the authority figure, who then changes, omits, or expands what the ghostwriter has already composed. The book then goes out under the name of the prominent figure.

ghostwriting: When a person other than the author of a book is the primary writer of the book—the author only agreeing and modifying what the writer has written on his or her behalf.

Some scholars turn to the idea of "ghostwriting" in order to explain the sometimes significant differences in style and thought between Paul's earlier letters and letters like Colossians, Ephesians, and 1 Timothy. They suggest that someone like Timothy or Luke was the primary composer of these letters and that Paul then approved the content before the letter was sent. Perhaps Paul was in chains and unable to write in his normal way. The same suggestion is sometimes also made to explain the differences in style between 1 and 2 Peter.

One candidate for such a situation is 1 Peter. Scholars have sometimes wondered how an Aramaic fisherman from Galilee could have written the Greek of 1 Peter. This is not a question of intelligence or of Peter's ability to learn Greek. Even in our day of cassettes and language courses, you can usually tell when English is a person's second language—occasionally they will phrase something just a little oddly because of how their original language works. However, it is very likely that Greek was a first language for the one who composed the actual words of 1 Peter. Books like Mark and Revelation frequently let their Aramaic-speaking origins peek through, but 1 Peter gives us no indications of that—its language is really good Greek.

At this point, 1 Peter helps us out by informing us that Silas helped compose the letter (1 Pet. 5:12). It would not in any way diminish the authority of 1 Peter to suggest that Peter asked Silas to help him compose the letter in Greek, allowing him to draft the actual words. The fundamental message would thus be Peter's. Peter would know what Silas wrote and would approve of it, but Silas would be the one to phrase it a particular way.

You will have to decide what you think on this matter. Many conservative scholars have turned to this idea in order to explain a number of situations in the New Testament where the writing style of one document differs from that of other writings by the same individual. Second Peter, for example, differs in style from 1 Peter. Some conservatives have explained this fact by suggesting that Peter actually wrote the second letter or, even better, that he used yet a different amanuensis than Silas to write 2 Peter.

We have the same situation with some of Paul's letters. Colossians differs in style from Paul's earlier writings, leading some conservative scholars to suggest that Timothy was its principal composer (cf. Col. 1:1). Others use this concept to explain why the Pastoral Epistles differ so much in style from Paul's earlier writings and yet are very consistent with one another. Paul simply switched amanuenses, they might say. This approach allows us to preserve Paul and Peter as the literal authors of these writings, yet also explain why the style and thought differ so much from their other writings.

Pseudonymity

A number of "pseudonymous" writings have survived from the ancient world. We have already alluded to the book of 1 Enoch, which certainly was not written by the Enoch of its title. The Old Testament does not mention such a writing even once. Indeed, the oldest parts of the book probably do not go back much earlier than the year 200 B.C., and all the evidence indicates that it was first composed in Hebrew. We conclude that its authors drew on the authority of Enoch in order to address their own times, a common feature of a group of writings known as "apocalyptic" literature.[2]

Are there such writings in the New Testament? The majority of conservative scholars have long been opposed to the suggestion, finding it difficult to see the practice of pseudonymity in anything but a negative light. Indeed, most conservative scholars make a direct equation between pseudonymity and forgery.[3] However, in some cases the evidence is striking, so we should probably at least consider the possibility. A solid majority of scholars are amazingly united in considering books like 1 Timothy, Titus, and 2 Peter as pseudonymous. You will need to decide whether you think there is any truth to their conclusions.

On the one hand, arguments about style and vocabulary do not hold as much force as some scholars used to think. Style can change from occasion to occasion and, potentially, *from amanuensis to amanuensis*. Further, some argue that the Pastoral Epistles in particular (1 and 2 Timothy, Titus) are a different kind of writing, written to individuals with whom Paul was on extremely close terms. Many conservative scholars find these considerations strong enough to affirm Paul as the author, even though the styles and vocabularies differ significantly from his other letters.

On the other hand, a small number of conservatives have recently argued that it is wrong to think that the Bible's truth or inspiration rises or falls on this issue. They would say that we cannot judge the "honesty" or "dishonesty" of a pseudonymous writing by *our* standards, but rather that we must consider what was appropriate when these documents were written. Given that the practice of pseudonymity continued for hundreds of years across numerous generations, we must suppose that the dynamics of the practice were generally known—at least by the types of individuals who composed such writings.

It is at least possible that a learned individual could recognize, in most cases, when a document was literally written by an author and when it was written pseudonymously.

If authorship in general was more about the *source of the ideas* in a document—the *autho*rity behind a writing rather than the actual person who composed the words—we can conjecture that a person could in some sense be the "author" of a writing *even if he or she was already dead.* Indeed, some evangelicals have argued that it would have been dishonest *not* to write under the name of the dead authority figure if you believed the ideas you were presenting originated from him.[4] If this was possible, a pseudonymous writing could potentially be as "true," "inspired," and even as "inerrant" as any other book of the New Testament. The truth would just come from the text in a different way than it comes from a book actually dictated by the person whose name it bears.

However, most conservatives do not find such arguments convincing. The Christians of the second and third centuries seem to have had a negative view toward books they suspected were not actually written by the person whose name appeared on them. In fact, a minister in the 100s was removed from ministry for pseudonymously composing *The Acts of Paul and Thecla*, despite the fact that he claimed to have had only good and honorable intentions.[5] These observations seem to imply that the early church rejected the practice of pseudonymity.

Conversely, we saw in chapter 4 of this book that God sometimes worked out His will with regard to the canon, despite the misunderstandings of the early church. For example, Hebrews probably found its way into the canon to a large degree because the church believed Paul had authored it. Yet few scholars believe this today. If canonicity depended on the church's accuracy in identifying authorship, we probably would have to remove Hebrews from the canon.

The case of 2 Peter gives us a good sense of the basic issue. Both "conservative" and "liberal" scholars alike agree that 2 Peter is the most likely candidate for a pseudonymous writing of all the New Testament documents in question. The Christians of the first few centuries seem to have agreed, for of all the New Testament books, 2 Peter had the greatest difficulty finding acceptance into the canon. It is reasonable to think that its final inclusion coincided to a high degree with the church's acceptance of Peter as its writer.

Many argue for the pseudonymity of 2 Peter because its style and vocabulary differ significantly from that of 1 Peter. Second Peter uses a number of words from the writings of the Greek poet Homer, as well as some that were typical of Greek religion and philosophy ("savior," "divine nature," "virtue")—not terms an Aramaic-speaking fisherman from Galilee would likely use. But none of these arguments are decisive against Peter as the actual author, since he probably would have used an amanuensis to compose his letters in Greek anyway (cf. 1 Peter 5:12). We can simply claim that Peter used a different amanuensis for each letter and allowed each a great deal of freedom in composition.

However, the fact that 1 and 2 Peter seem to differ significantly in their approaches to various *ideas* raises the stakes. Just how much freedom are we to suppose Peter's amanuenses had? For example, 1 and 2 Peter seem to have contrasting perspectives on Christ's return to earth. First Peter, just as Paul's writings do, gives us the sense that Christ will return to earth soon—in fact, that the final judgment has already started (1 Pet. 4:17). "The end of the world is coming soon," 1 Peter 4:7 says.

Second Peter, on the other hand, implies that Christ's return will not happen for some time. It also does not have the sense of current suffering that 1 Peter conveys. Because of the delay, Peter foretells of some time in the future after his death when some even will question whether Christ is coming back at all (2 Pet. 3:3). He rebukes someone who would scoff, "Jesus promised to come back, did he? Then where is he?" (2 Pet. 3:4).

While these comments do not necessarily contradict each other, they are certainly different in their orientation to a significant degree. First Peter is not only filled with the expectation of Christ's imminent return, it even sees the current time as the beginning of the end. Second Peter, on the other hand, almost implies that Christ's second coming could be thousands of years away (2 Pet. 3:8).

One interesting element in the debate is the way 2 Peter refers to other New Testament writings as Scripture. Second Peter 3:15-16 indicates not only that people were collecting Paul's letters, but that they considered them to be authoritative Scripture. We do not find anyone referring to New Testament books again as Scripture until around A.D. 150.[6] What is even more interesting is that 2 Peter does not consider Paul's letters to be letters written to specific communities. Instead, it considers them to be Scripture written to all Christians. Those who argue for pseudonymity do not think such shifts likely took place within Peter's lifetime.

Another interesting verse is 2 Peter 3:1: "This is my second letter to you, dear friends." Given the way our Bibles are arranged, it is natural to think Peter is referring to 1 Peter. But 1 Peter does not address the same audience as 2 Peter—1 Peter has a specific audience while 2 Peter addresses all Christians. In other words, if Peter wrote 2 Peter, he was probably referring to some letter we do not have. Those who think 2 Peter is pseudonymous would say our first impression was right—2 Peter now viewed 1 Peter as Scripture. First Peter was no longer read as a letter to specific communities but as Scripture for all Christians everywhere.

For many, these and other considerations are significant enough to conclude that 2 Peter is pseudonymous.[7] On the other hand, those who oppose pseudonymity can respond to each of the arguments used in its favor. In the end, you will have to make up your own mind as to whether a pseudonymous writing could legitimately be in the New Testament. What is most important here is to know that many argue for it and that there are those on both sides of the issue who believe in the inspiration and authority of Scripture.

Things to Think About

Key Terms
ghostwriting
pseudonymity

1. Does the suggestion that a "secretary" wrote down Paul's words affect the inspiration or authority of Scripture for you? What about the suggestion that Timothy might have had more to do with the composition of Colossians than Paul? What about the idea that Silas wrote most of the words of 1 Peter?

2. Is it possible that the Bible contains pseudonymous writings? Could such writings be inspired or authoritative? Using 2 Peter as a test case, argue for or against its pseudonymity.

endnotes

1. While most conservative scholars reject altogether the idea of pseudonymity in the New Testament, most scholars in general consider Ephesians, 1 and 2 Timothy, Titus, and 2 Peter as pseudonymous. Fewer argue for the pseudonymity of Colossians, James, 1 Peter, and Jude. Some argue for the pseudonymity of 2 Thessalonians.

2. The book of Revelation does not seem to share this characteristic, although some have suggested that it tells about the events of the A.D. 90s by putting a prophecy in the mouth of John in the early A.D. 70s.

3. For example, P.J. Achtemeier, J.B. Green, and M.M. Thompson, *Introducing the*

New Testament: Its Literature and Theology (Grand Rapids: Eerdmans, 2001), 380.

4. For example, D. Moo on 2 Peter in *2 Peter, Jude* in the *NIV Application Commentary* (Grand Rapids: Zondervan, 1996), 24.

5. Although it may be significant that those who removed him strongly disagreed with the ideas he had written in Paul's name.

6. In a writing known as 2 Clement. Those who argue for the pseudonymity of 2 Peter usually consider it the last New Testament book written, perhaps even written in the second century.

7. One scholar, R. Bauckham (*Jude-2 Peter*, vol. 50 of *Word Biblical Commentary* [Waco, TX: Word, 1983]), has argued that an educated reader of ancient times would have recognized 2 Peter as a writing from a genre known as a "testament," a writing that, he claims, was usually pseudonymous. According to this theory, a learned reader would have known not to take Peter as the literal author of 2 Peter. The actual writer would not be using Peter's name to deceive. He would expect his audience to know that his words represented what God would say to the church through Peter if he were alive, not that these were literally Peter's words. After all, the writer might say that Peter and s/he both spoke through the same Holy Spirit.

CHAPTER 48

1 and 2 Thessalonians:
Paul's Earliest Preaching

Paul's message of judgment and salvation did not focus on the dead but on the living, for Paul expected this judgment to occur in the near future.

The New Testament has thirteen letters that bear Paul's name, letters sent to various places around the ancient Mediterranean. Of these, 1 Thessalonians was probably the first he wrote.[1] If so, it was in all likelihood the first New Testament book written.

It is sometimes hard for us to imagine what Christianity would have been like without a New Testament. The Bible Paul used was what we call the Old Testament—it was the whole Bible for him![2] Paul knew some of the things Jesus had said while He was on earth, but perhaps not too many. He rarely quoted Jesus or referred to His teaching. He also had heard what some of Jesus' earliest followers

At a Glance

• First Thessalonians was probably the first book of the New Testament to be written.

• Paul wrote 1 Thessalonians from Corinth on his "second" missionary journey (ca. A.D. 51).

• Paul wrote as Timothy returned from Thessalonica with the good news that the Thessalonians were remaining true to Paul and to their faith.

• In his first letter to them, Paul reminds the Thessalonians of appropriate Christian sexuality, brotherly love, and diligent work.

• First Thessalonians also deals with what happens to Christians who die before Christ returns—they will rise from the dead.

• Second Thessalonians deals with things that will take place before Christ's return, including the coming of a "man of lawlessness."

were preaching, but what was most important for him was the revelation he had received directly from God. He was convinced that God had appointed him as an ambassador to non-Jews. This belief led him to travel thousands of miles on foot during his lifetime, preaching the good news of Jesus around the Mediterranean world.

Paul first visits the city of Thessalonica on what is usually called his "second missionary journey." It is one of the first cities he visits when he leaves Asia Minor and launches into Europe for the first time. About one hundred miles west of Philippi, Thessalonica was on the main road that crossed Macedonia, the region north of Greece. (See **Map 11**.) As the capital of Macedonia, Thessalonica was thus a somewhat large city. Accordingly, it was a logical place for Paul to stop and preach the gospel.

Acts gives us the impression that Paul did not stay very long in Thessalonica because of some fierce opposition that arose toward him in the Jewish synagogue. But his letters sound as if he has been with them longer than just two or three weeks (e.g., 1 Thess. 2:9). Philippians 4:16 tells us that he stayed there long enough to receive help from the Philippian church "more than once."

> "God wants you to be holy, so you should keep clear of all sexual sin. Then each of you will control your body and live in holiness and honor—not in lustful passion as the pagans do, in their ignorance of God and his ways."
>
> **1 Thessalonians 4:3-5**

No matter the exact length of time, he is forced to leave town in the face of strong opposition (1 Thess. 2:1-2). The Christians send him away under cover of nightfall (Acts 17:10). Similar things happen in the next city as well (Berea), leading Paul to travel south to Athens in Greece. But he remains concerned for the infant churches he left in Macedonia. Finally, he sends Timothy back to Thessalonica to strengthen and encourage the Christians there in their faith, and to make sure

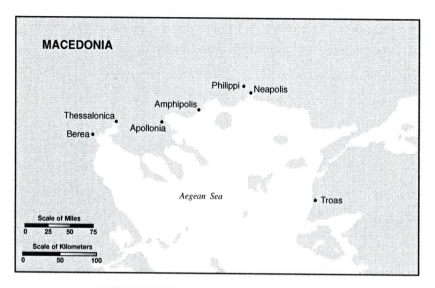

THESSALONICA, CAPITAL OF MACEDONIA
MAP 11

that the opposition he faced has not discouraged their commitment to his message (1 Thess. 3:2).

By the time Timothy returns to Paul, Paul has moved even farther south to the bustling city of Corinth. Timothy brings good news; the Thessalonians continue to hold Paul and his teaching in high regard. It is in this context that Paul writes the first letter of the New Testament, 1 Thessalonians. He writes both in celebration of the good news he has just received from Timothy and to give them some basic reminders of how to live. Perhaps of greatest interest to us is his instruction about Christ's coming return to earth from heaven.

Miscellaneous Instructions

Jews associated two sins in particular with Gentiles: idolatry and sexual immorality. They took both of these to be signs of ignorance on the part of such non-Jews. Thus, it is no surprise that sexual immorality is one of the main issues Paul deals with in his letter to the Thessalonians. While Paul does not specify the exact nature of the particular sexual sins he has in mind, adultery certainly would qualify as one that would "wrong his brother or take advantage of him" (1 Thess. 4:6 NIV). It is also conceivable that Paul might have in mind someone who would wrong a brother by sleeping with a virgin promised to him.

Paul also encourages the Thessalonians to show "brotherly love" to one another (1 Thess. 4:9). Later in the letter he tells them to "live peaceably with each other," to respect their hardworking leaders, and to be patient and kind to everyone (5:12-15). The letter closes with a number of miscellaneous exhortations, including some words to those who are lazy (5:14)—a theme 2 Thessalonians also takes up.

What About Christians Who Die?

First Thessalonians 4:13–5:11 might not strike a modern Christian reader as odd at first. These verses present us with some basic teaching on Christ's return to earth and the resurrection of the dead that will take place at that time. Paul tells the Thessalonians that Christians who had died will rise from the dead to meet Jesus in the sky (1 Thess. 4:14-16). Then those who are still alive will also ascend into the sky to meet Jesus—an event Christians often call the **rapture** (4:17).

Day of the Lord: The Day of Judgment when God judges the earth.

rapture: A popular Christian term for the ascent of Christians both dead and alive from the earth to meet Jesus in the sky.

In explaining when this would happen, Paul uses the analogy of a pregnant woman (5:3). On one level, such a woman can feel that the time is approaching; she experiences labor pains! In that sense, Christians who are "sons of the light and sons of the day" will be ready for Christ's *parousia*, His "arrival" back to earth (5:5-11).[3] On the other hand, this "**Day of the**

Lord" is also like the coming of a thief—it is unannounced (5:1). So it is also with the birth of a child. While the mother knows it is coming soon, the exact hour comes unexpectedly.

As we said, most modern Christian readers are not too surprised to find this teaching in 1 Thessalonians. Conservative Christians talk a lot about "the rapture," and certainly most Christians believe that death is not the end of our existence. Of particular interest is realizing that Paul was writing these things to a city where he had spent at least several weeks, perhaps several months. How could the Thessalonians be "ignorant" (1 Thess. 4:13) about what happens to Christians after they die if Paul had spent several weeks with them?

For many Christians, the issue of heaven and hell is basically what Christianity is all about. One approach to evangelizing non-Christians is initially to ask them where they would go if they were to die suddenly. Would they go to heaven or hell? However, Paul

> "Always be joyful. Keep on praying. No matter what happens, always be thankful, for this is God's will for you who belong to Christ Jesus.
>
> "Do not stifle the Holy Spirit. Do not scoff at prophecies, but test everything that is said. Hold on to what is good. Keep away from every kind of evil."
>
> **1 Thessalonians 5:16-22**

does not mention anything about Christians going to heaven or sinners going to hell in 1 Thessalonians. Indeed, all his writings taken together do not even mention hell; we get only a few hints anywhere in his writings that Christians might go to heaven when they die.[4] When he was in Thessalonica for all those weeks, Paul apparently said little or nothing about what happened to Christians after death.

Thus, while Paul likely believed in heaven and hell, his perspective had quite a different focus than we do today. As with many Jews, Paul thought much more in terms of the future resurrection of bodies than in terms of the immortality of the soul. He spoke of the time between death and this future resurrection as a time of "sleep" (1 Thess. 4:13-15). At the resurrection, not before, God will provide us with "spiritual bodies" (1 Cor. 15:44) and will clothe us with a heavenly "tent" (2 Cor. 5:1-2).[5]

What was Paul thinking about, then, when he spoke about salvation—is not salvation about going to heaven? First Thessalonians powerfully demonstrates that the heart of Paul's early preaching concerned the coming Day of the Lord, the day when God will come to judge the earth. Accordingly, Paul's message of judgment and salvation does not focus on the dead but the living, for Paul expected this judgment to occur in the near future (cf. 1 Cor. 7:29; Phil. 4:5). Salvation for Paul focused on the fact that Christ had made it possible for the Christians *on earth* to escape God's wrath when He came to judge the world. The fate of the dead may have been an afterthought—Paul probably did not expect many Christians to die before that day came.

Salvation for Paul was primarily about the fact that Christ had made it possible for the Christians *on earth* to escape God's wrath when He came to judge the world.

With these things in mind, we can reconstruct the situation in this way. Paul comes to Thessalonica with the message that God was soon going to judge the world for its sins—both Jew and Gentile. To a Jew, this message might not have been very surprising. However, Paul proclaims that through Jesus Christ, God has provided a way of escape. He probably preaches that Jesus' death was like a sacrifice that atoned for sins. Many Jews may even have found this message acceptable.

Where Paul probably got into trouble with the Jews of the city was preaching that this sacrifice was valid both for Jews *and Gentiles*. The Gentiles do not need to become circumcised or start following the Jewish Law to escape punishment, he says. Paul, Silas, and Timothy no doubt ate with Gentiles and crossed boundaries of purity, which might have infuriated some

Jews. He may also have attracted a group of Gentiles that the book of Acts calls "God-fearers," Gentiles who were sympathetic to Judaism but for whatever reason did not fully convert. If Paul drew such individuals away from the local synagogue, we can see even more reason for the Jews of the city to be angry with him.

You can see that if Paul's message were primarily about the fact that God was soon coming to judge the world, the fate of the dead might not come up. Paul wrote 1 Thessalonians at least in part to address the question of Christians who might die before Christ returned. Interestingly, however, Paul never discusses the fate of the wicked in any of his writings, nor does he address the question of those who died in the Old Testament—he writes only of the dead "in Christ." These are important things to consider. They help us realize the extent to which we read our beliefs into the Bible rather than get our beliefs out of Scripture.

One final instance of this practice comes with 1 Thessalonians 4:17. This verse comes after Paul tells his audience that the dead in Christ will rise to meet Him (Jesus Christ) in the sky. Paul then says, "Then, together with them, we who are still alive and remain on the earth will be caught up in the clouds to meet the Lord in the air and remain with him forever." Most Christians assume that the place where we remain with Christ forever is heaven. This conclusion may indeed be correct, but it illustrates how often we "fill in the blanks" of Scripture with things that are not exactly said by the text of the Bible. First Corinthians 6:2-3 indicates that Christians will help Christ judge the world—both humans and angels. As mentioned earlier, we will meet in the air for battle and then come back to earth as an army. Paul never says where we will remain forever.

Second Thessalonians

The second letter to Thessalonica in the New Testament is very similar to the first. Its opening language and style often mirror 1 Thessalonians, as do some of its topics. The last chapter of 2 Thessalonians deals with the problem of laziness just as 1 Thessalonians does. It is in 2 Thessalonians that we find what is sometimes known as the **Protestant work ethic**: "Whoever does not work should not eat" (2 Thess. 3:10).

Second Thessalonians contrasts slightly with 1 Thessalonians regarding Christ's second coming. While 1 Thessalonians talks about Christ returning at any time, like a thief at night, 2 Thessalonians talks about a series of events that need to happen before He can return. The first letter implies that the Thessalonians should be prepared now for Christ's return; the second argues that things are not yet ready. Of course, these

the Protestant Work Ethic: "Whoever does not work should not eat" (2 Thess. 3:10).

two emphases do not necessarily contradict. As we saw above, 1 Thessalonians uses the imagery of a pregnant woman to discuss Christ's parousia (1 Thess. 5:3). She may not know the exact day or hour, but she can sense that it is coming soon.

What is interesting about 2 Thessalonians is the fact that some evidently thought the Day of the Lord had already occurred (2:2). In our current Christian mind-set, it is difficult to imagine how anyone could mistake something for Judgment Day or Christ's return to earth. Some popular Christian images of the rapture involve driverless cars crashing into one another or airplanes plummeting to earth because their pilots have suddenly vanished. If the Day of the Lord is like this, you will hardly be in doubt about whether it has happened or not.

The people 2 Thessalonians mentions must have viewed the Day of the Lord somewhat figuratively. To them it must have referred to some cataclysm or to some horrific event that had already taken place. They interpreted such an event or events as the judgment of God on the world or on Israel. Clearly, they must not have interpreted the kingdom of God as a transformation of their bodies or of the world. Perhaps they viewed it as a spiritual matter, something inside a person rather than something that would literally come to the earth. They remind us a little of the people mentioned in 2 Timothy who believed that the resurrection had already taken place (2 Tim. 2:18).

Paul warns the Thessalonians not to be alarmed by teaching of this sort. He tells of some events that must happen before Judgment Day arrives, events that have not yet happened. Unfortunately, the letter is very cryptic and vague about what these events actually are. The audience clearly understood what Paul was talking about (e.g., 2 Thess. 2:5-6), but he does not make things very clear for those of us who are listening over their shoulders.

The letter says, for example, that a rebellion must come before the Day of Judgment, and during this rebellion a "man of lawlessness" will be revealed (2 Thess. 2:3-4). This person will set himself up in the "temple of God" as if he were a god. He will perform counterfeit miracles and signs (2:9). Paul affirms that the Thessalonians know about these things, in addition to knowing what was keeping the man of lawlessness from coming (2:5-6).

It is here that the letter reaches its most cryptic point. Paul says that they know *what* was now keeping this man from being revealed (2 Thess. 2:6), but after *he* was taken out of the picture, the man of lawlessness would be revealed (2:7). In the course of two verses, the thing holding the man of lawlessness back changes from an *it* to a *he*. Many suggestions have been made about what this mysterious it/he might be, but scholars have never reached any clear agreement.[6]

Christians often relate the man of lawlessness in 2 Thessalonians to the beast of Revelation 13 or an individual called the Antichrist (based on a particular interpretation of 1 John 4). However, we should be very careful because it is not clear that these verses all refer to the same thing. First John, for example, never speaks of a single Antichrist—it speaks of many antichrists who were around back in John's day (1 John 4:3). These were people who believed Jesus had not taken on human flesh (4:2), possibly members of a heresy called Docetism, which believed that Jesus had only *seemed* to become human. Ironically, the Bible never uses the word *antichrist* in the way we do today.

When Revelation talks about various beasts, on the other hand, it is speaking highly symbolically and may not even be referring to specific individuals. For example, many scholars think that the second beast of Revelation 13 is a symbol for Roman emperor worship and that the first beast represents the Roman emperor, perhaps even Nero. Nevertheless, since the first beast has some interesting traits in common with the man of lawlessness in 2 Thessalonians, some relationship could exist between the two.

One final issue relates to the statement that the man of lawlessness would set himself up in the temple.[7] Certainly no Jew would do anything like this, although we know of several instances in history when a Gentile ruler did. In 167 B.C., for example, the Syrian ruler Antiochus Epiphanes desecrated the temple by having a pig sacrificed there—the event to which Daniel 9:27 probably refers. The Roman general Pompey similarly violated the temple in 63 B.C. In A.D. 40 the Roman emperor Caligula tried to have a statue of himself set up in the temple but thankfully died before this order could be carried out. Finally, in A.D. 70 the temple was destroyed. During this invasion, the Roman soldiers sacrificed to the Roman gods within the precincts of the temple, perhaps the event to which Mark 13:14 refers.

The problem with the passage in 2 Thessalonians is that for someone to set himself up as a god in the temple, there has to be a temple. For this reason many Christians think that someday the Jews will rebuild the temple in modern-day Jerusalem. Unfortunately, when read in its original context, very little in the Bible seems to relate to this issue.[8] We can find prophecies that seem to relate to its destruction in A.D. 70, but not to its reconstruction.

In fact, the book of Hebrews indicates strongly that no earthly temple could ever have God's future approval—Christ's death has definitively put an end to all earthly sanctuaries and sacrifices (Heb. 8:1-2; 10:5-9, 26). Therefore, if we are to maintain the truthfulness of 2 Thessalonians, we probably will have to take its reference to a temple as symbolic or relate it to one of the events mentioned in the previous paragraph.[9]

Things to Think About

1. Do you agree that Paul has very little to say about heaven or hell in his writings?

2. What do you think the "Day of the Lord" is? When do you think it will occur?

Key Terms

Day of the Lord

Protestant work ethic

rapture

3. Do you think that the Jewish temple will ever be rebuilt or has the situation about which Paul was writing already occurred?

endnotes

1. Some scholars think Galatians was written first.
2. Since Paul was raised in a Greek-speaking environment, he probably would have considered some of the books of the Apocrypha to be Scripture—like the book of Wisdom—in addition to the Law and the Prophets.
3. Paul uses some language here that is fascinatingly close to terms used in the Dead Sea Scrolls by Essenes: "sons of light," "sons of darkness."
4. For example, 2 Corinthians 5:3, 6-8; Philippians 1:23-24. Even these comments

refer to the intermediate state of the dead between death and their future resurrection. Paul never speaks of an eternity in heaven or hell.

5. See chapter 43 of this text.

6. Suggestions have included the Roman Empire, the Roman emperor, Paul's need to complete his ministry, the Holy Spirit, etc.

7. Since the temple was destroyed not too long after Paul's death, the presence of this statement is probably an argument in favor of Paul as the literal author.

8. The temple of course was already rebuilt once by Zerubbabel in 520 B.C., the event to which the Old Testament prophecies of rebuilding refer. From the perspective of a Christian, Ezekiel's temple (e.g., Ezek. 43:5) can never be built. According to Hebrews, God's glory could not now be a part of any earthly sanctuary. Christ has definitively reoriented sacred space around himself and the heavenly realm.

9. The problem with relating it to the events of the preceding paragraph is that we would then have to say that the man of lawlessness has already come. This would contradict the more important fact that the Day of the Lord in 2 Thessalonians seems to be the second coming of Christ as Christians have traditionally conceived it.

CHAPTER 49

1 and 2 Timothy, Titus:
Passing on the Torch

*The Pastoral Epistles give advice to two "pastors" about how to
"shepherd their flocks."*

In categorizing Paul's writings, it is customary to refer to the two letters to Timothy and the letter to Titus as the "Pastoral Epistles" because they give advice to two "pastors" about how to "shepherd their flocks." Both Timothy and Titus were Paul's traveling companions and were useful to him in his extensive missionary activities. More than once he sent them in his place to take care of problems in the churches of Greece and Macedonia. Timothy served as Paul's representative on various occasions to Thessalonica and Philippi (1 Thess. 3:2; Phil. 2:19). Titus similarly went to Corinth on Paul's behalf (2 Cor. 7:6; 8:16-18).

However, the Pastoral Epistles represent a somewhat different "mission" that Paul had in mind for Timothy and Titus. It was the mission of directing

At a Glance

• 1 and 2 Timothy and Titus are called the "Pastoral Epistles" because of their concern with how to lead the church.

• Their main concerns include the correction of false teaching and the order of relationships in the church, not least the qualifications of church leaders.

• Most conservative scholars believe these three letters were written in the last days of Paul's life, just before and during a second imprisonment in Rome.

• Other scholars believe they were written pseudonymously to address Pauline communities of the late first/early second century.

579

the church after Paul himself was no longer around. The majority of conservative scholars believe that Paul gave this message in the very last year or two of his earthly life. If Paul was the literal author of these letters, he probably wrote them just before and during his final imprisonment and subsequent death in Rome.[1] Accordingly, these letters show a strong concern for the church to maintain "sound teaching" in the days to come.

However, many other scholars believe these letters were written to invoke Paul's authority a number of decades after his death.[2] In this scenario, some of Paul's churches have gone astray in their beliefs, leading someone to write under his name to redirect them toward sound teaching. We will discuss these two basic ways of reading the pastorals at the end of this chapter.

Whatever conclusion one reaches, it is clear that the pastorals present us with Paul as the supreme model of Christian faith. While he often encourages his churches to view him as a model to follow (e.g., 1 Cor. 4:16; 11:1; Phil. 3:17; 4:9), in these letters he speaks more than once of himself as a "prototype."[3] In 1 Timothy, he speaks of his "conversion" as the supreme example of God's graciousness (1 Tim. 1:16)—he had been the worst sinner of all.[4] In 2 Timothy it is his teaching that is the supreme model to follow (2 Tim. 1:13), a "deposit" of teaching he is trusting Timothy to guard and pass on accurately to future generations.[5]

Paul's primary role in these letters is thus as a teacher (1 Tim. 2:7; 2 Tim. 1:11)—something he never calls himself in his earlier writings. His primary concern is accordingly that Timothy and Titus faithfully preserve his teaching. While it is not exactly clear, it is possible that all three pastoral letters address the same basic "heresy" or false teaching. Titus especially addresses a Jewish teaching that involves keeping aspects of the Jewish Law (e.g., Titus 3:9). The false teaching Paul refers to in 1 Timothy seems similar and involves asceticism—an extreme form of self-discipline (e.g., 1 Tim. 4:3). Second Timothy mentions some Christians who believe that the resurrection has already taken place (2 Tim. 2:18). Whatever the specifics of the false teaching, the pastorals show a strong concern for orthodoxy (correct belief) to prevail in the days after Paul passes from the scene.

A second main concern of the pastorals is for proper order in the church—an understandable issue, whether penned by Paul just before his death or written several years later by someone else. On the one hand, the pastorals are the only New Testament writings to provide extensive qualifications for specific kinds of church leaders. Yet they also give extensive directions for individuals like older men and women, young men, widows, and slaves. Indeed, one of the most infamous verses in the New Testament regarding the role of women appears in 1 Timothy (1 Tim. 2:12). We see in the pastorals the plotting of a course that would eventually grow into the church as an institution with established roles and well-defined boundaries.

1 Timothy

We have already mentioned the dual emphases of the pastorals: (1) they warn against false teaching, and (2) they give instructions for appropriate order in the church. Certainly 1 Timothy reflects these dual emphases well. Paul provides clear guidelines for church order and instructions with regard to false teaching.

In contrast to Paul's "sound" teaching, 1 Timothy hints at some false teaching of a Jewish nature, perhaps the same teaching Titus addresses. Paul mentions a preoccupation with "myths and endless genealogies" (1 Tim. 1:4) and seems to connect it with the Jewish Law (1:8). Beyond these comments, we are not told the nature of these stories or genealogies. Whatever this heresy was, it forbade marriage and involved certain restrictions on what one could eat (4:3). Perhaps some teachers of this heresy took money for their instruction, perhaps even from churches. For whatever reason, the situation leads Paul to warn, "the love of money is at the root of all kinds of evil" (6:10).

Most of 1 Timothy relates to the appropriate roles of various individuals in the church. First Timothy discusses the qualifications of an **"overseer"**— the word that later would come to mean bishop (1 Tim. 3:1-7). Given the organization of churches today, it would be tempting to see this role as that of head minister over an individual congregation, what some churches call a "senior pastor" and others a "priest." However, a good argument can be made that Paul did not have in mind a *single* individual but a group of several *men* who together would lead a house church (e.g., 1 Tim. 5:17; Titus 1:5).

overseer: Perhaps the same as an elder (cf. Titus 1:5, 7), one of the leaders of a church.

deacon: A lesser role of leadership that involves serving the church.

It does seem certain that Paul or the author of 1 Timothy had only men in view as the leaders of a church. In contrast to most of what we might assume about Paul from his earlier writings and the book of Acts, 1 Timothy strongly asserts, "I do not let women teach men or have authority over them. Let them listen quietly" (1 Tim. 2:12).[6] Somehow it seems significant that this statement appears in a book that is strongly concerned with false teaching. Since the author views women through the lens of Eve (2:14)—someone many Jews viewed as the prototypical gullible woman—we see that this prohibition has everything to do with the belief that women are easily misled and thus make bad teachers. The next chapter will discuss the issue of how this passage might relate to the church today.

Another church role 1 Timothy discusses is that of **deacon**, a word that in general means someone who serves. Paul refers to a woman named Phoebe by this term in Romans 16:1 (although women seem excluded from this role in 1 Timothy), perhaps implying that she was one who provided material support for the church in Cenchrea, the port village of Corinth.[7] Many of the qualifications for a deacon are the same as those for an overseer. Men in both roles were to manage their households and children well (1 Tim. 3:5, 12). They were to have only one wife (3:2, 12);[8] and any drinking should be done with moderation (3:3, 8; cf. 5:23). In general, they were to be respectable first-century individuals (cf. 3:2, 8).

First Timothy has interesting things to say about other individuals in the church, most notably widows. Paul draws a distinction between "true" and "false" widows. Evidently, when a woman agreed to be supported by the church as a widow, she committed herself never to remarry. Many young widows, Paul points out, did not keep this vow but remarried because of their "physical desires" (1 Tim. 5:11). Paul tells Timothy to wait until a widow was sixty before "enrolling" her as a widow (5:9). Her female relatives should take care of her (5:8, 16) until she remarried (5:14).

The social roles that 1 Timothy encourages differ little from what non-Christians of the first century in general believed to be respectable behavior—there is little that is distinctively Christian about them. While this fact is clearest with regard to the subservient role women play throughout the letter, it is also apparent with regard to slaves. Far from encouraging Christian masters to free their slaves, 1 Timothy urges slaves to "work all the harder" because they are benefiting a Christian (1 Tim. 6:2). While comments like these may have been appropriate for the audience of 1 Timothy, it is hard for us today to read them and not believe that God intended for us to move the church forward on such issues—as it were, putting the spirit of Galatians 3:28 into action.

2 Timothy

Second Timothy has the most "concrete" feel of all the Pastoral Epistles and differs the least from Paul's earlier writings. It mentions more names and specific situations than both 1 Timothy and Titus combined. Second Timothy reads like Paul's "last will and testament," his farewell letter. As Paul victoriously says in 2 Timothy 4:7-8, "I have fought the good fight, I have finished the race, I have kept the faith. Now there is in store for me the crown of righteousness, which the Lord, the righteous Judge, will award to me on that day . . ." (NIV).

The setting is Rome (2 Tim. 1:17). Paul has already successfully passed his first defense before Nero, but almost all his associates have deserted him (4:16). Demas, mentioned in Philemon 24 and Colossians 4:14, especially seems to have turned his back on Paul, perhaps even on Christianity (2 Tim. 4:10). Others from Asia, Phygelus and Hermogenes, have similarly abandoned him (1:15). Perhaps even Crescens and Titus have left Rome to escape persecution (4:10).[9] Only Luke remains with Paul (4:11).

Of the two preoccupations of the pastorals—sound teaching and order in the church—2 Timothy focuses primarily on the first. It does, however, give us hints at how a proper chain of authority helps to maintain truthful teaching. Paul notes that he himself has laid hands on Timothy so that he could receive the Holy Spirit (2 Tim. 1:6-7).[10] Timothy knows "what I teach . . . and how I live, and what my purpose in life is. You know my faith and how long I have suffered. You know my love and my patient endurance. You know how much persecution and suffering I have endured" (3:10-11). The implication is that Timothy is an authorized bearer of Paul's authority—he knows Paul's mind and can speak for Paul. Paul encourages Timothy to pass on this same teaching to "trustworthy people" (2:2).

As we have already mentioned, we see Paul's teaching in 2 Timothy to be the "prototype" of Christian truth (2 Tim. 1:13). It has become a "deposit" (1:12, 14) that he is trusting both God and Timothy to guard after he has passed from the scene. He encourages Timothy to be a "good worker, one who does not need to be ashamed and who correctly explains the word of truth" (2:15). Timothy knows the Scriptures and he knows that "all Scripture is inspired by God" (3:16).

In contrast to Paul's deposit of truth and the correct teaching passed on through Timothy, Paul also warns Timothy about false teaching. For example, two individuals named Hymenaeus and Philetus were teaching that the resurrection had already taken place (2 Tim. 2:17-18). Second Timothy, on the other hand, affirms that salvation and resurrection are both things yet to come (2:10-11; 4:1).[11] These two men are examples of "godless, foolish discussions that lead to more and more ungodliness" (2:16). Timothy is encouraged not to quarrel with such individuals. Rather he should "gently teach those who oppose the truth" (2:25).

Paul notes that we should expect false teaching like this to rear its ugly head "in the last days" (2 Tim. 3:1). "People will no longer listen to right teaching. They will follow their own desires and will look for teachers who will tell them whatever they want to hear. They will reject the truth and follow strange myths" (4:3-4). If 2 Timothy is pseudonymous, these comments no doubt picture the writer's own time in the late first/early second century, and he was writing to invoke Paul's authority against these perversions and misinterpretations of the Scriptures.

Titus

The short book of Titus has much in common with 1 Timothy and presents some of the same basic advice for proper order in the church. "Elders," leaders of a church who are called "overseers" in 1 Timothy, are similarly allowed only one wife and should have obedient children (Titus 2:1-3). As in 1 Timothy, to older men and women are given advice on how to conduct themselves, as well as on how to train younger men and women (2:4-8). Slaves are encouraged not to talk back to their masters (2:9-10) and, just as in 1 Timothy, people are told to obey the political authorities (3:1).

Titus may also have the same heresy in mind as 1 Timothy does, although it is clearer about the Jewish nature of the false teaching. It makes warnings about the "circumcision group" (Titus 1:10) and connects the heresy with the Jewish Law (3:9). Like 1 Timothy this teaching involves myths (cf. 1 Tim. 1:4), although we hear in Titus that they are Jewish in nature (Titus 1:14). A preoccupation with genealogies is also common to these heresies (1 Tim. 1:4; Titus 3:9), as is the prospect of financial gain in some way (1 Tim. 6:5; Titus 1:11).

One difference between 1 Timothy and Titus, however, is the audience addressed. The context of 1 Timothy is Ephesus (1 Tim. 1:3) while that of Titus is the island of Crete (Titus 1:5). This difference might imply some distinction between the heresy of 1 Timothy and that of Titus. In particular, Titus quotes a Cretan proverb that would not seem to apply very well anywhere else:

Christ's divinity: The fact that Christ is God.

"The people of Crete are all liars; they are cruel animals and lazy gluttons" (Titus 1:12). In a manner consistent with ancient group culture, Paul affirms that this saying is true.[12]

Perhaps the most significant contribution that Titus makes to us as Christians has to do with the way it refers to Christ. This letter seems to refer to Christ as "God our Savior" four times (Titus 1:3; 2:10, 13; 3:4 cf. 1:4; 3:6). The best example is Titus 2:13 where Paul says, "We look forward to that wonderful event when the glory of our great God and Savior, Jesus Christ, will be revealed." This direct equation of Jesus with God is one of the clearest statements of **Christ's divinity**—the fact that He is God—in the New Testament. The New Testament often refers to Christ as the *Son of* God, but very rarely does it directly equate Jesus with God in such a straightforward way.[13]

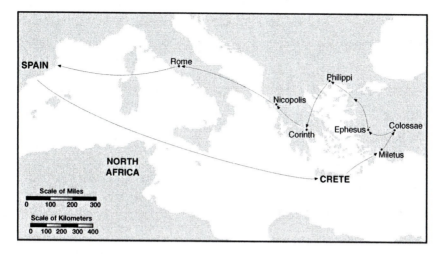

**PAUL'S HYPOTHETICAL "FOURTH" MISSIONARY JOURNEY
MAP 12**

The Authorship of the Pastorals

We have already mentioned that scholars debate whether Paul wrote the Pastoral Epistles or whether they are pseudonymous. We have discussed some of their unique characteristics and noticeable shifts from Paul's earlier writings. While both of these viewpoints can fit with the belief that the pastorals are inspired and authoritative, they do lead to slightly different interpretations of these letters and possibly to somewhat different ways of applying them today. Our respect for the Bible and its authority for the church today should lead us to consider the options carefully.

One of the challenges the pastorals give us comes from the book of Acts. How do the various places Paul mentions in these three letters fit with his life as Acts presents it? The majority of those who argue for Paul as the literal author suggest that after the two years of house arrest mentioned in Acts (Acts 28:30), Paul was released from prison and continued with his ministry. Perhaps Paul did make it to Spain as he intended (Rom. 15:24).[14] Perhaps he

Some Shifts between the Pastorals and Paul's Earlier Writings

Pastorals	Paul elsewhere
1. Paul considers himself the prototypical sinner (1 Tim. 1:15), the worst ever.	Paul considers himself blameless in keeping the Law before coming to Christ (Phil. 3:6), rarely uses words like repentance/forgiveness, speaks of his prior accomplishments as a Jew rather than his failure (Phil. 3:7,13).
2. Paul primarily refers to himself as a teacher (*didaskalos*; e.g., 1 Tim. 2:7), his teaching as prototypical doctrine (*didaskalia*; e.g., 2 Tim.1:13); he emphasizes "sound" teaching (1 Tim.1:10) and "trustworthy sayings" (e.g., 1 Tim.1:15).	Paul never refers to himself as a teacher or to his thought as doctrine; he never uses the terms "sound" teaching or "trustworthy sayings."
3. "Law" refers to moral core— don't murder, commit adultery, lie—1 Tim. 1:8-10.	"Law" refers to practices that divide Jew and Gentile (e.g., circumcision, food laws).
4. Paul says women cannot teach or have authority over men; the shame of Eve's sin remains in force until a woman bears children (1 Tim. 2:12-15).	Paul speaks of a female deacon (Rom. 16:1) and probably apostle (16:7); presumes that women prophesy in church (1 Cor. 11:5); blames Adam for sin and notes that in Christ the distinction male/female does not apply at least in regard to sin/sonship (Gal. 3:28).
5. Paul tells Timothy that he is not lying about the fact that he is an apostle (1 Tim. 2:7).	Timothy is perhaps Paul's most frequent associate as an apostle—why would he feel a need to reassure him of this fact?

returned to the East, visited Crete (Titus 1:5), and saw Ephesus once more—even though he had been so sure he would not (cf. Acts 20:25).[15] He then traveled through Macedonia again (1 Tim. 1:3) and wintered at a place called Nicopolis (Titus 3:12). (See **Map 12**.)

Following this hypothesis, however, Paul did not fare so well when he returned to Rome. He was imprisoned again, and some of his closest associates deserted him (2 Tim. 4:16). But Paul was ready to die for Christ. In some of the most confident language in the New Testament he says, "I have fought the good fight, I have finished the race, I have kept the faith. Now there is in store for me the crown of righteousness, which the Lord, the righteous Judge, will award to me on that day" (2 Tim. 4:7-8 NIV).

This reconstruction accounts well for various comments scattered throughout the pastorals. The strongest objection to it comes from the impression Acts gives us that Paul did *not* return to the East after his trip to Rome. We mentioned in chapters 19 and 29 of this text that it was very likely Acts was written after the destruction of Jerusalem in A.D. 70 because of how Luke presents Jesus' prophecy of Jerusalem's destruction.[16] Luke thus would have known what happened to Paul in the years after his house arrest in Rome. Therefore, if Paul returned to Ephesus, it is a little surprising that Acts would record Paul telling the Ephesians that "none of you to whom I have preached the Kingdom will ever see me again" (Acts 20:25). This difficulty is not insurmountable, but it does cast some doubt on Paul's return to the East in the time period after Acts.

Throughout our discussion in this chapter, we have noted a number of shifts in the language of the pastorals from Paul's earlier writings. For example, Paul never refers to himself as a teacher elsewhere (cf. 1 Tim. 2:7; 2 Tim. 1:11), and he never refers to his instruction as a body of teaching (e.g., 1 Tim. 6:1; 2 Tim. 3:10) or a "deposit" (1 Tim. 6:20; 2 Tim 1:12) like the pastorals do. While he considers himself an example for others to follow, he never speaks of his teaching as the "prototype" (2 Tim. 1:13) of true teaching or his conversion as the greatest example of God's mercy (1 Tim. 1:16). These words and others like them either do not occur at all in Paul's earlier writings, or Paul never uses them in the same way. However, they occur consistently throughout the three Pastoral Epistles.

Several shifts seem to go beyond style and language. For example, Paul does not think of himself as the greatest of all sinners in his earlier writings (cf. 1 Tim. 1:16), as we have seen in earlier chapters.[17] On the contrary, he believes himself to have kept the Law blamelessly (Phil. 3:6) before his vision of Christ. Although he believes with his head that everyone is a sinner, the absence of terms like "repentance" and "forgiveness" from his writings probably reveals that he had not experienced in his own life a sense of moral failure. Even in his most famous discussion on the inevitability of sin, he lets himself off the hook—"I am not really the one doing it; the sin within me is doing it" (Rom. 7:20). In the end, it is not his sin that he lays aside as he presses on as a Christian—it is his *honorable accomplishments* as a Law-keeping Jew that he sets aside as worthless in comparison to Christ (Phil. 3:7-8). The statement of 1 Timothy 1:16 thus presents an unknown side to Paul or a significant change in his attitude toward his previous life.

Another difference between 1 Timothy and Paul's earlier writings seems to be the role of women in the church. Those who believe that women cannot teach men often note how absolute Paul's prohibition seems in 1 Timothy 2:12. He bases his argument on the story of creation rather than on a problem in a specific community. Yet in Paul's earlier writings women seem to have done the very things Paul is forbidding here. In 1 Corinthians 11:5, for example, women appear to pray and prophesy in the presence of men. While 1 Timothy 3:12 only may allow men to be deacons, Romans 16:1 refers to a woman named Phoebe as a deacon, using the same masculine form of the word that appears in 1 Timothy. Paul mentions a woman named Priscilla before he mentions her husband in Romans 16:3, calling her a "co-worker." Later on in the chapter, he even seems to refer to a woman named Junias as an apostle (16:7).

One interesting shift that seems to take place in the pastorals is similar to what we saw in chapter 47 of this book as we were discussing the authorship of 2 Peter. The shift we have in mind is the ever so slight change from viewing truths in a context to viewing them on universal terms. The things for which Paul argues in his earlier letters relate consistently to specific churches with specific situations and issues. Even Romans, Paul's most systematic letter, carries with it the sense of his concrete struggle between his Jewish heritage and the inclusion of Gentiles as full Christians.

In the pastorals, however, not only Paul's teaching but Christian teaching in general has become a body of belief, a set of standardized ideas rather than ideas fitted to specific contexts. While we have seen that early Christianity was a somewhat diverse movement consisting of a number of different groups with contrasting ideas, the pastorals assume that the boundaries of Christian belief are relatively set.[18] We can now clearly distinguish "sound doctrine" from heresy.

Those who argue that Paul wrote these letters believe that these shifts took place within Paul and Peter's lifetime, or even that true teaching was clear from the very birth of Christianity. Those in favor of pseudonymity believe this shift took place decades after Peter and Paul had passed from the scene. When these men were alive, they might say, the strength of Paul's personality and his personal experience of the risen Christ provided the authority for his teaching. It was after the death of such figures that a body of standardized belief and practice emerged. In the absence of such foundational personalities, a set of teachings became the standard (cf. Eph. 2:20; 2 Pet. 3:2).

We could mention a host of smaller items in the debate. Why would Paul need to assure Timothy that he really was an apostle? After all, Timothy was a convert of Paul's and a long-time coworker. Yet after mentioning his role as

591

apostle, Paul says, "I am telling the truth, I am not lying" (1 Tim. 2:7 NIV). Were the roles of elder and deacon this well defined in Paul's lifetime? We certainly know they existed well before Paul's death (cf. Phil. 1:1). And what about the clarity with which Titus refers to Christ as God (e.g., Titus 2:13)? Only the Gospel of John, traditionally dated in the 90s of the first century, approaches such a clear understanding of Christ's divinity.

No single argument seems decisive against Paul as the actual author. A person's style can change over time or in a different setting. Or perhaps Paul used a different amanuensis to write these letters and gave that person a good deal of freedom. Yet we must admit that the weight of all these factors taken together is significant. We can understand why most scholars have concluded in favor of pseudonymity. But the vast majority of *conservative* scholars insist that Paul is the literal author. Individuals will have to make up their minds in terms of their own faith and understanding.

Things to Think About

Key Terms
Christ's divinity
deacon
overseer

1. In what way do the Pastoral Epistles address the need for order and a chain of authority in the church?

2. What aspects of the Pastoral Epistles relate to the need for correct doctrine in the church?

3. Do you think that the Pastoral Epistles are pseudonymous? Using the material from this chapter, argue for a position.

endnotes

1. The idea that Paul was imprisoned twice in Rome comes from our attempt to fit various comments throughout the Pastoral Epistles with data from the book of Acts. We have no explicit statements in any of Paul's writings to indicate that he was imprisoned there more than once.

2. See chapter 47 of this text.

3. This Greek word (*hypotyposis*) occurs only in 1 and 2 Timothy in the New Testament (1 Tim. 1:16; 2 Tim. 1:13).

4. It is interesting to compare this statement in 1 Timothy 1:15 to what Paul says in 1 Corinthians and Ephesians. In 1 Corinthians, he merely calls himself the "least of all the apostles" (1 Cor. 15:9). Then in Ephesians he becomes "less than the least of all God's people" (Eph. 3:8 NIV). Now in 1 Timothy he has become the worst of all sinners! The heightening of Paul's greatness by intensifying the significance of his "conversion" is not only typical of what happens to individuals as they become more and more legendary, but it stands in contrast to how Paul views his pre-Christian self in his earlier writings. Philippians 3:6 indicates that Paul sees himself as *blameless* in his keeping of the Jewish Law—something he speaks of as an accomplishment, not as a disgrace (Phil. 3:7). It is the *honor* of his Law-keeping that he discards in Philippians, not the shame (3:7-9). In other words, his perspective toward his pre-Christian self in Philippians is not one of failure but of accomplishment. He sees that while his accomplishments are noteworthy from a human perspective, they pale in significance next to Christ.

5. As we will see repeatedly, many of the key words used in the pastorals do not occur anywhere in Paul's earlier writings. Even when they do, they are used in different ways. The word *deposit* (*paratheke*) used here, for example, appears nowhere in the New Testament except in the pastorals (1 Tim. 6:20; 2 Tim. 1:12, 14). Similarly, Paul never views his instruction as this kind of teaching (*didaskalia*) in his earlier writings. It is a term that implies a body of teaching rather than specific teachings.

6. The other famous passage is 1 Corinthians 14:34-35. These verses interrupt the flow of the chapter and are actually found in different places in different manuscripts. Given that they seem to contradict 1 Corinthians 11:5 and use the concept of Law in a way atypical of Paul, it is possible that these verses were not originally in 1 Corinthians at all. They may have been added by someone else or by Paul himself at a later time. The manuscript evidence would make sense if the comments were first placed in the margins of a manuscript of 1 Corinthians and later copied into the text at different places by different copyists.

7. In fact, Paul uses the masculine form of the word in Romans 16:1. Some have taken 1 Timothy 3:11 to be about female deacons rather than the wives of deacons.

While this interpretation is attractive for those of us who believe women can hold such roles, such an interpretation does not fit with 1 Timothy 2:12. As well, 3:12 seems to presume that a deacon is male. Shifts like these from Paul's earlier writings lead most scholars to believe that Paul was not the actual author of 1 Timothy.

8. This is an interesting statement! Does Paul mean that some in Asia Minor had more than one or does he mean one in the course of a man's lifetime?

9. The implication that Titus had been with Paul in Rome and had left for Dalmatia presents a problem for those who believe the pastorals were written at the same time as a unit. The context of Titus itself seems to place Titus on the island of Crete.

10. In slight contrast to 1 Timothy 4:14, where a group of "elders" or overseers laid hands on him.

11. For those who believe Ephesians and 2 Timothy to be pseudonymous, some speculate whether the author of Ephesians is one of the "Pauline" Christians with which 2 Timothy is in dialogue, since Ephesians speaks of our resurrection in the present tense (e.g., Eph. 2:6; compare also 1 Cor. 15:12 and 2 Thess. 2:2).

12. See chapter 9 of this text.

13. Titus even differs from 1 Timothy in this regard. We have every reason to believe that when 1 Timothy 2:3 refers to "God our Savior," it is referring to God the Father, especially in light of 1 Timothy 1:1 and 2:5.

14. First Clement 5:7, a letter probably written in the late A.D. 90s, states that Paul reached the "limits of the West." Some take this statement to mean that he was released after a "first" imprisonment and went on to Spain. It is not entirely clear, however, that Clement meant this—Rome could very well have been considered the limits of the civilized West.

15. If Philippians and Philemon were written from Rome—perhaps the opinion of most scholars—it seems that Paul's ordeal had brought a significant change in his plans to go on to Spain. Now he was looking back to the East, expecting to visit Colossae (Phlem. 22) and perhaps Philippi (Phil. 1:26) in the near future. These observations support the hypothesis that Paul was released after a first imprisonment and then returned to the East.

16. Compare Luke 21:20 with Mark 13:14. Since Luke was probably writing his version of the prophecy on the basis of Mark, it is very likely that the vividness of his wording comes from the fact that the event was past and he was describing the fulfillment of Jesus' prediction as it actually took place. In keeping with this, he removed almost all the aspects of Mark 13 that were not fulfilled in A.D. 70.

17. See chapter 37 of this text, for example.

18. See chapter 35 of this text.

CHAPTER 50

Paul's Later Writings and Society

When doing what the Bible commanded "back then" would mean something different today, God might not want us to do exactly as He commanded the original audiences to do.

Many Christians use the Bible as a blueprint for how to live today. Since almost all Christians believe on some level that the Bible is inspired and holds authority over our lives, it makes perfect sense to go to it to find out how we should conduct ourselves in this world. This inclination makes even more sense for the person who reads the Bible as a single book without really considering the historical context of its words. To the extent that someone reads the Bible as a direct word from God to that individual, s/he will, of course, make life decisions exactly as the Bible tells that person to do.

But what happens when we realize that these words were spoken *first* to individuals of ancient times whose world was quite different from ours? As we said back in chapter 2, it does the doctor no

At a Glance

- The New Testament largely does not aim at changing the structures of ancient society, but addresses respectable Christian behavior within them.

- New Testament social teaching at times may reflect a defensive strategy to avoid persecution.

- The New Testament assumes the existence of slavery, although it values freedom.

- The roles the New Testament lays out for women and children are very similar to how non-Christians in the ancient world viewed these roles.

- Even more than we see demonstrated in the New Testament, it may be possible for us today to move society's structures closer to what they will be in heaven.

service for a patient to take someone else's prescription. When what God did back then corresponds closely to our world's realities, it makes sense to do exactly as the ancients did. But when doing what they did would have a completely different significance in our world—perhaps even one completely opposite to its significance in the ancient world—it seems doubtful that God would want us to do exactly as He commanded them to do.

We should not read the Bible so that we can do exactly what the people of Bible times did; we should read the Bible with a view to *why* God commanded what He did, so we can do things that work toward the same goals. We should not use this as an excuse to get out of doing what the Bible says. Indeed, at times we may find that this truth makes it wrong for us to do things that the Bible allows (e.g., slavery, polygamy). However, sometimes we will find commands in the Bible that simply would not mean the same thing today if we practiced them (e.g., "Greet all the brothers with a holy kiss" [1 Thess. 5:26 NIV]). At those times, God may suggest to us through His Spirit or the church alternative ways of accomplishing His purposes (e.g., handshakes).

> We should not read the Bible so that we can do exactly what the ancients did; we should read the Bible with a view to why God commanded what He did, so we can do things that work toward the same goals.

One area in which these considerations seem most significant is in the matter of how to live in society. Not too long ago, Christians struggled with the matter of slavery: should Christians own slaves or work against the institution of slavery? Here is an issue where in the end it was the character of God that won the day, not the specific commands of Scripture. We will search long and hard for a condemnation of slavery in the pages of the Bible.

Many conservative Christians are deeply involved in political issues today and form a strong lobby on Capitol Hill. For many, American patriotism and spirituality seem to go hand in hand. Yet it would be hard to justify something like the American Revolution from a New Testament perspective. The early church largely seems to have taken an isolationist/defensive approach to its interaction with the powers that be. Evidently, many Christians see

> ⌕
> **household codes:** Sets of instruction regarding the appropriate roles of individuals in relationships such as wife-husband, slave-master, and child-parent.

something in the nature of Christianity that plays itself out differently in our democratic world than it did in the autocratic world of the Roman Empire.

Perhaps the most sensitive issue relating to the New Testament and society is the role of Christian women in the world today. Many use certain verses from Paul's letters—particularly 1 Corinthians 14:34 and 1 Timothy 2:12—to ban women from any leadership roles in the church or home. Similarly, many consider the **household codes** of Ephesians, Colossians, 1 Timothy, Titus, and 1 Peter as models for Christian homes today.[1] Those who use these passages in this way make a strong case, particularly if you read them without considering their original contexts. Others think the character of God points us toward "a more excellent way" (1 Cor. 12:31 KJV), one in which men and women can serve in any role to which the Holy Spirit calls them.

This chapter briefly discusses some of these issues. Its basic conclusion is that while the New Testament certainly views Christian relationships through the lens of Christ, the specific *roles* it assigns usually do not differ significantly from what the ancient Mediterranean world in general thought was respectable and appropriate. In other words, to a great extent the roles it lays out are not specifically Christian. Pagan "moralists," for example, would have agreed with the role 1 Peter lays out for wives. If this is true, then it is legitimate to ask how the character of God might play itself out in our world today.

Slavery

Slavery is a good issue to start off with since it is one on which most Christians seem to agree. I do not know of any Christians who argue that we should revive the practice of slavery. We feel comfortable with the idea that "all are created equal" even if we do not practice it. While America no doubt could have done a better job in the process of emancipating its slaves, a world in which there is no slavery clearly comes closer to heaven than a world in which slavery exists.

Yet the Bible itself never questions the institution of slavery. It never says it is inappropriate to consider another person as property or that it is wrong for one person to have such extensive authority over another individual's life. In fact, if we are really honest with ourselves, those who argued for slavery in the 1800s had more explicit scriptural support on their side than those who argued against it.

Look at some New Testament verses relating to slavery:

"Are you a slave? Don't let that worry you—but if you get a chance to be free, take it . . . Whatever situation you were in when you became a believer, **stay there** in your new relationship with God."

1 Corinthians 7:21, 24

"In this new life, it doesn't matter if you are a Jew or Gentile, circumcised or uncircumcised, barbaric, uncivilized, **slave or free**. Christ is all that matters, and he lives in all of us.

Colossians 3:11

"You slaves **must obey** your earthly masters in everything you do. Try to please them all the time, not just when they are watching you. Obey them willingly because of your reverent fear of the Lord."

Colossians 3:22

"You who are slaves must accept the authority of your masters. Do whatever they tell you—not only if they are kind and reasonable, but even if they are harsh . . . Of course, you get no credit for being patient **if you are beaten** for doing wrong . . ."

1 Peter 2:18, 20

"Now he [Onesimus] will mean much more to you, both **as a slave** and as a brother in the Lord."

Philemon 16

On the side of those who oppose slavery, Paul does say that in Christ there is no longer slave or free (cf. Gal. 3:28). Yet Paul is referring to what we are in God's eyes—to the fact that we will all experience salvation without any distinction among us. In the world to come, the categories of slave and free will not exist.

Despite this fact, Paul does not teach that we should work to abolish the institution of slavery here on earth. Paul probably thought Christ would return very soon; thus, it was more important to spread the good news than to reform society. Colossians may say that it does not matter whether you are slave or free anymore (Col. 3:11), but it also tells slaves to obey their masters (3:22). Although it is easy for us to read into Philemon a plea from Paul to set Onesimus free, the letter itself never says anything of the sort.

Far from opposing the institution of slavery, the Bible *assumes* it. It tells Christians how to conduct themselves within it, not how to undermine it. Indeed, if Christians and abolitionists had followed 1 Peter 2:18-25 literally, they would not have helped slaves escape their masters on the Underground Railroad. These verses teach that a slave should submit respectfully to his or her master, even when that master is harsh and beats them unjustly.

I would agree with those scholars who think that 1 Peter reflects a "defensive strategy" to some degree, a strategy to avoid persecution.[2] To the Christians of the late first century, a group often hated and misunderstood by those around them, the thought of changing the institutions of society at large was hardly on their minds.[3] They were more concerned with avoiding persecution and the all-too-common perception that they were troublemakers. If this is the case, we should not be surprised to find that the household codes of the New Testament present us with behavior that the ancients considered "respectable."

Yet many Christians in the 1800s saw something in God's character that surpassed the respectability of ancient culture. They saw the opportunity to change not just individual lives on the inside, but to change the outside world as well. Our world today is a world in which Christians hold significant power, power that can make a difference in society. Further, the New Testament does value freedom over slavery; that much is clear. Paul told slaves who might have an opportunity for freedom to take it (1 Cor. 7:21).

But Paul and the early Christians did not even think to dream of the possibility of abolishing it altogether. We might say that when we abolished slavery, we moved farther along a trajectory Christ started, one towards which the early Christians themselves did not take significant steps. In the modern world, we have been able to move farther along this "Christ trajectory," bringing society just a little closer to what heaven will be like. To use Paul's words, we saw a "chance" for all slaves "to be free" (1 Cor. 7:21) and we took it.

Women

You can probably see where the previous discussion points us with regard to women. In a number of ways, the issue of a woman's role in society is similar to the issue of slavery. In Galatians 3:28 Paul not only indicates that the category of slave/free does not apply in heaven, he words this in such a way as to undo the distinction between the sexes made at creation.[4]

Just as with slavery, this fact did not mean that Paul felt that the traditional roles of men and women were invalid. For example, he still considers the husband to be the "head" of the wife and tells women to veil their heads when they pray or prophesy in the presence of other men (1 Cor. 11:3-5).[5] Some have argued that

> "All who have been united with Christ in baptism have been made like him. There is no longer Jew or Gentile, slave or free, male or female. For you are all Christians—you are all one in Christ Jesus."
>
> **Galatians 3:27-28**

Paul did not mean by headship that the husband was the leader of the wife or that he had greater authority than a wife, but this argument probably does not work. While Colossians does think of the head as something that nourishes the body (e.g., Col. 2:19), Greek literature in general makes it clear that the ancient world could think of the head as the "ruler" of the body.[6]

Look at the following verses from the New Testament relating to the role of women in Christian society:

> "You wives must submit to your husbands, as is fitting for those who belong to the Lord."
>
> **Colossians 3:18**

> "**In the same way** [as the slaves just mentioned], you wives must accept the authority of your husbands, even those who refuse to accept the Good News. Your godly lives will speak to them better than any words . . . Don't be concerned about the outward beauty that depends on fancy hairstyles, expensive jewelry, or beautiful clothes . . . For instance, Sarah obeyed her husband, Abraham, when she called him her **master**."
>
> **1 Peter 3:1, 3, 6**

> "Women should be silent during the church meetings. It is not proper for them to speak. They should be submissive, just as the law says. If they have any questions to ask, let them ask their husbands at home, for it is improper for women to speak in church meetings."
>
> **1 Corinthians 14:34-35**

> "Let a woman/wife learn in silence in all subjection. But I do not allow a woman to teach or hold authority over a man but to be in silence. For Adam was formed first, then Eve. And Adam was not deceived, but the woman, because she was deceived, has come to be in transgression. But she will be saved through childbearing, if they remain in faithfulness and love and holiness with modesty."

1 Timothy 2:11-15 (author's translation)

At some points these verses are difficult to read. Some might argue that they are difficult for only those who resist the truth, those who do not like the roles God has set out for men and women on earth. Others might suggest that these verses are hard *precisely because* they seem to contradict the character of God, particularly what He has done for the world through Christ. Far from eliminating the category male/female, these verses reinforce the category along the lines of ancient culture.

For this reason, some well-meaning Christians try to soften the force of these words in one way or another. For example, they might try to reinterpret the words *submission* or *authority* so that they do not carry as strong a connotation. One rendering of 1 Timothy 2:12 reads, "I am not *currently* permitting a woman to teach or *hold absolute* authority over a man." This translation makes the verse sound less offensive to women.

Some may notice that I have not quoted Ephesians' version of the household codes, the favorite of those who wish to soften the implications of verses like these. Ephesians reads:

> "You will submit to one another out of reverence for Christ. You wives will submit to your husbands as you do to the Lord. For a husband is the head of his wife as Christ is the head of his body, the church; he gave his life to be her Savior. As the church submits to Christ, so you wives must submit to your husbands in everything. *(continued on next page)*

> "And you husbands must love your wives with the same love Christ showed the church. He gave up his life for her to make her holy and clean, washed by baptism and God's word . . . In the same way, husbands ought to love their wives as they love their own bodies."
>
> **Ephesians 5:21-28**

These are beautiful verses that compare the husband-wife relationship to that of Christ and the church. You will often hear Christians say that if every husband loved his wife to this degree it would be a joy for wives to submit to them and obey them. The passage also begins with a statement that Christians are to submit to one another, which many take to mean that the husband must also submit to his wife in some way.[7]

I have intentionally focused on the other household codes of the New Testament so you can see that the softer approach in general probably waters these statements down a little too much. First Peter does not picture a husband who loves his wife as Christ loved the church. It pictures a husband who not only is an unbeliever, but one who is unjust and who treats his wife harshly.

The section on husbands and wives in 1 Peter follows the section on slaves and masters, in which Peter commands slaves to obey their masters—even when their masters beat them unjustly. Peter uses Christ's unjust suffering as an example of what slaves may have to endure as Christians. The section on wives and husbands continues this train of thought when it says, "*in the same way*, you wives must accept the authority of your husbands" (1 Pet. 3:1). Peter's use of the word "master" implies that he thinks of the husband-wife relationship in similar terms to the master-slave relationship (1 Pet. 3:6).

Perhaps the most difficult passage for us is in 1 Timothy 2. These verses seem to indicate that women cannot teach or hold authority over men, not only because God planned the world that way,[8] but also because women are easily deceived and thus make bad teachers. It holds the shame of Eve's sin over women past, present, and future, even though Christ has taken away *all* the shame of our sin.

Many Christian groups find in these verses the most important biblical words on the role of women in the church, using this passage more than any other to argue against women holding ministry roles in the church. Of course, these verses potentially ban women from *any* situation that would involve teaching or authority over a man—high school teacher or college professor, any job position that would place a woman in authority over a man. If we were to enact its words fully, Christian society would begin to look more and more like that of some Middle Eastern countries today.

Considering the Contexts

So what are we to do with the New Testament's teaching on women? At this point it is important to realize that these verses give us only half of the puzzle. When we are reading the Bible as a single book, it is easy to ignore the positive leadership and teaching roles women seem to have played in some segments of the early church. Many Christians use the preceding passages above to "trump" other passages that present women in a more active role in the church.

Therefore, it is very important to consider the contexts in which these statements appear. All the household codes, for example, appear in the later books of the New Testament. Arguably, many of these were written as Christians began to come under persecution and at a time when the importance of structure and order was increasing.[9] When someone is looking for an excuse to beat you up, you generally try not to be noticed. Similarly, many early Christians seem to have moved in the direction of "respectable" behavior during this period.

However, in the first thirty years of Christianity and in some segments of the later church, women seem to have played a much more active role in ministry, teaching, and leadership. Paul seems to have called a woman named Junias an "apostle" in Romans 16:7. He calls a woman named Phoebe a "deacon" in the same chapter (16:1), using the same masculine form of the Greek word he uses of Timothy in 1 Timothy 4:6. He sometimes mentions Priscilla before her husband when speaking of the churches that meet in their houses (e.g., Rom. 16:3), as Acts also does (e.g., Acts 18:18, 26). In fact, Acts mentions her name first in detailing how this couple *instructs* Apollos in the truth of Christianity.

Acts, perhaps one of the later books of the New Testament, has a consistently positive view of the role of women in the early church. Luke regularly mentions the fact that women support both Jesus' earthly ministry and the mission of the early church (e.g., Luke 8:2-3; Acts 17:4, 12, 34). As we saw earlier, Lydia seems to have been a wealthy woman in whose house Paul stayed while he was in Philippi. Her house may even have been where the church at Philippi met (Acts 16:15). Luke is careful to point out that both men and women function in the role of prophet in the early church (e.g., Luke 1:41-42, 46-55; 2:36-38; Acts 2:17-18; 21:9).

This last observation is important because Paul also seems to believe that women can pray and prophesy in church. Paul's instructions in 1 Corinthians 11:2-16 deal with holding the sensitive balance between the husband-wife relationship and a situation in which a woman is praying or prophesying in the presence of other men. What is important to realize is that these verses assume that a woman *can* speak and prophesy in church. Those who oppose women teaching in church often "trump" this verse with Paul's later comments about the need for women to be silent in church (1 Cor. 14:34-35; 1 Tim. 2:11-15). But the trump might just as well go in the other direction—you might argue that whatever Paul meant when he said women should be silent, it was nothing like an absolute statement.[10] He did not mean *all* women, just the uneducated and uninspired ones.

While we cannot ignore the male orientation of Paul's later writings, there are some aspects to their situations that seem significant. As you may recall, 1 Peter's comments on society seem to reflect a defensive strategy against persecution. We also saw that Paul believed Christ would return soon and accordingly oriented his teaching around "holding the fort" until that day. He probably did not think we would have enough time to begin revolutionizing society.

It is probably important also to remember that the overwhelming majority of women in ancient times had no education whatsoever. Since 1 Timothy is a book about sound teaching, we can thus understand why it turns more to men as teachers.[11] In fact, 2 Timothy 3:6 may imply that the false teaching Paul was addressing made its way into the church when certain women allowed traveling teachers to stay in their homes, using them as a base from which to spread their teaching.

All in all, the roles these passages lay out for women are not too different from the roles ancient society thought were "respectable." Take the following passages from the ancient world:

"The primary and simplest elements of the household are the connection of master and slave, that of the husband and wife, and that of parents and children.

"The head of the household rules over both wife and children, and rules over both as free members of the household . . . His rule over the wife is like that of a statesman over fellow citizens . . . The male is naturally fitter to command than the female, except where there is some departure from nature."

Aristotle (Greek philosopher),
***Politics* 1.3.1; 1.12.1**

"Let her, therefore, be obedient to him; not so that he should abuse her, but that she may acknowledge her duty to her husband; for God has given the authority to the husband."

Josephus (Jewish historian),
***Against Apion* 2.201**

"The husband appears to be a master, endowed with sufficient authority to explain these laws [Jewish Law] to his wife, a father to teach them to his children, and a master to his servants."

Philo (Jewish philosopher),
***Hypothetica* 7.14**

As you can see, the New Testament household codes fit in nicely with these excerpts from ancient literature. While the New Testament places these roles within the context of Christian belief—like the relationship between Christ and the church (Ephesians) or the submission of Jesus to unjust suffering (1 Peter)—the roles themselves are not distinctly Christian. It was the norm of ancient society for women to submit to their husbands.

As with the issue of slavery, we can legitimately ask whether God might have a "more excellent way" for us today, one that fits even better with His character and the work of Christ as Scripture reveals them. We must remember that just as there will be no distinction between slave or free, there will be no distinction between male and female in the world to come. In the kingdom of God, "They will be like the angels in heaven" (Mark 12:25), who do not marry. The roles of husband and wife will not apply. What is now true of us in terms of our salvation—no difference between male or female— will then also be true of us in terms of our roles. In fact, this comment may even imply that we will have spiritual bodies that do not distinguish gender (1 Cor. 15:35-50).

The Christ trajectory thus is not toward the subordination of one gender to another but to the complete equality of the two in every way. Indeed, we should be very careful how much weight we give to verses like 1 Timothy 2:12, for they can be used to negate the work of Christ if we push them too far. Would Paul really want us to model Christian society around the idea that women still bear the shame of Eve's sin? After all, Christ's sacrifice atoned once and for all for *all* sin (Heb. 10:14). Therefore, those who would position women on the basis of Eve's sin are implicitly rejecting Christ.

Children

Christians sometimes debate today about the appropriate way to raise children. "Spare the rod and spoil the child" is a well-known saying based on Proverbs 13:24. Most Christians have wisely steered the interpretations of verses like this away from the idea of beatings. They interpret them in terms of the general need for parents to discipline their children, rather than as a divine sanction of physical abuse. I believe that this approach to such verses comes from the Holy Spirit and reflects the character of God and Christ.

Suffice it to say that this approach is not really true to what many of the original authors of the Bible had in mind. Take Proverbs 23:13-14: "If you beat them with a rod, they will not die. If you beat them with the rod, you will save their lives from Sheol" (NRSV). A quick trip to some third-world countries would give you a fair idea of what such a beating might entail. While the New Testament clearly places such discipline in the context of love (e.g., Eph. 6:4; Heb. 12:5-11), it is all too easy for us to "sterilize" these verses so that they do not play out as harshly as they probably did play out among Christians of the early church.[12]

All the considerations we have discussed so far in this chapter also apply to this issue. It is not even that the church has a *right* to consider afresh the issue of parenting today. It is the *responsibility* of the church in every generation to listen prayerfully to the Holy Spirit and wrestle with such issues. In the process of decision, it is to our detriment to ignore the genuine growth that has taken place in our understanding of child development and child rearing.

With this knowledge in hand, we must ask what Christ would do today, given what the New Testament reveals of His character. And what does the character of God have to say on the matter? How does God's character as love play out in our world today? What will the kingdom of God look like? After we have asked such questions together, we plot our course as a church on the trajectory of heaven.

Things to Think About

Key Term
household codes

1. This book argues that we should not assume that every command of Scripture applies directly to today. What are the dangers of such a claim? Could someone use this idea as an excuse to get out of obeying God? Does God critique culture—is it possible that our culture is wrong and that we need to become more similar to the ancient world on some of these issues?

2. Compare the issues of slavery and women. How are they alike? How are they different? Do you think total equality for women and the abolition of slavery are essentially the same issue, or does some fundamental difference distinguish them? Explain.

3. Do you agree with this book's position regarding the issue of women? What are its strong and weak points?

endnotes

1. I will include the household codes of 1 Peter in the discussion of this chapter for convenience, although Paul obviously did not write them.

2. For example, S. McKnight in *1 Peter* of the *NIV Application Commentary* (Grand Rapids: Zondervan, 1996), 131.

3. See chapter 34 of this text.

4. Galatians 3:28 is worded in such a way as to echo Genesis 1:27. While Paul says "neither Jew *nor* Gentile, neither slave *nor* free," he says "not male and female." He does this to imply that the distinction God made in creation is abolished in Christ.

5. A fair amount of disagreement exists over exactly what Paul's reasoning entailed. See chapter 41 of this text.

6. Plato, for example, who wrote well before the time of the New Testament. He used the relationship between the head and the body to illustrate the relationship between the rulers of society and everyone else (*Republic*).

7. In my opinion, however, the verse serves as an introduction to the whole section of 5:21–6:9 and does not imply that husbands also should submit to their wives.

8. Actually, Paul's argument here is from birth order, another idea that fits well with ancient culture. Adam was formed first, Eve second. The firstborn conventionally held the position of authority in the ancient world.

9. It is of interest to realize that all the books in which the household codes appear are candidates for pseudonymity.

10. As we mentioned in chapter 41, some manuscripts do not place these verses at this point in the text, leading some to argue that 1 Corinthians 14:34-35 was not even a part of the original text of 1 Corinthians.

11. Of course, most men were illiterate and had no education either.

12. And, unfortunately, in the homes of some Christians today.

For Further Study

Paul in General

- Dunn, James D. G. *The Theology of Paul the Apostle.* Grand Rapids: Eerdmans, 1998.

- Malina, Bruce J. and Jerome H. Neyrey. *Portraits of Paul: An Archaeology of Ancient Personality.* Louisville: Westminster John Knox, 1996.

- Sanders, E. P. *Paul and Palestinian Judaism.* Minneapolis: Fortress, 1977.

- Wright, N. T. *What Saint Paul Really Said: Was Saul of Tarsus the Real Founder of Christianity?* Grand Rapids: Eerdmans, 1997.

Romans

- Dunn, James D. G. *Romans.* 2 vols. in Word Biblical Commentary. Dallas: Word, 1988.

- Fitzmyer, Joseph A. *Romans: A New Translation with Introduction and Commentary.* New York: Doubleday, 1993.

- Moo, Douglas. *The Epistle to the Romans.* NIV Commentary on the New Testament. Grand Rapids: Eerdmans, 1996.

- Stott, John. *Romans: God's* Good News *for the World.* Downers Grove, IL: InterVarsity, 1994.

The Corinthian Correspondence

- Fee, Gordon D. *The First Epistle to the Corinthians.* NIV Commentary on the New Testament. Grand Rapids: Eerdmans, 1987.

- Martin, Dale B. *The Corinthian Body.* New Haven, CT: Yale University, 1995.

- Witherington, Ben III. *Conflict and Community in Corinth: A Socio-Rhetorical Commentary on 1 and 2 Corinthians.* Grand Rapids: Eerdmans, 1995.

Paul's Other Writings
- Donfried, Karl P. and I. Howard Marshall. *The Theology of the Shorter Pauline Letters.* Cambridge: Cambridge University, 1993.

- Lincoln, Andrew T. and A. J. M. Wedderburn. *The Theology of the Later Pauline Letters.* Cambridge: Cambridge University, 1993.

- Mounce, William D. *Pastoral Epistles.* Nashville: Thomas Nelson, 2000.

Issues in Paul's Letters
- Green, Joel B. and Mark D. Baker. *Recovering the Scandal of the Cross: Atonement in New Testament and Contemporary Contexts.* Downers Grove, IL: InterVarsity, 2000.

- Hays, Richard B. *The Moral Vision of the New Testament: Community, Cross, New Creation: A Contemporary Introduction to New Testament Ethics.* San Francisco: HarperSanFrancisco, 1996.

- Matera, Frank J. *New Testament Ethics: The Legacies of Jesus and Paul.* Louisville: Westminster John Knox, 1996.

- Meade, David G. *Pseudonymity and Canon: An Investigation into the Relationship of Authorship and Authority in Jewish and Early Christian Tradition.* Grand Rapids: Eerdmans, 1986.

- Witherington, Ben III. *Women and the Genesis of Christianity.* Cambridge: Cambridge University, 1990.

Unit 6:
Hebrews, General Letters, and Revelation

Chapters 51–53

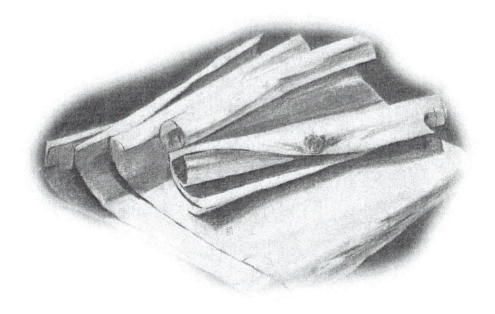

CHAPTER 51

Hebrews: Don't Give Up the Race

Despite the uncertainties of Hebrews' background, its basic message is clear enough: keep going, stay confident in Christ, remain faithful, do not drift away.

A great deal of mystery surrounds the book known as the Epistle to the Hebrews. We do not know the identity of its author, where it was written, or to whom it was sent. Without specific knowledge of the situation it addresses, Hebrews has been the playground of speculation. Scholars have suggested almost every conceivable situation to explain its unique mixture of imagery, without reaching any definite conclusion. Despite these uncertainties, the basic message of this early Christian sermon seems clear enough: keep going, stay confident in Christ, remain faithful, do not drift away.[1]

At a Glance

- Hebrews was probably a sermon sent to encourage a particular community to stay faithful to its Christian commitment.

- This community may have faced potential persecution and seems to have wavered at the prospect.

- The primary alternative to faith seems to be reliance in some way on the Old Testament sacrificial system for atonement.

- Hebrews proclaims that Christ is a high priest whose single offering in the true, heavenly sanctuary has definitively cleansed sin once and for all.

- Conversely, the Old Testament system of atonement was only a shadowy example of the reality provided by Christ.

The Bottom Line

Hebrews encourages its audience a number of times to remain true to its "confession" (Heb. 3:1; 4:14; 10:23). This letter may actually be referring to a specific Christian confession the believers made when they were baptized, something like "Jesus is the Son of God."[2] Whether or not it was a specific confession, however, it is clear that the author of Hebrews wishes his[3] audience to stay true to Christianity, to keep going, to lay aside anything that might hinder them from finishing the Christian race.

Hebrews is somewhat vague about what might have been hindering its original audience. Were they facing persecution? Were they beginning to doubt that Christ was really going to return to earth? Were certain Jews or Jewish Christians tugging at them in some way, perhaps denying that Jesus' death on the cross was enough to take away *all* their sins? Some even suggest that they simply had not matured as Christians and needed to move on to the next level in their understanding. These are all positions for which someone has argued at some time or another.

The bottom line, however, is that these believers were lacking confidence in their faith (e.g., Heb. 10:35). This lack of confidence seems to have involved questions about what was true, as well as some pressure they were experiencing from outside their community. As far as their questions about truth, they were wondering whether Christ's death was enough to take care of all their sins. At the same time, some element in their environment was raising the stakes of being a Christian. Perhaps persecution was looming on the horizon or perhaps they had become outcasts in the eyes of their families and friends. Whatever the specific context, the author of Hebrews affirms powerfully that they have something secure to trust in and that they can boldly approach God for help because of what Christ has done.

The Basic Story of Salvation

The basic point of Hebrews—keep going—appears throughout this early Christian sermon. Every so often the author will stop his argument and remind the audience of this "bottom line." The argument itself, however, is focused on the superiority of Christ. Throughout Hebrews the author shows the audience that what Christ has done is far superior to anything possible in the days of the **old covenant**—the Old Testament time when the Jewish Law was in force. If the audience's basic need was to have confidence, Hebrews meets this need by showing that what Christ did was something absolutely dependable, and that God guaranteed it with oaths and promises.

> **old covenant:** The arrangement between God and Israel made at Mt. Sinai; the Jewish Law.
>
> **new covenant:** The new arrangement between God and humanity through the blood of Christ.

The second chapter of Hebrews gives us a good overview of the whole story of salvation by way of Psalm 8. This psalm, as many early Christians understood it, indicates that God initially intended humanity to rule the earth. God's intention was for us to have "glory and honor" in His creation, for everything to be in submission to us (Heb. 2:6-8). Unfortunately, however, this was no longer the case (2:8). Presumably because of sin, we not only do not rule, we are slaves to death and to the one who holds power over death, the devil (2:14).

> "What is man that you should think of him, and the son of man that you should care for him? For a little while you made him lower than the angels, and you crowned him with glory and honor. You gave him authority over all things."
>
> **Hebrews 2:6-8, quoting Psalm 8:4-6**

According to Hebrews, Christ took on flesh and blood to defeat the power of the devil (Heb. 2:14-16). He became lower than the angels for a little while

Levitical priests: Priests who descended from Levi, one of the twelve sons of Jacob in the Old Testament.

tabernacle: The portable tent constructed by Moses in which sacrifices were offered in the period before Solomon built the temple.

Holy Place: The outer room of the Jewish tabernacle/temple (the Holies).

Most Holy Place: The inner room of the Jewish tabernacle/temple (the Holy of Holies) where the high priest offered a sacrifice on the Day of Atonement. The Ark of the Covenant was housed here.

Day of Atonement: The one day in the year when the high priest entered the Most Holy Place to atone for the sins the people had committed in ignorance that year; Yom Kippur.

(2:9), partook of the human experience with its temptations, yet did not sin (4:15). He became the sacrifice to end all sacrifices (10:14), a merciful and faithful high priest for God's people (2:17). Now He can lead us to the glory we were supposed to have in the first place (2:10).

With this basic story in mind, it is appropriate that Hebrews begins by celebrating Christ's superiority over the angels. While Christ's mission to save us required Him to become lower than the angels for a little while, He has now returned to heaven, and God has enthroned Him as king of the universe. Hebrews 1 is like an opening hymn that celebrates the fact that Christ has now made salvation possible. It reads like the announcement of the old newspaper salesperson standing on the corner shouting, "Extra, extra, read all about it!" Today's paper reads, "Christ accomplishes salvation—God exalts Him above the angels!"

Christ, the High Priest

As we mentioned in the previous section, the way Hebrews reinforces the confidence of the audience is by showing the superiority of Christ. By the time the author finishes his main argument, he has shown that Christ is greater than

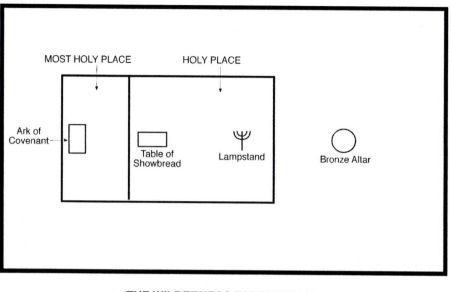

THE WILDERNESS TABERNACLE
Figure 5

angels, Moses, Old Testament priests, and Old Testament sacrifices—not to mention the fact that He has entered into a superior sanctuary. When we look closely at these individual contrasts, we see that they all connect to Hebrews' overall contrast between the old covenant (= the Jewish Law) and the **new covenant** brought about by Christ.

It is important to notice that Hebrews does not just argue that Christ is great in general. It argues that Christ has canceled and replaced the old covenant. Under the Jewish Law, atonement—the process of getting right with God by offering Him something—involved an endless number of animal sacrifices. Only certain priests were qualified to offer such sacrifices to God; namely, individuals who descended from Levi, one of the twelve sons of Jacob. They offered these sacrifices in a single, authorized location, which at the time of Moses was a portable tent, a sanctuary we sometimes call the wilderness **tabernacle**.

The Israelites worshiped God at this tabernacle while they wandered in the desert for forty years. The tabernacle had two basic chambers: an outer room called the **Holy Place** or the "Holies," and a smaller inner room, the **Most Holy Place** or the "Holy of Holies." Although priests from the tribe of Levi— **Levitical priests**—entered the outer chamber on a regular basis, only one priest was qualified to enter the innermost room of the tent (see **Figure 5**). This individual was the high priest, the highest office of priest, and he entered that room only once a year on the **Day of Atonement**.

Hebrews indicates that Christ is the decisive replacement of all these elements of the old covenant with its system of sacrifices. In fact, Hebrews argues that none of these things actually got you right with God even in the time of the Old Testament! They could not truly atone for sins; they could not "clean" them or take them away (Heb. 10:1, 4). According to Hebrews, the sacrificial system of the old covenant simply provided shadowy illustrations of what Christ eventually was to do for real (3:5; 8:5).

The fact that Hebrews reinforces the confidence of the audience in such a specific way—arguing for the superiority of Christ over the Jewish sacrificial system—makes us suspect that this sacrificial system in some way was part of their problem. In some way that Hebrews does not go into, the Jewish sacrificial system must have been the main competition to the audience's reliance on Christ. For this reason, some think the audience consisted of Jews who were tempted to return to mainstream Judaism. Or perhaps they were God-fearing Gentiles who had associated with Jewish synagogues before they accepted Christ. Whichever the case, the author of Hebrews found a way to argue that Christ is the reality behind every component of the old covenant.

Angels and Moses

Of all the contrasts Hebrews makes, the contrasts of Christ with angels (Hebrews 1) and with Moses (3:1-6) seem least related to the overall contrast between the old and new covenants. However, when we remember that Moses delivered the Jewish Law to Israel, we see that a contrast between Moses and Christ—the giver of a new law (8:6, 10; 10:16)—fits in well with the old/new covenant contrast. While Moses was a *servant* in God's house and his words were prophecies about Christ (3:5), Christ is God's *Son* (3:5-6).

Similarly, many Jews at the time of Christ believed that angels had brought the Law to Moses (Heb. 2:2; cf. Acts 7:38, 53; Gal. 3:19) and that they were its enforcers and guardians

> **mediator:** A go-between, an intercessor or arbitrator.

on the earth (cf. 1 Cor. 11:10; Col. 2:20-21). Like Moses, they were also *servants* of God (Heb. 1:7, 14), not a *Son* like Christ (1:5). Under the old covenant they served as God's ambassadors to the world, God's principal messengers and **mediators**—God's "go-betweens."

Now, Hebrews indicates, Christ has become the new mediator between God and humanity (Heb. 8:6). When the first chapter of Hebrews begins by showing that Christ is superior to the angels, it announces powerfully that salvation is now possible. Christ became lower than the angels for a little while (2:9) and offered the sacrifice to end all sacrifices (10:14). Now Christ has taken His place as *king* next to God in heaven, far superior to the servant angels of the old covenant (1:3-4).

Levitical Priests, Sacrifices, and Sanctuaries

Christians long before the time of Hebrews had considered Christ's death to be a kind of sacrifice (Rom. 3:25). Of course, a crucifixion was quite different from killing an animal and sprinkling its blood in a temple. A crucifixion was an act of capital punishment, putting someone to death. More recent forms of capital punishment have included electrocution, lethal injection, or hanging. At the time of Christ, the Romans crucified non-Roman criminals and enemies to make an example of them. They nailed such people to crosses and hoisted them up so everyone could see the shameful result of opposing the Romans and their laws.

From very early on, Christians began to see Christ's crucifixion *metaphorically* as a sacrifice. The normal or literal use of the word *sacrifice* was about offering animals in a temple or on an **altar**—usually a stone, table-like structure on which the animal was killed. People made offerings to a god to secure his or her good will or to atone for something that might have made the god angry. The early Christians saw Christ's death in this way—it was like a sacrifice that atoned for Israel's sins and thus would bring restoration to God's people.

altar: The structure on which an animal was killed as a sacrifice; usually a pile of stones or stone table of sorts, often in a temple.

However, Hebrews is the first Christian writing that clearly considers Christ not only a sacrifice, but a priest as well.[4] Again, this is a metaphor—the words are not being used in their normal, literal way. Try to picture Christ both as the one killing/sacrificing and as the one being killed/sacrificed. Hebrews creates this metaphor to show that Christ is the reality behind every aspect of the Old Testament system of atonement and sacrifices. The old covenant had priests, individuals from the tribe of Levi. Hebrews demonstrates that Christ is also a priest, but a far superior priest to any of the Old Testament priests.

Melchizedek: The first priest mentioned in the Old Testament. According to Hebrews, a "priest after the order of Melchizedek" is a priest who lives forever, yet who does not come from a priestly family—in other words, Christ.

Hebrews shows Christ's superiority by way of another priest mentioned in the Old Testament; in fact, the very first priest mentioned in the Bible. This priest's name was **Melchizedek**, and Genesis 14 tells how he blessed Abraham after a battle. Since he lived at the time of Abraham, he existed before the time of the Levitical priests. After all, Levi was Abraham's great-grandson. Hebrews argues that since Melchizedek was a priest to Abraham, he was a greater priest than any descendant of Levi could be (Heb. 7:4, 7, 9).

The main characteristic of a priest "after the order of Melchizekek" seems to be that he never dies (Heb. 7:3, 8, 16, 25). A great deal of debate has surrounded this figure in Hebrews. Is this an appearance of Christ in the Old Testament, a "Christophany"? Is he an angelic being, such as the figure mentioned in one of the Dead Sea Scrolls?[5] What makes it hard for us to understand Hebrews 7 is the fact that the author is using a method of Jewish interpretation that seems strange to us.

In asking what constitutes a priest like Melchizedek, Hebrews turns to Genesis 14 and focuses not so much on what the text says as what it does *not* say. For example, Genesis does not say that Melchizedek came from a priestly family, like the Levitical priests did (Heb. 7:3, 6). Genesis does not mention Melchizedek's death either. Therefore, Hebrews can conclude that a priest like Melchizedek does not have a priestly genealogy and does not die. Christ fits such a role perfectly.

Hebrews 7 now comes to its bottom line. The old covenant and the Jewish Law were founded on the system of sacrifices and atonement provided by Levitical priests (Heb. 7:11). If God turned from the Levitical priests to a priest like Melchizedek, Hebrews argues, then the entirety of the old covenant and its Law has been replaced (7:12). Thus, since Christ has arrived, the Old Testament sacrificial system has come to an end. While the blood of bulls and goats could not take away sin (10:4), Christ has offered His own blood through the eternal Spirit (7:24-25; 9:14), actually cleansing us.

For this extended metaphor to work, Christ not only must be a priest, He also must have a sanctuary in which to offer himself. Hebrews speaks of a *heavenly* tabernacle in which Christ offered himself—the model on which the earthly tabernacle was based (Heb. 8:5). A great deal of debate has also surrounded this heavenly sanctuary. Is it similar to what Plato called the ideal models behind the shadowy things in the world? Is it like the heavenly temples we read about in some Jewish literature, actual buildings up in heaven? Or is it the universe itself, with heaven as the Most Holy Place? This last option probably comes closest to what Hebrews is saying—Christ's entrance into heaven was like a high priest entering into the Most Holy Place on the Day of Atonement.

Hebrews is thus unique in the New Testament because not only does it consider Christ to be a priest, but it also considers Him to be a *high priest*. And while the New Testament elsewhere compares Jesus' death to the Passover sacrifice (e.g., 1 Cor. 5:7) or to a sacrifice in general (e.g., Col. 1:14), Hebrews is the only place where Christ's death is clearly compared to the sacrifice made on the Day of Atonement.[6] Just as that sacrifice was only offered once a year, Hebrews argues that Christ's sacrifice also was only offered once (Heb. 9:25-26). That one sacrifice has effectively done what no other sacrifice has ever done—it has taken away sins forever.

Following Good Examples

One of the ways in which Hebrews both encourages its audience to keep going and discourages them from turning away is by giving examples of each alternative. For instance, Abraham is a good example of someone who kept going even though he died before he saw his descendants inherit the land God had promised him (Heb. 11:8). Moses could

Hebrews is the only book in the New Testament to refer to Christ as a priest.

have enjoyed all the privileges of royalty in the palace of Pharaoh in Egypt, but he chose instead to be faithful to God and to suffer with God's people (11:25).

Hebrews 11 is filled with examples of individuals who faithfully kept going, even "without receiving what God had promised them" (11:13). They endured in faith, even though the things they were trusting God to fulfill were invisible to them.

> Hebrews 11 is the "faith chapter" of the New Testament.

Hebrews also provides its audience with scary examples of individuals who turned away from God. The most obvious are the Israelites who died in the desert after they escaped Egypt with Moses. These

> "What is faith? It is the confident assurance that what we hope for is going to happen. It is the evidence of things we cannot yet see."
> **Hebrews 11:1**

individuals had left Egypt under God's protection; they had been given the assurance that they would enter the Promised Land (Heb. 3:16). But in the end they did not make it due to of their lack of faith (3:19). Hebrews' audience did not miss the point. You have become Christians all right, and God has extended to you the promise of entering into His rest at that heavenly city (4:2; 11:16; 12:22). But if you abandon your faith, God will judge you just as He judged them.

Hebrews notes several times the possibility of becoming a Christian and yet not making it to the end (e.g., Heb. 3:14; 6:4-8; 10:26-27; 12:16-17). In fact, Hebrews seems to teach that once you have crossed a certain line, it is even impossible to return. Christians of all denominations find it hard

> "Therefore, since we are surrounded by such a huge crowd of witnesses to the life of faith, let us strip off every weight that slows us down, especially the sin that so easily hinders our progress. And let us run with endurance the race that God has set before us. We do this by keeping our eyes on Jesus, on whom our faith depends from start to finish."
> **Hebrews 12:1-2**

to accept this teaching. For some, the idea that you could "lose" your salvation is unacceptable. For others, the idea that you cannot return after losing it is unacceptable. Whatever our interpretation of Hebrews, we can take comfort in the fact that mainstream Christianity has always affirmed that anyone who wants to come to Christ can—whether for the first, second, or fiftieth time. It is not just any sin in general that the audience of Hebrews was in danger of committing; they were in danger of publicly shaming Christ by rejecting Him and the atonement He has provided.

"For it is impossible to restore to repentance those who were once enlightened . . . and who then turn away from God. It is impossible to bring such people to repentance again because they are nailing the Son of God to the cross again by rejecting him, holding him up to public shame."

Hebrews 6:4, 6

The Who's, When's, and Where's of Hebrews

We mentioned at the beginning of this chapter that Hebrews provides much fuel for guessing games. Who was its author? To whom was it sent? We simply do not have enough information to answer questions like these with certainty.

The church accepted for over a thousand years that Paul had written Hebrews, although almost no scholar would argue for Paul today. Hebrews' style is quite different from anything we see in Paul's writings. Some key words in Hebrews are also used differently than Paul would have used them. When Paul talks about the Law, he largely refers to things like circumcision and dietary laws; Hebrews almost exclusively refers to the Law's sacrificial system.[7] When Paul talks about faith, he generally means trust; Hebrews speaks primarily of faithfulness. One of the strongest arguments against Paul as author is the fact that Paul likely would not have said that he heard Christ's message of salvation from the apostles (Heb. 2:3), as if he were not an apostle who had seen and heard from the Lord himself!

Although the church probably accepted Hebrews into the Bible because it finally agreed on Paul as its author, other names had been suggested earlier, like Barnabas. In the end, an early Christian named Origen put it best when he wrote, "Who the author is, God knows." While the author probably knew Paul and may have been in his circle of ministers, it is unlikely that any new evidence will surface to settle this question once and for all.

The fact that the author was with some Italians and that he included them in his greetings to the recipients of this letter or sermon might provide us with a little more basis for guessing this sermon's destination, but not much more (Heb. 13:24). It could mean the author was writing from somewhere in Italy and those with him sent greetings to the audience, or it could mean that the author was writing back to Italy from somewhere else. The fact that Timothy had been in prison nearby could indicate the sermon was written from Asia Minor, perhaps Ephesus (13:23). The letter is first quoted from Rome, which might tip the scales in favor of Italy as the destination.[8] Once again, we simply do not know for sure.

A man named Clement quoted Hebrews in the late A.D. 90s, so it must have been written before then. The mention of leaders who apparently had died may indicate a time after Peter and Paul were put to death in Rome in the mid-60s A.D. (Heb. 13:7). Scholars are divided over whether Hebrews was written before or after the Jerusalem temple was destroyed. Hebrews refers to the offering of sacrifices in the present tense (e.g., 9:9; 10:2), but never refers to the temple in Jerusalem. Other Jewish authors after A.D. 70 write in the present tense about offering sacrifices, making it difficult to pin a date regarding the comments in Hebrews. Overall, our opinion is that the flavor of Hebrews better fits the period after the temple was destroyed than before, but it is difficult to conclude for certain.

Things to Think About

1. What strategy does Hebrews use to demonstrate that Christ has replaced the entirety of the Old Testament sacrificial system?

2. Do you think Hebrews goes one step further in its understanding of the significance of Christ's death than do the writings of Paul and the rest of the New Testament? Does the author of Hebrews differ in his understanding or does he have the same understanding but just expresses it in different imagery?

Key Terms

altar

Day of Atonement

Holy Place

Levitical priests

mediator

Melchizedek

Most Holy Place

new covenant

old covenant

tabernacle

3. Do you think it is possible to "lose your salvation," that is, to go from being "saved" to "unsaved"? Why or why not?

endnotes

1. Hebrews calls itself a "word of exhortation" in 13:22 (NIV), a phrase used in Acts 13:15 of a short sermon. However, Hebrews 13 indicates that this sermon was sent somewhere other than where the author was located. We might think of Hebrews thus as both a sermon and a letter.

2. Cf. 1:2, 5-6; 3:6; 4:14; 5:5, 8; 7:28.

3. Although we cannot see it in English, the author refers to himself as a male in the Greek of Hebrews 11:32. Therefore, it is almost certain that the author was a man.

4. Romans 8:34 may hint that the idea was around before Hebrews was written.

5. The document known as 11QMelchizedek.

6. Romans 3:25 may imply that Jesus was a sacrifice like the sacrifice offered on the Day of Atonement.

7. Acts 21:24 also indicates that Paul offered a sacrifice in the Jewish temple—something the author of Hebrews probably would have strongly advised a Christian against doing.

8. In 1 Clement, ca. A.D. 96.

CHAPTER 52

James, 1 and 2 Peter, 1-2-3 John, Jude: The General Letters

The General Epistles are a group of miscellaneous writings by important early church figures like James, Peter, and John.

Introduction

The letters mentioned in the title of this chapter are often called the *General* or *Catholic* Epistles because they seem to address much broader audiences than those of Paul's letters. In this context, the word **catholic** means "universal," implying that these letters were addressed to everyone, not just to specific churches. Of all the books in the New Testament, the church debated most vigorously over these when it was working out what writings should be included in the canon.

However, most of these letters do not have universal audiences in view. According to one interpretation, James was

At a Glance

- The books of James, 1 and 2 Peter, 1-2-3 John, and Jude are called **General Epistles** because they address broader audiences than Paul's letters do.

- James deals with the temptation to rely on the rich and on earthly things. This letter affirms that God is our only legitimate patron.

- First Peter addresses Christian suffering. It encourages its audience to be holy and to exercise respectable conduct on earth.

- Second Peter addresses skeptics who question whether Christ is going to return again.

- First John encourages a community that has lost a significant number of members.

- Second and 3 John address a fellow church and a man named Gaius, encouraging them.

- Jude addresses false teaching and heresy.

catholic: Universal, relating to all people everywhere.

addressed to "Jewish Christians scattered among the nations" (James 1:1). First Peter addressed "exiles of the Dispersion in Pontus, Galatia, Cappadocia, Asia, and Bithynia" (1:1 NRSV)—perhaps referring to individuals the Romans had literally sent into exile from Rome. Third John is written to a single individual, a man named Gaius (3 John 1:1). In the end, the General Epistles are really a group of miscellaneous writings authored by important figures in the early church. If for no other reason, they fit together because they do not go with any other group of writings in the New Testament.

James: Who Is Your Real Boss?

At first glance, the book of James appears to be a collection of loosely related advice to a Jewish Christian audience. If we look a little more closely, we see that most of its teaching relates to the fact that "every good and perfect gift is from above, coming down from the Father of the heavenly lights" (James 1:17 NIV). Because God is the true source of everything we need, we should not rely on the rich. James reads like instructions to various Christians, telling them to have their priorities in order.

One of the reasons we might not see how James' teachings fit together is because the world of James was structured around the relationships of *patrons* to *clients*.[1] Patrons were the "haves" of that world and clients the "have nots." As such it was customary for the "haves" to supply some of the basic needs of the "have nots." In return, the "have nots" showered the "haves" with praise and honor. In this way clients received their basic needs while patrons gained prestige and glory through their generosity. We will probably fail to understand New Testament words like *grace* and *gift* unless we know a little something about patron-client relationships in the ancient world.

When we look at James from this perspective, we can see that it primarily addresses the matter of who should be our "patrons" and "clients." Clearly God is the one on whom we are to depend, in contrast to the rich and their reliance on the world. On the other hand, the poor and downtrodden are those to whom we should show favor.

> "Look here, you rich people, weep and groan with anguish because of all the terrible troubles ahead of you ...You have spent your years on earth in luxury, satisfying your every whim. Now your hearts are nice and fat, ready for the slaughter."
>
> **James 5:1, 5**

When we have priorities like these, we will likely face trials and hardships from the rich (e.g., James 1:2; 2:6-7). It is hard to be teachers and leaders under such circumstances (cf. 3:1). But God promises wisdom to the person who remains resolved and committed to the right priorities (1:5; 3:17).

The Rich

The New Testament has almost nothing good to say about money. In a world where goods more than money were exchanged, those who relied on money were often seen as greedy and selfish. As the Arab proverb goes, "Every rich man is either a thief or the son of a thief." Further, we mentioned earlier in chapter 10 that the ancients thought in terms of a limited amount of good in the world. When you look at possessions from this perspective, the only way to gain is to take from someone else.

It is no surprise, therefore, that the New Testament virtually equates wealth with sin and evil. James is no different: "They [the rich] will fade away like a flower in the field" (James 1:10). James presents a hypothetical situation in which two men come into a synagogue, one who is rich and one who is poor (2:2). The temptation, James indicates, is to give the rich man the finest seat and make the poor man stand. To do so, however, would be wrong. James asks, "Isn't it the rich who oppress you and drag you into court?" (2:6).

James probably has temptations like these in mind when he says that God never tempts us (James 1:13). Such temptations, James says, come from "the lure of our own evil desires" (1:14). The focus of such desires is clearly possessions and "worldly" gain. "You want only what will give you pleasure" (4:3). "You are jealous for what others have, and you can't possess it, so you fight and quarrel to take it away from them" (4:2). In contrast, James encourages his audience to "humble yourselves before God" (James 4:7). "Resist the Devil, and he will flee from you. Draw close to God, and God will draw close to you" (4:7-8). The bottom line is that "friendship with this world makes you an enemy of God" (4:4).

The Poor

Back in the 1500s, the father of Protestantism, Martin Luther, called James "an epistle of straw." He did so not only because it says very little about Christ, but also because it appears to indicate that good deeds are necessary to be acceptable to God. Since Luther interpreted Romans to mean that we become acceptable to God *by faith alone*, he did not like James. In fact, he did not even translate it into German at first. His interpretation of Paul hardly fit together well with statements like James 2:24: "We are made right with God by what we do, not by faith alone."

It is difficult for many to read James and Paul's writings without concluding that these two men flatly disagreed with each other. James says we are made right with God by what we do, our "works," in addition to our faith. In contrast, Paul says that "people are declared righteous because of their faith, not because of their work" (Rom. 4:5). Indeed, both men use the same Scripture to draw opposite conclusions. Genesis 15:6 says that "Abram believed the Lord, and the Lord declared him righteous because of his faith." For Paul this verse means that we get right with God by faith (e.g., Rom. 4:3;

Gal. 3:6). For James it is the fact that Abraham *did* the right thing when God told him to sacrifice Isaac (James 2:23), not some abstract faith that did not show itself in his actions.

In the end, we probably take both Paul and James out of context when we read Luther's debate into their words. For example, Paul's argument is not primarily about whether good deeds in general can get us right with God, whether we can *earn* our salvation. Rather, it is keeping the *Jewish Law* that Paul says cannot make anyone right with God (Rom. 3:20).[2]

Further, Paul never teaches that it is acceptable for a Christian simply to believe and never produce any "fruit" in his or her life (cf. Gal. 5:22-23). In fact, Paul indicates he could be "disqualified" at the end of the race if he did not conduct himself appropriately (1 Cor. 9:27). If it is necessary for Paul to live a certain way in order to attain salvation in the end, then even he believes "works" of a sort to be involved in salvation. He is thus not really that far from James when James says, "Faith is dead without good deeds" (James 2:26).

We probably get James' comments out of focus as well when we read them in this way. In its broader context, James is concerned with the person who thinks only of increasing his possessions and does nothing to benefit those who are truly in need. The rich person says, "Today or tomorrow we are going to a certain town and will stay there a year. We will do business there and make a profit" (James 4:13). Such a person thinks s/he is in control of his or her own fate and does not give God His proper place. Such a person claims to have faith, but that individual's life does not show it.

James soundly rebukes such a person. "You believe that there is one God. Good! Even the demons believe that—and shudder" (2:19 NIV). On the other hand, "Pure and lasting religion in the sight of God our Father means that we must care for orphans and widows in their troubles, and refuse to let the world corrupt us" (James 1:27). The true concern of an individual submitted to God is not accruing possessions or staying on good terms with the rich. The proper

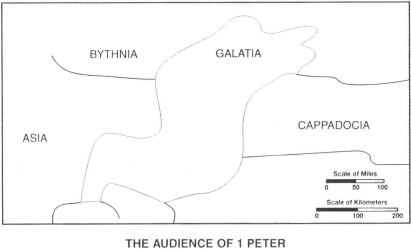

THE AUDIENCE OF 1 PETER
MAP 13

concern is with the poor and downtrodden of the world. "Christians who are poor should be glad, for God has honored them" (James 1:9).

James in Context

Although the author of James does not clearly identify himself, it seems almost certain that he was the half brother of Jesus (cf. Mark 6:3). This James became the leader of the church in Jerusalem (cf. Acts 15:13, 21:18) until he was martyred (put to death) in A.D. 62. The flavor of this book fits very well with the Jewish Christianity of which James was a part. If this James wrote it, we should probably date it sometime in the A.D. 50s.

1 Peter: Christians and Suffering

Like James, 1 Peter also addresses an audience that is suffering in some way. "Don't be surprised at the fiery trials you are going through," Peter says (1 Pet. 4:12). He thinks of their sufferings as the beginning of God's judgment on the earth: "For the time has come for judgment, and it must begin first among God's own children. And if even we Christians must be judged, what terrible fate awaits those who have never believed God's Good News?" (4:17). The bottom line is to "keep on doing what is right, and trust yourself to the God who made you, for he will never fail you" (4:19).

Because 1 Peter was written in the context of persecution and suffering, it is no surprise that it seems somewhat defensive in nature—it encourages Christians to live in ways that most ancients thought were respectable. When someone is watching you closely, just waiting for an excuse to pounce on you, you try to do the kinds of things that will keep you from being pounced on. Accordingly, 1 Peter encourages Christians to live in an orderly, respectable way. Christians were to "live such good lives among the pagans that, though they accuse you of doing wrong, they may see your good deeds and glorify God on the day he visits us" (1 Pet. 2:12 NIV).

The Living Hope

First Peter has the same fervent expectation that Christ's return was near that Paul's writings have in general (e.g., 1 Pet. 4:7; cf. Phil. 4:5), although the fact that the audience was suffering heightened the hope that He would return soon. It is no surprise that, like Hebrews, Peter encourages his audience to think of themselves as "foreigners and aliens" on the earth (2:11; cf. Heb. 11:13), individuals who

> "If you are asked about your Christian hope, always be ready to explain it."
>
> **1 Peter 3:15**

do not really belong down here. Rather, our inheritance is in heaven, and we are just waiting down here for our salvation—our escape will appear when Jesus is revealed on earth for a second time (1 Pet. 1:4-9).

Nevertheless, the audience had been **born again,** this time by God's word.

If they drank the milk from this word, they would grow up to have salvation (1 Pet. 2:2).[3] God **redeemed** us, paid for our freedom, by way of Christ's blood (1:19). "He [Jesus] personally carried away our sins in his own body on the cross so we can be dead to sin and live for what is right" (2:24). As a result, Christians were to "be **holy** in everything you do, just as God . . . is holy" (1:15). We are to act as if we belong to God, which means we must not "slip back" into our "old ways of doing evil" (1:14).

First Peter presents us with some unique images of Christians as a "holy priesthood" (1 Pet. 2:5 NIV). We are a "spiritual house," Peter says (2:5), with Christ as the cornerstone (2:6-7; cf. Eph. 2:20). Peter redefines God's people in terms of Christians in general, not just Jews. The Gentile Christians of the audience were a "holy nation" of a new sort (2:9-10). Martin Luther used some of these verses to speak of a **priesthood of all believers**, the notion that all Christians are priests, not just specific individuals. While 1 Peter does not really address such issues directly, it does indicate that all Christians are priests who offer spiritual sacrifices to God.

Submit to the Proper Authority

After Peter tells his audience to live model lives for non-Christians to see, he gives a number of examples of what that might mean. For example, he encourages Christians to submit to Caesar and his governors (1 Pet. 2:13-17). He tells slaves to submit to their masters—even those who are harsh (2:18)— giving Christ as an example of someone who suffered undeservingly (2:21). He says that wives should submit to their husbands "in the same way" (3:1)— they should call their husbands "master," as Sarah did to Abraham (3:6). Husbands were encouraged to be considerate of their wives as the "weaker partner" (3:7).

It is in passages like these that we see clearly how connected 1 Peter is to its context in the ancient world. If we followed these words without considering ancient culture and the defensive position in which Peter's audience finds itself, we would have to say that the American Revolution was immoral and that we had no real basis for abolishing slavery in America. Still closer to home is the implication that wives whose husbands abuse them are to submit to them so they will be "won over by watching your pure, godly behavior" (1 Pet. 3:2). God's Spirit has rightly led the church to recognize that these verses should not be applied in these ways today.[4]

redemption: A payment made to set someone free in some way.

born again: A phrase used by many Christians to refer to becoming a Christian; used in 1 Peter to speak of the spiritual birth of a believer.

holy: Belonging to God, often with the sense that such a person lives appropriately.

priesthood of all believers: Martin Luther's teaching that all Christians are priests, not just particular individuals ordained by the church.

Yet the principles of mutual respect and submission to authority are certainly things we should continue to encourage. Peter tells his audience, "Humble yourselves under the mighty power of God . . . Give all your worries and cares to God, for he cares about what happens to you" (1 Pet. 5:6-7). They are to "be of one mind, full of sympathy toward each other, loving one another with tender hearts and humble minds. Don't repay evil for evil. Don't retaliate when people say unkind things about you. Instead, pay them back with a blessing" (3:8-9). Here are instructions that relate to the very core of Christian values.

The Who's, When's, Where's of 1 Peter

The traditional understanding of 1 Peter flows rather easily from the text. The apostle *Peter* identifies himself in the first line and mentions in 5:1 that he witnessed Christ's death. *Rome* was the most likely place from which Peter wrote, since he says in 5:13 (although not in the NLT) that the church in "Babylon" greets the audience. It is very likely that "Babylon" here is a nickname for Rome, both because we have no reason to believe Peter ever traveled so far east to the site of Babylon and because we know some Jews referred to Rome as "Babylon." Like Babylon, Rome destroyed Jerusalem and its temple.

The audience of 1 Peter was made up of "God's chosen people who are living as foreigners in the lands of Pontus, Galatia, Cappadocia, the province of Asia, and Bithynia" (1 Pet. 1:1). All these places are in Asia Minor, modern-day Turkey. [See **Map 13**.] At least one scholar has argued that these individuals were literally exiled from Rome, taking the word "foreigners" in its more literal sense, "exiles" (e.g., NRSV).[5] Since Peter apparently wrote it from Rome in a time of persecution, the mid-60s seems an appropriate date for the letter. According to tradition, Peter was crucified upside down in Rome during the reign of Nero.

Some scholars have argued that 1 Peter is pseudonymous. The fact that the letter is written in good Greek is not relevant. Although Peter the Galilean fisherman probably could not have composed such good Greek, the Greek-speaking Silas—whom 1 Peter 5:12 tells us was Peter's amanuensis in writing the letter—no doubt could have. We should look to Silas thus as the one who actually composed most of the words of 1 Peter.

The strongest argument that 1 Peter is pseudonymous comes from the reference to Rome as "Babylon." If Jews called Rome "Babylon" mainly because Rome had destroyed Jerusalem, the letter would have to date from after A.D. 70 when Jerusalem was destroyed. Peter died several years before this event. If pseudonymous, this letter was written at some point after Peter's death to encourage Christians who were suffering. The author would have used Peter, therefore, as an appropriate voice to address such individuals, since Peter had died as a martyr to the faith. On the other hand, it is certainly possible that

Jews referred to Rome as Babylon even before Jerusalem was destroyed. If this was the case, then we have no significant reason to think the author is anyone other than Peter.

2 Peter: The Lord Is Not Slow

Second Peter has a number of interesting features. For example, Peter draws most of 2 Peter 2 from the book of Jude. Second Peter is the only New Testament book to refer explicitly to New Testament writings by other authors. Not only does it refer to a collection of Paul's letters, but it considers them to be Scripture—the first reference we have to a New Testament book as Scripture (2 Pet. 3:15-16). Second Peter alone speaks of the destruction of the world by fire (3:10), although Hebrews may imply this end as well (Heb. 12:29). Because of these unique features, this short book of only three chapters has much to offer us.

The main focus of 2 Peter seems to be on false teaching, particularly with regard to the future judgment of the world.[6] As we have seen a number of times in the preceding chapters, the earliest Christians generally expected Christ to return to earth in the near future. Even 1 Peter mentions that the coming of the Lord is near (1 Pet. 4:7). Second Peter indicates that some had begun to doubt whether Christ was ever going to come back and if there really was going to be a judgment of the earth. "Jesus promised to come back, did he?" they scoffed. "Then where is he? Why, as far back as anyone can remember, everything has remained exactly the same" (2 Pet. 3:4).

In response Peter reminds his audience that "a day is like a thousand years to the Lord" (2 Pet. 3:8). "The Lord isn't really being slow about his promise to return, as some people think" (3:9). Rather, Peter indicates that God is being patient so that as many as possible could be saved—"he is giving more time for everyone to repent" (3:9). Assuredly, though, He would come, "as unexpectedly as a thief" (3:10). On that day, "the heavens will pass away with a terrible noise, and everything in them will disappear in fire" (3:10). "The elements will melt away in the flames" (3:12).

Chapter 47 of this text discusses the question of 2 Peter's authorship, so we will not address it here. The majority of conservative scholars affirm Peter as its author. As such they would date it to the late A.D. 60s. The majority of scholars in general believe it is pseudonymous, perhaps even the last book of the New Testament written. These individuals would date it sometime in the early second century (the A.D. 100s).

1, 2, 3 John

1 John

Although the Gospel of John and 1-2-3 John are all technically anonymous, they share enough in common to suggest that they come from a common source.[7] For example, compare 1 John 4:9 to John 3:16 in the text box on the next page. Both share an emphasis on believing in Jesus as the Christ (e.g., 1 John 5:1; John 20:31), and both emphasize that the consequence of such belief is eternal life (e.g., 1 John 5:13; John 3:16). While the other authors of New Testament books probably agree with John on this issue, none of them put it quite this way. It is thus reasonable to assume that the Gospel of John and 1-2-3 John all come from the same basic community and that the same authority figure stands behind all four documents.[8]

The Situation

First John gives us several hints about the situation it addresses. It mentions that a number of individuals have departed from John's community.[9]

[See **Map 14**.] "They went out from us, but they did not really belong to us. For if they had belonged to us, they would have remained with us" (1 John 2:19 NIV). The reason John gives for their departure is that they did not believe that Jesus was the Christ (2:22).

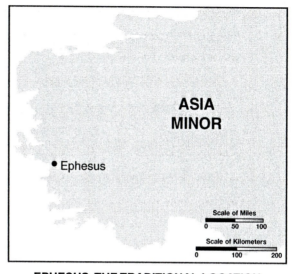

EPHESUS, THE TRADITIONAL LOCATION
OF JOHN'S COMMUNITY
MAP 14

It seems fairly likely, however, that they did believe Jesus was the Christ in some way—just not in a way that John found acceptable. If they had not at least been Christians in some sense, it is hard to explain why they would have joined with John in the first place. It is important, therefore, to look a little more closely at what John means when he says that Jesus is the Christ.

First, to John it is very important for someone to believe that Christ had truly been human. According to John, anyone who does not

"God showed how much he loved us by sending his only Son into the world so that we might have eternal life through him."

1 John 4:9

"For God so loved the world that he gave his only Son, so that everyone who believes in him will not perish but have eternal life."

John 3:16

believe that "Jesus Christ has come *in the flesh*" (1 John 4:2 NIV) is an antichrist. The gospel reflects this same concern when it says, "The Word *became flesh* and made his dwelling among us" (John 1:14 NIV). Related to this concern is the stress 1 John 5:6 puts not only on believing that Christ came "by water"—presumably that Jesus was Christ at His baptism—but also "by blood," that the Christ shed His blood on the cross.

Many scholars see similarities between what John was combating and what another Christian named Ignatius challenged in the early second century (A.D. 100s). Ignatius said, for example, "What benefit does someone bring me if he praise me and blaspheme my Lord by not acknowledging that he wore flesh?"[10] and, "He suffered all these things for us . . . not as some unbelievers say—that he *seemed* to suffer."[11] Indeed, when writing to Ephesus, the traditional location of John's community, Ignatius mentioned that some individuals with evil teaching had stayed there for a while (cf. 2 John 10). He commended the Ephesians for the fact that they did not listen to such individuals.[12]

We had occasion in some earlier chapters to mention the second-century movement known as Gnosticism. In Gnostic belief, matter is evil and spirit is good. Therefore, salvation is a matter of freeing our spirits from our bodies so they can soar to the spiritual realm. This salvation comes by way of true knowledge and wisdom. While Gnosticism did not become a fully developed movement until the second century (A.D. 100s), we see some of these ideas in the first century in much more basic forms. At various times scholars have suggested that some kind of "proto-Gnosticism" could have been behind the false teachings at Colossae, or in the Pastoral Epistles, or even at Corinth.

Two early forms of Gnostic teaching that are frequently mentioned when discussing 1 John are Docetism and the teachings of **Cerinthus**. Docetism was the heresy that Ignatius addressed in the quotes above. The word *Docetist* comes from a Greek word that means "to seem" (*dokeo*)—a name given to the Docetists because they believed that Jesus had only *seemed* to have flesh. Because they believed that flesh was evil, they did not accept the idea that Christ had truly taken on flesh.

Cerinthus was also one of the earliest Gnostics. A Christian named Irenaeus passed on a story that John had refused to bathe at the same bathhouse as this man because of his false teaching.[13] Cerinthus made a sharp distinction between the human, fleshly Jesus and what he thought of as the spiritual "Christ." He taught that the spiritual Christ had descended on Jesus at His baptism but had left Him before He suffered on the cross.

Cerinthus: An early Gnostic who believed that the spirit-being Christ had descended on the human Jesus at His baptism and that Christ did not really die on the cross. Rather, Jesus cleverly changed places with Simon of Cyrene, who was carrying the cross for Him. Simon, not Jesus, died on the cross.

It is reasonable to think that the "antichrists" of 1 John believed something similar to what Cerinthus or the Docetists taught, although it is hard to be completely certain. Cerinthus held a number of strange beliefs that 1 John says nothing about. Docetism seems to have had a strong Jewish element that we also hear nothing of in 1 John. What we know is that these false teachers did not believe that Christ had taken on flesh, and they did not think that they needed His death to cover their sins (cf. 1 John 1:8-10). They seem to have departed from John's community with a spirit of hatred toward those who disagreed with them (cf. 2:9-10).

The Message

The key claim with which 1 John leads off is the statement that "God is light and there is no darkness in him at all" (1 John 1:5). First John has one of the strongest statements about Christians and sin to be found in the New Testament: "Those who have been born into God's family do not sin, because God's life is in them. So they can't keep on sinning, because they have been born of God" (3:9). One of 1 John's main points is to urge its audience not to sin. As 1 John 2:1 says, "My dear children, I am writing this to you so that you will not sin."

However, it is important that we know just exactly how John defines sin. On the one hand, he gives us two general definitions: "All sin opposes the law of God" (1 John 3:4) and "Every wrong is sin" (5:17). But if we really want to understand what the heart of sin is to John, we will have to look at his repeated command to love one another. For John, as for the rest of the New Testament, love sums up everything that God requires of us.

The "new" command John gives in this letter/sermon is the "old" command that Jesus also gave and lived while He was on earth—"love your brother" (1 John 2:5-10). Those who left the community did not love their brothers—they were like Cain who killed his brother (3:12). Those who were in the light, on the other hand, were like Jesus, who laid down His life for us (3:16). Those who left loved the world (2:15). They were the sort of people who do not help their brothers and sisters in need (3:17). One of the best-known passages in 1 John sums it up nicely: "Dear friends, let us continue to love one another, for love comes from God. Anyone who loves is born of God and knows God. But anyone who does not love does not know God—for God is love" (4:7-8).

First John gives us many statements that can become skewed if we do not think of them in context. John's repeated commands to love surely relate to the fact that some had just left the church in a most unloving way. John's words against sinning thus were his pleas for Christians not to act like some so-called Christians had just acted. His commands were not so much abstract theological statements about Christians and sin; they come out of the divisive conflict from which his community had just emerged.

Similarly, some Christians ironically have taken John's comments about *having* sin in a way that actually contradicts John's overall message. First John 1:8 says, "If we say we have no sin, we are only fooling ourselves and refusing to accept the truth." First John 1:10 also says, "If we claim we have not sinned, we are calling God a liar." John would be shocked to know that some Christians think these verses teach that we cannot help but sin every day in word, thought, and deed—exactly the opposite point he was making in his overall message!

The false teachers who left John's community did not believe that Christ had come in the flesh or had suffered on the cross. They did not believe that Christ had come "by blood" (1 John 5:6). Therefore, they did not think they needed the atoning death of Jesus to make them acceptable to God. It was as if they were saying they "had" no sin for Christ to cleanse.

Far from affirming that all Christians continue to sin, 1 John 1:8 and 10 relate to individuals who did not believe they needed Christ's atoning death— they thought they had no sin for Him to cleanse. First John certainly does not teach that Christians are helpless against sinning. On the contrary, John's desire is that those who have already trusted in Christ will *not continue* sinning (2:1; 3:9). "But if you do sin, there is someone to plead for you before the Father. He is Jesus Christ, the one who pleases God completely. He is the sacrifice for our sins" (2:1-2).

2 John

Second John is a short letter addressed to "the chosen lady and to her children" (1). While some take this lady to be some unknown female, it seems more likely that John is addressing a sister church.[14] Once again, the author does not give his name, although he does refer to himself as "the elder," a title that may be significant for figuring out the identity of the author.

Much in 2 John is similar to the message of 1 John. For example, it mentions the "new" command that we had from the beginning, to "love one another" (2 John 5; cf. 1 John 2:7-10). It warns against false teachers who do not believe Christ came in the flesh and calls such a person an antichrist (2 John 7; cf. 1 John 4:2-3).

However, some scholars believe that 2 John was written before such individuals had fully left the communities under John's influence and, thus, that 2 John was written *before* 1 John (see 2 John 10). Second John gives us the impression that these individuals were traveling teachers who went from place to place. With such little information to go on, it is difficult to know for sure.[15]

3 John

Third John is a personal letter from John the elder to an individual named Gaius, although once again the letter is technically anonymous. While some have suggested that false teaching is still the problem, the letter is far from clear on this. More important, John writes to encourage Gaius to receive into his home individuals that John had sent, "even though they are strangers to you" (3 John 5).[16] This letter urges hospitality (8) toward traveling teachers who receive no help from non-Christians, but rely on Christians alone for their food and living (7).

Apparently, a man named Diotrephes rejected these traveling teachers and the authority of John himself (9). It is not clear that he rejected them because he disagreed with their teaching, although this is possible. More likely, he saw himself as the leader of his church and believed that John and these teachers were intruding on his authority. Many think that 3 John was written at a time when single, authoritative men were increasingly becoming the leaders of individual churches. In the early 100s, the Christian Ignatius wrote, "Clearly we must consider the bishop to be like Christ himself."[17] Perhaps we are seeing in 3 John the growing conflict at the turn of the century between traveling teachers/prophets and local church leadership.

Who was John?

Since the earliest centuries of the church, Christian tradition has held that the Gospel of John and the three letters we call 1, 2, and 3 John all come from John the apostle, the son of Zebedee, the beloved disciple of John 13:23. Unfortunately, none of these letters actually name John as the author. The only clues we have are the mention of the "beloved disciple" in the gospel and the fact that he calls himself "the elder" in 2 and 3 John. Nevertheless, the strength of early Christian tradition is enough for some to affirm that the author is John, the son of Zebedee.

On the other hand, a good case can be made that the author is another John who had also been a follower of Jesus, just not one of the twelve core disciples. For example, there is the fact that Jesus seems to prophesy the martyrdom of John, the son of Zebedee in Mark 10:38-39. The author of John, on the other hand, seems to have died of old age (John 21:22-23). The use of the term "the beloved disciple" in and of itself is somewhat curious in the gospel, especially since the sons of Zebedee are mentioned in John 21:2. It is almost as if the gospel is deliberately ambiguous about who this beloved disciple was.

The matter gets even cloudier when we realize that Jesus had more than one follower named John. The Christian Papias, writing in the early 100s, mentioned not only John the apostle, but also someone he called John *the elder*. The fact that John actually identifies himself in 2 and 3 John as "the elder" makes this possibility particularly enticing. The Christian Eusebius, writing in the early 300s, noted the differences in style between the Gospel of John and the book of Revelation and brought up the two individuals named John we have just mentioned. Although he preferred to think of the apostle as the author of the Gospel (he did not like Revelation), he suggested that John the elder had written 2 or 3 John.[18] Perhaps he was correct.

Jude

The short book of Jude is directed against individuals who were teaching false things in the church. These individuals were participating in the activities of the church—they had "wormed their way in among you" (Jude 4). They "join you in fellowship meals celebrating the love of the Lord," perhaps a reference to *communion* or the *Eucharist*, but they spoiled these meals (12). In fact, they seemed to try to "shepherd" the churches, perhaps meaning that they claimed to have authority (12). Perhaps they were traveling teachers similar to the ones we saw in 1 and 2 John. Maybe they were the false teachers mentioned in 1 Timothy.

In contrast to them, Jude encourages his audience to "contend for the faith that was once for all entrusted to the saints" (Jude 3 NIV). These individuals apparently had "evil desires" (16 NIV) and used the idea of God's grace as an excuse for immorality (4), perhaps of a sexual kind (7). One curious aspect of their belief involved slandering angelic beings in some way (8).

A number of Jude's features are interesting. First, there is the name Jude itself. Jude tells us that he is "a brother of James." Most likely, he is telling us that he is the brother of James, the leader of the Jerusalem church, and thus the half brother of Jesus himself (cf. Mark 6:3). It is also interesting that 2 Peter seems to have used almost all of Jude in the composition of its second chapter, although we should not conclude from this fact that the false teaching it addresses is the same as what Jude attacks.

One of the most interesting things about Jude is the way it seems to quote non-biblical writings as authoritative. It seems to treat as history a story told in a writing known as the Assumption of Moses. It also quotes a book known as 1 Enoch, whose various parts were written over the period from about 200 B.C. to the first century A.D. Not only does it seem to quote Enoch as Scripture, but it also treats Enoch's words as if Enoch really said them. At the very least this shows us that we can find truth anywhere. It may also affirm to us that

God reveals truth to us from within what we understand—He does not always correct us on the details.

Things to Think About

Key Terms

born again
catholic
Cerinthus
holy
priesthood of all believers
redemption

1. What is the "bottom line" for each of the General Epistles? Write a sentence or two summarizing each one.

2. How well do you think the ancient patron-client system or the concept of limited good helps us to better understand the message of the New Testament?

3. First Peter advocates submission to oppression rather than civil disobedience or social reform. When we can actually have an impact on our society and social structures, do you think God would still advocate passive submission?

4. Why do you think God has allowed 2,000 years to pass without sending Christ back to earth?

5. What do you make of the fact that Jude seems to consider books that are not in the New Testament as authoritative? Did God work around Jude's misunderstanding or was the church wrong not to include such books?

endnotes

1. See chapter 10 of this text.
2. For this reason it seems that James is not contradicting Paul himself but a certain interpretation of Paul made by others.

3. The NIV and NLT probably skew the sense of this verse somewhat. First, the word they translate as "spiritual" is actually related to the word for *word* used in 1:23 and 25. It is the milk of this word that the believers were to crave. Second, 1 Peter 2:2 translates best in terms of growing up "into salvation." First Peter generally thinks of salvation as something that is yet to come, something that will be revealed in the last time (1:5).

4. See chapter 50 of this text.

5. J. H. Elliott, *A Home for the Homeless: A Sociological Exegesis of 1 Peter, Its Situation and Strategy* (Philadelphia: Fortress, 1981).

6. See the discussion of Jude below for the material in 2 Peter 2.

7. Although not all scholars agree. When we say they come from the same source, we do not necessarily mean that "John" composed all of these without help. The Gospel of John seems to derive from the same person as 1 John, but other individuals probably helped edit his teaching into its current form in the gospel (notice the way John 21:24 talks about the beloved disciple in the third person).

8. As we will see in chapter 53 of this text, Revelation differs in a number of respects from the Gospel of John and these three letters. For this reason, most scholars believe that a different John authored the book of Revelation than the John of the gospel.

9. I will refer to John as the author without implying a definite conclusion on the identity of the author.

10. Ignatius *To the Smyrnaeans* 5.2. The translations of Ignatius are mine.

11. Ibid., 2.1.

12. *To the Ephesians* 9.1.

13. *Against Heresies* 3.3.4, written in the late 100s.

14. The Greek word for church is feminine—it would thus be natural to refer to a fellow church as a sister or a woman.

15. Some suggest 2 John is pseudonymous because of its deep similarities to 3 John in style and 1 John in content.

16. Third John seems to mention one—a man named Demetrius.

17. *To the Ephesians* 6.1.

18. *Ecclesiastical History* 3.39.1–11.

The Apocalypse: Jesus Revealed!

While so much of Revelation is difficult to follow, its bottom line comes through loud and clear: God wins in the end, and He wins through Jesus Christ.

The Genre of Revelation

You would not get very far into the book of Revelation before you realized how different it is from the other writings of the New Testament. Its fantastic images of dragons, beasts, and destruction are unparalleled in the other books, as is the heavenly trip its author takes. Yet for all its uniqueness, it also has many features in common with other books in the New Testament. Like Paul's writings, Revelation addresses specific situations in specific churches (Rev. 2–3). Like some of the gospel material, it contains prophecies of the future (1:3).

Part of its singularity is the fact that it partakes of more than one genre.[1] It is both a letter meant

At a Glance

• The book of Revelation fits three genres: (1) a circular letter, (2) a prophetic writing, and (3) an apocalypse.

• There are at least four basic approaches to Revelation, ranging from the belief that it was written about ancient Rome to the belief that Revelation deals completely with things yet to come.

• Some think its middle section lays out a series of chronological events, while others think it portrays the same basic messages over and over.

• Its basic images relate to (1) a time of great trouble for Christians, (2) forces that will persecute Christians, and (3) the ultimate salvation of the persecuted/judgment of the persecutors.

• The author of Revelation is a man named John, perhaps not the John of the gospel.

to circulate to a number of places and a book of prophecy. However, the things that puzzle us most about Revelation arise from its inclusion in a third genre, the genre of apocalypse. For this reason, Revelation sometimes is known as "The Apocalypse."

We have a number of apocalypses from the ancient world. As the word *apocalypse* suggests in Greek, their main feature is the fact that they "reveal" what is going on in heaven and what is about to happen on earth. They also tend to have a number of other characteristics in common. For example, they typically begin with a visit to earth by a heavenly being such as an angel. They are usually written during a time of crisis and are meant to bring hope to their audiences. No matter how bad things might look now, these writings insist, everything will soon be all right. While Revelation probably is not pseudonymous, most apocalypses are—their writers talk about the present through the voice of some authority figure from the past. They imagine this person from the past having a vision of the author's time.[2]

preterist: Someone who believes all or almost all of Revelation is about events in the first century A.D.

futurist: Someone who believes that most of the events of Revelation are still to come and relate to the end of time.

historist: Someone who believes Revelation is about events throughout all of history.

idealist: Someone who believes that Revelation is a symbolic portrayal of the eternal struggle between good and evil, not a book with predictions about specific events in history.

The book of Revelation shares many of these features with the other apocalypses of the period. In Revelation, Jesus is the first "heavenly being" who visits the earth (e.g., Rev. 1:9-20), followed by another angel who leads John into heaven (e.g., 17:1). The book reveals visions of heaven and the future (e.g., 4:1), and believes that a time of great trial is on its way (e.g.

3:10). Despite the trials to come, it proclaims emphatically that good will triumph in the end (e.g., chapters 20–22). The only feature Revelation does not seem to share with other apocalypses is that of pseudonymity. Most scholars believe that the John who identifies himself in Revelation 1:4 is the author of the book.[3]

Revelation is one of the most difficult books of the New Testament to interpret. All in all, there are four basic approaches to its meaning. **Preterists** believe that all or nearly all of the prophecies of the book are directed at the time period in which they were made. In other words, the book is entirely or almost entirely about events in the late first century A.D. **Futurists**, on the other hand, believe that almost all its prophecies are still to come and relate to the end of time. **Historists** combine these two positions and believe that Revelation prophesies about events from the past and the future, including events throughout the last two thousand years. **Idealists** believe the book is mostly about the continual struggle between good and evil. Its images thus are symbolic of all time rather than predictions of specific events in history.

The Revelation of Jesus Christ

You can often tell what is most important in a book by the way it starts and ends. This seems to be true of the book of Revelation. While so much of its imagery is difficult to follow, its beginning and conclusion come through loud and clear with the bottom line of the book: God wins in the end, and He wins through Jesus Christ.

The first sentence of the book very well may have had a double meaning: "The revelation of Jesus Christ" (Rev. 1:1 NIV). On the one hand, Jesus does reveal a number of things in the course of the book—it thus presents revelations *from* Jesus Christ. On the other hand, some early Christians talked about Jesus' second coming as the time when He would be "revealed" (e.g., 1

Cor. 1:7; 1 Pet. 1:7, 13; 4:13). For this reason, the phrase "the revelation of Jesus Christ" might have made this book's audience think of Christ's return to earth, when He would be revealed.

It is no surprise thus to find that Revelation both begins and ends with mention of Christ's return (Rev. 1:7; 22:7, 12, 20). In a time of crisis, Jesus reassures the churches of Asia that He will soon come back to earth and everything will be set straight. No matter how we interpret the various pictures the book gives us of God's salvation and judgment, we should not forget that it is primarily about what God has done and will do through Christ.

trisagion: "Holy, holy, holy"—calling God holy three times. We find this phrase in both Isaiah 6 and Revelation 4.

What Christ already has done was to die as a sacrifice for God's chosen people. The image of Christ we see most often in Revelation is that of the Lamb of God (e.g., Rev. 5:12). It is because He died that Jesus is worthy to set in motion the judgment. It is because He died that He is qualified to rule the world.

Another interesting feature of the book of Revelation is the way in which Christ is worshiped (e.g., Rev. 5:14). Revelation presents us with the worship of Jesus more clearly than any other book in the New Testament. Yet even here, God is the primary object of worship (e.g., 19:10; 22:9). In a scene that reminds us of Isaiah 6, Revelation 4 depicts four living creatures worshiping God, saying, "Holy, holy, holy is the Lord God Almighty—the one who always was, who is, and who is still to come" (4:8). This set of three "holys" is sometimes called the **trisagion**—calling God holy three times.

Some of the most fantastic images of Christ in Revelation, however, are those that depict Him coming to the earth in judgment. Revelation 14:14-16, for example, pictures Jesus sitting on a cloud with a crown on His head and a sharp sickle in His hand, with which He reaps the earth. In 19:11-16, He is the Word of God riding on a white horse. Jesus' eyes blaze with fire and He has many crowns on His head (19:12). A sharp sword comes out of His mouth (19:15), and the titles "King of kings and Lord of lords" are written on His robe and thigh (19:16). As He comes, He treads the "winepress of the fierce wrath of almighty God" (19:15), an allusion to the blood that will flow on the Day of Judgment.

This imagery brings us to some important conclusions. First, these two images of Christ probably refer to the same event—Christ's second coming to the world with salvation and judgment. What this means is that we cannot assume Revelation offers anything like a chronological sequence of events. It much more likely gives us a number of pictures of the same basic events of judgment and salvation—a kaleidoscopic view of the judgment from many angles rather than a storyline of how each event will unfold.

Second, John clearly does not expect us to take this imagery literally. He does not give us a literal picture of what Jesus will actually look like on Judgment Day or even of what He looks like now in heaven. Surely no one thinks that Jesus in heaven right now really looks like a slain Lamb with seven horns and seven eyes (Rev. 5:6). With this comes a strong word of caution about how literally we take Revelation's imagery of such things as beasts and marks on foreheads. We cannot rule out the possibility that these are symbols for things like governments and allegiances.

Signs and Seals

Although a great deal of debate surrounds the meaning of the images in the central part of Revelation, they seem collectively to make three points, each of which shows up several times: (1) a time of great trouble is coming, (2) evil will oppress Christians in an unparalleled way, and (3) eventually

Christ will return, bringing judgment to the wicked and salvation to the righteous. Revelation unfolds this message by a series of different images.

Seven Seals

After John's spirit goes up into heaven and sees God on His throne (Rev. 4:1), he witnesses a crisis. There is a scroll that symbolizes the solution to the problems of the world and of God's people, but no one is worthy to open it. John weeps to think that the world's problems will not be solved, but is consoled when someone in heaven points out Jesus to him (5:4-5). Because of Jesus' death as the Lamb of God, He is worthy to open the scroll!

The next two chapters (Rev. 6–7) involve a number of images of judgment that take place as Jesus opens each of the seven **seals** on the scroll—seven pieces of wax keeping the scroll shut—one by one. After Jesus opens the sixth seal, John witnesses 144,000 Jews on earth (7:5-8), probably a symbolic rather than an actual number. A "vast crowd, too great to count, from every nation and tribe and people and language" (7:9), follows the 144,000. All these individuals are right with God, although they have experienced "**the great tribulation**" on the earth (7:14).

seal: A piece of wax with which a scroll was sealed shut.

The nature of this great tribulation is highly debated among Christians. Many Christians think of this as a specific seven-year period at the end of time during which a figure they call the **Antichrist** will rule on the earth. While we cannot say that they are wrong about how God will end things, it is important to realize that Revelation itself nowhere discusses such a seven-year period. While it does mention a three-and-one-half-year

The great tribulation in Revelation is a period during which God's people will undergo a time of intense suffering on earth.

656

period when Jerusalem will undergo siege (11:2-3) and a three-and-one-half-year period when God's people will be protected from Satan (12:6, 14), these seem to be the same period of time. Not only is this a time when God's people are protected (not persecuted, as in the great tribulation), but Revelation never associates the beast with this time of persecution. The idea of a seven-year period actually comes from the book of Daniel (Dan. 9:24-27)—it does not feature in the teaching of Revelation.

Further, modern Christian prophecy often uses a number of other terms differently from their original use in the Bible, if these terms appear at all. For example, the word *antichrist* appears in the New Testament in 1 John 2:18, but it does not refer to the evil figure of Revelation or the "man of lawlessness" mentioned in 2 Thessalonians 2:3. In 1 John it is used in the plural to refer to a number of individuals who deny that Jesus Christ came in the flesh, false teachers who lived at the end of the first century A.D. The phrase "*the* antichrist" used by many translations (e.g., NIV, NLT) does not actually appear in the Greek. The original does not put the word *the* in front of antichrist.

Another non-biblical term often used in relation to this hypothetical seven-year period is the **rapture**, the "seizing" of Christians from the earth as mentioned in 1 Thessalonians 4:17. Some futurists think that the vast crowd of Revelation 7:9 refers to the "rapture" of Christians from the earth *before* a seven-year period of tribulation begins, a **pre-tribulation rapture**. Others think that since these individuals have come out of the great tribulation, Christians will be removed from the earth three and one-half years into the seven-year period, a **mid-tribulation rapture**. Still others do not see Revelation as a straightforward sequence of events and so believe that these people are removed from the earth—if they manage to survive—*after* the tribulation, a **post-tribulation rapture**.

It is important to realize how little this contemporary language seems to really connect with the book of Revelation itself. While it is possible that God

Contemporary Views of Tribulation

the tribulation (great): Some Christians speak of a seven-year period of difficult times that will precede the final judgment, often called the Tribulation or the Great Tribulation. During this time it is thought that an evil leader, the Antichrist, will rule the earth. However, the idea of a seven-year period comes solely from the book of Daniel (e.g., Dan. 9:27) and may relate to events that took place around the years 167–164 B.C. Revelation itself never refers to a seven-year period, although it does draw on Daniel when it speaks of a three-and-one-half-year period (e.g., Rev. 11:2-3). Whether or not John wanted us to think of a specific forty-two-month period is unclear, although Rome did lay siege to Jerusalem for exactly forty-two months. The statement in Revelation 7:14 about individuals who have come out of "the great tribulation" (NIV) does not mention a specific length of time (e.g., a seven-year period), but refers in general to a time of intense persecution and suffering.

Antichrist: Usually connected to the beast of Revelation 13:1-10, the word antichrist is never used in Revelation. For preterists, this beast is a Roman emperor from the first century or represents the Roman imperial system in general. For futurists, it will be the final oppressor of Christianity, the "man of lawlessness" from 2 Thessalonians 2:3. For idealists, it represents all those who oppose God and His church at any point in history.

rapture: Not a term used in the Bible, but one that refers to the removal of Christians from the earth when Jesus returns in judgment (cf. 1 Cor. 15:51-52; 1 Thess. 4:17). The New Testament relates this event to the time when Jesus returns in judgment.

pre-tribulation rapture: The belief that Christ will remove Christians from the earth before a seven-year period of "tribulation" in which the earth will undergo great distress.

mid-tribulation rapture: The belief that Christians will undergo three and one half years of a seven-year "tribulation," but will be removed from the earth before the most intense suffering of the last three and one half years.

post-tribulation rapture: The belief that Christians will be present on earth throughout a seven-year "tribulation" period. If any survive, they will be taken up to be with Christ when He returns in judgment.

has inspired modern prophecy teachers to see the future correctly by reading the Bible "spiritually," Revelation itself did not seem to involve any of these schemes. *The great tribulation in Revelation is a period during which God's people will undergo a time of intense suffering on earth.* The book does not give a specific amount of time for this suffering, nor does it give us any reason to think that the removal of Christians from the earth will take place at any point other than when Christ returns in judgment. In other words, we have no reason to believe that Revelation gives us any different message with regard to Christ's second coming than the other books of the New Testament.

Seven Trumpets

After the seventh seal is opened, a series of events featuring seven trumpets begins (Rev. 8–11). Once again, some interpret the events that accompany each trumpet blast as things that will take place sequentially, following the events of the seven seals. Indeed, the devastating things that happen as the trumpets are sounded are worse than the destruction that accompanies the opening of the seals. However, others believe that these images have the same basic meaning as the opening of the seven seals; namely, that things will get worse and worse as the final judgment approaches.

After the sixth trumpet sounds, just as happened after the opening of the sixth seal, Revelation stops to give us several pictures of the witness, persecution, and triumph of God's people. In Revelation 11, two witnesses appear on earth. These two individuals prophesy while the Gentiles trample on Jerusalem for forty-two months (three and one-half years). At the end of the forty-two months, a "beast" rises from the dead and kills them (11:7). But the two witnesses are also raised from the dead (11:11), leading to the final trumpet (11:15). After the final trumpet, Revelation once again makes us feel that we have reached the point of salvation and ultimate judgment.

A great deal of debate surrounds the meaning of the two witnesses of Revelation 11. Because the miracles the two witnesses perform are things that Moses and Elijah did (Rev. 11:6), some futurists believe that Moses and Elijah themselves will literally return to the earth during the first half of a seven-year tribulation.[4] On the other hand, some preterists believe that Revelation is referring to Peter and Paul, both of whom were put to death by the emperor Nero, a popular suggestion for the identity of the beast. Indeed, the Romans did lay siege to Jerusalem for a period of forty-two months in the years between A.D. 66–70. However, Peter, Paul, and Nero all died well before this siege was over.

Another interpretation that fits more with the idealist interpretation is that these two witnesses symbolize the church, modeled after the Jewish sense that two or three witnesses were essential to assure the certainty of something (e.g., Deut. 19:15; cf. 2 Cor. 13:1). Indeed, in Matthew 18:20 Jesus says, "Where two or three gather together because they are mine, I am there among them." In this interpretation, the two witnesses represent all Christians who faithfully preach Christ's return to earth. Revelation indicates that they will undergo a time of intense persecution.

Dragons and Beasts

Before the final series of sevens, Revelation presents us with some more controversial images. The first is that of a woman and a dragon (Revelation 12). The dragon is clearly Satan (12:9), and the woman appears to represent the people of God—initially Israel but later on the whole church. The woman is protected from Satan for three and one half years. A preterist might see this as a picture of the protection the Christians of Jerusalem enjoyed during the time that Rome laid siege to the city in A.D. 66–70. According to tradition, they fled to a desert city called Pella during that time (cf. 12:6).

end times: A way of referring to the events that will happen at the end of time on Judgment Day and in the days right before it.

beast from the sea: The arch-persecutor of God's people in the book of Revelation. For futurists, he is the Antichrist of the end times; for preterists, he represents either the emperor Nero or the Roman Empire in general.

beast from the land: A figure who orchestrates the worship of the beast from the sea; also known as the false prophet. According to futurists, he sets up a world religion around the Antichrist in the end times; preterists say he represents emperor worship in Asia Minor in John's day.

mark of the beast: A mark in one's right hand or on one's forehead, without which one cannot buy or sell. Futurists take it as a tattoo the Antichrist will require in the end times; preterists take it as allegiance to Rome, perhaps even the use of money proclaiming the divinity of emperors.

Revelation 13 continues with more evil forces that are the enemies of God's people. The "**beast from the sea**" and the "**beast from the land**" have given rise to much speculation among Christians. According to futurists, they refer to the Antichrist of the **end times** and a "false prophet" (e.g., Rev. 16:13) who will set up a world religion around the Antichrist, forcing everyone everywhere to worship him. Unless you have the "**mark of the beast**" on your right hand or on your forehead, you will not be able to buy or sell (13:16-17).

Preterists, on the other hand, see this imagery in relationship to the Roman Empire and emperor worship. Asia Minor, the area to which Revelation was written, was particularly known for the way it worshiped the Roman emperors, sometimes even while they were still living. In the years that followed the writing of the New Testament, Christians sometimes got into trouble for refusing to offer sacrifices to the emperors—a refusal that was seen by non-Christians as disloyal and unpatriotic.

One interesting preterist interpretation of the mark of the beast is that it refers figuratively to the use of Roman money. Some of the Roman coins in John's day celebrated the divinity of the emperor whose face they bore. It is understandable that some Christians may have struggled with using such coins, effectively keeping them from buying or selling unless they had the "mark of the beast" in their "right hand."

Since Revelation seems to revisit the same themes over and over, it is no surprise that Revelation 17 returns to the topic of the beast, this time in more detail. Revelation 13 speaks rather vaguely about this figure, mentioning ten horns and seven heads, a fatal wound that had healed, and the "number of his name"—six hundred and sixty-six (Rev. 13:17-18 NIV). Revelation 17 expands on the first two images, equating the seven heads with seven hills and the ten horns with ten kings.

In Revelation 17, a woman is sitting on a scarlet beast. This woman has on her forehead: "Babylon the Great, Mother of All Prostitutes and Obscenities in the World" (Rev. 17:5). Even if you believe the beast to be a figure yet to come in history, a good case can be made that John was thinking heavily of ancient Rome as he wrote these chapters about the beast. For example, his readers almost certainly would have thought of Rome when they read that the "seven heads are seven hills on which the woman sits" (Rev. 17:9 NIV). The starting point for understanding the woman of Revelation 17, therefore, is the Rome of John's day.[5]

One clue that this woman represents Rome is the fact that John refers to her as "Babylon" (Rev. 17:5). After the Romans destroyed Jerusalem in A.D. 70, Jews began to call Rome "Babylon" (cf. 1 Pet. 5:13), since the Babylonians had also destroyed Jerusalem several centuries previously. In fact, some have unfortunately identified the woman of Revelation 17 with the Roman Catholic Church and the beast with a future Pope. While this hateful identification is most certainly wrong, it shows how clearly Revelation's imagery connects with the city of Rome.

Given that John's readers had Rome in mind, they almost certainly would have thought of Roman emperors when he mentioned seven kings in association with the seven hills. Since Revelation was written in the Asia Minor area, it made sense to think of Rome as "from the sea" (Rev. 13:1)—Rome was in that direction. "Five kings have already fallen," John says, "the sixth now reigns, and the seventh is yet to come" (17:10). The beast, John tells us, "was alive but isn't now . . . The scarlet beast that was alive and then died is the eighth king" (17:8, 11). What is startling is that this eighth king was also one of the first seven (17:11), an individual who had been fatally wounded (13:3, 12).

Although a great deal of debate surrounds the meaning of these statements, the view that commands the most support is that John was referring to the emperor Nero. A good case can be made that even if the beast represents someone still to come, Nero provided John with the prototype of this individual. On one reckoning, the five dead emperors were: (1) Augustus, (2) Tiberius, (3) Caligula, (4) Claudius, and (5) Nero. If we omit the tumultuous year A.D. 69, during which Rome had three different rulers, the sixth would be Vespasian and the seventh Titus. If we take the number eight straightforwardly, Domitian becomes the eighth king—the emperor reigning at the time John wrote Revelation according to tradition.

This approach raises a number of questions. Is it valid to omit the emperors of A.D. 69? Should we start with Julius Caesar rather than Augustus? Must we then redate Revelation, since the imagery places its writing during the time of Vespasian? Or is Revelation pseudonymous after all, placed back in time for stylistic reasons? Does John wish us to view Domitian as the beast?

Nevertheless, the idea that Nero was the basis for the symbolism of the beast fits well with other imagery Revelation gives us. For example, Nero committed suicide in A.D. 68, which corresponds to the fact that the beast was fatally wounded (Rev. 13:3, 12). Nero was also a fitting prototype of one who persecutes the church, since he was the first to put Christians to death on any large scale.

The figure of 666—the "number of the beast" (Rev. 13:18)—has long been intriguing to those interested in Revelation. Before the symbols we now use for our numbers existed, languages used their letters for numbers as well as for letters. You could thus add up the letters of a word. Christians have long pointed out that the name Caesar Nero adds up to 666 if you use Aramaic letters. Of course, Christians have also found ways to make the names of everyone from U.S. presidents to Popes fit as well. Given the context of Revelation, however, Nero seems a fairly probable candidate for the origins of the 666 number.

A final factor makes Nero the most likely prototype for the beast. A legend existed in John's day that Nero would return one day with armies from the East to exact his revenge on Rome (cf. Rev. 16:12). A writing called the *Sibylline Oracles* tells of Nero fleeing "Babylon" (= Rome) for the eastern empire of Persia.[6] Eventually, he would return and exact judgment on the Roman world, including Asia Minor: "All Asia, falling to the ground, will lament for the gifts she enjoyed from you . . . But the one who obtained the land of the Persians will fight, and killing every man he will destroy all life so that a one-third portion will remain for wretched mortals."[7]

If this legend stands behind the puzzling imagery of Revelation 13 and 17, we do not need to think that John thought Nero himself would literally return from the dead. A futurist might see Nero simply as the prototype for the Antichrist to come. Similarly, a preterist might say that John thought of Domitian as a Nero-type individual. An idealist might suggest that figures like this have "revived" throughout history and will continue to appear from time to time.

The Final Showdown

In between the two chapters on the beast that we have just discussed, Revelation gives us one last picture of its basic themes. Revelation 14, for

> **Armageddon:** Whether literal or symbolic, the place where the final battle between good and evil takes place.

example, again mentions the 144,000 righteous, those Jews who have remained faithful to God throughout persecution. We probably should not take literally the comment that these individuals have never defiled themselves with women (Rev. 14:4). It may echo both Old Testament and Qumran beliefs that warriors were not to sleep with their wives before battle—in other words, this section of Revelation may finally be gearing us up for the final showdown, the final battle between good and evil.[8]

Following this mention of the 144,000, we have two more series of seven. The first involves six angels and Christ, who is placed in the middle of the series. Christ and the last three angels are pictured "harvesting" the earth (Rev. 14:16), which seems in this instance to be a harvest of judgment, since blood flows from the harvest (14:19-20). The actions of the angels and of Christ all seem to be pictures of the same event, the final judgment.

Revelation 16 gives us the final series of seven—seven bowls of wrath. After the sixth bowl, the dragon and two beasts gather for the final battle at a place called **Armaggedon**. It is not clear exactly what place John might have had in mind by this name. There is an important place called Meggido in Palestine, but it is a valley, not a "har" or mountain. Thus, we cannot say for certain where Armaggedon is located. John may not even have had a specific location in mind.

Final Salvation and Judgment

Revelation 16–19 really support the idea that what we have been seeing throughout the book over and over again is the same event of final salvation and judgment. Revelation 14:16, 19-20 all seem to be the judgment of the earth, but we find ourselves at this point in the story once again in 16:17-21. If you thought Babylon had fallen in 16:19, you might be surprised to find her falling again in 18:2—and again in the final battle with the beast in 19:19-21. Christ rides a white horse in judgment in 19:11 and performs the same judgment already pictured in 14:16.

Revelation 18 has the starkest picture of Babylon's fall. It makes clear that economic sins are a part of her offenses. John rails against the orientation of Babylon around wealth (e.g., Rev. 18:19) and against all the merchants who take advantage of the opportunities she brings (18:11-13). These comments remind us of how severe the book of James is on the rich, as well as the merchant who goes from place to place in search of money (James 4:13). A preterist might find in these verses a critique of how the materialism of Rome brought hardship on the everyday person of Asia Minor.

Yet the preterist interpretation runs into some of its greatest difficulties in Revelation 18–22, events that hardly seemed to be fulfilled in John's own day. Unless you are willing to conclude that John's prophecies did not come true, the historist, futurist, and idealist perspectives become attractive from this point on in Revelation. A historist, for example, might understand Revelation 18 to be about the fall of Rome in A.D. 410. An idealist might say that all such persecutors of Christians will fall—not just Rome but any oppressive empire. A futurist might say that regardless of the overtones of the Roman Empire, the truest fulfillment of these words will take place at the end of time.

Revelation 20 is yet another chapter with imagery over which a great deal of debate has occurred. This debate has centered largely on the nature of the **millennium**—a period of a thousand years mentioned in Revelation 20:2, 4, and 7. After the dragon (Satan) is destroyed, he is thrown into the Abyss for a thousand years. At this time, all those killed for their faith come back to life in the first of two resurrections from the dead. It is quite possible that this group includes the 144,000 and the others in Revelation 7:14 who come out of the great tribulation. These individuals reign with Christ for a thousand years on earth.

After the thousand years is over, Satan is released for one more battle. He loses, of course, and is consigned to a lake of fire forever. At this point, all the dead from all of history are raised and brought before a great white throne for judgment. Following this event, God makes a new heaven and earth, then a new Jerusalem comes down to that earth from heaven (Rev. 21:1-2). There is no temple in that city, for God Almighty and Christ are its temple (21:22). Similarly, there is no need for a sun or moon because of the light these two bring (21:23). Interestingly,

millennium: A thousand-year period during which Christ will reign on earth with those Christians who have been martyred for their faith.

premillennialism: The belief that the millennium has not yet occurred but will happen after a time of world crisis during which things get worse and worse.

postmillennialism: The belief that the millennium either already has taken place or is currently taking place. Things will get better and better until Christ returns.

amillennialism: The belief that the millennium is symbolic of any time when Christ rules "on earth as it is in heaven."

Revelation does not picture Christians going off to be in heaven forever—rather they find their place on a renewed earth on which there is no longer a curse (22:3). The book concludes with Christ's promise that the time for all these things is near (22:10).

The most natural reading of Revelation's millennium is futurist. Revelation seems to imply that things will get really bad for Christians in a time when most of those Christians will die for their faith. These individuals will be raised when Christ returns in judgment and they will rule on earth for a thousand years—perhaps not an exact number but a number symbolic of a very long period of time. This perspective is called a **premillennial** view because it would say that the millennium is still to come.

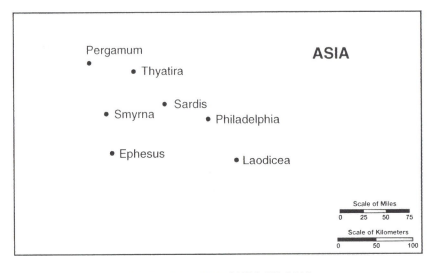

THE SEVEN CHURCHES OF ASIA
MAP 15

On the other hand, Revelation would likely have given its original readers the sense that it was speaking of Rome and that all these things would happen soon. "The time is near," Jesus says to the audience of this ancient time (Rev. 22:10). For this reason, most Christians up until about the 1800s were **postmillennial** in their view—they believed that Christ's rule roughly corresponded to the rule of the church on earth. In this view, the millennium is either something we are currently experiencing if we are part of God's church or it concluded some time ago. Unlike premillennialism, postmillennialism tends to believe that things will get better and better until Christ finally returns.

The difficulties with the two positions we have just mentioned have led others to what we might call an **amillennial** view—the view that Revelation is not really about a specific period of time that will take place in history. Rather, Christ rules at any point when His people are serving him faithfully. It is important to remember that Christians of all stripes, both liberal and conservative, have been able to hold to all of these positions. That is to say, you cannot presume a person to be liberal or conservative simply on the basis of which interpretation he or she takes. We should not use "end time" views as a litmus test for whether or not a person is a Christian.

The Who's, When's, Where's of Revelation

The traditional view of Revelation's background is very specific. According to this view, the apostle John wrote Revelation while he was exiled on the island of Patmos during the reign of the emperor Domitian in the 90s. By this time you will not be surprised to find out that several aspects of the traditional view are far from certain.

Some have suggested that John might have written Revelation much earlier than the 90s. If one connects the seven kings of Revelation 17 with the emperors of Rome, then John would have written during the time of Vespasian (Rev. 17:10). On this reckoning, John wrote Revelation just after the Romans had destroyed Jerusalem.

Since the earliest years of the church, various Christians have also realized that the style and orientation of Revelation are quite different in many respects from that of the Gospel of John. A man by the name of Dionysius noted as early as the 200s that the style of Revelation was dramatically different from that of the gospel, as did the church father Eusebius in the 300s. This difference does not seem connected to the imagery of Revelation; the book simply seems to come from one for whom Greek is a second language.[9]

Further, Revelation seems to have a strong sense of imminent judgment and salvation. John, on the other hand, has very little emphasis on Christ's second coming and focuses more on the presence of God's Spirit on earth at that time. For these reasons, while most scholars accept that the author was a man named John from Asia Minor, a man on the island of Patmos at the time of writing, many do not think this John was the same individual responsible for the gospel and Johannine epistles.

At the same time, Revelation does share a number of commonalities with John's gospel. Both seem to come from Asia Minor, traditionally from about the same time period. Both uniquely use the image of Jesus as the Lamb of God and Christ as the source of living water. They both make reference to Christ as the Word of God; Jesus also makes "I am" statements in both. It is thus difficult not to see some connection between Revelation and the Gospel of John.

Things to Think About

1. Do you think Revelation is about John's time, the end of time, all time, or some combination of these possibilities?

2. Notice that Revelation uses very few of the terms associated with the interpretation of the book. Does this fact imply that most of our interpretations of Revelation have little to do with the book itself?

3. Does Revelation support the idea of a seven-year tribulation with an Antichrist and a rebuilt temple?

Key Terms

amillennianism
Antichrist
Armageddon
beast from the land
beast from the sea
end times
futurist
historist
idealist
mark of the beast
mid-tribulation rapture
millennium
postmillennianism
premillennianism
preterist
post-tribulation rapture
pre-tribulation rapture
rapture
seal
tribulation (great)
trisagion

endnotes

1. R. Bauckham, *The Theology of the Book of Revelation* (Cambridge: Cambridge University, 1993), 1–2.

2. For a discussion of pseudonymity, see chapter 47 of this text. Because apocalypses are often pseudonymous, they are usually easy to date. The authority figure from the past tells history accurately until he gets to the time frame for which the apocalypse is being written!

3. Although many do not believe it is the John of the gospel. Some have suggested that Revelation assumes a point of view in the A.D. 60s to prophesy about events in the 90s.

4. On the other hand, both of these individuals are said to do the things that both Moses and Elijah did in the Old Testament. In other words, both witnesses have the power to shut up the sky and turn the waters to blood. Moses and Elijah here, therefore, probably symbolize the fact that the church's witness rests upon the foundation of the Law and the Prophets.

5. This woman is clearly not the same woman as we saw in Revelation 12.

6. The Persian Empire was administrated by fourteen governors—perhaps that to which the ten horns of Revelation 17:12 refer.

7. *Sibylline Oracles* 5.93-110 from *Old Testament Pseudepigrapha*, trans. John J. Collins, vol. 1 (New York: Doubleday, 1983), 395.

8. For example, Deuteronomy, Qumran. This interpretation broadly fits with what seems to be Paul's understanding of the final events. According to Paul, Christians participate in the judgment of the world (1 Cor. 6:2-3).

9. Some have pointed to what might normally be considered Greek grammatical errors, although other explanations have also been offered (e.g., that Revelation reflects a Jewish-Greek dialect).

Epilogue

Where Do We Go from Here?

If you have read very much of this book, you have crossed a bridge you can never go back over. You realize that for the most part the Bible was not written in your categories of understanding, but in those of the people to whom it was first written.

The Bible as Scripture

At the very start of this book we discussed a number of different ways to read the Bible. In general we pointed out two basic approaches to its words: (1) reading them in their original historical context, and (2) reading them against some other context. The chapters of this book have focused heavily on the words of the New Testament in their original contexts, although from time to time we have mentioned significant "community readings" of Scripture—interpretations that have been important to various Christian groups and traditions throughout the centuries.[1]

If you have read much of this book, you realize that the Bible's original meaning is not something you can arrive at very easily without a knowledge of ancient language, history, and culture. In other words, without this knowledge you would only get a superficial sense of what Matthew, Paul, or any of the other writers of the Bible were really trying to say, even if you have an excellent English translation. In fact, there are enough gaps in our knowledge of the historical context of the Bible for even scholars to often disagree on its original meaning. These observations at least *seem* to contradict the belief of many Christians that anyone can understand the Bible correctly as long as s/he has a good translation.

For some, the Bible becomes less relevant and less meaningful when they begin to read it for what it meant originally. In most religions, the very idea of "Scripture" is that the words hold *direct* and *immediate* authority over you: "God said it; I believe it; that settles it for me." But when you begin to read Paul's words in the light of the situations he was addressing, it becomes less clear that his words are actually directed at you. You may begin to feel that you are reading letters written to someone else in a faraway place and that you are just looking over someone else's shoulder.

> At this point we can no longer question that what Paul and his audiences understood his words to mean was a function of what words and ideas could mean 2,000 years ago.

> Many conservative scholars believe that while the Bible was indeed written to ancient contexts, the way it addresses those contexts reflects certain timeless principles and the timeless character of God.

At this point in the game we cannot question that Paul's words were in fact written to the audiences of ancient times and that they addressed situations at the various places to which he wrote. We cannot question that what *he and his audiences* understood his words to mean was a function of what words and ideas could mean *two thousand years ago*. Nor can we now question that frequently there are significant differences between what our words mean and what theirs did.

In other words, if you have read very far into this book at all, you have crossed a bridge you can never go back over. You recognize the difference between then and now. You know that, at least in the first instance, the words of the Bible were written to someone other than you and that they were written in *their* categories of understanding rather than in yours. Is this the end of the Bible as Scripture? Does the Bible now become a dated book? Or is there a way to achieve what one philosopher called a "second naïveté," a way to see the Bible once again as a word to me directly?[2]

I would say, "Yes!" Most conservative scholars have reclaimed the Bible for today by slightly modifying their understanding of what it means to call it "Scripture." Many conservative Christians would say that while the Bible was indeed written to contexts quite different from ours today, the way it addresses those contexts reflects certain timeless *principles* that in turn reflect the timeless *character of God*. In other words, while the specific commands and statements of the Bible may not always relate directly to today (e.g., the command not to eat pork), the principles *behind* those commands and the unchangeable nature of God always apply directly to us today.

For some this approach is enough to maintain the Bible as Scripture. For others, it may still seem like a lot of work and thinking—more work than you would expect of a message directed at you. Still others may ask whether the various portraits of God in the Bible even reflect the worldviews of ancient culture at times. To put it another way, will we always be able to find a principle behind every command? Or does much of it boil down to the fact that God always meets people wherever they are—and within whatever understanding of the world they have?

The Bible as a Witness to Saving Events

In some ways, crossing the bridge to the Bible's original meaning does us a favor—it potentially places our faith on something far more solid than words. Words mean different things to different people in different contexts; they are slippery things. But when we read the Bible in context, we begin to see Jesus, Peter, and Paul not as words on a page, not as characters in a story, but as real people who lived in history. We shift from words to events.

Surely the rock bottom foundation of Christianity, at least traditional Christianity, is the saving death and victorious Resurrection of Jesus Christ. Ironically, the focus of so many Christians on the *words* of the Bible can sometimes cause them to lose sight of Jesus as a real person who really lived and who really rose from the dead. It is on this *event* in history that Christianity stands, not on the *words about* that event.

> The rock bottom foundation of traditional Christianity is the saving death and victorious Resurrection of Jesus Christ— real events in history rather than words about events.

When we read the Bible in context, we begin to see its books as a part of God's constant workings in history, just a few examples of the way He has repeatedly met His people wherever He might find them. Each of its books represents just one instance of His ongoing relationship with the world. When we read the Bible in context, the story of this relationship becomes

> Each of the books of the Bible represents just one instance of God's ongoing relationship with the world. We might say that the individual books of the Bible are in the story of God even more than that the story of God is in the Bible.

much bigger than the stories *within* the Bible. Rather, we see that the books of the Bible are *within* the story of God's relationship with the world. We might say that the individual books of the Bible are *in the story of God* even more than that the story of God is *in the Bible*.

Reading the New Testament in this way leads us to some important breakthroughs in our understanding. For example, when we read the Bible out of its historical context, we usually view it as a single book with a single message. To a high degree, we assume that each book has fully "arrived" at a final understanding of truth. For example, some Christians even have difficulty listening to the New Testament when it changes aspects of the Old!

However, reading these books in their historical context leads us to wonder whether there is not in fact some dialogue that takes place within them. Do Matthew and Ephesians represent two different groups of Christians, each listening to God as they seek what He requires of them? Do genuine developments in understanding sometimes take place in the course of its pages? It is just possible that reading the Bible out of context causes us to miss the richness of God helping His people "unpack" the momentous events they had witnessed.

We know that the early Christians themselves experienced these events as such a process. Take Peter, for example. You would have expected him, of all people, to have it all figured out from the very beginning. After all, not only had he been with Jesus for His whole ministry, but he was also one of the chief apostles, one of the first witnesses to the Resurrection. Yet we see him struggling with the most fundamental issues of Christian truth throughout the New Testament.

Take the matter of Jewish food laws. Mark tells of an incident in Jesus' ministry in which Jesus implies that "every kind of food is acceptable" (Mark 7:19). Yet this truth apparently was not obvious to Peter, who decades later refused food that God offered him in a dream. "Never, Lord," he told God. "I have never in all my life eaten anything forbidden by our Jewish laws" (Acts 10:14). Still later Peter would refuse to eat with Gentiles, in order to preserve his ritual purity (Gal. 2:12). Although I think Peter probably "came around" eventually, we have no hard evidence to prove it. Indeed, it is possible that Peter never fully agreed with the idea that Christ's death had "ended the whole system of Jewish Law that excluded the Gentiles" (Eph. 2:15).[3]

What we see is that the people in the Bible were real people who did not always have it all figured out. When we view the books of the New Testament as moments in a process of God helping His people to "figure it all out," we at least have to consider the possibility that at points these books, rather than being the final word itself, are on a trajectory *toward* the final word. Take the notion of the Trinity. It took several hundred years *after* the books of the New Testament were completed for Christians to work out the details of what was appropriate to believe about the divine status of Jesus and the Holy Spirit. The seeds for these beliefs are in the New Testament, but they are far from "worked out."[4]

The New Testament in no way questions the institution of slavery. Contrary to popular belief, Paul did not tell Philemon to free Onesimus the slave—he only told Philemon to take him back after he had run away (Philem. 17). Paul affirmed the goal of freedom but did not consider it a high priority (1 Cor. 7:21). Far from encouraging civil disobedience or anything like an Underground Railroad, 1 Peter 2:18-25 commands slaves to submit to masters even when these masters beat them unjustly. Yet surely we would all agree that the abolition of slavery has moved human culture just a little closer to what the Bible implies heaven will be like.

These observations lead us to realize just how important the church and the Holy Spirit are for us today. When we read these books for their original meaning, we realize that they say different things in different contexts. But if they say different things, then we need some way of prioritizing and connecting them to *our* situations. This process is bigger than any one individual. We dare not trust ourselves to apply the Bible appropriately without other Christians around to make sure the Holy Spirit is with us.

The Bible as Sacrament

I mentioned earlier in this chapter that I believe it is possible to attain a kind of "second naïveté" with regard to the Bible. I believe it is possible for its words to speak directly to us today even after we have passed them through the fires of their ancient meanings. Of course, not all Christians want to go back to reading the Bible without a view to its original, historical contexts. They may prefer to look for principles behind the things God commanded back then and then reapply the *principles* directly to today. Indeed, because of the historical orientation of our Western culture, it may be very difficult for some to suspend the idea of context long enough to read the Bible in this way again.

It is possible, however, to view the words of the Bible "sacramentally," as we mentioned way back in chapter 2. Baptism is considered a Christian sacrament—a divinely appointed way of meeting God in which some ordinary medium like water comes to have extraordinary significance. God may have set up the words of the Bible to work in this way.

Words are ordinary things—we use them all the time. In a sense, God could speak to you through any words anywhere. Potentially, you could hear God's voice through the words of a newspaper. Yet, the history of the church seems to tell us that God has set aside these particular words of the Bible as a place where He can meet His people.

How the Holy Spirit accomplishes this feat is, of course, a mystery, and we know many people claim to hear God's voice when they probably do not. But if we are open, if we are in tune with God through prayer, who is to say that God will not authentically speak to His people through these words by way of the "dictionaries" in their heads, regardless of how close their understandings come to the original meanings? It is indeed possible for us to see ourselves in the stories of the Bible, regardless of what those stories meant to their original audiences. The very process of trying to understand the Bible's words in English leads us to hear them in ways that make sense to us in our lives.

Because the Bible treats the most important topics of human existence— the meaning of life, the possibility of existence after death, the problem of evil in the world—its words consider the very questions for which we are seeking answers. Because by faith we believe that the One with the answers was the

One inspiring the people in its pages, we believe its words are the most appropriate place to go to hear the right answers. The Holy Spirit, working through individuals and the church, can do the rest.

Things to Think About

1. As you finish this book, to what extent do you think the Scriptures were written for their own times and to what extent do you think they were written for all times?

2. What is the best way to read the words of Scripture? In terms of their original meaning? Prayerfully, in whatever way the Spirit leads you? In terms of your church's interpretations?

3. Does any particular teaching in Scripture give the "final word" on any specific belief or practice? To what extent is it legitimate and/or necessary to move beyond its words? Regarding things the Scriptures originally prohibited, is it legitimate to allow these things in new contexts? Regarding things the Scriptures originally allowed, is it legitimate to prohibit these things in new contexts?

endnotes

1. It would be helpful now to go back and reread chapter 2. What at that point might have seemed somewhat vague to you should be fairly clear now.
2. P. Ricoeur, "Biblical Hermeneutics: The Metaphorical Process" *Semeia* 4 (1975): 75–106.
3. Some of you might suggest that I have not yet heard my own words—that I have still presented this case from an out-of-context perspective. You might suggest, for example, that Mark and Acts were written from a segment of Christianity that largely did not believe the food laws were still in force, and that they were written

long after these Christians had come to these conclusions. Peter, you might argue, came from a community more like Matthew's, a Jewish Christian community that never agreed the food laws were void. This reconstruction would be a good example of the shift to seeing the books of the Bible as a part of the story rather than looking for the story in the Bible.

4. Take Colossians 1:15, which calls Christ the "firstborn over all creation" (NIV)—in other words, it places Christ on the creation side of things rather than on the uncreated side. A heresy known as Arianism was very prevalent in the A.D. 300s and used this Scripture to argue that Christ was the first created being. The church, on the other hand, rejected this idea, moving beyond the Scripture to affirm that Christ was "begotten, not made" (Nicene Creed).

For Further Study

Hebrews
- deSilva, David A. *Perseverence in Gratitude: A Socio-Rhetorical Commentary on the Epistle "to the Hebrews."* Grand Rapids: Eerdmans, 2000.

- Schenck, Kenneth L. *The Thought World of Hebrews.* Louisville: Westminster John Knox, 2003.

General Epistles
- Donelson, Lewis R. *From Hebrews to Revelation: A Theological Introduction.* Louisville: Westminster John Knox, 2001.

- McKnight, Scot. *1 Peter.* NIV Application Commentary. Grand Rapids: Zondervan, 1996.

- Moo, Douglas J. *2 Peter, Jude.* NIV Application Commentary. Grand Rapids: Zondervan, 1996.

Revelation
- Bauckham, Richard. *The Theology of the Book of Revelation.* New Testament Theology Series. Cambridge: Cambridge University, 1993.

After the New Testament
- Richardson, Cyril C., ed. *Early Christian Fathers.* New York: Collier, 1970.

Glossary

Adam: The first human being (Genesis 1–3). Paul's writings indicate that Adam's moral failure resulted in the power of sin over the world.

altar: In the Bible, the structure on which an animal was sacrificed; usually a pile of stones or stone table of sorts, often in a temple; in some Christian denominations today, a kneeling board at the front of the church where a person can pray.

amanuensis: A scribe; someone who actually wrote down an author's words on paper.

amillennialism: The belief that the millennium is symbolic of any time when Christ rules "on earth as it is in heaven."

Antichrist/antichrist: In 1 John 2:18, anyone who does not believe Jesus came into a human body, a charge John seems to direct at late first-century Docetists. For many Christians today, the term is connected to the beast of Revelation 13:1-10, although the word *antichrist* is never used in Revelation. For preterists, this beast is a Roman emperor from the first century or represents the Roman imperial system in general. For futurists, it will be the final oppressor of Christianity, the "man of lawnessness" from 2 Thessalonians 2:3. For idealists, it represents all those who oppose God and His church at any point in history.

Antinomians: Individuals in the early church who believed that as Christians they could do anything they wished—they believed that Christ had freed them from all moral obligations.

anti-Semitism/anti-Judaism: Hatred of Jews.

apocalypse: A type of writing in which a heavenly being brings a revelation to an authority figure, both about things going on in the heavenly realm and about things that are going to happen in the near future. Usually these were written in a time of crisis and were placed on the lips of a famous figure from the past, who foretold how God would make everything right in the world.

apocalyptic: Viewing events on earth as the playing out of spiritual conflicts in the invisible realm, conflicts that will eventually lead to the judgment of the world and the restoration of the righteous.

Apocrypha: A group of writings included in Roman Catholic and Orthodox Bibles but not in the Bibles of most Protestants.

apostasy: Abandoning or rejecting Christianity after having previously been a Christian.

apostle: Someone who is sent on an official mission, an ambassador; in the New Testament, someone who saw Jesus after He rose from the dead. The New Testament primarily refers to Jesus' disciples by this term, but the word can also be used of others like Paul who took leading roles in the spread of Christianity.

Aramaic: A language that evolved from Hebrew. It was what most Jews in Palestine spoke as their first language.

Armageddon: Whether literal or symbolic, the place where the final battle between good and evil takes place.

Ascension, the: Jesus' passage up to heaven forty days after His Resurrection; described in Acts 1.

ascetism: Involving extreme self-discipline or even the abuse of one's body.

atonement: The process of getting on good terms with God ("at-one-ment") by offering Him something.

Babylon: The nation that destroyed Jerusalem and Israel's first temple in 586 B.C., taking many Jews as slaves. Hundreds of years later, Jews and Christians would also use the word "Babylon" to refer to Rome, which destroyed Jerusalem and its second temple in A.D. 70.

baptism: A dipping in water that symbolizes the washing away of one's sins.

baptism with the Holy Spirit: The *inner* cleansing of your heart when your sins are forgiven and you become a Christian. It corresponds to the *outer* cleansing of baptism in water.

beast from the land: In Revelation, a figure who orchestrates the worship of the beast from the sea, also known as the false prophet. For futurists, he sets up a world religion around the Antichrist in the end times; for preterists, he represents emperor worship in Asia Minor in John's day.

beast from the sea: In Revelation, the arch-persecutor of God's people. For futurists, he is the Antichrist of the end times; for preterists, he represents either the emperor Nero or the Roman Empire in general.

Beatitudes: The blessings Jesus pronounces on the poor in spirit, mourners, the meek, and others in Matthew 5:3-10.

biography (ancient): Ancient biography aimed at presenting the overall *character* of an individual. Biographers generally assumed that a person remained the same throughout his/her whole life from birth to death. They did not focus on factors that might have *caused* a person to become a certain way. Rather, the events of a person's life *revealed* who that person had been from birth.

body of Christ: A metaphor Paul uses to signify all Christians. Each of us has a different function and the Holy Spirit dwells in the whole body.

born again: A phrase used by many Christians to refer to becoming a Christian; used in 1 Peter to speak of a believer's spiritual birth.

brokers: Those who served as go-betweens for patrons and clients in the ancient world when the gap between them was significant. See **patron-client system**.

Calvinism: A theological view that typically believes in individual predestination and "eternal security."

canon: The group of writings that Christians consider to be authoritative on the level of Scripture.

Capernaum: A village on the Sea of Galilee where Peter and perhaps Jesus seem to have had their homes.

catechism: Basic instruction in the teachings of Christianity.

catholic: Universal, relating to all people everywhere.

Cerinthus: An early Gnostic (see **Gnosticism**) who believed that the spirit-being Christ had descended on the human Jesus at His baptism and that Christ did not really die on the cross. Rather, Jesus cleverly changed places with Simon of Cyrene, who was carrying the cross for Him. Simon, not Jesus, died on the cross.

Christ: The Greek word for Messiah, meaning "anointed one." See **Messiah**.

Christ's divinity: The fact that Jesus is God.

church: A group of believers who *assemble* together (church means "assembly" in Greek). See **house church**.

circumcision: The cutting off of the foreskin; a sign of the special relationship between God and the sons of Abraham.

civil disobedience: Disobeying the law of the land because you disagree with it on principle.

clients: Those who received patronage/resources in the ancient world in return for the honor and prestige they gave their patrons. See **patron-client system**.

collectivist culture: Cultures where identity is primarily a function of the groups to which an individual belongs—such as one's race, family, or gender.

communion: See the **Lord's Supper**.

community meanings: The meanings that various groups of Christians see in the Bible.

confirmation: For churches that baptize infants, the process of personally affirming or *confirming* the faith your parents affirmed for you when you were a child.

conversion: The process of changing from one religion to another; the process of becoming a Christian.

covenant, the: The solemn agreement between God and Israel. He would bless them if they kept His commandments.

creed: A statement of basic belief.

Cynics: Believed that the rules of society had no basis in reality and that one should live life without worrying about possessions or human rules. Some scholars have dubiously suggested that Cynic thought influenced Jesus' teaching.

David: The second king of Israel and the first of a long-ruling dynasty. For many Jews at the time of Christ, he symbolized the ideal king.

Day of Atonement: The one day a year when the high priest entered the Most Holy Place to atone for the sins the people had committed in ignorance that year; Yom Kippur.

Day of the Lord: The Day of Judgment when God judges the earth.

Day of Pentecost: Also known as the Feast of Weeks and the Feast of First Fruits, Pentecost celebrated the end of the grain harvest, fifty days after Passover. For Christians, it represents the birthday of the church.

deacon: A lesser role of leadership involving the service of the church.

Dead Sea Scrolls: Writings found at Qumran that probably represent a wide variety of Essene communities from the two centuries before Christ. The most distinctive documents probably come from a community that split off from the broader Essene movement.

demythologize: To remove aspects of the New Testament that seem foreign to our current worldview.

deterministic: Holding that everything that happens is predetermined beforehand. See **fatalistic**.

deuterocanonical: In a "second canon," a term used for the authoritative status of the Apocrypha for many Roman Catholics and Orthodox churches.

Diaspora: The scattering of Jews throughout the Mediterranean world and away from their geographical point of origin.

disciple: One who is a follower or learner; in the context of the gospels, a follower of Jesus while He was on earth, someone who attached him or herself to Jesus in order to learn from Him and become like Him.

Docetism: A late first-century/early second-century movement that believed Jesus only had *seemed* to be human when He was on earth; He was really a spirit being. Because Docetists believed flesh was evil, they could not believe Christ could take on human flesh. It was thus an early form of Gnosticism.

dynamic equivalence: The attempt to catch the spirit of the original meaning in readable English that makes sense on our cultural terms.

Ebionites: Jewish Christians of the second century who continued to observe the Jewish Law and did not view Jesus as divine.

elders: A group of individuals, probably older men, who oversaw the direction of individual churches.

election: With regard to the Old Testament, God's choice of Israel as His special people out of all the peoples of the earth; with regard to the New, God's choice of Christians to be His people. Some Christians understand this on an individual level: God chooses which individuals will be saved.

emperor worship: The practice in the Roman empire of venerating the emperors as gods, usually after their deaths. In many places, however, emperors were worshiped prior to their deaths (e.g., Asia Minor), and a few emperors actually demanded worship before their deaths (e.g., Caligula and Domitian). Such worship at least involved offering sacrifices to them as gods.

end times: A way of referring to the events that will happen at the end of time on Judgment Day and in the days right before it.

Epicureans: Did not believe in an afterlife; one's soul atoms disintegrated at death just like one's body. By the time of Christ, they believed that one should "eat, drink, and be merry, for tomorrow we die."

epistle: Basically, a letter, although some scholars only use the word to refer to a somewhat official letter that circulates to a broad audience.

eschatological Jesus: The reconstruction of the historical Jesus that sees Him as someone oriented around the end of the current period of history, perhaps even of the world.

Essenes: Probably the Jewish group that followed the Jewish Law most strictly. They were often celibate and lived communally, holding their possessions in common.

eternal security: The belief that once people have become right with God, they cannot fail to be saved on the Day of Judgment.

eternity: Forever.

ethical Jesus: The reconstruction of the historical Jesus that sees Him as someone oriented around how to live in the present time.

Eucharist: Often called "communion," it literally means "thanksgiving." It is a celebration in memory of Jesus' atoning death on the cross. Bread represents His body, while wine represents His blood. See the **Lord's Supper**.

evangelism: The practice of telling others about the possibility and need to escape God's wrath.

exodus: The victorious departure of Israel from Egypt to freedom.

exorcism: Causing an evil spirit(s) to leave the body of someone it was controlling.

faith: Primarily *trust* in something. It also involves *belief* in that thing and *faithfulness* or commitment to it.

fatalism: The sense that nothing happens by chance, that everything that takes place is determined by forces beyond human control.

fatalistic: Having a sense that whatever happens was meant to happen. See **deterministic**.

flesh: On the most basic level, skin. By extension, the part of a human being that is under the power of Satan because it is a part of the earth; the "sinful nature."

foreknowledge: Knowledge of something before it happens.

formal equivalence: The attempt of a translation to stick closely to the wording and sentence structure of the original languages.

Four Pillars of Judaism: One scholar's way of summarizing the basic elements of Jewish self-understanding at the time of Christ: (1) **monotheism** (one God for Israel), (2) **election** (one people for God), (3) **covenant** (the solemn **patron-client** relationship between the two parties), and (4) **land** (the focus of blessing if Israel was faithful).

free will: The idea that God has allowed humans freedom to some extent to make choices and that God has not already decided who will be saved.

fruit of the Spirit: The natural result of having God's Spirit within—love, joy, peace, patience, kindness, goodness, faithfulness, gentleness, and self-control.

futurist: Someone who believes that most of the events of Revelation are about the futuristic end of time.

Galilee: The region in which Jesus grew up and conducted much of His earthly ministry. It included Nazareth, Jesus' hometown; Capernaum, a village in which Jesus may have had a house at one time; and the Sea of Galilee, where Jesus "called" some of His first disciples.

Gehenna: The Aramaic way of referring to the Valley of Hinnom, the trash dump of Jerusalem. The location became a metaphor for hell.

genealogy: A family tree. In Matthew, the genealogy starts with Abraham and moves forward to Jesus. In Luke, it starts with Jesus and moves back to Adam.

general history: An ancient genre of history writing that presents the story of a nation or people from its origins to contemporary times; Luke-Acts may have fit in this genre.

genre: A type of literature or literary form, such as a novel, a personal letter, an eviction notice, a diary, etc. Such forms create certain expectations in a reader before s/he even starts to read.

Gentile: Someone who is not a Jew.

ghostwriting: When a person other than the author of a book is the primary writer of the book—the author only agreeing and modifying what the writer has written on his or her behalf.

gift of prophecy: The ability to present messages from God about the church and its future.

gift of tongues: The ability to speak in angelic languages.

Gnosticism: A movement—both Christian and Jewish—that believed that the salvation of our spirits from our physical bodies came from hidden knowledge. Gnostics saw flesh as evil, and some believed the God of the Old Testament was an evil being.

good works: Good deeds, doing good things.

gospel/Gospel: (1) From our perspective, the genre of the four presentations of Jesus in the New Testament, Matthew, Mark, Luke, and John, whose aim was to present the gospel of Jesus Christ. In their own world, however, most of them come closest to the genre of ancient biography, although Luke may be considered history. (2) In the ancient world in general, good news of an extraordinary sort, such as the birth of a future emperor or an important military victory. (3) In Jesus' ministry, He used the word to refer to the good news that the kingdom of God was about to arrive on earth "as it is in heaven." (4) For Paul and the early Christians, it was the good news that God had provided salvation for the world through the death and Resurrection of Jesus Christ. We come closest to Paul in our use of the word today—the gospel as the "good news" message that through Jesus Christ God has provided a way of escape from judgment.

grace: God's willingness to serve as the supplier of our needs, our divine patron. In return He expects honor and obedience. Unmerited favor.

Great Commission, The: Jesus' command to make disciples from the peoples of every nation; found in Matthew 28:18-20.

Griesbach hypothesis: The suggestion that Matthew was written first, Luke second, and that Mark used both to create his gospel.

group culture: See **collectivist culture**.

Hanukkah: The Jewish feast that celebrates the rededication and purification of the temple after the Maccabeans freed the Jews from foreign rule.

Hasmoneans: The actual family name of the Maccabees. Israel was somewhat self-governing for about a hundred years under their rule.

hell: The place of eternal torment for the damned.

Hellenistic Jews: Greek-speaking Jews.

heresy: Incorrect teaching according to the Christian mainstream, as opposed to orthodoxy, which is correct teaching; inappropriate belief.

Herod Antipas: The son of Herod the Great, he ruled the regions of Galilee and Perea from 4 B.C. to A.D. 39. This Herod beheaded John the Baptist, and Jesus referred to him as a "fox" (Luke 13:32).

Herod the Great: The king the Romans appointed to rule Israel just before Jesus' birth. The New Testament tells us that he put all the male infants in Bethlehem to death in an attempt to kill Jesus.

high priest: The highest rank of priest in Judaism. The high priest's most significant religious responsibility was to enter the Most Holy Place of the temple once a year and offer a sacrifice for the sins of the people. At the time of Christ's death, he was the most powerful Jewish political figure in the land.

historist: Someone who believes Revelation is about events throughout all of history.

history (ancient): Ancient history varied in terms of historical reliability, with some authors being more careful than others. The emphasis was more on the big picture than on precision. For many, a creative, artistic presentation that led to true inferences was more valued than accuracy.

Holies, the: See **Holy Place**.

holy: Belonging to God, often with the sense that such a person lives appropriately.

Holy of Holies, the: See **Most Holy Place**.

Holy Place: The outer room of the Jewish tabernacle/temple (the Holies).

Holy Spirit, the: Primarily a way of referring to God's (or Jesus') presence and action in the world. However, the New Testament often speaks of the Holy Spirit as a person distinct from God the Father and Jesus. The church spelled out His identity more clearly in the years following the writing of the New Testament.

honor/shame culture: Culture oriented around the approval or disapproval of your group rather than around being true to yourself as an individual.

house church: A group of believers that meets together in the house of a particular person. See **church**.

household codes: Sets of instruction regarding the appropriate roles of individuals in relationships such as wife-husband, slave-master, and child-parent.

idealist: Someone who believes that Revelation is a symbolic portrayal of the eternal struggle between good and evil, not a book with predictions about specific events in history.

idol: A physical representation of a god, such as a statue or figurine that is used to worship the god.

immaculate conception: The Roman Catholic belief that not just Jesus, but also Mary was born without sin.

incarnation: The idea that Jesus was God made flesh, that He came from heaven and became human.

individualistic culture: A culture where one's identity is determined by each person as an individual.

inerrant: With regard to the Bible, without errors, including scientific or historical errors.

infallible: With regard to the Bible, without error in any matter of faith or doctrine.

inspiration: The process by which God conveyed truth through human authors to the written text of the Bible.

Israel: Originally the name of Abraham's grandson, it would become the name of his descendants and the nation they constituted.

Jerusalem Council: The name often given to the meeting where it was decided that Gentiles could be Christians without being circumcised.

Jesus movement: A way of referring to the earliest followers of Jesus, both before and after His crucifixion.

Jesus Seminar: A group of scholars who voted to decide what they thought Jesus *really* said. In general, they eliminated all of Jesus' sayings in which He viewed himself as a part of world-changing events or in which He preached the coming of God's judgment on Israel or the world.

Jewish War: Took place from A.D. 66–73. This attempt of the Jewish people to free themselves from Roman rule resulted in the destruction of Jerusalem and the temple in A.D. 70.

John the Baptist: A first-century reformer whose proclamation of coming judgment and restoration provided the launching point for Jesus' own mission.

Judah: After the kingdom of Israel was split into two parts, Judah was the name of the southern kingdom. Since the northern kingdom was obliterated, the Israelites that survived this destruction were largely from Judah. It is thus from this word that the later term "Jew" derives—a descendant of Judah.

Judaizers: Christians in the early church who insisted that Gentiles must become Jews and follow the Law of Moses in order to be acceptable to God.

Judea: The southernmost region of Palestine where Jerusalem and Bethlehem were located.

justification: Legally considered innocent; declared "not guilty"; for it to be "just-as-if-I'd" never sinned.

justification by faith: The idea that the only way to be found "not guilty" by God is through trusting in what Jesus Christ has done for you on the cross; getting right with God by trusting in Christ.

kerygma: The basic Christian message.

koinonia: The Greek word for "fellowship," often used to indicate how Christians should get along with one another.

kingdom of God: The reign or rule of God, on earth as it is in heaven.

last Adam: An image Paul uses of Christ as the counterpart to Adam. Adam sinned, brought death, and prevented his family from ruling the earth. Christ brings life to those "in Him" and enables them to attain to the glory God originally meant humanity to have.

Last Supper, the: The final meal Jesus had with His disciples, the Passover meal the evening before His crucifixion. The Christian celebration of the Lord's Supper mirrors this final meal.

Levitical priests: Priests who descended from Levi, one of the twelve sons of Jacob in the Old Testament.

limited good: The idea that there was only a certain amount of wealth, goodness, and value in the world. If one person gained, therefore, it was assumed that someone else lost.

Lord: A term that implies Christ's kingship over heaven and earth and that He is the ruler of all.

Lord's Supper, the: Also called communion or the Eucharist (meaning "thanksgiving"), this was the weekly meal early Christians had on Sundays to remember the significance of Christ's death. It mirrored the Last Supper Jesus had with His disciples, the Passover meal.

Maccabees: The Jewish family that successfully freed the Jews from Syrian rule, resulting in about a hundred years of freedom.

Magi: "Wise men," often thought to be astrologers or star watchers. The similarity of the Greek word to "magician" is obvious.

manuscript: An ancient document written by hand. Over five thousand handwritten Greek manuscripts, copies of portions of the New Testament, have survived until today.

mark of the beast: A mark in one's right hand or on one's forehead, without which one cannot buy or sell. Futurists take it as a tattoo the Antichrist will require in the end times; preterists take it as allegiance to Rome, perhaps even the use of money proclaiming the divinity of emperors.

martyr: Someone who dies for what s/he believes.

Mary's perpetual virginity: A belief among many Roman Catholics that Mary remained anatomically intact throughout childbirth and then remained a virgin her entire life.

mediator: A go-between, an intercessor or arbitrator.

Melchizedek: The first priest mentioned in the Old Testament. According to Hebrews, a "priest after the order of Melchizedek" is a priest who lives forever yet does not come from a priestly family—Christ, in other words.

messiah: Translates as "anointed one" and was originally used to refer to someone such as a king or priest who was set apart for a special, divinely appointed role. This person often was installed into office by being "anointed" with oil.

mid-tribulation rapture: The belief that Christians will undergo three and a half years of a seven-year "tribulation," but will be removed from the earth before the most intense suffering of the last three and a half years.

millennium: A thousand-year period during which Christ will reign on earth with those Christians who have been martyred for their faith.

monotheism: Belief in only one God.

Most Holy Place: The inner room of the Jewish tabernacle/temple (the Holy of Holies) where the high priest offered a sacrifice on the Day of Atonement. The Ark of the Covenant was housed here.

mystery religions: Religions that involved secret rituals relating to the death of a god, secret knowledge, and the guarantee of a happy afterlife.

mysticism: Practices and beliefs that relate to achieving a oneness of one kind or another with the divine realm.

Nazareth: The village in Galilee where Jesus grew up.

new covenant: The new arrangement between God and humanity through the blood of Christ.

New Testament: The second part of the Christian Bible; literature relating to God's people after the coming of Christ.

old covenant: The arrangement between God and Israel made at Mt. Sinai; the Jewish Law.

Old Testament: The first part of the Christian Bible; literature relating to God's people before the coming of Christ.

original meaning: Reading the Bible's words for what they meant when they were first written, using the meanings of words and concepts from 2,000 years ago.

orthodoxy: Correct teaching as it is understood by mainstream Christians, as opposed to **heresy**, which is incorrect teaching.

overseer: Perhaps the same as an elder (cf. Titus 1:5, 7), one of the leaders of a church.

pagan: Worshiping many gods (polytheistic) as opposed to one god (monotheistic).

parable: A rather wide category of figurative speech that includes such types as riddles, similes (x is *like* y), and even allegories (where several elements in a story are given symbolic meanings).

parousia: The arrival of Jesus again to judge the earth.

Passover: The most important Jewish festival, it celebrates the day when the death angel "passed over" the sons of the Israelites before they escaped from Egypt.

Pastoral Epistles: 1 and 2 Timothy and Titus, so called because they give instructions to two "pastors" on how to shepherd their "flocks." Timothy and Titus were two of Paul's most trusted "trainees."

patron-client system: Ancient networks of informal arrangements between those with money, power, and resources (**patrons**) and those without (**clients**). Patrons would provide clients with resources in return for the prestige and influence it brought them. Clients in return did patrons various favors and generally honored them.

patrons: Those with power, influence, and money who were able to assist those with less power. See **patron-client system**.

Pentateuch: The first five books of the Old Testament—Genesis, Exodus, Leviticus, Numbers, and Deuteronomy. According to Jewish tradition, Moses authored all five of these books.

People of the Land: The common person in Israel going about his or her day-to-day business. Most farmed for their subsistence.

personal meaning: Finding meaning in the Bible's words without regard to their original meaning; interpreting the Bible from the "dictionary" in your head, as if its words were written directly to you and not to people who lived 2,000 years ago in a far different historical and cultural context.

Pharisees: A group of Jews known best for their careful keeping of the Jewish Law as it was interpreted in the traditions of the elders. Unlike the Sadducees, Pharisees strongly believed in the resurrection of those who died noble deaths in faithfulness to God's covenant with Israel.

plan of salvation: A brief explanation of why and how you become a Christian.

Platonists: Platonists believed that earthly things were simply copies, images, and shadows of heavenly realities and that the only way to access these truths was through the mind. They believed in a soul that survived death only to migrate to another body.

poor: Displaced from your inherited place in life, from your possessions, etc.

postmillennialism: The belief that the millennium either already has taken place or is currently taking place. Things will get better and better until Christ returns.

post-tribulation rapture: The belief that Christians will be present on earth throughout a seven-year "tribulation" period. If any survive, they will be taken up to be with Christ when He returns in judgment.

predestination: The idea that God has already decided who will believe and be saved; God decides/determines who will be saved and then plans history so that it happens accordingly.

premillennialism: The belief that the millennium has not yet occurred but will happen after a time of world crisis during which things get worse and worse.

preterist: Someone who believes that all or almost all of Revelation is about events in the first century A.D.

pre-tribulation rapture: The belief that Christ will remove Christians from the earth before a seven-year period of "tribulation" in which the earth will undergo great distress.

priesthood of all believers: Martin Luther's teaching that all Christians are priests, not just particular individuals ordained by the church.

priests: Those from the Israelite tribe of Levi whose role was to administer the Law to the people. This included such things as offering sacrifices in the temple, settling disputes, and declaring individuals ceremonially clean.

Prison Epistles: The letters of Ephesians, Philippians, Colossians, and Philemon. According to tradition, Paul wrote these letters while under house arrest in Rome.

prophet: Someone through whom God speaks messages of challenge and hope to human beings. A prophet's messages usually addressed contemporary situations rather than the distant future.

Protestant Work Ethic, the: "Whoever does not work should not eat" (2 Thess. 3:10).

pseudonymity: The practice of writing under the authority of someone else's name, usually an authoritative figure from the past who has long since died.

Quest for the Historical Jesus: The attempt to determine as much as is possible about the life, teachings, and aims of Jesus of Nazareth—the one from whom Christianity originated.

Qumran: The location of the Dead Sea community where the Dead Sea Scrolls were discovered. This community was thought to be one branch of a group of Jews known as the Essenes.

rapture: Not a term used in the Bible, but one many use today in reference to the removal of Christians from the earth when Jesus returns to judge the world (cf. 1 Cor. 15:51-52; 1 Thess. 4:17).

redemption: A payment made to set someone free in some way.

repentance: Changing decisively from one attitude or way of life to another.

resurrection: Coming back to life from the dead, usually involving a body of some sort.

resurrection of the dead: The bringing back to life of the dead when Christ returns. At that time God will provide the dead with "spiritual" bodies.

Resurrection, the: Jesus' miraculous return from the dead.

revelation: Truth conveyed or "revealed" from God to humanity.

revolutionaries: Jews who sought to throw off the yoke of Roman oppression and who were the primary fuse of the Jewish War. Individuals from all three main Jewish sects participated in the Jewish War. Some revolutionary groups that arose in the Jewish War included the Zealots and the Sicarii.

rich: Generally thought of as someone who had stolen the goods and possessions of someone else or descended from someone who had.

righteousness: In a legal context, one's innocence or acceptability in the eyes of the law; in a Christian context, acceptability before God, the righteous judge.

righteousness of God, the: The fact that God not only is faithful to His covenant with Israel, but is also a merciful God in general who wishes to save people of all kinds.

Roman Road: A series of four verses from Romans (3:23; 6:23; 5:8; 10:9) that explain the "plan of salvation"—the basic reasons for becoming a Christian and how to do so.

Sabbath: The period from sundown on Friday to sundown on Saturday during which Jews did not work.

sacrament: A "means of grace," a divinely appointed path by which to meet God and experience His love (e.g., communion, baptism).

Sadducees: A small group of aristocratic Jews who held political power in Jerusalem. They did not believe in an afterlife.

salvation: In Paul's writings, escaping God's wrath, which is the consequence of our sins; being "saved" from our sins. In the gospels, the word also can have the sense of freedom from Israel's enemies or from demonic forces, as well as physical liberation from disease and sickness. For many churches it has become a shorthand way of referring to becoming a Christian—"getting saved."

Samaritans: Those who lived in the region formerly known as the northern kingdom of Israel. They were of ethnically diverse origins, including the race of Israel.

Sanhedrin: The Jewish ruling council, made up of elders from the Jewish aristocracy.

Satan: The prince of demons, leader of demonic forces and the epitome of evil, also known as Belial, Beelzebub, and the devil.

scribe: One whose function was to copy documents—primarily the Jewish Law. Scribes were thus closely associated with the Pharisees.

Scripture: A writing or collection of writings considered to be authoritative in some way for a particular religious group.

seal: A piece of wax with which a scroll was sealed shut.

Sea of Galilee: A sea in northern Israel around which Jesus conducted much of His earthly ministry. Here Jesus called some of His first disciples to follow Him.

second coming: Christ's return to earth on the Day of Judgment.

sign: An indication of something. In John, signs indicate Jesus came down from heaven. In the synoptics, Jesus refuses to give "signs" on demand to prove that He is the Messiah, although He performs many miracles.

sin: In general, any wrongdoing, particularly intentional wrongdoing. For Jews it primarily meant breaking the Old Testament Law.

sinful nature: The way that some Bibles translate the Greek word for *flesh* (see **flesh**). It refers to that part of a human being (i.e., the physical part) that is subject to the power of sin if a person does not have the Holy Spirit within.

sinner's prayer: A prayer in which you admit that you are a sinner in need of God's forgiveness.

Solomon: The third king of Israel. He built the first temple to Yahweh in Jerusalem.

Son of David: A descendant of David who occupied the throne. In the New Testament, Jesus is referred to as the "Son of David," meaning He is the king that Israel had been awaiting.

Son of God: A term used for the anointed kings of Judah. It indicated that they were in a special relationship with Yahweh, like that of son to father, and that their earthly authority mirrored that of God himself.

Son of Man: One of the main ways in which Jesus referred to himself. The phrase can be taken in several different ways. It can simply mean "a human being." It also was used of a king God would send from heaven to judge the nations and rule Israel.

sovereign: Having absolute control.

spirit: The heavenly part of our nature that God's Holy Spirit can enter.

Stoics: Stoics believed that the *Logos*, the divine Reason that was in all things, directed and ordered the world. Since one could not possibly overcome its direction, one should accept his/her fate and not be concerned with pain or emotion. One should listen to the small seed of *logos* that is the human spirit. This seed returns to the *Logos* of the world at death.

syncretism: A mixture of religions.

synoptic gospels: Matthew, Mark, and Luke, so called because they present similar portraits of Jesus.

synoptic problem: The question of how the synoptic gospels have come to be so similar in content, wording, and arrangement.

tabernacle: The portable tent constructed by Moses in which sacrifices were offered in the period before Solomon built the temple.

table fellowship: The matter of whom it was appropriate to eat with.

Teacher of Righteousness: The founder of the particular Essene community that lived at Qumran on the Dead Sea.

textual criticism: That branch of New Testament studies that aims at recovering the exact wording of the original texts of the Bible.

theological: Pertaining to our beliefs about God and related issues.

tongues: Languages. In Acts 2 these are human languages, while 1 Corinthians 14 seems to refer to angelic languages that some Christians can speak.

tradition of the elders: Oral traditions that arose about how to keep the specifics of the Law. The Pharisees are best known for keeping these traditions.

Transfiguration, the: Jesus, along with Moses and Elijah, was transformed into a heavenly state in front of the disciples Peter, James, and John.

tribulation, the: Some Christians speak of a seven-year period of difficult times that will precede the final judgment, often called *the* Tribulation. During this time it is thought that an evil leader, the Antichrist, will rule the earth. This idea of a seven-year period comes from the book of Daniel (e.g., Dan. 9:27), since Revelation itself never refers to such a seven-year period. The statement in Revelation 7:14 about individuals who have come out of "the great tribulation" (NIV) does not mention a specific length of time (e.g., a seven-year period), but refers in general to a time of intense persecution and suffering.

trisagion: "Holy, holy, holy"—calling God holy three times. We find this phrase in reference to God in both Isaiah 6 and Revelation 4.

TULIP: An acronym for remembering the basic beliefs of Calvinism, namely, Total depravity, Unconditional election, Limited atonement, Irresistible grace, and Perseverance of the saints.

two-source hypothesis: The idea that Matthew and Luke based their presentations on Mark and a collection of some of Jesus' sayings called Q.

Valley of Hinnom: A valley outside Jerusalem where Jews burned their trash.

virgin birth: Jesus' miraculous birth; His mother Mary gave birth to Him even though she had never slept with a man (more accurately called the virginal conception).

Way, the: The term Christians themselves seem to have used to refer to themselves as a group in the first century A.D.

(to) witness: To tell others about the possibility of salvation; to "evangelize," share the "gospel."

Word/*Logos*: Many Jews at the time of Christ talked about God's actions in the world by speaking of His word doing things. The world was created through His word, for example. It represented His will and purpose for the creation.

Yahweh: God's proper name in the Old Testament, usually translated LORD in all capital letters.

Index

pharaoh 55-56, 64, 255-256

Pharisees 19, 59, 61, 75, 78, 80-83, 86, 134, 152-154, 161, 164, 166, 171, 174-176, 179, 193, 199, 234-235, 270, 282, 301, 329, 340, 362, 371, 377, 387, 393, 399, 404-405, 414, 475, 512, 515, 701, 705, 707

Philemon 24, 106, 345, 403, 408-410, 412, 415, 428, 537, 539, 541, 543, 545, 547-553, 584, 594, 599, 680, 703

Philippi 227, 316, 318, 343, 345, 349, 371, 410, 537, 541, 568, 579, 594, 605

Philippians 24, 93, 113, 118, 388, 403-405, 408, 410, 412, 414-415, 460, 531, 537, 539, 541-543, 545, 547, 549-553, 568, 577, 593-594, 703

Philo 89, 96-97, 352, 517, 607

Phoebe 443, 493, 582, 590, 605

plan of salvation 448-450, 460, 702, 704

Plato 41, 114-116, 119, 121, 215, 222, 384, 511, 610, 624

poor 24, 35, 77, 107-109, 151, 153, 170, 178, 197-198, 201-202, 206, 223-226, 228, 235, 238, 258-261, 298, 313-314, 316-317, 458, 502, 523, 529, 631-632, 634, 688, 702

post-tribulation rapture 657-658, 670, 702

postmillennialism 667-668, 702

power 40, 57, 64, 70, 75-78, 99, 101, 103, 105, 107, 109, 113-116, 128-129, 131, 152, 154, 158, 189, 203-204, 211, 226, 245, 247-248, 267, 269, 301, 314-315, 317-319, 325-326, 328-329, 336, 351, 353, 356, 363, 365, 368-372, 396, 417-419, 424, 426-427, 429, 431-432, 435, 439-440, 444, 447, 453-454, 469-470, 475-476, 480, 482-483, 487-488, 491, 502, 533-534, 552, 600, 617, 637, 671, 686, 693, 701, 704-705

prayer 40, 105, 169, 197-198, 203-204, 231, 233, 238-239, 258, 270, 287, 313-314, 317-319, 334, 348, 363, 371, 419, 448-449, 460, 506, 681, 705

predestination 75, 80, 118, 441-442, 444, 470-477, 482, 538, 688, 702

premillennialism 667-668, 702

preterists 652, 653, 658, 660-661, 662, 664, 666, 670, 686, 688, 699

pre-tribulation rapture 657-658, 670, 702

priesthood of all believers 636-637, 649, 702

priests 61, 76-79, 86, 88, 115, 123, 234, 300, 329, 371, 399, 500, 503, 618-623, 628, 636-637, 698, 702

Priscilla 228, 317, 344, 443, 590, 605

Index